Richard,
With my warm
thanks for much.

Brian 04/03/08.

Landscapes, Documents and Maps:
Villages in Northern England and Beyond
AD 900–1250

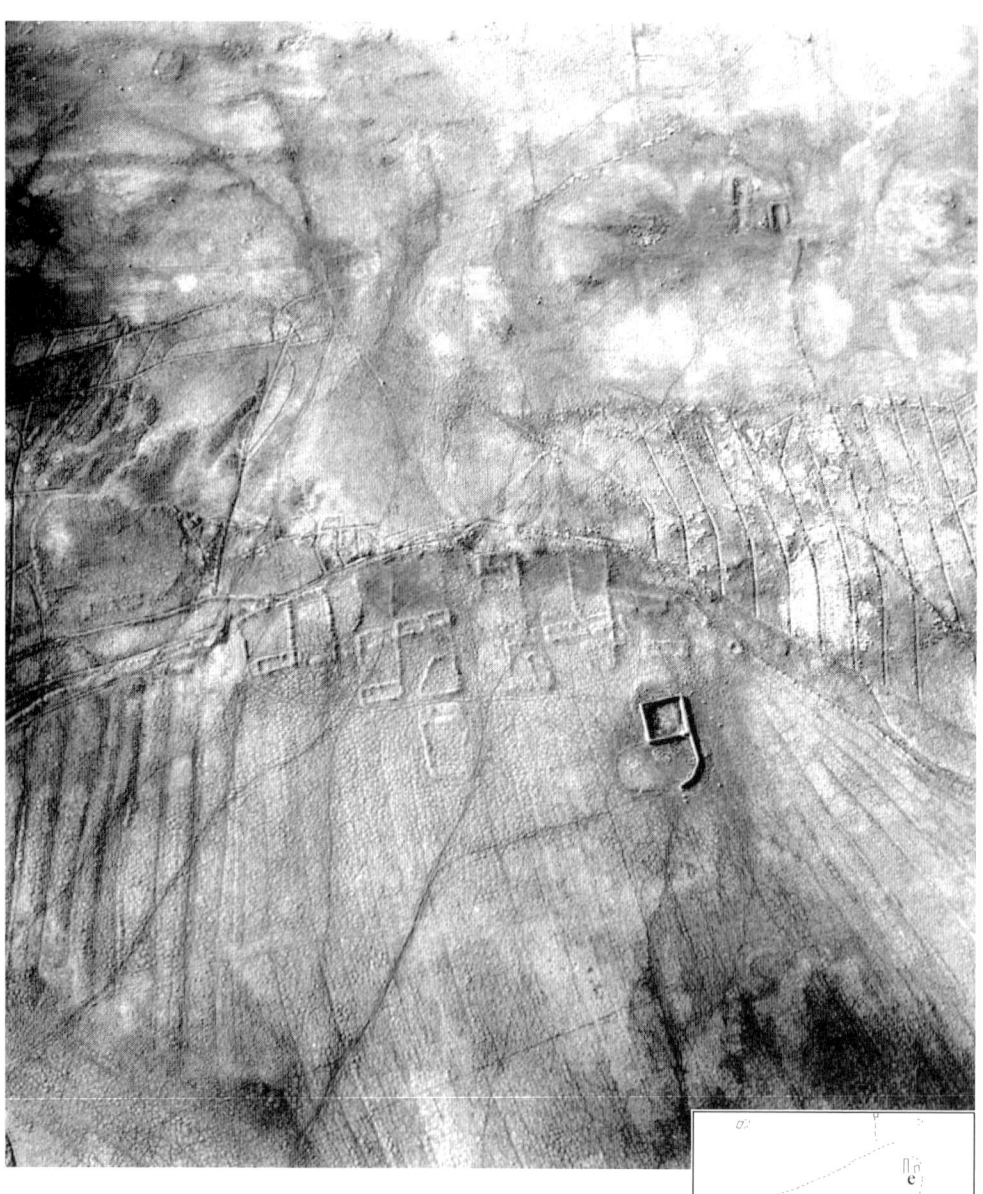

Frontispiece: The site of Hartside, Northumberland, from a photograph taken 1st June 1979 by Tim Gates (copyright reserved).

Lines of modern hill drainage score slopes at (a); in the foreground (b) the strips of a foothold furlong, some 400 m long, appear to pass beneath a planned hamlet at (c); behind the settlement, between a small topographic bench and rising ground, is a former roadway, now followed by a stream (d); at (e) two massive buildings pose questions, while at (f) is an outlying enclosure. A sheepfold is seen at (g). There are, furthermore, many traces of antecedent enclosures and structures, probably linked to the use of the site as a shieling.

These traces indicate a long history of occupation at this physically marginal site.

To my wife Jan,
a constant companion on many journeys.

'Geography and chronology are the two eyes of history.'

Giambattista Vico
New Science 1744 [17]

Published by
Oxbow Books, Oxford, UK

© Oxbow Books and the authors, 2008

ISBN 978-1-84217-237-7

A CIP record for this book is available from the British Library

This book is available direct from

Oxbow Books, Oxford, UK
(Phone: 01865-241249; Fax: 01865-794449)

and

The David Brown Books Company
PO Box 511, Oakville, CT 06779, USA
(Phone: 860-945-9329; Fax: 860-945-9468)

or from our website

www.oxbowbooks.com

Printed in Great Britain by
CPI Anthony Rowe, Chippenham

Landscapes, Documents and Maps:
Villages in Northern England and Beyond
AD 900–1250

Brian K. Roberts

Contents

	Preface	xii
1	The Nature of Rural Settlement	1
2	Of Patterns and Forms – Settlement in Northern England	29
3	Settlement Plans – Regular Forms	58
4	Settlement Plans – Variations and Complexities	88
5	Interpreting the Morphological Record	122
6	Estates and Shires – The Articulation of Local Settlement	151
7	Village Plantation – Problems and Questions	188
8	Of Drengs and Plans	223
9	Planned Villages in Europe and England	248
10	Planned Villages in England – a National Perspective	279
	Appendices	301
	Bibliography	313
	Index	325

List of Figures

Frontispiece: The site of Hartside, Northumberland (photograph)

Chapter One
Figure 1.1	Settlement patterns and forms	5
Figure 1.2	Settlement territories and plan antecedents	7
Figure 1.3	The classification of village plans	9
Figure 1.4	Rural settlement in England in the mid-nineteenth century	15
Figure 1.5	Presences of woodland in pre-Conquest England	16
Figure 1.6	Mid-nineteenth century settlement in northern England	20
Figure 1.7	The terrains of northern England	21
Figure 1.8	Presences of woodland in pre-Conquest northern England	27

Chapter Two
Figure 2.1.a	The rural settlement of the North York Moors (W)	30
Figure 2.1.b	The rural settlement of the North York Moors (E)	31
Figure 2.2	The settlement history of Stanhope, County Durham	36
Figure 2.3	The anatomy of north Yorkshire settlement plans	39
Figure 2.4	The distribution of common pastures in County Durham in about 1600	46
Figure 2.5	The distribution of medieval farms in County Durham in about 1350	47
Figure 2.6	The morphology of rural clusters – villages and hamlets – in County Durham	49
Figure 2.7	Processes of plan development	51
Figure 2.8	The analysis of settlement sites and locations	55

Chapter Three
Figure 3.1	Regular northern village plans: Appleton, Newby, Melkinthorpe, Middridge, Carleton and Carlton	59
Figure 3.2.a	The village of Acklington, Northumberland	74
Figure 3.2.b	Analysis of the village of Acklington 1248–1616	75
Figure 3.3	Maulds Meadburn, Westmorland: a field map	77
Figure 3.4	Some northern village plans: Newby, Newton, Byers Green and Escomb	79

List of Figures ix

| Figure 3.5 | Schematic model of a 'sun-divided' village | 85 |
| Figure 3.6 | Fiscal tenements in England: a summary map | 86 |

Chapter Four

Figure 4.1	The village of Cockfield, County Durham	89
Figure 4.2	Two Cumbrian villages, Great Asby and Kirkbampton	92
Figure 4.3	Two long-tofted villages in Cumberland, Hayton and Cumwhitton	95
Figure 4.4	Four examples of Cumbrian villages, Gamblesby, Melmerby, Newton Reigny and Waitby	96
Figure 4.5	Long tofted plans: two cases and a model, Little Asby and Scale Houses	98
Figure 4.6	The village and township fields of Middleton by Pickering	100
Figure 4.7	The villages and fields of Hutton Buschel and Normanby	102
Figure 4.8	The reconstructed territory of Coxwoldshire	105
Figure 4.9	Coxwoldshire settlement and tenurial profile: Coxwold, Carlton Husthwaite and Husthwaite	106
Figure 4.10	Coxwoldshire villages: Low and High Kilburn and Yearsley, with Ampleforth township	112
Figure 4.11.a	The township and village of Hutton Sessay	116
Figure 4.11.b	The township and village of Hutton Sessay (*contd.*)	117
Figure 4.12	Appleby and Helmsley town plans	119
Figure 4.13	Durham City and a chronology of planted towns in England	120

Chapter Five

Figure 5.1	Some excavations of northern villages	126
Figure 5.2.a	The basic elements of rural settlement	130
Figure 5.2.b	The diagnostic features of a planned village	131
Figure 5.3.a	The Merringtons, County Durham	136
Figure 5.3.b	The Merringtons, County Durham (*contd.*)	137
Figure 5.4	The village and township of Wheldrake, Yorkshire	141
Figure 5.5	Social structure and tenurial composition of Bishopric vills	145
Figure 5.6	Village plans in Cumberland, northern Westmorland and Durham	148

Chapter Six

Figure 6.1	County Durham, parishes, townships and terrain types	153
Figure 6.2	The estates of St. Cuthbert, County Durham	155
Figure 6.3	The estates of St. Cuthbert, County Durham	156

Figure 6.4.a	The multiple estate model	164
Figure 6.4.b	Food rents and geography: the primitive kingdom	165
Figure 6.5.a	Medieval settlement in Aucklandshire, County Durham	174
Figure 6.5.b	Medieval tenurial structures in Aucklandshire, County Durham	175
Figure 6.6	The Durham commons: a time dimension	176

Chapter Seven

Figure 7.1	Settlement in Heighingtonshire, County Durham	197
Figure 7.2	Devastation in England 902–1156	201
Figure 7.3	Woodland and waste in northern England in 1086	202
Figure 7.4	Scottish raids into northern England 1315–1345	204
Figure 7.5	A theoretical basis for settlement chronologies	206
Figure 7.6	Durham vills with a dreng, Boldon Book 1183	211
Figure 7.7	Durham vills with a probable dreng, Boldon Book 1183	213
Figure 7.8	Durham vills with a dreng, Boldon Book 1183	217
Figure 7.9	Durham vills with *firmarii*. Boldon Book 1183	218
Figure 7.10	Durham vills with a probable dreng on the estates of the Cathedral Priory	221

Chapter Eight

Figure 8.1	Settlement and social structure in Bishopric vills, County Durham	227
Figure 8.2.a	The Durham estates of St. Cuthbert 647–1183	230
Figure 8.2.b	The Durham estates of St. Cuthbert 647–1183 (*contd.*)	231

Chapter Nine

Figure 9.1.a	Traditional rural settlement forms in northern Europe	252
Figure 9.1.b	Traditional rural settlement forms in northern Europe (*contd.*)	253
Figure 9.2	Nucleation, dispersion and field systems: a model	255
Figure 9.3.a	Generalised European settlement contrasts	256
Figure 9.3.b	Generalised European settlement contrasts (*contd.*)	257
Figure 9.4.a	Major landscape types in Europe	262
Figure 9.4.b	Major landscape types in Europe – key	263
Figure 9.5	Early village plans from Europe, Körbisdorf, Vorbasse, Gasselte and Kootwijk	264
Figure 9.6	Boroughs and village origins	274
Figure 9.7	The land and sea empire of Cnut	275

List of Figures

Chapter Ten

Figure 10.1	The distribution of royal demesne in England, 1066–1086	281
Figure 10.2.a	Aspects of settlement in Yorkshire	282
Figure 10.2.b	Aspects of settlement in Yorkshire (*contd.*)	283
Figure 10.3	The genesis of the English village – one	287
Figure 10.4	The genesis of the English village – two	288
Figure 10.5	The genesis of the English village – three	289

List of Tables

Table 1.1	A brief retrospective model of settlement evolution in England	22
Table 3.1	Carlton and Middridge: patterns of fiscal tenements from 1183 to the early 17th century	69
Table 3.2	Carlton and Middridge: summary of areal context	70
Table 4.1	Lords of the Honour of Mowbray *c.* 1066–1223	103
Table 4.2	Stewards of the Honour of Mowbray *c.* 1147–1175	104
Table 7.1	Devastations in County Durham 969–1138	203
Table 8.1	Relative sequence of tenurial types on the bishopric estates in County Durham	225

Abbreviations

DB *Domesday Book*, General Editor John Morris (Phillimore and Co. Ltd., Chichester, 1975–1992); qualified by county, volume and index detail.

EHD *English Historical Documents, c. 500–1042* Whitelock, D. (ed.) 1955 (Eyre and Spottiswoode, London).

EYC *Early Yorkshire Charters*, William Farrer and C. T. Clay (eds) (Yorkshire Archaeological Society Record Series, 12 vols., 1914–1965).

NCH *A History of Northumberland*, issued by the Northumberland County History Committee, vol. 5 (Newcastle upon Tyne, 1899).

VCH *Victoria County History*; qualified by the county, the volume and the relevant pages.

Preface

This book originates in an assumption. When I moved to Durham in 1963 it was assumed that I might continue work first undertaken in the late 1940s by Harry Thorpe and encapsulated in a single paper entitled *The Green Villages of County Durham* (Thorpe 1951). My aims, so far as they were defined, differed, but in those far off days there was a robust practice in the Department of Geography at Durham of sending out all new members of staff to lead a field excursion for the new students. This has sadly been discontinued. Knowing nothing about the area other than the generalised history of the coalfield culled from the writings of that excellent geographer Arthur Smailes, and given my interests in historical geography, I was forced back to 'green villages', for I had actually read Harry Thorpe's paper on this subject and was thus an 'expert'. The acquisition of a car a year or two later, thanks to the labours of my wife – for university salaries were as pinched then as they are now – took me out into the landscapes, generally at my own charge, but eventually aided by small grants from the University of Durham. What emerged from these excursions, from fieldwork linked to third year teaching, and eventually weeklong field classes in the local region, was a sharp awareness of the presence of repetitious regularities found throughout northern nucleated settlements. The same or similar plans appeared again and again, repeating themselves with minor differences and some variations in size, while work in Yorkshire by June Sheppard, Margaret Allerston and Mary Harvey showed me that regular and part-regular plans extended into that county. While they are by no means wholly absent such forms are generally less visible in the Midlands and elsewhere, although they are often present, concealed amid more complex plans. The best exemplar of what was discovered is that of the well-known children's play-tool, *Lego*™, in which standardised square and rectangular shapes can be assembled to create a host of new forms, from model houses to dogs and even spacecraft. In fact, villages and towns proved simpler, but the presence of both underlying regularities and a uniform structural geometry provided clear *prima facie* evidence of 'planning'. This observational data, seen in cultural landscapes and on maps, remains the most cogent evidence for events and activities that, as subsequent studies have revealed, lie at the edge of active documentation. There is indeed a limited amount of material that allows the presence of plan-regularity in some Durham villages to be documented by the earlier twelfth century. Nevertheless, the bulk of the evidence is found in the villages themselves, in their plans, in the limited number of excavations of deserted sites but above all in the presence of numbers of geometrically regular plans throughout Durham, Northumberland, Cumberland and

Westmorland and Yorkshire. These pose questions that cannot readily be resolved. Were all of the plans that can be categorised as 'part regular' once wholly regular? Over what time period were the plans created? Was this short or was it long, or are we seeing the result of several waves or cycles of planning activity? Who did the planning? Why was it done? From what context or contexts did it emerge? Is it really 'planning' in the full sense, or the result of the repetition of convergent logical steps? Here were a series of research questions deeply lodged in the realities of northern landscapes. This book is a re-exploration of some of them. Further, the study is planned as a demonstration of how the methods of village plan analysis pioneered by Chris Taylor, the present author and many others, can be applied to a large region. The view though the train window seen in author's *The Making of the English Village* – the words of June Sheppard's sharp but kindly criticism – must be replaced by a slower excursion, often, as Carl Sauer noted, 'interrupted by leisurely halts to sit on vantage points and stop at question marks' (in Leighly 1963, 400).

One thing is clear: geometrically regular settlements are present throughout northern England in very, very, large quantities. There is a parallel in another area of settlement study. In spite of debates over the chronology, distribution and economic significance of village desertions, amounting to a national total that must be in excess of 2500 sites, the economic significance of what are essentially archaeologically attested changes would not now be challenged by any serious scholar. The work of Maurice Beresford, John Hurst (now both, sadly, no longer with us) and many others, has thrown light upon what was once a dark corner of economic and social history. Yet village depopulation and desertion represents only a part, perhaps 25%, of a wider rhythm of village development, florescence and change. At the present time even gross national figures are difficult to provide. Nevertheless, figures presented by the author in a *post mortem* Festschrift prepared for Harry Thorpe in 1982 suggested that while in Warwickshire about one third of 221 village plans could be classified as regular or part-regular, in Durham the figure was over 80% of some 205. It is inevitable that such figures adjust as more and more elements of a settlement pattern are identified, analysed and interpreted, but an overall figure of 80% may not be unrealistic for the proportion of regular town, village and hamlet plans of the north of England. By any measure this is an amazing total, and the present review is designed to provide a substantive foundation for future work in both Durham and the rest of England. Beginning simply with the characteristics of settlement patterns and forms, the argument proceeds, more controversially, to an examination of some of the more obscure aspects of pre-1200 land-ownership and tenure. Ultimately all rural settlement reflects rural economy, social structure and tenure interacting within the contexts provided by terrain, land quality and farming systems. These factors underlie the substance, maintenance and destruction of settlement arrangements. Beyond such pragmatics, however, there are possibilities, even visions, for the advent of the computer as a tool for data storage and research has yet to be brought to full fruition. The potential is vast, and this both fuels the imagination and sets a course for the methodology of future research in historical geography. This study incorporates and gains immeasurably from recent work based on research funded by Arts and Humanities Research Board on the wastelands of County Durham between 1150 and 1350 and from work done for, and funded by, English Heritage. My gratitude to these bodies and to my co-workers – Stuart Wrathmell, Richard Britnell, Helen Dunsford and Simon Harris – is great. To Richard I owe, *inter alia*, my careful weeding of the use of the term 'medieval' throughout the text, attempting to replace this with more specific dates, even when these are only approximations, for the seamless robe of settlement does not lend itself to easy dating.

Nevertheless, all settlements possess a through-time trajectory. They come into being; each generation then inherits what has been created and uses and adapts it before passing it on to succeeding generations. Sometimes, destruction takes place, so that only a few archaeological traces are eventually transferred. In contrast, wholly new settlements may also be added. Time, as has already been said, is a seamless robe, a continuum, and those punctuations we recognise, critical events, stages, and phases, and even centuries, are merely cultural interpretations of a single fundamental dimension within which all things exist. For the author there are conspicuous problems about how to present, indeed how to write, this book. Evidence from several disciplines needs to be integrated. Experts have to be mollified, technical terms used and defined, yet there is no reason why such a study should not be available to that 'wider' audience, who one way or another have footed the bills for the underlying research. We are not here in the realms historical linguistics, textual criticism, calendarial adjustments, or the many obscurities of the by-ways of history, where the language used necessarily forms a barrier to the uninitiated. Thus, attempts to 'make clear' do account for elements of explanation and indeed repetition in the text that some may find irritating. In addition, throughout the study there is a progression from the relatively simple and descriptive to the more intricate and complex, in which professional assumptions, embedded in all scholarship, can be less penetrable to readers, both professional and general. Nevertheless, and attempt has been made to build bridges. Furthermore, the multitude of maps and diagrams used in this study may be daunting, and the numbers used by the author in previous publications have indeed been subjected to *sotto voce* but rarely open criticism. Yes, they do indeed present a challenge, but they are the equivalent of the vast numbers of footnotes present in any serious historical study. They 'footnote' landscapes and distributions, and in spite of their many limitations they are 'evidence' that requires the reader to study, absorb and ultimately assess: they can then be accepted or rejected but, uncomfortable as it may be for some, they cannot be ignored. Where older maps are not available, plans are based upon the earliest available Ordnance Survey six inch to the mile maps, and the place-name and county plus the National Grid Reference provides adequate documentation (Harley 1964 and Oliver 1991).

This study, focusing on the evidence for village planning in the centuries before about 1250, seeks to do two things: first, to integrate the relatively new techniques of morphological analysis, used by historical geography and landscape archaeology, with the techniques of rigorous documentary analysis used by many generations of historians. Second, within this frame, the investigation will seek to demonstrate the potential of cartographic analysis, at local, regional and national scales, as a powerful research tool, particularly when aided by computer-generated graphics. Furthermore, throughout the whole study what Graeme Snooks has aptly termed *existential models*, *i.e.* empirical models of reality, will loom large as ways of generalising from specific cases (Snooks 1996, 433–4). These have the advantage that they can be tested, and paradoxically, because they are based upon many individual cases and professional experience over many years, the models may transcend even errors and misinterpretations in the particular examples cited. The ingredient of reiteration found in using the same case in different contexts reveals in measure the author's own process of testing and re-evaluation of evidence. The argument is illustrated by numerous maps and diagrams, and these fall into three categories; first, the models generalise and draw together much empirical evidence, second, the distribution maps both describe and pose questions, while third, the numerous settlements plans correspond to the footnoting of conventional historical presentations… 'Here be evidence' for what the author believes is happening. I would not be honest if I did not say that this study, while ostensibly being an analysis of the macro-region of northern England, really seeks to demonstrate the checks and opportunities on the bridge between generalisations at a national, or even a continental, scale and often elegant, accessible but essentially myopic local studies. The ground between these two scales is fertile soil, worthy of tillage and with great potential, although there is much wood felling and stone-clearance needed before the rich but often intractable soils of the middle scales can produce their latent harvests. Perhaps a rather ponderous analogy, but in this I am, undoubtedly, presenting a challenge, to geographers, historians and archaeologists alike!

A word is needed on terminology: where highly technical terms are used an effort is made to define them at the first time of use, and then the simplest version is adopted to continue the chain of the argument. This is to make this study as accessible as possible. Some consistency has been imposed. More particularly the subtle distinctions between *villan, villein, bondsman* and the like are not dwelt upon. The terms villan and bondsman are seen as essentially interchangeable, while the term 'villein' is in general avoided, as it is more applicable to a thirteenth and fourteenth century contexts. A definitive study of the regional and temporal ranges of these terms has yet to be created. In the broad temporal framework treated in the study even the word 'farmers' becomes loaded, but I have used this in its most general sense, men and women who farmed the land in order to survive, retaining the Latin *firmarii* for those rent payers so described in the documents. Even such words as 'village' and 'town' can give rise to confusion, and there are instances where I use the word *town* in its older sense of 'a village', *i.e.* a *-tun*, as seen most clearly in *township*, a territory smaller than a parish, indeed part of a parish, but often supporting a nucelated hamlet or village. Finally, for the metrically minded an English acre is two fifths of a hectare, namely there are two and a half acres in a hectare. However, a Durham acre, measured with a 21–foot land rod rather than a 16.5–foot standard rod was larger. In other cases rods could have been 18 or 20 feet in length. Where possible I have been specific. Where necessary I have given in-text conversions to metric units. Somewhat anachronistically I have retained the use of the pre-1972 English counties. A map in the Appendices shows these. Historically the former have been units of administration, of taxation and of record keeping, so that they still retain a historical integrity.

Finally, it remains to acknowledge the many scholars whose work I have plundered to create this volume. I alone am responsible for misinterpretations and misuse of this material. When I use their work, and am even gently critical of giants, F. W. Maitland, F. Seebohm, Sir Paul Vinogradoff, M. M. Postan, Sir Henry Clifford Darby, Maurice Beresford and John Hurst, and – as the charters say – 'and may others', I am all too aware that I stand upon their shoulders. To name more names would be invidious, but the Bibliography attests the depth of my debts. For June Sheppard there is a lasting gratitude: I owe her more than I can tell, while my long hours of discussion with Stuart Wrathmell, Richard Britnell, Helen Dunsford and Simon Harris have helped me formulate my ideas over the last decade. Paul Harvey and Chris Taylor have also often been present with quiet support. To English Heritage, in the person of David Stocker, I owe another lasting debt, for the work he contracted allowed, indeed forced, my horizons to open to the national scene, and this is evident in the content of this volume. In fact the basic analysis of the Durham tenures was done over thirty years ago, following work I did with David Austin, and it has taken a third of a century to create a matrix within which those materials can, at last, be presented. The perpetrators of the Research Assessment Exercise, seeking 'scholarship' as instant as 'A hamburger and chips, fast as you can!' need reminding of this simple fact.

Finally, but by no means least, I wish to thank two groups of people: first, the many academic, secretarial and technical staff of the Department of Geography in Durham. Over many, many, years I have been given sustained support and friendship and provided with much merriment. For this I am deeply grateful. Second, the debt I owe the farmers and rural communities of England is vast. Their open-handedness has been without parallel and I find in many of the working farmers I have met a 'scholarship', seen in an understanding of field and place, which cannot be equalled. Finally, my thanks are due to the 'ladies of Oxbow' for their patience, kindness and support.

Chapter One

The Nature of Rural Settlement

One of the characteristic features of rural settlement throughout the whole of the north of England is the presence of 'green villages', hamlets, villages, or even market towns, whose interior is, or was once, dominated by a large open space. Sometimes, particularly in those rather larger places that have crossed the threshold to become a town, the open area is now surfaced, cobbled or paved, to provide a hard stand for markets or car parking. In the large majority of rural cases, in the damp climate of Britain, the surviving open spaces are now given over to grass with some surfaced roadways and many unsurfaced, muddy and potholed tracks. Nevertheless, once an 'eye' for plan analysis has been cultivated, the presence of long-destroyed open spaces can often be detected. Perhaps most villages and hamlets once possessed interior greens, but in the north the greens are often strikingly rectangular and formal. Of course, some rural greens have been wholly enclosed, with gardens pushed forwards onto the former open area, while in others buildings, cottages, public houses, a school, almshouses and even the village church, have been intruded into the former space, resulting in a network of small lanes, garden plots, dwellings and outbuildings. Nevertheless, this internal irregularity is often edged by the shadowy survivals of more structured arrangements of houses, farms and cottages, marking the limits of a former open space.

It is the large numbers of such greens throughout the north of England that raise questions. Although the green is undoubtedly important, varying in size, shape and function, the real issue lies in the character of the boundaries that limit and contain the open area. In practice standard units of building land, *compartments,* each comprising six, eight, ten or more standard house plots, *tofts or garths,* are – in settlement after settlement – assembled to create a variety of plans. These important configurations are the basic blocks of the 'Lego' system noted in the introduction to this study. Each settlement is unique, yet plan families can be identified, all possessing an underlying unity, inviting comparison with others of similar form. There can be little doubt that at root, somewhere, there is a 'village idea', a concept that in some way defines a 'normal' layout. Indeed, there are powerful parallels here with the architectural elements of churches, in which chancel, nave, transepts, tower and porch, represent elements that can be variously combined to give a multitude of plans. Much of the author's early work was concerned with discovering, defining and providing the terms for this 'grammar' of settlement construction. Of course, classification and terminology should never be ends in themselves, but they do create valuable tools, ways of grasping and manipulating the immense complexity of the observable features of the real world. For this reason classification, the means of handling a very large sample and moving towards general concepts, will be discussed below. In the case of churches we are indebted to nineteenth century scholars such as Rickman for providing modern scholarship with both a fundamental terminology and a basic chronology. Later work has modified the original definitions and concepts, but a contemporary paper discussing a fine adjustment in chronology, such as the precise date of the west front of the Norman Leominster priory, builds upon earlier studies (Hillaby 1993). In fact, while a great deal of foundation work has been done upon rural settlement, terminology remains rather rudimentary, while the deeper questions of developmental chronology have only been tackled during the last thirty or so years. This book is a contribution to an exploration of settlement forms and patterns that aims to provide explanation rather than mere description. In this it is a contribution to both historical geography and economic history.

Questions of Terminology

Further discussion must use technical terms and these need to be defined. First, throughout this discussion traditional, 'historical', pre-1974 county boundaries and names have been used. There is no easy answer to this question because, while the post-1974 administrative counties are now embedded and widely used, the older counties, with some minor changes, persisted for over a thousand years, and all surviving historical materials, both governmental and local, relate to the framework they provide. For this reason they have been used here, and to assist the reader a final map of this study (Appendix III), shows 'traditional' and modern northern counties superimposed within a framework of the National Grid. More particularly, there are no simple definitions of villages and hamlets, although even though most of us, indeed well over eight out of every ten live in towns, we all have an idea of what is meant when the term 'village' is used. Villages are 'a self-contained group of houses and associated buildings, usually in a country area… larger than a hamlet but smaller than a town' (*Oxford English Dictionary*): a neatly circumlocuitous definition that begs many questions. A church is usually, but by no means invariably, present. Certainly when compared with towns villages tend to cover less ground, have fewer people, and today have few public buildings, no banks, no large stores and generally no markets. In short, at present villages differ from towns in their physical extent, their population and their function, but drawing a line between the two is never easy and will depend upon where and when the observations are being made (Roberts 1996b, 15–19). In historical terms definitions are even more difficult, for a place that today is no more than a village may, two hundred or so years ago, have been a thriving if small market town. Similarly, at the other end of the scale there are problems of distinguishing between a village and a hamlet. This lower threshold can be arbitrarily set in terms of the number of people, the number of houses, or the presence of a church, a shop or a garage but once again the passage of time may result in growth or contraction (Thorpe in Watson and Sissons 1964, 359; Everson *et al.* 1991, 28–41; Roberts 1987, 10.9). Without labouring definition, a village in this study comprises a cluster of dwellings, mainly inhabited by farmers. By way of qualification the terms 'small' and 'large' will be applied where appropriate. Where a place subsidiary to a village is definitely involved, or there is a need to portray the concept of a smaller, simpler, cluster, the term 'hamlet' will be used. The word 'town' is applied to a settlement sufficiently large to possess urban characteristics, *i.e.* a significantly more complex plan, larger area and more buildings, generally a settlement in possession of market rights (Beresford and Finberg 1973). To complicate matters further it is necessary to point out that Pevsner was wholly correct when he created the elegant term 'townish villages' to describe some settlements of north-eastern England. These are settlements sufficiently large to embrace the area of a small town, and indeed may once have had market rights, but for much of their history they have been of no more than very local administrative importance. Similar questions of definition also occur at the level of the individual farmstead. While it is not proposed to reiterate arguments presented elsewhere about the nature of 'linked farmstead clusters', 'linked hamlet clusters', 'shrunken settlements' and the like, these are all part of any complex and deeply rooted settlement pattern (Roberts 1987). This diversity reflects two powerful forces. On one hand the creation and growth of differing types of settlements at different periods of time, in response to local or regional economic needs, and on the other the break-down of earlier settlement forms and patterns as depopulation, desertion and adjustment take place. Nevertheless, the use of such terms as settlement *pattern* and settlement *form* shows that when thinking on the broader scale, county or national levels, other concepts concerning the relationships between individual settlements and others within a given local area become important. We must now turn to these more general definitions.

Patterns and Forms – Some Definitions

The idea of a 'pattern of settlement' is an abstraction. It is only seen clearly on a map or in a low altitude flight across the countryside such as can now be seen in 'Getmapping's' *Photographic Atlas of England*. Such views have been largely invisible to all but the most recent generations, although hilltops sometimes gave a wide perspective. More familiar are the characteristics of villages as distinct places, made up of roads, dwellings, outbuildings, open spaces and churches, the shop and the pub, seen as living spaces or holiday locations. Further, an individual settlement can take the form of dwellings strung out along a street, arranged around a green or clustered tightly around the junction of several roads. In practice the study of village settlement focuses upon many aspects of its character and must use several scales of investigation. The location (or *situation*), the ground plan (or *form*), the character of the *site* (the land upon which the settlement is placed) and the nature of the buildings – the *vernacular architecture* – are all concerned with physical aspects. Features of a settlement's *function* are seen in its population, demographic structure and the work the inhabitants do, while the degree to which they interact, are related, quarrel, make merry or work together touches social dynamics (Cohen 1982, 1–24). All of these characteristics exist today, but all possess a dimension in deep time, *i.e.* a village might have existed for many hundreds of years. Of the earlier Norman village, however, little may survive other than a few fragments of stone incorporated into the church, while traces of the people may survive in the churchyard, but also in the genetic make-up of contemporary families (Howell 1976, fig. 1). More pragmatically, the inventory represented by the words *site*, *situation*, *form*, and *function*, together with *architecture* form an essential mnemonic when out in the field, and is applicable in any settlement anywhere in the world. To these five words must be added the all-important dimension of *time*, for as is being stressed, all settlements, occupy locations in time as well as space. Though time they change and within time they are adapted for the use of new generations.

Figure 1.1 provides an illustration of the links between patterns and forms and suggests that several scales of enquiry are possible when dealing with the structural aspects of settlement. First, the top row in the figure represents a generalised model of the distribution of settlements throughout the landscape. These create distinctive and complex patterns on the land, and tell of presence or absence, frequency or scarcity and if this is in a regular distribution or a random scatter. In practice even the most 'random' of scatters may have an underlying cause, and in fact is by no means random, being closely related to a particular set of drainage conditions or the existence of a productive soil type. Second (Fig. 1.1, middle row), each pattern is made up of individual units of settlement, towns and single farms as well as villages and hamlets and scattered dwellings. Here they are shown separately as three patterns, which are then combined in the last model. A third level of resolution is to be found in a detailed study of individual plans (Fig. 1.1, bottom row), settlement forms, extending to the examination of individual settlement plans and even the arrangements within individual dwellings and other buildings. These varied levels provide a framework within which the links between settlement characteristics, culture, economy and land can be evaluated. No longer need this be mere exhortation, lacking an accessible context, for the *Photographic Atlas of England* now provides a direct view of the reality in question, of the substance of this study – the settlement landscape of England. Many approaches are possible. In this study, adopting an historical geographical approach, the broad distinction between patterns and forms is used as a framework for discussion.

Of course, a given settlement does not by any means have a single function. In England, most rural settlements, farmsteads, hamlets, villages and market towns developed to serve the needs of the countryside, as bases from which the land could be farmed, with the market towns forming trading centres for the exchange of both basic and luxury goods. In the last century, however, there was a steady transformation into

The Nature of Rural Settlement

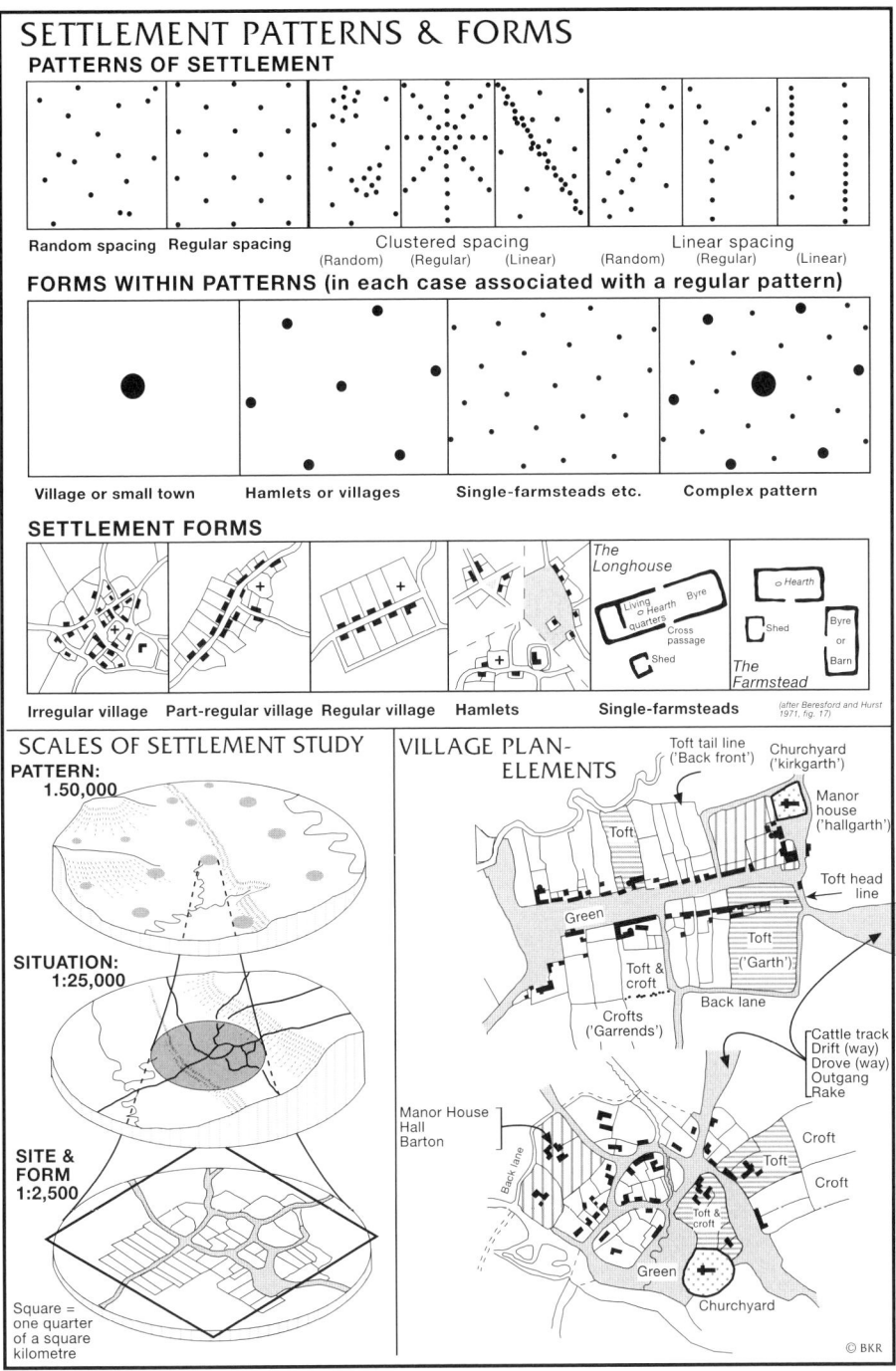

Fig. 1.1 Settlement patterns and forms

commuter and dormitory settlements, and as farms change and lands are consolidated, this change is extending to individual farmsteads and cottages, with second homes and holiday conversions pervading all. This is interesting in itself because of the complex processes of change involved. Nevertheless, in historical terms these processes are normally highly destructive, for while buildings are often subject to statutory protection, even during restoration and reconstitution, many subtle details of the surrounding lands, yards and gardens are easily and regularly destroyed. The pace of this destruction is accelerating steadily. Barely visible earthworks are as much a part of a settlement's history as are Norman stones in the church or seventeenth century probate inventories relating to village farmsteads. Slight platforms or hollows, traces of the continuation of a boundary, the physical qualities of a boundary, or a slight change in level, can all acquire historical meaning when placed within an appropriate context.

Of Space and Place

At this point one tricky problem must be defined. In Figure 1.2 the circle represents a 'settlement territory'. In the south of England this would often be a *parish*, an area of land able to support a parish church, but in the north it would normally be a *township*, land supporting a local unit of settlement, usually comprising a group of farmers. In the south of England the township, or *tithing*, often corresponds with the parish. Initially, in the far distant past, this grouping is likely to have involved bonds of kinship or marriage, but as population grew and lords grew more powerful, tenancies developed. In some areas, and notably in the north and west, a single parish may comprise several townships (Winchester 1990; Sylvester 1969, 166–89) indeed as many as ten or more township units may be grouped together to form a parish. In practice such territories differ in shape, and as the small schematic diagrams at the top right of the figure show, township and parish shapes are apt to vary in response to the character and distribution of the underlying land resources. Turning to the top left of the diagram, the circle is divided so as to show eight possible ways in which the farmsteads of a single township can be distributed. These extend from wholly nucleated to dispersed, and the same number of farmsteads is present in each sector of the model. Effectively all classifications of patterns define jumps in what in practice is really a continuum of types. Here we have the nub of a key historical problem: just because maps created in the middle decades of the nineteenth century show a 'village', and a 'vill' or community appears in documentation before 1250, we cannot assume that the settlement was wholly or even partially nucleated. Early documents are not concerned with settlement forms: they deal with administrative units, which may support varied types of settlement pattern. Furthermore, we cannot even assume that villages are of that date, still less the details of their plans. Even when we have clear evidence for a church containing fabric from the twelfth or thirteenth century, the church may

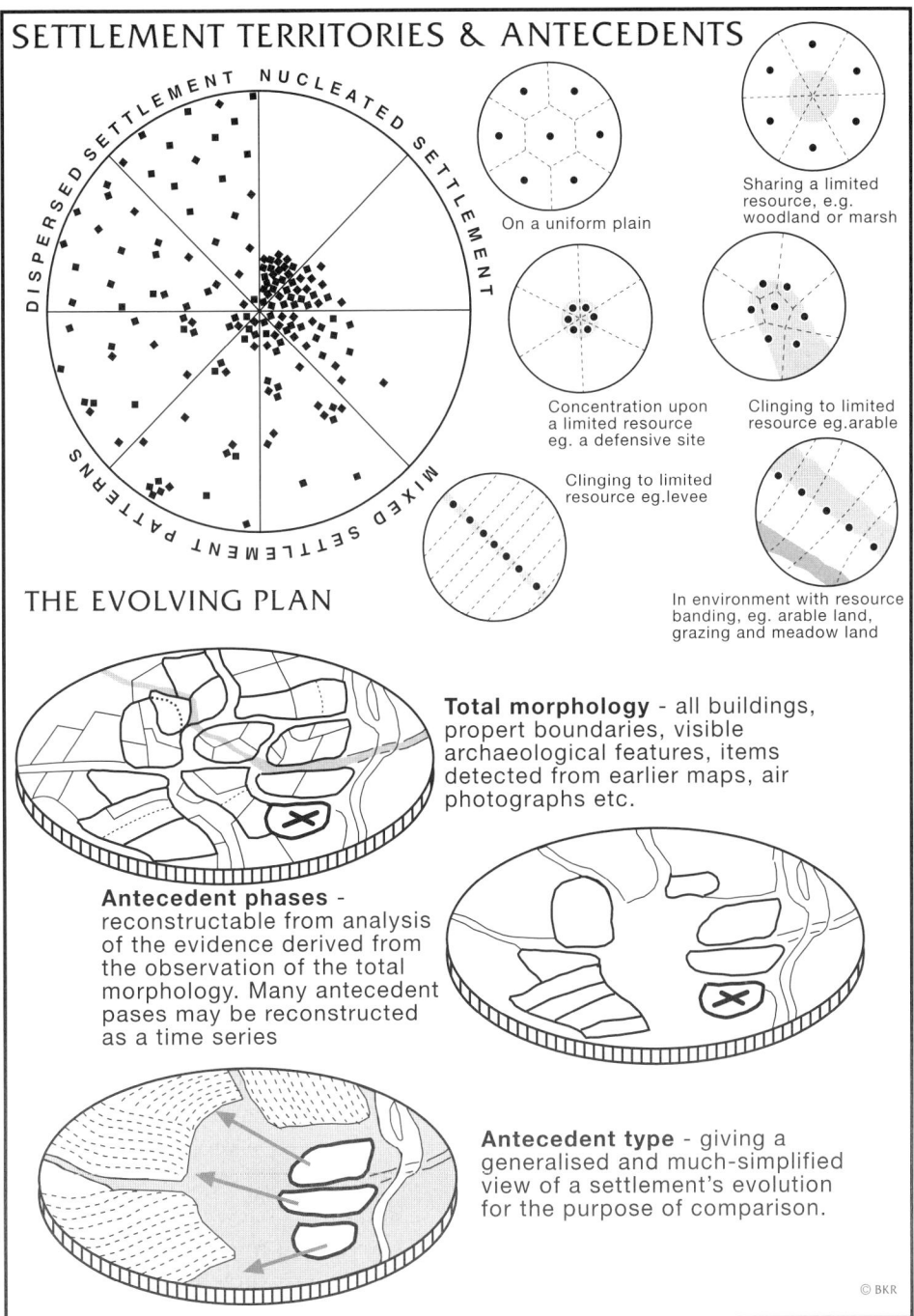

Fig 1.2 Settlement territories and plan antecedents

then have been set in isolation, or, as is more likely, been built near the dwelling – a 'hall' – of the principle landowner in the township, its 'lord'. In many senses this is a simple point, yet the fact that it has been taken on board by archaeologists, historical geographers and historians in the last three decades has added a necessary dimension to thinking about the on-ground realities of settlement. While it has to be admitted that there is increasingly concrete evidence for the existence of large numbers of villages by about 1200, it now appears likely that what we think of as 'nucleated villages' were only gradually appearing in the two or three centuries before and, indeed, even after that date. Thus, any settlement pattern we can see upon a map or an air photograph is the result of development through time. Questions always arise about its content, the ingredients or elements of which it is made – towns, villages, hamlets and scattered farmsteads and dwellings – and chronology, the time span during which these have developed. A glance at the *Photographic Atlas of England* reveals, as nothing else can, what is involved in these questions.

Further links between patterns and forms are shown in Figure 1.1. Beginning with the most complex settlement pattern, in this case mixed, comprising hamlets, villages and a small town, or farmsteads, hamlets and one larger village – either is possible, for the symbols are ambiguous – the diagram then moves on to suggest that there are fundamentally three distinctive types of village plan. These will be discussed later, but the fact that the shapes of individual settlements vary is a crucial if obvious observation. Some clusters are utterly irregular, lacking any semblance of a regular geometry – termed *agglomerations* – while others are clearly based upon assemblages of rectangles, with the compartments that carry the farmsteads and other dwellings – tofts – being largely rectangular in form. In these *regular* plans the compartments from which they are constructed form *rows*, and while most villages and hamlets are based upon two compartments, with a street or green between them, particular plans may be assembled from three, four five or even more compartmental building blocks. Inevitably, some settlements fall in between, and may be considered as *part regular,* while others exhibit no obvious structure and are perceived as *irregular*. Figure 1.3 shows a much more complex classification of village plans developed from three criteria, namely, the identification of a basic shape seen in rows or agglomerations, the degree of regularity present (for even agglomerations may be regular, for instance when arranged in a radial manner), and the presence or absence of an integral green. This allows the identification of eleven village plan types. This is a classification discussed in detail elsewhere (Roberts 1987). Nevertheless, this is a necessary part of understanding nucleated settlements, and while it need not be laboured excessively, it underlies the symbols used to depict villages and hamlets on all of the distribution maps discussed below. It represents a 'way of thinking about' and a 'way of seeing' what can be observed on the map, the air photograph and in the field. The significance of such observations will be assessed later: suffice at this stage to point out that many regular plans could result from a degree of deliberate planning, an ability and desire to organise and arrange

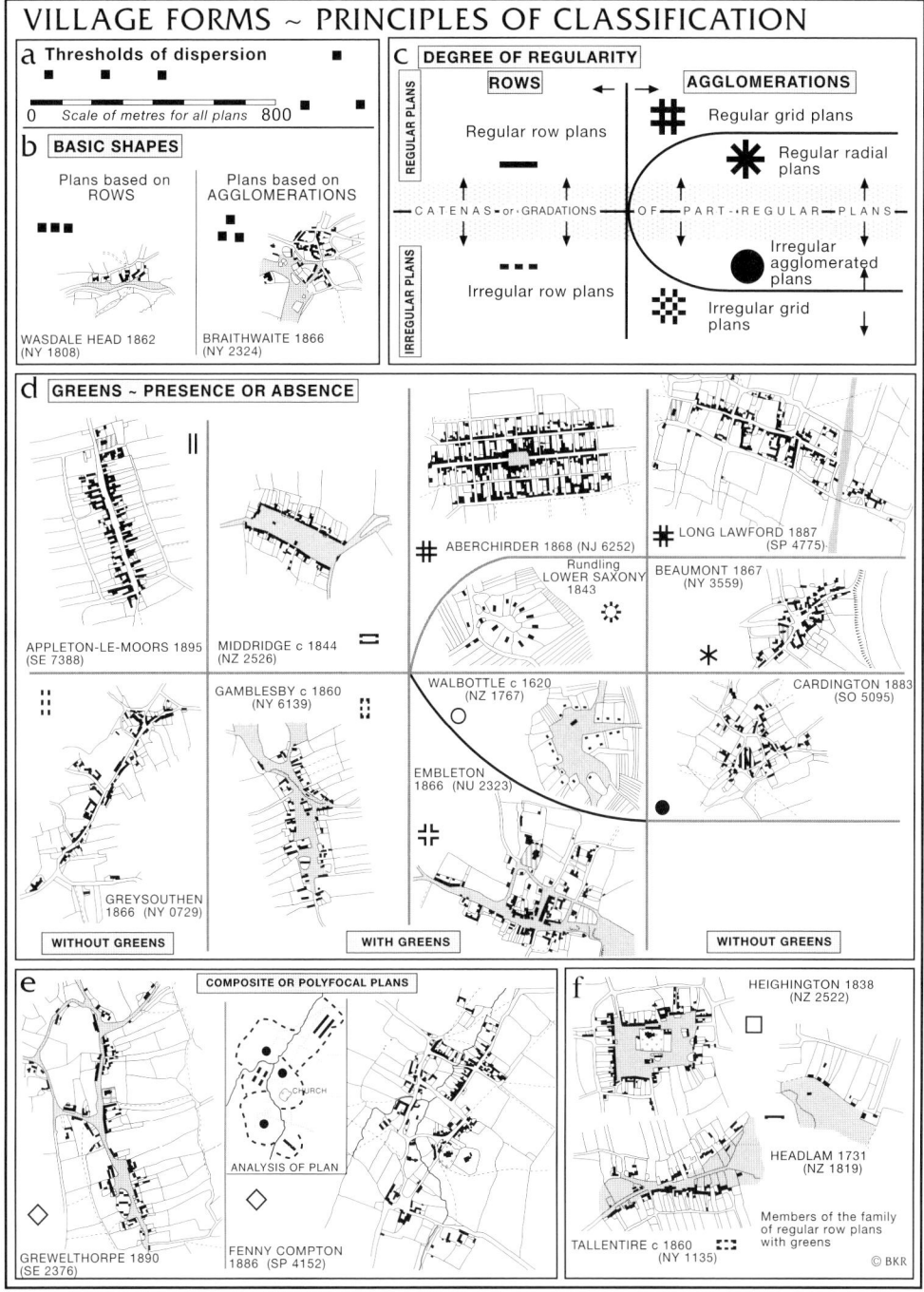

Fig. 1.3 The classification of village plans

space. Organised geometry can hardly be wholly accidental. In spite of David Sturdy's note with reference to town development that 'roads and lanes of various dates running off approximately at right angles to a spine road do not constitute "planning"', the accumulated evidence for regularities within the structured geometry of settlement plans, both urban and rural, cannot be ignored (Sturdy 1995, 191). But how can these 'regularities' be identified and, indeed, what can settlement forms really tell us?

Place and Shape – Village Plan Elements

The study of settlement forms has long been a traditional part of geography. Briefly, the study is of importance because in more primitive societies, settlement forms are often closely related to the social divisions and economic conditions (Fraser 1969). Furthermore, England's present settlement system, the basic distribution of settled places, undoubtedly owes much to the centuries immediately before and after the Norman Conquest of 1066. Our understanding of Anglo-Saxon society has been greatly enhanced by the emergence of a body of work upon their settlements (Rahtz 1976, 49–98; Hooke 1998, 105–38). This is not to denigrate the study of burial customs, place-names, social obligations and kinship ties, boat-building and other technologies, including agricultural techniques or even the deeper mysteries of sculptural styles: to each its place in a wider pattern of understanding. Settlement forms, as discussions in Chapter 5 will show, reflect a wider matrix of forces at work within a given society and are themselves the end-product of complex interactions between many factors. These are as diverse as the physical framework, demographic circumstances, proprietary and tenurial arrangements, the degree of social stratification present or the strength of kinship ties, inheritance practices, the types of farming practised, the nature of the field systems used and even the nature of plough technology. A thread running though all settlement studies, and evident within the discussion so far, is the question of how to make sense of the tremendous diversity found both in the present and in the past. What place does an individual settlement occupy within the larger scheme of things, be this a prehistoric hut-cluster, a Roman villa and its associated ancillary settlements, a village plan of the period between 1140 and 1300, or indeed the harshly serrated rows of a nineteenth century planted mining village?

There has been a tendency for classifications of rural settlement forms to be cumbersome to the point of being unusable or so simple that they merely serve as superficial generalisations. The generalisation used here, regular, part regular and irregular, derives from important insights communicated to the author by June Sheppard, and forms an essential basis for his own classification. All villages and hamlets are in practice made up of two distinctive sorts of space, private space and public space. They differ from each other in both their sites and situations and in the distinctive and individual ways in which these two categories of space are arranged (Fig. 1.1, bottom right). Private space is made up of the farmsteads, cottages and other houses, together with their outbuildings, yards, gardens, and home enclosures. The basic building-block is a dwelling, with yards, outbuildings and a plot of land bounded by a fence, hedge or stone wall, to which the author, with conscious archaism, has applied the word *toft*, although throughout the north of England the word *garth* is normally used. A convenient neutral term is house plot, but *toft* was chosen to be universally meaningful throughout England, the alliterative phrase 'toft and croft', *i.e.* the house plot itself with any other attached enclosure, is normal in documentation of the period 1150–1250. Hairs could be split further, concerning the dimensions of such a plot, the presence or absence of any internal divisions, but while entertaining for those closely involved, these create tedious discussions. Suffice to say, the toft or garth is usually clearly separate from the surrounding field lands, although on occasions this distinction can be blurred. In some cases a small enclosed piece of field land can be seen to have been added to the end of the toft, and such an intake is best termed a croft, although examples have been found called 'Garrends', *i.e.* 'garth end' in Durham. In Durham also, the line where the tofts end, to the rear of a settlement, and meet the arable of the fields was traditionally, succinctly and appropriately termed the 'backside'. There are in addition other special pieces of private land, together with their associated structures, namely the church and churchyard (kirk and kirk-garth), the manor house and manor farm (hall and hall-garth) together with such structures as the mill and the smithy. Finally, there was the ale house, now often the village 'local', a public house, still set upon the open space of the green (Roberts 1987, 20–21).

All of these plots of private land are set in a wider context. We may think of this as originally comprising public land, land formerly used by and in measure in the care of the group of farmers with rights in the territory, even if these were 'held' from a superior lord. Thus, footpaths, access lanes, public highways and open spaces or greens within a village or hamlet are features normally distinct from the wider context of communally cultivated field lands, the common grazings and those important routes for use by the general public, the kings' highways. The cattle drift, or outgang, leading from the common pastures to the green blurs this picture somewhat, for there will normally be no sharp distinction between the green, the passageway and the common pasture to which it leads. Nevertheless, the distinction is real enough and can still occasionally lead to lawsuits between local authorities and private landowners. These parts, let us call them *plan elements*, make up all villages and hamlets – and, for that matter, even single farmsteads – although all may not of course be present. Further, while each village is individual, the repetition of particular and distinctive arrangements of these basic ingredients permits the recognition of plan-families. This enables us to define a series of plan-types, each being representative of a wider plan-family that embraces the extended range of sub-types and variants that are found in the landscape. Classification does not explain what can be seen, but it is a useful beginning.

As noted earlier, the classification of plan-types shown in Figure 1.3 is based upon three principle variables in the arrangement of public and private space. First, all village or hamlet sized clusters tend to be made up of either *rows*, with buildings and tofts arranged more or less in a line, or *agglomerations*, with buildings and tofts grouped closely together in a roughly circular order. This is seen in box a. Some settlements (box e) are seen to be made up of both rows and agglomerations *i.e.* they comprise two, or sometimes more, distinctive plan-types, a fact of vital significance in understanding their nature, for such discontinuities may reflect growth phases or the presence of social or functional contrasts. A nucleation of this type, made up of two distinct but physically joined plans, is said to be *composite* or *polyfocal*. A second point, wholly crucial to the argument in this study, is the fact that the plots or tofts making up a settlement will vary in character. Rows or agglomerations may vary structural layout, and may be irregular or regular. This essentially means that the tofts of which the substance of the settlement is constructed can be haphazard in shape, with the buildings arranged randomly, or they may be rectangular (more rarely wedge-shaped), and the buildings ordered either in straight or gently curved lines or even in a circle. A regular agglomeration appears either when the roads and plots form a grid or are arranged in a radial pattern. Thirdly and finally, all of the types defined so far may or may not possess a substantial green, an area of open grassy ground incorporated as an integral part of the plan. This distinction is important. Throughout many parts of England, particularly in the east and the west, settlements are found which bear a place-name incorporating the suffix 'green', as in Saxstead Green, Danzey Green, Tile Green and the like (Roberts and Wrathmell 2002, 54–56). These green areas, residuals of once very extensive commons, often lie at the edge of settlements or even townships or parishes. They differ markedly from the central, integral greens present in the north of England and are *not* 'green villages'. They are settlements which grew up piecemeal on and around existing patches of common waste – greens – generally in the thirteenth, fourteenth and even later centuries, and normally they are neither parish nor township centres. In County Durham only one village, Byers Green, actually has the word 'green' as part of the place-name, and this, as will be shown in Chapter 5, is an exception that proves the rule. In practice, distinction between a wide street and a true integral green is a fine one and there is in fact a continuous gradation from one to the other. Particularly in the period before hard road surfaces the distinction between one tract of mud, stones, ruts and struggling grass and another tract of struggling grass, mud, stones and ruts, must have been difficult to ascertain. The pragmatic definition of local recognition may be crucial: if local people think they have a green, and it is enshrined in local terminology and custom, then they have a green. The issue is clouded by the fact that many have disappeared without trace, for not all have been formally registered as a green under the common land regulations (Denman *et al.* 1967, 202–12). Suffice to say that as with many aspects of settlement this question of definition is a troubled one, and a degree of pragmatism is required. In areas outside England, indeed outside Europe and particularly in sub-tropical and tropical regions, the open space need not be grassed and such plazas comprise no more than open, dusty, ground, largely free of vegetation (Uhlig 1972, 165–8). Greens and plazas are universal features of nucleated settlements, but nonetheless, their character, location and usage are important.

Eleven basic plan families can be defined on the basis of the three key variables, but there are of course others, such as size, complexity, building density and degree of plot fragmentation. Figure 1.3 incorporates examples of actual villages drawn from all over the British Isles, with one case from Europe. Clearly, this matrix uses 'good' examples, of rather clear-cut types. However, a subtlety of the matrix lies in the arrangement of the cases, for each plan-type defined here can be thought of as one end of a gradation of types. In this series, to which the term catena – generally used in soil science – can be applied, where each type grades gradually into the plan-type found in an adjacent cell. That is to say, examples of plans exist which are intermediate between the two plan types represented by a cell (Roberts 1987, 24–31). In this way the extended range of sub-types and variants that are found in the landscape can be incorporated into the matrix, indeed, all plans can be classified and allocated a location in the grid. This is most clearly to be seen in the examples of Appleton-le-Moors and Middridge: if the central street of the former were gradually widened, then at first a narrow street green would appear, and eventually a rather broad street green such as that at Middridge. These arguments have been presented with much visual detail in a previous book and will not be recounted at length here (Roberts 1987). Two points suffice: first, the matrix is and remains a powerful tool of analysis, allowing changes in plans to be grasped, discussed and analysed. The terminology used is insidious, and while the reader may not be enthused by 'a regular two-row street green' plan or 'an irregular agglomeration with an integral green', it remains a fact that these types can be identified and will appear in the discussions to follow. Second, the 'green villages' of County Durham that provide the initiating material for this study occupy distinct locations in the matrix (Thorpe 1951). Middridge is an absolutely typical example, a 'regular two-row street green plan' although less regular examples such as that at Gamblesby, in Cumberland, also appear in Durham. More complex and more simple layouts also appear, such as at Heighington, a 'regular multiple row green village', and Headlam, a 'regular single row green village'. The 'green villages' of Durham all tend to be examples of regular plans based upon rows, and built of compartments that while they are 'regular', nevertheless lack the rigid and formal layout to be seen in the planted eighteenth century settlement of Aberchirder (Lockhart 1980, 249–70). The compartments possess a large degree of Euclidian regularity, *i.e.* they approximate to a rectangle that has then been subdivided ladder-wise to create a series of tofts, and indeed Aberchirder was conceived as a town. The geometric layout is by no means inelastic, and indeed may be rather curved. Invariably the layout is 'softened', *i.e.* even the formal geometry of Appleton-le-Moors lacks wholly straight lines or sharp corners, but nevertheless, the underlying idea of the plan undoubtedly derives from an idealised version based on two compartments of tofts. It can hardly have arisen by chance. We may suppose that the translation of an idea to the realities of local terrain, plus the imprint of time, involving the constant replacement and slight re-ordering of property boundaries, underlies such softening. Subdivision of an original pattern of tofts must also have taken place. All these changes serve to blur the original concept. Of course, in this short overview there is much speculation. Can the antiquity of these plans be proved? Can the process of subdivision be documented?

To conclude this introduction, three key words, *pattern, form* and *function*, underpin the questions to be asked in this study of the historical geography of villages in the north of England. Ideal circumstances would be to be able to accumulate evidence that would enable a discussion of each of these aspects for time slices separated by perhaps two hundred years, 1800, 1600, 1400, 1200 and 1000. However, any study of the historical geography of settlement is inevitably limited by the availability of evidence, so that the exercise becomes a test of ingenuity. How far, given the limitations of what evidence is available and given its bias, its variable quality, its uneven distribution in both space and time, can we begin to assemble answers to fundamental questions concerning settlement patterns, forms, functions, and the processes of temporal and spatial change? This is the challenge. In this discussion, while some guidance concerning the wider issues is provided in the form of comparisons and references, the thrust of the argument will be concerned with the physical character of the northern village, and will range from Northumberland to Yorkshire and from County Durham to Cumberland and Westmorland. Further, the changing fortunes of buildings will not be considered, and nor, except for providing brief context, will the changing fortunes of the inhabitants. Nevertheless, the north of England cannot be understood in isolation. Placed as it is between England and Scotland, the area can only be understood in this wider context, while the European dimension provides a broader setting. The setting in England must first be explored.

National Contexts: Rural Settlement and Woodlands

Two maps, Figures 1.4 and 1.5 provide panoramic views and allow the settlement characteristics of northern England to be placed in context. The first is a representation of the distribution of settlement in the whole of England in the middle decades of the nineteenth century using the Old Series one inch to one mile maps (Fig. 1.4). This map provides a well-documented and important section across time. The second map reaches back in time, a thousand years and more, to explore the distribution of woodland and cleared lands at, and indeed before, the Norman Conquest of 1066 (Fig. 1.5)

The distribution of settlement in Figure 1.4 cannot be closely dated because its source maps, reproductions of the First Edition Old Series one inch to one mile maps published by Harry Margary (1975–1981) range in date from 1809 to1866. This version of the data downplays the importance of urban settlements, which are merely shown as small dots, but integrates two distributions relating to rural settlement. On one hand, a single dot is used to show the presence of individual nucleated settlements, be these hamlets, villages and towns, and these are subjectively size-graded in such a

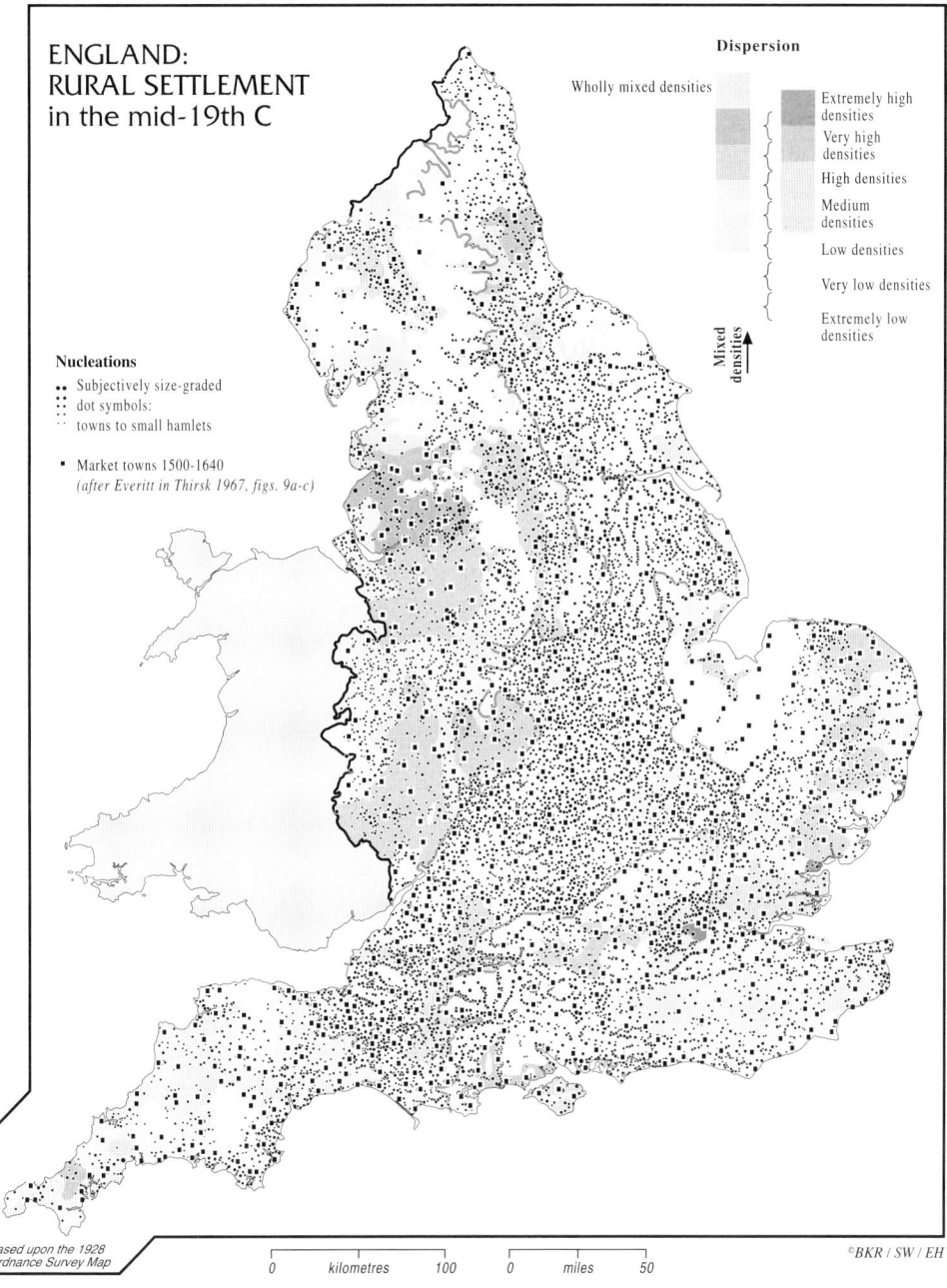

Fig. 1.4 Rural settlement in England in the mid-ninteenth century

16 *Landscapes, Documents and Maps*

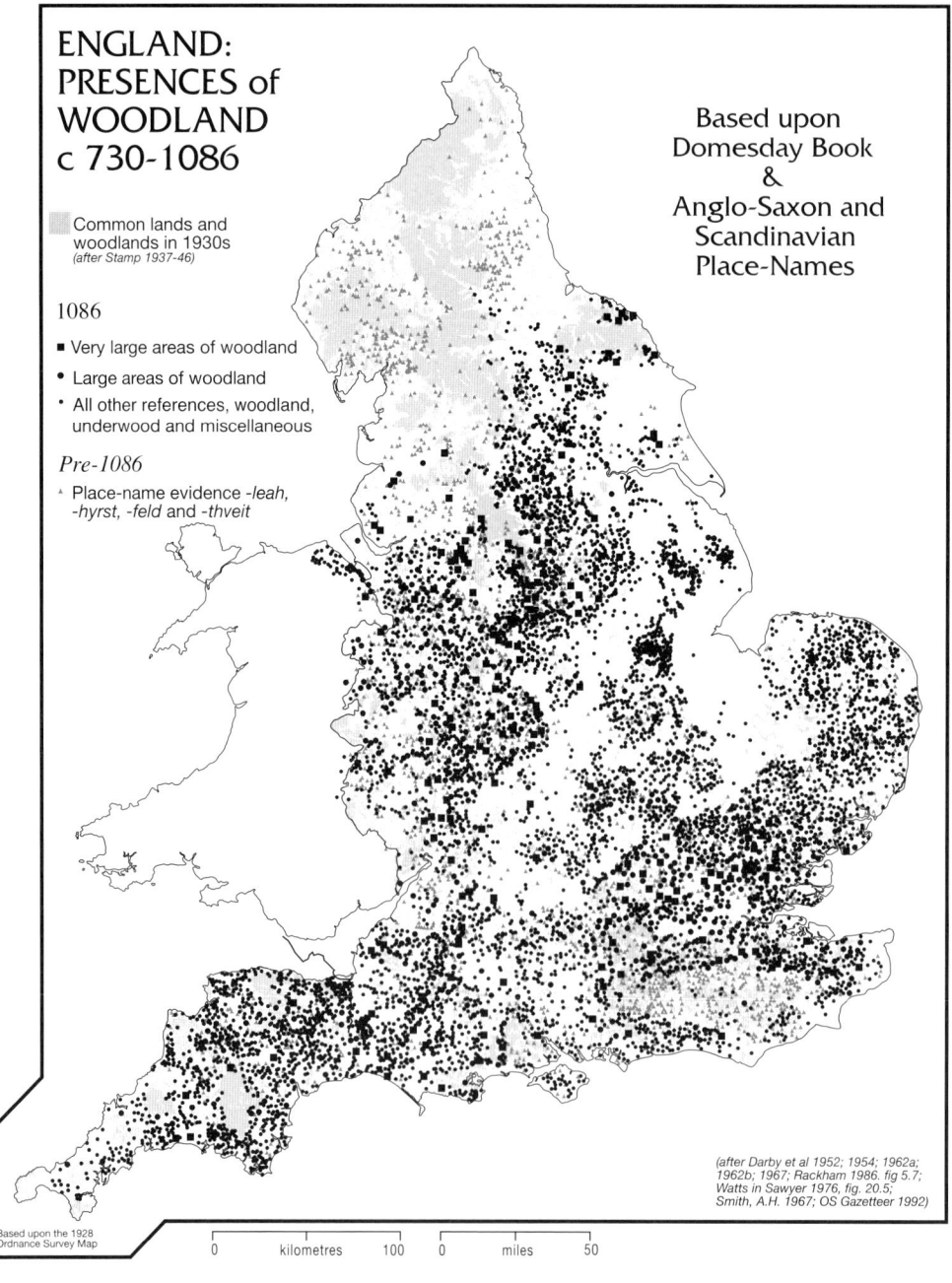

Fig. 1.5 Presences of woodland in pre-Conquest England

manner as to suggest the gradation. While there are undoubtedly small errors and omissions, this is a highly base-stable picture (the map has already been done twice) and would not be substantially altered by being re-done again unless larger scale maps were used. It shows a number of things: first, nucleated settlements concentrate in a band, extending from the Channel and Severn Estuary in the south to the North Sea, extending up the eastern side of the Pennines to the Scottish border. This zone, delineated by two lines, can be termed the *Central Province* and is lightly outlined in the figure. To the south and east and the north and west lie areas where, while a scatter of nucleated settlements does appear, the distribution is largely dominated by dispersion, with small hamlets and scatters of farmsteads and other dwellings. These cannot be shown is detail, but their intensity is indicated by using a simple range of shading, white for the lowest concentrations and darkest grey for the highest concentrations. Of course, some dispersed settlement appears in the Central Province, but this is generally of low or extremely low density. Only in a few localities, where the presence of a vigorously developing industry during the three centuries before the 1850s brought settlement intensification, are there high concentrations.

In fact three 'provinces' have been identified, and these are named in the inset map in Figure 1.6. As early as 1577 the Elizabethan topographical scholar William Harrison succinctly described the contrasts:

> 'It is so, that our soile being diuided into champaine grounde and woodland, the houses of the first lie uniformlie builded in euerie town togither, with streets and lanes; whereas in the woodland countries (except here and there in great market townes) they stand scattered abroad, eache one dwelling in the midst of his owne occupieng'
>
> (Harrison 1994, 217)

The Central Province was also, until the advent of the enclosure movements of the seventeenth, eighteenth and nineteenth centuries, dominated by great open communally cultivated field systems, with the arable of each township or parish being subdivided into hundreds, sometimes even thousands, of strips. Each farmer was the tenant of a number of these, and by the later stages in the history of these complex arrangements, two, three, four, five, six or even more fields were identified for the purposes of cropping. There is little doubt that the arrangements had antecedents long before 1500 (Baker and Butlin 1973). In contrast, to the south and east and the north and west of the Central province extend landscapes where, while villages and hamlets do appear, the countrysides were dominated by scatters of farmsteads and small hamlets. Some of this pattern may indeed be early, perhaps Anglo-Saxon or even earlier in date, but a great deal is undoubtedly post 1500. In fact, the internal settlement character of both the South-eastern Province and the Northern and Western Provinces fluctuates tremendously, reflecting both environmental variations and the degree of industrialisation. Some of the highest national concentrations of dispersed elements appear in Lancashire – a product of post seventeenth century industrial intensification

– while an almost complete absence of dwellings is found in the high Pennines and areas of the Fenlands. Parts of the western Midlands and Welsh borderlands and eastern England give some pause for thought: while industry has not been absent, it has never come to wholly dominate the landscape, but these largely rural areas carry high and extremely high densities of dispersion in the middle decades of the nineteenth century. In fact, the substance of this map requires analysis of book length. The way in which it was constructed has been discussed in Roberts' and Wrathmell's *Atlas of Rural Settlement* (2001) while the historical implications of the distribution has been examined in the volume *Region and Place* (2002). Versions of this general national map have been published before, but what differs here is that market towns present in the period 1500–1640 are shown using a square symbol (based on Everitt 1967, fig. 9 (a)–(c)). While some of these places are today little more than villages, most survived, some to become urban centres in the eighteenth and nineteenth centuries. Their distribution closely reflects basic agricultural prosperity and the need for rural markets in former centuries. What the map does reveal, however, is the rich diversity of local settlement regions present in northern settlement landscapes and, through the character of the distribution, the manner in which the presence of the uplands results in a series of major settlement cells, discussed below.

A second national map, Figure 1.5, draws together in one framework three categories of source material. First, the evidence for woodland in 1086, derived from Domesday Book; second, four categories of pre-Conquest place-name indicative of woodland; and finally, the distribution of common-waste and woodlands (not plantations) from the land utilisation survey of the 1930s. The latter is a surrogate for a map yet to be fully drawn, namely the distribution of common waste in the late eighteenth century before the enclosure of the commons, land largely unsettled and used as open common pasture or as wood-pasture. The first two distributions, based upon Domesday Book and place-names, correlate closely and together create an impression of woodland areas in 1086 and at some date before the Norman Conquest of 1066. Studies by Roberts and Wrathmell suggest that this impression may well reflect early eighth century conditions and even the situation in the Romano-British period (2002, *passim*). Comparison between Figures 1.4 and 1.5 shows that the Central Province was a zone with less woodland, and probably had less common pasture than the two outer provinces. Overall, however, these two maps show two things: first, highly developed regional contrasts at a national scale, ranging from extremely sharp to the greatly subtle, and secondly, when these distributions are analysed, the extent to which they are products of a great depth of temporal development becomes clear. The woodland map, with all that it implies in terms of open, partially cleared and wooded landscapes already present by 1086, with roots extending back to the Roman period and beyond, serves to inform any analysis of the distribution of settlement as it is finally recorded on the detailed mid-nineteenth century Ordnance Survey maps.

Settlement and Woodland in Northern England

Figure 1.6 is a simple extraction from Figure 1.4 and takes the argument to more detail, depicting the distribution of settlement in northern England between approximately 1840 and 1870 (Harley 1964, fig. 1). In south Lancashire, west Yorkshire, Durham and southern Northumberland, coalfield regions, the impact of the Industrial Revolution is seen in the emergence of nucleated elements and local increases in the intensity of dispersion. While, to a degree, rural industry does affect the remainder, lead and zinc in the Pennines and iron and alum in north Yorkshire and other minerals in the Lake District, the basal pattern is essentially rural. Villages and hamlets with intercalated dispersion spread across the plain of the Vale of York and northwards along the coastlands of Northumberland. In Figure 1.4 this eastern tract is delimited from the Pennines by a shaded line, and on a national scale this is the western boundary of the Central province. To the east is a landscape dominated by villages and with comparatively low concentrations of dispersion. An outlier of similar countrysides lies further west, where the Eden Valley of Cumberland and Westmorland bears similar densities of villages, hamlets and dispersion. A striking feature of the distribution seen at this scale of resolution is the way in which the dales of Yorkshire, Durham and Northumberland push fingers of settlement into the upland regions. The hill masses appear as white, because of the extremely low densities of settlement of any kind. The history of this pattern is complex, and cannot be related here (Roberts and Wrathmell 2000b; Winchester 2000), but two points must be emphasised. First, in southwest Yorkshire there is the peculiarity of a landscape seemingly dominated by villages yet lying west of the provincial boundary (Fig 1.4). This is because the nucleations of that area arose as a result of great increases in the populations of local settlement in the seventeenth, eighteenth and nineteenth centuries because of the presence of industries based upon coalmining, textile production and the rest. This led to the rise of village-sized aggregations of dwellings to landscapes once dominated by hamlets and dispersed elements (Defoe 1724–6, 491 ff.). Second, contained within the overall pattern are elements of great antiquity. While we cannot be certain that the hamlets and villages are themselves ancient, as the case of southwest Yorkshire exemplifies, their place-names are usually Old English and take their origin before the Norman conquest of 1066. Place-names, however, apply to townships and parishes, and apply equally whether the settlement of such a territory is settled by a concentration of farmsteads at one location or by scattered farmsteads (Fig. 1.2 top left). To complicate matters, some names appear to imply an origin in the name of a single farmstead, such as names with the suffix -*worth*. However, even those names that seem to imply a 'group' idea, *i.e.* those ending in -*ton* (originally -*tun*; Smith 1956, 188–98), may at root imply no more that a single-farmstead or a small farmstead group.

Within the broad framework provided by these synoptic maps we can postulate a

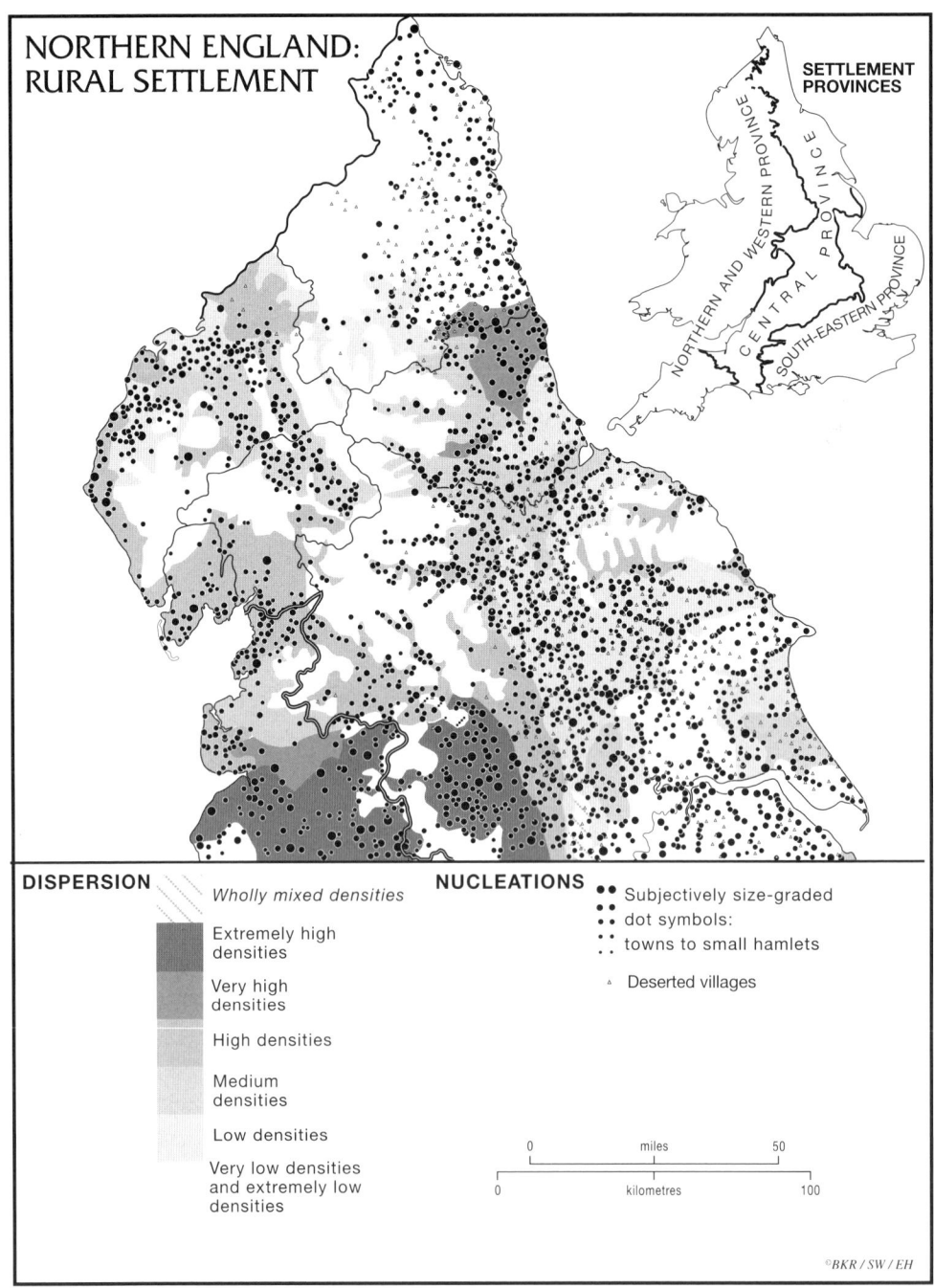

Fig. 1.6 Mid-nineteenth century settlement in northern England

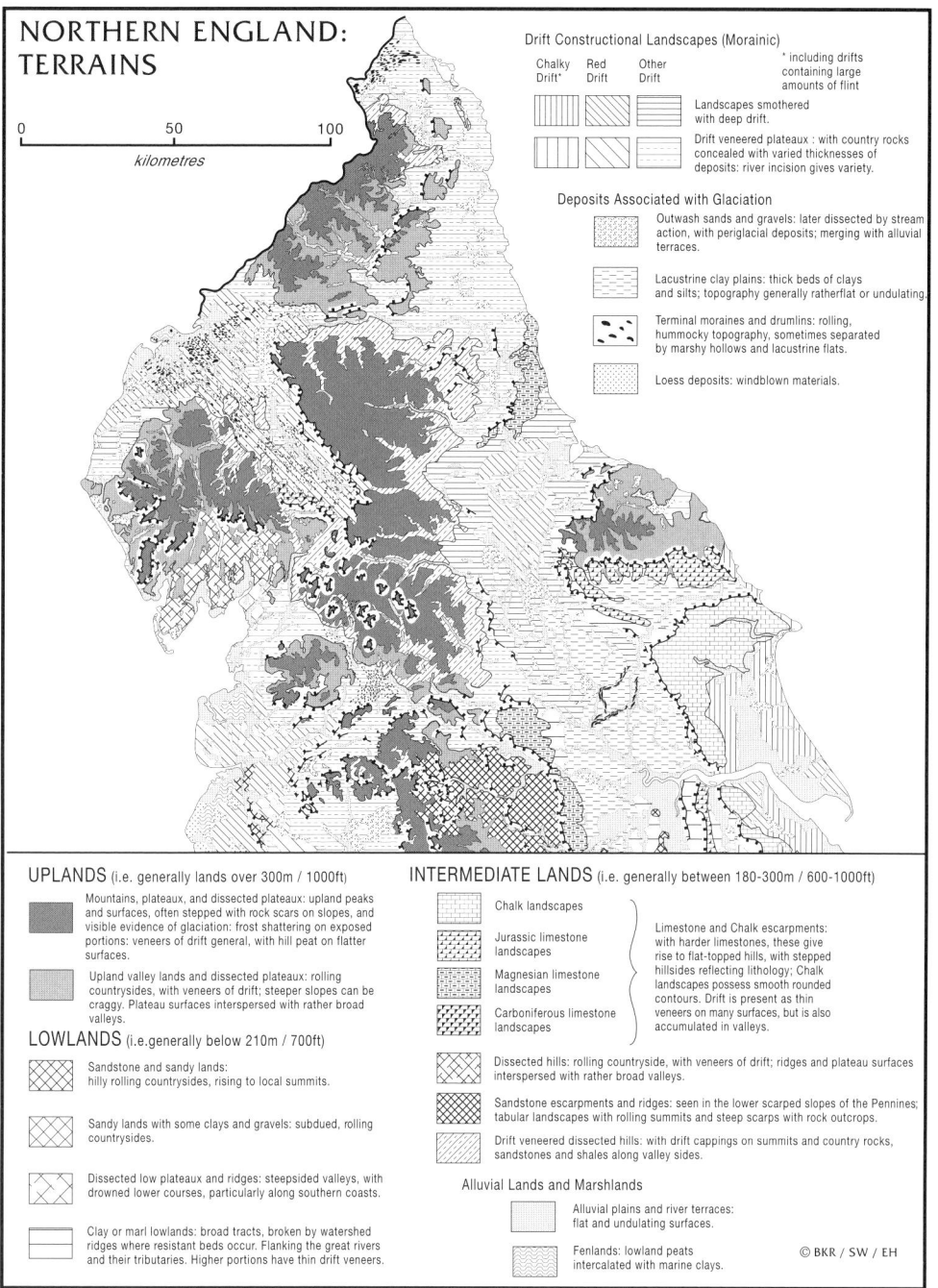

Fig. 1.7 *The terrains of northern England*

schematic general development sequence against which to assess developments within individual townships and/or parishes:

19th. Century – Stage 5:
- Subsequent developments preserve elements of the antecedent arrangements, although, *in some areas*, industrial activity brings a new wave of building and reconstruction,
- increasing existing hamlets to village or even town size,
- and bringing wholly new plantations such as mining villages and other specific industrial settlements to the landscape.
- In other areas, often those with villages, rural life continues
- until migration to the towns and the rise of sophisticated transport systems brings both emigration and new population influxes.
- Marginal zones preserve elements of antecedent settlement forms and patterns.

Stage 4:
- Established rural settlements respond to changing economic and demographic circumstances: in some, growth occurs,
- while others contract, shrink and may disappear;
- many others show signs of long-term physical stability, while experiencing changes in the number of farmsteads and/ or small holdings present.

Stage 3:
- The arrival of power centres brings seigniorial farmsteads, fortifications, churches to serve the local communities: *some* of these provide the foci for the appearance of tenanted clusters, villages and hamlets, but
- in other areas *some* isolated churches remain as elements of a pattern comprising a scatter of farmsteads and hamlets;
- throughout this stage competition, desertion and foundation are important themes.

Stage 2:
- Population increases lead to the multiplication of farmsteads:
- at first the clusters are kin groupings; some continue to expand by allowing strangers some rights in the community's lands.
- These developments are linked with a closer definition of territories as populations increase.

Stage 1:
- Settlement by sparse scatters of farmsteads, hamlets and their arable fields:
- their place-names become associated with adjacent land areas, where they graze their stock;
- 'the waste' forms a matrix within which all settlements and settlement regions are placed.

Table 1.1 A brief retrospective model of settlement evolution in England

This simple generalisation is a way of envisaging the long-term processes involved in the evolution of settlement: no clear chronological frame is provided, but broadly this postulated sequence extends from Anglo-Saxon times – Stage 1 – to the nineteenth century – Stage 5. However, this statement conveniently ignores the presence of pre-Anglo-Saxon settlements of Romano-British and prehistoric date, periods of extraordinarily complex transitions (Higham 1992). In some areas both of these earlier phases were probably associated with local population numbers at least as high as those present during the period between 1100 and 1300, higher indeed than during the nineteenth and twentieth centuries. This, if correct, provides a context in which a given landscape could go though not one but several cycles of development, from relative simplicity to developed complexity, reverting to a new simplicity (Stage 1) and then gradually developing to a new level of complexity (Stage 5). Within each cycle there will be great local complexity. Furthermore, the board has never been completely wiped clean and interactions between destruction, adaptation, change and inertia have preserved features from every succeeding century and decade. This underlying structure is glimpsed most clearly in place-names, which still carry traces of Stages 1 and 2 into Stage 5, but other elements, boundaries, land usage elements, sacred sites, harbours and fortifications, to name only a few elements, will also persist. This simple empirical model, in which much could be challenged, serves as window, and does no more than provide a brief glimpse of the complexities that certainly underlie all English, indeed European, settlement development.

This discussion stresses the need to understand the role of antecedent landscapes (Fig. 1.2), and the social and economic factors which moulded them, in affecting all subsequent developments, but that such landscapes are also affected by the nature of the land itself cannot be disputed. Figure 1.7 is a physical map of northern England. This summarises not merely relief, geology or soils but *terrain*, a synoptic picture of many physical elements. Complex as it is, it represents a great simplification. A glance at Figure 1.6 and comparison with Figure 1.7 confirms the general association between settlement and the nature of the land, its slopes, its climate and weather, its soil quality, its general habitability, and ultimately its suitability for intensive or extensive farming. There is inevitably a broad correlation between the two maps. It is comparatively rare for settlement to rise above 300 metres above sea level, and in fact the vast majority of lands dominated by villages and hamlets are seen to lie below 210 metres. A key linkage is found in the fact that latitude, altitude, land-characteristics and soil-quality all affect farming potential. Grain growing needs enough warmth for sufficiently long to allow the crop to ripen, while the clays and stiff loams, soils possessing high clay content, offer the best possibility for plant nutrition, particularly in the centuries before the advent of chemical fertilisers. There is no mystery in this, and all farmers have always had to negotiate with the quality of land available. The 'best' lands have long been found adjacent to the great rivers, where river gravels, and slopes covered with a downwash of alluvial materials, and lying somewhat above the danger of any regular flooding, have attracted farmers. The poorest lands lie on the high and windy uplands where forest clearances over millennia have exposed the soils to rainfall, eluviation, downwash and degradation. Nevertheless, advances in technology, pressures of population, demands from industry, the availability of imports, and the potential for expansion beyond the restraints of communal cultivation, have all helped distort any simple land quality-farming type linkages. The issues become complex when it is appreciated that the settlement patterns seen in Figure 1.6 contain elements that are 500, 1000, or even 1500 and more years old. Furthermore, the very farming systems that supported former settlements have themselves altered the land, wearing away soils, leading to the flow of detritus, alluvium and minerals in solution down the slopes, streams and rivers, to be deposited in basins of accumulation and whenever rivers flood and drop their loads. Finally, these reach the sea and estuarine mudflats. The soil is the thin skin of the land, between the underlying rocks and the atmosphere. This is never stable, and movement is exacerbated by all human activities. A key advantage of temperate western Europe is the speed with which most soils renew themselves, although even then this is radically affected by altitude, mineral and organic composition and farming practices applied.

The terrain of the north east of England can be understood in terms of a broad eastern corridor of lowland, extending northwards from the Humber marshlands. Across this run rivers, largely west to east, but while most of the drainage of the Vale of York is drawn southwards to the Humber, further north the Tees, the Wear, the North and South Tyne and the smaller systems of Northumberland form separate entities. The North York Moors constitute a discrete mass of upland touching the east coast. However, further north the line of the Magnesian Limestone escarpment forms a subtle but important division, running at first west to east from near Bishop Auckland to Ferryhill, and from there northwards until it reaches the coast at Tynemouth (Figs 2.6 and 6.1). To the south and east of this line, the land is very much an extension of the great lowland tracts of central England. To the west and north lie more broken scarp-and-vale countrysides and the low plateau of the outcrop of the Durham coalfield. Further north the coastal plain of Northumberland is a rolling landscape dissected by east to west running rivers, while north of Alnwick sharp ridges of Fell Sandstone reach towards the coast. Most of this lowland is, in broad terms, sound farming country, although to the north of the Magnesian Limestone in Durham the quality is more variable than further south. It is, however, worth reflecting on one simple fact: before the construction of bridges each river, each major river, or indeed stream, presented a barrier, particularly at certain times of the year. Crucial crossing points, with some of the early ones being still visible as *-ford* names, have affected the eventual location of bridges, the formalisation of route ways, the siting of castles and eventually the growth of all of the region's major towns. A slight gorge on the Tyne, with reasonable access down the slopes on each side for wagons and armies, allowed determined Roman engineers to impose their own bridging point affecting the eventual growth of the regional capital at Newcastle. That such decisions did not always have a great and long-lasting effect is shown by the decay and disappearance of substantial Roman bridges at Piercebridge and Corbridge.

To the west the land rises and each major river cuts deep valleys – dales – into the hill masses. In practice there is an intricate transition between lowland and upland, sometimes with distinctive foothills. Sometimes, as in Northumberland, the rise is more gradual. The high, windy and often desolate landscapes of Pennines are wetter, more backwards in terms of the arrival of spring – hence possessing a shorter growing season – and in colder spells prone to snow. In winter conditions the routes through the Aire Gap, the pass of Stainmore and the Tyne Gap, assume a great significance, allowing contact with the more discontinuous lowland tracts to the west. On the western flanks of the Pennines and Cheviots the rivers flow to the great soft, sand- and mud-filled estuaries of the Solway and Morecambe Bay. These present both the economic possibilities for seafood as well as great dangers to travellers and the unwary who seek to cross the sands. The mountains of the Lake District form a distinctive mass, relatively high, yet interpenetrated by deep valleys. In this discussion there will be less emphasis on Lancashire villages, because the area's settlement problems require a discussion of the whole of western England. However, between the Lakeland mountain country and the high western edge of the Pennines, extending north and westwards along the English side of the Solway Firth there is a lowland tract comprising the Vale of Eden and the Solway Plain. Separated from the main English lowlands by uplands and narrow passes, the Eden valley forms a corridor for routes between the Lancastrian lowlands, the Solway fords and bridges of the lower Eden and Irthing and the route ways of eastern Scotland. Rolling, with areas of great fertility intermixed with heathy ridges and lowland mosses, the area retains a rich local texture. Effectively this is an outlier of the village landscapes of the eastern plain. To the north and west it merges gradually with the Solway Plain, where islands of clay drift rise above surrounding moss lands and coastal estuaries to provide footholds for village settlements. Like north eastern England, this area has long been traversed by important north to south routes, as many former fortifications attest, but the east differs in that due south lies London, while due south of the Eden Valley lies Lancashire, Cheshire, and the Welsh border country. No disrespect is intended, but the difference can be appreciated in the location of Catterick. This locality, a word chosen with care, had a vast prehistoric complex of fortifications at Stanwix – whatever these imply – an important Roman site, and to this day remains an important base for the British army. It was, and is, strategically located where the important and near direct north to south route between London and Scotland meets a second route, through the easy pass of Stainmore, leading north and west to Carlisle and eventually western Scotland.

These points are mere reminders of nature's diversity and the subtleties of cultural evaluation. The north is richly varied – and no mention has yet been made of the softer chalks, lacustrine and glacial clays of the east, extending from the Corallian limestones that cap the southern edges of the North York Moors, and run south and east to Flamborough Head and Spurn Point. Since the departure of the glaciers many possibilities have existed for negotiations between human communities and the land, between upland and lowland, wold and sand, marsh, fen and clay plains. In this region, where activity occurs has always been important, making generalisation both difficult and often misleading. In human terms, the changing nature of the distribution of vegetation has also been crucial. It is probable that in earlier prehistory forest covered most of the region, except for the very highest parts of the Pennines and perhaps the Lake District, although it is doubtful if for many centuries past the squirrel could pass unhindered from coast to coast. What we cannot yet know is how much open rough grassland there was in earlier centuries, but Figure 1.5 has a sharp reminder of the importance of this category of land in the form of the commons and rough pastures recorded in the Land Use Survey of the later 1930s (Stamp 1937–44: 1962). As later maps of Durham will show (Figs 2.4–2.6), the vast extent of rough grazing land in the mid-twelfth century was wholly astounding, and most of it must have been utilised as common pasture by the lowland villages and hill farms. Camden in his *Britannia* notes of Northumbria that

> All over the *Wasts* (as they call them) as well as in Gillesland [*i.e.* Gilsland in Cumberland] you see as it were the ancient Nomades; a Martial sort of people, that from April to August, lye in little Hutts (which are called *Sheals* or *Shealings*) here and there dispersed amongst their Flocks.
>
> (Gibson 1695, 851)

This note, whose substance there is no reason to doubt, records the remarkable survived of a system that must once have been more widespread (Ramm *et al.* 1970). Distances between useful upland grazing and the permanent settlements were so great that temporary settlement was linked to the movement of stock to the more distant lands. It is probable that these survivals represent the last evidence for a system that was once prevalent throughout the whole of northern England. At an earlier time such movements must have taken place at far lower altitudes, when the concentration of permanent occupation was limited to more limited areas of even the better quality soils.

This brief introduction to the grammar and language of settlement and its physical spatial context has been geared to what is to be found throughout the north of England. The chapters to follow begin with an analysis of the settlement, emphasising different scales of investigation, and then to consider in more detail the character of particular villages, hamlets and small towns. The character of settlement can only be understood by using such scale jumps, from the general to the particular and back again to the general. In geographical terms national studies lead to regional studies – not merely the administrative county – and thence to local studies, and vice versa.

Furthermore, the series of maps presented here are in themselves tools: a close study of Figure 1.8, a map of northern woodland extracted from Figure 1.5, gives a local regional view. If we accept that Figure 1.8 is indeed a useful guide to the distribution of early woodland, and supportive evidence will be assessed in Chapter 2, then it is

The Nature of Rural Settlement

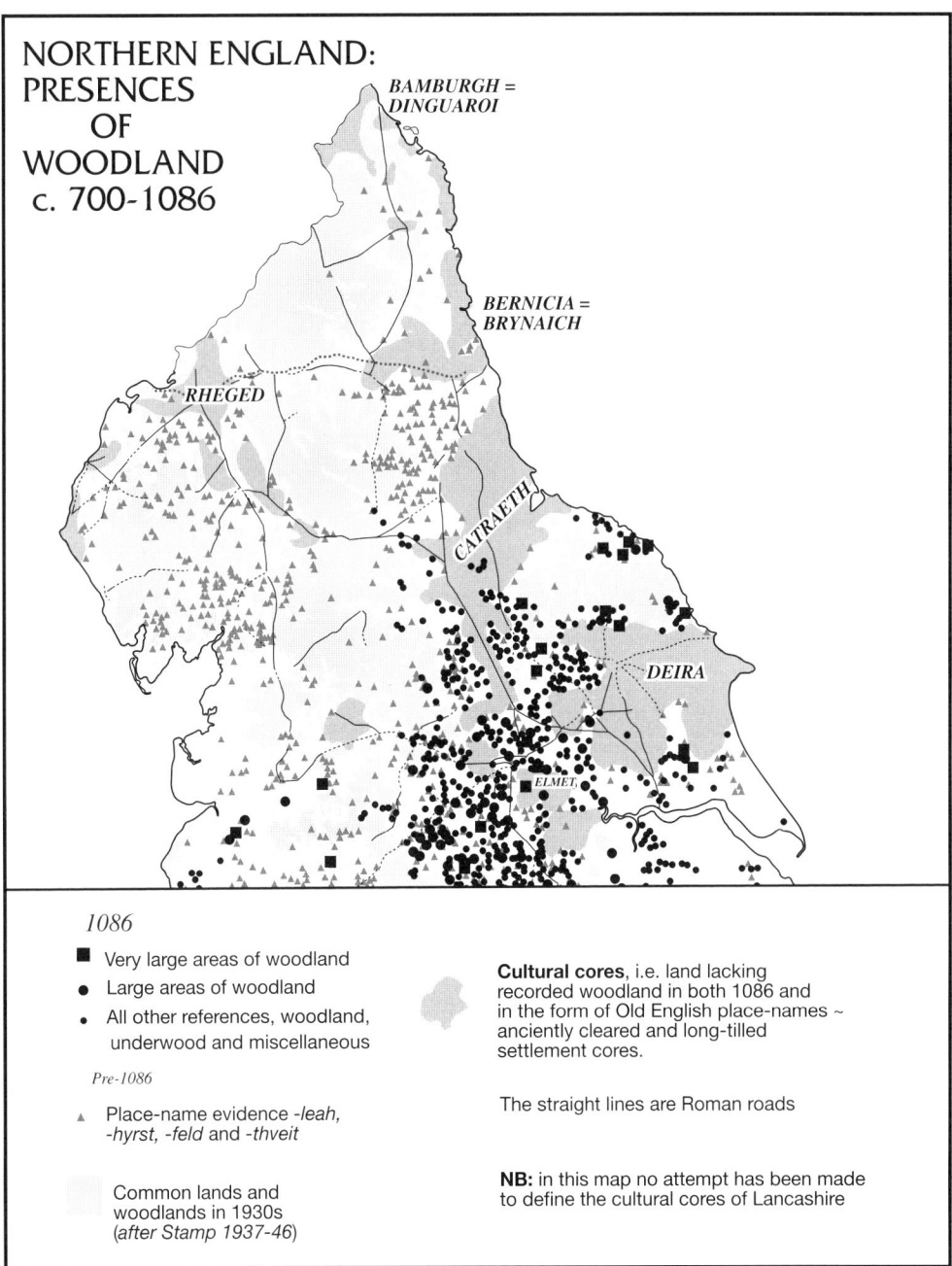

Fig. 1.8 Presences of woodland in pre-Conquest northern England

possible to define and outline those lowland areas that were wood free – or relatively so – defining a series of core areas of anciently cleared land. Comparative study of this map and other distributions, such as the earliest Anglo-Saxon burials and habitation names and prehistoric and Romano-British sites, suggests that in these cultural cores, in Figure 1.9 projected onto the terrain map, we have indications of the ancient polities of *Deira*, *Catraeth*, *Bernicia/Brynaich*, *Bamburgh/Dingayroi* and *Rheged* with *Llwyfenydd* (Higham 1986, fig. 6.2; Roberts 2007). This by no means exhausts analysis of these complex issues, but serves to illustrate the use of maps as tools. This is an underlying leitmotiv of this study.

Chapter Two

Of Patterns and Forms – Settlement in Northern England

The settlement maps used so far have been greatly generalised. If Figure 1.6 is compared with Figure 2.1, it can be seen that while in both cases every nucleation is recorded, in the second map all dispersed elements, such as halls and hamlets and scattered farmsteads, are also present. This example, a very detailed picture of the settlement characteristics of a local region in north Yorkshire, creates a bridge between the study of patterns and the study of the plans and character of individual places.

The North Yorkshire Moors – a Case Study

The double page spread (Figs 2.1.a and 2.1.b) summarises the settlement within the area of the North York Moors, an area approximately 40 by 25 miles. On this map pecked lines along the watersheds suggest relief, with some hachures indicating other key slopes. The forms of individual villages and hamlets are shown in a generalised way using symbols, and halls, single farmsteads, deserted villages and possible deserted villages and even isolated churches, are included. Based upon an even more detailed research map, this level of resolution assists understanding of the geographical characteristics of settlement. The evidence was drawn from six inch to the mile (1:10,560) nineteenth century maps, but the area selected is exactly that shown upon the old one inch to one mile Ordnance Survey Tourist map of the North York Moors. While the uplands dominate the core of the map, the surrounding lowlands are also well represented.

Three things are apparent: first, because there are no large conurbations to obfuscate the pattern, small towns, villages and hamlets are seen sweeping around, and occasionally into, the upland masses. Middlesbrough appears only as a blank in the northern edge of the distribution, none too subtly concealed beneath the title. In large, as the land rises and farming conditions become less attractive nucleated settlements give way to a pattern of dispersed farmsteads and small hamlets, while the high grazing lands of the watersheds are largely devoid of permanent settlement. Second, villages and hamlets have a clear tendency to form distinctive lines in the landscape. This can also be seen in Figures 1.4 and 1.6, but in the case of Figure 2.1 sufficient topographical detail is present to appreciate why this is happening. A classic case is to

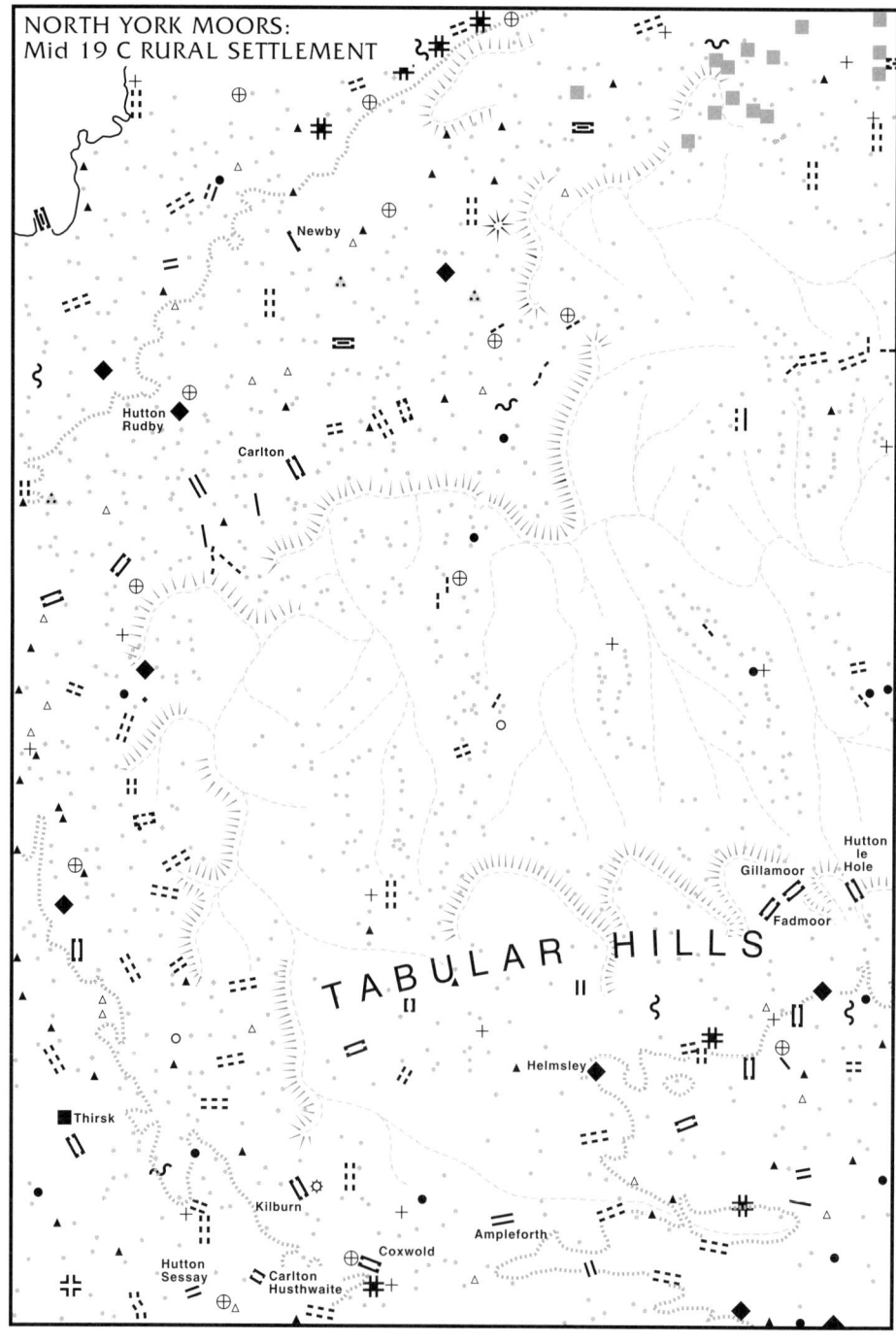

Fig. 2.1a The rural settlement of the North York Moors (W)

Of Patterns and Forms 31

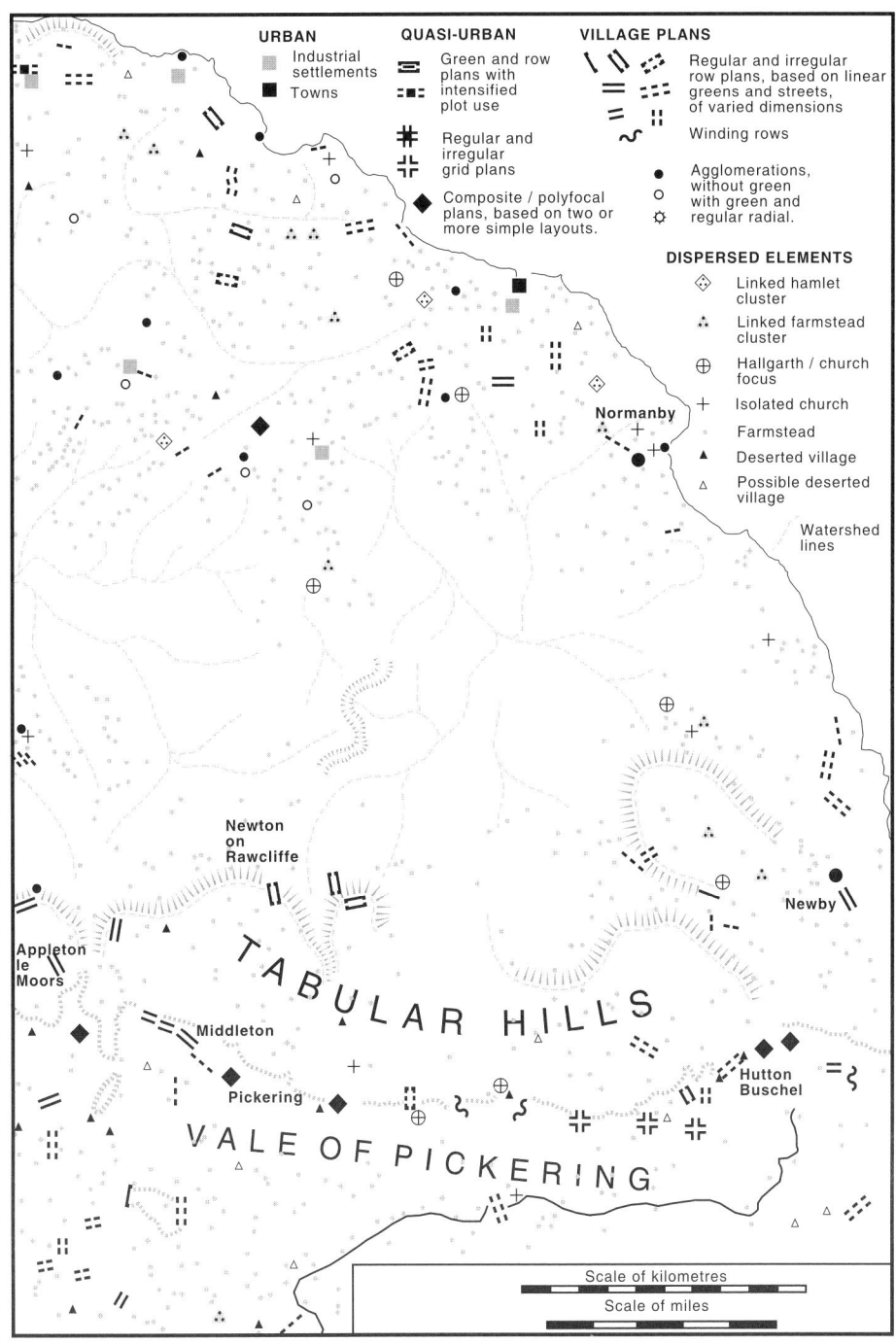

Fig. 2.1b The rural settlement of the North York Moor (E)

be seen along the northern edge of the Vale of Pickering, where the dip-slope of the Corallian Limestone scarp of the Tabular Hills runs beneath newer, softer deposits of the former glacial lake basin: along, at, or near this boundary villages and hamlets are concentrated, from Hutton Buschel and Pickering to Helmsley. While the need for a water supply cannot be ignored, for springs or streams are more permanent at this point, the heterogeneous and well-drained soils associated with geological variety, local glacial drifts and downwash, are particularly concentrated along this line. This is what Domenic Powlesland has termed a 'preferred settlement zone'. His excavations along the southern edge of the Vale of Pickering – just beyond the southern limit of Figure 2.1.b – have shown that what is visible in the landscape and on the map are settlements that are emerging in the later Anglo-Saxon period (Powlesland 1999, 44–65). They are but the final phases of successive chapters of activity which extend back, though the middle and early Anglo-Saxon centuries, to Romano-British times, to the Iron Age, the Bronze Age and even the remoter ages of prehistory (*ex inf.* Powlesland). This valuable and varied tract of sloping land, with great arable potential because of a continuous renewal of the soils linked to limey downwash and good drainage, has been continuously occupied for several thousand years. Of course, these localised discoveries beg many questions about what remains to be discovered in all other parts of the map. We have no reason to assume that the area of scarp-foot excavated differs in any respect in from scarp-foot slopes to be seen elsewhere. These recoveries present archaeological questions of great national significance. Third, while a scatter of single farmsteads is fairly evenly intercalated between the villages and hamlets of the peripheral lowlands, those in the uplands are by no means randomly scattered. There is a clear tendency for them to form two lines, one on each side of a dale, sited upslope, away from the floods and frosts of the valley floors. They are in fact placed where, when they were established, dung could be carted downhill to manure the arable, while the stock, cattle and sheep, could be walked uphill to the grazing of the higher slopes. Some of these are actually documented in 1086 (*e.g.* Thirley Cotes, see below), but the names of others suggest that they originated as temporary settlements set amid extensive tracts of grazing land (*e.g.* Airy Holm, see below).

But what does a map like this actually mean? We can picture the map's flat surface as a representation of one phase of time, *i.e.* the middle decades of the nineteenth century. Powlesland's work shows that below this, concealed and so to speak 'beneath' the map, are many further sheets, in what can be termed 'the deeps of time', lie centuries, indeed millennia, of complex maturation during which the present settlement arrangements have been developing. The picture is one of subtle and complex patterns of movement and change, stability and quiescence (Roberts 1996, fig. 6.3). How then can the map be grasped, understood and used as an attribute of both space and time? Two facts illuminate this question: first, the majority of the place-names associated with the villages and hamlets appearing on this map are documented in Domesday Book, compiled in 1085–6. They are at least Old English (Anglo-Saxon), Scandinavian or Anglo-Scandinavian in origin, although the settlement areas to which the names are attached may be very much older. However, one of the problems of dealing with Yorkshire is that Domesday Book and other sources reveal that regions of the county were terribly devastated during the Norman Conquest, particularly during 1069–70. However severe this was, and as will be shown throughout this study this is a much-debated issue, it looks as if the settlements present before this event, in large, recovered, to provide the foundations for later settlements, even if the antecedent place-names only gave their nomenclature to territories associated with what came later. This in no way excludes the possibility of fundamental changes in settlement form and character. Second, this general conclusion is confirmed by the fact that remarkable numbers of the region's parish churches contain Norman stonework (Pevsner 1966). No doubt the bulk of this is post-1072, but it suggests that post-devastation re-development took place on, at or near, former pre-Conquest settlements implied by the survival of pre-Conquest place-names. As Taylor and Taylor showed, numerous pre-Conquest architectural survivals – with few exceptions as dense as anywhere in the country – speak of on site-continuity of church building (1979, xxxii–xxxiii). The changes associated with conquest and sometimes devastation during the later eleventh century will be reconsidered in later chapters of this study. There is no doubt that the Norman Conquest of the north, the theme of a book by an eminent American scholar, was a cataclysmic event: this is amply attested by the numerous great and small castles, by the region's social characteristics, and less directly by many the vast and splendid church buildings (Bishop 1934; *ibid.* 1935; Kapelle 1979). The cathedrals at Durham and Carlisle, and that recovered by excavation at York, the multitude of great and rich monastic houses, and the scatter of parish churches, some humble, others richly ornate, still attest the impact (Phillips 1985). If the changes led to Norman artistic and organisational success, they can hardly have been comfortable to experience at the level of the peasant farmer. Each and every great structure needed the labours of rustic cultivators to support the aristocratic laymen and churchmen and their households who commissioned and used the buildings, as well as the many artisans involved in their construction. The food to feed the local populations and the skilled artisans came from the local land, the good soils of the northern lowlands and the extensive poor-land grazings of the uplands.

The Components of Settlement Patterns

Analysis of this particular settlement pattern must begin with a review of the ingredients of the settlement systems shown at three scales in Figures 1.4, 1.6 and 2.1. These extend from scattered farmsteads to market towns. Where the character of the distributions has been generalised using shading this also includes the cottages resulting from common-edge squatting, a settlement type closely associated with the rise of industrial activity in rural areas, as well as the industrial sites themselves. The basic mixtures of towns, villages and single-farmsteads vary from region to region, with environmental factors, notably the presence of lowlands and uplands, playing a significant part because they affect land quality and farming potential. Coalfields have a powerful effect because by the middle decades of the nineteenth century industry and population were moving to them. The discussion that follows, focussing on Figure 2.1, will be 'bottom to top', beginning with dispersion and then moving up the hierarchy. Nevertheless, the points developed are generally applicable to the north as a whole.

Dispersed Elements

Farmsteads, usually single-farmsteads, but sometimes groups of two or three – the smallest of hamlets – are scattered widely though all northern lowlands and upland. In the lowlands (Figs 1.4 and 1.6), where they are intercalated between the nucleated villages and hamlets, farmsteads often represent movements out of the villages during the last two or three centuries, the result of the enclosure of the communally organised townfield systems (Harris 1961, 61–96). The vast majority of the symbols simply represent farmsteads, houses and their outbuildings – or 'offices' to use an older word – set amid enclosed and ring-fenced fields. Some, however, are of higher status, great houses, halls, manors or granges, and sometimes halls with churches set adjacent to them. All of these have other attributes: most are surrounded by some parkland, a proportion bear township or parish names, while some undoubtedly occupy the sites of depopulated and destroyed villages (Beresford 1954, 391–3; Beresford and Hurst 1971, 207–212). A proportion of the dispersed farmsteads in the lowlands are moated, *i.e.* surrounded by a substantial and wide wet ditch (Aberg 1978). This means that the symbols used on the map cannot be wholly exclusive without complicating the key even more. Thus, in a few cases, an open version of the small black triangle used to symbolise a deserted village has been used to show a hall or farmstead possessing unusual features, where the author's professional experience suggests that what is there may be more than merely a large house. A degree of subjectivity cannot be excluded. Nevertheless, it is clear that some of these lowland farmsteads are more than secondary dispersion following enclosure, and this fact raises important research questions. The deserted villages amongst them will be considered below, but old, single-farmsteads, sometimes with early documentation, sometimes bearing a township or parish name, and often with no indications that there was ever a nucleated village or hamlet beg many questions. Some may be specialist structures such as demesne farms of aristocratic landholders, others may be properties granted to monastic corporations, while others may be locations where exceedingly ancient farmsteads have survived. In eastern County Durham a region eventually populated by villages, Edderacres (GR NZ 40 39) remains today as a single-farmstead, is mentioned in Boldon Book in the later twelfth century, and bears a name, 'Æthelred's fields', of Anglo-Saxon origin (Watts 2002, 37). As a settled place, howsoever altered through time, 'Edder Acres' is a reminder that patterns dominated by nucleated, clustered settlements, may contain older less obvious features that are of equal importance to an understanding of the development of regional settlement as are the hamlets, villages and towns. Another case is seen at Amerston, also in east Durham: no more than a farm in the nineteenth century, not known to be a deserted village site, it nevertheless bears a name of pre-Conquest origin, the 'farm of *Eymundr*', a personal name of Norse origin (Watts 2002, 1). Nevertheless, it is not documented until the third decade of the thirteenth century. Amid a landscape dominated by nucleated villages and hamlets such survivals conceivably represent 'windows' into older, perhaps pre-village, landscape levels.

This is an important point: any distribution map brings together within a single plane surface settlement ingredients of varied date. In an early stage of analysis the research questions must focus upon teasing out the layers likely to be present and assigning dates to them. This is the purpose of this section of the present study. As the case of deserted villages shows, the task can rarely be done with any precision, because of the vagaries and imperfections of the historical record. Nevertheless, there is a further step, to focus in on the discordant ingredients present within a pattern, treat them as features for special study, and place them into a context through which they can be seen as part of the developing system. These questions were examined at greater length by Roberts and Wrathmell (2002), concentrating on townships in which scatters of farmsteads were nonetheless part of communities closely involved with the cultivation of limited areas within ring-fenced arable areas (Roberts and Wrathmell 2002, 83–118).

An examination of the distribution in Figure 2.1 shows that it includes two settlement categories that lie at the threshold between dispersion and nucleation. The category termed *linked farmstead clusters* comprises farmsteads that are either set in close proximity, sometimes at or just beyond the 'hailing distance' of about 150m that bear associative names. For instance, in east Durham the place-name *Hurworth*, appears in four farms, Hurworth Burn, White Hurworth, Black Hurworth and Red Hurworth. Meaning 'hurdle enclosure', the term possibly implies an enclosure for settlement set within woodlands. It has a frequent appearance of the suffix -*worth* as an element in township and parish names (Watts 2002, 64; Smith 1956, 273–77, endpaper map; Roberts and Wrathmell 2002, fig. 7.2). This is perhaps an extreme case, as these are all approximately a mile apart, but such cases raise questions. Sometimes, each element of the group is more than a single farmstead, comprising two, three or four, with associated cottages. Effectively these are small hamlets. In Figure 2.1 these are mapped as *linked hamlet clusters*. The example at Normanby, 'the -*by* of the Norwegians', is included in Figure 4.7 (Smith 1928, 117 and 57). It must be admitted that a single symbol for these categories that appears in Figure 2.1 may well conceal an as yet unrecognised settlement type. Any mapping involves taking classificatory judgements, using experience to generalise and the limited range of evidence on Ordnance Survey Old Series six inch to the mile maps. In short, a distribution map is by no means an end product: it initiates research. Nevertheless, these enigmatic farmstead and hamlet groupings are important.

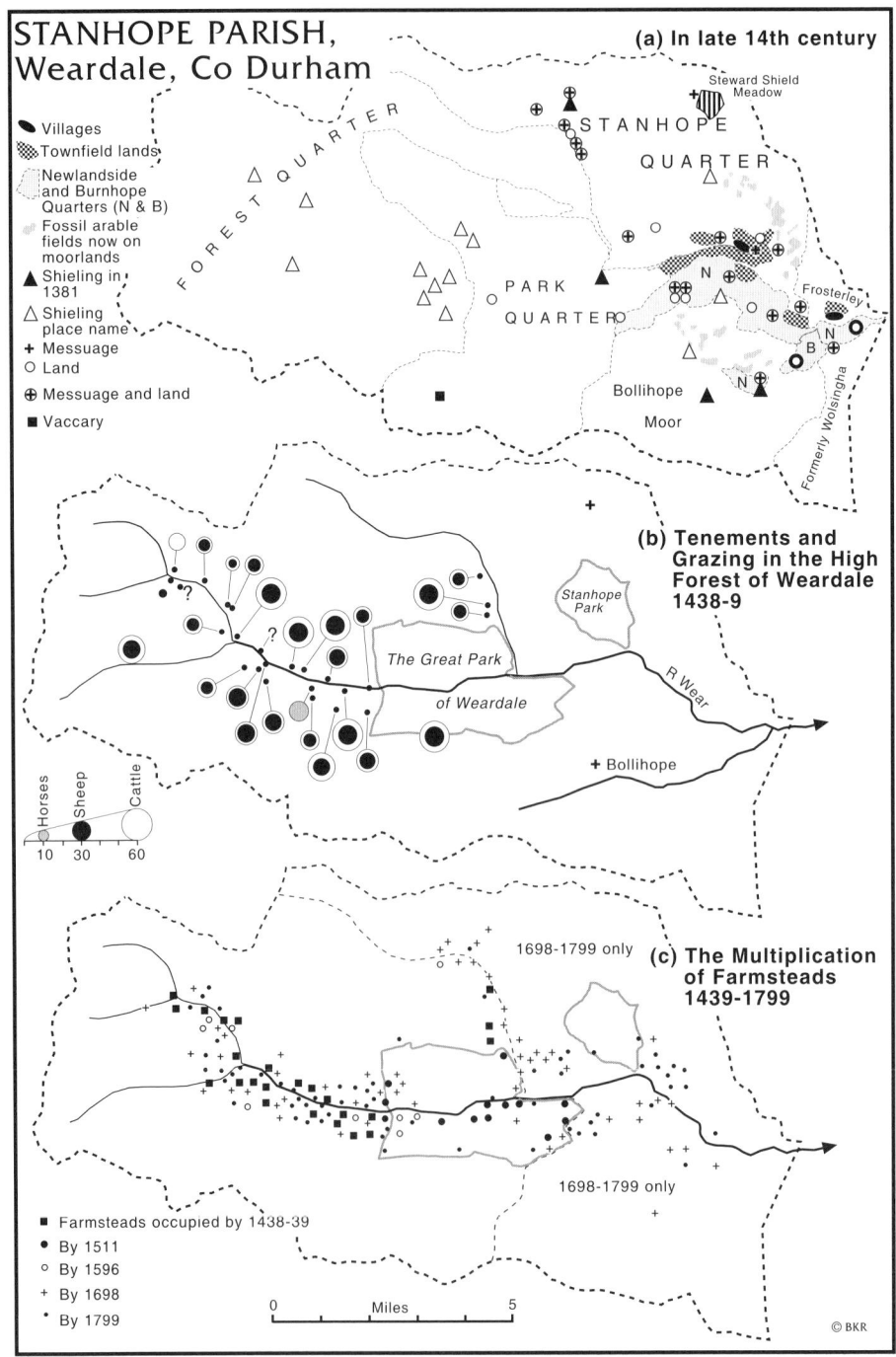

Fig 2.2 The settlement history of Stanhope, County Durham

While they may originate at many periods of time there is more than a suspicion that they can be seen as one stage in a developmental sequence from a single farmstead to a full village. Thus a linked farmstead cluster experiencing sustained expansion could generate first a linked hamlet cluster and eventually even a large composite village of a type common in the Midlands. This, as the author suggested in 1978, could explain the growth of irregular agglomerations, seemingly formless clusters (Roberts 1987, 126–50).

The impact of land quality is much in evidence in the uplands where, as was noted earlier, there is a strong tendency for each major valley to contain two strings of farmsteads, strung between the fells upslope and the better drained lands of the valley sides. There is little doubt that this is an ancient arrangement, but once again the farmstead sites seen on the map must date from many periods, namely, the occupation of individual sites must date from many periods. The buildings will be even more varied. Some undoubtedly grew from shielings, areas with huts used for the summer pasturing of cattle. In the North Yorkshire Moors this is seen in the Norse-Irish place-name element *arigh* – pronounced 'airey' – as at Airy Hill (Whitby) and Airy Holm (Great Ayton), and the old Norse *skale*, as at Laskill (Helmsley) and Scaling (Roxby; see Harrison and Roberts in Spratt and Harrison 1989, 95). This is the same word as *shele* and *shield*. In the mountains of the Lake District such names cluster thickly (Whyte in Baldwin and Whyte 1985, figs 8.1 and 8.2; Winchester 2000, 84–93, fig. 4.4). In Northumberland and Cumberland, amid the headwaters of the North Tyne, Liddle Water, the Lyne and the Irthing physical traces of many shieling huts have been recovered (Ramm *et al.* 1970, map 2). Of course, by no means all shielings decayed, many developed into permanent farmsteads. Figure 2.2 documents the chronology of farmstead development in upper Weardale, Durham, where strings of farmsteads of many periods sprawl along the valley sides. In this case, because of evidence provided by the Master Forester's account rolls of the fifteenth century, together with a succession of rentals from later centuries, allows a glimpse of the very complex chronologies involved in the establishment of scatters of upland farmsteads. The earliest documentation of each steading is noted in the map and gives an impression of the temporal dynamism of the process, yet in detail this analysis is at best crude. At one farmstead, Steward Shield Meadow, the pollen record of a small bog suggests that the initial foothold may be a seasonally occupied shieling with roots in the Iron Age, although the actual farm is likely to have been established after 1150 (Roberts *et al.*1973, 207–221)

A glimpse of the antiquity of some upland farmsteads may be seen in two other areas: first, in the eastern portion of the North York Moors Arnketill had his single plough and two carucates of taxable in 1086. Today the valley contains several farmsteads, but Troutsdale Hall seems the likely focus of this pre-Conquest activity (DB Yks. 1N45, note: SN, D13). Similarly Thirley Cotes is documented as part of the sokeland of Falsgrave at the same date (DB Yks. 1Y3: SN, D2). We have no real measure of its size at that stage: it may indeed have been a small hamlet, but it is today a single farmstead set at the lower end of Harwood Dale. In Westmorland, an area lacking a record in Domesday Book of 1086, there are clear indications of greater antiquity in some of the farmsteads of the upper Lyvennet valley where it is possible to trace a small string of former steadings appearing as earthworks (RCHM We.1930, 78–90; Roberts 1993a). Once again these are set somewhat upslope of the valley floor. To the north, down the Lyvennet valley, these earthwork sites give way to functioning farmsteads whose buildings bear traces of construction in the last three centuries, and these must surely be developed upon even older sites. These earthworks have long been interpreted as Romano-British, and indeed they may have been occupied in that period. Nevertheless, careful field examination suggests that some of them bear traces of long, rectangular dwellings, and the few available radiocarbon dates from this category of site in the north suggest that occupation may have continued into the tenth century A.D. (O'Sullivan in Baldwin and Whyte 1985, 21; Dickinson *ibid.* 86–88; Roberts 1993). All of these dispersed steadings are likely to *pre-date* the region's system of villages and hamlets and some indeed may have been those 'lovely homesteads' linked to 'comely *Llwyfenydd* (Lyvennet)' given by Urien of Rheged to his bard Taliesin (Pennar 1988, 64). It is probable that in Westmorland the final depopulation and desertion of what are now seen as archaeological sites took place when the farmers who lived there were – probably forcibly – resettled in the developing hamlets and villages established in the later eleventh and early twelfth centuries, a development to be discussed in later chapters. While it must be emphasised that such antiquity cannot be attributed to all dispersed farmsteads, the recognition that in some cases deep-time continuity may be present represents a useful and constructive way of thinking. Some sites may reflect continuous occupation from Anglo-Saxon, Romano-British, or indeed prehistoric periods (Hodges 1991). In the uplands such ancient steading sites intermingle with farmsteads developed during the colonisation of the marginal wastes by farmers in centuries both before and after 1500.

To conclude: a glance at the modern 1:50,000 or the Explorer 1:25,000 maps shows that similar patterns of dispersion are universally present throughout the north, lightly intercalated between the villages and hamlets of the lowlands and but spreading thickly along the upland flanks and valleys. There is a danger of seeing them as relatively unimportant in comparison with the more strident presences of nucleated villages and hamlets, but as Figures 1.4 and 2.1 reveal, a given area can be farmed just as successfully and productively from a scatter of farmsteads as from hamlets or villages. They represent important elements in the settlement system of northern England and in origin range from the nineteenth century back to the mists of prehistory.

Villages and Hamlets
The distinction between a village and a town is as much legal as it is one of mere physical size. Paradoxically, in northern England we must begin by defining towns: early towns possessed distinctive tenurial, jurisdictional and trading rights that separated them from

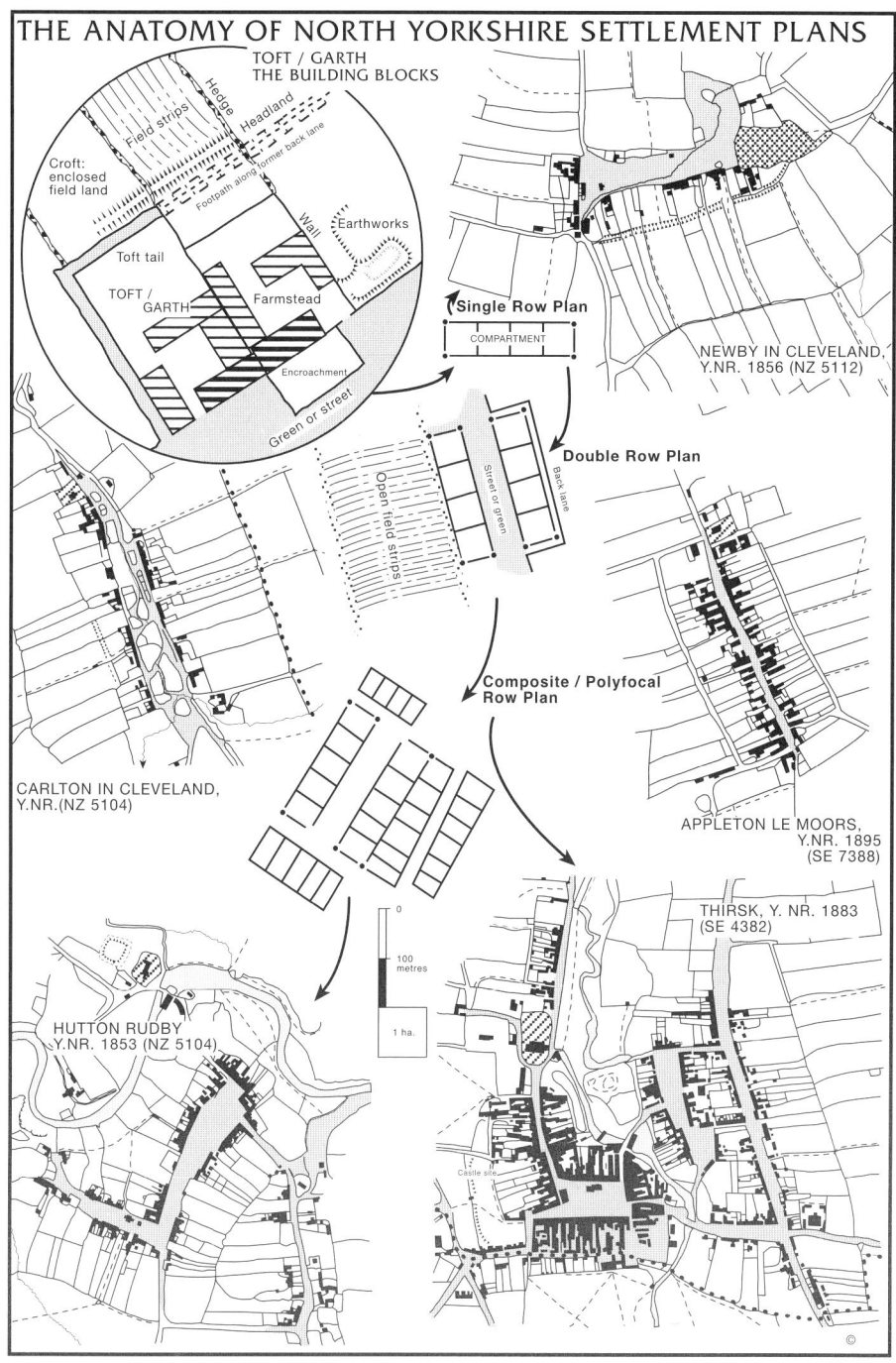

Fig. 2.3 The anatomy of North Yorkshire settlement plans

the rural settlements from which they derived support. These differences were expressed in burgage tenure, the town charter and the grant of a market, and sometimes a fair, by the crown. The town burgage – a town-house plot – was held subject to a money quit rent and free alienation – the right to create a will – while the charter from the crown or lord of the manor gave rights to self-regulation. It allowed the inhabitants to administer their own justice, and the rights to create assemblies for the purposes of trading, both retail and wholesale. This circumlocuitious definition is used because throughout the north, the largest and most complex village plans are more complex than many town plans, while even Newcastle, Carlisle, Durham, Penrith and Darlington reveal an underlying structural logic that bear a clear relationship to the region's village plans. Indeed, in terms of plans, distinguishing between a large village and a small town is not easy. Nevertheless, even these legal definitions do not provide the whole picture. There are cases where a plan suggests an attempt to found a town where no documentary evidence is forthcoming. Brancepeth, County Durham, is a case in question: a straight street, running northwards from the castle precinct with the ancient church nearby runs for nearly half a mile, and on an eighteenth century map has traces of long plots. Set adjacent to thus, on the other side of a small beck is the site of Stockley, now a deserted village, and ploughed out (Ingleson 1972). It is hard to interpret the layout at Brancepeth other than an attempt to establish a borough by the castle gate, conceivably by the Fitz Meldreds, Hansards or Nevilles, great secular landowners and conjoined families holding lands of the Cathedral Priory (Offler in Piper and Doyle 1996, study XIII, 10–16). A date in the first half of the thirteenth century is perhaps likely. The Bishop of Durham was probably not well-pleased, and this may account for the undocumented darkness enveloping these interesting topographical arrangements.

Figure 2.3 gives some examples of specific plans and creates an illuminating bridge between the rural and the urban plans in Yorkshire. As was argued in Chapter 1, basic house plots or tofts were combined to create a compartment, comprising a single simple row. In turn, these compartments may be variously combined: as a single row, in the case of Newby set alongside what may be the oldest focus of the settlement, the oval of the hallgarth or manor house enclosure. First mentioned in 1236 this is, as the name implies, a post 1086 plantation (Smith 1928, 169). The next two cases show how rows, with varied types of toft, some short and some long, have been combined to create two-row plans. At Carlton, in Cleveland a plan with a narrow and rather steep-sided stream-green that has subsequently been enclosed, was in 1086 assessed at eight carucates (DB Yks. 5N28), but at that time its lands were described as 'waste'. Appleton-le-Moors, a very regular street-green plan by the nineteenth century, in 1086 was a two-carucate vill (DB Yks. SN, D21 and SN Ma 14). These entries raise two questions. Was the plan at Carlton created after the devastation of the north in 1069–70 and does the fact that the two settlements appear as the same size in mid-nineteenth century maps suggest that both achieved, at a later stage in their development, the same fiscal size? These are points to which we must return for no easy answer is forthcoming.

At Hutton Rudby a hall-church complex on one side of the river bears a single name with a polyfocal village of three two-row entities. We need no documentation to postulate this, but sure enough, Hutton and Rudby appear in 1086 as wholly separate entities (DB Yks. 5N29). Finally, in Thirsk there is a true market town, in which it is possible to detect in its structure a series of distinctive compartments, one of which must post-date the destruction of the castle, present by the 1130s, but destroyed in 1174 (Renn, 1968, 322.). There are other northern towns, Bishop Auckland, Appleby in Westmorland, Pickering, Yarm and Easingwold, whose plans are no more complex than that at Hutton Rudby, yet Hutton was never a town. It is in fact a polyfocal or composite plan. In 1086 Hutton is mentioned as the *caput* of a manor to which Rudby is a sokeland appendage, and the former, with the church, is the manor house focus, with post-1086 tenancies appearing at the latter. In Thirsk, still purely rural in 1086, the 'tofts and crofts' of the borough of East Thirsk are mentioned by 1145. It seems possible that this was the focus around St. James' Green, with the development of western Thirsk on the older castle site. The easternmost compartment, with the strong north-to south axis and beheading an arable furlong to the east, must be later (DB Yks. 1N112, 23N5).

Villages and hamlets occur in substantial numbers and Figures 1.6 and 2.1 emphasise their concentration throughout the better soils of the lowlands. The symbols used on the latter map are generalised, but relate to the classification exemplified in Figure 1.3. The problem with all such mapping is how to select and then depict characteristics that can be rendered meaningful by further discussion and analysis. Thus, the presence or absence of a back-lane within row plans may have 'significance', perhaps reflecting when the village plan was established, but such chronological subtleties have so far escaped the author. The fact remains that some villages have strong back lane systems, as at Appleton le Moors, while in others they have decayed, as at Carlton, yet in other cases there is no trace at all. Further, a practical threshold must be set upon the detail a map can carry at a given size of page. Figure 2.1, using concepts explored in Figure 1.3 concerning the plan elements combined to make villages and hamlets, shows how the settlement plans to be found on mid-nineteenth century Ordnance Survey 1:10,560 maps can be recorded and analysed. Inevitably it includes a rather complex yet much-simplified key. Circles and hash shapes show agglomerated settlements, which may either lack any clear structure or be based upon a regular grid, while the other symbols show varied settlements plans based upon rows, sometimes very structured, 'regular', sometimes less so, hence 'irregular'. All categories may or may not possess an interior open space or green. This daunting detail – in itself much simplified from the original version – is designed to allow more subtle levels of analysis and questioning (Roberts 1990, 107–25, fig. 4). However, if a series of plans depicted on the map are traced both on the map and in the field, it will be seen that that row plans tend to dominate, that regular row plans are common, and that row plans with an interior green are frequent. Better still, if this map is compared with the contemporary Ordnance

Survey 1:25,000 maps of the North Yorkshire Moors, then the problems of mapping will be appreciated. In fact, any distribution can be simplified. In Figure 5.6 the plan types are reduced to basic essentials to create a striking contrast between Durham and Westmorland, and shows how detail can be simplified and generalised to establish a broader picture. Clearly, the allocation of a settlement layout to a plan type category involves an element of subjectivity thinly disguised as 'professional judgement', not least because plan types are not static, but evolve through time, experiencing expansion or contraction which can substantively alter the pristine geometry of the original layout. Nevertheless, once the likelihood of an underlying regularity is appreciated, it can be sought and confirmed by map and field evidence. In fact, as has already been suggested, all the evidence points towards the existence of a sub-stratum of regular, possibly planned, villages throughout northern England, and while they are most certainly not all of the same date – a complex issue to be examined below – many clearly date to the centuries before 1350.

Whatever the implications of the local variations, whatever the complexities of local and regional chronologies, whatever the circumstances of origin, development and the variations in size, there is in this mass of material clear evidence for formalized layouts that are surely indicative of *planning*. This involved the application in the landscape of what may be termed a 'village idea', an idealised conceptual framework of what a village should be. Furthermore, this is by no means abstract, theoretical or academic: it *has* been applied, again and again, throughout very large tracts of northern England, with great thoroughness and great persistence. Again and again the recovery of additional pre-nineteenth century map evidence, or the close examination of earthworks attached to a surviving village reveals the presence of once unsuspected regularities (Roberts 1993b; 1996). The cumulative volume of evidence is now vast. In fact concentration of actual cases far exceeds any other available set of archaeological evidence for the period between 1150 and 1350. The widespread distribution emphasises one further fact: planning was in no way confined to one category of estate. It appears that existence of a conceptualised village layout was an idea that thoroughly permeated the medieval mind and the landscapes of the north. In this there are, as has already been noted, close parallels with the well-known sequence of architectural styles, Norman, Early English, Decorated and Perpendicular. No building stands in isolation, but manifests parallels, in its plan, in the details of its building practice, elevation, structure, decorative ornament and even siting, with edifices elsewhere, in the region and in this country and abroad. Settlement plans show the same tendencies, and this is at once a simple yet exciting observation.

The emphasis upon row-based plans needs some comment. Other plan types *are* indeed present and agglomerated plans do appear. From this latter category grid plans must be excluded, although they represent a form of agglomeration, because they are variants of row plans, with more streets developed (Fig.1.3). Anomalies such as highly irregular clusters, wholly radial plans, loose tangles of lanes and tofts set with no apparent order, are all part of northern landscapes (*e.g.* Figs 3.4 and 4.10). In all of this work complete, detailed and comprehensive data collection is impossible. The landscape is richer than even the best of maps can reveal and the principles of analyzing less-regular plans were outlined in 1977 (Roberts 1977, 63–86).

Towns

The composite or polyfocal plans of Figure 2.1 reveal a set of higher status places. Helmsley has a clear-cut and rectangular market place, still used as a street market and recently for the assembly of bikers! Nearby is a Norman church, set to the north of the market place (Fig. 4.12). An exploration of the land on the west, or castle side, of the square shows that a stream flows from up the hill and runs down a street to the north-west of the church, round the churchyard (where it is now in a culvert and underground), down to the rear of the market place, and thence down the hill. A Norman castle lies on a low ridge to the west of the town. Once this layout is interpreted in terms of the grammar of 'village' settlement plans, the reason for the layout becomes clear. The northern extension of the settlement, along the stream is a 'two row street green' plan, and once a rural village; the Norman church is set at the lower end of this and down-slope of the church was once a large market area, taking in all of the in the settlement's interior. The rather irregular plots and alleys to the south and west of the open market area today result from the process of 'market colonisation', *i.e.* the establishment of permanent buildings in the former open space (Conzen 1960, 34–8; Whitehand 1981, 30). Originally there was one long inward facing row to the west of the stream and one to the east. This open space was very large. The upper end of the open market square has been 'closed' by a *head row*, extending eastwards from the church. All other elements are accretive growths around this focus, except for the castle, which must surely be associated with the planning of this little town and may predate – perhaps by days, perhaps by months, perhaps by some years – the laying out of the market area below the church. The castle is Norman in origin, attributed to Robert de Roos (1186–1227), while the church is documented before 1166 (EYC I, 147) and shows details such as can be seen in Durham maybe 50 more so years earlier (Renn 1973, 204). These details hint at the developmental context of this little planted borough. Paradoxically it does not matter if this particular analysis is 'wrong' or 'right'. What it does is, in the context of a broad understanding of settlement in northern England, establish hypotheses that can eventually be tested, and either rejected or accepted. Helmsley is but one of a group of such plans, and this short analysis owes much to the groundbreaking work of Maurice Beresford on planned towns of the period 1086–1400 (Beresford 1988; Beresford and Finberg 1973, 187). This mode of thinking, exemplified in Figure 2.3, shows important linkages between town, village and hamlet plans in Yorkshire.

This argument can be extended throughout the north. As will be discussed in Chapter 4 Appleby in Westmorland, set within its river loop, sweeps downward from the great standing Norman keep of the 1180s as a broad rectangular market street, now partially given over to gardens, while set at the bottom is a church established in the Norman period (Fig. 4.12). A similar plan appears at Warkworth in Northumberland. At Whorlton, North Yorkshire is a remarkable survival; the earthworks and ruins of a great castle – again of Norman origin – and the arches of a Norman church stand amid fields, all being set on a high ridge. Traces of a limiting bank suggest that this was an unsuccessful effort to establish a small borough. The success of market towns was eventually subject to rules of competition that governed success or failure, but the decision to plant a town, to provide the land and obtain a grant from the crown of market and fair rights lay in the hands of local landowners and their stewards (Beresford 1988). Of course, initiative and luck also played a part, because a soundly based market town needed to be established in an area which was sufficiently wealthy to provide a degree of basic support, and located on route ways which allowed travellers from further afield easy access. These were crucial factors in sustaining success. Furthermore, location at the junction of contrasting countrysides enhanced economic potential, drawing in stock, wool and woodland products from the foothills and uplands, and grains and vegetables from the lowland fields and gardens. On larger scales regularities in the spacing of successful market towns can be detected (Coates 1965). These are linked to the distance of six to ten kilometres, say 4 to 6 miles, representing a day's journey to and from market for those wishing to buy and sell.

Towns, then, were an integral part of the countryside. They provided focal points where local produce was assembled and exchanged, and where items obtained via long-distance trade were available to those who could afford them. The peasant who took surplus grain, a calf, a pig, poultry and eggs or garden vegetables or fruit to market could purchase country cloth, trenchers, dried fish, squirrel skins, crafted metal and leather goods and local and regional pottery. Salt and spices, fine cloths and exotic pottery were brought in by itinerant traders, members of a wider national or even international community, and through these transactions flowed talk and gossip, spreading rumours, ideas and new attitudes. Rural culture was underpinned by such exchanges, all meditated by the use of an increasing volume of currency in circulation. These were not closed worlds, even for the peasantry. For the lords, both churchmen and knights, and their stewards, travel to the discrete elements of great estates, involvement in regional and national affairs and attendance at markets and fairs held beneath the towers of castles and religious houses must have created opportunities to compare, contrast, exchange and engage in weighty matters and business. Camille uses a quotation from Stallybrass and White (1998, 269) to express the excitement of these contacts for ordinary folk:

> Even the smallest fair juxtaposed "both people and objects which were normally kept separate and thus provided a taste of life beyond the narrow horizons of town or village. Part of the transgressive excitement of the fair for the subordinate classes was not its 'otherness' to official discourse, but rather the disruption of provincial

habits and local tradition by the introduction of a certain cosmopolitanism, arousing desires and excitements for exotic and strange commodities. A fair 'turned the world inside out' in its mercantilist aspect, if not more so than it 'turned the world upside down' in its popular rituals".

Talk lay at the root of this social intercourse. In this way, in a society where reading skills were limited, flowed some of the knowledge that helped create contexts for the diffusion of new concepts as diverse as, architectural styles, the possibilities for migration and betterment, and, perhaps, some of the perspectives needed for village planning.

Distribution Maps: Comparing and Contrasting

The distribution of towns, villages and hamlets in County Durham is shown in Figure 2.6. These concentrate in the south and east of the county, on the better quality lands of the Tees valley and along the eastern seaboard. In effect they encircle the Magnesian Limestone plateau, concentrating both on its seaward side, where the limestone is drift-covered but appear in greatest numbers along its western edge. This is where the varied soils of the scarp and waning lower slopes of the limestone provide that soil variety so attractive to settlement. Like the edges of the Vale of Pickering this is a preferred settlement zone. For the moment ignoring the varied forms, the desertions in east Durham appear to have taken place gradually as much as cataclysmically. Hodgson's work on sixteenth century ecclesiastical census material, the Compton Census of the later seventeenth century and the household returns of the 1801 national census suggests gradual declines, the result of the accumulation of tenancies in fewer and fewer hands leading to the decay of unwanted steadings (Hodgson 1989, figs 5.1–3). It will be noted how these depopulations complement the pattern of successful, surviving villages. Overall, however, the pattern, as Thorpe suggested, is a delicate response to small local variations in terrain that affect soil quality and potential for arable farming (Thorpe 1951). Watts has demonstrated that in this zone are concentrated the forms of Anglo-Saxon place-names indicating habitation, names ending in *-tun*, *-ham*, *-worth*, *-wic* and *-burh*. In contrast, further to the west and north-west is a zone dominated by place-names indicative of woodland, names in *-leah*, *-hyrst*, *-rydding* and *–wudu* (Watts 2002, xi–xix; Fig. 2.4, inset). Nucleated settlements do appear in this western zone, but they are more thinly scattered and as will be shown in Chapter 4 do have plans that are subtly different to those further to the east. Furthermore, two differing types of countryside are involved, but in this case, unlike the North York Moors these cannot be easily explained by using underlying bold terrain contrasts. While there are at core undoubted environmental differences between east and west Durham, these change gradually as one moves from east to west across the basin of the Durham coalfield, a low plateau broken up into blocks by incised drainage networks finding grade with the

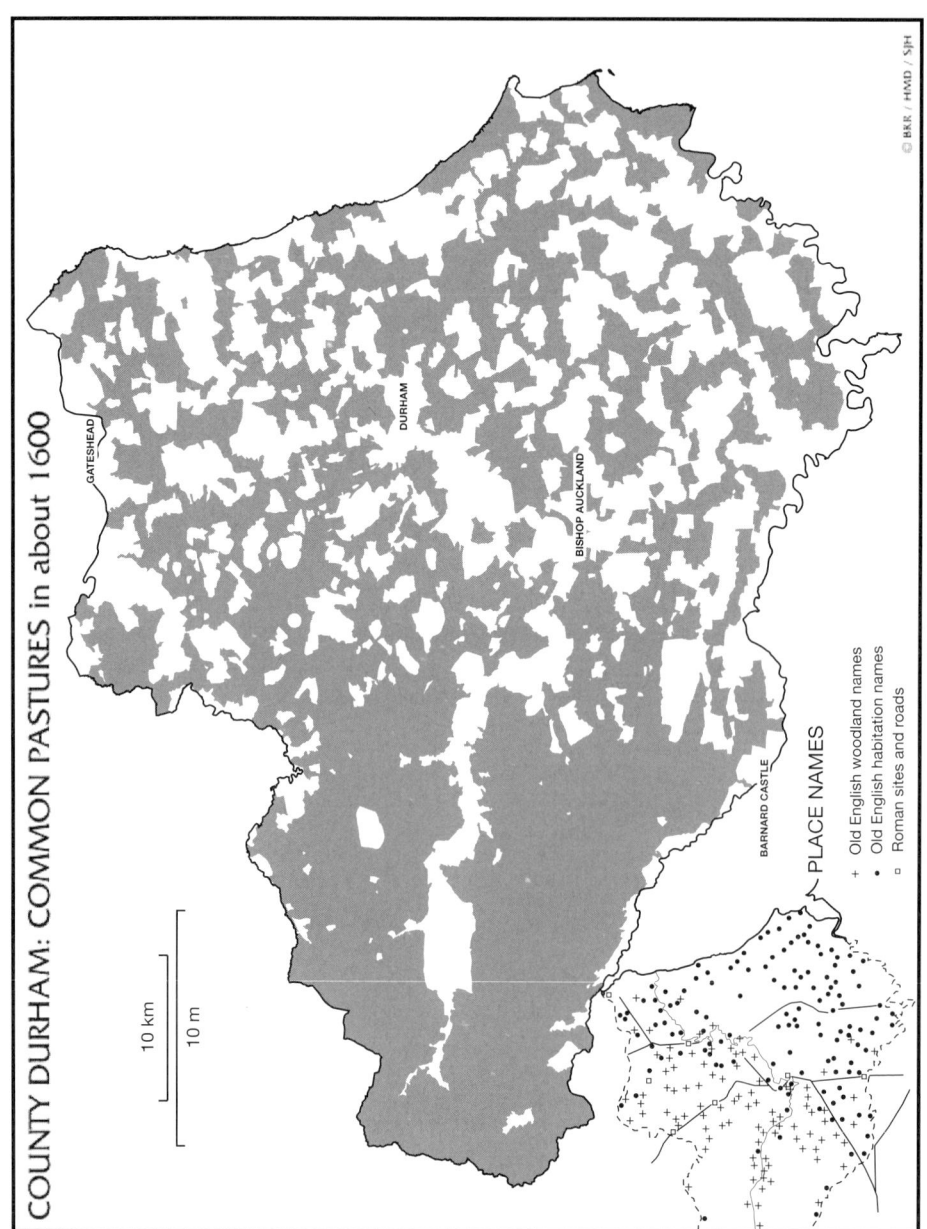

Fig. 2.4 The distribution of common pastures in County Durham in about 1600

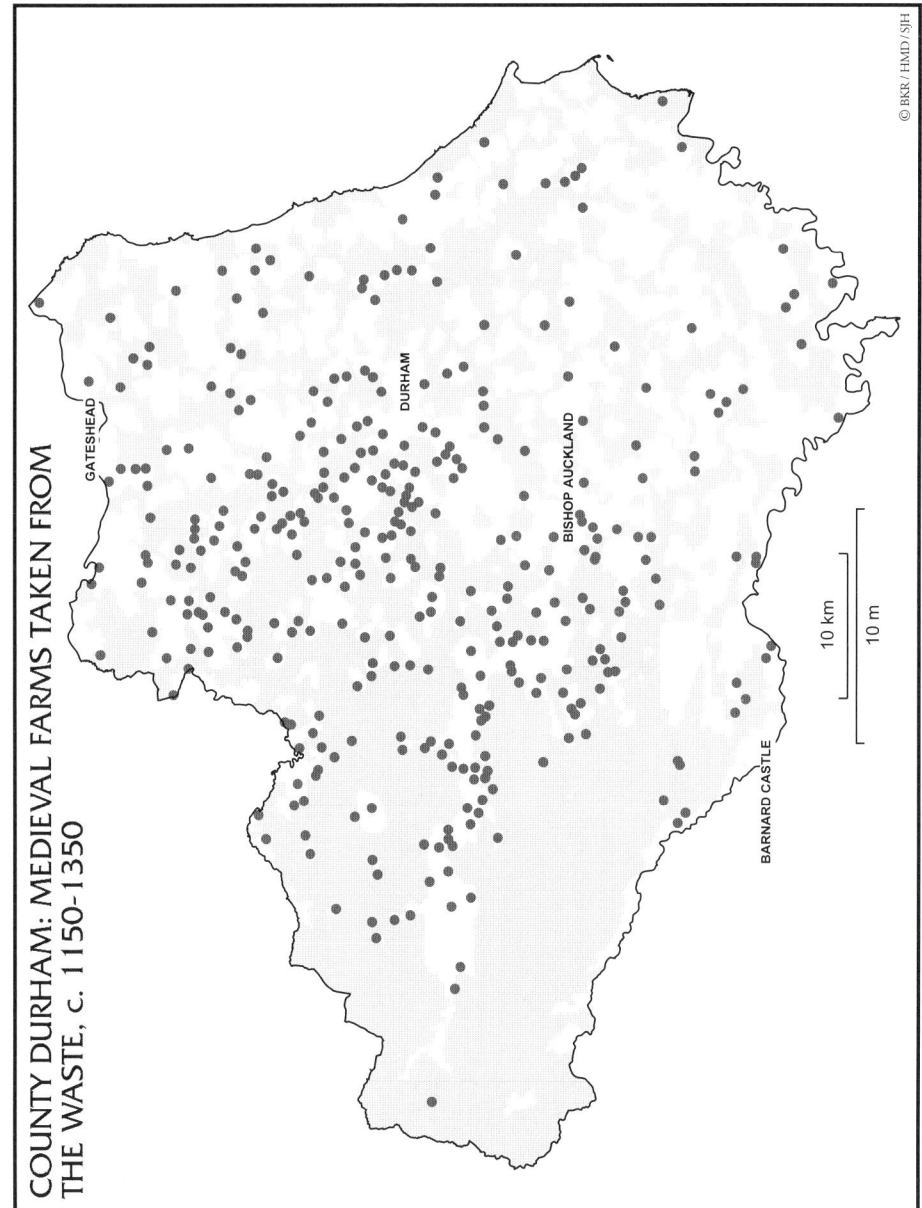

Fig. 2.5 The distribution of medieval farms in County Durham in about 1350

River Wear. The slopes to the rivers are separated by flat or rolling plateau surfaces. In general no sharp lines like the northern edge of the North York Moors or the edges of the Vale of Pickering are detectable in the Durham landscapes. However, the line, from Barnard Castle to Bishop Auckland, thence to Durham, thence north via Chester-le-Street to Gateshead is a cultural boundary of great subtlety and importance. It may be no accident that one is forced to describe this boundary in terms of towns, for these represented exchange points, where the produce of varied countrysides were brought to market, but this is by no means the whole story.

Figure 2.6 has to have been considered out of sequence, but an exciting map of County Durham appears as Figure 2.4. This depicts the common wastes of the county, as they may have appeared in about 1600, on the eve of a major cycle of seventeenth century enclosures (Dunsford and Harris 2003). In this respect County Durham was a century earlier than many English counties because of its quickening economy as a result of coalmining (Hodgson 1989, figs 6.1–6.4 and 6.7–9). There is, however, a disadvantage in this, because the enclosure measures, by surrender and admittance in the Halmote Court of the Bishopric, followed essentially medieval procedures. On a given day the tenants all came to court, and surrendered their properties to a named individual. The next day these were re-granted to each individual tenant, thus effecting the change from scattered strips to consolidated block holdings. No maps were produced. However, the Ordnance Survey maps of the 1850s retain the names of the former common wastes, probably because the area was a coalfield and the land-rights were important, indeed a land-ownership map of about 1840 survives for the whole portion of the county underlain by coal. Though a careful examination of the field patterns, supplemented by some local studies, eighteenth century maps, Victor Watts' place-name studies and the evidence from charters and surveys falling between 1150 and 1400 it has proved possible to create a distribution map of the wastes and commons in about 1600. The compilers, Helen Dunsford and Simon Harris and the present author believe it to be accurate at least to the 80% level, and greater precision is not improbable. The picture it provides is stunning. Anyone familiar with the surviving wastes of upland Durham, now divided into large pasture blocks and true communal common pastures, is aware of their vast extent, even today. One comes upon them as one travels above the 300 m contour line, above the valley bottom meadows and enclosed fields of the dale sides, set on the high rolling ridges and plateau of the west. However, in the earlier decades of the seventeenth century such open common pastures, probably comprising mixtures of coarse grasses, heather and bracken, with galleries of trees along the most sloping land, spread to the gates of Durham city and were present as great swathes amid the well-farmed landscapes of the south and east.

This simple mapping procedure has deeper methodological implications. Those portions of the land surface *not* mapped as common waste essentially comprise improved lands, within the head-dykes of the uplands and ring-dykes of the lowlands. In 1600 much of this was largely townfield arable, together with a variety of enclosed farms

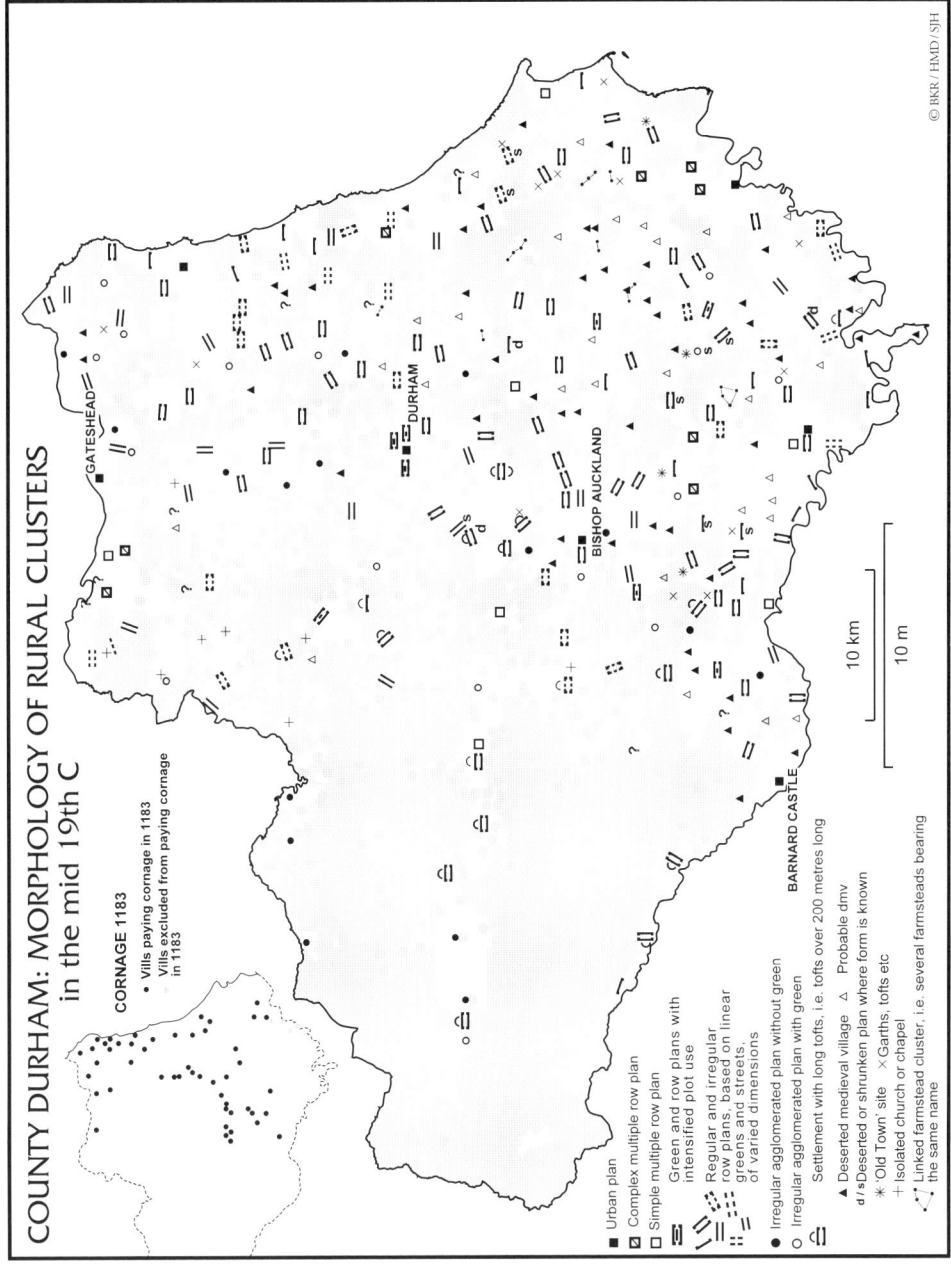

Fig. 2.6 The morphology of rural clusters – villages and hamlets – in County Durham

of ancient foundation. In addition there were parklands. It was into this framework, whose lineaments we can now see, that coalmining was intruded, bringing pits, wagon ways and railways, and the closely packed rows of mining villages. As Hodgson has shown, the earliest mining villages were loose clusters, resembling disordered squatting settlements, set upon the common wastes of north-west Durham (Hodgson 1989, fig. 5.5). However, Figure 2.5 incorporates another element, a scatter of simple dots. Each and every one of these represents a farmstead created as a result of a grant of wasteland in the period between about 1150 and 1350 (Dunsford and Harris 2003). These tell of piecemeal reclamation and are a further reminder of the need for studies of dispersion. To obtain this picture, Simon Harris, building on initial investigations by Richard Lomas, searched no less than ten thousand charters in the Durham archives. In size these grants range from a few acres to over 300 acres, but often fall into groups, 20 acres, 40 acres, 60 acres, 80 acres, 120 acres, 240 acres, reflecting the concept of the carucate of 120 acres. These figures have not been metricated – they need to be divided by 2.5 to give hectares – but neither are they necessarily statute acres based on a 16.5–foot land rod. These may be acres measured with an eighteen-foot land rod or even a twenty-one foot land rod, making them larger pieces of land than at first sight.

What this mapping indicates is that in west Durham the common wastes of 1600 must be extended by adding to them lands intaken between 1150 and 1350. We arrive at a picture – developed though Figures 2.4 and 2.5 – in which it is likely that in 1150 to the west of the Barnard Castle – Durham – Gateshead line at least 80% of the land surface was open land, rough grazings and residual woodlands. Containing both Roman roads and other tracks this was undoubtedly accessible, but it was still wolf-haunted, with deer, wild cattle and boar, and no-doubt at times bandit-ridden; later generations would call them rievers (Watts 2002, 167; Fraser 1971). In contrast, to the east approximately 50% of the land surface was common pasture, grazed by the beasts from the villages. These are indeed approximations, but the essential picture is valid, and we have a remarkable image of landscapes that are far removed from those of today, in which cultivation and improvement appeared as islands within a vast sea of waste. In retrospect we can see that there were hints already in the generalised picture seen in Figures 1.5 and 1.6, supporting the value of such overviews or 'top down' approaches. In the south and east communally organised townfields, open, and in some way divided into strips, tended to occupy most of the improved land, or to use the northern term, the inby land (Hodgson 1989, figs 6.1–2, 6.7). In sharp contrast, to the north and west these formed no more than tiny islands of cultivation set amid a vast sea of waste. The research programme that resulted in Figure 2.6 is as yet incomplete. Maps are to be created using the Hatfield Survey, showing the county as it was in the later fourteenth century, and using the Boldon Book to show it as it was in the later twelfth century (Greenwell 1852: 1857). As yet there are substantial uncertainties about the degree of detail that can be achieved, and all we have at this stage is a glimpse of what may be possible and establishing a real time context for the

Of Patterns and Forms 51

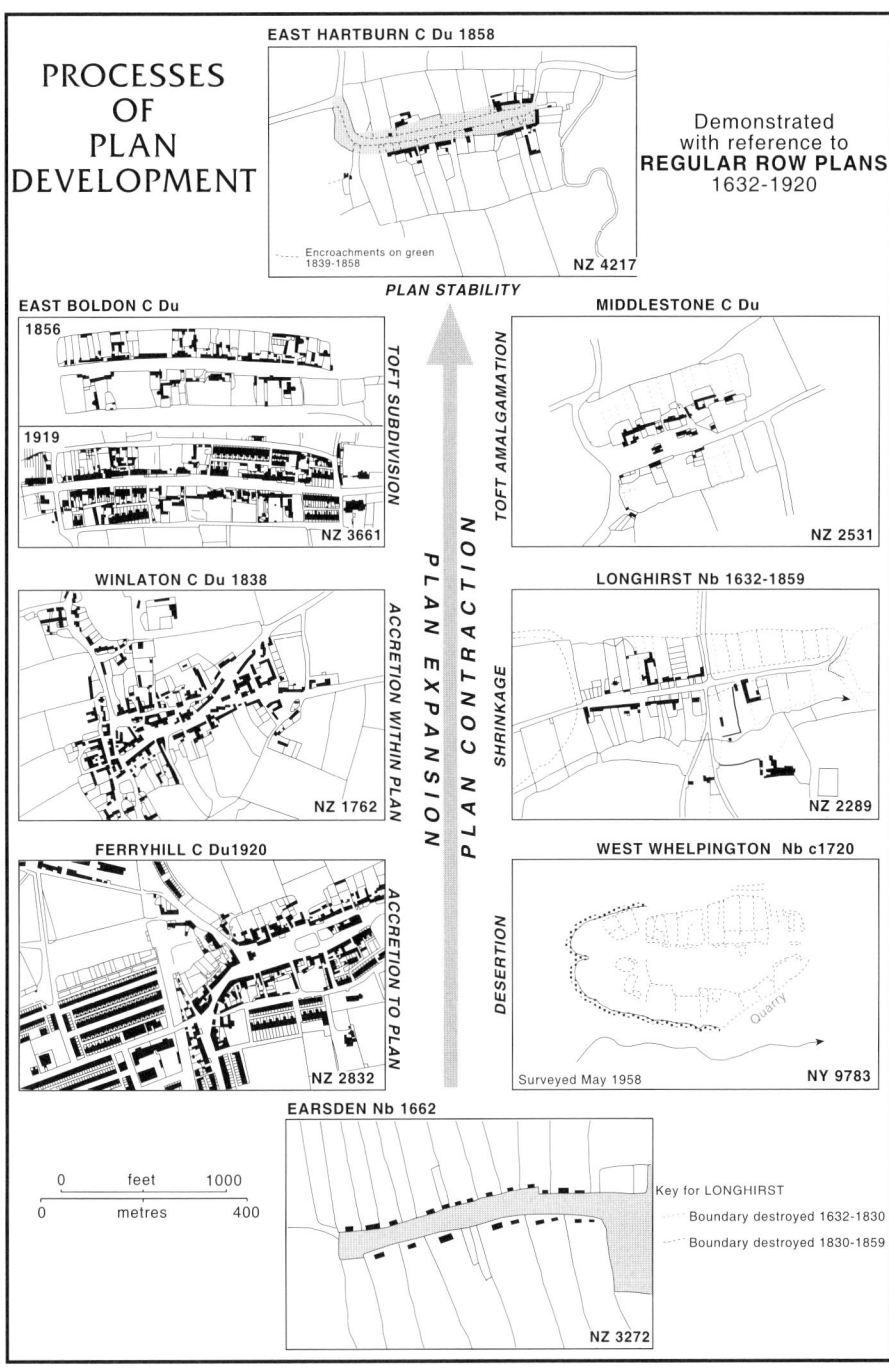

Fig. 2.7 Processes of plan development

settlement data, single-farmsteads, hamlets, villages and towns, incorporated in Figure 2.6. The precise vegetation of the western woodlands and wastes can be much debated (Innes *et al.* in Huddart and Glasser 2002, 351–65). The bulk of earlier settlement lay to the south and east of the Barnard Castle – Bishop Auckland – Durham – Chester-le-Street – Gateshead line (Figures 2.5 and 2.6). This defines one boundary of the early, perhaps British, territory of Catraeth that was postulated in the discussion of Figures 1.7 and 1.8. A close examination of Figure 1.7 shows that there were indeed significant internal terrain variations, in geology, soils and relief, within each of the polities. Both the Durham enquiries and the regional projections are based upon the concept of positive and negative analyses: the commons and wastes can be mapped, giving a positive distribution, while the residual landscapes, in fact those which were economically the most important, appear as negative images. The interplay of county and region allows scale to be manipulated as a further tool of enquiry, the whole procedure allowing the formulation of new questions and the testing of hypotheses using other data sets.

Village Plan Elements and Processes of Change

This listing of some of the ingredients of the settlement patterns of northern England provides a measure of the fundamental question raised by this study: we must make sense of landscapes replete with evidence of settlements. Before continuing, however, we must return to the problem of how individual settlements can be analysed, interpreted, dated and understood as historical source materials. The classificatory grid seen in Figure 1.3 serves as a reminder that the present study concentrates upon a group of plans that are based upon row structures: other forms will be treated only incidentally. Examples of row plans range from highly regular through to distinctly irregular, but many exhibit what can best be termed part-regular arrangements, namely that the experienced eye detects in them traces of what may have once been a regular layout that has become deformed through time. This, it can be argued, is the result of a succession of gradual adjustments and changes, each relatively insignificant, but cumulatively resulting radical alteration in a village's layout. This is well illustrated in Figure 2.7. Using eight village plans, all versions of a 'regular two row street green' layout, the diagram presents them in a way designed to raise questions about the varied processes of change that have affected such settlements in the last four hundred years. Earsdon in 1632 exhibits a basic and uncomplicated layout with two rows of farmsteads aligned along the frontages associated with a green. Admittedly, in this case the tofts are rather longer than in usual with northeastern green villages, but as will be shown later in this study, this type is not uncommon (Fig. 3.1). In the other cases, all of which are to the same scale, are to be seen the ways in which one type of plan can mutate as the result of expansion and contraction. East Hartburn shows the way in which a largely stable plan like Earsdon might appear by the middle-decades of the nineteenth century. In contrast, Ferryhill has not only been altered by infill, but a new mining village has been grafted to one side. At another extreme, West Whelpington has been wholly depopulated. Without analysing these cases in detail, this diagram suggests that the basic processes of expansion and contraction, and paradoxically, the emergence of a state of relative stability, can result in the same type of plan appearing in several different configurations or disguises. Sometimes, of course, all of these processes operate together within a single plan, although to explore this would require a detailed analysis of a single place.

Nevertheless, while classification is the foundation of all settlement study and mapping, there is rather more to classification than shoehorning a perceived plan into an appropriate cell of a classificatory grid. The system seen in Figure 1.3 is applicable throughout the north of England, indeed can be used on a world scale (Roberts 1996b, fig. 5.2). The professional judgements involved in classification are contingent upon specific criteria, and the identification of these criteria depends upon detailed observations made upon maps, air photographs or on the ground. The process depends, in short, upon the correct recognition of *plan elements* (Fig. 1.1). Discussion of these, the ingredients making up the two-dimensional plan seen on the map and air photograph and the three-dimensional reality of the field, must begin with something that is obvious: villages are often alike. They can possess similar arrangements of their elements, streets, lanes, footpaths, open spaces, farmsteads, enclosures, cottages, a hall and a church. Hamlets, simpler and smaller, tend to lack the last two elements. In practice there are three types of space present within all village plans, private space and communal and public space, so that in effect villages differ in the distinctive and individual ways in which these three sorts of space are arranged. These are universals in the content of rural settlement space, and drive the logic of the classificatory grid seen in Figure 1.3.

These ingredients – plan elements – make up all villages (although all of them may not be present) and the possibility of identifying groups of villages having broadly similar arrangements of these basic ingredients underlies the definition of the series of plan-types in Figure 1.3. Of course, all is not this simple. Features such as the mill, the smithy and the ale house (now often the village 'local'!), widows' cottages, the pound for strayed stock, sometimes a lock-up, and a host of smaller elements such as wayside crosses, pant houses (where the spring or well appears) may all be ingredients. Mills, set by streams or on a hill-top are usually outside the village, but examples can be seen in many northern villages of dwellings, houses and cottages, set upon the public space, such that to step outside the front door is to be on the public space of the green. A public footpath may even pass though a back yard or toft, indicating a cottage encroaching on former communal space. In other settlements garden space has obviously been carved out of the former green. Some of these are former smithies and alehouses, *i.e.* communal services, but many can be interpreted as later arrivals, placed on the communal land as populations rose in the last three centuries. Older farmsteads characteristically occupy locations between communal open space and the field land, for ease of access to both. There are in addition other special pieces of private land, together with their associated structures, particularly the church and churchyard (*kirk* and *kirkgarth*). In this the community undoubtedly has a share, and may be responsible for part of the structure. However, the owner of the living, the rector, also has an interest, while the location, often near the hall or manor house, or the site of a former hall, shows that the lord of the manor once had a strong association with the power represented by the church. Indeed, church-hall foci are a recognisable ingredient of settlement patterns.

If there is pedantry in this analysis, contained within these material differences are important social divisions, between the great house and the tenancies, between the holders of farmsteads and the holders of cottages, and between the humbler cottagers and the landless. Such social contrasts are fundamental to understanding the English village. However, repeated observations reveal other, less obvious but none-the-less conceivably important details about village and hamlet plans. Further categories of information can be detailed as follows:

- the shapes and sizes of individual tofts, regular, irregular, oddly shaped, *e.g.* a dog-leg shape, with an angled body
- the details of the land within tofts; *e.g.* garden space, showing ridge and furrow, or the presence or absence of earthworks
- the nature of the toft tail line, between the outer limit of the tofts and/or back lane and the arable fields, which may be regular or irregular
- the nature of the toft head line, between the tofts and the street or green, which may be regular, irregular or stepped
- the character of toft boundaries joining the village enclosures, seamless or with a slight discontinuity
- relationships between villages and field systems
- the road, lane and footpath systems
- 'soft and hard shapes', sharp angles or gentle curves
- the character and location of the open greens
- the character and scale of enclosures, hedge-banks, walls, their composition and the ground level of each toft relative to its neighbours
- the presence, or indeed absence, of substantive earthwork remains.

This listing is hardly definitive or all embracing, but each point constitutes a set of observations that can be made: all are part of the story the ground has to tell even before excavation or documentation. Such observations provide the foundation of plan-analysis, both on the map and in the field.

Sufficient evidence has been presented to show that from the basic ingredients it is possible to use observation to define a series of plan categories, effectively sub-groups of those appearing in the four cells of the grid allocated to regular and irregular rows, with

Of Patterns and Forms 55

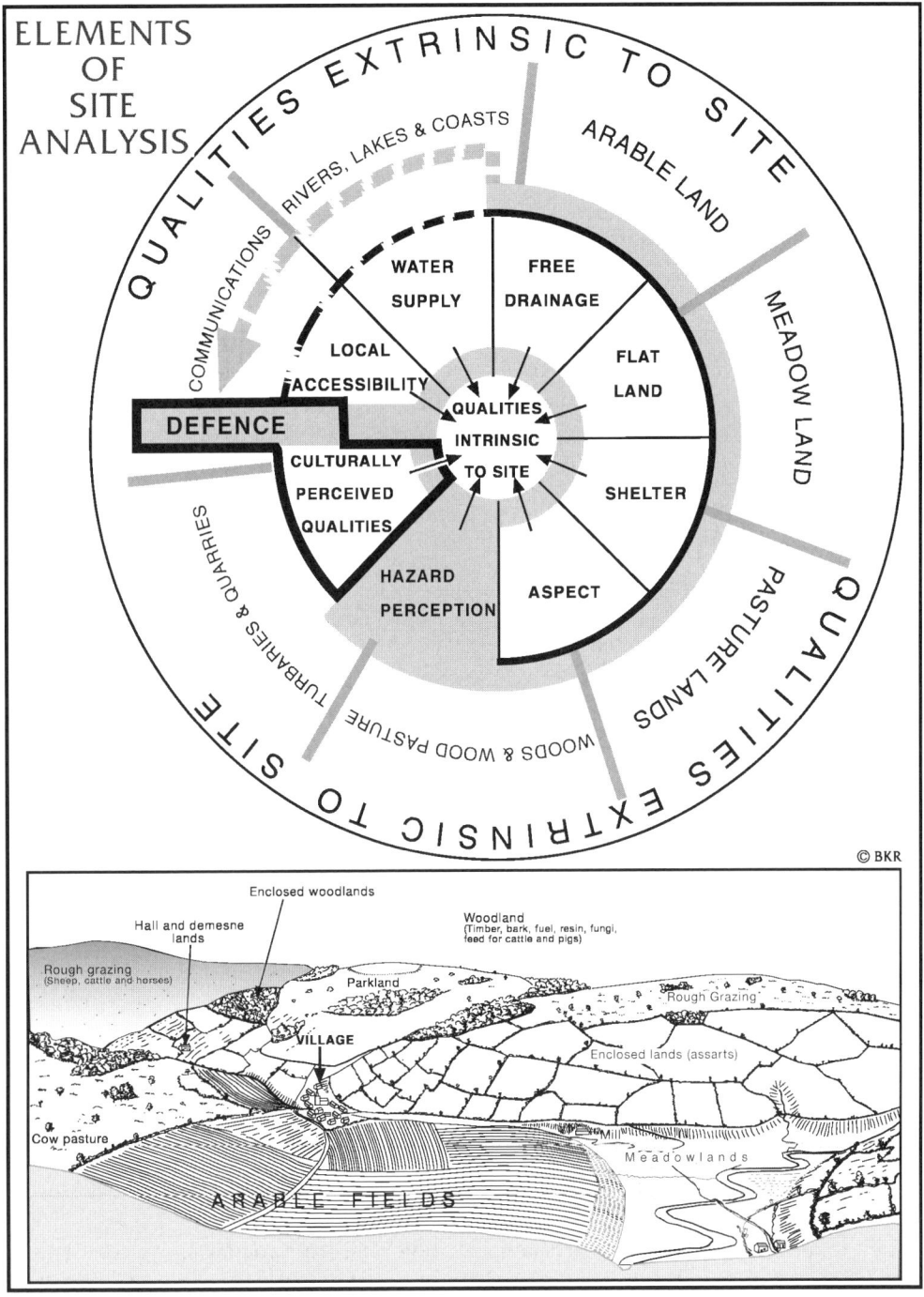

Fig. 2.8 The analysis of settlement sites and locations

and without greens. These can then be mapped. There are some signs that the categories so devised are historically significant because they appear frequently, and undoubtedly have genetic, functional and possibly spatial and temporal implications. Property boundaries, while they retain elements of stability, were nevertheless mutable. While these points have been described rather mechanically at this juncture, the importance of being able to suggest and identify the presence of these features in the evolution of particular plans will be demonstrated in Chapter 3. However, before turning to more specific discussions it is helpful at this point to reflect on the nature of settlement sites, the pieces of land upon which the houses, gardens and other structures of each village are placed.

Settlement Sites

Figure 2.8 identifies the categories of information that can be assembled. While many of these are, or were, qualities intrinsic to the site itself, others reflect a settlement's situation. In practice nucleated rural settlements occupy sites that were selected so as to give easy access to the labour-greedy arable and meadowlands, to permit access to the grazing, building materials and fuel of the unimproved wastes and woodlands. A balance of decisions was involved: a place possessing excellent site qualities (and these are listed in Figure 2.8) could well be ignored if it lay remote from excellent potential arable land. On the other hand, a poor site adjacent to particularly good arable would often be tolerated. This is necessary information for two reasons: first, those settlements that grew organically from a single farmstead or a small group rapidly outgrew the constraints of the site originally selected, with new outward growth having a less comfortable relationship to the terrain. It is as if each of the upland farms seen in Figures 2.1 formed a nucleus for expansion. In contrast the planned settlements of northern England by no means always occupy 'the better' sites. This is something rapidly revealed by the most superficial fieldwork. Numerous examples occur of regular planned settlements that are sited upslope, on level surfaces, sometimes even being located on flatter surfaces that were more logically part of former common grazing land. Site drainage and exposure are problems. Second, many northern settlements are composite or polyfocal in character, with the constituent plan types occupying different sites, selected at different times. The quality of polyfocality occurs when a single settlement (Fig. 1.3) contains two or more distinctive plan types. This can reflect many things: growth phases both planned and unplanned, social distinctions, manorial divisions, as well as ultimate origins in a linked farmstead or linked hamlet cluster. At times the physical contrasts in the siting of each part can be startling: in many settlements it is quite subtle (Roberts 1987, 105–26)

This way of thinking is more productive than analysing 'site' in general, defined by a rather large symbol on a small-scale map, in terms of location upon a particular geological outcrop. It is demanding, for there are few quick answers. That broad scale correlations can and do occur between settlement and solid geology is not to be denied but even the most detailed geological maps do not, indeed cannot, reflect local soil conditions. Thin drift, the alluvium and gravels of hill-wash, even the manner in which former small streams – *sykes*, *sikes* or even *sikets* – have been managed, in new channels and more recently in culverts or pipes, can affect local micro-terrains and the character of the soils that occupy them. In practical terms understanding settlement sites can rarely be achieved quickly because an essential ingredient of their qualities involves an appreciation of time. From one year to the next, as occupation occurs, roadways erode and deepen as rain and melting snows wash at their surfaces or as they are scoured for manure. As erosion occurs there are changes in level, while surfaces may also rise or be consolidated as fieldstones are added to give purchase to horses and wagons. Above all, the slow drift of climatic variations, bad winters and good, wet seasons and dry, reveal new site qualities, some disadvantageous and others tolerable. Site is undoubtedly important in understanding settlement, but what can be determined from both regional and local scale analyses must be treated with great caution and subjected to careful local evaluation. To give one specific example, Kirk Merrington, County Durham: the main axis of the settlement lies along the top of a high and exposed ridge (Fig. 5.3.a). To the south, tucked into a small hollow and thus protected from the winds coming from the north-west, north and north-east – 'lazy winds', for they blow right though you rather than round you – lies the settlement of *Shelom* or *Shelam*, 'at the huts', originally inhabited by the bond tenants. At its centre lay a small pond, an attractive point on this dry limestone ridge, and surely a critical factor in the location of the settlement?

This review of northern settlement draws together patterns, forms and terminology to provide a foundation for a series of case studies to follow. Such an alteration in viewpoint, and a change of scale from the general to the specific, is necessary. The intention is to show how individual places, individual plans, can be analysed, dated and explained in the light of the generalisations developed in chapters one and two. In the absence of full excavation and a full exploration of all surviving documentary material this is never complete, but plan-analysis poses questions worthy of pursuit.

CHAPTER THREE

Settlement Plans – Regular Forms

When dealing with the details of northern village plans, the size of tofts or individual farmstead plots is a practical issue that cannot be ignored. Pragmatically it appears that three types of regular toft can be identified throughout the north. First, 'short tofts' are generally less than 150 metres in length; second, 'long tofts', generally falling between about 150–250 metres and third, 'strip tofts', in excess of 250 metres in length, sometimes reaching the vast length of 600, 800 or even 1200 metres. Here already are contradictions. The longest strips are not mere house plots. They are field strips. Nevertheless, if it is recalled that a standard furlong is 220 yards or 200 metres in length, then it can be seen that the intermediate group designated 'long tofts' bridge the gap between true house plot and field strip. Short tofts are rarely square, and a proportion of 1:2 and 1:3 is usual. The proportions of long tofts fall between 1:5 to 1:10, while strip tofts may reach the exaggerated proportions of 1:100 or more. Furthermore, when these plots are seen upon late maps their width may bear no relationship to what was there originally because of centuries of splitting and amalgamation. Nevertheless, these functional spaces are the building blocks of nucleated villages and hamlets.

There are of course other qualities. When these features are observed, on maps or in the field, they are normally enclosed. However, the author has seen examples in Poland of broad field strips, each open to its neighbours and with no more than a furrow between two properties. The house-plots, each with a wicket fence, were placed as islands at each strip head and set back a little from the roadway. Pragmatically, the terms (normal) 'toft', 'long toft' and 'strip toft' are merely convenient labels to describe what can be observed on maps and in the field and as such they are of proven value. Furthermore, the term 'croft' normally means an enclosed plot, but throughout the early seventeenth century Northumberland was specifically applied to the bundles of open field strips set in a block behind the tofts and also at right angles to the street axis (NCH, 5 map, facing page 204; Roberts 1987, 46–7). In some cases each farmstead is found to be backed by one broad strip, co-terminal with the width of its toft: in other cases the core furlong – for this is what it was – was divided into a multitude of strips with each farmer possessing a scatter (Roberts 1987, 58–9). A careful study of air photographs of Newby shows that the long crofts are in fact former field strips stitched onto a set of short tofts once demarcated by a back lane (Fig. 3.1). This is revealed, indeed proven, by a succession of small irregularities in the pattern of enclosure boundaries at the junction between the tofts and the former field strips, along the line of the former lane. This observation generates a number of further possibilities, for some long tofts, as at Cockfield, Co.

Settlement Plans – Regular Forms 59

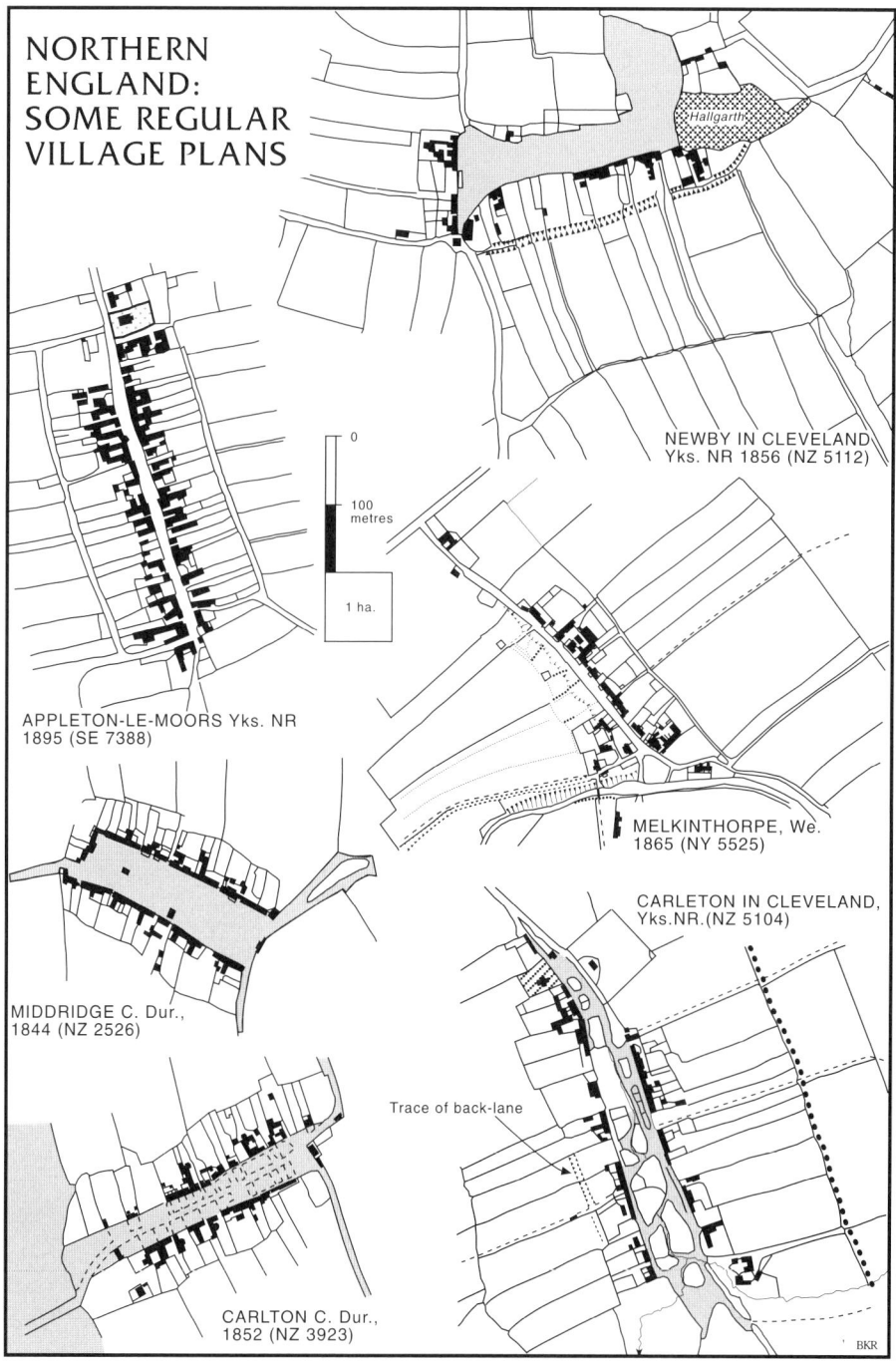

Fig. 3.1 Regular northern village plans

Durham (Fig. 4.1) may well have originated as single unitary strips, comprising toft and field-strip, and in this case there is no back lane. In all discussion, the quality of the maps used and the dates when the changes were made all play a part in survival of sufficient material remains to elucidate the story. Classification must be tempered by common sense. Basically a tool, it becomes an instrument of research when applied with imagination and experience. However, there is little doubt that this plot diversity, detectable in the landscape and on the region's earliest estate maps, was already present in earlier centuries. Selecting randomly ten tofts in northern villages mapped in the author's study *The Making of the English Village,* these vary from about 9000 square metres (about 1.25 acres) to 1000 square metres (about one quarter of an acre). Sizes of the order of 2000, 3000 and 6000 square metres appear. An acre, originally 22 × 220 yards – a shape linked to ploughing – can also be thought of as a square with sides of somewhat under 70 yards, namely 63.6 metres, or approximately 4000 square metres, some 4840 square yards. Thus a toft of the order of 150 metres deep and 50 metres wide would give 7500 square metres, somewhat under two acres. By the standards of those of us who live in semi-detached dwellings, these are not small plots, but the gradual descent into 'imprecise accuracy' is necessary. What is required is a grasp of the general dimensions involved, not spurious precision.

Taking as sample the first three volumes of Farrer's *Early Yorkshire Charters* and selecting those where toft sizes are specified, and citing only references before 1200 and assuming an 18 foot perch (Jones 1979), confirms these points. We have:

- in Settrington a toft 4 perches by 12 perches in *c.* 1185–1200, about 1445 square metres (EYC i, document 625);
- in Kirby Grindalythe 3 perches by 9 perches and five feet, about 1008 square metres, and 4 perches by 10 perches in *c.* 1180–1201, about 1206 square metres (*ibid.* ii. 1080 and 1083);
- a toft in Wilberfosse 4 perches in width by a furlong (*quadragenam*) in length in *c.* 1180–1193, about 4816 square metres (*ibid.* ii, 914);
- in Huggate a toft in width 4 perches and in length between two roads in 1178–1190 (*ibid.* ii, 1255);
- in Swaythorpe a toft 6 perches in width by 16 in length in 1190–1210, about 2889 square metres (*ibid.* ii, 850) and
- in Tollesby a toft 8 perches by 40 long in 1170–1188, approximately 9632 square metres (*ibid.* iii, 1849).

Even if we assume a perch of 16.5 feet or even 20 feet – and we can rarely be certain – then these fall within the size ranges and dimensions of those noted upon nineteenth century maps, excluding only the very longest strip tofts extending over several hundred metres. This documentation provides justification for using the word *toft* to embrace all plots with a dwelling set at the head, even when they incorporate the strip of an arable furlong backing onto the row dwellings. Of course tofts are also measured by statute measure, if indeed a 16.5–foot rod was used. We read of

- a toft of half an acre in Nun Coton (EYC iii, 1309);
- a toft of one acre in Liverton (*ibid.* i, 892);
- a toft of one and a half acres in Linthorpe (*ibid.* iii, 1851),
- a toft of two acres in *Frisemareis* (*ibid.* iii, 1403) and
- a toft of four acres in Bramley in Handsworth (*ibid.* iii, 1291).

There are also subdivisions: a half toft (*ibid.* iii, 1555), a third of a toft (*ibid.* iii, 1644) and a quarter part of a toft (*ibid.* iii, 1283). These examples show that the classification described above is empirically grounded, and not only in map sources of the eighteenth and nineteenth centuries but also in pre-1300 documentation and that these often imprecise measurements nevertheless relate to real world situations.

The case of Appleton-le-Moors (Fig. 3.1) shows how back-lanes can be carefully integrated into a village plan, establishing a clear-cut termination to the toft tail line. However, today they are often seen with tarmac upon them and this, with the enclosing boundaries on each side, ensure that their presence as a strip of what is now public space is preserved. Others – perhaps the majority – survive only as bridleways, footpaths or even as farm tracks, a categorisation that crosses the threshold from public to private space. Others survive as no more than slight earthworks (see Carlton in Cleveland, Fig. 3.1). In this case they may be virtually indistinguishable from the headland that inevitably ran along the toft tail line when the adjacent furlong was ploughed using mouldboard ploughs and ridged lands (Fig. 2.3, model). Often set slightly higher than the field ridges which ran up and into them, these represented turning grounds, access points and plough cleaning locations, using a clod beetle or mallet, a necessary operation when plough frames were wooden and bulky. For the farmers of the settlement such rights of way – and one must suspect these were originally wholly for the use of the community and not the general public – gave access to the rear of the toft, for wagons, ploughs and for bringing in hay and grain harvests. There is an inevitable tendency to see these as wholly functional plan elements, and in many senses that is precisely what they are. Nevertheless, in some Swedish regulated villages, *i.e.* villages formally planned so as to integrate tenemental structure and the settlement plan, it is clear that back lanes could be present and planned as part of the whole concept and layout (Göransson 1958). But there is here a hint that a back-lane could be also be seen as the line defining space formally divided and used in one manner, the toft lands, *i.e.* the inner living space of the community's land, together with paddocks, gardens, orchards and vegetable plots. Beyond this line lay the extensive field lands, where rather different divisions and management practice prevailed. In practical terms this arrangement was sensible: the back-lanes form liminal space between the arable fields and the private spaces of the tofts, allowing individuals to move freely around the settlement with their ploughs and carts and wagons. It eliminated the tensions that could have arisen if fieldstrips had directly abutted the toft lands.

Of course, when such villages were fully functioning, inhabited by a farming tenantry, surrounded by open fields, meadows and common pastures, they must often have appeared as small blocks or islands set amid extensive open arable spaces. Enclosed in some way, with fences and hedges, perhaps with timber and fruit trees, they presented a sharp contrast to the grain, hay and grass produced in their surroundings. Further, they accommodated wealth, stored harvests, grain and other produce, with beasts in the byres, pigs in the sties and horses in the stables. They were attractive to raiders and rievers, and in small measure their toft tail lines must have been defensible. The formally structured green village, with its interior for stock – and the function of greens has yet to be considered – its farmsteads and tofts, while never planned to be defensive, was in fact defensible. Kurosawa's *Seven Samurai* provides an indelible image, with the outer boundary of a small agricultural village being attacked by mounted bandits while being valiantly defended by the peasantry whose capacity to resist was stiffened by the presence of six hired *samurai* and a peasant impostor. In this there were strong echoes of the north at various times in its history. The alternative was to pay the bandits off, and no doubt this strategy was commonly adopted (Fraser 1971, 192–5).

Simple Row Plans

Generalisations are useful in creating frameworks in which particular examples can be examined, but the discussion in the remainder of this chapter will follow a format in which studies of particular plans are used to inform and extend the synoptic arguments. The methodological questions involved have been well exemplified by Peter Ryder in his study of medieval church fabrics in west Yorkshire (Ryder 1993, 3–6). He identifies three levels of assessment. Level 1 is essentially general, derived from an initial examination using the classificatory framework of architectural style; in contrast, Level 3 comprises a full architectural and archaeological investigation, revealing as much as can currently be learned through such a process. Level 2 is an intermediate level between the superficial assessment and a full examination. Essentially it is based upon a full and informed visual inspection, using an accurate ground plan, drawings of elevations and photographs. It embodies a compromise between time, cost and scholarly needs. While it would be tedious to draw lines between the three levels in terms of the analysis of village plans, the three steps are represented amongst the varied cases used in this study, with the majority being of Level 2. Inevitably, working in this manner means there are many threads that cannot be relentlessly pursued to their conclusion. In all cases, however, the object is to provide material evidence that can illuminate the fundamentally more complex discussions of the later chapters of this study. To structure the arguments a simple classification is adopted, based upon the framework modelled in Figure 1.3.

Newby in Cleveland

Newby, in the parish of Stokesley, in the North Riding of Yorkshire (Fig. 3.1) has already been introduced. First documented in 1236 (EYC I, 445) the name itself speaks of a *niwe-by* or 'new farm' (Smith 1956, 50–51; Smith 1928, 169). There is no hint of its existence under the Stokesley entry in Domesday Book, and while we cannot be absolutely sure the presumption is that the settlement developed at a date between 1086 and 1236. The present village comprises a single row, with a compartment facing an open green on the northern side and formerly delimited by a back-lane to the south. To the west a short head-row appears, to be interpreted as expansion over former west to east field strips, while to the north of the green cottages are planted on its edge. However, to the east a complex of earthworks fill an approximate oval whose area is approximately half that of the toft compartment. This is a classic example of the frustrations of plan analysis, for this argument presents a likely chronological sequence, with the earthworks, probably a manorial enclosure, representing the initial settlement. To this was eventually added the tenant row, involving the enclosure of plots along the head of furlong running westwards of the hall-garth, creating the toft compartment, with the former field strips eventually becoming attached as 'garrends' to the tofts. A back-lane separates the two, and, as noted earlier, a slight irregularity is evidence for the later attachment of the garrends. These extensions took place at a time when any original equality of share – once represented by equal sized tofts, although this is an assumption – had long disappeared. It must be admitted that this hypothesis, floating in time, is compounded by the absence of a church, because the township of Newby was in the parish of Stokesley. Newby is here used as an example of a single-row plan. The fact that there is in Northamptonshire a similar single row plan, Newton Bromswold, documented as a tenanted settlement in 1086 (Roberts 1978, 88–9), permits the suggestion that such single row compartments *can* be of at least late eleventh century date. Nevertheless, it is probable that they continued to be established well into the thirteenth century and there are dangerous traps here, not least because the foundation of a single row plan at East Thirston, Northumberland, took place as late as the sixteenth century (Roberts 1977, 204–5). In Newby there are some accretions at the western end of the compartment, caused by intruding small plots into the communal space of the roadway. On balance, however, the way that the compartment is adapted to the landscape, with gentle curves, indicates that this is a plan of ancient rather than early-modern foundation. The irregular shape of the green is in measure explained by the drainage sike and pond, while the existence of at least three footpaths and other private access lanes echoes the situation to be seen in Melkinthorpe, We. (Fig. 3.1 above), whose regularity is such that we must be close to the idealised version of an underlying conceptual model.

Melkinthorpe, Westmorland

Melkinthorpe is, however, not entirely a comfortable case. To the northeast of the street there is a very regular compartment, but to the southwest are a group of buildings, perhaps indicative of the surviving end of a row, with traces of a former road or green edge and fossilised plot boundaries. The presence of highly distinctive Shap granite boulders, interpretable as field clearance stones, in some of these do hint at considerable antiquity for the boundaries of the small toft-like enclosures. One of these clearly continues the line of a surviving field boundary, and three of them cut, at an approximate right angle, across what seems to be the bank of a former green or street edge, now set within the present enclosures. Cumberland farmers, undoubtedly a hardy breed, did not move Shap granite boulders around without good cause. Once in place, they were left in place!

This plan offers several possibilities for interpretation: first, the compartment between the back lane and the street green of the north row may be 'original'. The traces of structures along the south row need be no more than cottages, perhaps associated with the smith, the common herd, widows and the like, intruded into the end of a former furlong. However, the erosion of the street level must raise questions. A second possibility is that the 'original' row may have been the south row, with the north row being established later, when the settlement re-organisation took place. Further, some of the boundaries *within* the northern toft compartment appear to be extensions of the boundaries seen within the former furlong to the northeast. These are also associated with 'through-gangs' or 'toft vennels', former ways through the toft compartment from green to back lane and thence out to the fields. In this there are hints that the back lane, and hence the tofts, may have been laid out over a pre-existing arable furlong, corroboration that we are dealing with a two-phase settlement. However, the issue is more complex because the boundary wall bases of the southern row run down across the street edge and thus post-date the underlying earthwork structures, with concordance between one of the boulder strings and an existing field boundary. This boundary's relationship to the others on the south side indicates that we are dealing with a field system that overlies slight earthworks and may well be liked with the reorganisation associated with the northern row. Such details, producing evidence that is often inconsistent, are nevertheless a salutary reminder of the archaeological complexity present beneath the visible land surface. The fact that alternative hypotheses can exist in no way detracts from the evidence of remarkably similar regular plans, in two northern counties and over 60 miles apart as the crow flies. Surely, we have here, in the careful layout, evidence for an underlying concept, a village idea. Like Newby, Melkinthorpe is chronologically ambiguous: *Melkan's-thorpe* is first documented in *c.* 1150, or rather a person bearing the name of the settlement appears in the records at that time, with the actual place being documented in *c.* 1199. The element *-thorp* may mean a farmstead or a hamlet (Smith 1956, 205–12; Smith 1967, 183). There is no sign here of a manor house, and although once in the possession of the Melkinthorpe family, the village has been absorbed by the Lowther estate and remains a part of Lowther parish. *Melkan* may derive from an Old Irish or Old Welsh personal name.

These arguments, relating to two simple plans, indeed both could be termed hamlets rather than villages, illustrate something of the reasoning processes underlying plan analysis, the degree of detailed observation needed, some of the questions which can be asked and indeed, it has to be admitted, some of the inadequacies of the technique.

Appleton le Moors, East Riding, Yorkshire
Appleton-le-Moors, on the Tabular Hills of North Yorkshire, provides a stark contrast to Newby, for there are no obvious earthworks, and the village is a powerful reminder of the degree to which a plan may possess geometric regularity (Fig. 3.1: Beresford and St. Joseph 1979, 139–41). Two symmetrical back lanes frame a regular street layout. Pamela Allerston and Margaret Allison have provided evidence from the fourteenth and early fifteenth century for the presence of the two compartments of tofts set on each side of a north-south orientated street (Allerston 1970, 102: Allison 2003 17 and 86). While evidence from Northumberland does show that early nineteenth century *in situ* re-planning can occur, there are no grounds in this case for not accepting that the plan was present long before 1300 (Fig. 3.2). Unfortunately, the church is wholly Victorian for Appleton is in fact a township in the ancient parish of Lastingham. Nevertheless, it is mentioned in 1086, apparently twice, once under *Dic* Wapentake and once under *Manshowe*, in each case being held by 'the Abbot' and rated at two carucates (DB Yks. SN. D21, note. SN, Ma 14). Do we have here four carucates or two carucates? This is not clear. Kirkby's inquest of the later thirteenth century tells us that *Appilton* is in the liberty of St. Mary's Abbey, York, where it is preceded by the unidentified name *Dueld* (Skaife 1866, 123) and no carucage figure is given. *Dueld* must surely be attached to the name Appleton, and correspond to the mysterious '*Duueld*', noted by the editor of the North Riding volume of the *English Place Name Society*, that the settlement appears as '*Duueld Appilton*' in the Lay Subsidy Roll of 1301 (Smith 1928, 59). That of 1334 merely lists *Apelton* (Glasscock 1975, 380), but does securely locate it in the Liberty of St. Mary and St, Leonard. *Dueld* may derive from 'Duggal', a personal name, perhaps of Old Irish origin, although Allison suggests that that it could be a corruption of the word 'wood' (2003, 42). This is possible. The element 'le Moors' that replaces it was as necessary as the *Dueld*, *i.e.*, because five Appletons in the North Riding of Yorkshire necessitated administrative and postal differentiation. However, the attachment of personal names to village plans is considered in detail in Chapter 8.

Margaret Allison notes early-mid-thirteenth century documents which mention tofts of 20 perches in length (Allison 2003, 18–17) and this, and the regularity of the visible plan, encourages speculation on the units of measurement that may have been used. If an approximation of one hundred metres is accepted for the toft depth, *i.e.* about 330 feet, then this, if divided by a twenty foot perch, gives 16.5 units, and divided by 18 feet gives 18 units and by 16.5 feet, gives 20 units. All are rod lengths used in the medieval period

(Grierson 1972, 20–24). Allison opts for a 16.5–foot perch, but can this be tested given that centuries of sub-division and boundary replacement have destroyed the details of any pristine layout? The length of the toft compartments is less easy to determine for the map suggests that additions could have been made to either end. Nevertheless, the western compartment, delimited by two lanes, appears to be of the order of 450 metres, namely the 100 metres of toft depth multiplied by 4.5, *i.e.*, let us say 1476 feet. If in 1086 the assessment was two carucates (DB Yks. ii, SN, D 21 and SN, Ma 14), with eight bovates to the carucate this gives an overall assessment of sixteen bovates. Experiments with figures and this fiscal assessment produces the reasonable hypothesis that the length of each compartment was 80 × 18 feet, giving 1440 feet, or 439 metres, then the depth would represent 18 × 18 feet, 324 feet (99 metres). In both bases on-map measurements vary a little from this ideal, perhaps always tending to be slightly larger than the model. This was to be expected when simple techniques were used to lay out the units of length. However, if the widths of the back lanes were added in to the toft-depth figure, a not unrealistic surveying procedure, then the toft-depth plus lane-width equals 20 × 18, or 110 metres, give or take. The length of each compartment can be divided into eight units, each of 10 × 18m in all some 1440 feet. This would give an underlying plan based upon two compartments each 80 × 18 rods long and 20 × 18 rods in width, each divided into eight bovate units, in all, sixteen. These measurements could also fit were the village rated at four carucates. That the measurements are not precise, even within such a clear-cut plan, need occasion no surprise with anyone familiar with land survey, the more so when reality is filtered through an Ordnance Survey map and measurements are made from a reproduction of an old map. Cynics may suggest that such measurements could be massaged to fit any preconception, but anyone with even a modicum of practical experience of land survey and the creation of and measurement from maps will grasp the difficulties. Furthermore, it is distinctly possible that the eastern row contains slightly shorter tofts than those on the western side, for this difference appears on the Tithe Map although it is less apparent on the First Edition Ordnance Survey six inch to the mile map (Allison 2003, map 9). This difference could hint at two growth phases.

In fact, the more the plan is examined, the more it is appreciated that a general 'sharpening' of the geometry could have taken place at enclosure, straightening roads that could once have been slightly more sinuous (Roberts 1987, 14–5). No enclosure award is listed (Turner 1978), but the trend of the field boundaries relates to an underlying structure of long, very broad, strips, suggesting enclosure by agreement and Allison dates this to the seventeenth century. These strips are likely to have extended for at least 600 metres to the west, and those to the east of are the same order of length, indeed, is not impossible that both were once part of one system, running essentially west to east, following gentle curves for in excess of 1200 metres. Careful observation shows that the street axis is set essentially at right angles across the curve of these broad strip holdings, fossilised in the enclosure patterns, just at the point where there is a flexure in the system. The village street axis is in fact set not quite north to south, but lies 32 degrees west of south on a low swell on the limestone surface. While suitable for a planned village site this has few obvious attractions for old settlement, not least it must have relied upon the ponds and springs at the southern end. One is left wondering where the original steading from which the village took its name – the 'apple *-tun*' – was located. Allison's research shows that there was a potential focus, with a manor house and chapel just to the south of the present rows, where Philip Rahtz excavated what may have been a parish oven (Allison 2003,19–24). The expansion of demesne may be indicated by the appearance of the term 'tofts' in field names (Allison 2003, endpaper map). A lost settlement of *Baschebi* probably lay to the north of the present village so that re-planning may have integrated two, or if we think of the two manors held in 1086 called Appleton, three earlier steadings. There is no evidence at all to suggest that the village plan is pre-Conquest.

Appleton is but one example of a number of villages strung along the shoulders of the Tabular Hills (Fig. 2.1), many of which show clear signs of clear-cut regularity. If the dimensions of strips some 1200 metres in length seem improbable, surviving examples, running north to south, appear at Wrelton, Aislaby, Middleton and Pickering, and Figure 4.6 shows the strips at Middleton. As will be argued in Chapter 4, these are likely to have been the result of land breaking with a large primitive plough and in Cumbria it has been argued that such features date from the Norman period (Roberts 1996 a). In the case of Middleton the presence of a Norman royal borough at Pickering, established in or before the first third of the twelfth century, is a key focus (Beresford and Finberg 1973, 187). The nearby village of Middleton by Pickering (Fig. 4.6) has a very similar plan to Appleton, and was clearly laid out *over* pre-existing arable strips whose aratral curves are also reflected in the eastern boundary of the township. Consultation of the Ordnance Survey North York Moors 1:25,000 Outdoor Leisure map (sheets 26 and 27) will confirm many of these points. There can, of course, be no proof that Appleton was a planned, two row street green village developed on the lands of St. Mary's Abbey York – perhaps by 'Duggal' – before 1300, but the probability appears to be high. It may well be that more evidence exists, in both archive and field. Further investigation may either confirm or destroy the hypotheses constructed here.

One final point: Allison suggests that each house had a side access lane leading from the green through to the back lane. In Sweden the author has seen plans on the ground and on maps where rectangular tofts are each separated from the other by what may best be called 'vennels', a term used in Durham dialect and derived from the Latin *venella*, a lane. If tofts were laid out in this way, the splitting of some tofts, the closure of some of the vennels, the degeneration of some to the status of footpaths and the preservation of vehicle access in only some cases would result in the landscape patterns now seen. In Milburn, Westmorland, local inhabitants still recognise the presence of these 'through-gangs' even though they are barely detectable on the nineteenth century maps. In fact traces of this interesting arrangement can be noted in many plans and, as Chapter 9 suggests, may be of considerable antiquity (Fig. 9.5).

Carlton in Cleveland

After these analyses two others fall into place. Carlton in Cleveland (Fig. 3.1) is a parish, mentioned in 1086, when the Count of Mortain held an eight-carucate manor (*DB* 5N28; SN, L43). By the later thirteenth century, in Kirkby's Inquest, the lands had passed to the Maynill family, tenants of the church of Canterbury (Skaife 1866, 126). The place-name, an Anglo-Scandinavian version of the Old English 'Charlton', implies, as Finberg has revealed, that this settlement of farmers, *ceorls* – with a soft 'c' but Scandinavianised to a hard one – provided crucial labour services for the demesne of the estate (Finberg 1964, 144–60). In 1086 this settlement lay in Seamer and Tanton, the latter *-tun* name today being no more than a small farm hamlet with slight and ambiguous earthworks around it. But we learn more: while in 1086 there were five tenants (*villani*) at the estate centre, the outlying soke was, with the exception of three tenants at Middleton upon Leven, merely *waste*, although the Commissioners record that '13 ploughs [are] possible' (DB. Yks. 5N28, SN, L43). The plan at Carlton reveals two clear components: first, there is east row, backed by long tofts, of the order of 200 metres in length, and abutting the parish/township boundary to the east. In this case, fieldwork produced no evidence at all for a back lane. On the western side of the village lie a similar set of long tofts, but in this case, there are slight but unmistakable earthworks associated with a former back lane. As at Newby we have crofts added to the back of the village tofts at a later stage in the settlement's history of development. To the north of this compartment lies a manor house and churchyard. Unfortunately the church of St Botolph was wholly reconstructed in 1896–7 and there are no apparent survivals of earlier material.

In this case a green is present although now wholly enclosed, with farmsteads and cottages being set at the edge of what has always been a small ravine, opening out and becoming shallower to the north. This ravine was the green, with steeply sloping sides. A stream through the centre gave a water supply, while the setting of the village, where the moor lands to the south meet the drift-covered shelf of the Lower Lias, represents a preferred settlement zone now occupied by a succession of surviving, shrunken and deserted villages (Fig. 2.1) with some of the latter appearing as halls and church hall foci. In the case of Carlton there is no dating evidence, but recording of the area as *waste* in 1086 hints that what can be seen represents re-development after the regional devastation of 1069–70. To describe this interesting and distinctive settlement as a regular or part-regular – and here opinion may differ – two row stream-green plan perhaps over-emphasises mere terminology. But this is exactly what is present, and the most cursory glance at the Ordnance Survey 1:25,000 Outdoor Leisure maps not only reveals examples of other two row plan types in the area, but two row plan types in all of the stages of development and decay depicted in Figure 2.7. They are, in short, and as Figure 2.1 reveals, as common as loaves in a bakery!

Middridge and Carlton, County Durham

When the author first explored Middridge, Co. Durham it was a settlement of cottages and a few active farmsteads, but is now wholly transmuted into a suburb of Newton Aycliffe, so that historically and archeologically the settlement has been devastated. When those first visits were being undertaken in the 1960s, the author, he must admit, knew very little of what he was looking for amid the landscape of a living village and can now only regret that he cannot re-examine Middridge in its pre-development stage. Much may have been missed! Be this as it may, the plan (Fig. 3.1) is a regular two row green village with, in this case, a flat pasture-green. No back lane has been recorded, but one remarkable fact can be noted: the village has three roads entering it, and two of these are clearly continuations of what is still essentially a northeast to southwest route way.

Table 3.1 Carlton and Middridge: patterns of fiscal tenements from 1183 to the early 17th century

Carlton				Middridge		
1183	1381		1638	1183	1381	1638
Drengage	***Drengage***		**Free**	***Drengage*?**	**Free**	**Free**
1 carucate William son of Orm	4 bovates plus 4 bovates (one carucate)		4 oxgangs plus 4 oxgangs	4 bovates 1/2carucate Vekeman *	60 acres (4 bovates)	4 oxgangs
Firmars (leaseholders)	**Bondages**		**Copyhold**	**Bondages**	**Bondages**	**Leasehold**
	Messuages	Bovates	Oxgangs		Messuages Bovates	Oxgangs
23 firmars hold 46 bovates	2	4	2	15 bondsmen each with 2 bovates	1 3	2
	1	1	5		1 2	1
	3	6	4		1 2	4
	1	1	1		1 2	5
(23 messuages each with 2 bovates or some variation of this pattern)	2	4	2		1 3	3
	1	2	5		1 3	3
	2	4	1		1 3	4
	1	2			1 3	3
	2	4	1		1 3	
	2	4	5		1 3	**Copyhold**
	1	2	4		1	1
	1	1	3		1 2	4
Others	2	4	4	Others	Others	2
4 bov.	1	3	4	2 bovates*	2 bovates	
2 bov.	1	2	7	1 bovates	1 bovates	
2 bov. (Miller)	2	4	6			
2 bov. (Widow)	1	2				
	1	2				
	2	4				
	Messuages 29+2?				Messuages 11+1?	
64 bovates	**64 bovates**		**64 oxgangs**	**37 bovates**	**37 bovates**	**37 oxgangs**

The * indicates Vekeman's holding.

However, the village green and toft compartments are not set along this road, for there is a slight but wholly clear skewing to give the plan a greater east to west orientation, so that the road enters from the north-eastern corner of the green, and leaves via the south-western corner. Indeed, this could be the result of fitting the plan into a slight hollow. However, work on the Tithe map does suggest that this orientation may in fact cut across a series of rather long and broad north to south long strips, which result from the enclosure of open townfields in the seventeenth century (Hodgson 1989, fig. 6.1b, 283). For this process no maps were created, and the procedure of surrender and admittance' was used in the Halmote, or manorial court, of the Bishop of Durham. With these early enclosures, unlike the classic late-eighteenth century remodellings, there was a tendency to use existing townfield structures, *e.g.* an underlying pattern of long, broad strips, as the basis for much of the new layout and this has helped preserve shadows of the more ancient patterns.

It is possible to trace the number of fiscal tenements in Middridge up to and before this enclosure in 1638. In Table 3.1 Middridge is compared with Carlton, County Durham, and a rather larger two-row green plan. Both are in County Durham (Fig. 3.2).

A number of points can be made. The numbers of fiscal tenements in 1183 are perceived to be those present at enclosure in 1638: this was an assumption made by the bishops' officers. There is no reason to believe these bovates varied in size between the three dates or the two places. Tabulating the figures available we get:

Table 3.2 Carlton and Middridge: summary of areal content

	Carlton	Middridge
(1) Total Acreage (OS: statute acres)	1500.5	1132.1
(2) Total Acreage (GIS: statute acres)	1495.9	1129.2

(i.e. derived from measurement on the Old Series Ordnance Survey maps using a Geographical Information System in a computer.)

(3) Townfields (bovates each of 15 statute acres)	960	555
(4) Townfields (bovates each of 15 Bishopric acres)	1628	899
(5) Waste in c 1600 (GIS: statute acres)	779.5	652.1
(3) plus (5)	1739.5	1207.1

In neither case is the acreage of the settlement, roads, waters etc. taken into account. We must conclude that there are three possibilities of error: first, that the measurements of total acreage are wrong, and this is not likely given the closeness of the Ordnance Survey and GIS calculations, the latter being computed automatically within ArcGIS, used as a recording system. Second, that the estimates of the acreage of the waste in about 1600 could be wrong; this is possible but is unlikely to account for all of the discrepancy in the case of Carlton. Finally, we can conclude that while the gross number of bovates is correct, converting them to on-ground acreages is the most likely source of error and that their real size was smaller than the assumption of fifteen statute acres to the bovate allows. This discrepancy makes it difficult to conclude that between 1183 and 1382 there was no expansion of the townfield arable. The majority of the tenancies are customary and for both settlements lists of labour services exist. In time some tenancies changed their character slightly and the *firmars* – a form of leaseholder owing only light services – became bondagers, and then bondages became copyhold. In short, through time the terms applied to tenancies have mutated, although this does not necessarily imply that their essential character changed. In detail, the distribution of the bovates or oxgangs between tenants varies somewhat through time, and in both cases there are traces of one or two a significantly larger holdings. In both cases these form a single farm in 1183, and are then held by a single named tenant.

There is, in addition, a sense of an underlying regularity in both villages. As will be demonstrated later, many northern villages possessed completely regular tenemental arrangements as well as regular plan geometry. The distinction is important. There were eight bovates to the carucate, then $8 \times 8 = 64$, and $4 \times 8 = 32$. In both villages tenurial structures show an approximation to such regularity. It will be recalled that in 1086 Carlton in Cleveland, discussed earlier, was an eight carucate village, and physically it is of the same general dimensions Carlton in Durham. What is wholly clear, in the Durham context, is the continuity of tenemental arrangements between the twelfth and the seventeenth century, two cases of remarkable conservatism even if they conceal 'on ground' changes, such as adjustments in the size of the acre and the bovate. These points lead the argument in an important direction, that in practice settlement planning involved more than a regular plan for a village. 'Regulation' could also be present, with plan, tenemental structure and field system forming a coherent whole. This forms an underlying motif for all analyses of regular settlement plans.

Boldon, County Durham
Boldon is a complicated case (Fig. 2.7): the plan at East Boldon comprises a regular spindle shape, a crisp layout of two symmetrical and rather narrow compartments, and was in fact closely paralleled in Durham at St. Helen's Auckland, where plan survival is more fragmentary. In 1183 twenty-two villans, bondsmen, each held two bovates, in all forty-four, while twelve cottagers, held 12 acres. In addition 'Robert' holds a further two-bovate holding of thirty-six acres. There is a demesne, where four ploughs are working. The problem is that there are today two villages at Boldon, East and West, and we have no real indication which one is recorded in 1183 (Greenwell 1852, 3, 45). The ancient church is located at West Boldon, a small rather irregular agglomeration in sharp contrast to the regularity of East Boldon. In 1183 the entry for 'Boldon' is

followed with a further settlement called Newton, and while this is normally thought to be East Boldon, this is clearly not the case, for about a kilometre to the north of East Boldon mid-nineteenth century maps record 'Newton Garths'. This is plainly the Newton of 1183 and the '*villa de Newton*' of 1381 was then in the hands of Lord Neville (Greenwell 1856, 98). This is relevant because a careful count of the messuages and attached bovates present in 'Boldon' in 1381 shows that there are in fact 23 (*sic*) messuages, each with two 30 acre bovates attached. The two bovates owned by 'Robert' in 1183 are also traceable in 1381, when they were held with a single messuage; the 23 plus one makes 24 messuages, each with two bovates attached, to parallel the twelve cottage holdings present in both 1183 and 1381. That an extra bovate has appeared between 1183 and 1381 merely suggests a slight error in the copying of the earlier account. A perfectly regular tenemental structure is being described, important because of the next level of analysis.

There are three points: first, it is probable that the demesne lands of 1183 lay at West Boldon, at some sort of seigniorial centre, with the church and the glebe; by 1381 this had, as the Hatfield Survey records faithfully, been broken up (Greenwell 1856, 98–100). It is the location of a stately early thirteenth century church. Second, it is clear from the Hatfield Survey that there had been extensive wastes present at an earlier stage, evidenced by farms taken from the waste and pieces of waste added to cottage holdings. This is also supported by the general complexity of the township boundaries in this whole neighbourhood revealed by the work of Dunsford and Harris: thus Newton has ended up in the township of Whitburn. In conclusion, if the demesne lay at West Boldon and if the regular tenemental structure described in both 1381 and 1183 does apply to East Boldon – and this is likely – then we must presume that the regular plan of this village was indeed already present by 1183. It represents a plantation of tenants in a new settlement established in the waste. This may have been the result an expansion of the Bishop's demesne, because – as will be shown in a later chapter – East Boldon is unusual because it bears a full complement of services associated with bondage. It is likely that some tenants were moved from West Boldon to East Boldon when the new village was planted. Further, the services at Boldon were used as an exemplar for other villages: this gives a name to Boldon Book, because of repetition in 1183 of the phrase 'and they render as they of Boldon'. In this matter, it has to be admitted, assumptions are present, not least the important one that the documented patterns of these ecclesiastical records bear a relationship to the on-ground reality of settlement. However, this assumption appears to be supportable, both in terms of *prima facie* argument and in the many cases where on-ground reality conforms to the surviving documentation (see Fig. 5.3). While the precise date of the plantation of East Boldon cannot be ascertained, it must be probable that when it took place the bondage services attached to the older focus at West Boldon were transferred to the new plantation.

Acklington, Northumberland

Radical reorganisation is also to be seen in the Northumberland village of Acklington but in this case it is recent enough to be documented with some clarity. Northumbrian villages, however, present a particular set of problems. For the estates of the Duke of Northumberland a fine set of early seventeenth century maps survives. When these were compared with the landscapes the 'fit' was found not to be good. Figure 3.2.a shows two maps of Acklington: that of 1864 indicates a village that had experienced *in situ* reorganisation, probably in the earlier decades of the nineteenth century. An undated map in the Duke's collection, stylistically of about 1800, shows the earlier village, and the shape of this corresponds much more precisely with the outline on the map of 1616. The schedule that accompanies this map provides a strip-by-strip breakdown of the furlongs in the arable fields, and allows the settlement's tenemental structure to be mapped onto the village plan. The survey begins ' at the West end of the South Rowe and goeing east', the crosses 'the gate [road or lane] into Southfield, breadth one pole and a half', then continues along the south row before 'Goeing over the streete to the North Rowe and goeing west, the street fower poles in breadth'. Note how even the widths of the streets are given. Along the north row the progression is from east to west, crossing the 'Church way to Warkworth, breadth one pole and a half', before surveying a short 'headrowe going south' (Northumberland Estate Surveys, Acklington; NCH V, 362–76). The seventeenth century surveyor even provides us with a clear picture of the village as it then was. Figure 3.2(b) places it at the centre of a schematic plan of the village, shaded, and notes the messuages or steadings then present. Then, using other evidence published in the Northumbrian County History, the diagram (Fig. 3.2.b) works backwards in time from 1616 to more remote documentation (NCH V, 382–376). It can be seen that not only did a major structural reorganisation of the plan take place in the late eighteenth or early nineteenth century, there was a major re-organisation of its tenemental structure between 1498 and 1567, essentially making one new fiscal farm from two older smaller units. Inquisitions *post mortem* allow more speculative reconstruction in the 1350s and 1360s, and a final one in 1248. Evidence from 1309 shows that all is by no means uncomplicated, and it would have been surprising if the village had not suffered in some measure from the increased Scottish raids of the first half of the fourteenth century. This diagram summarises much evidence and undoubtedly involves some 'professional judgements'. Nevertheless, the limited thirteenth century data indicates that we have here a 'quartered' plan, with the south-eastern quarter being the former hallgarth, the demesne, with some cottages and tenements attached; across the street this was faced by a cottage row. The western end of the settlements comprised two rows of tofts facing each other: some cottages are intermixed, but essentially these are farmsteads associated with substantial holdings in the arable and meadow and there were status variations between the tenants on the north side and those on the south side. In this case the husbandland holders probably represented an older category of tenant, while those of the south side, *firmars*, or

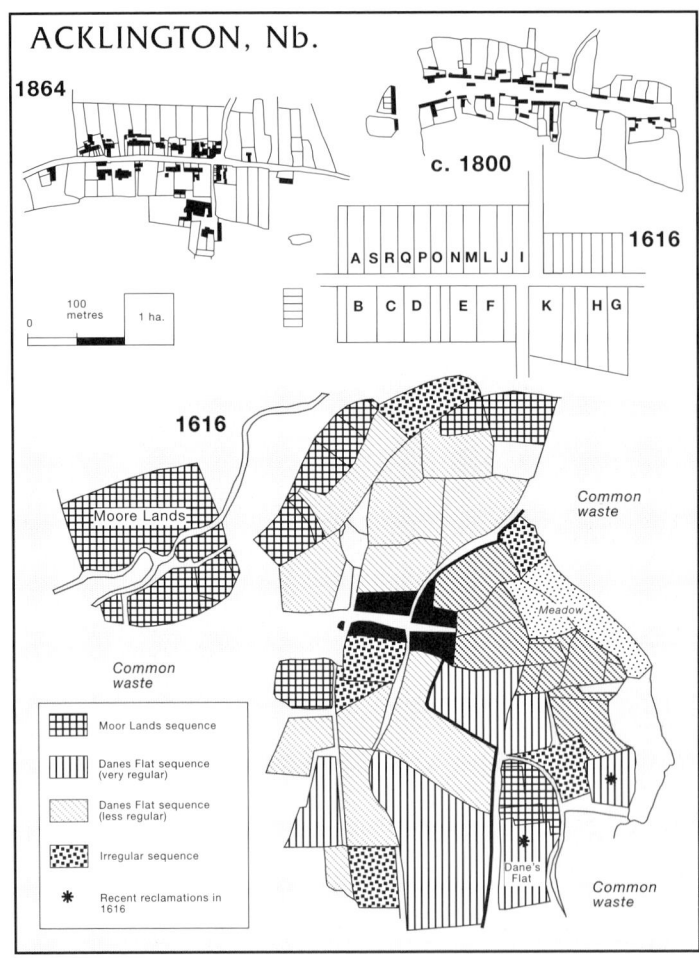

Fig. 3.2.a The village of Acklington, Northumberland

leaseholders, represented a newer category of tenant. This interpretation conforms to the known facts (Roberts 1978, 49–51). Appropriately, the small head row, surely set upon former common waste, contains only five cottages (Fig. 3.2.a). Acklington was initially rated at 35 fiscal farms, a wholly peculiar case because while regular fiscal sequences of eight, twelve, sixteen and twenty four are known, together with five ten, fifteen and the like, in Northumberland a sequence based upon sevens occurs, seven fourteen, twenty one, twenty eight and thirty five!

The field book for 1616 shows that in some furlongs the individual strips followed the sequence of houses in the village. These are keyed to the lettered toft sequence in Figures 3.2.a and 3.2.b and three separate sequences can be identified:

Settlement Plans – Regular Forms

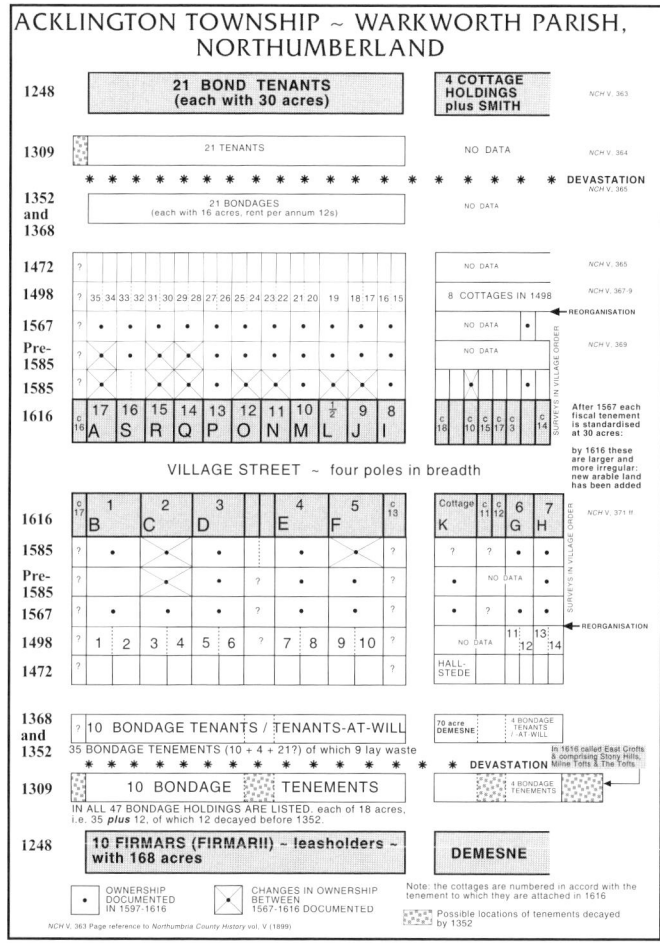

Fig 3.2.b Analysis of the village of Acklington 1248–1616

- first, a partition cycle related to toft order, with each partition sequence running from A to S, sometimes with a cottage strip inserted into the sequence. The strip beginning each furlong is chosen randomly but the first partial partition unit is always completed even when additional strips have clearly been added at a later stage. The 58 acres 0 rods and 27½ and ¹⁄₁₆ perches of Moore Furlong are a case in question:

JKLMNOPQRS(Y),ABCDEFGHIJKLMNOPQRS(V),ABCDEFGHIJKLMNOPQRS(X), ABCDEFGHIJKLMNO<E>PQRS(Y), ABCDEFGHIJKLMNOPQRS(Z), ABCDEFGHI(*)S(Y)(X), [ABCDEFGHMJHLMNOPQ]

A simple bracket (X) is a cottage strip, a pointed bracket <E> is a strip for some unknown reason out of sequence, the square bracket is an aberrant sequence and (*) marks the end of the formal sequence, picked up again at the beginning JKL etc.

- second, a sequence related to toft order, but with K (the demesne holding) missing and with L, a half farm, appearing alternatively, and beginning each cycle randomly, as in Danes Flat (23 acres 3 rods 8 ½ ¹⁄₁₆ perches):

    MNOPQRSABCDEFGHIJ,   CDEFGHIJLMNOPQRSAB, BCDEFGHIJMNOPQRSA, QRSABCDEFGHIJLMNOP

- third, there are a group of irregular furlongs, perhaps reflecting an earlier system of partition.

Figure 3.2(a) shows that the 'Moore Lands' sequence relates to furlongs peripheral to the townfields, while versions of the 'Dane's Flat' sequences form the bulk of the remainder of the fields. In all cases however, there are anomalies and slight irregularities, to be expected when imposing a conceptualised sequence upon the realities of a farming landscape. Nevertheless, a glance at Acklington's village plan would classify it as 'part-regular', yet concealed beneath this part-regular layout, not only is there a conceptualised ordering of settlement space, this same settlement space has been used as a paradigm for laying out the orders of strips in the townfields. Clearly, this documentation is largely post-thirteenth century, but the sophistication of the arrangements, indeed the pattern of regularities and irregularities present, indicates that it does not represent a recent innovation. The term *regulation* is applied in Scandinavia to such villages where plan and fiscal – *i.e.* rent and tax paying tenements – are locked into an organised spatial system (Göransson 1961). Of course, few northern villages are as fully documented as are those on the estates of the Dukes of Northumberland, and indeed the presence of regularity may be 'documented' only in the surviving characteristics of a settlement's plan.

Maulds Meaburn, Westmorland

So far this account has been based upon maps and documents and there has been an emphasis upon the eastern lowlands of Northern England. Maulds Meaburn, Westmorland, (Figure 3.3) is a reduction of a quite remarkable field map, compiled by the author, of a regular two-row green village, bisected by the River Lyvennet, a south bank tributary of the Eden. The valley floor, much scarred by former river channels, is sufficiently wide to form a tract of valuable meadowland amid this dry limestone area, indeed the name 'Meaburn', 'meadow stream', implies recognition of this fact in Old English nomenclature. The river name 'Lyvennet', as was noted in the previous chapter, is British. The Maulds Meaburn plan is mostly earthworks, with the few remaining working farmsteads in the village either being rather small or set at its edges. Several things are important to understanding this plan:

Settlement Plans – Regular Forms

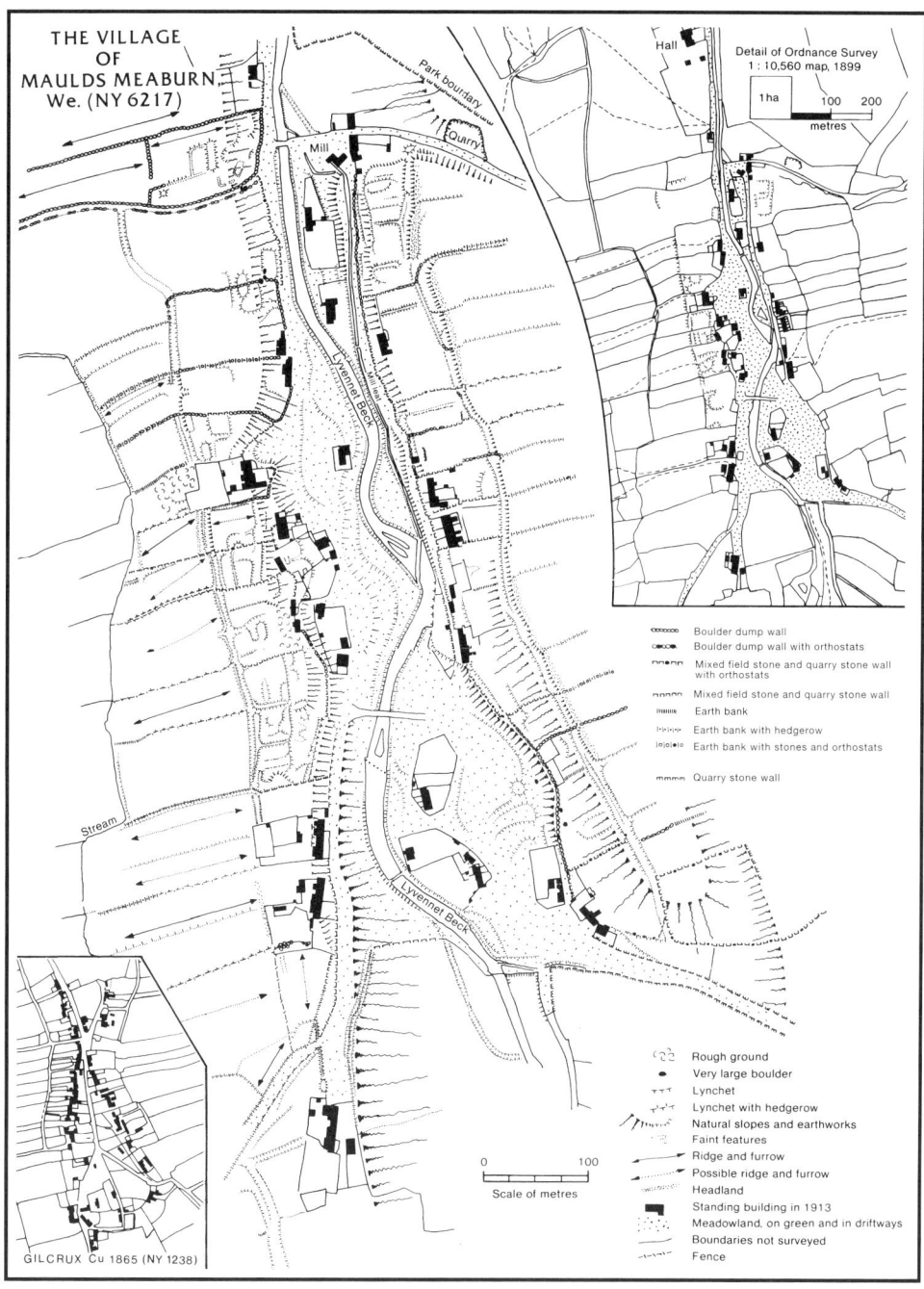

Fig. 3.3 Maulds Meaburn, Westmorland: a field map

- first, Maulds Meaburn consists of two long, sinuous toft compartments, occupying low benches and rising slopes set above each side of the valley. Two back lanes frame these compartments. It will be noted that on the western side the earthworks vary from toft to toft, suggesting that maintenance of the lane was incumbent upon the toft-holder. While clear in the field, these are no longer rights of way;

- second, earthworks define a succession of tofts, and many of the lateral boundaries contain substantive boulders. Some of these are sandstone, but a significant portion are rounded Shap Granite, erratic blocks, left on the land by ice-flows. These latter must be interpreted as field clearance stones, and a significant number are visible in the toft head lines between the compartment and the green. Effectively there must once have been a wall of boulders enclosing the whole green. This stone fence could have been used to protect the vital meadowland for mowing and controlled grazing. In this context the back lanes assume great significance, offering passage for people, cattle and carts when the meadow was closed;

- third, many of the field boundaries abutting the village are coincident with the toft boundaries set within the compartment, suggesting that the back lane was, in this instance, superimposed *over* pre-existing clearance boundaries, and that in this stone-rich landscape, the original 'strips' were – as the inset map shows – of the general order of 150 metres in length. This is undoubtedly the result of topography, for throughout Cumbria villages of this character tend to have long field strips, sweeping into the village right to the toft head line (see Figs 4.2 and 4.3). Drainage sikes to the east and west of the village give definition to the boundaries of this inner core of tofts and crofts. The doglegs in field boundaries to be seen in the south-eastern quarter of the inset map are a reminder that the strips once extended further across this drumlin landscape and that the creation of enclosed fields, as opposed to strips edged by clearance stones, has led to adjustments;

- finally, the whole complex is set south of and peripheral to an area of parkland around Meaburn Hall, apparently with its own enclosed field system.

In Maulds Meaburn we have a careful adaptation of a generic type of plan to a specific site, showing evidence of both a careful layout and a complex history. Once again it is reasonable to suggest that the whole pattern is too regular, too organised to be accidental, although elements of organic growth cannot be wholly excluded. The available documentary evidence is limited and there is no Domesday Book for Westmorland. If it is assumed, as is likely, that Meaburn Hall represents the most ancient focus of activity then at what stage did the estate acquire a sufficiently large number of tenants to need toft compartments of the dimensions we now see? By 1240 the settlement was a large one, a moiety – one half – comprising four and a half ploughlands of land (*culturae*) – being the demesne, together with meadows, pastures and woodland. In addition there were some twenty-eight bovates and nine acres of tenant land, two cottages and eight

Settlement Plans – Regular Forms

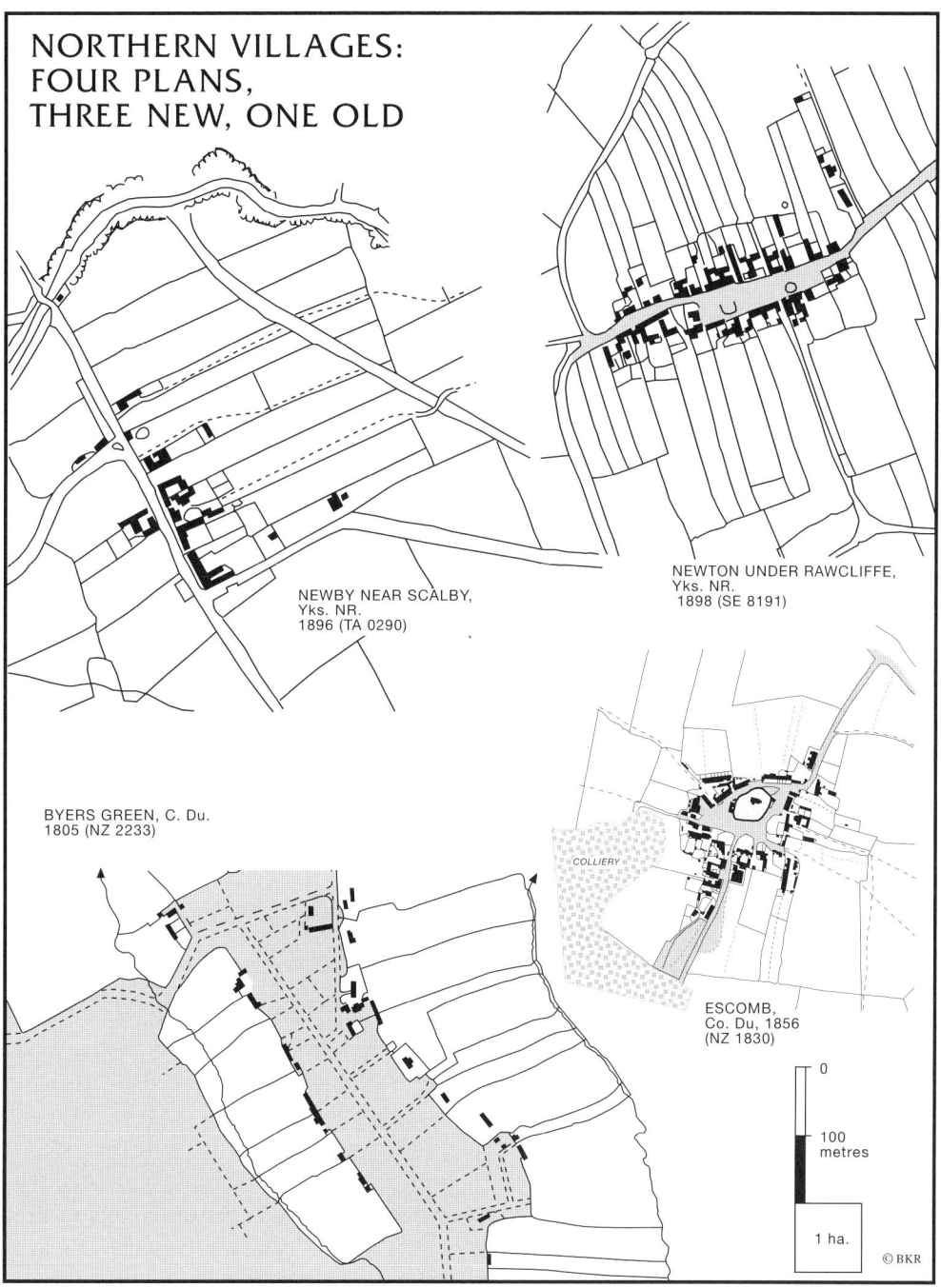

Fig 3.4 Some northern village plans

holdings, all broadly free tenements, together with three servile tenants (*nativos*) with their broods (*sequela*) (Roberts 1996a, 48–49). Doubling these figures makes a very large village indeed. Fifty-six bovates and eighteen farms, what in Northumberland in the early seventeenth century would be termed a 'great towne'. Of course, this raises many questions; what was the origin of these tenants? Whence did they come? Why did they come? What attracted them? Above all, when did this expansion from a putative origin in the single high status farmstead, represented by the hall, take place? There is nothing in the plan to hint at chronological variation between the two compartments. In the name, Maulds Meaburn, is to be found a slight clue. Maud de Veteripont, wife of William de Veteripont, Lord of Appleby, was given the estate in *c.* 1174 and as the first specific reference to Maulds Meaburn is in *c.* 1210, this gives a pointer to foundation in the last quarter of the twelfth century (Smith 1967, 156).

The case of Maulds Meaburn has edged the argument away from the short-tofted villages of the north-east, to settlements in which the farmsteads appear to have been located at the head of very long field strips, longer than the normal 220 yards or 200 metres of the standard furlong. Maulds Meaburn is a rather exceptional case, with doglegs appearing at the point where the field strips attach to the village closes. However, a documented example of a hybrid village in County Durham provides a bridge to the more complex plans discussed in the chapter to follow.

Byers Green, County Durham

When Byers Green common and green were enclosed in 1805, the village was a two row plan, orientated approximately north to south, with a large green and sprawling across a north-facing plateau surface (Fig. 3.4). The plan is self-explanatory and two facts are of salient importance. First, in Bishop Hatfield's survey of about 1381 many of the cottages and farms are described as lying on the east side or the west side of the settlement (*ex parte orientali* and *ex parte occidentali villae*). Given the demonstrable use of these terms throughout the north to place individual farmsteads within the plans of villages (Roberts 1972) this is sound confirmation that the plan seen in the nineteenth century was present in the later fourteenth century. Second, Byers Green appears in Boldon Book in 1183 merely as the *assart of Byres* (Greenwell 1852, 27 and 63). To the north of the present village, on sloping land on the south side of the Wear Valley, a large house called 'The Park' may represent a nucleus in association with which the tenanted village was established. It was the likely place of residence of Richard Park in 1381, the tenant of a two-carucate freehold estate (Greenwell 1857, 43–44), possibly a significant point in the light of the importance of named tenants to be discussed in Chapters 7 and 8. Within the village the structure of the tenancies seems to have been very irregular, comprising only cottagers and rent payers (the holders of *terrae scaccarii* or Exchequer lands) but no bondage tenants. Cottages and substantial exchequer messuages appear in both rows, sometimes with croft appended, and significantly all the cottages with crofts specified appear on the east side where the plots are longer in

1806. The arable is often described as scattered in various locations but in this case no clear links can be established between the geometry of the plan and the holdings. Byers Green is wholly unusual in that the suffix 'green' had become attached to the place name by 1562 (Watts 2002, 22). Once known as 'Bires Geoffrey', it shows all the signs of being planned, being located upon a distinctively unfavourable site set high on an unsheltered plateau surface. This took place at a date between 1183 and 1381, probably in the half-century after 1183 and once again the association with a personal name is worthy of note. The reference to an assart does suggest that woodland may have survived to ameliorate, initially at least, the site qualities, set on a sloping but north-facing plateau surface, although its survival may have been longest along the valley sides rather than on the plateau surface itself. This is a late village, probably one of the last nucleated villages to be established in the county. Its lavish dimensions bear witness to this fact. It name, from the Old English *byre*, a 'cow shed', probably implies the use of the area as cattle grazings before the settlement was developed.

These vignettes provide us with no sustained regional picture but all point towards three conclusions: first, that many northern villages show layouts that are likely to have been planned; second, that likely *teminus ante quem* is the later twelfth century; third, there are sometimes underlying and complex linkages between a plan, the tenancies it contains and the fiscal system imposed. None of the evidence is wholly satisfactory, being disjointed in both space and time, but cumulatively – and many, many more cases could be cited – it is impressive and challenging.

The Regulated Village

Writing on the sociology of the thirteenth century English village in 1941 the American scholar George C. Homans, noted that while bovates or oxgangs were conceived to be structured units of a given number of acres, there is evidence that *forlands*, additional pieces of assart land, were added to them. At Spaldington in Yorkshire in the time of Henry II (1154–1189) the nuns of Ormsby were granted an oxgang with the following provision:

> If it happen that the bounds of the tilled land be extended further than they now are, their oxgangs will be increased as much as the other oxgangs are increased
> (Homans 1960, 84).

This reveals a fundamental problem of the scattered strips associated with the townfield systems. This is not the place to discuss the nature of these arrangements in detail, still less the troubled questions of their origins. The case of Acklington, already considered, provides a useful illustration of the inherent complexities. The fundamental arrangement was clearly one of creating equal, or approximately equal, shares in the arable and meadow of a community. That these arrangements were by no means wholly standardised and could vary from village to village is shown both by the variations in the length of the land-rod used and by variations in the number of acres in a bovate. That a land rod was used is shown by some medieval illustrations (Camille 1998, fig. 76). The term bovate, of Latin derivation, or oxgang, from the vernacular, are used in this study of the north. In the south and midlands the virgate, or yardland, was the usual measure (Adams 1976), and was undoubtedly based upon the use of a rod – Latin *virga*. A virgate was 30 statute acres while a bovate was 15 acres, so that the northern peasant farmer tended to hold two oxgangs as a standard arable holding. The scattering of the strips making up the individual bovate farms throughout the townfields ensured a spread of the risks brought by varied soils, varied fertility, the hazards of pests and the animals of rough pastures and wild-wood, and misfortunes brought about by human agency. In practice two parallel systems emerged for dealing with the scattering of strips. First, there was the structural system, in which individual strips were ploughed as groups forming blocks, furlongs or *culturae*, sometimes in the north *wongs* or *flatts*. Furlongs, in this case implying the block not the length, were in turn grouped into larger units for the purposes of cropping, so that each settlement was organised with, in general, two or three great open fields. Second, bovates were organised into larger groupings, eight combining to form a carucate or ploughland, of approximately 120 acres, and it is likely that this represented a year's tillage, including fallow ploughing, for a team of eight oxen, two from each peasant holding *i.e.* one from each bovate.

Homans noted that when specific oxgangs were transferred by grant then the individual strips needed locating in the fields. While in practical terms the new owners or their representatives were no doubt shown the locations of the varied strips making up each oxgang – and he cites an example of this – the adoption of a regular sequence made this process easier. He found examples of oxgangs that were said to lie 'against the sun', 'on the sunny side', 'near the sun' (*versus solem, ex parte solis, propinquior soli*) or 'against the shade' (*versus umbram*). While this may mean no more than 'to the south' or 'to the north', to achieve a deeper understanding he brought into the argument evidence from Denmark and Sweden.

> 'There it was called *solskifte,* which may be translated as *"sun division".* The tofts, the house sites, as they might lie in two rows on either side of the village street, were considered to fall in order in a clockwise direction about the village. The clockwise ordering of tofts is significant, because the course of the sun as seen from any point toward the northern parts of the earth is clockwise, an a belief common in folklore is that the lucky way to make any circular motion is clockwise'
>
> (Homans 1941, 94–101; *note that the modern spelling,* solskifte*, has been adopted. See* Göransson 1961, 80).

Furthermore 'the order of tofts in the village was that of the strips belonging to these tofts in the fields.' (Homans 1960, 97) This is summed up by the Danish proverb 'the toft is the mother of the acre' and Homans summarises his discussion as follows:

'The following, then, seem to have been the important characteristics of the *solskifte*:

- The holdings of the different villagers in the land of the village were arranged in a regular order of rotation.
- In particular, the order of the arable strips in the furlongs was that of the tofts in the village to which the strips pertained.
- The direction in which this order was applied was applied was that of a conventional direction and the course of the sun'.

Homans noted that the documentation available to him for England, largely northern England, suggests that two of these were indeed present, notably, the regular order of the strips of the holdings and the link between this and the conventional direction of the sun; in contrast the close link with the tofts is rarely documented. He cites a document by which Robert de Tolebu granted to the Canons of Guisborough, in Cleveland, Yorkshire, a ploughland (*carucate*) in Yarm, comprising:

> one ploughland in the township of Yarm, of my demesne, that is to say, that one which lies nearer the land of Robert de Lestria, with half my meadow which lies next to the meadow of the same Robert, and with a toft which is next to the toft of the said Robert.
>
> (Homans 1960, 98)

He concluded by making two important points. First, there is evidence that oxgangs need not always be comprised of scattered strips, commenting in a footnote that 'there is much to be considered about the field systems of the North of England', where he also cites a case at Salton, Yorkshire,

> *Sunt etiam ibidem xvj bovatae terrae dominicae arabilis; quarum quaelibet cont. ix acres terrae: unde octo bovatae jacent in quatuor flattes... Istae praedictae flattae... sunt separales. Et caeterae viij bovatae terrae jacent discontinue per diversas partes inter tenentium ibidem.*
>
> (Homans 1960, 426, n. 31).

> There are in the same 16 bovates of demesne arable: each of which contains 9 acres of land: of which 8 bovates lie in four flatts (furlongs) ... which said flatts are in several... and the other 8 bovates lie scattered in varied in varied parts between the tenancies.

Second, in a masterly conclusion he noted that

> 'a properly guarded statement might be that in certain English villages of the thirteenth century the existence of the debris of a scheme resembling in some respects the Scandinavian *solskifte* may be inferred from phrases used in charters and final concords'
>
> (Homans 1960, 100).

Figure 3.5 presents a model, developed from a drawing by Homans (1960, 99) of a sun-divided village containing two ploughlands or carucates, each comprising eight oxgangs, sixteen in all. There are sixteen furlongs, eight lying to the north and eight to the south of an east to west orientated planned village. In 1951 Thorpe, with no reference to *solskifte,* noted that a large proportion of the Durham green villages possessed this same orientation. In this diagram we glimpse one 'village idea' that must surely underlie many of the examples already examined. Writing in 1961 Göransson assembled evidence to show that terminological evidence suggestive of a the clockwise allocation of strips appears, although he concludes that impact of sun-division upon village plans 'is uncertain' (Göransson 1961, 98). Nevertheless, his distribution map, built into Figure 3.6, is a *tour de force* and makes the fundamental point that while the terminology is widely scattered, the most notable concentrations occur in Yorkshire. They appear in the northern portions of the North Riding, in the Vale of York, in and around the Vale of Pickering, with extensions southwards across the Wolds, then into Holderness, with a thinner scatter throughout Lincolnshire. He concludes that:

> The bulk of the evidence suggests that the Scandinavian *solskifte* was in fact derived from England during the period of close political, ecclesiastical and cultural contact between these countries (10th to 12th centuries). By the time the system was well-developed in Denmark and in Sweden, however, it was already, as Homans suggests, in full decay in England, vanishing in consequence of land division, transfer and consolidation. It origin lies in the obscure organisational processes of the Dark Ages.
>
> (Göransson 1961, 101).

In fact both Homans and Göransson tend to ignore the fact that the best evidence for the regularities upon which they are commenting occurs relatively late. What was happening in the period before 1300 and indeed 1200 depends upon the interpretation of documents that are normally rather opaque in locational details. For instance, the vast majority of early charters cast too little light upon topographic detail and organisation. In practice, Göransson's final conclusion probably touches the truth for we cannot be certain of the direction of the earlier information flows between England and Scandinavia. Brian Hope-Taylor in his analysis of his excavation at Yeavering, Northumberland, raises important questions when he argues that the meticulous measurement he found in the seventh century royal halls that may have influenced the great royal Viking sites in Denmark at Trelleborg, Fyrkat and Aggersborg (Hope-Taylor 1977, 271–75). In this matter architectural details are physical evidence for the transmission of ideas.

As is often the case, some of these arguments had been foreshadowed by the work of an earlier scholar. Vinogradoff in 1911 when commenting on the distribution of strips added an extensive footnote that drew upon Scandinavian experience to throw light on the deeper questions underlying what could be discovered in England (Vinogradoff

Settlement Plans – Regular Forms

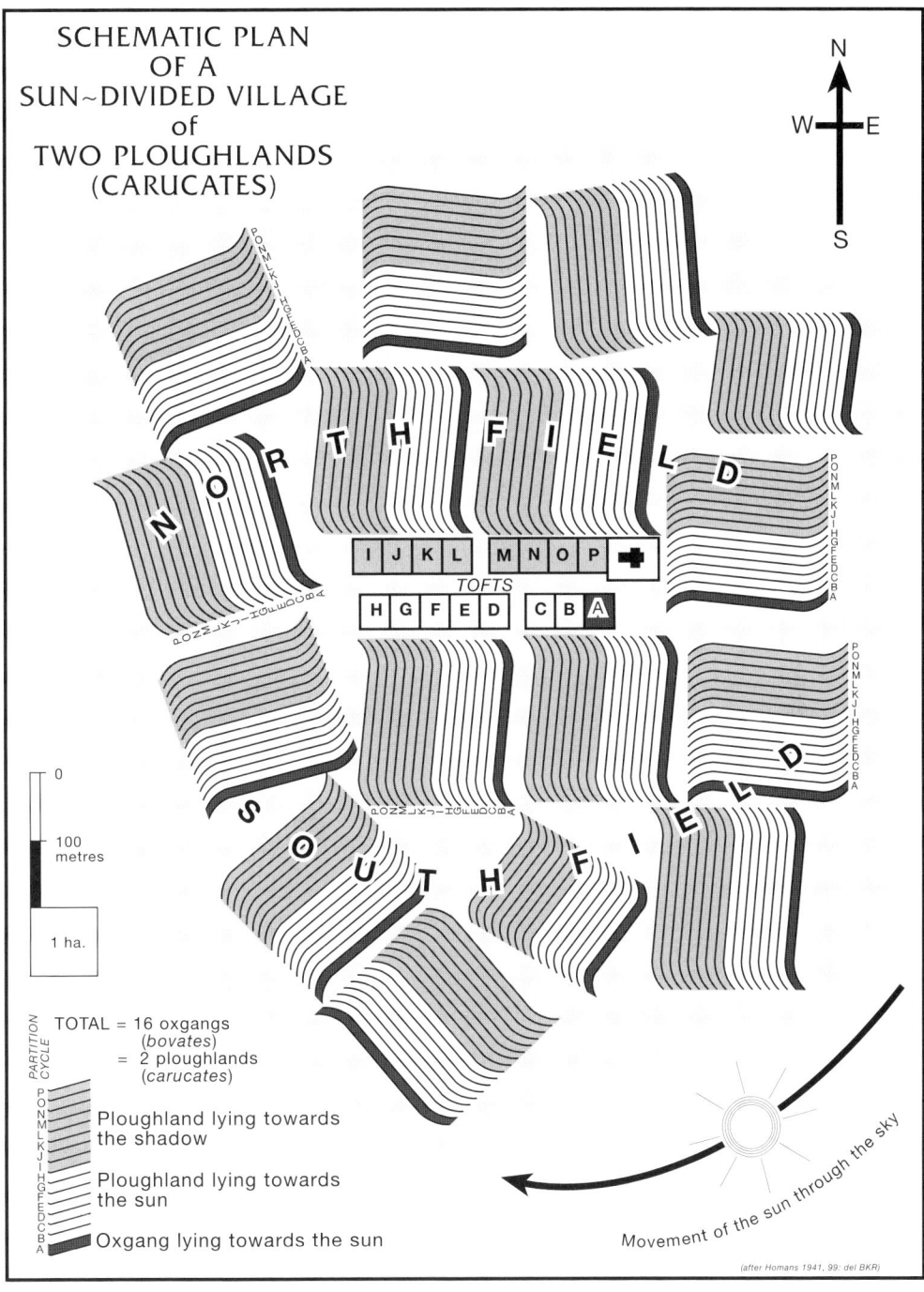

Fig 3.5 Schematic model of a 'sun divided' village

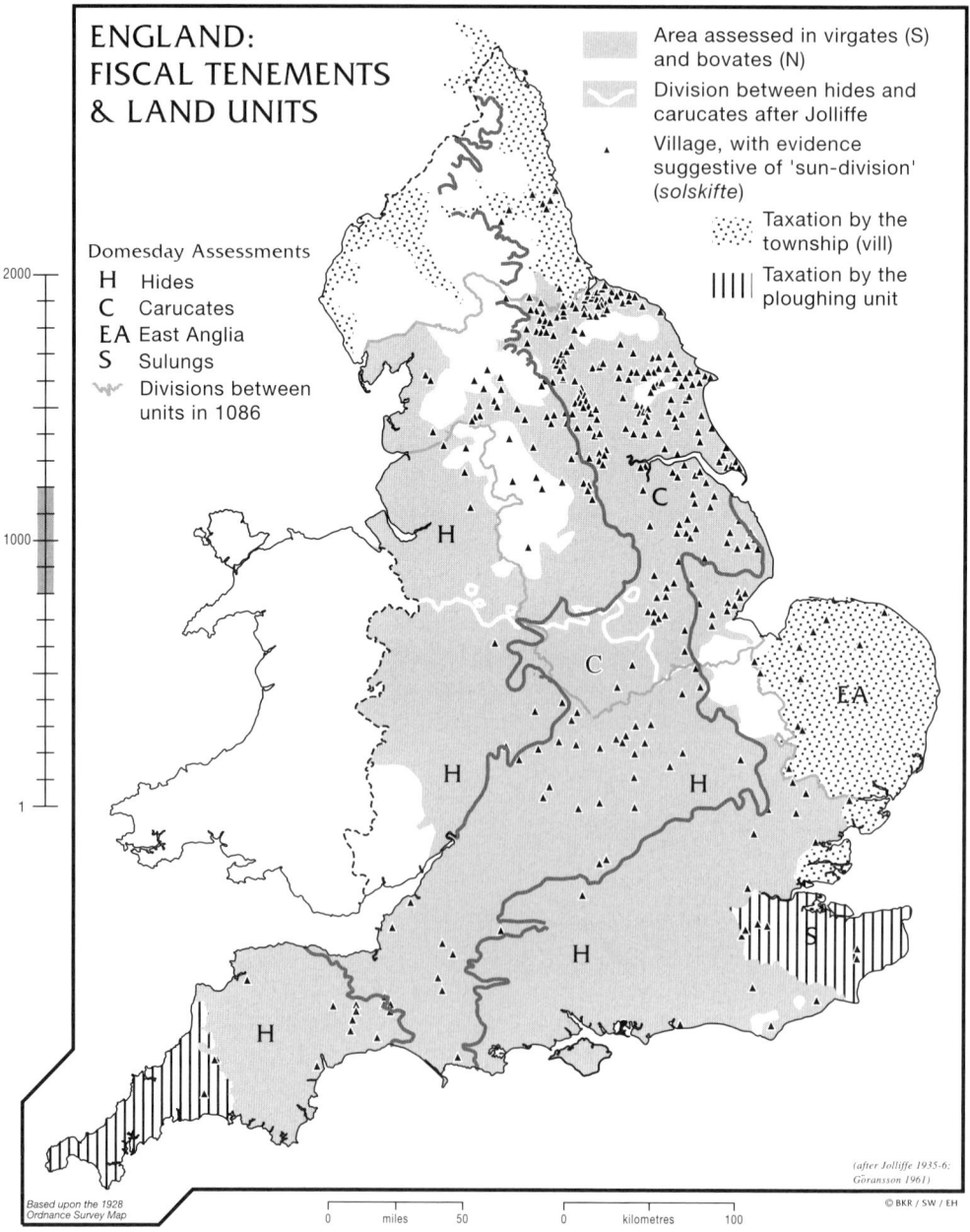

Fig. 3.6 Fiscal tenements in England: a summary map

1911, 179, n. 33; 263–67). In this he also raises a troubled question: did the 'planning' of villages and their fields originate with lord or peasant? Further, he pointed out that there were inevitably tensions between the pressures to maintain the equality of shares following their imposition and forces engendering change. Even in Scandinavia much of the clearest evidence is post-medieval, and it is clear that the identification of examples dating from thirteenth and fourteenth centuries did not render re-organisations in the sixteenth and seventeenth centuries superfluous or impossible (Sømme 1968, 304–7). In fact, the possibility of episodic re-organisations cannot be excluded, and the case of Ackington, noted earlier, shows that the imposition of regularity need not be a wholly one-off activity but might be a rolling process as new land was taken in and as tenemental re-organisations or even devastations occurred.

The variety of examples presented so far in this study serve to emphasise the existence of formally structured settlement plans. There are strong indications that this formal structure permeates not only the physical layout of plans but also their tenemental and social structure. Two fundamental issues must be kept in mind. On one hand, not only is the evidence essentially limited and often intractable and difficult to interpret with absolute certainty, we should never forget that it is inevitable that it contains, and sometimes via the imposition of a uniform terminology conceals, both spatial and temporal variations. Thus, it is inevitable that in published studies of limited scale, the need to communicate, the need to generalise, the need to tell – dare one say – a story, encourages a synthesis that may draw together what are essentially disparate elements, from different times and places. In this there are great dangers, but a preliminary statement needs making. We must also keep in mind that changes of scale, from fragmentary generalisations to local studies, inevitably revealing the disparities and limitations of local documentation and landscape survivals, are of equal importance. Even if we assume that fully regulated villages were indeed being established – planned – in the period before 1300, perhaps even 1200, certain latent forces for change were always present. Population dynamics, the demographic fortunes of individual families, the land market, a steady encroachment upon the waste, the catastrophes of recession and retreat and particularly the powerful filter of post-medieval developments, all had the potential to deform and distort any imposed pattern. Furthermore, in spite of some indicators, the key questions of origins, dates and diffusions all remain unresolved. These are all in the plural. At root all of these systems bear the hallmark of the need to create aliquot shares in a community's land resources. The links between these aliquot shares – bovates – and the fiscal systems – the carucates – upon which royal taxation was usually based, carry us away from the needs of the peasantry towards the interests of the landholders and the king. The issues raised here cannot be resolved at this stage of the argument, but will be returned to in the later chapters of this study. The following chapter uses the same approach as this one, examining a range of cases, landscapes and documents in order to generate a corpus of plan evidence with which to buttress arguments to be developed later.

Chapter Four

Settlement Plans – Variations and Complexities

To summarise and generalise as a foundation for the argument in this chapter, throughout the eastern lowlands of Northern England, from Yorkshire to Northumberland, two row village and hamlet plans with short tofts are the norm. However, as the land rises westwards, towards the foothills of the Pennines, field observation shows that settlements with long tofts appear, although normally intermingled with other plan types. To the west of the Pennines the latter plans appear as the regional dominant, intermixed with both short-tofted and strip-tofted layouts and more irregular types. In the East Riding of Yorkshire, notably in the eastern portions of the Vale of Pickering and southwards into the Wolds and Holderness, strip tofts appear as the dominant type. Let us face it, these are unlovely statements, but they encapsulate many hours of study, driving, exploring and archive work. What do such observations mean? The formidable but essential jargon serves both to describe with some degree of precision and draw attention to the regional variations in northern village and hamlet plans, thus creating a mechanism for analysis. This chapter begins with a view of some transitional types and then considers examples of long- and strip-tofted plans, once again using particular cases to illuminate a more general picture.

Cockfield, County Durham
Cockfield is a village with distinctive long tofts still surviving as dramatic landscape features, but the analysis in Figure 4.1 documents several stages of development. First, the present village is located adjacent to an area of some 850 acres (344 ha.) of common waste. It remains a stinted pasture, still used for rough grazing. Earlier usage is attested in the form of many traces of former coal mining and at least four earthwork sites (Roberts 1975). None of these have been excavated, but one takes the form of an oval enclosure with a bank and external ditch. Except for the fact that it is set upon a shelving surface, it resembles a nothing less than a small Iron Age hill-fort and may well date from that period. Two others are much slighter structures and are wholly impossible to date. The fourth, over an acre in area, however, is less visible at ground level, rectangular, with slightly rounded corners, and once possessed a massive rampart built of fieldstone, with facing stones that may have been roughly squared. It is probable that this rampart has been robbed to build the village walls. There are no signs of a ditch and there is one possible entrance on the eastern side. It is not a

Settlement Plans – Variations and Complexities

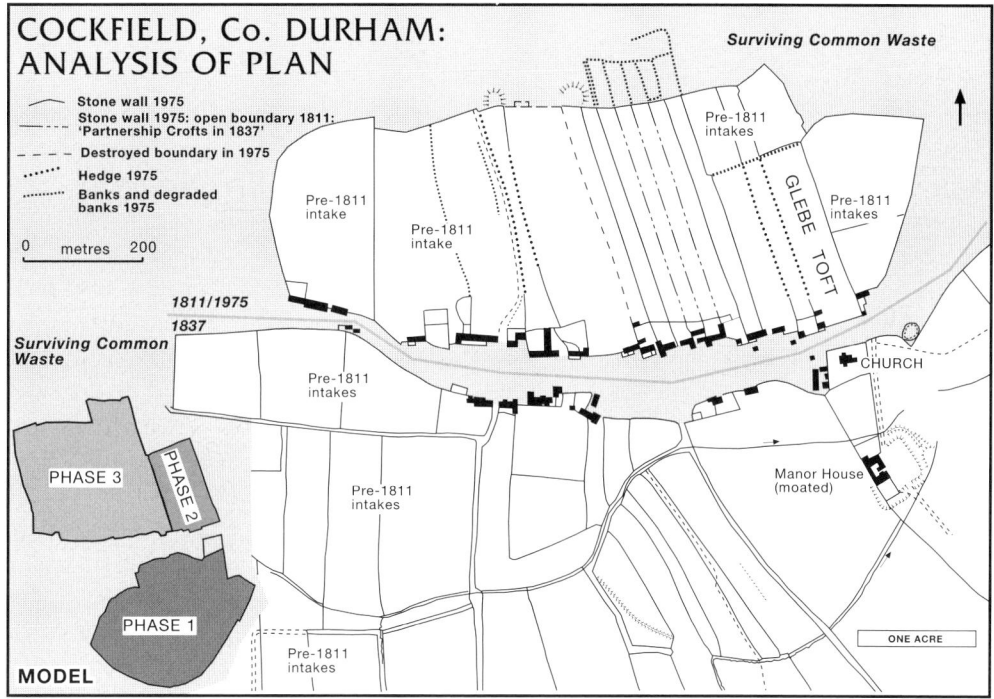

Fig. 4.1 The village of Cockfield, County Durham

Roman fort, and while a Roman date has been postulated, this is an exceptional field monument. The closest parallels are to be found in two equally enigmatic sites. A first appears at Hamsterley Castles, several miles to the north-west of Cockfield, with a second site up-valley from Richmond, Yorkshire, North Riding, where a similar stone-built structure, in this case with an annex, lies at the foot of a 50 metre cliff (Nat Grid. NZ 103331 and NZ 137019). Such massive structures may have been expressions of status as much as defence and undoubtedly took great amounts of labour to construct. For reasons that will become clear, the present author would opt for a date between the end of the Roman period and the Norman Conquest – in this case truly the 'Dark Ages'. The use of this marginal upland environment for hunting may give a pointer to the origin of all three of these sites, but the presence of shieling grounds is also possible. A context for the construction of the rectangular structure at Cockfield, and perhaps even the putative Iron Age site, is to be found in the building services of the bondage tenants of Aucklandshire, to be discussed in Chapter 6. Whatever their precise chronology and purpose these earthworks are tangible evidence for a long-term usage of this area of Pennine spur fell country.

Second, there are charters from the 1220s and 1230s for two unidentified places in Durham issued in the name of Robert de Cockfield, the antecedent of the Vavasours, the owners of Cockfield (Roberts 1983, 39–40). Before 1226 he was granted waste land in *Statheleg* and by 1234 had founded a church in a place called *Beaurepayr*. The presumption is that both of these could have been at Cockfield, for one name is Old English in origin, the other Norman French. In fact, the Vavasours held no other property in Durham. The de Cockfield family, with lands in Norfolk and Suffolk, may well have taken their name from the eponymous Suffolk village and transplanted this as a third level of naming to the Durham site. If this is so then in Figure 4.1 we have a date for the planting of the manor house, and the associated oval field enclosure – although both site and field could be older – together with the church and the glebe toft to the north. At about the same time, or soon after, the oval enclosed field area was divided into two portions, the easternmost becoming the demesne, and this necessitated the addition of further tenant tofts adjacent to the glebe. Finally, the establishment of a few tenants led to the creation of a further set of long tofts in excess of 400 metres in length that were added to the western end of the northern row. Between these developments and the older manor house nucleus with its oval field there lay an irregular green, opening, as in measure it still does, to the fell grazings. The intrusion of mining cottages and rows into this old plan has deformed its rural character but the earlier lineaments still survive.

Again, there are many questions here. Was the southern oval field really associated with the manor house? The gently domed and sheltered ridge it embraces was suitable for arable and is now gently lynchetted, still with traces of tenant strips at the western end. Was this merely the original field associated with the manor house, or was it earlier? Where did the original tenants come from? When was the large informal green, where the common waste swept between the original hallgarth enclosure and the settlement's north row, substantively enclosed? Only part of the large green in fact survives. Fossil traces of former extensions of the long tofts appear out on the present fell; why and when did this slight retreat at the northern end of the long tofts occur? An early nineteenth century map hints that the strips were originally open, and as there is no trace of a back lane, were the original house enclosures at the head of each broad strip, as was described earlier in this study? To add to these complications and questions, mining has gone on in and under this village for many centuries, and surface subsidence of as much as one or two metres has taken place. The earliest fieldwork sessions by the author, in the 1960s, introduced him to old miners and there is no reason to disbelieve their view. Nevertheless, in spite of these and many other questions – which should be noted, even if they cannot be answered – the picture is essentially sharp. A single-farmstead was developed in the waste before 1226: by 1234 there was a church, Early English, with the documentation being wholly in accord with the structural remains. Presumably tenants were present by that date. The long tofts are to be interpreted as a new foothold furlong – in fact set on a quite desperately exposed north-facing slope

Settlement Plans – Variations and Complexities 91

– in part replacing land lost to an expanding demesne, and in part for newcomers. In fact there are other villages with this type of plan found throughout the Durham foothills, as at Iveston and Frosterley (Roberts 1972, 54). All are associated with the breaking of new land from the great tracts of former 'waste' that in 1200 dominated the landscape of all of west Durham and a great deal of the east (Fig. 2.5). The story of Cockfield emerged gradually over many years and while the landscape detail is rich, the documentary references are scanty. Nevertheless, the fact that Cockfield is one of a particular category of plan, definable and significantly different from the general run of northern short-tofted plans exemplified by Carlton and Middridge, allows this intractable evidence to be manipulated within a broader context. In this is the essence of using plan morphology as historical evidence. In Durham (Figs 2.6 and 5.6) villages of this 'Cockfield' type concentrate in the west of the county, a zone of active agricultural colonisation, where the century and a half after 1150 brought expansion to long-established nuclei, and new farmsteads to the favoured portions of the dales sides and plateau surfaces (Fig. 2.2).

Cumbrian Villages and Hamlets

The case of Great Asby, Westmorland (Fig. 4.2) carries the argument to the west of the Pennines. Here the southernmost row of the village contains a series of strip tofts: these are somewhat over five hundred metres (550 yards) in length, and vary considerably in width. There are traces of others on the western side of the village at its southern end, and yet a third group in a detached small hamlet to the southeast – note here the re-orientation of the plan in Figure 4.2 to fit it on the page. On both map and ground, two things are striking about the strips: they are enclosed, but they undoubtedly possess aratral curves, reflecting the continuous passage of ploughs along arable lands. The boundaries of the strips sweep into the village, and indeed are continuous with some of the toft boundaries. The enlarged field detail included within the circle reveals a number of interesting and important facts. At point (a) a toft vennel, passing alongside the vicarage – the building contains traces of a fifteenth century bastle house – continues along the strip as a field vennel (Perriam and Robinson 1998, 255). The slight hollowing and the way it follows the aratral curve suggests this is an ancient feature. At points (b) and (c) are the traces of headlands associated with the ploughing of the strips, but between these and the toft tail line lie the remains of a former back lane. Surviving stiles show that this was once a footpath, although it has now decayed. However, the eastern lateral boundary of the field strip and the toft, are continuous (point d) and contain *inter alia* Shap Granite boulders, interpretable as field clearance stones. This arrangement can be interpreted as follows: first, the land was broken by being ploughed, and the headland of this ploughing must have lain along what is now the toft head line or building line, edging the village green. Second, as ploughing continued the debris taken from the land was lodged within the substantial

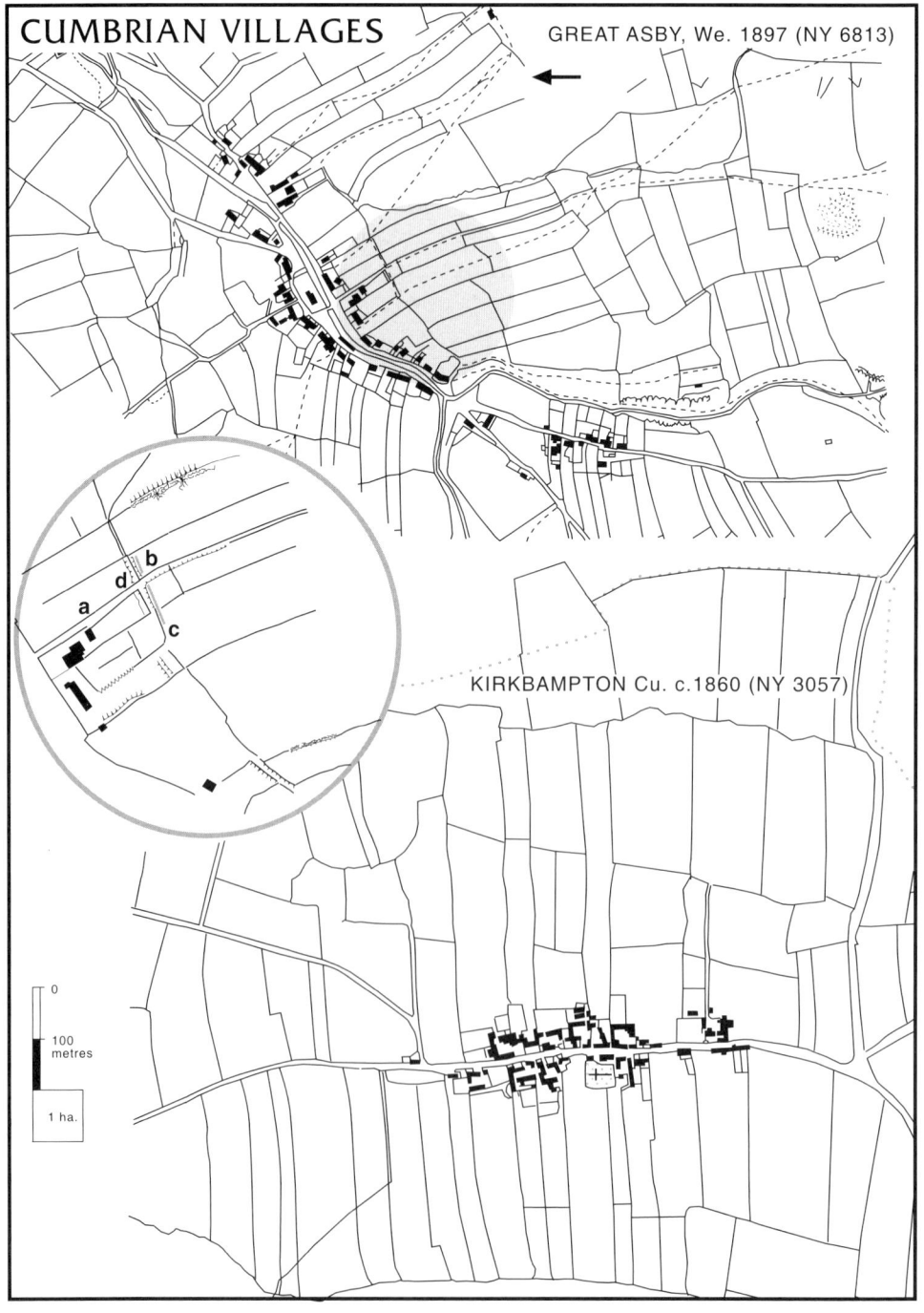

Fig. 4.2 Two Cumbrian villages

lateral boundaries, demarcating a series of broad strip properties. Third, tofts were established *over* this ploughing, and a back lane to service these existed for a time, eventually falling into disuse. Very faint traces of this can be identified along much of the southern compartment of the settlement, but unlike Maulds Meaburn the whole system has not been mapped although 'binocular access' from footpaths suggests few other surviving earthworks.

This analysis begs further questions. Great Asby by no means stands alone because long and strip tofts, closely attached to the village farmsteads and hence intimately associated with the settlement's core arable, are particularly frequent throughout Cumbria (Fig. 5.6). Most are enclosed, but the example of Hayton shows that some at least of the strips were once open (Fig 4.3). The aratral curve, a giant reversed-S shape, shows that their underlying structural geometry derives from ploughed strips. The length, however, is quite remarkable. In order to explain these observations the author has postulated the use of a 'great plough', a roughly made and massive tool, which could be drawn by many beasts, oxen, men and women, to break new land for sustained arable use (Roberts 1996 c). The resulting rough tilth could then have been stone-picked, accounting for the boulders and stones in the lateral boundaries. This suggests haste, the need to reclaim at speed, and may have swept beneath the imposed new patterns all traces of smaller plots resulting from earlier activity on the site. It is the sheer length of many of these Cumbrian strips that implies an exceptional process, for they can be four, five, six or even eight hundred and more metres in length. Like many of the points raised in this chapter, this will be returned to, but a post-Norman Conquest date is likely. However, this hypothesis raises questions about the physical traces of this 'ploughing'. Many years of examining traces of medieval ploughing seen as ridge and furrow and/or lynchets on hill-slopes shows that these present a remarkable picture of regularity and smoothness of form. Such strips are emphatically moulded by powerful draft through cultivated and husbanded soils, and this morphology is both distinctive and sustained throughout the landscape. Close examination of the fields at Maulds Meaburn raises further interesting questions (Fig. 3.3). In this village a set of drumlin-like features run essentially north to south along the valley sides, with drainage sikes between them running parallel to the main valley and this physical arrangement seems to have discouraged the appearance of very long strips. Nevertheless, the Ordnance Survey map shows a succession of aratral curves appearing as the enclosed field boundaries. When these are carefully examined, indeed surveyed and mapped at a scale of 1:500, they prove to be singularly irregular in detail, sometimes of earth with a drainage ditch, sometimes set with clearance boulders. This irregularity can only appear in a very large-scale map, and when the detail is subsumed in a map of 1:10,000 or even 1: 2500 the small-scale irregularities disappear and a clear aratral curve emerges. In short, the field boundaries, probably established over earlier land-breaking ploughing, are old, very old, having had time to become deformed as side ditches were re-cut and the banks added to by further field stones. In this complex local morphology the effects of time are clear.

Hayton, Figure 4.3, offers a measure of support for these arguments. It is located on the kinder land near the junction of the Eden and the Irthing. A map of 1603 in the Howard of Naworth in the Department of Palaeography in Durham collection shows that at that date, and in this particular settlement, the strips were essentially open. Each strip constituted the plot of a single landholder and lengths of up to 600m are found. Tenements sat near the head of each strip but the map is insufficiently detailed to show with any precision how the buildings and yards were arranged. The church is placed at the head of three narrow strips in such a position as to suggest that it is *later* than the layout of the strip system. In this case the church dates from 1868, replacing one constructed in about 1780. However, the parish is an ancient one, and the church was given by Robert de Vallibus to the convent of Carlisle in the second half of the twelfth century (VCH Cu. II, plate facing page 320: Parson and White 1829, 427). We can only assume that the site is the original one. Further north, at Kirkbampton, a gem of a Norman church, still retaining its decorative programme (Fig. 4.2), is probably pre-1150 in date and yet sits on or over the heads of a similar series of strip tofts. Cumwhitton is a contrast (Fig. 4.3), for while a series of rather long tofts lie at the heart of the village, these may even be secondary and later than the less regular series seen in the south row, where the church, containing Norman work, and its glebe toft, forms an integrated unit. Around the core has developed a radial pattern of enclosed fields.

In Figure 4.5 a simple model shows how slight morphological changes can lead to the detachment of a foothold furlong from its base village. Kernel Type A comprises long tofts with the farmsteads set on their heads, often with a fenced yard area. Type C comprises a planned village in which a toft furlong is sharply detached from the tofts proper by means of a back lane, while Type B is a less formal structure, the 'back lane' being no more than a toft tail/headland line. Type D suggests that farmsteads may, in some cases be placed on the green space at the head of the field strips, as can be seen in Scale Houses. The point is that through time all of these mutate, and the crisp differences visible here are concealed amid later changes and accretions. Furthermore, the toft and primary strip can be separated by reallocation, so that a given toft may have two, three or more strips scattered through the kernel of the toft furlong. A splendid photograph by Tim Gates of a village at a stage of 'decision-taking' in Paul Frodisham's volume on the archaeology of the Northumberland National Park appears as the frontispiece to this study. At Hartside, whose name suggests development from a shieling site, orientated long-houses and tofts are seen to be developing in the liminal area between the arable strips and a drainage sike (Frodisham 2004, fig. 7.15). Further variations can be seen in other cases (Fig. 4.4). At Waitby a small two-row concentrated hamlet is surrounded by long broad field strips that survive as earthworks. These are post-Roman, for they over-ride the small Romano-British site, and their association with the hamlet's field system is clear (Roberts 1993 a). Their antiquity is attested by the notched township boundary to the north. Gamblesby is a complex street green,

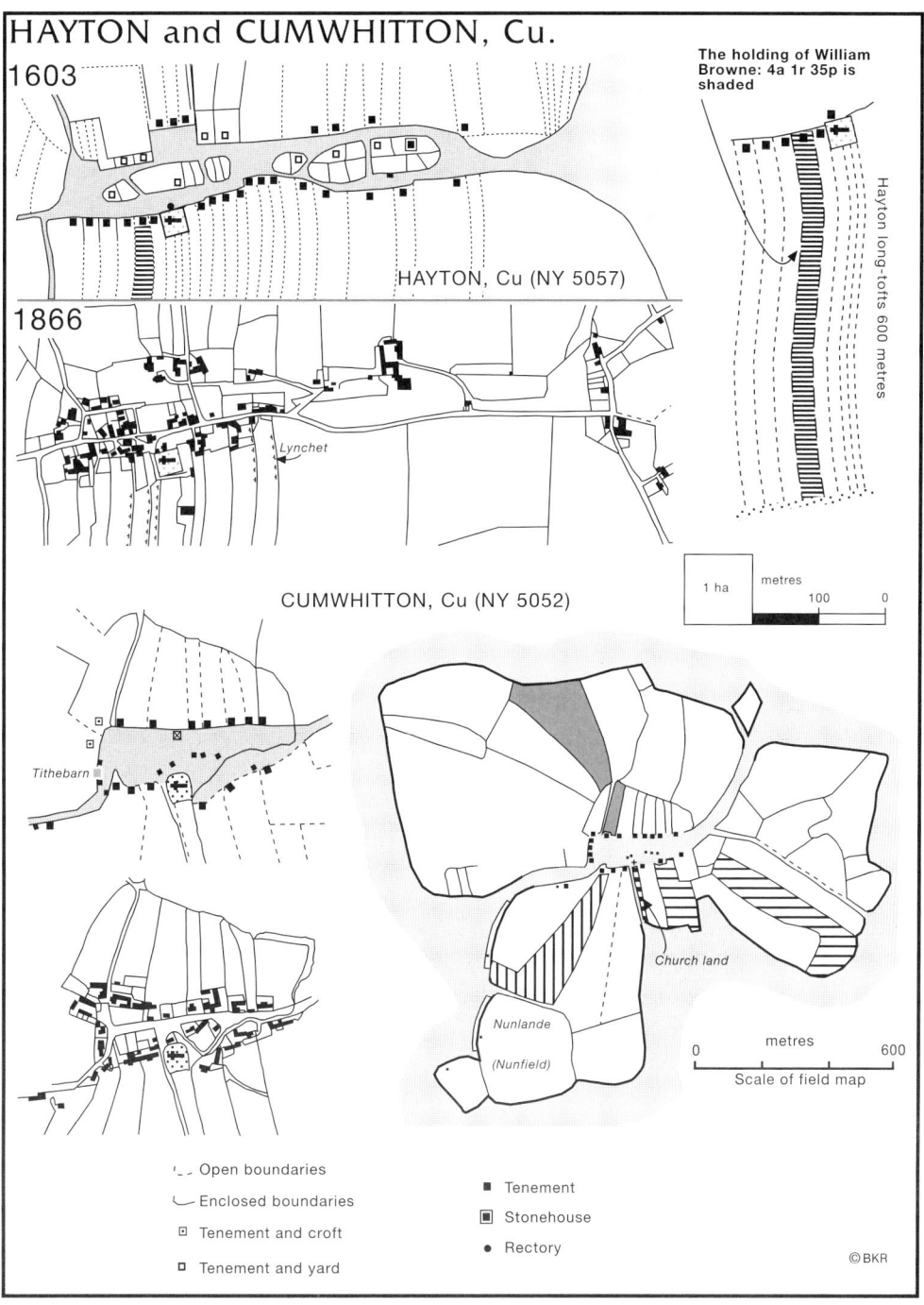

Fig. 4.3 Two long-tofted villages in Cumbria

Fig. 4.4 Four examples of Cumbrian villages

lacking a clear-cut building line where cottages and outbuildings have accreted by moving forward into the open space, a process seen in its early stages at Cockfield (Fig. 4.1). At the present day numerous structures intrude onto the green in front of the building line of 1812. Gamblesby is interesting because village takes its name from the Gamel son of Bern who appears in a writ of Henry I described as a *dreng*, a member of a ministerial group to be discussed more fully in Chapter 8 of this study. This man, bearing an Old Norse personal name, and whose father bore an Old English name, is likely to have been associated with the planting of this settlement (Roberts 1989), an issue to be examined in Chapters 7 and 8.

Melmerby is an even more striking case, with four independent single-row plans with long or strip tofts conjoined within a single plan. In one, that to the south-west, a 'back lane' footpath indicator is present; in another, a straight toft tail line is a possible indicator; in another the toft furlong must have terminated in a headland, while in the last case the irregularity is such that a back lane is unlikely. This is a frustrating example: it ought to be possible to work out a developmental sequence, additions to an older core, but apart from suggesting that the north row may be the earliest to go further is not possible and the questions remain. *Melmor* was yet again a personal name of twelfth century provenance in the region (Armstrong *et al.* 1952, 223–4; Roberts 1989). In contrast, Newton Reigny is as 'neutral' a plan as one could wish to find. Its tofts lie at the maximal length for a normal toft, but in the core of the village a Norman church lies in a kirkgarth integrated into the present north row, suggesting a *terminus ante quem* date for that row. To the north of this a small earthwork enclosure could well be an earlier north row that has never developed, or perhaps a planned addition that was never used. The relationship to the rest of the plan certainly suggests this, while the place-name with its manorial affix places this into the same general chronological context as Gamblesby, Melmerby and other settlements of Cumbria to be discussed further in Chapter 8. While the author views these, and Newton Reigny, as new plantations of the earlier twelfth century, the different morphology of the settlement nucleus at Waitby may imply a twelfth century restructuring of an older focus, indeed an older steading site may be incorporated into the village's structure (Roberts 1989). Nevertheless, even in Newton Reigny there are slight hints that the village has been laid out over a pre-existing set of long strips, indicated by the congruence of a few north to south field boundaries from one side of the settlement to the other.

Two final Cumbrian cases emphasise the way in which settlement formalisation extends down the hierarchy to the smallest hamlets. Little Asby (Fig. 4.5) is today a small hamlet of two working farmsteads, one with an extensive caravan park, and when last visited some of the older buildings were experiencing improvement and one new dwelling was under construction. Slight earthworks in empty enclosures along the street tell the practised eye that former buildings have utterly decayed. Little Asby is a village in embryo. Common grazing land still sweeps though the centre of the settlement to form a narrow green. Until recently the eastern end possessed a great

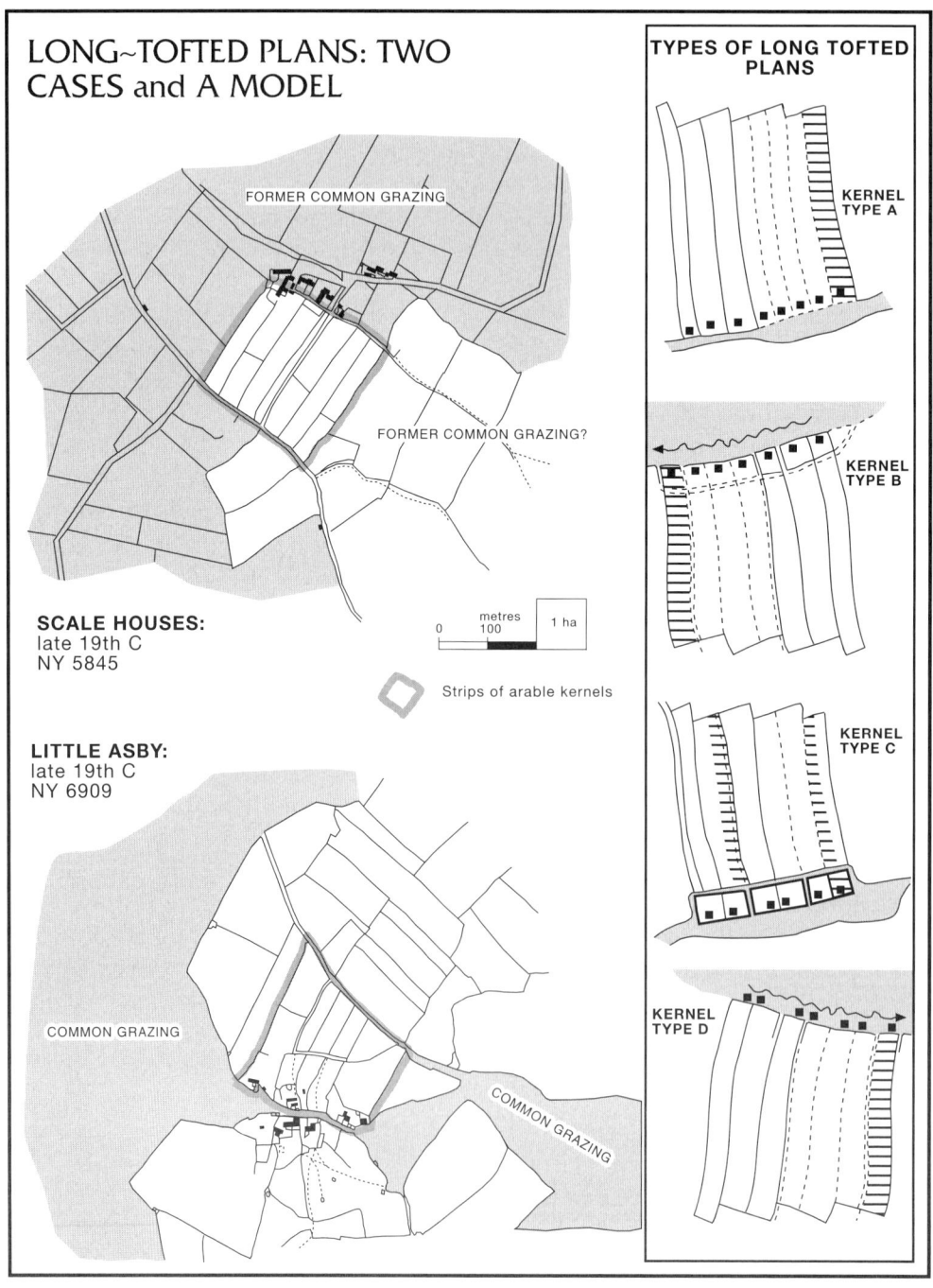

Fig. 4.5 Long-tofted plans: two cases and a model

rarity, a surviving village gate, often seen recorded on eighteenth century maps. Little Asby is likely to have been a daughter settlement of the larger village of Great Asby. *Asby*, 'the farmstead with the ash-trees', is a Scandinavian name-form, *i.e.* originating before the Norman Conquest and, in this county lacking Domesday Book, Little Asby is first documented in 1185 (Smith 1967, 54). Clearly we have no means of knowing if this settlement plan was completely reorganised at some point between 1185 and the later-nineteenth century, but the experience throughout northern England is that ancient plans do tend to persist as elements in the landscape. If the identification of the old arable kernel, the arable field that supported the initial settlers is correct, then we have at Little Asby a compartment incorporating field strips of the order of 250 metres in length. Scale Houses carries the argument one stage further. Here the kernel field is remarkably regular and was carefully planned, and it is postulated that the original farmsteads were set in common grazing land at the head of the strips. This may also have been the case at Little Asby. First mentioned in 1531 *Scailhouses*, in the township of Renwick, may well be the successor of *Rauenwykchales* mentioned in 1278 (Armstrong *et al.* 1952, 236). What the place-name – *Scales* – and the settlement morphology make wholly clear is that we have here a former shieling, a summer grazing area for stock, and that at some stage in its history an arable field developed on the site. This must have been placed where manuring had enriched the soils, perhaps adjacent to the booths associated with milking the animals, so that permanent farmsteads could be established, in this case laying out a 'field compartment' and placing the steadings adjacent to these on the common pasture. It is no accident that Little Asby has a similar form, for it probably developed in the same way. In the light of these two examples, both representing hamlets set near agricultural margins and both likely to have been established on the site of seasonally occupied locations, we see examples of small but nevertheless highly organised plans. Many questions remain, not least about an absolute chronology. There is no inherent reason why Little Asby was not a twelfth century development and Scale Houses one of sixteenth century date, for plans of this nature while tending to be pre-1300, do appear in sixteenth century contexts (Roberts 1987, 204–5). That there are errors of interpretation here is probable, but the strength of this argument builds upon the richness and diversity of the evidential base. The plan variations are real, even if the author has not been able to draw together the obvious evidence that could be available as a result of lengthy and more focussed enquiry.

Yorkshire – Three Cases

Figure 4.6 shows Middleton-by-Pickering and the striking thing about this plan is the curve of the township boundary on the eastern side, reflecting great sweeping curves of fieldstrips. When these are measured we are dealing with field strips of the order of three thousand metres, three kilometres in length! Yet they show all the features of a gentle plough structured curves, running seamlessly across the landscape. There are indeed cross-divisions, but these in most cases have the appearance of breaking up the

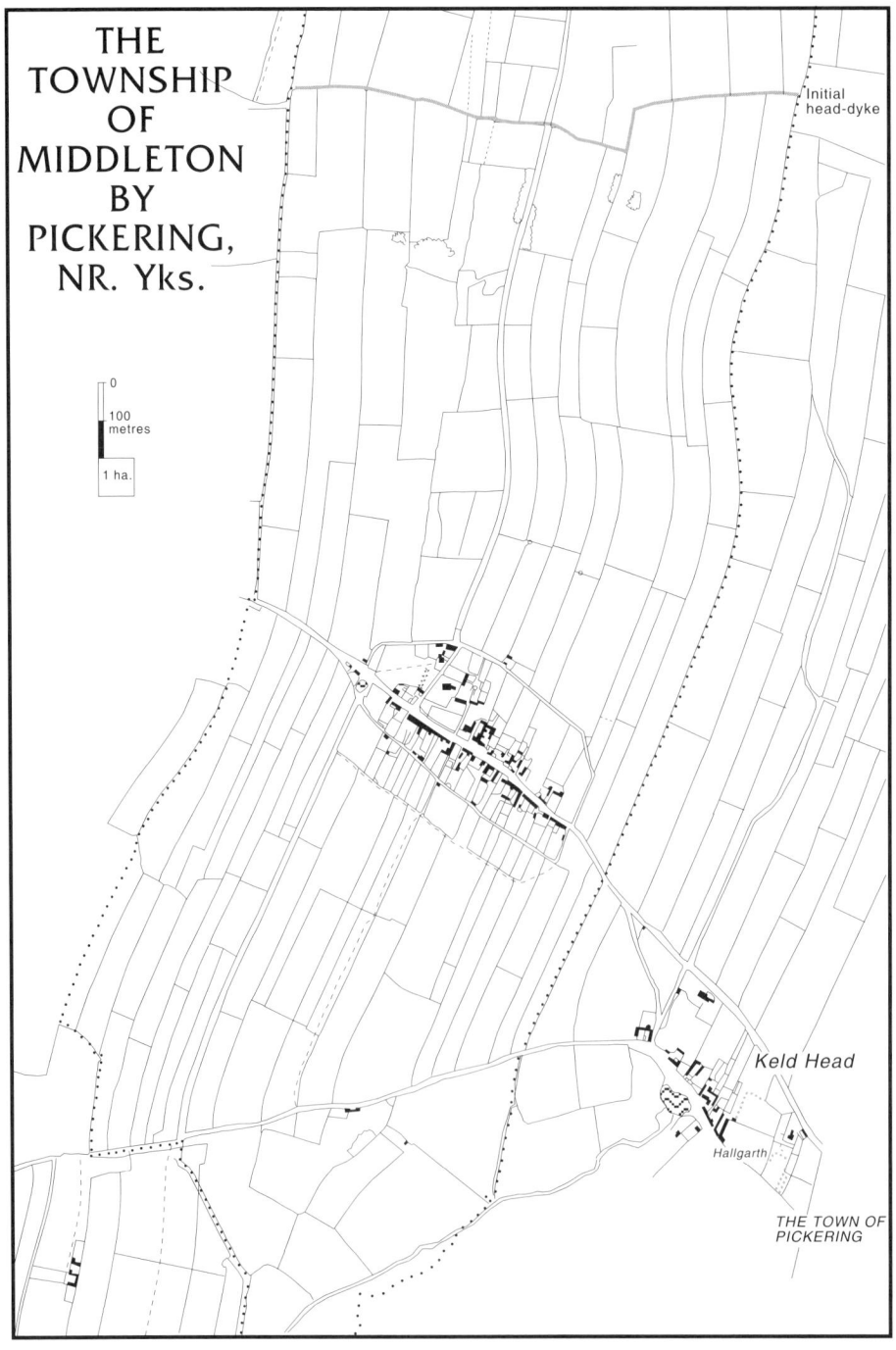

Fig 4.6 The village and township fields of Middleton by Pickering

large sub-structural system. The same types of long strip fields continue westwards into the next two townships, and with variations and in less striking forms eastwards along the dip-slope of the Corallian escarpment beyond Pickering (Fig. 2.1; Ordnance Survey 1:25,000, North York Moors, sheet 27). The village appears to overlie the strips although it has to be admitted that few, if any, of the strip boundaries flow directly into the toft lands. On balance superposition of the village plan seems likely, with slight discord appearing in the north-western sector of the settlement in the form of an angled cross-lane; the churchyard and possibly a manor toft further to the west, perhaps indicators of an antecedent settlement in this location. The line of additional small closes on the settlement's south side suggests either garden crofts or an attempt to add a further row, but modern development excludes real field investigation. There is also the possibility that the north row is the original, with the south row being a set of cottage tofts added at a later stage. While the main entry of Domesday Book merely lists Middleton as part of the soke of Pickering, and describes it a 'waste' in terms that can hardly be queried in this essentially accessible location adjacent to a royal centre (DB Yks.1Y43, see also SN,L39 note), the contemporary summary entry notes that the king has five carucates there (DB Yks., SN,D18). The scale of these great strips is noteworthy and parallels are found in Holderness, where Mary Harvey thought them to be of ninth century origin (Harvey 1982; *ibid.* 1983, 103). In contrast are the notably different rather irregular and broad large strips at Hutton Buschel (Fig. 4.7). Field names attached to the First Edition 1:10,560 Ordnance Survey, and indeed also appearing on the modern 1:25,000 maps, are linked to several hamlets making up the village. All are mentioned in Domesday Book, Newton, Preston, Hutton and Martin (Garth), and all were sokelands of Falsgrave and Northfield, but it is not feasible to sort out their carucage because of grouped entries (DB Yks., 1Y3, SN,L18 note, SN, D7). These strips in Hutton correspond most closely to woodland clearing strips, or *Waldhufen*, found on the continent (see Figs 9.2 and 9.3). Normanby, a linked farmstead cluster, has been intruded into this image as a further reminder of topographic variety, for it was in 1086 assessed at two carucates (DB 1N1: SN,L3), emphasising that an assessment in carucates need not be associated with landscape regularity.

These three cases show the ways in which individual settlements seen on the map or in the landscape can be used to initiate lines of enquiry. All of them are variants on the range of types defined in the classification developed in Chapters 2 and 3 and stretch the limits of present generic knowledge. They are different. The examination now moves away from individual cases to look at the diversity present within a single small territory. This allows a greater depth of documentary context to be established leading towards the detailed analyses used in the remainder of the book. The third case in Figure 4.7, Normanby is a powerful reminder that settlements lacking the dramatic impact of plans such as that at Middleton by Pickering and Hutton Buschel were present in the same landscapes.

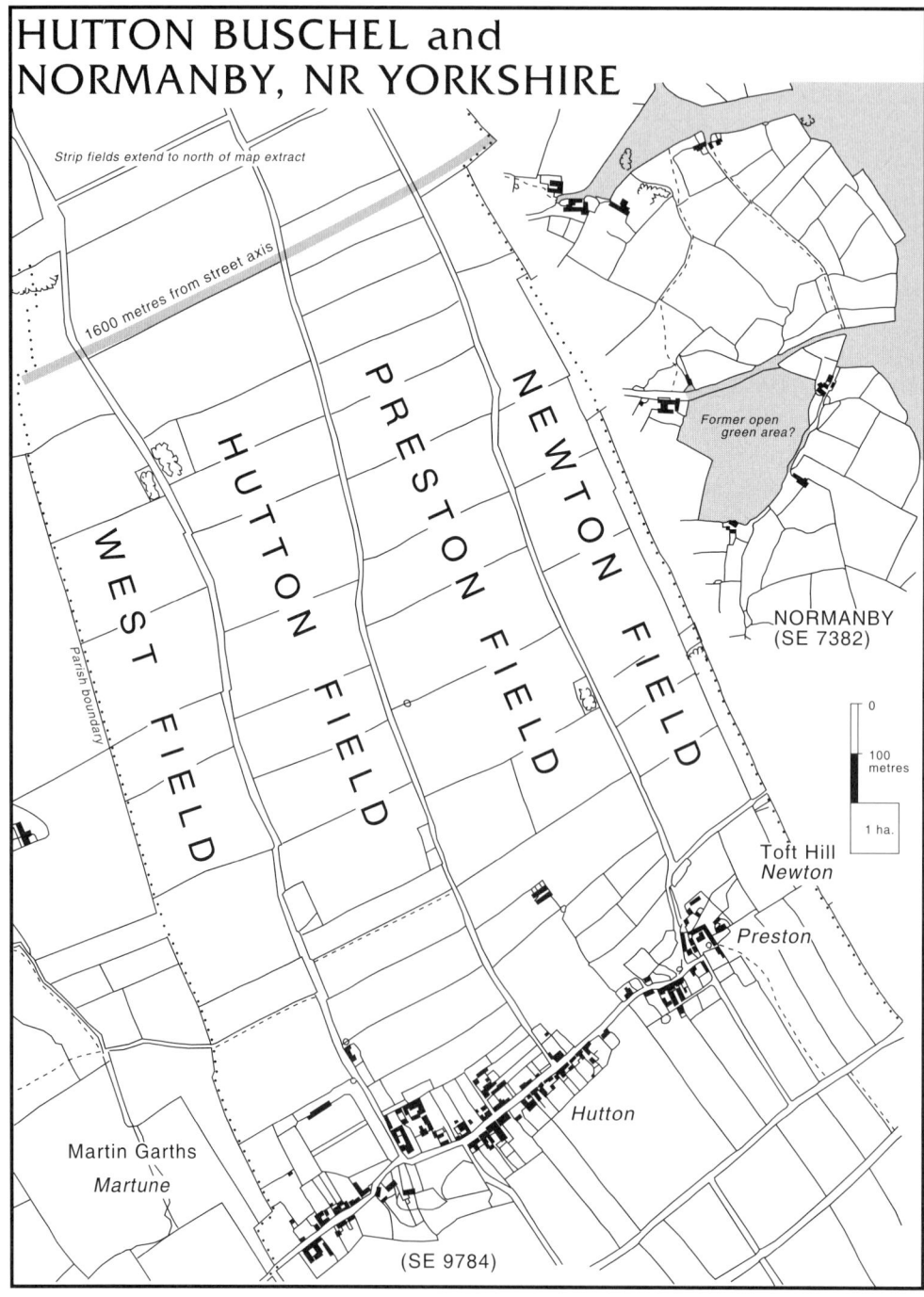

Fig. 4.7 The villages and fields of Hutton Buschel and Normanby

Settlement Plans and Feudal Structures – Coxwoldshire, Yorkshire

The group of settlements seen in Figure 4.8 are likely to have been a small shire, territorial associations of functionally variable settlements to be considered more fully in Chapter 6. The group are a part of the Mowbray estates for which there is charter material (Greenway 1972). In Domesday Book the Coxwold estate actually shows a doubling in value between 1066 and 1086, a rare trend for Yorkshire (DB Yks. C.36, 23N1). The presence of the shire is attested in charters of the twelfth century (EYC ix, 115, 117–8), but Domesday Book provides substance to the territory, by linking Coxwold with Yearsley, Ampleforth, Osgodby, Thirkleby, Baxby (now deserted, in Husthwaite) and finally *Ireton* (now wholly lost). However, it would be wrong to see the shire of 1086 as having wholly fixed and rigid boundaries; rather there was a core of settlements, surrounded by areas of indeterminacy represented by administrative inter-relationships, indicative of antecedent complexity, within the sea of rough grazings used as commons. The estate was in the hands of Hugh Fitz Baldric, the Norman sheriff of Yorkshire, and had formerly been held by Kofsi. It then passed then Robert de Stuteville, to Nigel d'Aubigny in 1106, eventually becoming part of the Mowbray fee. The Cistercians arrived at Hood in the 1130s, followed by the building of Byland Abbey in the later 1170s. These latter grants established a distinctive development trajectory for approximately half of the shire which contains great settlement diversity, with surviving plans, shrunken plans, depopulated villages, monastic foci, monastic granges and other types, and ranges from manors under wholly secular control to manors under wholly ecclesiastical control. The territory, a diamond shape, with a long axis east to west, approximately some fifteen by twelve kilometres, is vastly complex: analysis of the administrative framework reveals a tremendous intermixing of parishes and townships and varied settlement types. Figure 4.9 summarises the tenurial structure and shows examples of settlement plans.

The history of the Honour of Mowbray is admirably documented by Greenway (1972, xvii–lxx). After the confiscation of Robert de Stutville's properties in 1106 these lands passed to Nigel d'Aubigny. His son, Roger, after a minority of nine years, took charge in 1138 and adopted the name de Molbraio, 'de Mowbray' or 'Mowbray'. The late eleventh to the early thirteenth century may thus be divided into several stages in terms of lordship:

Table 4.1 The Lords of the Honour of Mowbray c. 1066–1223

		Years
c.1066–c.1087	Hugh fitz Baldric	c.11
c.1087–c.1106	Robert de Stuteville	c. 9
c.1106–1129	Nigel d'Aubigny	c.23
1129–1138	Minority of Roger de Mowbray	c. 9
1138–1188	Roger de Mowbray	c.40
1188–1192	Nigel de Mowbray	c. 4
1192–1223	William de Mowbray	c.31

It is perhaps inevitable that far more charters survive for the period of Roger's tenure of the estate than for that of his father, Nigel d'Aubigny, but there is no inherent reason why a short phase of tenure need be less important in terms of policy implementation than a long one. Nevertheless, while it has to be admitted that the vigour of mid-twelfth century activity on the estate is noteworthy, particularly the grants to monastic houses, it is necessary to consider other evidence. The 1166 return of knights fees suggests that of the hundred fees then present in the Honour only sixty had been present before about 1114 (by which date the assembly of royal grants to form the Honour was complete). Some 28 of these were established by Nigel d'Aubigny, while Roger added only eleven and three-quarter new fees. After 1166 only four further enfeoffments to knight service took place and these were for fractions of fees. A presumption must be that the granting of estates for knight service normally involved lands already productive, but must also have afforded a powerful stimulus to further development, particularly the extension of farming, the acquisition of new tenants and the development of settlement. The knights' fees of the north were the result of 'settling household knights on the land' and few of the fees owed the service of more than one knight (*ibid*. xxxiv). In Greenway's view they tend to date from the lordship of Nigel d'Aubigny or Roger de Mowbray, and represent development after the first decade of the twelfth century. In Coxwoldshire, however, this conclusion must be set against the important increase in value of the estate between 1066 and 1086, suggesting a sustained process of development extending from the later 1060s to the mid-twelfth century.

This short discussion provides a compressed view of the context in which the estate's settlements must have been evolving. However, when a manor or manorial grouping was held in demesne, policy would be implemented through decisions taken by lord and steward (*ibid*. lxiv–lxv; English 1979, 63–9). It is worth recalling that Roger de Mowbray alone had no less than four stewards:

Table 4.2 Stewards of the Honour of Mowbray c. 1147–1175

c.1147–c.1154	Hugh Malebisse
c.1154–c.1157	William de Wyville
pre 1169/ 1175–6, after 1182	Ralph de Belvoir (possibly)
c.1174/5	Roger de Cundy (joint)

Further, once subinfeudation of a manor had taken place, decisions passed to the administrative control of the mesne lord, the knightly sub-tenant. The point here is that it was within this complex framework of lordship, subinfeudation and stewardship that settlement developments took place. Within this crucial period of development policies were implemented involving three essential areas of decision taking: the management

Settlement Plans – Variations and Complexities 105

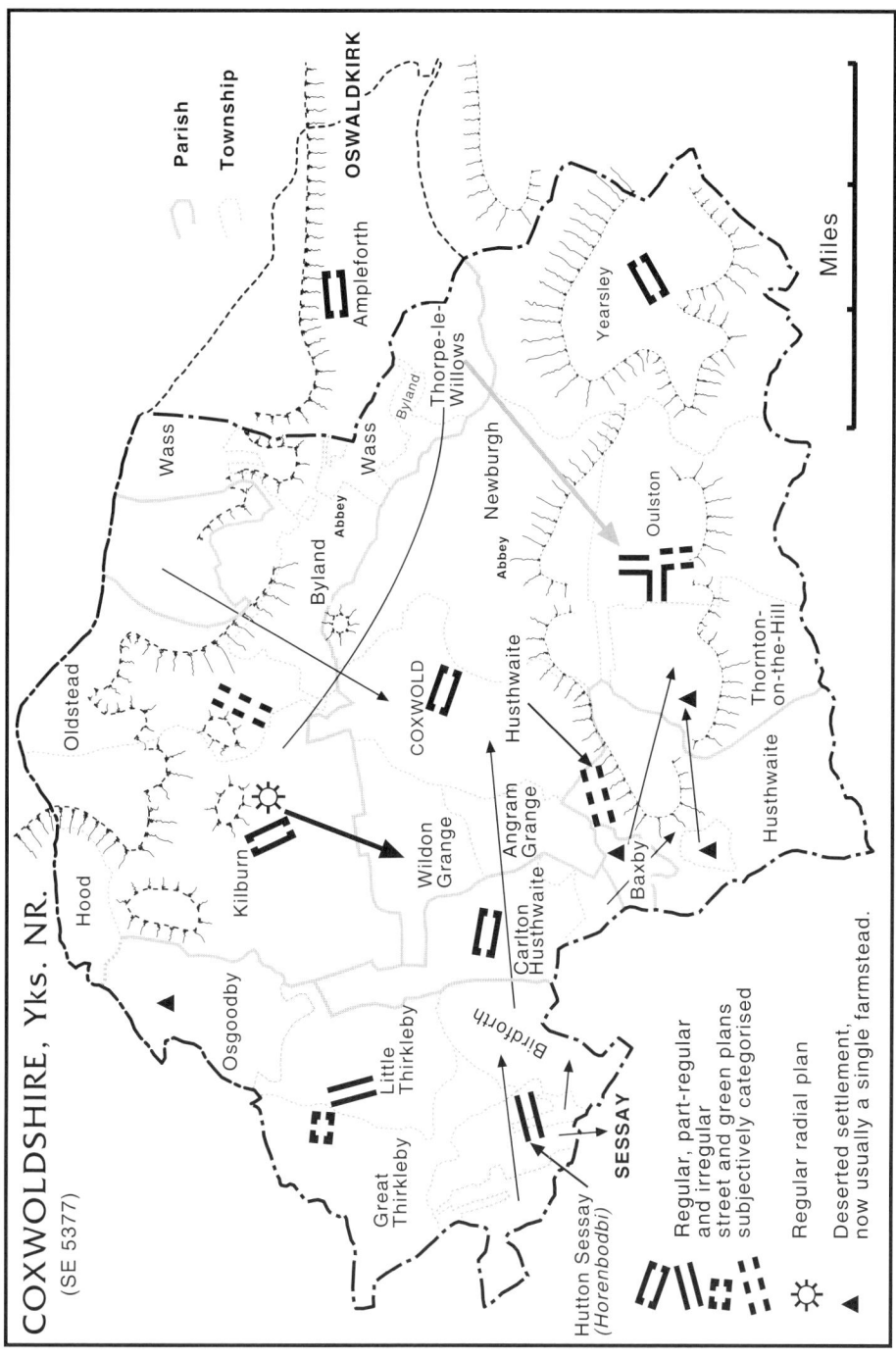

Fig. 4.8 The reconstructed territory of Coxwoldshire

106   *Landscapes, Documents and Maps*

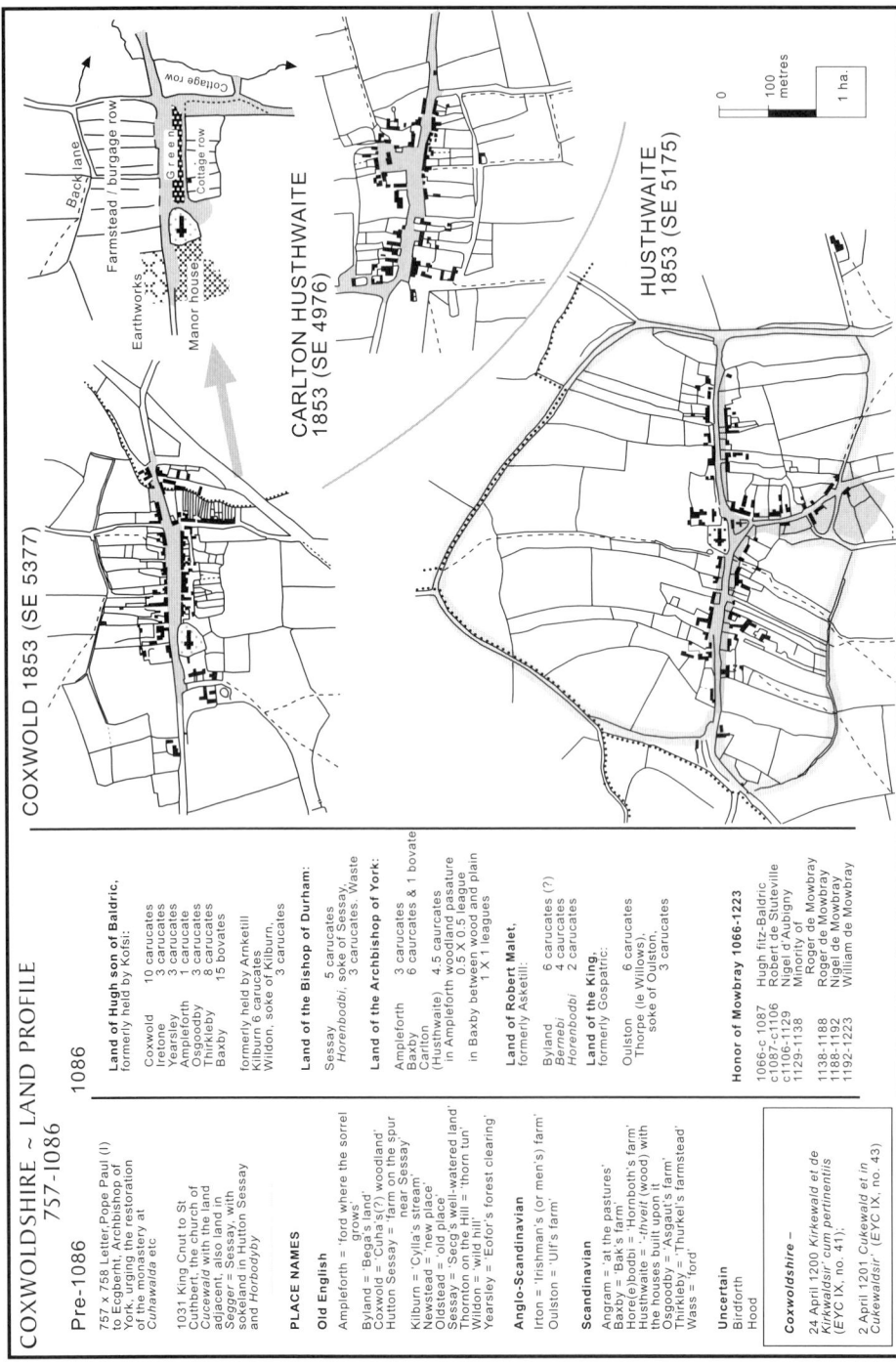

Fig 4.9 *Coxwoldshire settlement and tenurial profile with some villages*

of the demesne holdings (in the broadest sense), subinfeudations to enfeoff knights, and grants to ecclesiastical foundations and monastic houses. Is it then possible to tease out of this complexity the links between the settlement forms found in this territory and the evolving feudal context?

The landscape of today, essentially that depicted upon nineteenth century maps, shows some remarkable contrasts, between the broken wooded country of the Corallian Limestone scarp edges, the scattered large farmsteads developed from former monastic granges and the formal, clear-cut two row structure of the shire's surviving villages. Figure 4.8 emphasises two points; first, the shire is dominated by wholly regular or part-regular two-row street or street green plans, with a few depopulated villages. Second, villages are virtually absent from those townships completely under monastic control, Oldstead and Wass being mere hamlets, although monastic townships do contain actual or reputed deserted village sites. In the light of this several questions must now be defined: how old are Coxwoldshire's village plans and is there any discernible relationship between lordship and village plans? *Cuhawalda*, appearing in the mid-seventh century as the name of a former monastery (Hart 1975, no. 153) suggests the presence of a wooded tract in the possession of Cuha, an Old English personal name. Oulston ('Ulf's farm'), Thornton ('Thorn farm'), the lost *Ireton* ('Irishman's farm'), and perhaps even the enigmatic lost *Twattleton* between the townships of Coxwold and Wildon ('wild hill' – OS 6 1st. Ed.), represent settlements within this wooded zone. Woodland survived late on the scarp faces of the Lias uplands; Yearsley, 'Eofor's forest clearing', Byland, 'Bega's land' and Kilburn, 'Cylla's stream', reflect a more general absence of Old English settlement names in *-tun* and *-ham*. To the west, names such as Thirkleby 'Thurkel's farmstead', Osgodby 'Asgaut's farmstead', and the lost *Hore(n)bodbi* 'Hornbod(th)'s farmstead' reflect Scandinavian influence (Smith 1928, 280; Fellows Jensen 1972, 30). At Carlton while the second element is undoubtedly the Old English *-ton*, the first, the Scandinavian genitive plural *karla* probably replaced the Old English *ceorla* (Finberg 1964, 144–60; Fellows Jensen 1972, 113–4).

Coxwold is a classic part-regular plan (Fig. 4.9). From the church and manor house at the crest of a gentle hill-slope a two row green plan sweeps down, eastwards, towards the valley floor, and although settlement now extends into this the original limit was probably the north-south road. Along the southern arm of this the nineteenth century map shows cottages that once faced a smaller green where the smith and pinfold were sited. Because of the activities of the Belasis family, who acquired the site of Newstead at the Dissolution, the present appearance is very much the 'estate village', with a late seventeenth century hospital and tidy cottages. Nevertheless, the broad, sloping street is paralleled in many northern planted towns and townish villages – Hesketh Newmarket in Cumberland, Appleby in Westmorland and Bedale, in the North Riding of Yorkshire, to cite but three. It is no surprise to find a market and fair in 1257/1304 (VCH Yks, NR. ii, 157), although Beresford and Finberg do not include it in their list of boroughs. There is indeed an indication of trading rights in 1086, for before 1066

Kofsi had "full jurisdiction, market rights and all customary dues' (DB Yks, C.36). Nevertheless, there is the possibility that the name of Newburgh Priory derives from the recognition of the new plantation. The founding of religious houses at Newburgh and Byland together with competition from other small local centres may have curtailed the little town's development, perhaps preserving the simplicity of an early layout. The plan suggests that on the south side of the village, buildings have intruded into the green, and this argument is reinforced by the fact that today there are no historic relationships between ownership or tenancy of the buildings at the street frontage and the tofts behind. The mid-seventeenth century date of the hospital gives *terminus ante quem* for the encroachment of this row of buildings into the green area. The asymmetry of toft length, longer on the north, hints at a social contrast between a farmers' row and a cottagers' row (Roberts 1987, fig. 3.8). The church/village relationship is important. The present fabric is fifteenth century and the D-shaped churchyard is not integrated into the structure of the toft compartments, suggesting it may pre-date these, perhaps occupying the eastern end of an earlier hall-garth enclosure site on the crest of the spur. If the arguments concerning the intrusion of buildings onto the green were correct, then as at Bedale, the church and yard would have sat at the head of the original broad street layout, in effect a plan appropriate for a small proto-borough.

As is so often the case, no evidence exists to secure a firm date, but the author would argue that the antecedent of the present plan came into being between 1066 and 1086. Kapelle (1979, 167–178) has argued, convincingly, that the 'Howardian Hills and vicinity' were one region where the Normans made a systematic attempt to increase agricultural production in the years between 1070 and 1086. In 1086 Coxwold was rated at 10 carucates, with the remaining vills of the shire accounting for slightly fewer than 20. Thirkleby, with 8 carucates was closest in potential size, and while we have no measure of how the 54 villagers with their 29 ploughs were distributed though the territory, that a proportion were already concentrated in Coxwold seems probable. The whole estate was rated at 15 ploughs, but was in fact overstocked, carrying 33. Particularly telling is the increase in value between 1066 and 1086, from £6 to £12. It is possible that the harrying of 1069–70 displaced thousands of peasants, and destroyed their grain and seed, plough beasts and dwellings, creating a reserve of 'colonists' seeking havens where political security was assured. One such haven was to be found on the estates of the Norman lord of Coxwoldshire, Hugh Fitz Baldric, who was made sheriff of the county in 1069/70 following the devastation. He held office until late in the 1070s, possibly up to the time of king William's death in 1087 (YDB, 23N1 note). If this analysis is correct, then these events define one critical stage in the evolution of the landscape of Coxwoldshire and possibly saw the establishment of Coxwold's plan.

Yearsley affords an instructive contrast (Fig. 4.10). It is mentioned in 1086, part of the shire, being rated at 3 carucates, the same as are noted in 1285. At that date it was in the hands of the Colville family, who held it from Roger de Mowbray. An earlier Thomas de Colville had in fact been placed in possession of Coxwold, Oulston and Yearsley for the service of one knight before 1157, the record of the enfeoffment surviving as a copy in a Patent Roll of 1354–8 (Greenway 1972, 228). The plan is characteristic of Corallian escarpment villages, very regular and rather spacious, in this case with the green firmly enclosed, but very similar to layouts at Cold Kirby, Fadmoor and Gillamoor (Fig. 2.1). There are signs that the green once opened at each end directly onto the common wastes, namely the formal late enclosure road running through the former green and the distinctive late enclosure roads on the east. Was the antecedent of the present settlement begun in the period 1070–1087, or was it begun after 1154? The plan is essentially similar to that of Coxwold, with formal toft head lines, one or more lanes – now footpaths – leading from the middle of the village to the toft tail line, toft tail lines which are never wholly regular, and lacking back-lanes. Yearsley, 'Eofor's forest clearing' was settled and taxed by 1086, but is the village a product of development within the demesne manor of Hugh Fitz Baldric, Robert de Stuteville or Nigel d'Aubigny? At the moment we cannot tell. Little Thirkleby – not illustrated – is also a regular street plan, shows slight signs of a rather narrow former green and is of the same general dimension as Coxwold and Yearsley. If the arguments concerning Coxwold are correct, namely that it was a manor and estate revitalised after the devastation of 1069–70 to provide a nucleus of resources for Hugh Fitz Baldric, then it is possible that the other two plans are of the same period. On the other hand the stimulus to village development and the importation of tenants could have been the grant of a knight's fee to Thomas de Colville in c. 1154–1157, in Coxwold, Oulston and Yearsley. This created a situation in which the formalisation of the settlement on the plateau surface could take place. However, and this is a useful conclusion, in all these cases a post-Conquest formalisation of plans appears probable.

Carlton Husthwaite, however, is smaller, a neat, compact two-row village, formerly with a narrow street green but now possessing a small green at one end (Fig. 4.9). This is best interpreted as a late creation, the result of removing the heads of one or more tofts to establish a rather enigmatic chapel generally considered to be of seventeenth century date. Once again there is a suggestion of toft vennels – communal ways – down the sides of some of the tofts. The southern back lane is now destroyed at the west end of the settlement by the emergence of a very large farmstead, and is visible in the field as three banks, across the head of the surviving ridge and furrow, representing both headland and lane. It seems likely that this tight plan, with its constrained layout and traces of back-lanes delimiting the toft compartments to the north and south, is a different 'style' to that found in the other plans so far examined. Part of a group entry in 1086, the settlement had four and a half carucates taxable and was held by the Archbishop of York. In this case there are, however, interesting complications, for Carlton lies in the parish of Husthwaite, itself possibly originating as a chapelry of Coxwold (VCH, Yks. NR. ii, 38) but whose church is Norman of about the 1140s. The Victoria County History suggests that Husthwaite was used as an endowment for a prebend of York by the first Norman archbishop. The essential point is that Husthwaite has been in church ownership since 1066 and represents a very different context for development than the secular manor at Coxwold.

Reference to Figure 4.8 will, however, show a very curious situation; Carlton Husthwaite is separated from Husthwaite by the township of Baxby, now containing a deserted village, and in 1285 is linked with Thornton on the Hill. Given the small size of Baxby township, and the fact that 15 bovates there in the possession of Hugh fitz Baldric were part of Coxwold, there must be a strong presumption that the six carucates and one bovate held at Baxby by the Archbishop in 1086 are the lands that became the township of Husthwaite. This settlement plan (Fig. 4.9) is less regular, with a strong east-west axis met in the middle by a shorter north-south axis approaching from the south. The Norman church lies at the junction. However, the nineteenth century Ordnance Survey map preserves a remarkable pattern of field boundaries comprising a series of rather irregular north-south strips set within an ovoid enclosure, partially demarcated by field boundaries, partially by roads and partially by the township boundaries. The contrast with the formal layouts at the other settlements could hardly be greater, and significantly, this is the only one where the evidence points to the recolonisation of depopulated land. In the place-name, Husthwaite, the element -*thveit* suggests elements of marginality, originally meaning 'meadow' but in English dialect 'fenced forest clearing', not incompatible terms, for forest meadows were vital nuclear areas from which settlement expansion could take place. This ring-fenced arrangement is a widespread form, found most characteristically in areas of woodland clearance (Roberts and Wrathmell 2002, chapter 4). Husthwaite is perhaps an example of the chimera involved in dating settlement plans. The basal structure, the ring fence, and perhaps even the strips, are likely to be pre-Conquest – for all we can prove to the contrary they could be Iron Age – and perhaps originated as the fields around a magnate farmstead, which became a hall-garth/church focus, to which tenant farmsteads were gradually added at a later stage. There may even be two plan-types integrated within the Husthwaite enclosure, one to the west of the church, the other to the east

Kilburn has been included in the 'shire' for several reasons. First, the parish, including an outlier at Thorpe le Willows interlocks with the Coxwold territory granted to Byland in such a way as to emphasise the geographical coherence of the unit. Second, Wildon Grange, part of Coxwold parish, was a soke of Kilburn in 1086, and third, a source of 1389, citing earlier material refers to Kilburn as a chapelry of Coxwold (see below). The village in fact comprises two separate elements, Low and High Kilburn. The former is a regular two row green village, with the green now infilled with an inserted extra row, while High Kilburn is a small rectangular green from which toft boundaries radiate to an almost circular toft tail line surrounding a small hill. A quite remarkable degree of regularity is present (Fig. 4.10). In 1285 the three carucate vill was divided into two manors, two carucates held of Roger de Mowbray by John d'Eyvill and one carucate held by Newburgh priory (Skaife 1867, 104). An Inquisition *post mortem* of 1275 gives a summary extent of the d'Eyvill holding, revealing a manor dominated by bond and cottage rents, with 57 acres of demesne arable and 14 acres of meadow. Newburgh was in fact given 'all the assarts made by their men in Kilburn' by Roger de Mowbray in *c.* 1147–54 (Greenway 1972, 142). In a charter nominally dated *c.* 1154–1157, Newburgh is granted the chapel of Kilburn 'one carucate of land in the same vill and certain assarts within the dense wood they are assarting there, and cultivated by the men of the same church'. This may be a later interpolation, but a charter of *c.* 1147–54, derived from the Byland cartulary, confirms the process. The church at Low Kilburn is Norman, and what is particularly interesting is that it is set within a square churchyard integrated into the east row. It is indeed possible that it was grafted onto the northern edge of a distinctive block of older tofts, containing the manorial enclosure to the south, but that they are broadly contemporaneous seems more likely. Given the fact that in 1086 there was only one settlement with one villan and two ploughs in Kilburn, a manor rated at 6 carucates, there must be a presumption that Low Kilburn village was established between 1086 and the middle years of the twelfth century, when assarting was still in progress. Once again, neither of these plans is likely to be of pre-Conquest foundation.

In these analyses there are undoubtedly many uncertainties. This territory had been settled long before the record of Domesday Book, and the Old English landholding and administrative arrangements within it had already become complex before the Norman Conquest, with Coxwoldshire already being divided amongst numerous landholders. The patterns of parish and township boundaries are powerful indicators of this. Yet there was still land to colonise. To this complexity came the overlay of knight service and feudal tenure, while the severance of large tracts to create monastic estate has barely been touched in the preceding account. Further, the processes of land settlement, involving the development of anciently established centres, and the creation of new settlements in 'old' places, evidenced by indications of devastation even in this developing estate, added yet another layer of visible complexity to the landscape. Amid the mosaic there were woods and heaths, still to be reconstructed. All of these are statements of facts, not supposition, and to the author at least, this attempt to bring limited documentary evidence to bear on the visual evidence of landscape is less than satisfactory. To state that more work is needed is evident enough, yet two further examples suggest that the hares started here may be worth pursuing.

Ampleforth parish presents an extraordinarily complicated picture with its village and fields divided into three townships and two parishes by the late nineteenth century. As Figure 4.10 shows the division took the form of strips and blocks, strips in and around the village and blocks to the north and west, the boundaries being taken from the Ordnance Survey maps of mid-nineteenth century. This pattern clearly has a story to tell, and is illuminated further by selected documentation. *Kirkby's Inquest* of Yorkshire vills was compiled in the reign of Edward I by the King's Treasurer, John de Kirkby, and lists the fees held immediately of the king and of others who held of the king *in capite*. It was broadly compiled between 1283 and 1286, and the date of 1285 is here adopted. The diagram

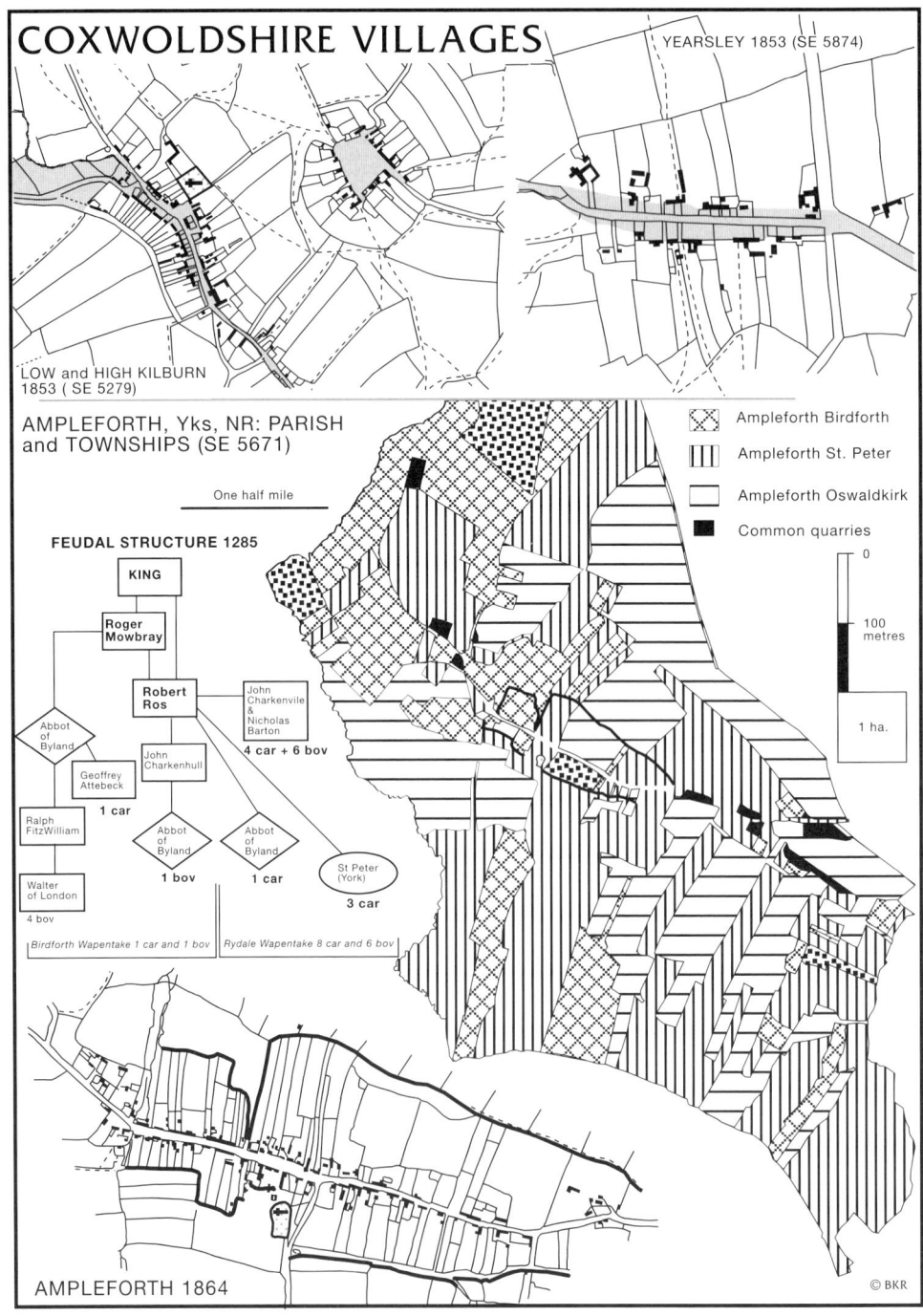

Fig. 4.10 Some Coxwoldshire villages and Ampleforth township

appended to the map affords a view of the parish's feudal framework at than time (Skaife 1867, 106, 110, 114, 115, 123). The nineteenth century townships clearly relate, in some measure, to the feudal structure: the holding of St. Peter in York, described as a 'liberty' by Kirkby, was in Ryedale Wapentake, as was the substantial holding of de Charkenull and Barton and a carucate of the Abbot of Byland, in all some eight carucates and six bovates. These holdings appear in Figure 4.10 as Ampleforth St. Peter and Ampleforth Oswaldkirk (the adjacent parish to the east). Ampleforth Birdforth, in the wapentake of that name, is clearly the remaining one carucate and one bovate and in Figure 4.10 is notably smaller in area. Looking at the map and its patterns the presumption must be that we have the ancient arable in the south of the parish, while to the north and west the former waste has been variously, but not necessarily proportionately, divided between the three townships following later enclosure. The village lies between these two landscapes, in fact on rather sloping land. The division of the toftlands is by no means easily explicable, but a number of blocky plan components are present.

In this matter Domesday Book brings disappointment! The largest holding listed comprises:

> Ampleforth – the Archbishop of York 3, carucates taxable: Ulf had one manor

Under the Carlton Husthwaite entry

> In Ampleforth – meadow 8 acres, woodland pasture half a league long and as wide.

This accounts for Ampleforth St. Peter, but there is a further entry:

> Ampleforth – the land of Hugh son of Baldric, one carucate, in Birdforth Wapentake (DB 23N1)

There is no other entry, but when we turn to Oswaldkirk we have:

> Oswaldkirk – land of the Count of Mortain, Uhtred, one manor of one carucate
> Oswaldkirk – land of Berenger de Tosny, one carucate taxable. Land of half a plough. (DB 5N38, 8N19)

Returning to Kirkby's Inquest, we have the 'Ampleforth and Oswaldkirk' reference to de Charkenull and Barton's land, so that one of these Oswaldkirk entries must account for some land in Ampleforth parish, a circumstance easily explicable on a frontier of colonisation where administrative boundaries are in process of definition. It can hardly be accident that the main toft lands of Ampleforth St. Peter and Ampleforth Birdforth lay at the western end of the village, while those of Ampleforth Oswaldkirk lie to the east. From this we can conclude that the village was probably actively accreting tofts in 1086. The core units to the west were older and in the hands of the Archbishop and the Birdforth manor, while those to the east must, in the main, be later additions linked to carucated lands not present in 1086. Once again this is a story of which there is much more to be told, and the township is worthy of an extended exploration.

A final example from this small shire touches singularly convoluted questions concerning the links between settlement forms and feudal fiscal structures, and once again focuses upon a divided administrative territory. The nineteenth century township of Hutton Sessay was split between the Birdforth township of Coxwold parish – the wapentake centre – and the parish of Sessay to the south (Figs 4.8 and 4.11). This place is not specifically mentioned in Domesday Book, but clearly represents a redevelopment of a lost vill, *Horenbodbi*, for the feudal structure of the place of that name in 1086 can be traced through Kirby's Inquest of 1285 (Skaife 1867, 95). The township division appears on the mid-nineteenth century Ordnance Survey map. There are two entries for *Horenbodbi* in 1086: one notes that the Bishop of Durham had a holding rated at 3 carucates, soke of Sessay and entered as waste; a second, held by Robert Malet, again waste, comprised two carucates and two bovates of land once held by Asketill (DB 3Y12: 11N19: SN Bi4). This lost settlement is likely to have been the antecedent of the present hamlet of Hutton Sessay, for the following reasons, which incidentally also confirm the association with Coxwold. The argument is complex enough to be formalised as a series of bullet points:

- Birdforth was an outlying township of the parish of Coxwold held by the Bishop of Durham (VCH, Yks. NR. ii, 16, 22).
- By 1285 Birdforth was held in chief by the Earl of Cornwall as part of the Honour of Eye, while Sessay was held in chief by the Bishop of Durham.
- In 1285 Hutton Sessay was divided between three manors, two (totalling 2 carucates) held of the Earl of Cornwall, and one (3 carucates) held of the Bishop of Durham, in all five carucates.
- In the 1850s the township of Hutton Sessay was divided into two parts, one portion being part of Sessay parish, the other part of Birdforth township of Coxwold parish.
- The *Horenbodbi* property in a document dated 1100 – *c*. 1115 was noted as a 'gift of ancient kings and chiefs belonging of old to St. Cuthbert' – a splendid phraseology – and comprised 3 carucates (EYC II, 269). As late as 1128–1135 it was being referred to as 'Horemoteby' in a Durham record (EYC ii, 283–4).

The feudal breakdown of 1285 appears as a diagram in Figure 4.11. The nineteenth century village comprised a rather small regular two-row street plan, but the division between two townships, and presumably the two lordships, extends into the structure of the village, some of the tofts lying in Birdforth, some lying in Sessay (Fig. 4.10 (1), (2) and (4)). The proportions of this division are broadly correct in the light of the Birdforth-Sessay carucage ratio of 2:3, for Sessay clearly had more land. In this case it is reasonable to see the village as a post-1086 re-foundation replacing *Horenbodbi*, with two lords, one secular, one ecclesiastical, each possessing a portion of a unitary planned settlement. As Kirkby's Inquest of 1285 shows, there were numerous sub-tenants on all three entities, but the *in capite*, in chief, division seems to be the important one.

Looking more deeply at this division, Figure 4.11 (3) shows what may be the morphological structure of the plan. This may be structured as follows:

- 'settlement space' lies at the core, comprising short tofts, a street green, and to the south and beyond a possible back lane are a series of short closes. There are parallels here with Middleton by Pickering (Fig. 4.6).
- north and south of this are two toft furlongs, arable strips closely linked to the tofts of the settlement, labelled A and B in Figures 4.11.a and b.

The evidence upon which the plan analysis to follow is based must be stated without equivocation: it is grounded upon the author's professional judgement brought to bear upon the curious irregularities in a township boundary (*e.g.* Roberts 1987. fig. 3.7). There can be no certainty in such an opinion, but this synthesis of experience, once expressed, can then be tested. The publishing of the plans and the analysis lays bare the limited evidence, something of the assumptions and allows others to evaluate and test. In this case Figure 4.11 item 4 and item 5 examine in detail the enigmatic patterns made by the boundaries between the two estates as they pass through the hamlet. They are hardly random patterns, and must be interpretable as historical evidence. It is crucial that the angled kinks in the north to south township boundaries (Fig. 4.11, item 4) undoubtedly represent the inclusion of small blocks and strips within each manor at break points that often show accord with other lines parallel to the west to east orientation of the plan.

Concentrating first on the toft furlongs A and B (Fig. 4.11, item 3), Figure 4.11 item 4 shows where a series of measurements were taken: a, b, c, d, e and f. When these are allocated to the two estates we have a, c, e and b, d, f, and within the degree of accuracy we can expect from such land to map measurements it is clear that these toft acres were divided in the ratio 2:3, reflecting the carucate assessments of the two estates. The differences between ace as *c.* 260 metres and the averaged measurement of 268 metres, and between *c.* 410 metres and 402 metres for bdf are not significant given the map scales involved and the difficulties of measurement. That there are further uncertainties here cannot be denied, for instance the measurement at 'f' is problematic, but Euclidian precision is not to be expected with such land measures. Figure 4.11, item 5 shows the hamlet in greater detail. In the analysis of the layout of the plan there is a further assumption, that the back lane demarcates the tail of the toft row, the north row being cottages. While measurement 'y' is limited by the current eastern end of the compartment, in terms of landownership the boundary is unlimited, and could be extended eastwards. Accordingly, 'w' plus 'v' and 'x' provide two measurements, and together give +/-251 metres, approximately 823 feet. The proportion x : w+v is equal to 2:3, once again the same proportion as the carucage ratio, and the analysis extended in Figure 4.11, item 5 suggests that an eighteen foot land rod was possibly used.

Where does this take us? It appears that the 2:3 proportionality of the documented carucage ratio between the two manors, present in both 1285 and 1086, is also to be

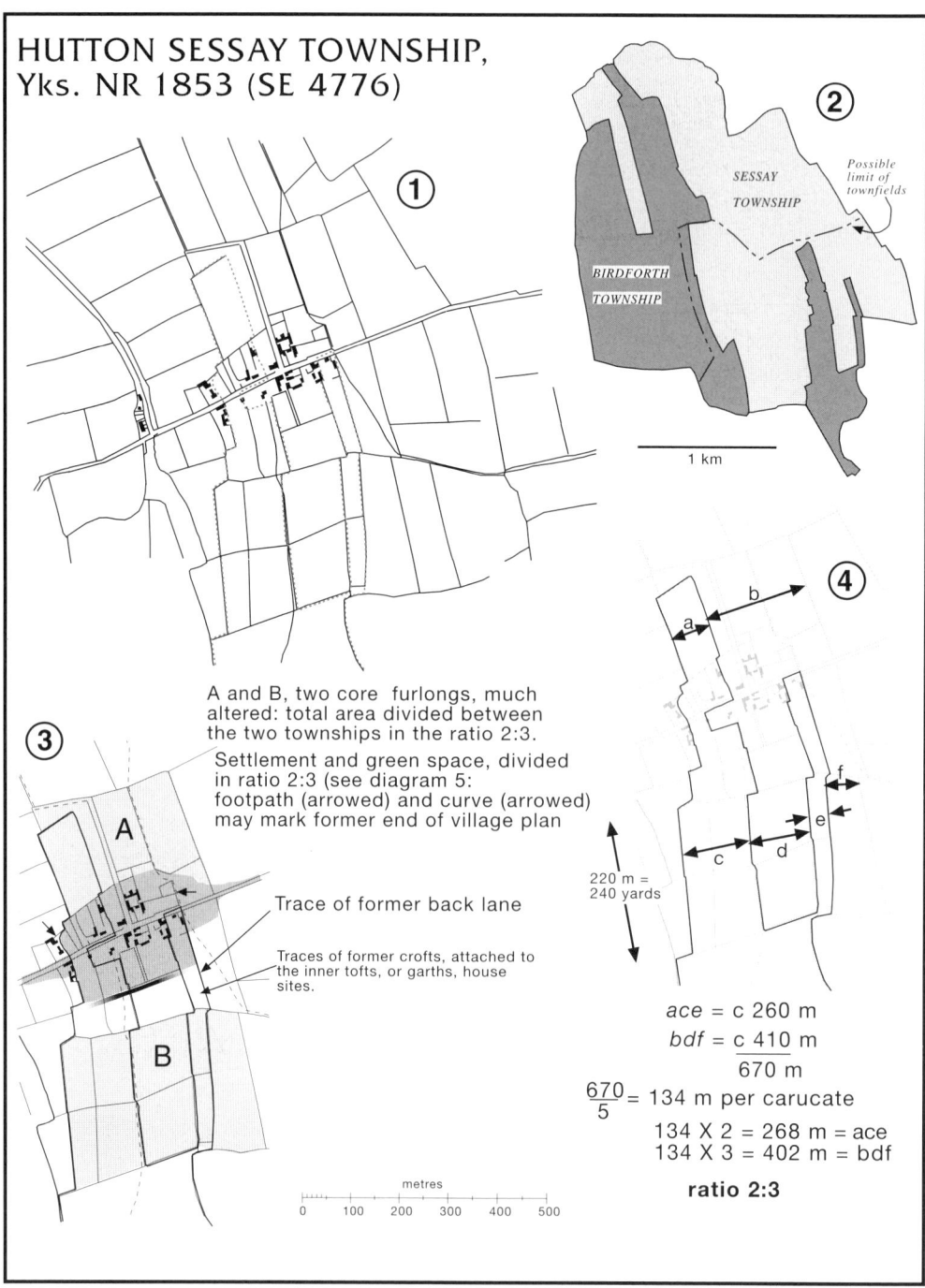

Fig. 4.11.a The township and village of Hutton Sessay

Settlement Plans – Variations and Complexities   117

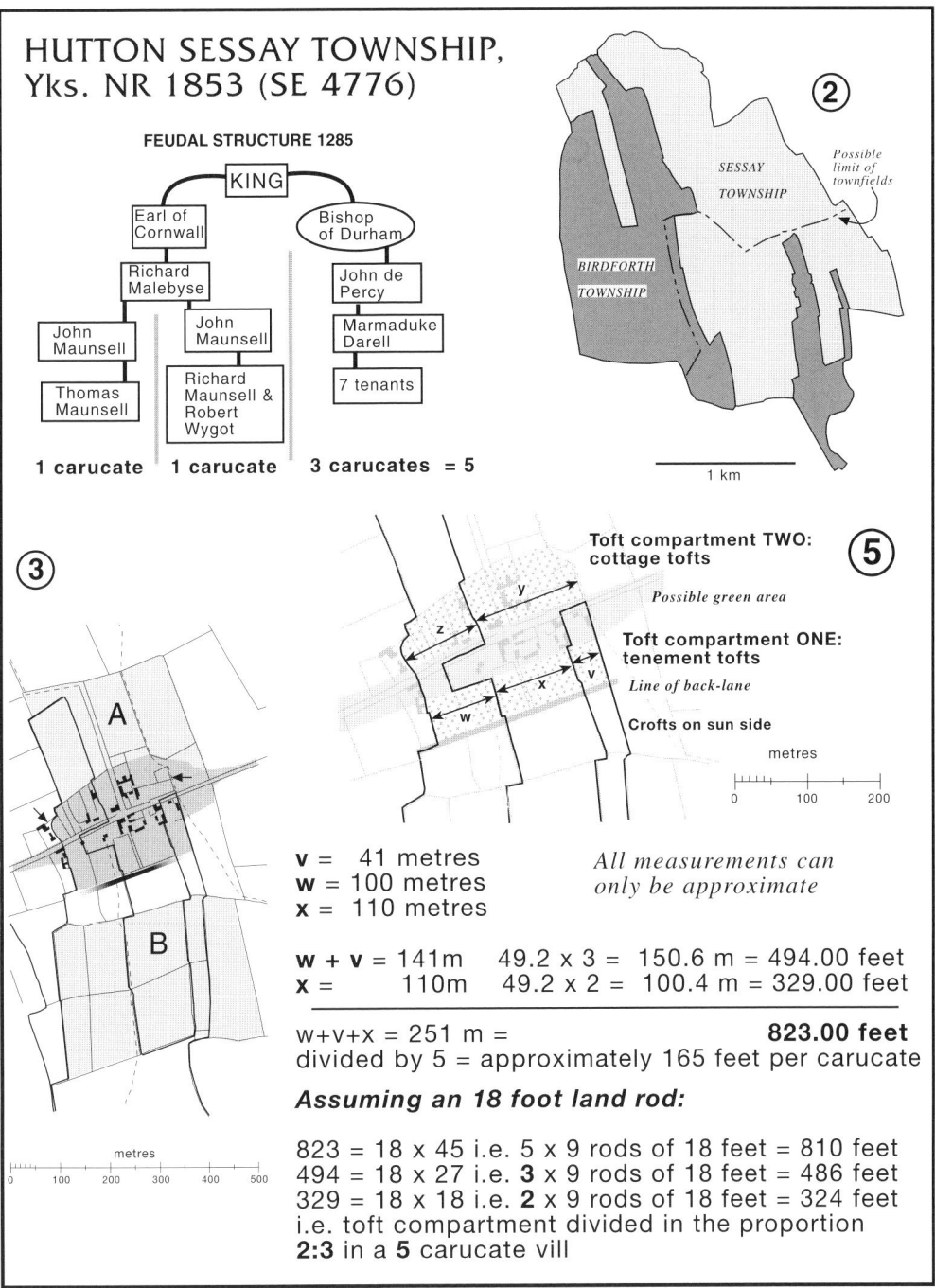

Fig. 4.11.b *The township and village of Hutton Sessay*

found in the plan-structure of the surviving hamlet, or to put it another way, that the hamlet was planned with the carucage ratio in mind. In this the extra two bovates of 1086 are being ignored as indeed they were in Kirkby's Inquest (Skaife 1867, 95). Whatever has emerged, this analysis, whose results could not have been foreseen before the measurements were taken, do suggest that a 'conceived plan' underlies what is still visible on the mid-nineteenth century Ordnance Survey map, a plan very similar to that at Carlton Husthwaite (Fig. 4.9). Before analysis began, the case looked wholly unpromising, and was selected because of the visible evidence of a tenurial fossil seen in the internal division of the township. Of course, there is here no evidence of the date of the planning, but the change from *Horenbodbi* to Hutton, 'the farm on the spur of land near Sessay', suggests that it was after 1086 (Smith 1928, 187). Thus in both Ampleforth and Hutton Sessay there are indications of a restructuring of township boundaries in the half century or so after the Norman Conquest. While we cannot prove beyond all doubt that this involved settlement reconstruction, the probability that this was taking place is high.

In this analysis of a group of villages an attempt has been made to show that many types of evidence must be brought to bear when attempting to analyse and explain individual settlements. Plans and feudal structures undoubtedly interlock, and there are signs that fiscal assessments may also bear a relationship to the on-ground layouts. However, one group remains for comment: Coxwold lies at the lower urban threshold, but regular layouts are also to be found amid town plans.

Composite Row Plans and Towns

Three final cases effectively cross the urban threshold. Appleby in Westmorland, the former county town, is a plan of the same general dimensions as that of Coxwold (Figs 4.9 and 4.12). The little town undoubtedly received in 1179 a grant of the liberties and free customs of York from Henry II (Beresford and Finberg 1973, 176), and is to this day dominated by the site of the great castle, with its Norman keep, rising high above the Boroughgate. Directly to the east of the castle, on the other side of the river, Bongate, with its separate church reveals a rural plan, with a single compartment and contrasts with Boroughgate, the main town street. A little to the north lies a second compartment with clearer evidence for a toft furlong. A baronial *caput*, the little town was never much more than village size, and unfortunately lies beyond the coverage of Domesday Book. Helmsley, already briefly examined, is in contrast is notably larger, and is once again a castle borough, being granted the liberties of York by Robert de Ros in 1186 x 1227. Like Thirsk (Fig. 2.3) the plan is constructed of a series of compartments. The Norman church, of earlier twelfth century date judging by its architectural similarities with the work at Durham, lies at the break point between a street green 'Bondgate' component to the north-west and the main urban plan to

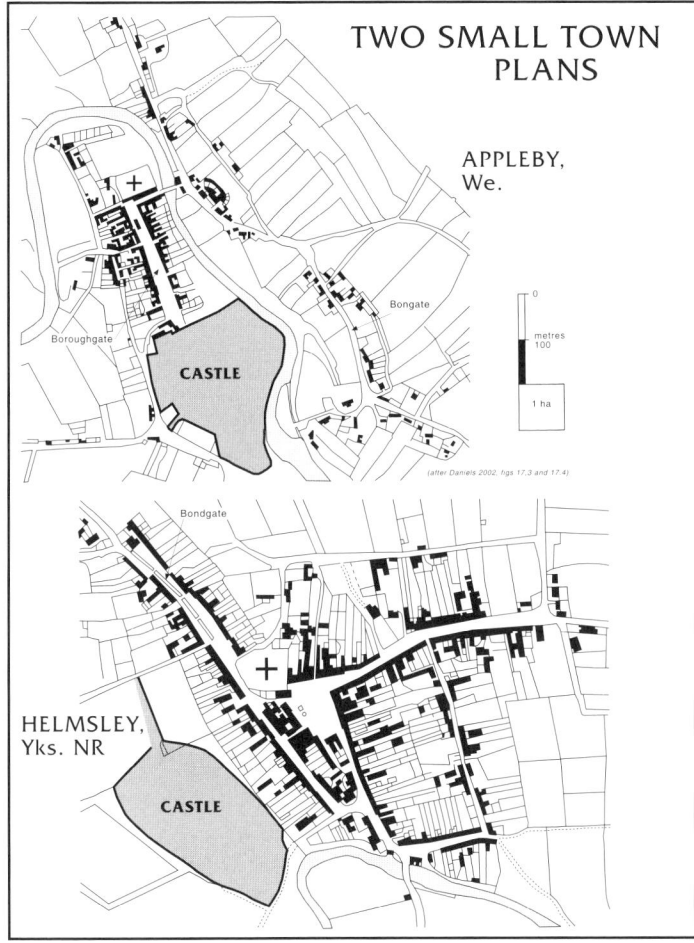

Fig. 4.12 Appleby and Helmsley town plans

the south and east. There is, further, clear evidence of what Conzen termed 'market colonisation' infilling what was once a large market area with a stream flowing down the west side (Conzen 1960, 34–8). In both of these cases it is appropriate to infer an earlier twelfth century origin for the plan, possibly a decade or so earlier, but there are no suggestions of any substantive pre-Conquest roots.

Nevertheless, these two cases do illuminate a larger issue already touched upon. The town plans of the north of England are in all cases merely larger versions of the regular row plans found in purely in rural contexts (Daniels in Brooks *et al.* 2002, 185–96). This is seen at Newcastle (Conzen in Whitehand 1981, 25–53), Alnwick (1960),

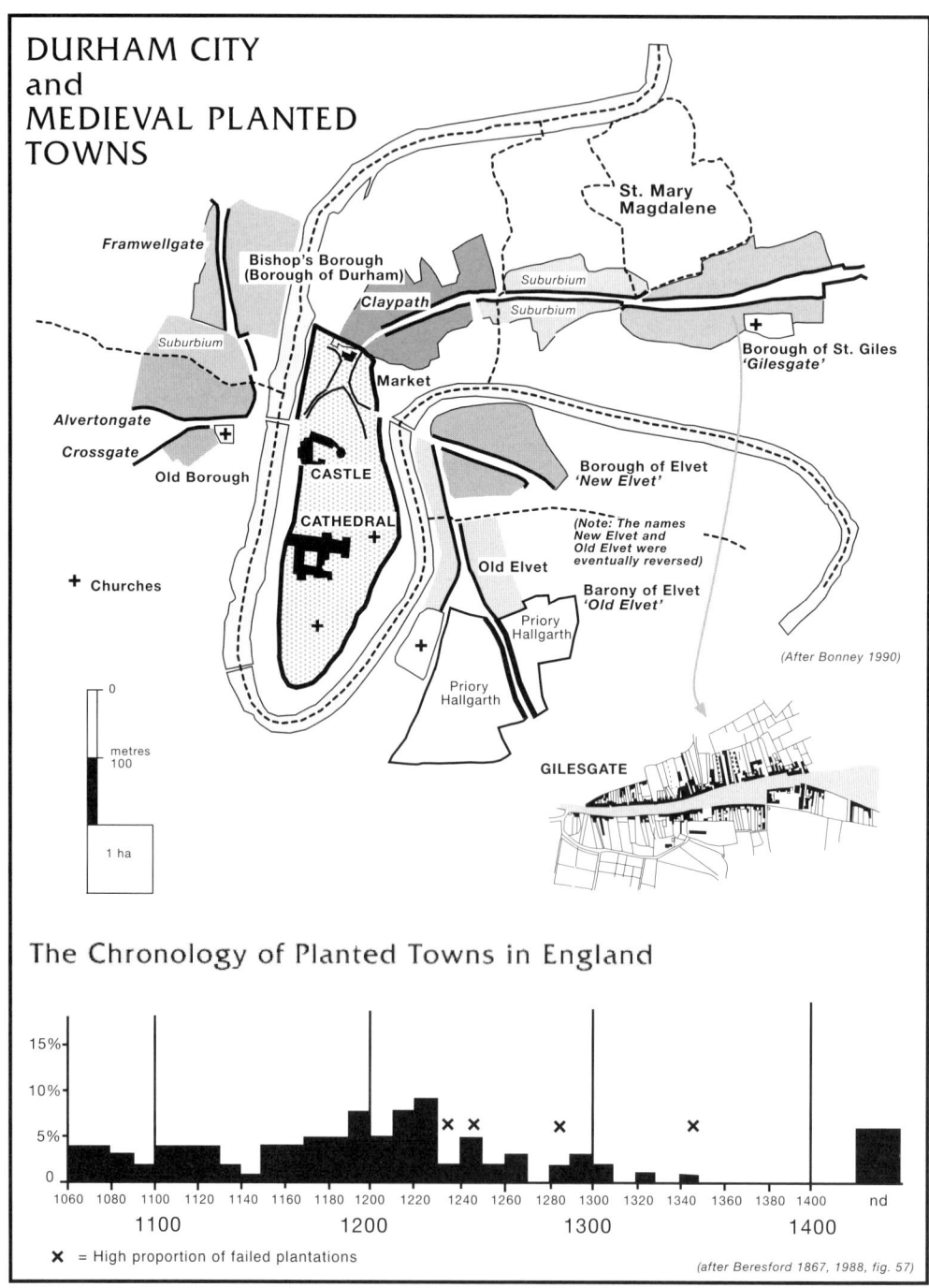

Fig. 4.13 Durham city and a chronolgy of planted towns in England

Carlisle (Gosling in Clack and Gosling 1976, 165–80, and Jones *ibid.* 181–5), and in Durham itself, where (Fig. 4.13) the plan can be seen to comprise a series of village scale units, in fact a series of separate borough entities (Bonney 1990, 41–49). These northern plans have been studied and ordered by Robin Daniels, while the magisterial studies of work by Maurice Beresford and David Palliser (Beresford 1988; Palliser 2000) provide essential contexts. In many of these studies plan persistence is often assumed, even where it cannot be directly established. Beresford's important work has provided the chronological framework seen at the base of Figure 4.13. New town plantations, often, indeed normally based upon regular compartments, were appearing throughout England steadily from the 1160s to the later decades of the thirteenth century, although after 1230 failures were commonplace. There is furthermore evidence of the emergence of a succession of pre-Conquest towns (Palliser 2000), many of whose surviving plans show traces of regular geometries that may be attributable to deliberate planning. There are deep roots in Mercian boroughs such as *Hamwic* (Rahtz in Dornier 1977, 107–29; Hill 1981, 226–36; Hodges 1989 a, 69–114; Hodges 1989 b, 47–86; Zaluckyj 2001, 193–222). All involve the establishment of either an informal or formal degree of regularity of property plots along one or more street axes, a sharing out of the commercially valuable town spaces. In this we see one pragmatic source of the village planning idea, the establishment of approximately aliquot rent producing plots. In towns deeper, subtler, forces were at work, because a smaller, 'poorer', plot set in a location of high potential public access in a town could be vastly more valuable than a larger plot in a less commercial location. In this, absolute equity of division was less important than in rural contexts, so that burgage lengths can be very variable. Further, we cannot know how urban concepts of plot regularity, reflecting aliquot rent shares, and aliquot rights in the resources of the community, passed from the town to the countryside, but lords and their stewards are likely to have been important agents of diffusion. It is at this juncture that the origins of regular rural settlement plans merge with the history of planned towns, castle and church, market place and burgage.

CHAPTER FIVE

Interpreting the Morphological Record

During discussion of the case studies in the previous two chapters careful attention was paid to evidence that could have a bearing on the chronology of the plans. Varied techniques were used, and the first section of this chapter will focus more specifically on questions of dating. It is now apparent that villages and hamlets cannot be dated easily: their continued existence through many centuries is only adequately documented if historic maps exist, but these are rarely earlier than the later sixteenth century (Howell 1983, figs 8–13; Harvey 1980, 167–8; Smith 1988, 36–49). To complicate matters further all settlement can be linked with several interlocking chronologies, involving (1) the visible landscapes, (2) the rents, renders and services, (3) the place-name, and (4) the absolute archaeological chronology, were the site to be completely excavated. Settlements are part of an ongoing continuum of *being* and are rarely susceptible to the label of a single date. Normally only the church will contain elements which can be as much as nine hundred, a thousand, or even more years old. Dating the property boundaries and plots is more problematic, for the former will have suffered many changes, involving maintenance, destruction or addition, with each generation affecting the features they inherit. Nevertheless, the previous chapters have indicated that the framework of old, even ancient, plans can survive for many centuries. The problem of interpretation is to disentangle the varied chronological levels present. In fact, it is normal that only some of these be identified, for as Clive Gamble reminds us 'the past is closed to travellers. We visit it in our imaginations. We reconstruct its processes from the evidence that survives. We interpret the results according to our principles and purposes. But we can never experience the past' (Gamble, 1996, 241). Thus, even our most detailed analyses are mere summaries, highlighting a few facets of the temporal development of a succession of infinitely complex real worlds of the past.

Dating Village Plans

A settlement's place-name is likely to be far older than any of its surviving material substance. In England the majority of names are Old English in origin, derived from the language spoken by the Anglo-Saxons. Place-names, however, appear in documents and in England Domesday Book presents an important datum line across both time and space. As Peter Sawyer has shown, by no means all the places in existence in 1086 are mentioned in the Great Survey because their resources are subsumed under the heading of a more important place (Sawyer 1976, 1–7). In practical terms, however, the date when a place-name appears in the documentary record bears a relationship to its place in the settlement hierarchy: important places tend to get mentioned before small places, although both may possess equal antiquity. Furthermore place-names have meanings, and while no exact chronology can be established it is widely recognised that there are 'early' and 'late' elements and name forms (Gelling 1978, 106–29; Watts 2002, xii–xvi). In general, however, place-names may well be earlier than the particular settlement forms to which they eventually become attached, indeed many of the Old English names need not refer to the precise location of a village if the principal cluster was established long after the period of name formation. Names carry a territorial meaning. Of course, in theoretical terms at least, if a settlement were to be wholly excavated, then archaeological techniques could reveal a site's earliest phase of occupation. Nevertheless, this must also embrace the settlement's territory, for site moves did take place, particularly in the centuries before the Norman Conquest (Beresford and Hurst 1990: Aston and Costen 1994).

The associations of rents, renders and services attached to particular places present a particular and difficult challenge. Payments, in kind, in service and in labour, the latter ranging from agricultural work, ploughing, harrowing, reaping and carting, to renders of eggs, building services, or the keeping of hunting dogs or hawks were fundamental to earlier medieval life. Only gradually were these commuted to cash payments, and this was never a universal, continuous nor irreversible process, but varied from period to period and from estate to estate (Postan 1973, 103–6). At root, particular combinations of renders and services differ from place to place, from village to village, and this variation must often have chronological implications and well as social ones. In Durham, for instance, Bishop Hatfield's Survey of 1381 organises the returns for each place in terms of the obligations of the tenants (Greenwell 1857). Not only can we then compare 1381 with the materials listed in Boldon Book of 1183 (Greenwell 1852), it is evident from in-text 'asides' that the compilers of the Hatfield Survey did precisely the same. The 'lands of the bondsmen' (*terrae bondorum*) tend to be those lands cleared and settled by 1183, indeed the entries in 1381 sometimes relate to exactly the same amounts of land as are recorded in 1183. In contrast 'exchequer lands' (*terrae scaccarii*) generally pay only a money rent, and can most reasonably be interpreted as those lands reclaimed from the waste between 1183 and 1381. In this way the documentation provides a temporal datum line that also has spatial implications, for the estates with the most exchequer land lie, as might be expected, in the west of the county (Fig. 2.5 and 2.6). The value of such details in establishing relative chronologies for the development of particular places will be explored in the later chapters of this study, where an attempt is made to use them to sift out the relative sequences of settlements. However, these theoretical discussions lead towards more pragmatic issues concerning dating plans. It is inevitable that the various ways of dating overlap, but the sequence to be followed below allows a logical structure for presentation and discussion.

Historical Cartography

The processes of change affecting the plans of villages and hamlets are most readily achieved though the use of maps. Figure 2.7 incorporates examples of time series mapping. East Boldon, County Durham, is seen as portrayed on Ordnance Survey maps of 1919 and 1856, while at Longhirst, Northumberland, a single map has been used to draw together the changes between 1632 and 1859. Both settlements are versions of regular two row plans and in both cases the green is little more than a slight broadening of the street. However, the ecclesiastical estates of Durham religiously adhered to medieval estate practice until the latter years of the nineteenth century, *i.e.* essentially using no maps before the advent of Ordnance Survey but relying upon land transfer via surrender and admittance in the Bishops' courts. In contrast, the region's great lay estates, notably of the Duke of Northumberland, Howard of Naworth and the Earl of Newcastle, had maps created by the early decades of the seventeenth century (*e.g.* NCH v, 136, 180, 376 and 416; Pal and Dip. Du.; Nb. CRO, Alnwick Cas Ms. O; Univ. of Nottingham, Welbeck Mss.). While some simplified versions of this evidence has been incorporated into the author's own diagrams, much remains to be done. For instance, the Welbeck maps of the middle Coquet valley, above Rothbury, suggest the presence of rather large toft compartments that are no longer, if they ever were, filled with farmsteads. This is, both literally and metaphorically, largely unexplored territory.

In general, map evidence from the seventeenth to the nineteenth century allows us to see the ways in which settlement plans already long established were adapted to changing economic and social circumstances. The outcomes of this process are well exemplified by Figure 2.7, so that further discussion is not needed. The techniques of cartographic analysis involved were described in great detail in *The Making of the English Village* where it was emphasised that the comparison of maps from varied periods using 'eyeballing' techniques is wholly unsatisfactory. Analysis must employ transcription, *i.e.* using a nineteenth century Ordnance Survey map as a base, and carefully transcribing the detail from the earlier map to this accurate master (Roberts 1987, fig. 1.8). 'Goodness of fit', or not, becomes immediately discernible, and small details that confirm or refute the survival of the earlier plan into the nineteenth, and eventually the twentieth and twenty-first century landscape, become verifiable by using fieldwork. This action, methodical, even pedantic, in character should never be by-passed, for by presenting challenges it sharpens perceptions, leads to further questions and stimulates more fundamental analysis of the plan. This was how the major changes at Acklington and other Northumbrian villages were first detected. Because of the radical early nineteenth century changes, it was often impossible to achieve a close fit between the early seventeenth century maps and those of the nineteenth century (Figs 3.2).

Archaeological Evidence

Excavations really fall into two categories; those which are extensive, such as those at Wharram Percy, East Riding of Yorkshire, West Whelpington in Northumberland, and Thrislington, County Durham, West Heslerton in the East Riding of Yorkshire, and those that are more limited in scale (Fig. 5.1). At Wharram Percy over thirty years of excavation have resulted in a picture of a regular row plan, incorporating what is essentially a two row structure with a head-row, set around a steeply sloping green that incorporates the side of a deep valley cut into the chalk (Beresford and Hurst 1990, fig. 2). A terrace forms the site for a church, a parsonage and some tofts, while three large compartments, two set in a line and one at right angles to these, are associated with substantive tenements and two manor houses, for this village incorporated two manors. Prehistoric, Roman and Anglo-Saxon settlements were antecedent to the village that took shape by the end of the twelfth century. While the evidence is by no means wholly clear, it appears that the Anglo-Saxon landscape was essentially one of hamlet settlements, at least two, and nucleation, the creation of the visible village, probably took place between the ninth and the twelfth century (*ibid.*, 79–8; Wrathmell *ex inf.*). It is important to grasp that this is a picture, whatever its limitations, revealed by extensive excavations over a very long period of time. In contrast, Austin's work at Thrislington, a rescue excavation prior to quarrying, took place in a comparatively short time. The site was an example of a small two-row village, focusing upon a street rather than a green. Toft tail banks lie essentially parallel to the street and a 1947 vertical air photograph shows that several phases of development were present. At the western end of the village was a large sub-rectangular manorial enclosure, containing the manor house and a chapel, but at the northern edge of this there is some ambiguity, effectively covering the whole north-western sector of the village, because the later hall farm developed at that location. The air photograph raises doubts as to whether the manorial rectangle extended that far north and there are signs that the original village – more a hamlet – comprised a smaller rectangle grafted onto the eastern side of the manorial enclosure. Ridge and furrow abutted this development, both to the north and the south, but at the southern side an eastward extension of the boundary around the manor, over the heads and headlands of a set of ridges, effectively created a series of crofts. The whole effect is 'informally rectangular' rather than geometrically rigid, and David Austin's reconstruction suggests a rather short irregular tenant row with little, if any, clear-cut regularity (Austin 1989, 167–173). Nevertheless, his conclusion is that 'regularity of form seems to have some direct relationship to a positive act of measured planning as a conscious transformation of the landscape' so that the term 'part-regular' seems appropriate.

The documentation and excavation combine to suggest that in Thrislington there were never more than six freehold farmsteads in a village of perhaps eight, perhaps twelve in all (Austin 1989, 174), plus the substantial manor house. The freeholds were often substantially larger than the two-bovate unit of 30 acres regularly described in the

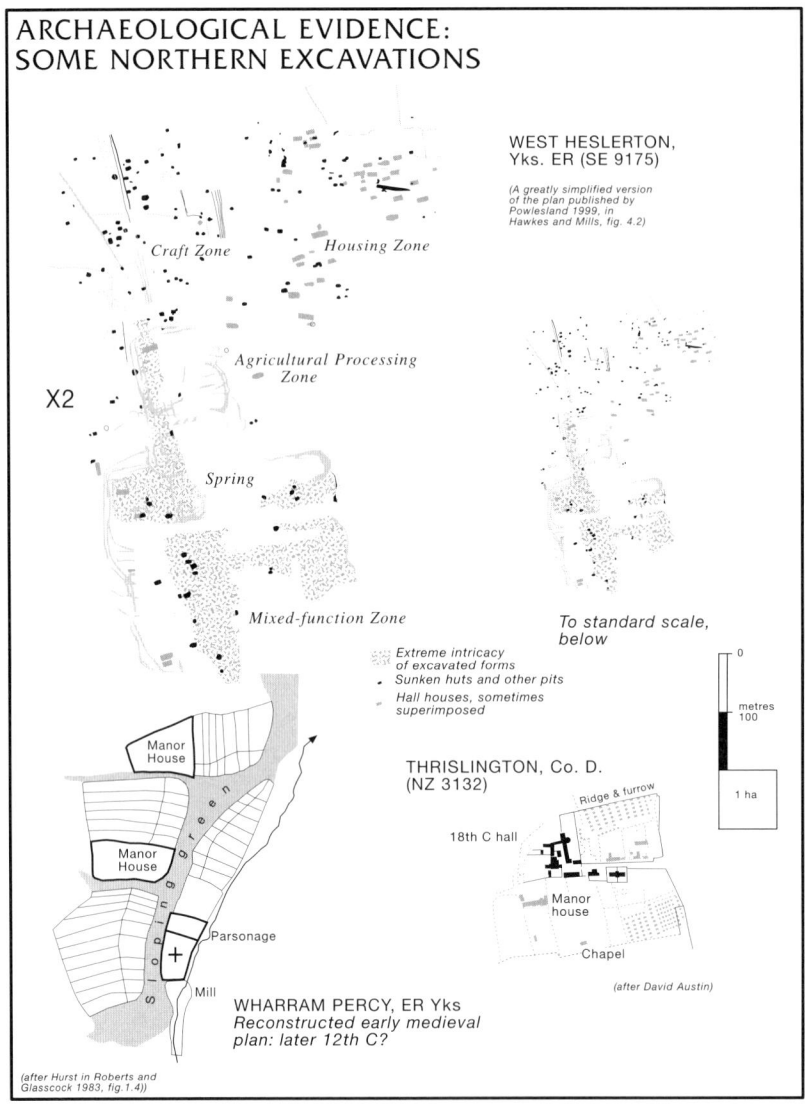

Fig. 5.1 Some excavations of northern villages

Durham records, approximately 50 statute acres if we take account of the Durham land rod of 21 feet (Austin 1989, 12–13). Austin concluded that the visible plan came into existence at some stage during the twelfth century, a uniform start date being suggested by the fact that most of the tofts he excavated produced late twelfth/ early thirteenth century material. Occupation of the peasant tofts seems to have ceased by about 1500.

The hall standing on the site when it was excavated dated from the seventeenth-century and may have been constructed in about 1625. It is unlikely to have been the successor to the manor house as it was built by one of the village's free-holding families. Desertion appears to have been a product of the engrossment of farms by the more powerful farmers of the settlement, a number of which were absentee landlords (Austin 1989, 10–14, 191–2 and 197). In this careful work is a salutary reminder of the gulf between two approaches. The relative precision of the micro-exploration of the detail of this single site sits awkwardly amid the compromises present in a scale of enquiry used in this study that takes as its canvas the whole of northern England. The latter inevitably paints a broad-brush picture. Nevertheless, the fact that Thrislington emerges as a part regular, two row plan established in the late twelfth to early thirteenth century adjacent to a substantial hall-garth enclosure with an aisled hall of the Norman period or twelfth century can be seen as representing a regionally significant conclusion (Austin 1989, 16–17).

While Austin excavated some 5,600 square metres, this was only a limited portion of the site, and the work left unanswered the question of the location of '*Thorsteinn's* farm', the meaning of this Grimston-hybrid place-name, with it's Scandinavian personal name attached to the Old English element *-tun* (Fellows Jensen 1972, 195–204). However, as Austin notes, the settlements associated with this phase could have been anywhere in the township. As the work at Wharram has shown, success in the recovery of pre-Conquest material needs more than careful and professional excavation; it needs the good fortune to strike the right part of the site. It follows that limited excavation can only provide a limited picture, and may not even provide a clear-cut *terminus post quem* date for the development of a plan-type. Jarrett, Wrathmell and Evans' final analyses of the site at West Whelpington (Fig. 2.7), where 14,000 square metres were excavated (approximately 20% of the whole) emphasise that while the evidence they unearthed is consistent with occupation 'from the 12th or even the late 11th century' the lack of well-dated local pottery sequences make precision impossible (*ibid.* 1987–8, 140). Even the structures they were able to place in Period I were only a small part of a more extensive settlement. They suggest that 'the frontages on the north and south sides of the green, which were to persist as long as the village, had been established before the end of Period I, and they may have been original features of the plan'. Interestingly, they continue 'There was also a rudimentary croft system whose extent and layout remain uncertain. Some of the crofts were cultivated, and boundaries may not have been permanent' (*ibid.* 140). Never more than seventy-five metres in length, these plots, sometimes a single unit, sometimes subdivided near the dwelling, would be termed tofts in this present study, and the settlement is 'green-centred', to use the excavator's neat phrase. It is in fact an example of a settlement type wholly normal throughout the north, a plan with two rows that is part regular. On the other hand, the excavators do not doubt that it was 'a planned green village' (*ibid.* 183–4). Of course, this begs many questions about which elements of the layout were indeed planned, and which have developed during the centuries between its foundation and the final abandonment of the site in about 1720.

These extensive and painstaking excavations create pictures that derive from the infinite details of material remains. In such contexts preconceptions become dangerous, and the careful phrasing of the written reports is necessarily conservative and cautious. However, the approach adopted in this present study, of grasping what is apparent in the whole of the north, classifying it, defining the elements that are present, and then deriving from these an analysis of broad brush conclusions of general applicability is in no way at variance with this archaeological evidence. All three of the cases discussed here are regular villages based upon rows; all three contain varied sizes of compartments; all three have greens, although that at Wharram took many years to be recognised because of the steep slopes involved. In no case do we have a blueprint or the putative original plan. There are, of course, fundamental differences in scale between archaeological and morphological evidence. Although the extensive programmes of work at West Whelpington, Thrislington and Wharram are exceptional, it is the morphological analysis of regional and national plans that allows this work to be set in broader spatial contexts. Nevertheless, with a limited sample of three it is hardly special pleading to note that the late-eleventh and twelfth centuries emerge as the period when, with all the qualifications we can muster, these regular plans appear to be emerging.

With this in mind we can turn to two further excavations. At West Heslerton, East Riding, Yorkshire, Dominic Powelsland has excavated an extensive site occupied between the late fourth and the middle of the ninth century and extending over 32 hectares (Fig. 5.1). While the layout does include a remarkable degree of internal spatial variation, with distinctive areas for housing, craft and industry and agricultural processing, with a more mixed zone, there appears to be no evidence for the imposition of a formal plan. The southern portion, a vastly complicated multifunctional zone, contains an extensive network of ditched and fenced enclosures, spanning the complete period of occupation (Powelsland in Hawkes and Mills 1999, figs 4.1 and 4.2). In contrast the northern zones were without any signs of internal divisions or property boundaries. There are a large number of buildings, at least 220 structures, including 130 *Grubenhäuser*, sunken huts, and 90 post-hole structures. Preliminary analysis suggests that the earliest phases embraced virtually the whole site, with contraction in the Middle Saxon period. In contrast, Thirlings, Northumberland, was much smaller, comprising ten substantial buildings and traces of others (O'Brien and Miket 1991). The six largest, all built using deeply cut continuous foundation trenches to support timbered wall planks, were arranged with their axes approximately east to west. Only two of the settlement's buildings were surrounded by enclosures, one being oval and the other rectangular, and no traces of the settlement's boundary were recovered. Traces of *Grubenhäuser* on the periphery of the excavated site suggest that the latter was only the core of a more substantial settlement, and in the suggestion of spatial zoning echoes the discoveries at Heslerton. Calibrated radiocarbon dates fall between AD 454 and 590.

The excavators interpreted the settlement as being perhaps for reception and storage, the provider for the nearby *villa Regis* at Yeavering (Hope Taylor 1977).

Antecedents and Antecedent Forms

With such a limited sample, and this is not the place to explore at a national scale the recovery of Anglo-Saxon settlement sites, significant generalisations are impossible. It is, however, worth reflecting upon what features one could expect to find in the morphology of a relatively simple agriculturally based settlement. Figure 5.2 (a) pulls these together, and the author must admit this draws heavily on his experience of maps and field evidence in Sweden (Helmfrid 1994, 20; Sporrong *et al*. 1995, 78–7, 130). The model depicts a small hamlet surrounded by its arable fields and meadows. The existing settlement is seen at A, but the site has already had an antecedent arrangement that took the form of a scatter of dwellings on the up-slope side of an earlier arable field. This arable has been expanded up the slope, over the former steadings, with their manure-enriched soils. The dwellings and outbuildings of the cluster are now arranged near a higher status farmstead, between the settlement land and the arable there must be a fence, to provide protection from straying cattle. Around all of the arable and meadow is an out fence, a ring dyke (D), needed to protect the crops and grass from the depredations of both cattle pastured on the common grazing lands and deer from the woodlands. In this we see the full significance of the doom of Ine of Wessex in about AD 690 that states

> If *ceorls* have a common meadow or other land divided into shares to fence and some have fenced their portion and some have not, and [if cattle] eat up their common crops or grass, those whose are responsible for the gap are to go and pay to the others, who have fenced their part, compensation for the damage that has been done there.
>
> (Whitelock 1955, 368–9)

Good fences, it is evident, make good neighbours! In Figure 5.2.a the expansion of the core fields has resulted in the formation of an outgang or drift (B), leading from the settlement land to the common pastures. At this stage we can picture a senior farmer, some of his kin, and some household slaves making up the nucleus, and a date would be some centuries before the Norman conquest of 1066, although arrangements like this persisted in marginal environments right into the nineteenth century. Should the settlement be able to acquire more tenants, perhaps slaves, and expand by adding some new dwellings, these could be organised to fill in the settlement space (A), although any substantial increase would of necessity spill outwards, sometimes along the drift, but sometimes into the area of the early arable lands. Were this substantive expansion done in a carefully considered manner, then a planned settlement layout could be imposed, perhaps set alongside or opposite the original high status farmstead of the

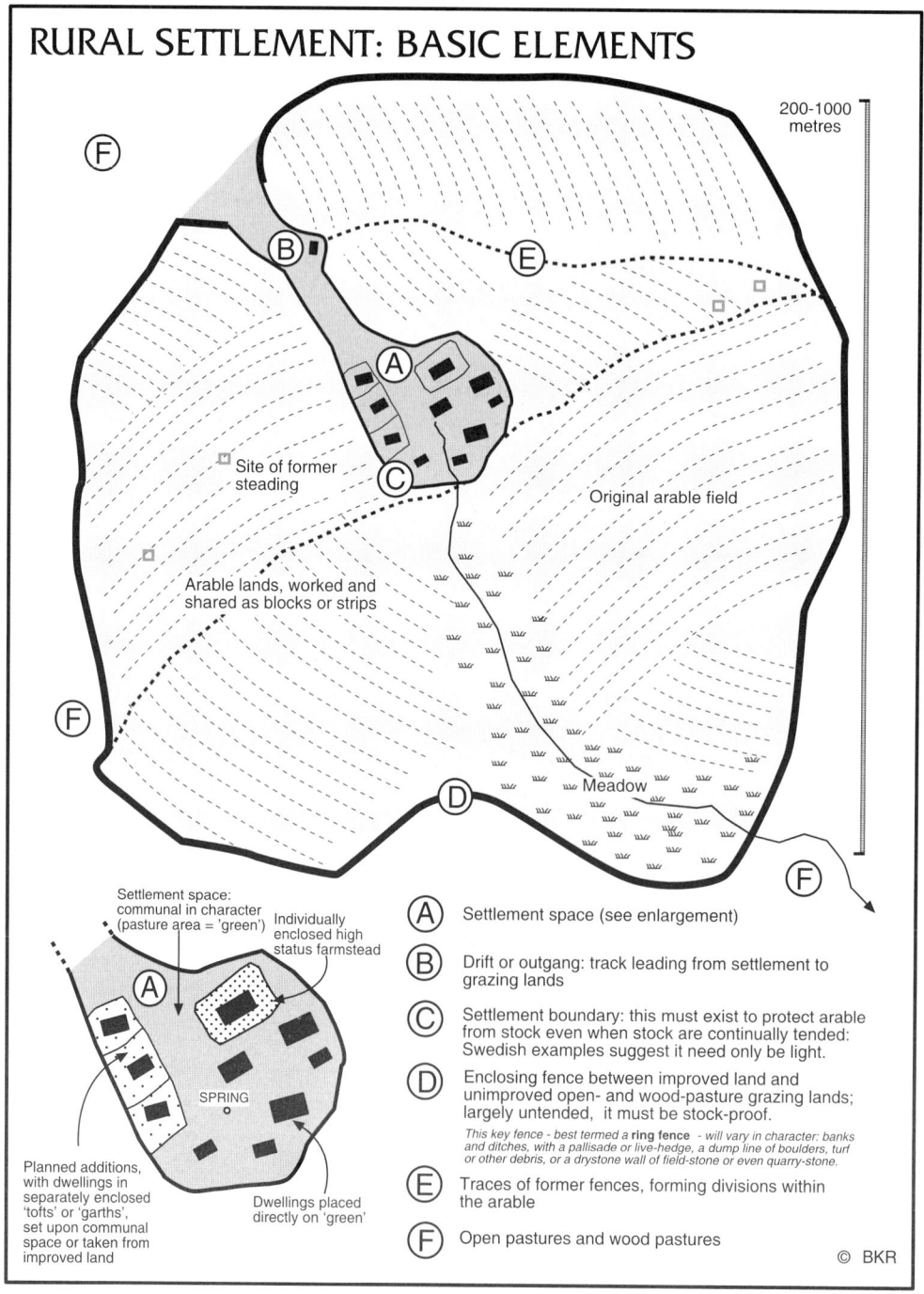

Fig. 5.2.a The basic elements of rural settlement

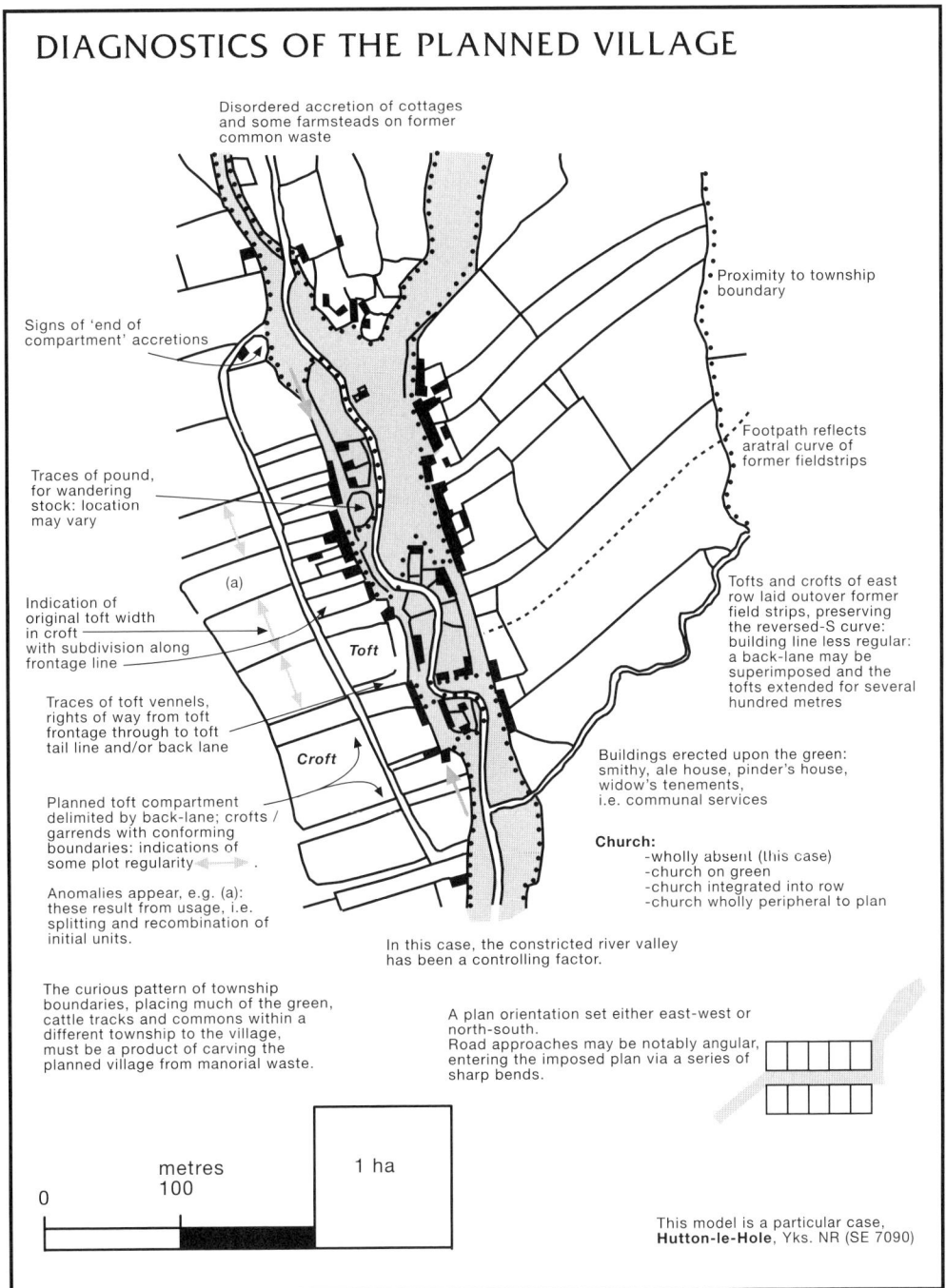

Fig. 5.2.b The diagnostic features of a planned village

132   *Landscapes, Documents and Maps*

former 'senior farmer'. This person might be of Anglo-Saxon or Anglo-Scandinavian stock, or eventually, an incoming Norman knight. In this simple model we glimpse the beginnings of many villages.

The model in Figure 5.2.b contrasts such relative simplicity with a version showing the varied features indicative of a planned village. This is by no means as geometrically regular as that seen at Appleton le Moors, where the formality is singularly sharp, but is characteristic of hundreds of northern village and hamlet plans – it is in fact merely Hutton-le-Hole, Yorkshire, North Riding, annotated generally. Effectively, two types of planning are included. The west row is built around a compartment, back-lanes and a set of small crofts or garrends, while the east row has clearly been established over a former arable furlong, in fact a foothold furlong, so that the enclosures reflect the shapes of the arable strips. This suggests a relative sequence, but caution is necessary, for the east side could contain the original farmsteads (Fig. 4.3 model) while the west row represents later cottages. Such questions are often irresolvable. In effect, each of these models can form an antecedent for settlement plans whose individual trajectories have evolved in many different ways. Like all of the models in this study these are not mere static images. They are in fact existential models, 'empirical representations of dynamic timescapes' … 'that can set free the imagination to range over the actual patterns of existence'. In these arrangements we glimpse those 'dynamic processes of reality' identified by Snooks (*ibid.* 1996, 433–4).

Documents – Kirk Merrington and Middlestone

The existence of compartments or 'rows', 'raws' to use the Durham pronunciation, is explicit in many northern documents. In particular the landed property of the great Benedictine monastery and Palatinate Bishopric at Durham encouraged the creation of numerous records, a proportion of which do survive. Associated with this religious corporation special offices were created for the keeping of alms money and the like, and to provide the holders of these with adequate funding small sums were made available though endowments. One of these, *gillycorn* – originating in a render of grain – was paid to the almoner of Durham. While the surviving schedule of this payment dates from 1424, in her careful study of its contents Constance Fraser concluded that tenancies created after about 1200 were excluded, *i.e.* the assart lands, and that the substance of the render was incumbent on farms and messuages created before 1200. Certainly only lands already liable in 1235 remained liable to pay in 1424. In fact, she concluded that the roots of the payment appear to lie in the 'first quarter of the twelfth century', *i.e.* 1100–1125. This chronology is important because for a number of the villages the farms that pay are located by using terms such as *Westraw, Northraw, Southraw* and *Eastraw*. These correspond with the orientation of the toft compartments found in surviving village plans, even the case of Wolviston, where the appearance of a *Northraw, Westraw* and *Eastraw* tells of a more complex type of layout arranged in an approximate rectangle (Fraser 1955; Roberts 1972). Important as is this conclusion, we are faced with an interesting problem. The uncertainties of establishing a precise chronology means that this documentation can only be used archaeologically, *i.e.* to establish *terminus ante quem* dates. There is a certainty that the plans were present by 1424, the date of the surviving document: reasonable certainty that they were present by 1235, and a strong possibility that they were present by the first quarter of the twelfth century. More than this cannot be said. Similar problems arise from the use of the *Feodarium Prioratus Dunelmensis* compiled in 1430 and treating the 'free rents and services belonging to the exchequer of the prior'. This in turn was based upon an earlier feodary compiled on the orders of prior Thomas of Melsamby (1233–44), in 1235, and frequently cites locations in terms of place in the row structures (Greenwell 1857, *e.g.* 21, 57–70). In every case these relate to what can be seen on the ground in surviving plans.

A 1972 analysis by the author of a number of Durham plans attempted to relate the precise structure of plans to the tenemental structures recorded in the documents. No high degree of success was achieved: a deep suspicion that an arrangement such as that at Acklington was likely to have existed is no way tantamount to proof. In 1989 Lucille Campey pushed the whole argument further by relating rental details of the lands of Durham Cathedral Priory to eighteenth century plans of the villages, although, perhaps wisely, she attempted no specific toft-to-record correlation. There is no question that her analysis of the complex plans of Wolviston, Aycliffe and Billingham represent a *tour de force*. Her general conclusions were threefold: (a) that the pre-1200 holdings display features which can be linked with a pre-Conquest estate structure; (b) that village growth is linked to the location of 'the residence associated with a particular drengage' (1989, 85) and (c) that the location of these freeholds within the village plans represent a 'surviving pre-conquest feature of settlement'. These are important conclusions and must be evaluated with great care, particularly her argument that the village plans contain pre-Conquest structural elements.

Kirk Merrington is the subject of analyses by both Campey (1989, fig. 7, 79–80) and by the present author (1972 fig. 21, 44–7). For this village, the relevant portion of the 1424 schedule is worth citing at length. The letters are added to assist discussion, and the bracketed smaller notes derive from the *Feodarium Prioratus Dunelmensis* that lists the freehold properties:

East (Kirk) Merrington

[A] In the vill of Est Merrinton [now Kirk Merrington] the Commoner of Durham [a minor monastic official] freely holds 2 messuages and 1 carucate of land, containing 80 acres, and renders yearly 1 thrave [a measure of grain].

[*FPD p. 68, n.1: '1 messuage next to the manor house' (juxta manerium); 4 bovates containing 60 acres; free tenure; by charter; {1. 13.Spec.2}: rendering one mark of silver; mill works; merchet; heriot; metreth (milch cow) and aid when it is levied}; held by William de Meryngton and Lord John Neville].*

[A* *FPD p. 68:* the Commoner of Durham; freehold; 1 messuage and 20 acres, for 20s; held by William de Meryngton and Lord John Neville; *location not specified.]*

[A and A* may represent the division of a former hallgarth: there are signs here of a split, although the gillycorn schedule may only record a gross total]

[B] Item, John Jakson of Elstob freely holds there 1 messuage on the Southraw and 2 ½ bovates containing 37 ½ acres called Cukeland and he renders yearly 15 sheaves.

[FPD p. 69: freehold; military service; suit of court.]

[C] Item, Richard Heghyngton freely holds there one messuage on the Northraw and 3 bovates containing 45 acres, and renders 18 sheaves.

[FPD p. 69: freehold; military service and suit of court; reaps for eight days with one man; plough half and acre in Boneher and Whetland.]

[D] Item there is 1 messuage there by the vicar's house [V] and 3 bovates of land, containing 45 acres, called Massamland, and lying among the 24 bovates of Shelam, it renders 18 sheaves.

Shelam

[W] In the vill of Shelam (Shelom) John Wyndilson freely holds 1 messuage on the Westraw at the end of the village and 2 bovates, containing 30 acres, and renders yearly a half thrave.

[FPD p. 68: freehold; military service; suit of court at Durham; reaping with one man for two days; ploughing one rood at Bonher: 'next to Denom's messuage' (see Y below); W and Y were originally in the hand of Robert son of John]

[X] Item, the same John freely holds there 1 toft and 1 bovate in exchange for land in Aycliffe, and renders nothing.

[This entry is included but bracketed in Figure 5.3, and illustrates a fundamental problem of all such analyses; is it a later inclusion or really a small toft within the village sequence? Should it be added to the gross total of village bovates, or are we seeing a sub-let from Denom? There is no answer to this!]

[Y] Robert Denome holds there 1 messuage and 2 bovates, containing 30 acres, and renders yearly a half thrave.

[FPD p. 68: a capital messuage: freehold; military service; reaping with one man for two days; ploughing one rood at Bonher: W and Y were originally in the hand of Robert son of John]

[Z] Item, in the vill of Shelam there are 8 tofts and crofts and 16 bovates of bondland, each of which bovates contains 15 acres and all render similarly by the year 8 thraves.

Figure 5.3.a contains two maps of this village: First a reconstruction of 1840, based upon a transcription of the Tithe Map to the scale of a mid-nineteenth century Ordnance Survey 1:2,500 map, the details of which have also been checked against an estate map of 1768 used by Lucille Campey. This is as close as one can get to a definitive plan of the village. Second, there is a reconstruction by Campey based upon the rental of 1400 and taking the form of a cartogram, integrating this with a reconstruction of the village morphology published in 1972 by the present author but strangely not used by Campey. A number of conclusions can be drawn from this evidence:

- first, the village is composite, with an east to west row and a north to south row; this is amply confirmed by the documentation;

- second, while the detail of neither reconstruction can easily be projected into the structural details of the plan, the presence of two rows in Kirk Merrington, beginning with the manor house at the south-eastern side of the village is securely attested. The church, first documented in 1157 (a date broadly confirmed by an engraving by R.W. Billings in the author's possession) is integrated into the north row;

- third, Shelam, or Shelom, is predominantly a bondage vill, and the Wyndleton and Denom properties represent a holding that was been split in half after 1235, the datum point for the compilers of the *Feodarium* in the early fifteenth century;

- fourth, this four bovate freehold, added to the sixteen bond bovates, makes twenty bovates that rendered gillycorn before 1200;

- fifth, a number of the freehold tofts, with their curious suite of services are best, as Campey notes, interpreted as drengages (Campey 1989, 80, 85–6), in which military service was linked with the servile renders of heriot, merchet and with the render '*metride*' or 'milch cow'.

The question of these rent forms is crucial to understanding the chronologies of village development. *Metride*, or 'milch cow' is likely to be a very ancient form of rent with close parallels to be found in Irish Law – to be discussed in Chapter 6 – while drengages are generally considered to be a pre-Conquest form of service. Nevertheless, the earliest date for which we can postulate the presence of the surviving plan from the documents is the first quarter of the twelfth century. In fact, as Chapter 8 will argue in detail, drengage is by no means always a pre-Conquest form of service and this has an important bearing on the chronology of settlement plans within which drengage tofts are integrated. From this analysis two key points emerge: the village layout is closely

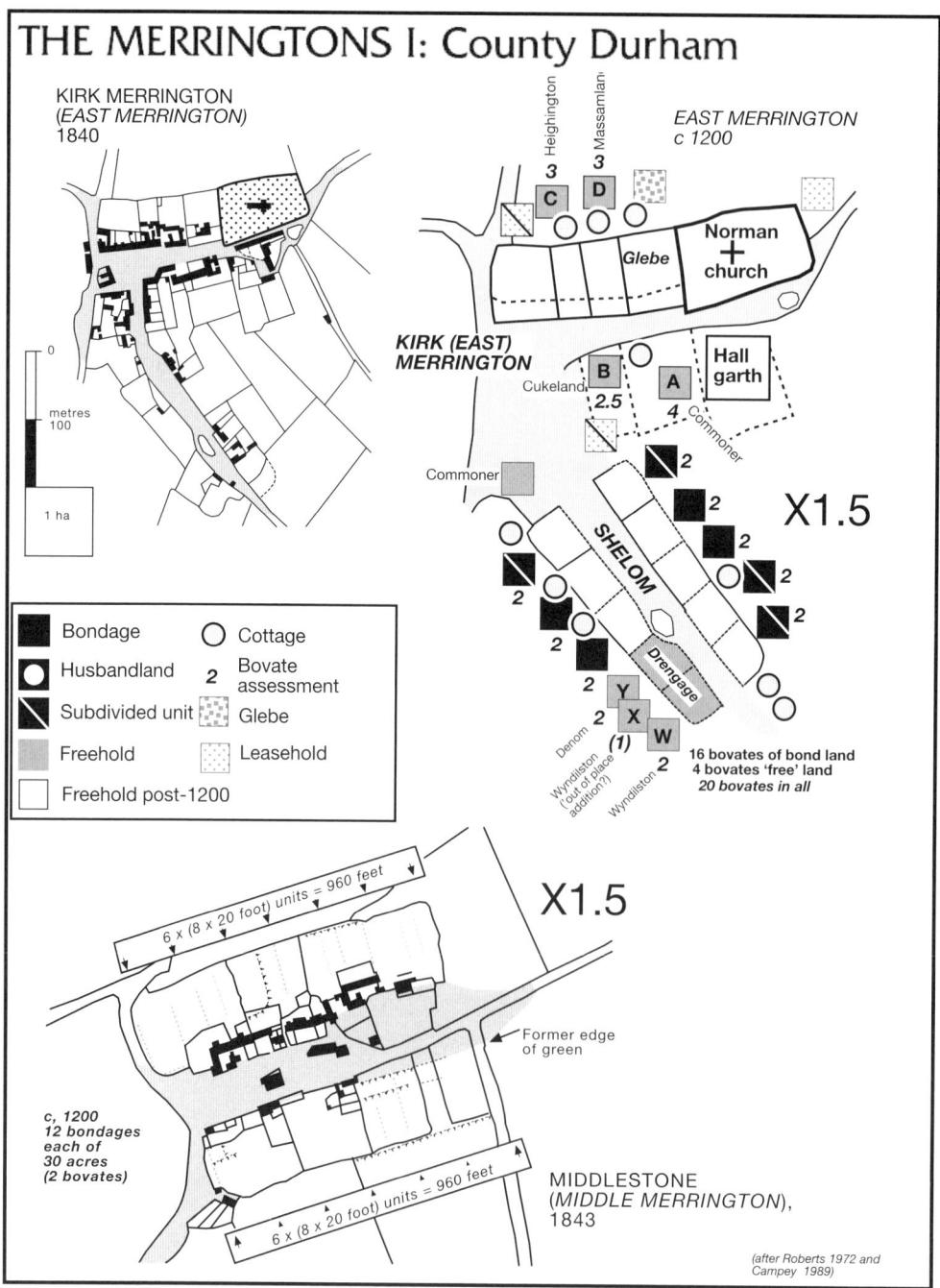

Fig. 5.3.a The Merringtons, County Durham

Interpreting the Morphological Record 137

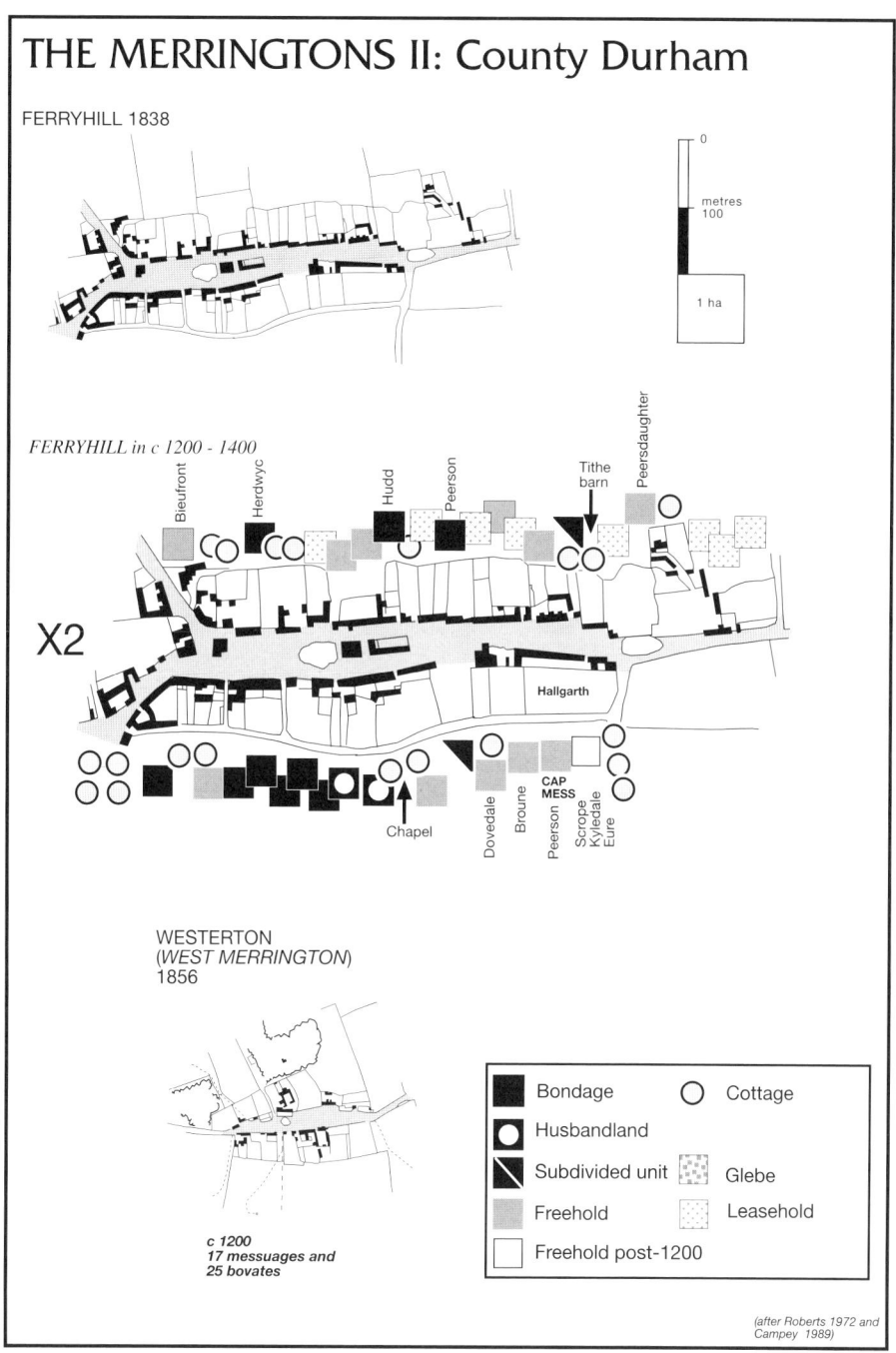

Fig. 5.3.b *The Merringtons, County Durham, (contd.)*

linked to the tenemental structure, and the plan of 1840 bears a relationship to that present by about 1125. Unless we believe that drengages are an indisputable indicator of a late Anglo-Saxon tenure then there are no indicators that the plan of this polyfocal village need pre-date the Norman conquest of the region between 1066 and 1070.

Middlestone and Ferryhill, both part of an ancient portion of St. Cuthbert's estates that may once have been *Merringtonshire* (see Chapter 6), carry the argument in two further directions. On one hand Middlestone, Middle Merrington to give it its original name, comprises two short rows, of east to west orientation (Fig. 5.3.a). The gillycorn schedule indicates that it was tenanted wholly with bondage tenants, twelve in all, each comprising two bovates of 30 acres (Fraser 1955, 59; Roberts 1972, 46–7). In this case a subsequent reduction of the number of tenant farms allowed the fossil skeleton of the ancient plan to survive to be visible on air photographs of the later 1940s (Roberts 1972, plate VII). On the basis of this the conceptual framework, in this case using a twenty foot land rod, can be tentatively reconstructed, although not without small inconsistencies. As with the case of Appleton le Moors it can be argued that given the practical exigencies of land survey, the measurements would as well fit 6 × (8 × 18), for land rods of that length appear in the Priory records. The differences between accumulative measurements, first toft A, then toft B, until' toft n' is reached, will always tend to increase the overall ideal length, while division of an established compartment will tend to lead to internal irregularities within the ideal standards (Roberts 1987, 196–7). Ferryhill, in sharp contrast (Fig. 5.3.b), shows the near impossibility of relating medieval documentation to the on-ground conditions, confirming Campey's wisdom of adhering to cartograms in her presentation of the material. What the data does reveal is the tenemental fragmentation and structural complexity of this plan by 1200, raising important questions about the length of time during which the plan had been subject to accretive change before that date. It is worth reflecting that Ferryhill lay on the main north – south route through Durham, the potential A1, and the plan alone might well suggest an urban plantation, effectively larger than Appleby the county town of Westmorland (Fig. 4.12). The substantial number of free tenants in Ferryhill in 1200 treads that thin line between free socage and burgage tenure, a feature to be found in Devon, the county with the greatest number of planted new towns according to Beresford and Finberg's lists (1973, table 4; Roberts 1987, 194–5) – new towns that are small enough merely to be new villages.

At this point, however, it is helpful to reflect upon a version of the author's map originally published in 1972, seen in this study as Figure 2.6. While this was, and is, inevitably built upon a succession of professional judgements concerning individual plans, the fact remains that additional local studies invariably tend to confirm the presence of regular compartmentalised layouts, often rather more regular in character than was first appreciated. As was noted at the beginning of this study over 80% of the two hundred or so villages and hamlets present in Durham in the middle decades of the nineteenth century possessed row plans constructed with compartments, and were either regular or part regular in layout. In fact 114 (56%) out of 205 were either single or two row plans, and 27 (13%) were multiple row plans of a more complex type. Large villages such as Billingham, Wolviston, Aycliffe, Heighington and the like only represent a small proportion of the total pattern and are simply concealed amid the selection of symbols used to create Figure 2.6. With few exceptions, possibly Wolsingham, Stanhope and Lanchester, they all lie to the south and east of a line that can be drawn between Barnard Castle, Bishop Auckland, Durham, Chester le Street and Gateshead, an ancient boundary separating the more developed portions of the county from the vast untamed spaces of the north and west (Roberts 2005, 221–37). The importance of this line is attested by the presence of the county's urban centres, with the remainder being either coastal or riverine ports. The multiple row villages fill in the intervening interior spaces of the pattern. As will be argued in the next chapter, they generally have a special place in the settlement hierarchy, being higher status administrative centres than the generally rather smaller two-row and single row plans, indeed as Chapter 6 will show, are often the centres of small administrative shires, comprising a central settlement with outlying dependencies.

Morphology and Plan Elements – Wheldrake, Yorkshire

The thinking supporting the historical analysis of plans – morphogenetic analysis – has been made explicit in the range of specific cases presented so far. Three ways of using this technique are to be found in recent literature. First, it is used as a way of formulating hypotheses both before and after an excavation; second, it is a way of analysing particular plans without excavation; and third, it is used in geographical analysis as a way of dealing with large numbers of plans at a regional scale. A crucial question touching the morphology of many villages, and a way of beginning morphogenetic study, is the way that the church is integrated into a plan. Both the architectural and documentary history of a church is normally to some degree recoverable, providing an approximate chronology. In Cumbria Bouch concluded that nine out of ten of the older churches of the diocese were rebuilt during the twelfth century, and in Yorkshire large numbers of the village churches contain at least a small portion of Norman fabric. The survival of even a small amount of fabric is a convincing demonstration that there was a church on that site at that time, thus sidetracking the fundamental issue of a possible change of church site when only documentary evidence is being considered. There are major problems, because of the frequency and radical nature of Victorian church restoration throughout the north: the Victorians were in effect replacing substantively decayed churches resulting from a Norman building campaign (Pevsner 1967, 18; Bouch 1948, 9). Thus Gamblesby, Glassonby and Melmerby (Fig. 4.4), have churches that suffered major reconstructions or were built in the eighteenth and nineteenth centuries yet the villages have undoubted medieval roots.

June Sheppard's study of Wheldrake is a fine example of morphogenetic analysis

(Fig. 5.4). In the later seventeenth century there were about 95 households in this rather large village, sustained by a core of communal arable fields, pasture closes, and an open common that occupied about one quarter of the township area (Sheppard 1966). In 1609 there had been 57 tenants, and the arable fields and meadows were divided amongst about 45 tenants, while the pastures were held entirely by 23 more prosperous yeomen and gentlemen farmers. Using the map she was able to create for the seventeenth century Sheppard was able build a reconstruction of the township in about 1300. At this stage there were two settlement nuclei, the village itself, and a to-be-deserted hamlet by the river Derwent at Waterhouses. There were then three types of arable area, covering virtually all of both the arable area and the pasture closes present in the seventeenth century:

- first, land assarted after 1234–5 embraced most of the area subsequently covered by pasture closes: this was probably divided into selions, shared amongst tenants and used for the corn, hay and pasture;
- a second type of arable land was divided into *culturae*, essentially forming a ring between the assart land and the third category of arable. This land was fragmented into parcels, and may have been divided between freehold and demesne;
- finally, an inner core of arable seems to have been more fragmented than in the *culturae*. This is likely to have been the core of the oldest arable land of the settlement.

However, the available maps, supported by field names, point to the existence of a walled core, embracing parts of the second and third categories of arable. The reference in a charter to the 'west Surdwall' suggest this may have been of sods, and that it once surrounded an inner core of ancient arable and settlement, some 425 acres (172 ha) in extent, of which approximately 75 acres (30 ha) were occupied by roads and village tofts. If it is assumed that a peasant bovate holding fell between 13 and 20 statute acres, then this arable would have been adequate for between 15 and 20 households, together with a demesne farm. In 1086 there were only six tenants, and Sheppard argues that the dyke may delimit the settlement's mid-twelfth century arable, although it could, she concedes, even be the pre-Conquest limit. The central portion of this land, backing onto the south row of the village itself, was termed the *Toft Acres*, and she speculates that this may have been the area cultivated in 1086. The strips located here would have ranged between 220 and 880 yards (200 to 800 metres) in length, dimensions well in accord with those of such core furlongs noted elsewhere.

Her analysis of the village plan itself reaches an interesting conclusion (Fig. 5.4). The compartment on the southern side of the village is much subdivided on late maps, but three angled kinks in its frontage hint at the former presence of six regular tofts, each approximately 100 × 130 yards, interpretable as (18 × 16.5 feet) × (24 × 16.5 feet). This number could correspond to the six tenancies in 1086. The north row looks like

Interpreting the Morphological Record

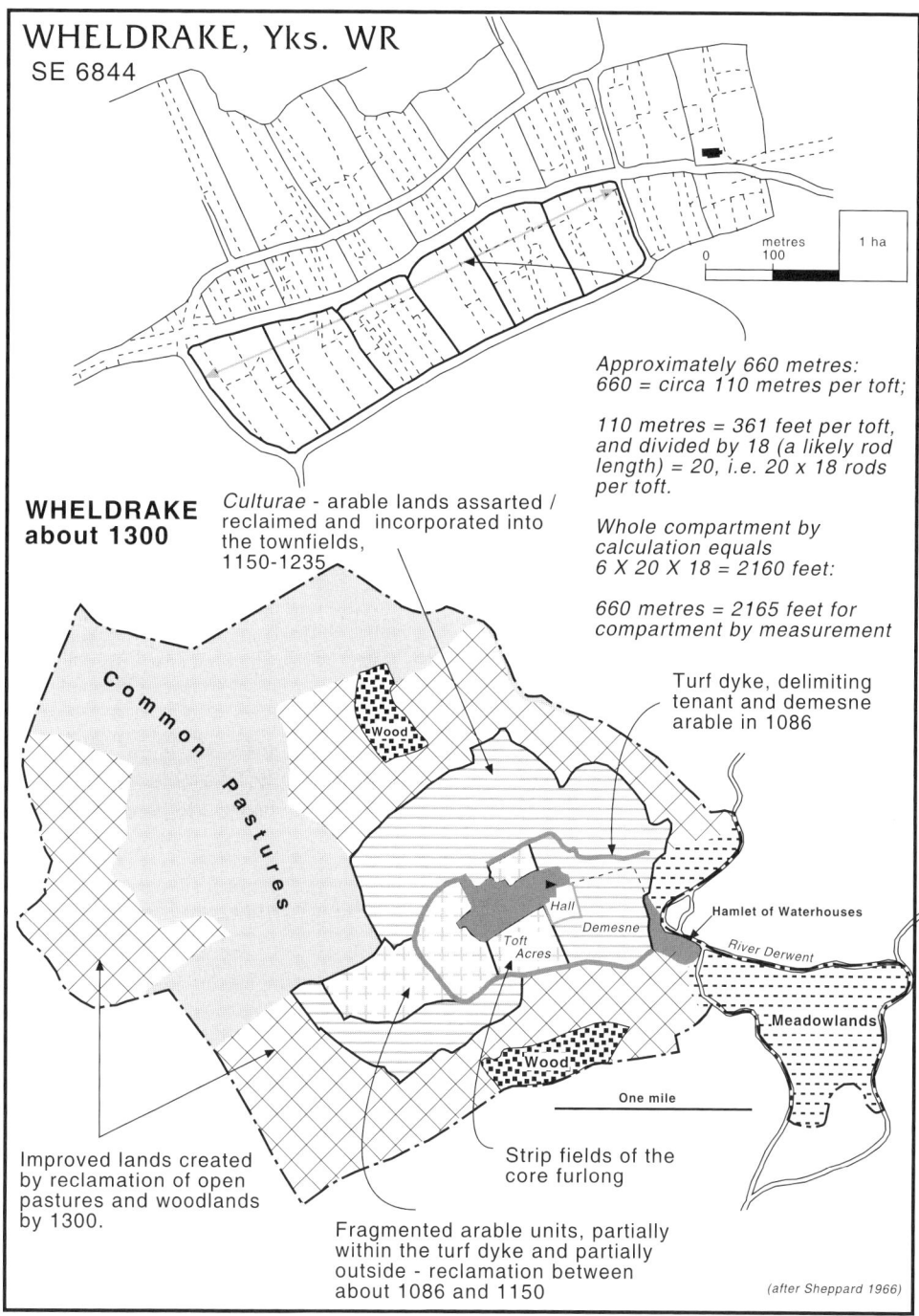

Fig. 5.4 *The village and township of Wheldrake, Yorkshire*

a less regular addition, although there are signs that the tofts there possess boundaries that cross the northern back lane – possibly a pre-existing route – while tofts certainly continue to the east of the village, where one contains the church and rectory. As is so often the case with such plans the hall is located at the village's south-eastern corner, opposite the church. In fact, the church is recorded in Domesday Book, and as these buildings tend not to change site, then there is a pointer here that the regular toft series may represent a pre-1086 layout. In fact this whole argument is brought to focus by one cataclysmic event – the Harrying of the North in the years 1069–70. Domesday Book, howsoever the entries be interpreted in detail, attests to the impact of this event. The 'waste' it records is not the natural waste of rough pasturelands and marsh, but the result of devastation caused by warfare or the deliberate movement of tenants from the outlying portions of estates to their more productive cores. It may indeed only record an inability to raise rent, and contain elements of an administrative fiction, but at the very least it speaks of an absence of 'normality'.

This is a crucial issue. In the North Riding as many as 217 places were wholly wasted and 150 were partly wasted, a total of 367 out of the 639 places recorded in the text. In the East Riding 67 places were wholly waste and 93 were partly waste, some 160 places out of the 424 places recorded. In the West Riding 196 places were wholly waste and 267 partly waste out of a total of 719 places (Darby 1962 b, 139, 212, 61). This devastation was an event of profound importance throughout Yorkshire, where the record of Domesday Book is available, but the Conqueror's armies reached the Tyne, so that Durham was by no means exempt. The Anglo-Saxon Chronicle is terse: *sub anno* 1069 it records 'the king went northwards with all of his army which he could gather, and wholly ravaged and laid waste the shire' (Swanton 2000, 204). As long ago as 1935 Sir Clifford Darby pointed out that 'although it was sporadic, local and relatively ephemeral… repeated devastation was an ingredient of no mean importance in the life of medieval England' (Darby 1951, 173). In her assessment of the developments at Wheldrake Sheppard took devastation into account. Was the sod dyke in fact the limit of pre-devastation cultivation? Does Domesday Book give a picture of the settlement at an early stage of post-devastation re-development? Was the formalisation of the plan a part of this process? It is interesting to note that Carlton in Durham shows traces of a similar ring-fenced 'inner arable core', marking perhaps one stage in the transition from an informal layout to a planned layout.

There are important issues here. There is no doubt that the present author in his early writings on planned villages used 'the 'Harrying of the North', the devastation caused by the Norman army, as a 'catch all' explanation'. Three issues emerge: first, David Palliser's important critique of the use of the term 'waste' in Domesday Book as an explanatory mechanism has shown the problem of such a simplistic explanation. Military devastations, literary exaggeration, the movement of populations to more economically viable sites, administrative concealment and write-offs, misinterpretation of instructions and lack of experience in assembling the record must all play a part in distorting the record of 1086 (Palliser 1993, 1–23). Second, even a great record such as Domesday Book, which had the effect of administrative fossilisation, *i.e.* it formed a reference framework to which all subsequent developments and enquiries were related, was only a part of a wholly dynamic historical continuum. That there were localised climactic events both before and after, of both local and regional impact, introduces troubled questions of scale and time. Palliser points out that the few regular plans that have been closely studied show no consistency of relationship to the presence of waste in 1086, but this is hardly surprising. The sample is very small. Third, this present study offers a new challenge: to grasp settlement and the records of settlement as part of a time-space continuum. On one hand a single explanation of planned settlements of the north must be rejected as highly improbable. The present author's use of this *deus ex machina* in 1972 was of its time; on the other, as is repeatedly emphasised in this study, the correlation of document-based 'historical' evidence, with on-ground morphological and archaeological evidence, *at any scale*, is fraught with many uncertainties. The mind seeks to correlate and construct, and a narrative must be framed from disparate materials, yet deconstructive arguments warn of issues that touch levels of greater difficulty. Thus, the fundamental problems of time, space and scale of enquiry endure, and an initial narrative must be created as a basis for informed and constructive criticism. For many years the author has been creating and publishing settlement models that are on the edge of viability, *i.e.* they are too complex to be understood without great effort and some experience, and indeed, some, like that line in Browning's poetry, are eventually a puzzle to him! Many appear for the first time in this study, and the multitude of studies appearing since the 1970s, a third of a century, are now creating pressures for more sophisticated contextual creations. A volume by the present author and Stuart Wrathmell represented one step. This study represents a second step. The term *vasta*, 'waste', with all its possible shades of meaning appears in the documentary record, and Latham (1965, 505) and the *Oxford English Dictionary* reveal something of this. 'Waste' is a term we must accept, even though it's meaning can vary. The range is from the wholly general to the wholly specific, from holdings from which it is not possible to raise rent or tax, from uncultivated but grazed land, to the sheer awfulness of burned steadings, slaughtered men and oxen, raped and enslaved women and children perhaps implied by record of Domesday Book and certainly by some chronicles entries. We can all agree that it must be interpreted with caution, but if this study reveals nothing else, it shows that no close or simple correlation between the presence of waste in 1086 and the final emergence of planned villages need be sought. Settlement evolution is by no means as simple as this as a later discussion will suggest. We may agree with David Palliser and Richard Fletcher that 'waste' does not necessarily mean 'devastated', but could also imply 'untenanted', 'information not available' or 'vacant' (Fletcher 2002, 138 and 181–3). Nevertheless, any reading of the sources and literature of the ninth and tenth centuries, with the passage of royal and aristocratic war bands and other freebooters shows that the stealing of food and stock, the killing and enslaving of men and women, and the stealing of valuable items was an accepted part of life, and indeed policy (Fletcher 2002, 100). We need not doubt that this extended into the centuries after 1066. Devastation by fire and sword offered *opportunity* for settlement planning but not the certainty of this taking place.

The villages with signs of imposed regularity throughout the north in fact fall into two extreme geographical groups. First there are those places set 'near the margins', surely colonising ventures, bringing into cultivation the natural 'waste' of lowland commons and former upland hill-pastures. A second group results from the restoration and revitalisation of places, sometimes places denuded of stock and tenants by the process of 'devastation', or, perhaps more usually, for we have no means of generalising with accuracy, resulting from the redevelopment of existing settlements. Often these are local 'central places'. Add to these factors two further components, namely those normal enlargements initiated by population increases and the presence of great estates and small estates within which varied policies were implemented. Together these provide dynamic settings within which the development of the regional patterns of village plan-types undoubtedly took place.

Graphical Analysis

Figure 5.5 draws together into one graph two major sets of source materials with a bearing on County Durham: the map appearing as Figure 2.6 allows the data on plan morphology to be assembled as a simple series of counts. In Figure 5.5 the sequencing of the ideograms representing these from left to right runs from complexity to simplicity and thence to question marks, and derives from professional judgment based upon the examination of maps and work in the field. The vertical axis comprises a sequencing of the tenurial character of the settlements as documented in the estate surveys created by Bishop Hugh de Puiset and Bishop Hatfield (Greenwell 1852 and 1857). At root, individual settlements are categorised according to the presence or absence of demesne land, bondage land, cottage land, exchequer land and free land. In fact, by no means the whole of County Durham is involved, for in the Norman period the estates of St Cuthbert were split between the Cathedral Priory and the Bishop. The acquisition of the wapentake of Sedberg late in the twelfth century brought secular lands into the county (Harvey 1994, 399–405) and consolidated the pre-1974 county unit. Nevertheless, the tenurial order used from the top to the bottom of the graph was arrived at experimentally, and there are some inevitable rough edges. The presentation of two periods of evidence led to the creation of two levels, 1183 and 1381, for each category of tenure. The final diagram is sufficiently structured to allow simple isochrones, lines of equal time, to be added. Two points must be kept firmly in mind; first, while many of the chronological pointers concerning plans discussed so far touch the thirteenth and even the twelfth century, this does not mean that all settlement plans are necessarily as early, or indeed that the bulk necessarily date from that period. As some cases show,

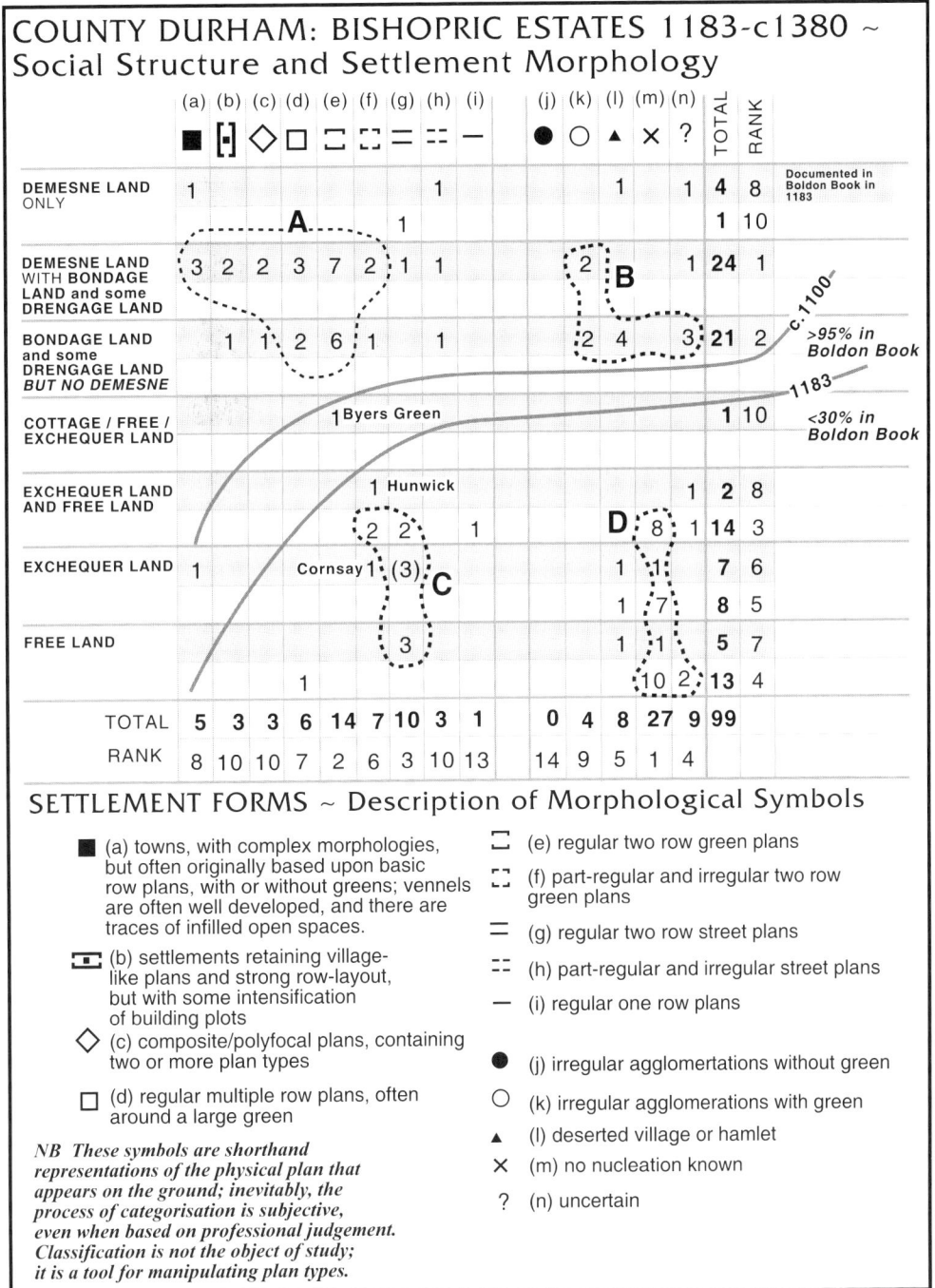

Fig. 5.5 Social structure and tenurial composition of Bishopric vills

post-medieval re-planning was possible. The case for dates before 1300 being normal must be securely established. Second, the plans of villages and hamlets are certainly not of one date: they surely originated at varied points in time. Even if they are to be placed, for instance, 'in the twelfth century', was this early, in the middle decades or in the last decade? Such dates must ultimately represent only a *terminus ante quem*. Much of the remainder of this study will be concerned with the nature of this time curve of foundation. Finally, one question must remain: how many plans, if any, do indeed pre-date the early twelfth century?

Essentially this diagram allows four groups to be identified. No group is large, but in this case the figures have the advantage of relating to a single, coherent estate, that preserved its character throughout the medieval period and long after. Group A, embodies settlements with varied combinations of demesne land and bondage land. These are all places where the hands of the bishops' officers rested heavily, growing produce for his table and utilising the work of the bondage tenants to work the demesne lands as well as to generate rents. It will be noted that the core of each group consists of correlations with more than a single representative case, but the picture of four groups would remain sharp even if the single cases were included within the dashed lines. The segregation is remarkably consistent. Group B contains the same mixture of tenancies, but in these irregular agglomerated plans, lacking rows, appear, as well as township centres where a deserted settlement is likely or where there may be nothing more than a farmstead. The isochrone of *c.* 1183 fits diagonally across the graph and above this line 95% of the settlements listed appear in Boldon Book. The position of Byers Green (Fig. 3.4) set between this and the isochrone for about 1100 needs little comment given the history of the plan sketched in a previous chapter. In spite of its rather regular two-row green plan this settlement has more in common with those of Group C than of Group A. Group C comprises largely part-regular plans, the bracketed case being where two names in the record are matched by three plans of the same type on the ground. Finally Group D is a residual group, with many uncertainties that were not resolvable when creating the original map, where nothing more than a hall may appear on the ground.

What do these data mean? On the estates of the Bishop of Durham the most regular and the most complex plans are to be found associated with those villages the Bishops had most directly under the control of their estate administrations. Less formalised and simpler plans, as is evidenced by their association with exchequer land, appear in situations where reclamation was still taking place after 1100. These deductions would be equally true even if the isochrones were completely misleading, and, for instance, in the unlikely event that the plans we can document were imposed as the result of estate re-organisation in the early decades of the sixteenth century. In fact, given the proof of the antiquity of the village plans on the estates of the Cathedral Priory, we have a *prima facie* case for the modal number of plan foundations being before 1200 and perhaps even before 1100 throughout the estates of St Cuthbert. There is nothing here to suggest that the Harrying of the North of 1069–70 may not have been a crucial marker, but given that most of the settlement / township place-names are Old English in origin, we must consider three further possibilities. First, the plans date from the foundation of the Anglo-Saxon settlement. Second, that the plans have evolved from anciently established nuclei, perhaps seen in the church and hall foci, and have accreted around these, either suddenly or gradually. Third, that one or more deliberate acts of formalisation have taken place, affecting each plan, and that this may have been a single event or a succession of temporally discrete events. The evidence of the cases discussed in Chapters 4 and 5 suggests that the first is inherently improbable and that a combination of the second and third scenarios is the more likely. This begs many questions, not least, how old are the plans, what factors brought them into being, and what was the real duration of their period, or periods, of foundation?

Analytical Cartography

Finally, we return to the distributions of plan-types: Figure 5.6 is a piece of analytical cartography created by the author at an early stage in his investigations but has stood the test of time. It both simplifies and generalises the distributions of plan-types and reveals that regular and part-regular plan with short tofts have a rather different distribution to regular and part-regular plans with long tofts and strip tofts. This can also be seen within Durham (Fig. 2.6), and settlements of the Cockfield type tend to appear in the west of the county, in the Pennine foothills and dales, in contrast to the short-tofted plans of the Middridge and Carlton type, which concentrate in the county's better agricultural areas. The examples from west Durham are all to be linked with settlements that were developing during the twelfth century, each set in what we now know was virtually a vast sea of savanna-like waste, with small islands of cultivation (Fig. 2.5). In contrast the east of the county was much more developed, and although extensive wastes were present, cultivation was much more extensive and while land-clearance was in progress this was in no way the raw pioneer fringe. In Cumbria, while Anglo-Saxon settlement had indeed been present since the seventh century (Stenton 1936, xlviii) the region was finally brought into the control of the English crown in 1092, when the Anglo-Saxon Chronicle records.

> In this year the king William [Rufus] travelled north to Carlisle with a very great army, and restored the town, and raised the castle, and drove out Dolfin who earlier ruled the land there, and set the castle with his men, and afterwards returned south here, and sent very many peasants there with women and with livestock to live there to till the land.
>
> (Swanton 2000, 227)

In this case military conquest, accompanied no doubt by a degree of devastation was followed by reorganisation and pioneer peasant settlement. This record, which there is

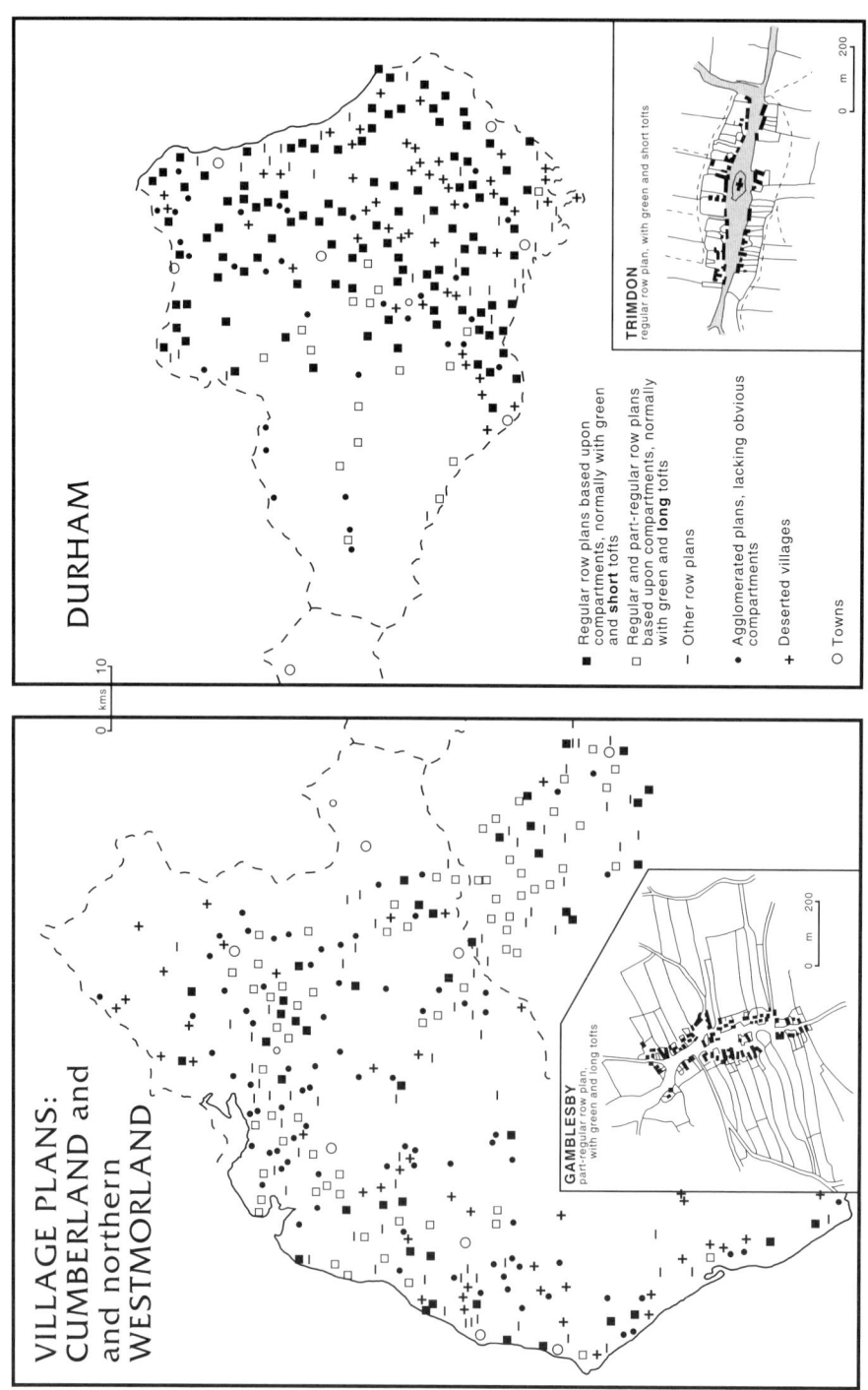

Fig. 5.6 Village plans in Cumberland, northern Westmorland and Durham

no good reason to doubt, creates one context to account for the villages and hamlets of Cumbria with their distinctive patterns of foothold furlongs, arable cores, from which other farmland was gradually extended as population expanded (Roberts 1996c). This was an active zone of colonisation right into the twelfth century encouraging the remodelling of older settlements. The antecedent settlements, both 'native' and Anglo-Scandinavian, may have been no more than farmstead clusters and hamlets (Roberts 1993a). But here one must ask if 'context' provided by an illuminating text is sufficient for explanation? In fact no single cataclysmic event needs to be involved. Effectively the conquest of 1092 initiated a series of processes that may have continued for a century or more. In this matter an important clue is provided by an entry in a *Curia Regis* roll of 1201, that cites a writ of Henry I (1100–1135) by which the king granted to Hildred of Carlisle and Odard his son *terram que fuit Gamel filii Bern et terram illam que fuit Glassam filii Brictrici drengorum meorum*… 'the land which belonged to Gamel son of Bern and the land which belonged to Glassan son of Brictric, my drengs' (VCH Cu. I, 313, note 2). Gamel is Old Norse and Bern possibly so, although it could also be Old English, while Glassan is Old Irish yet his father possessed Old English name, reflecting the mixture of peoples and names in this frontier zone. A Pipe Roll entry of 1130 refers, in retrospect, to *Gamel son of Ber'(n)*, providing a *terminus ante quem* datum (VCH Cu, I, 338). Gamel and Glassan gave their names to part-regular two-row villages, of which Gamblesby is illustrated in Figure 4.4. The possible links between drengs and the establishment of villages will be explored in Chapters 6 and 7 and it is of interest to note that the ancient rent of cornage – *servicio Gablum animalium* – was due from these lands (VCH Cu. 313, note 2). Nevertheless, in this case it is clear that Gamel and Glassan were linked with the two villages, and the name-element *-by* continued in use until the later eleventh or early twelfth century (Fellows Jensen 1985, 20–24; Roberts 1989–90, 25–38). Of course, there may have been an earlier generation of settlement, completely or partially depopulated when the new foundations took place. Unfortunately there is no ancient church in Glassonby to give focus to morphological analysis: the great curving plough strips are evident enough, but what is less visible, but seen with closer study, is that the plan is built from at least three, possibly more, units. These are not compartments in the full sense of the word; rather they are bundles of long strips, foothold furlongs, with buildings set almost haphazardly at their head. The green emerges as a mere patch of residual space between minor encroachments into it rather than the tightly formal structures seen in many villages to the east of the Pennines. The four plan units can be seen in two central elements facing each other across the central green, an additional block set on the north-eastern side of the plan, with a possible more nucleal focus at the southern end. That settlements could grow in this way, by adding plan units is seen at Melmerby (Fig. 4.4). This incorporates the name *Melmor*, a name appearing in a document of the later eleventh century (VCH Cu. II 1905, 232–33; Armstrong *et al.*, 1950–2, 223–4; Fellows Jensen 1985, 35), although in this case no definite association can be established. The village plan, already discussed in Chapter 4, is startling in its clarity of structure: at the centre lies an irregular green, partially enclosed, with a church set upon it. This latter is now mostly Victorian, but with a little surviving if indeterminate medieval fabric. No less than four great toft furlongs give form to the village, with lateral strip boundaries often sweeping in directly to the toft-head line, although as with Gamblesby, the buildings are arranged rather haphazardly. There can be hardly any doubt that these represent growth phases.

Review of Questions

In summary we must return to Homans' 'properly guarded statement'. There is indeed evidence in certain English villages of a system of plan organisation and strip allocation 'resembling in some respects the Scandinavian *solskifte*'. In the north of England these indications are present for a period falling between the early seventeenth and the mid- to late-twelfth century (Göransson 1961). This, however, raises a fundamental problem touching the nature of the sources available, particularly for the earlier period. We face a situation in which individual studies suggest that the very large numbers of regular village plans throughout the northern counties may have a medieval provenance. Furthermore, it is likely that large numbers of these had communally organised townfield systems supporting them and that these were intricately regulated. However, the charters, rentals and surveys containing significant indicators of the disposition of strips through the arable fields, of the presence of regular partition cycles, or the location of tofts within the village plan, appear to form only a small proportion of the *corpus* required to offer explanation. In short, much peasant reality was hidden beneath the surface of the formal and legal documentation, indeed much of the practical aspect of working and managing the village and fields lay in the minds of the farmers. We should perhaps not be surprised that the documentary debris is so often opaque and difficult to interpret. The written evidence affords no real measure of the vitality or otherwise of particular arrangements. In this respect Homans' conclusion was almost certainly wrong. The fact that arrangements 'resembling in some respects the Scandinavian *solskifte*' survive to be documented in the early seventeenth century is a strong indication that the twelfth century evidence is not merely the debris of a vanishing system. Nevertheless, this discussion still leaves open many questions about the origins and chronology of such arrangements. The plan analyses presented in Chapters 3 and 4 pointed towards the existence of some regular plans before the thirteenth century. They also point towards the origins of some of these in the processes of the colonisation of new land and the restoration and revitalisation of devastated land and the development of settled land. Before turning to the complex issue of village plantation, we must explore the context within which northern settlement evolved, namely the 'small shire'.

Chapter Six

Estates and Small Shires – the Articulation of Local Settlement

The argument so far has interleaved three levels of analysis. First, at a national and regional scale each individual pattern contains concentrations and absences, and can be described and analysed purely in these terms. Second, a countywide distribution or a local regional pattern invites comparison between the distribution and the physical environment, seen in the contrast between upland and lowland, and between biologically productive areas and areas with lower potential. Nevertheless, a third level is essential, for each and every village has particular qualities. In all of these analyses the settlements, objects of study, have been viewed as components of distributions, concentrations and absences, set within a framework that is effectively physical in character. However, all settlements are set within another matrix, that of landownership. This in turn contains zones of stability and zones of change, while throughout analysis the depth of time presents extraordinarily complex problems of study and manipulation. At any one point in time each place was owned and in the possession of a local landowner. Of course, landownership also has a regional and even a national perspective, providing contexts within which all settlement must be studied. In practice, in the medieval period rent flows from a single village could pass not merely to a single lord, but to two, three or even more (Fig 4.10). The landed estate was an important part of the matrix of space, place and time within which each and every town, village, hamlet or farmstead, and indeed virtually every person, existed. A hierarchy of crown, great barony, lesser fee, knight's fee, and local lord of the manor towered above each place, village, hamlet or farmstead, often affecting its character and development. Nevertheless, this in no way excludes the vitality of local communities (Hilton 1966, 124–7). Further, once we have recognised that secular estates in particular could be unstable, and that a single century, a few decades, even a few years could see often quite radical changes, then the kaleidoscope quality of the medieval cultural landscape can be appreciated. In contrast, the undying corporations represented by church holdings sustained existence and often written estate records through many centuries, indeed often until the dissolution of the monasteries in the earlier decades of the sixteenth century (*ibid.*, 26–65).

There is more. From long before the Norman Conquest of 1066, it is clear that individual settlements were in some ways grouped, so that individual centres possessed dependencies. Nowhere is this seen more clearly than in Domesday Book, where a single estate centre may have many berewicks or dependencies attached. Indeed this pattern of spatial dependency gives rise to the hundredal manor, in which the association of central place and attachments is sufficiently large to appear in the record as an administrative hundred (Cam 1944, 64–89). We can term these individual attachments 'hamlets', begging the question of their precise morphology and character, and recognise that while some were undoubtedly of village size and perhaps comparable with the village of post-Conquest centuries, many were undoubtedly smaller. Figure 5.1, by comparing pre-Conquest settlement layouts with medieval plans illustrates the problems of scale involved. Some settlements may indeed, have been very loose associations, linked hamlet clusters or linked farmstead clusters, all bearing the same name and occupied by farmers for whom that name implied 'home'. There is, however, evidence from throughout the north that individual places could be part of ancient territorial divisions larger than a parish but significantly smaller than a county. Generally these are termed 'shire' in early documentation, but Professor Offler very aptly termed them 'small shires' to distinguish them from those, perhaps rather younger, counties with the suffix *-shire*, as in Warwickshire, Northamptonshire and the like (Offler in Piper and Doyle 1996, XII, 4; Barrow 1973, 7–68; Jones 1971; Cam 1944, 91–106). Northern small shires could contain a dozen or so villages and hamlets, and have as a focus one, or sometimes or more, individual places. One of these central places normally gave its name to the shire, for example, Bedlingtonshire, Heighingtonshire, Gillingshire, Richmondshire all focus on settlements bearing the 'shire' name. These estates, providing evidence of both stability, and occasionally kaleidoscopic change, offer frameworks in which to explore the complexities of settlement development. James Campbell put the issue of the small shire quite squarely: 'what one is talking about here is not survival in comprehensive detail, but the persistence of enough elements of a system in fairly substantial outline and with pockets and patches of detail' (2000, xvi).

The Organisation of Space

Figure 6.1 contains example of a foundation map for all studies of the past, the parishes of County Durham as they were in the middle decades of the nineteenth century together with the local communities into which parishes were divided, the *townships*. The antiquity of these boundaries is by no means always certain (Winchester 1990; 2000). In the west of Durham the many straight lines show boundaries that were only finally established at the period of final enclosures and definition in the closing decade of the eighteenth and the earlier decades of the nineteenth centuries, and this accounts for areas of extreme parish fragmentation, far greater than can be depicted at this scale. These reconstructed boundaries are in themselves an important research theme, perhaps dismissed lightly in this map that took two years to assemble from the available data. Once it has been reconstructed the pattern can then be used to amplify more tenuous evidence. Thus, when Boldon Book notes that:

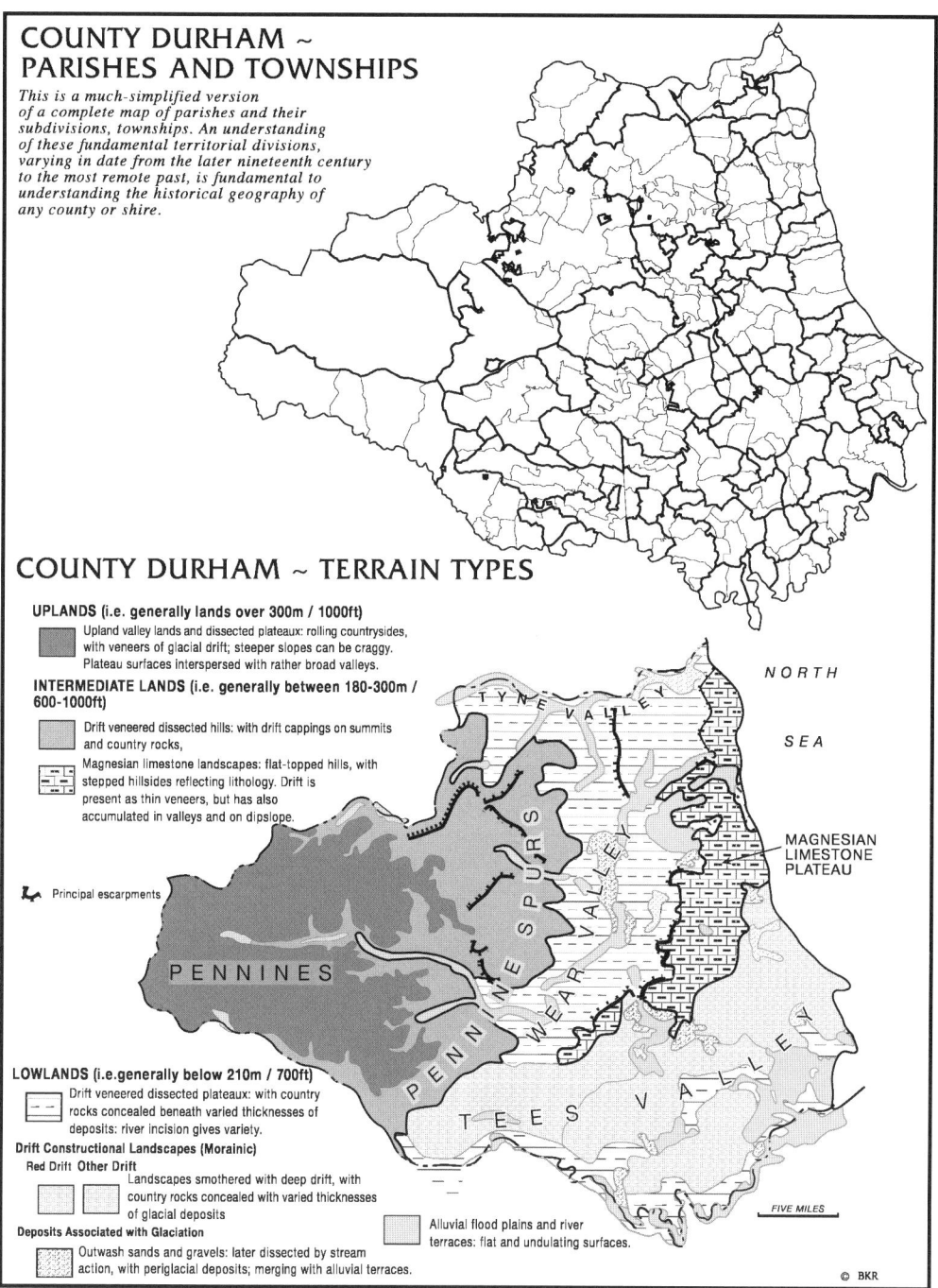

Fig. 6.1 County Durham, parishes, townships and terrain types

> All the villans of Aucklandshire, that is North [Bishop] Auckland and West Auckland and Escomb and Newton [Cap] provide one rope at the Great Chases of the Bishop for each bovate…

the point locations of these place-names – North or Bishop Auckland, West Auckland, Escomb and Newton Cap – can be converted into a view of *territory* by assuming that the township area of each named place is likely to have been, substantively at least, the land attached to the place in the twelfth century. Of course, such assumptions are not without dangers. In Durham it is fortunate that the arrangement of places in both Boldon Book and Hatfield Survey of 1381 bear a clear relationship to geographical space. In both texts places are grouped together in logical sequences, and this assists the reconstruction of earlier territories. Ultimately, professional judgement is necessary. The use of a map of townships and parishes, made explicit here, provides a powerful tool for reconstructing the cultural contexts in which settlement development took place. Even if it is not wholly accurate for medieval reconstruction, and we have no means of being wholly certain, its use has acquired a time-honoured respectability. A study of the pattern of parishes, church supporting territories, and townships, smaller economic divisions reflecting the presence of farming communities, emphasises that the nature of the network varies spatially (Figure 6.1 top). Parishes and townships tend to be smaller where the land was of good quality and are larger when the land is subject to limitations of topography, climate and soils. Nevertheless, the more that the detail of this mosaic or network is studied, the more that inconsistencies between the nineteenth century mapped evidence and the documented evidence from earlier centuries emerge. Places are found to change both parochial and township attributions. Nineteenth century maps can never be more than a guide.

Early Land Grants in County Durham

The estates of the Bishop of Durham were split from those of the cathedral priory in the later eleventh or twelfth century but they originated in grants of land to the deceased but undecayed St. Cuthbert, saint and former Bishop of Lindisfarne (Aird 1998: Hart 1975, 117–150). Figures 6.2 and 6.3, drawing upon the detail presented by William Aird and Cyril Hart record in a summary fashion the land transactions we know of between AD 700 and 1100, concluding with a synoptic view of the situation towards the end of the twelfth century. The appendices of this study tabulate much of the data upon which the maps are based. In these cases little attempt has been made to give the grants real spatial substance, except where very large blocks are involved (Dunsford and Harris 2003, map 5). The history of the estate may be briefly summarised as follows: before 716 grants of land made in the form of *familiae*, 'families', passed to the Lindisfarne community a block of coastal territory between the Tyne and the Wear. In the ninth century substantive rights were granted over lands

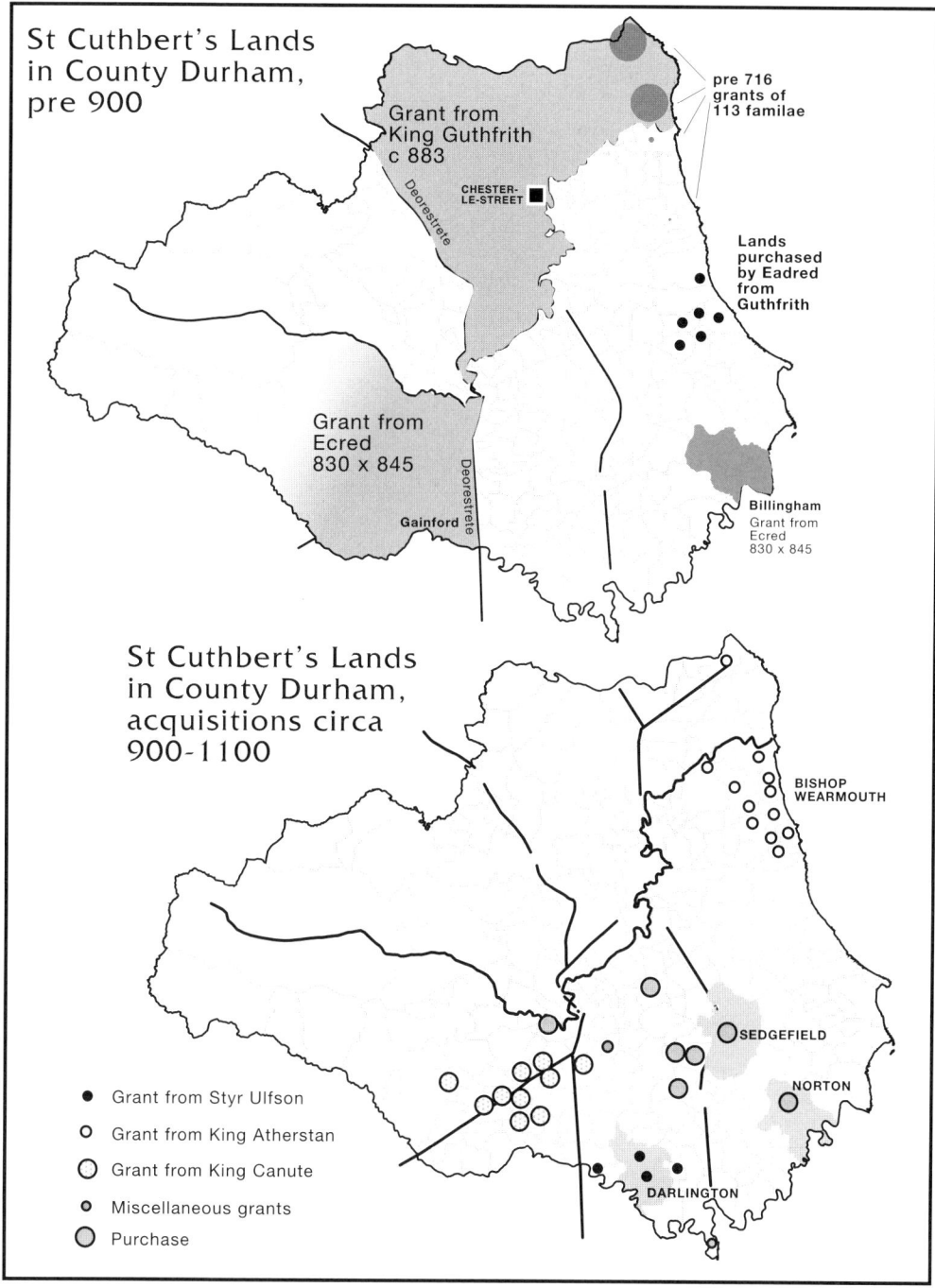

Fig. 6.2 The estates of St. Cuthbert, County Durham

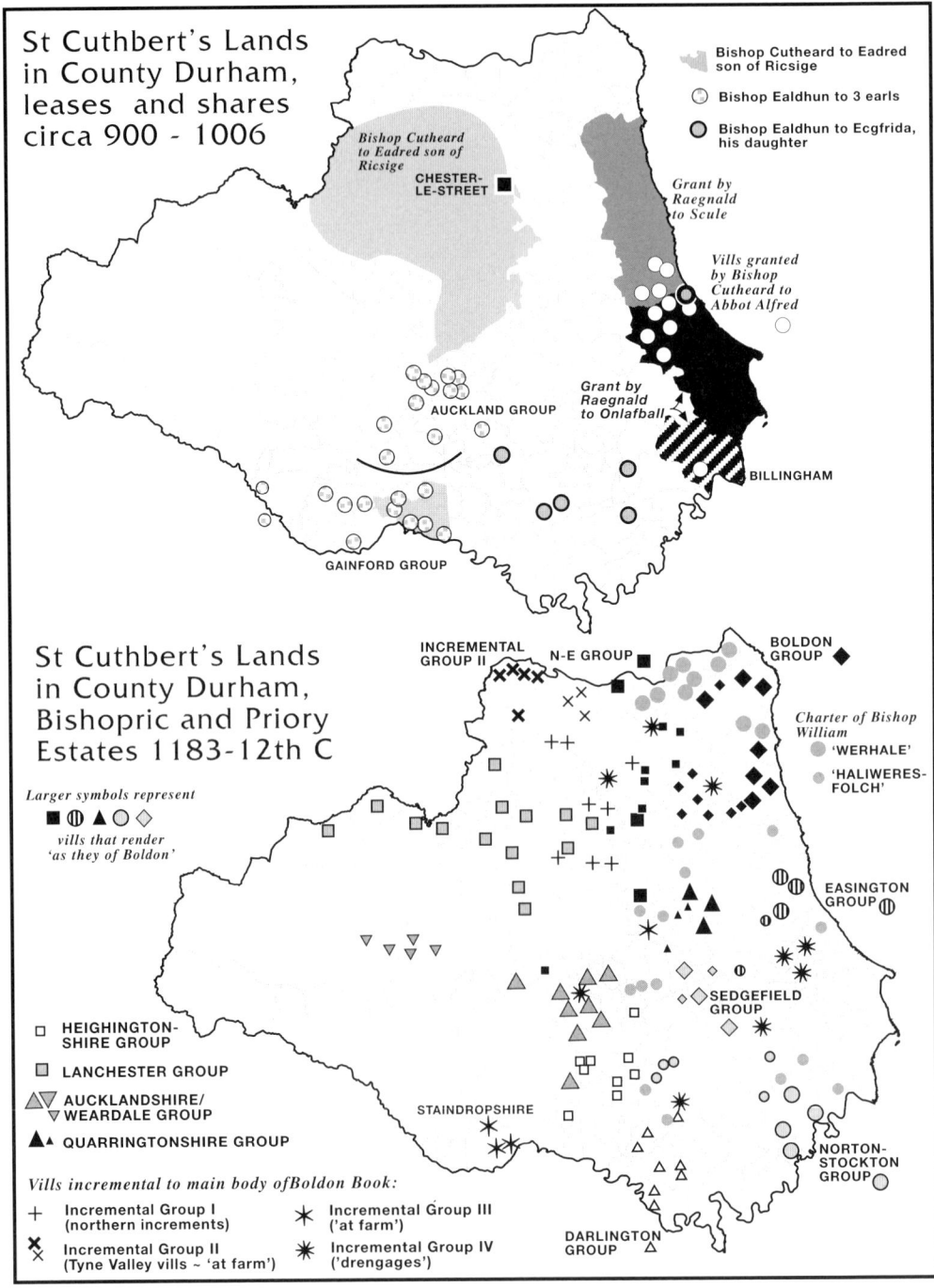

Fig. 6.3 The estates of St. Cuthbert, County Durham

in the west of the county, west of the River Wear and the Roman road called Dere Street, *i.e.* the road leading south to Deira. A comparison with Figure 2.5 suggests that this royal 'generosity' largely comprised uncultivated wastes, open grazings and wood-pastures on the foothills of the Pennines, although, if you could protect them, it was good cattle land, comprising both open land and wood-pasture. The southern portion, immediately to the west of the Roman road and the road heading to the south-west must have contained more cultivated land, while there is likely to have been some settlement and cultivation around the former Roman centre in the lower Wear valley around Chester-le-Street. In fact the Community of St Cuthbert, originally based on Lindisfarne, established themselves at Chester-le-Street in 883, and there was during the next century a complex pattern of acquisition, loss and re-acquisition throughout the eastern and southern parts of the county in the agriculturally most productive regions. Intermediate between expansive grants of 'Gainford and all that belongs to it from the River Tees to the River Wear' and transactions involving individual places, for instance, 'every fourth acre' in Ferryhill, lie other grants, comprising chief settlements and an indication of associated places or rights. Thus we have 'Sedgefield, and that which pertains to it', 'Bishop Wearmouth with its appendices', and Darlington with legal rights of 'sac and soc'. All of these transactions are presented in more detail in Figure 8.2, a diagrammatic view of the history of the Cuthbertine lands between 674 and the earlier twelfth century, so that in-text references will not be documented further. By 1183, some of the settlement groups in the county are termed 'shires' and it is to this term that we must turn.

Evidence and Questions

The term *-shire* in fact implies something severed from a large whole, a district or a kingdom (Smith 1956, 109–111; Palmer 1998, 87, 187–9). Sometimes in the documentation a list of constituent places is given in detail, sometimes it is merely generalised. As Professor Geoffrey Barrow notes, the formula usually consists of a place-name, indicating the chief hall, followed by the phrase *cum omnibus appendiciis suis*, 'with all its appendages', or, to use the splendid term favoured by Scots lawyers of a later age, 'with all its pendicles' (Barrow 1973, 24). Both Barrow and Craster cite material in which the Latin *appendicia / appendicium* is glossed by the Old English *geburatun(as)*, *i.e.* 'the *-tuns* of the *geburs*', 'the farmers' settlements'. This implies a contrast between the estate centre with its hall, administrative, craft and storage functions, and the outlying wholly rural dependencies producing grain and stock (Barrow 1973, 24, note 89; Craster 1954, 191–2). Craster's important and revealing reference is to a document in Thorpe's *Diplomaticum,* and is dated to AD 821. In a wide-ranging analysis of such estates in Scotland Barrow precedes his discussion with a review of the English evidence (Barrow 1973, 24–25). Small shires are widespread, from Essex to Somerset, but in particular the northern counties are rich in indicators of their presence. In Durham we have not only Aucklandshire, but Heighingtonshire, Quarringtonshire, Billinghamshire, Staindropshire (or Rabyshire) and in Northumberland Bedlingtonshire and Islandshire. In Yorkshire we have Hallamshire, based upon Sheffield, Howdenshire, Kirbyshire (based upon Kirby Malzeard), Gillingshire, Burgshire (based upon Aldborough), Riponshire and Allertonshire. In Lancashire Blackburnshire is but one of a number of similar territories. While the term 'shire' may not be specifically appended, Yorkshire also provides examples of estates in royal hands consisting of many components, berewicks or sokelands in Domesday terms, which 'lay to the chief manor'. This occurs at Pocklington, Driffield, and Kilham and along with Allertonshire and Howdenshire all formed wapentakes or hundreds at a later date. As Barrow notes:

> In medieval and later times, Aldborough wapentake took its name from Claro on the Great North Road, but in the eleventh century its name was 'Boroughshire', after the 'old borough', Aldborough, formerly *Isurium Brigantum*, cantonal capital of the Brigantes. Gilling represents what was evidently in the seventh century a *regio*, to which Bede gives the name *in Getlingum*, 'among the people of Getla'.
>
> (Barrow 1973, 25)

In these cases, and in more that Barrow was able to define in Scotland, there are clear hints of ancient territoriality. Basically there is evidence for a consistent and repeated pattern: a central place, of high status, where things happened and which is named in documents, to which are attached smaller, less important places as outlying dependencies. As the case of Aucklandshire to be discussed below shows, a list of dependencies within early documentation may not embrace all of the places that were present. Furthermore, to see shires as completely stable is to misunderstand their nature and while ancient territoriality is buried in the lists of vills recorded in some of the Cuthbertine land grants, it is clear that places were being detached and then reattached to different administrative centres. The case of Aucklandshire (pages 172 ff.) will illustrate this point.

A variety of terms have been applied to these arrangements: to Glanville Jones and Rosamund Faith they were 'multiple estates' and 'extensive lordships' (Jones 1971; Faith 1997, 1–14) to Joliffe and Barrow 'shires' (Jolliffe 1926; Barrow 1973, 1–68;), but Offler's term, 'small shire', is succinct, neat and accurate. However, one must stress that this term can also be applied where the suffix *-shire* does not necessarily appear in the documentation. Thus, the five hundreds of South Lancashire, namely, Salford, West Derby, Leyland, and Amounderness along with Blackburnshire, all show signs of being similar estates, although only the latter bears the specific designation. Furthermore, there is far more to small shires than the mere congregation of a group of settlements into a territory. It appears that shires represent a pre-feudal milieu within which flows of rent and service took place, and records we have involve the insertion of an intermediate high status tenant between the crown – be this a regional or a 'national' ruler – and the varied tenantry beneath. This intermediate lord intercepted much of what had once been royal revenue so that Jolliffe's term 'mediatised hundred' – yet another term, for many such small shires emerge into the light of documentation as hundreds – encapsulates the idea (Jolliffe 1926, 2). Renders of grain, stock and their products such as ale and cheese, agricultural work and personal services such as the keeping or dogs or the riding of errands were all drawn from these estates, while their grazing reserves supported the cattle of both aristocrats and peasant farmers. In Durham there is a tendency for the shires to be smaller in the agricultural east and south of the county, but in the uplands further to the west, where pasture reserves were vast, they become very large indeed. Welsh examples cited by Jones suggest that lowland territories were often paired with upland territories, so that a reciprocity of rents renders and services could be achieved, the grain of the lowlands complementing the stock of the uplands and the honey, timber, pig and cattle pastures of the intervening woodlands. It is likely that these small shires represent ancient local administrative units, essentially rather primitive in nature and yet having diverse origins, relics of a period when renders and work were the primary sources of landed income and tax. Once, at some stage preceding the Norman Conquest, such territories provided a local ruler with his *feorm* or food rents (Barrow 1973, 11, citing Davis 1954, xl, xlvi–xlvii). Indeed, as will be argued below, some of the dues and services seem to be exceedingly 'ancient' in origin while others undoubtedly merge with those owed by the peasantry in many parts of medieval England. In fact the latter dues and services may perhaps be of equally ancient origin even though they were absorbed into the 'manor' as perceived by Norman lawyers, and indeed there is a real need for a careful large scale re-evaluation of the services demanded in customals.

Paradoxically, but perhaps predictably, there appear to be no markers that are indisputable indicators of the presence of a small shire. Nevertheless, each small shire contained a variety of people performing diverse services and paying a mixture of rents and renders. In the north these were, at least at first, personal rather than attached to land holdings. This should be emphasised: the bonds were at first personal, between lord and man, rather than tenurial, between the lords and the tenant of the holding. The underlying thesis of the argument to follow is that if the small shire was indeed an ancient territorial arrangement, present before the Anglo-Saxon period and possibly even possessing Romano-British or even Iron Age roots (Campbell 2000, xvi), then the rents, renders and services present in these estates by the twelfth and thirteenth centuries evolved from those current in vastly earlier contexts. Establishing a chronological sequence for such accreted layers is by no means easy, but the challenge of this way of thinking can be brought to bear upon the real history of settlement. The rise of feudalism and feudal tenures after the Norman Conquest meant that there was a process that frequently involved shoe-horning the more ancient systems of rents and services into the non-ecclesiastical categories devised by Anglo-Norman lawyers, namely, knight service, grand and petty serjeanty, socage and bondage (Denman 1958, 84–88).

The appendices to this study comprise a series of tables based upon the Durham records (Appendices I and II). These lists take published archive materials, dissect them, and then reconstitute the material in a tabulated format. They are the foundation for this analysis.

The following paragraph is introductory to Boldon Book:

> In the year of the Incarnation of our Lord one thousand one hundred and eighty three, at the feast of St. Cuthbert in Lent, the Lord Hugh Bishop of Durham, in his own presence and that of his council, caused to be described all the revenues of his whole Bishoprick as they were, and the assised rents and customs as they then were, and formerly had been.
>
> (Greenwell 1852, 43)

In a powerful if belated analysis of this text Offler showed how the three versions of this survey we now have are in fact copies derived from an original that has not survived (Offler 1996, XII). The material incorporated within the surviving texts relates not only to the year 1183, the date of the compilation from diverse pre-existing documents, all of which have now disappeared, but also reflects numerous subsequent amendments and alterations. Boldon Book is in effect a working document treating a dynamic situation. Offler argues that the edition published by Greenwell in 1852, is the most authentic version and this has been used here. In addition to the character of the emendations, the sequencing of the text is crucial. Not only is there a group of settlements at the end of the manuscript treating Bedlingtonshire, part of Northumberland, but these are preceded by a group of settlements in Durham (Greenwell 1852, 69–71, from Great Usworth to Urpeth) that represent a group of 'special places'. These will be examined later. In discussion of the lands of St. Cuthbert and basing his analysis on the *Historia de Sancto Cuthberto*, an account of the estates in *c.* 1050, but drawing upon earlier material, Craster showed that the pre-Conquest documents allow groups of settlement loci, whatever their real character, to be identified. The individual places making up these will be termed *vills*, begging the question of whether they were villages or hamlets. This list included at least three places to which the suffix *-shire* was appended, and it is likely that concealed within the other entries are the substance of further small shires.

As was noted earlier the lands of St. Cuthbert suffered dismemberment in the tenth century as a result of Viking incursions and aristocratic take-over (Figs 6.2 and 6.3: Aird 1998, 9–59: Fig. 8.2 below). While there are only a limited number of place-names in *-by* indicative of colonisation by Scandinavian settler-farmers (Watts 1988–9), Hart assembled a formal listing of all the pre-Conquest documents whose texts can be reconstructed from the Durham records (1975). The Viking depredations were gradually overcome, and the church appears, gradually, to have regained control – if it ever really lost it – so that the vills that appear in Boldon Book represent those portions of these ancient Cuthbertine estates that fell into the hands of the Norman bishops.

There were, in addition, the lands of the Priory and while there are indications that these were surveyed, the key document has failed to survive (Greenwell 1872, i–iii; 119, note 2). The lower part of Figure 6.3 is a summary based on Boldon Book and some twelfth century charter materials (*ibid*. lii–lvi: lxxxiii; Fig. 8.2 below). The fundamental sequencing of Boldon Book is by 'vill groups' (Appendix II) and this fact, together with the surviving pre-conquest charters, allows the reconstruction of a mosaic of small shires. Undoubtedly, this picture must be hedged with qualifications and caveats, but the pattern is a useful reconstruction of the pre-twelfth century territorial structure of the county.

The Substance of the Small Shire

Clues regarding the spatial content of small shires come from a surprising source. Jolliffe, Barrow and Glanville Jones have pointed out that the rent forms and organisational characteristics found in the twelfth century records of all the northern shires show clear parallels with those of Wales and Scotland. This suggests not only a degree of common origin, but also, it is argued, an origin in the period preceding the take-over of the north by Germanic peoples. It was Glanville Jones who first gave material substance to the character of the estates involved, within whose territories and populations the transmission of the survivals took place. The model he created is recast as Figure 6.4.a and shows what he termed a 'multiple estate', effectively a small shire, at two stages of development. The top diagram he places in eleventh century Wales, and it draws heavily upon Welsh legal texts (Jones 1971, 251–67). At this stage there were already two categories of tenant, bondsmen and freemen, and these resided in mixtures of hamlets and scattered homesteads. An idealised picture of such a small hamlet is provided by a note in Welsh Laws that:

> This is the compliment of a lawful hamlet (*trefgordd*): nine houses and one plough and one oven and one churn and one cat and one cock and one bull and one herdsman.
>
> (Seebohm 1896, 36: see also Homans 1941, 26 and note 19).

This is a taxable unit, sharing agricultural resources and pooling labour, homesteads and neighbours acting together. All farmers, including those in the most remote dwellings, sought justice from the territorial lord, and in return the bondsmen paid rents in kind or cash and performed various services and works. This network of local obligations linked the various elements of the estate together. Physically we can imagine a settlement similar to that shown in Figure 5.2 (a), a basic agricultural hamlet, which could either be bond or free.

In Wales rents and services were rendered at the lord's dwelling or hall, in Welsh *llys*, often built of stone (*maen*), probably the root of the term given to the territory in Welsh, *maenor*. In close proximity to this court, but not necessarily in the same settlement, there was often a hamlet containing a church (*eglwys*) and the lands with which it was endowed (Jones 1971). These could be separate and distinct entities. Some farmers could owe building services for the upkeep of the court. Sometimes this involved freeholders, but the main burdens of the estate were carried by the bondsmen. Under the supervision of the reeve they cultivated the demesne lands (*tyr bawd*, table land or mensal land), which, like the *llys* itself, were usually located near a hamlet known as the reeve's settlement (*maerdref*). The bondsmen erected the court buildings that included a hall, a kitchen, a chamber, a chapel, and latrines, and in addition they constructed distant encampments and provided transport for, among other items, food supplies in time of hunting and war. The size of these estates, measured in terms of the hamlets or vills they contain varied considerably, and range between as few as four to as many as thirteen or fourteen. According to Jones there is slight evidence to suggest that a lowland *maenor* was often paired to an upland *maenor*, so that the better arable sources of the former could compliment the extensive summer pastures and hunting grounds of the latter. Furthermore, each *maenor* had its own refuge in the form of a hill fort, constructed by the labour of the bondsmen, and with the larger of the two in the uplands to accommodate the larger herds of cattle. The implication of this is that the estate was multi-centred, with the court settlement being separate from the church focus, and the vill with the lord's table land, under the control of a *maer* or reeve, hence *maerdref*. Each of these specialist centres tended to form a separate entity, although the degree of physical separation need not be great. Within the territory the social relationships took the form of services rendered to the 'chief' or 'lord' of the territory, and essentially there was a flow of edible renders, grain and ale, honey and stock, to support the aristocratic household, so that this residence formed a focus for activity. Ploughing, mowing and harvesting services were demanded from bond tenants, to assist the cultivation of the lord's table land, *i.e.* that geared towards produce for his household, the demesne in Norman-French terminology. Higher status service took the form of keeping horses and dogs, carrying messages – an essential part of administration – and rendering other duties, to the person of the estate's lord or to the officers who act as his intermediaries. These officers, the reeves, also serve, and organise and intercept the flows of rent for the benefit of the lord. Into this system the church was intruded. Normally located near the chief residence, but within its own nucleus, it may even take the form of a private venture under the control of a member of the ruling aristocrat's family.

The model seen in Figure 6.4.a shows an idealised, legalistic view, from which the real world frequently, indeed normally, departed, not least because all such static pictures can take no account of changes wrought by time. These arrangements arose in societies, as Koch reminds us, in which the primary institutions of political power were 'chieftain, dynasty, court and tribe', in which there was at the time no political entity which was even approximately co-extensive with the ethnolinguistic collectivity of the Britons nor with that of the Anglo-Saxons'. This was a warrior society 'in which there was a level of endemic intra-ethnic violence which equals or exceeds the inter-ethnic' (Koch 1997, xx). Effectively this was a northern society based upon clans, echoes of which survived into the seventeenth century amongst the riding families of the Scottish-English borders. Thus, to see the small shire as Welsh, British or Anglo-Saxon is to misunderstand its nature. It is a practical pre-feudal way of filtering surplus from an agricultural society, albeit based upon grain production, but in which cattle formed a primary component of moveable wealth and in which there were only limited amounts of coin in circulation. Urien of Reged, who may have died in about AD 570, is described by his bard, Talesin, as 'a battle-victorious, cattle-rich sovereign' (Koch 1997, xxvii). In praise of Gwallawg the same poet is equally concise

> *A beginning, my praise in verse,*
> *Of lords faultless in warfare;*
> *Men who fill byres with cattle…*
>
> (Clancy *et al*. 1998, 92).

These qualities gave local rulers the power to reward through gifts. As will be shown later there are even parallels between this northern British situation and that once present in Ireland.

In the second portion of Figure 6.4.a is what Jones describes as 'the settlement and administrative patterns likely to have developed by the eleventh and twelfth centuries'. This is an important component of the model, and in his dismissive criticism of Glan Jones' work Steven Bassett fails to appreciate the two temporal stages involved in the model (Bassett 1989 20, n. 51). This is a pity, although the publication of the thinking behind Jones's argument is widely scattered and his general model appears in a Continental conference volume. The empirical work upon which his arguments were based took place in Welsh contexts and more particularly, when treating manorialisation *within* a pre-exiting multiple estate, in 'the upland fringes of northern England' as the result of the 'economic development and fission … of ancient multiple estates' (Jones 1971, 261). Geoffrey Barrow's careful exploration of a substantial body of evidence extending over much of England and Scotland provides a cautious synoptic view of such extensive lordships (Barrow 1973, 25) and may be contrasted with powerful, if at times eccentric insights projected by Glan Jones. Implicit rather than explicit in his argument is the idea that 'multiple estates', to use his term, comprising focal settlements with appendices, could form enduring building blocks. Explicit in his account is the idea that this small shire, whole at some date in the indeterminate past, is modelled in a stage of fission, the result of post-Conquest manorialisation with subinfeudation of elements of the older estate. In short, Jones projected into his model many well-documented aspects of settlement evolution:

- the existence of outlying townships form parish of parishes located elsewhere,
- the existence of outlying members of manors, berewicks and sokelands, the appearance of Norton, Sutton, Eston, Weston and Middleton as place-names, reflecting their location within the original estate,

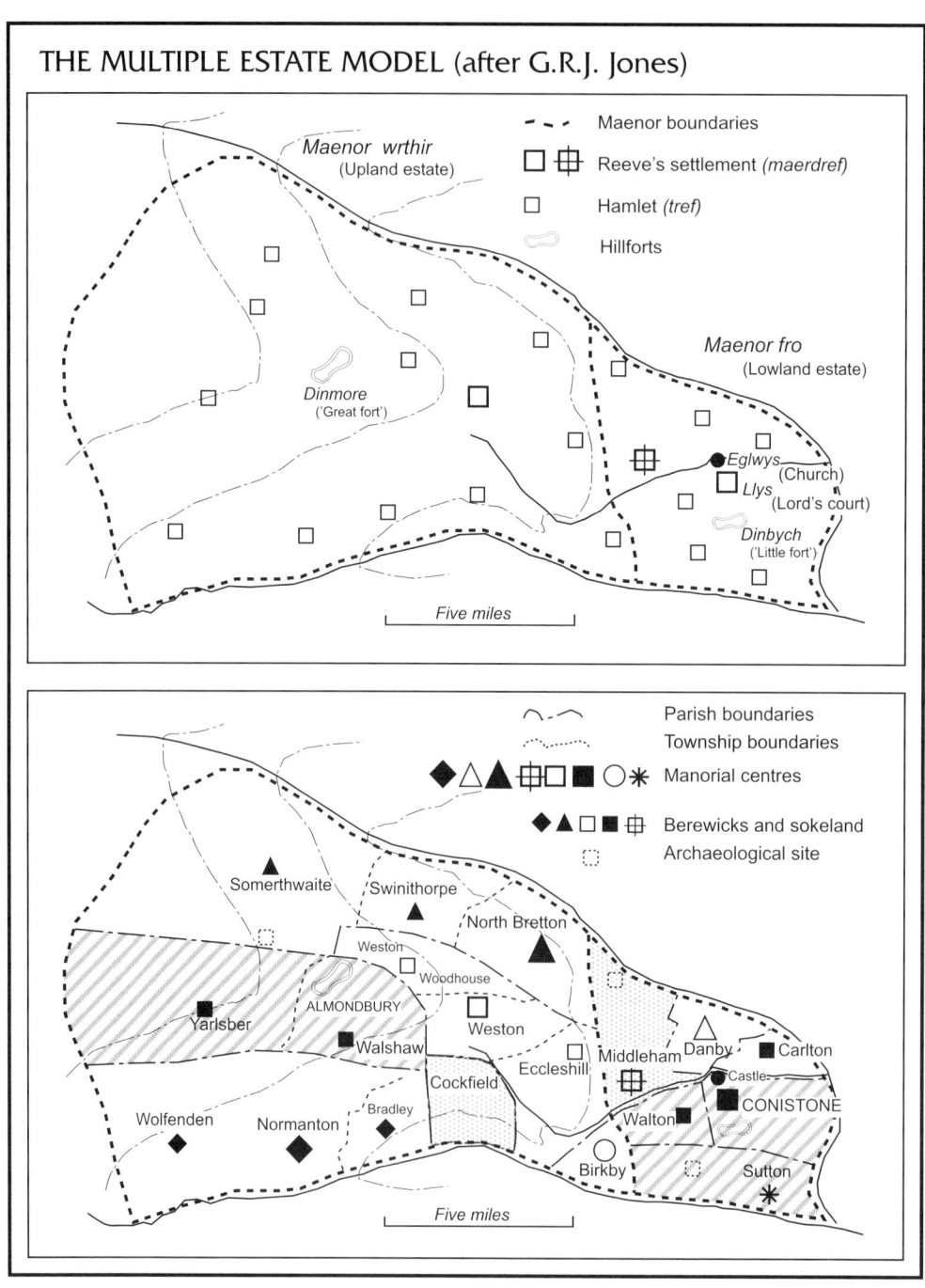

Fig. 6.4.a The multiple estate model

Estates and Shires 165

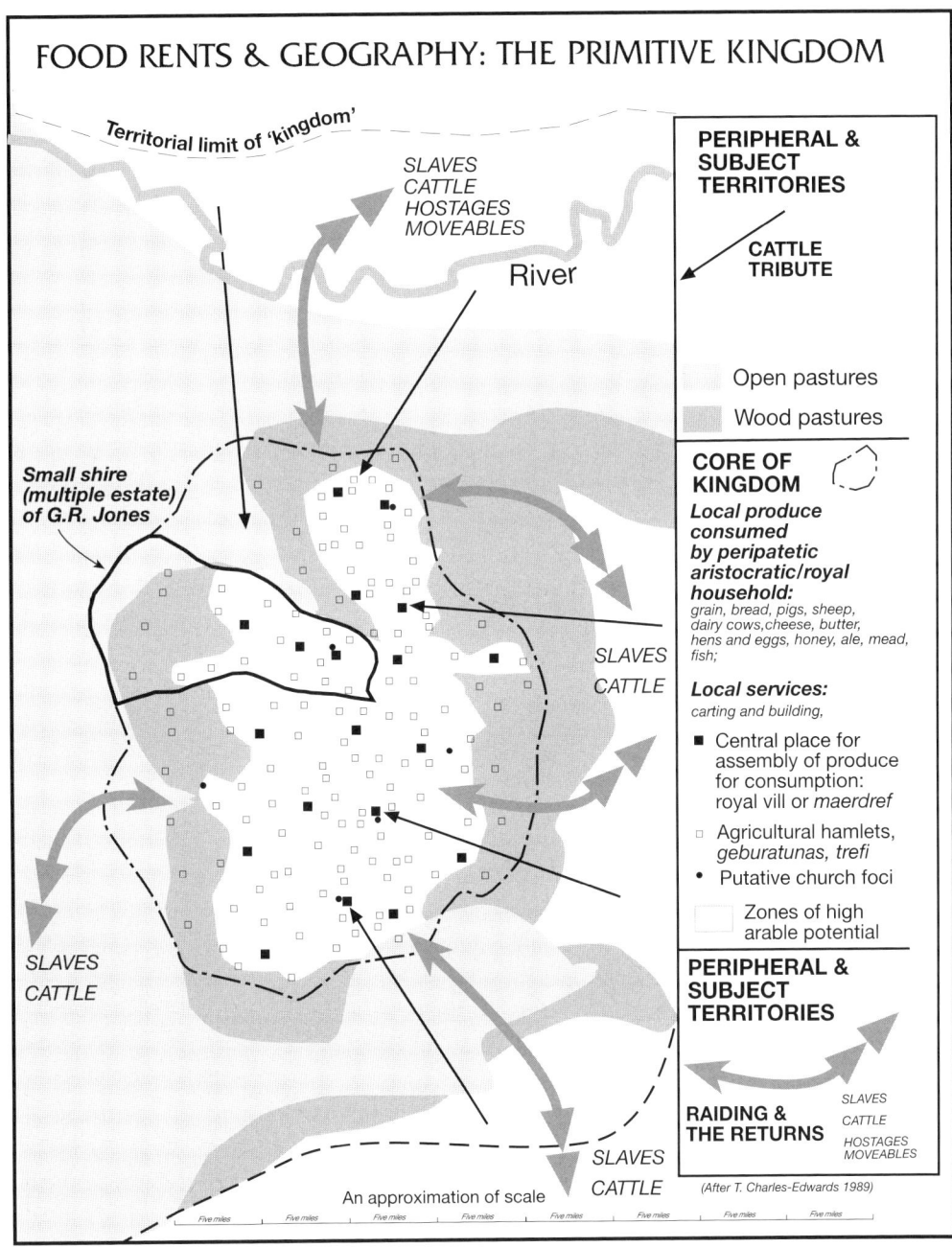

Fig. 6.4.b Food rents and geography: the primitive kingdom

- the survivals of place-names indicative of the presence of British or 'Welsh' populations;
- the interdigitation of Scandinavian place-names amid Old English names, the former taking over portions of the estate;
- and finally, the sustained importance of estate centres, reflected in place-names such as Conistone – the king's *-tun* – and the eventual development of a castle, market and important church focus in close proximity.

The economic elements of the former unitary estate are also reflected in the appearance of names such as Carlton – 'the *-tun* of the *ceorls* or farmers' – set near the chief vill to provide food and labour (Finberg 1964, 144–60). Place-names in *-leah* (ley), and names such as Wootton – 'the wood *-tun*' – or Woodhouses, indicative of woodland tracts, and the *-thweits, -thorpes* and *-sheles,* or upland summer pastures, are indicative of remoter tracts. Finally there are the commons. At first these were shared by the whole territory of the shire, but were gradually appropriated to individual parishes and townships. The question is not of the presence of manors or estates in earlier Anglo-Saxon times, but of the emergence of rights in land and rights over land. Thus, the territory seen in the upper part of Figure 6.4.a (1) may have been assembled by a powerful local leader over a short term, (2) may have been taken over from a Romano-British unit, (3) may originate in the remoter, tribal, prehistoric past, or (4) may even represent a feudal pastiche. The model seen in the bottom of Figure 6.4.a presents they way in which traces of the ancient arrangement survive when the frame has been adapted to feudal needs. These are all points to be debated, but this working model is an exceedingly useful concept, to be carried, used and tested. Furthermore, it is important to grasp that its creator never regarded it as static: rather we have in Figure 6.4.a two images of an ever-changing dynamic reality, and an empirical model designed to nourish the imagination rather than be used uncritically.

Thomas Charles-Edwards in an essay on early medieval kingship creates what he terms 'an over simplified' model of a 'kingdom'. In Figure 6.4.b this has been converted into a pictorial model incorporating indications of land quality and land usage (Charles-Edwards 1989, 28–33). This construct feeds directly back into Figure 6.4.a, and it underlies the estate development seen in Figures 6.1, 6.2 and 6.3 and Figures 7.1 and 8.1, and finally with the ideas formulated in Chapter 10. The core of the 'kingdom' (James 1989, 40–52) comprises a zone with a degree of agricultural potential. Within this local produce is consumed by the 'king', whose peripatetic household, or sometimes households, visited central places, 'royal *-tuns*', where collection had taken place. While Charles-Edwards did not incorporate the small shire into his model, the present author believes that such a core would contain numerous examples, only one of which is shown. Raiding outwards had several purposes: it could be planned to absorb other incipient polities into the central core, or may be for booty and/or as punishment for inward raiding. None of these are mutually exclusive, and while slaves, stock and moveables may be the result of initial raids, stabilisation leads to the giving of hostages and demands for tax in the form of cattle tributes, items that can move on their own feet into the successful kingdom's core. That wood pastures and open pastures initially formed 'no man's lands' between incipient proto-kingdoms is inherently probable. These are ideas that cannot be developed fully here, for the developments examined in this study occur when generally stable local regional polities had emerged, but the socio-economic relationships expressed in Figure 6.4 are radical issues for settlement development.

Those authorities which have given them close attention all tend to agree that the traces of small shires detectable in the north survive because the imposition of the practice and terminology of the manor and feudalism were both later and less completely imposed upon this region than in the midlands and south. Given that these documented traces are often of twelfth century provenance, and given that the roots of village planning appear in the documents of the same period, then the small shire clearly provides one context in which planned settlements could evolve. A second context was the feudal estates, comprising honours, knight's fees and manors, that were imposed upon the more ancient arrangements. These interwoven cultural patterns sit foursquare upon the geographical spaces of northern England, amid the castle-defended grain-lands and meadows of the lowlands, the enclosed farmsteads and woodlands of the rising spurs, and the cattle summering grounds and wild hill country of the uplands, safe routes for cattle rustlers and slave raiders. Further, the inherent conservatism of ecclesiastical estates ensured that the records retained traces of ancient pre-feudal rent forms. The Durham evidence offers rich opportunities for further exploration.

Rents and Renders Associated with Small Shires

This section sets out to establish a general structure within which examples of the rents and renders due from small shires can be evaluated. Nevertheless, it is the specifics that are wholly crucial. The manor, which looms so large in post Conquest medieval England, is a term that does not appear in England until 1067 and has been rightly described as 'confusion roughly organised' (Latham in Barraclough 1960, 29–50). It was primarily a legal and administrative unit, in which the rights of a private landlord implied seigniorial jurisdiction and economic control of shareholders, the rustics of a given area, whose labour, services and rents were directed towards the support of a feudal lord. It was based upon compulsory and direct cultivation of the soil, extracted in the form of heavy labour services, within a system of prescribed custom. Characteristically, a settlement, often a village or hamlet was divided between the home farm, demesne, of the lord, and the lands of the cultivators. These latter, of varied social grades and economic status, were tenants: there were no kinship links between them and the lord. The most characteristic feature of the manorial economy lay in the intimate link between demesne and tenant lands, and the main social characteristic feature of the manor lay in the dependent status of the tenants, who were perceived as either free or unfree (Postan 1972, 73–4). Effectively, one must conclude that the manor was a legal and administrative entity, defined by Anglo-Norman lawyers, and gradually superimposed upon indigenous vernacular farming communities (Denman 1958, 79–104). Of course, the manor was also a development that took place through time and whose origins are much debated (Postan 1972, 73–87; Aston 1957, 11–35). The appearance of the manor was undoubtedly preceded by an older system of contribution, involving the payment of food renders and other services for the support of a local chief or lord. These older elements that became absorbed into the manorial system are most clearly seen in the north and west of England, extending into Wales and Scotland, but can also be detected in the survival of more primitive elements in fully manorialised regions. The issue is a troubled one, and involves comparisons between terminology and the actual nature of rents and renders, and the identification of similarities, correspondences and resemblances, sometimes using linguistic evidence and sometimes the nature of social and /or economic characteristics. Professional judgements are necessary, and being wrong is easy.

For present purposes it is necessary to consider the renders and rents flowing between the 'lord' and the inhabitants of a small shire in a pre-manorial past. This is a step towards more complex questions considered in the next two chapters. In post-Conquest feudal contexts there was a flow upwards of rent and service: varied grades of tenants owed rents, in kind, in labour, in cash to the lord of the manor. This lord, in turn, owed service, most characteristically knight service together with other payments, either directly to the crown, or more often to a great secular baron or the owner of a great ecclesiastical estate. It was normal for a chain of three or four steps to exist in this ladder, and at each level a state of tenancy was involved. Ultimately, all were tenants of the crown, who had defined interests in each level of the ladder, and the capacity to obtain further revenue by means of taxation. Royal rents and revenue were generally collected on the basis of the shire or county, as in Essex, Worcestershire, Somerset and Nottinghamshire, and the king's officer in that shire was the sheriff, literally the 'shire reeve', that long-standing opponent of Robin Hood.

If, however, we turn to the northern shires and the royal record of revenue and expenses for 1130, we find Hildred, the sheriff, rendering account for revenue, for manors, mines and the town of Carlisle 'farmed', *i.e.* let to a tenant, in return for a fixed sum of cash. There are also notes of debts still due from the previous sheriff and others. The most substantial item of income was, however, £80 105s 8d of the 'geld of the animals', while it is clear that there are debts outstanding from the previous sheriff (VCH Cu I, 338). A similar record for Durham for 1130, when the Bishopric was in the king's hand, gives a figure of £110 5s 5d for the 'cornage of cattle in the Bishopric' (Greenwell 1852, Appendix i). In 1920 Rachel Reid noted that this render was paid throughout the north, in Durham as *cornage*, in Lancashire as *cougeld* and *oxgeld*, in Yorkshire as *coumale* (Reid 1920 186–7), and in Scotland as 'the *cain* of the animals', although to this list to may be added *cowgeld, geld of the animals and neatgeld* 'on the Welsh border' (Rees, in Lewis 1963, 148–68), *gab[u]lum of the animals* or *geldo vaccarium* (VCH Cu i, 314–5), *horngeld* (VCH Cu i, 315), *cowmael* in west Lancashire, and *noutgeld* in Cumberland (VCH Cu i, 306 plate, 315–6). At Singleton in Lancashire *beltancu i.e.* Beltane-cow, is recorded (Rees 1963, 161), no doubt payable on the ancient festival of Beltane, May 1st. Thus it corresponds to correspond to the Welsh *treth calan mai* (Rees 1924, 229; 1963, 162), According to Rees (1968, 40, 50) this was payable in Wales in alternate years, although in Wales some documents suggest that it was paid in every third or fourth year (Rees 1924, 229) and may correspond to the milch-cow payments of Durham. Wilson presents a neat summary, 'we have here a list of names linked together in a series, each of which indisputably refers to the same source of revenue'.

Both have been interpreted as representing a commutation of the *gwestfa*, or food rents to support the ruler and his household (Rees 1924, 229–34, 10–13), although as the discussion of Figures 6.4 showed, cattle tribute was an essential part of primitive state construction. The range of small variations suggests the influence of a host of local agreements and adjustments, although we may doubt if it was ever a wholly uniform payment, unless it found an origin in Roman taxation (Morris 1973, 220–2). Irish parallels suggest that if this is the case, the Romans may have adapted an even older system. There are hints that in Wales *commorth* was a render in lieu of *gwestfa*, for the distribution of the two payments was complementary (Rees 1924, 230), and it was paid by the free tenants, members of the *gwely* or kin group (Rees 1924, 231). Furthermore, on some estates *commorth* was divided into a 'Great Commorth', paid by free tenants, and a 'Small Commorth' paid by co-parceners, of uncertain status, but one might suggest these were bondsmen (Rees 1924, 232; 1953, xxxvi). Its origin clearly lay in the render of a fixed quota of cattle, a communal render, incumbent upon a place, involving both free and unfree tenants, and yet not appended to particular holdings of land. Rees cites a case at Welsh Penkelly where '*comhortha*' was 'payable every other year by the freeholders of the lordship, *and also for certain mountains*' (1924, 231). In some estates in Brecon, the *gwestfa* paid by free tenants was organised into 'cow units' (*vaccae*) with free family groups contributing towards the value of a cow, and while in some of these groups co-owners contributed equally, in another a common cow was rendered (Rees 1924, 232–3).

What do all of these terms suggest? It is clear that only one explanation is possible, viz. 'that noutgeld, horngeld, cornage, geld of animals, geld of cows, gavel or gafol of animals, was a rent paid in kind, that is, in cattle' (VCH, Cu i, 315). Perceptively, in the light of more recent work, James Wilson, writing in 1901 adds 'It is … probable that it was the survival of some archaic original, like the 'cumal of the cows' in the [Irish] Brehon laws, or the 'cane of the animals' in Celtic Scotland, and was utilised by the Norman conquerors for their own purposes'. In a footnote he comments:

> It has been suggested that the origin of cornage must be sought at some period when the four northern counties were under one government, previous to the dismemberment of the kingdom of Northumberland in the ninth century… but

> from its primitive characteristics and its existence outside the Border counties, it would be hazardous to ascribe any limit to its antiquity.

In spite of all subsequent work, no better summary can be achieved. In a nutshell, is this payment of Dark Age origin, does it indeed owe anything to Roman taxation or do the Irish parallels suggest roots in pre-Roman Iron Age Celtic custom and kingship? In Irish law, whose individual components are impossible to date, cattle formed a unit of currency, and this continued even after the Norsemen introduced coinage in the early tenth century. The basic unit was the milch cow normally accompanied by her calf, three of which were equal to the worth of one female slave (Kelley 1991, 115–6), significantly termed a *cumal*.

In contrast to these payments from free tenants, the estate owner's bond tenants, *taeogs*, had the far heavier duties of the upkeep of certain royal officials; the falconer, huntsmen, grooms and their horses, and the reeve. This was done though gifts of food: bacon, bread, oats (for the horses), butter, cheese, honey and ale, and in addition they had to construct and repair the chief dwelling, with hall, chamber, kitchen, chapel, barn, kiln, latrines, stable and dog kennel (Jones 1971). In time of war they provided packhorses, each *tref* also supplying one man with horses and hatchet to make encampments. Furthermore, where there was arable land in plenty, the *taeogs* of the neighbouring hamlets owed labour services, ploughing, mowing, harvesting, at first light, but as time went on heavier, and in some cases the tenants of a *maerdref* owed dayworks resembling those of an English manor. These duties were arranged though the court of the *maerdref*, the 'halmote' in Durham terminology (Rees 1924, 11–14). In origin then, cornage was an ancient rent. It was as Reid notes 'paid by all free landholders from baron to bondager', a subtle recognition that whatever burdens were imposed upon them the northern bondager was personally free (Reid 1920, 186). Linked with this is the fact that there are complex and subtle links, not to be examined at length here, between cornage payment and a form of pre-feudal military duty known as *endemot*, that appears to underlie the concept of border service (Reid 1920, 187–8; VCH Cu. I, 318 ff).

This diversion into Welsh and Irish sources must now be focussed upon the Durham evidence. In Durham *cornage* was owed on the feast of St. Cuthbert (September 4th) while another payment, *methreth*, probably implying a milch cow and her follower, paid on the feast of St Martin, November 11th. Martinmas was traditionally the time for the beginning of the autumn slaughter of stock that could not be carried through the winter. Cornage was paid by all tenants, while milch cow – a term to be used from now on – was due from the bondsmen of each vill. The Irish evidence gives us a glimpse of what must have been involved. Milch cow was a rent of cattle, mature cattle, over four years old, already having carried a calf. Productive of milk, cheese and butter, and with the capacity to generate more, they were stock at maximum value and proven fertility, so that these cows had the potential for continued production of more calves, butter and cheese until they were about seven years old (Kelly 1991, 113, note 97). These precious animals were associated with the husbanded care of the steading and inner pastures close to the inby lands. Cornage, in contrast, represented a payment upon stores, beasts from the outer pastures, running semi-wild amid the reserves of the wider grazing lands (Patterson 1994, 95–6). Some of the dry-heifers from this herd could eventually be put to the bull to bear calves, becoming milch cows, while the surplus males, castrated bullocks, were suitable for training as work oxen, with the residue representing beasts for slaughter, giving meat, hides, horn, and tallow. Such stock were no doubt the focus of cattle raids by young warriors from adjacent communities.

In such a cattle economy the control of the bulls was an important component, for if they were allowed to run in the wild grazings, then feral herds would emerge. Surplus bulls in the waste were no doubt deliberately hunted, for control of the bulls was crucial to the control of the cattle of the wildernesses unless the herd was to go feral. The white wild park cattle of Chillingham and other localities surely represent the final remnants of such herds, in this case selected with reference to their colour to create parkland cattle. Not only were such beasts paid in compensation for an insult to a Welsh king, they were also sacred to St. Bridget, while Hemming points out that 'Cnut's Forest Laws' refer to *bubali* (literally 'buffalo') and *vaccae, i.e.* cows. As there have never been buffalo in Britain the former were beasts of a different sort, perhaps the wild bulls of the forest, for some uncastrated bulls must have escaped to form a feral nucleus (Hemming 2002; Kelly 1998, 33–4). Significantly, in 1647 in the Bishop of Durham's park at Auckland there were 'Wild bulles or Bisons' (*sic*), *i.e.* beasts not obviously related to domesticated stock. Again these – two or three lonely animals – must have been survivors of the wild and semi-wild stock of the great waste pastures (Kirby 1971, 3).

In summary, cornage was a render from the wild lands and milch cow from the tamed lands. Both milch cow and cornage were, when coin was available in sufficient quantities, commuted to cash. However varied in detail, however adjusted to the local calendar, these were ancient payments, pre-feudal, and originating in a pre-monetary economy. Patterson, using Irish materials, provides a superb image of a settlement such as can be seen in Figure 5.2:

> there appears a classification of social space in terms of the likely frequency with which the settlement's inhabitants would venture there. The old classification begins with the house, then proceeds to the *cathair* (enclosure) and on to the *faithche* (fields), the *raite* (common pastures), the *rofida* (great forest, *i.e.* not coppice) and the *sliab* (moor or mountain). In the commentary, the pasture is referred to as *sechter faithche* (outer *faithche*): these lands were depicted as far as the limits of a cow's grazing before it turned home for milking, or as far as the sound of a bell could be heard (on monastic lands…), or the crowing of a cock. Lands that lay beyond, *i.e.* the forest, moor or mountain, were viewed as unsafe areas, into which livestock and implements should not be taken, and where animals were unlikely to be found if they strayed (1994, 111).

Of course, through these outer spaces came cattle and slave raiders, preying upon the established agricultural communities (Fig. 6.4.b). The location of the vills in the Bishop of Durham's lands that rendered cornage and milch cow in 1183, or which were specifically exempt, presumably because of local conditions or agreements (an interesting insight), form a distinctive swathe of settlements spread through southern and eastern Durham (Fig. 2.6 inset). Logically, whatever the archaeological evidence, and it is thin, this distribution tells of the settled lands at a remote period – by the later Iron Age? – and of cattle rendered to superior lords from hamlets and extensive rough pastures inhabited by free tribesmen and bond tenants. Significantly, Marijke van der Veen, using later prehistoric and Romano-British palynological evidence identified a contrast between intensive, small scale agriculture north of the Tyne and larger scale arable expansion in the Tees lowlands (Van der Veen 1992, 147–48). It is evident that with cornage and milch cow renders we are touching a period when the upland open and wood pastures were so massive that they dominated western Durham on a scale even greater than is seen in Figures 2.5 and 2.6. The settlement associated with this chronological level is, we may deduce, now wholly invisible, having largely disappeared from the long-ploughed landscape. However, in order to push this analysis further, a laboratory is needed, a shire whose geographical content can be subjected to more detailed dissection. Two of these will be examined: in this chapter Aucklandshire, one of the of the great western territorial blocks granted to St Cuthbert and in the next chapter, Heighingtonshire, set within the anciently settled and cultivated zone of the county (Figs 6.2 and 6.3).

The Nature of Aucklandshire

The place-name 'Auckland' is of Celtic origin (Watts 2002, 9–10), and while the actual territorial extent of the shire has never been fully documented it is evident that it did involve far more territory than the four vills listed in Boldon Book. The case for this conclusion is strong: in 1183 the bondsmen of the four Aucklandshire vills, North Auckland, West Auckland, Escomb and Newton Cap, had the collective duty of building a hall for the Bishop 'in the forest' (Greenwell 1852, 23–26, 60–62). This comprised a hall, 60 feet long and 16 feet wide between the posts, with a buttery and service hatch, together with a chamber, a privy, and a chapel 40 feet in length and 15 feet wide, with an enclosing fence around the buildings. This forest hall, was by 1183, a hunting lodge, built in the hill country of Weardale for the Bishop's use. However, the bondsmen of Aucklandshire were only building half of the lodge, and the suite of buildings was completed by the bondsmen of Stanhope in Weardale, who constructed 'a kitchen, larder, and dog kennel for the great hunts', added a settle in the hall, and found 'litter for the hall, chapel and chamber'. They also rendered carrying duties between Stanhope and Durham and Auckland, and between Wolsingham and the lodges, *logeas*, a plural word (*ibid*. 29, 64). The Aucklandshire tenants made their part of the fence around the lodges, they guarded the eyries of the hawks in the district of Ralph the Crafty (at Frosterley), and built 18 booths at the fairs of St. Cuthbert. In short, the services of the bondage tenants of Aucklandshire and Stanhope were complimentary. This strongly implies that Stanhope was a part of Aucklandshire, indeed the inclusion of Wolsingham in the carrying services strongly suggests that North (later Bishop) Aucklandshire extended up the Wear valley, from the great hall at Bishop Auckland to the hills of Weardale, embracing the territory that became the vast parish of Stanhope. In the light of the possible pre-Conquest origin of the shire, perhaps even pre-Anglo-Saxon, it is no surprise that this distinctive list of buildings is most closely paralleled in tenth century law codes from Wales:

> There are nine houses which it is right for the King's villeins (*sic*) to make: hall, chamber, food-house, stable, porch, barn, kiln, latrine, dormitory or sleep-house.
>
> (Jenkins 2000, 41)

In Wales as in Durham *taeogs*, villans, or bondage tenants did the work, but the slightly different assemblage of structures probably reflects time, local custom, the exigencies of translation and the fact that the *aulam*… in *foresta* was specifically for the *magnas cazas*, the great hunts in the forest of Weardale. A kiln was not needed. The Welsh structures were probably stone-girt courts, but by the twelfth century the Bishop no longer needed peasant skills to construct his residence – he used professional masons – and the tenant service was relegated to the building of a rustic lodge.

Figures 6.5.a and 6.5.b reconstruct the likely extent of Aucklandshire: the lowland section is taken to be the ancient parish of St. Andrew Auckland, and the upland portion involves the parishes of Wolsingham and Stanhope, in all some 273,200 ha (683,000 acres). This is not to argue that this territory has not varied through time. To give concrete cases, those sections of Evenwood and Barony, West Auckland and Lutterington and St. Helen's Auckland south of the Gaunless were probably acquired from Staindropshire between 1031 and 1183 (Hart 1975, 127). In a document of 1031 Evenwood, *Alclit* (in this case probably West Auckland) and Lutteringtun are described as dependencies of Staindrop (Hart 1975, 127). The Hatfield Survey confirms this link by revealing that part of Staindrop glebe, the parson's farm, lay in West Auckland (Greenwell 1857, 31). Significantly this latter village is the only major settlement of the estate core 'Auckland' to lie south of the Gaunless, and confirmation that such acquisitions were possible is found in adjacent place-name 'Copeland', derived from an old Norse technical term meaning 'the purchased land' (Watts 2002, 29). As Newton Cap (*i.e.* 'the new village') lies north of the Wear it may be that the heart of Aucklandshire once lay between the rivers Wear and Gaunless. Eldon and Thickley were also once linked to Staindrop and it is evident that we are here dealing with an area of debatable ground, probably largely common waste, between the territories

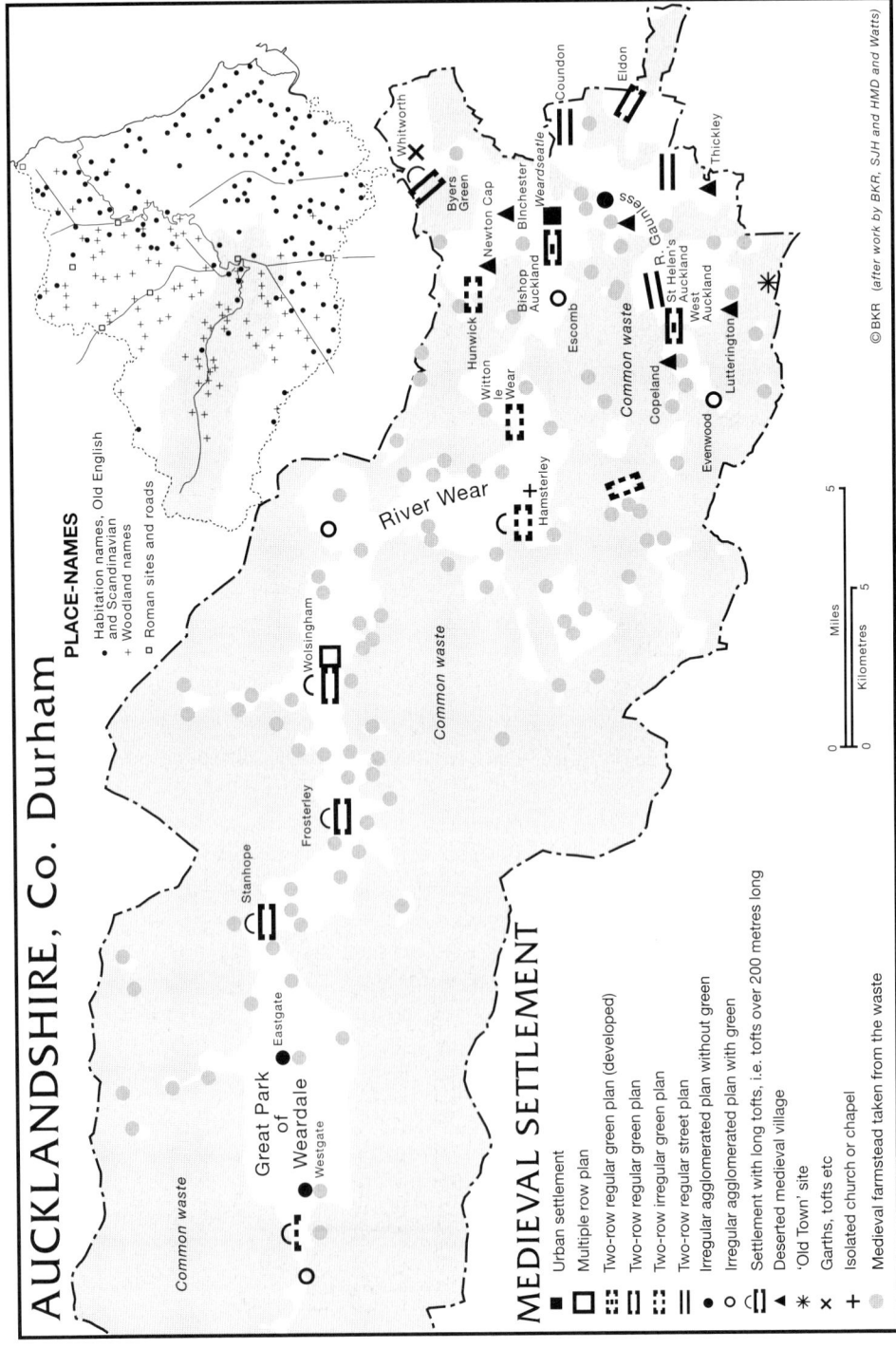

Fig. 6.5.a Medieval settlement in Aucklandshire, County Durham

Estates and Shires 175

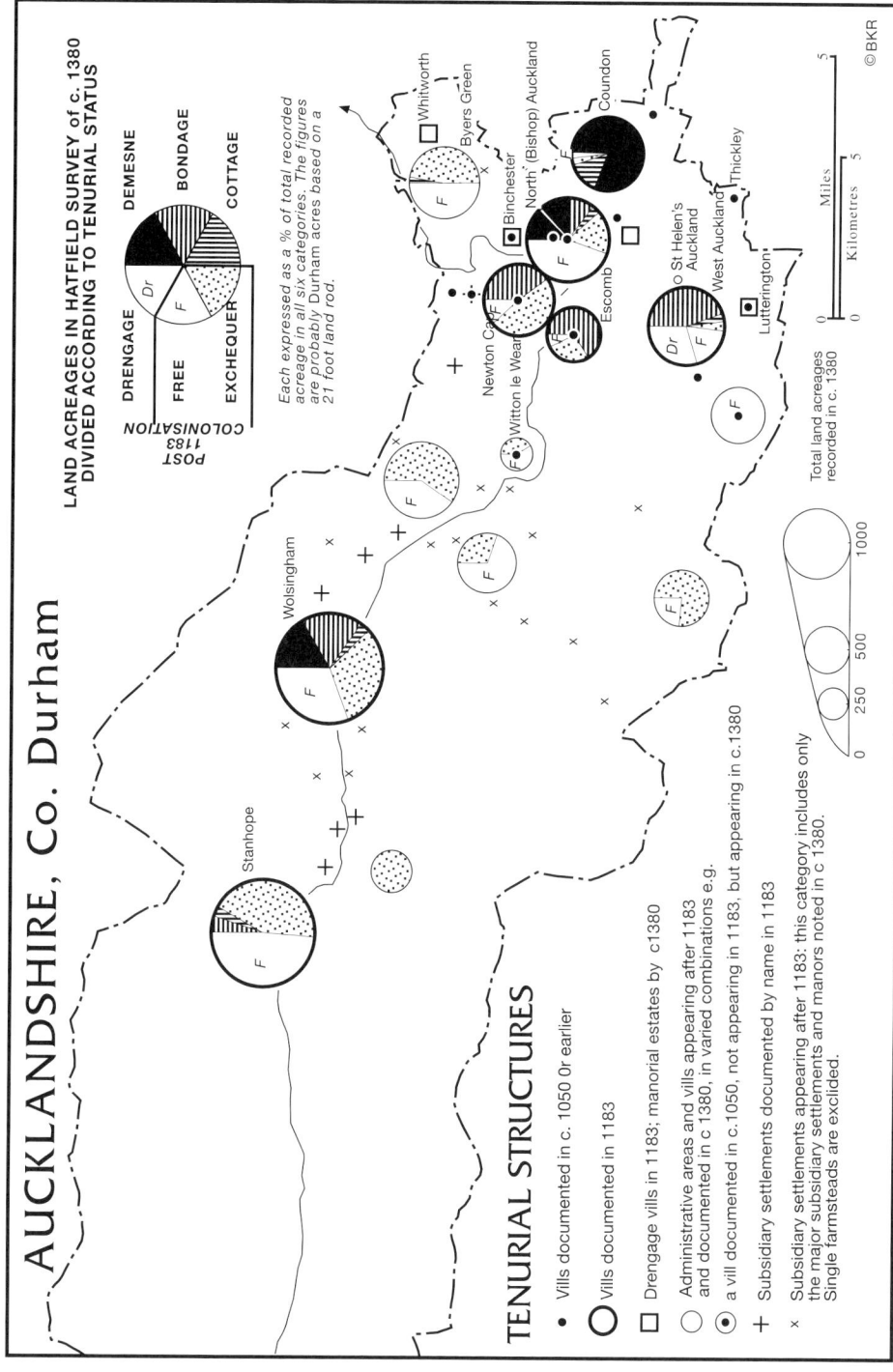

Fig. 6.5.b *Medieval tenurial structures in Aucklandshire, County Durham*

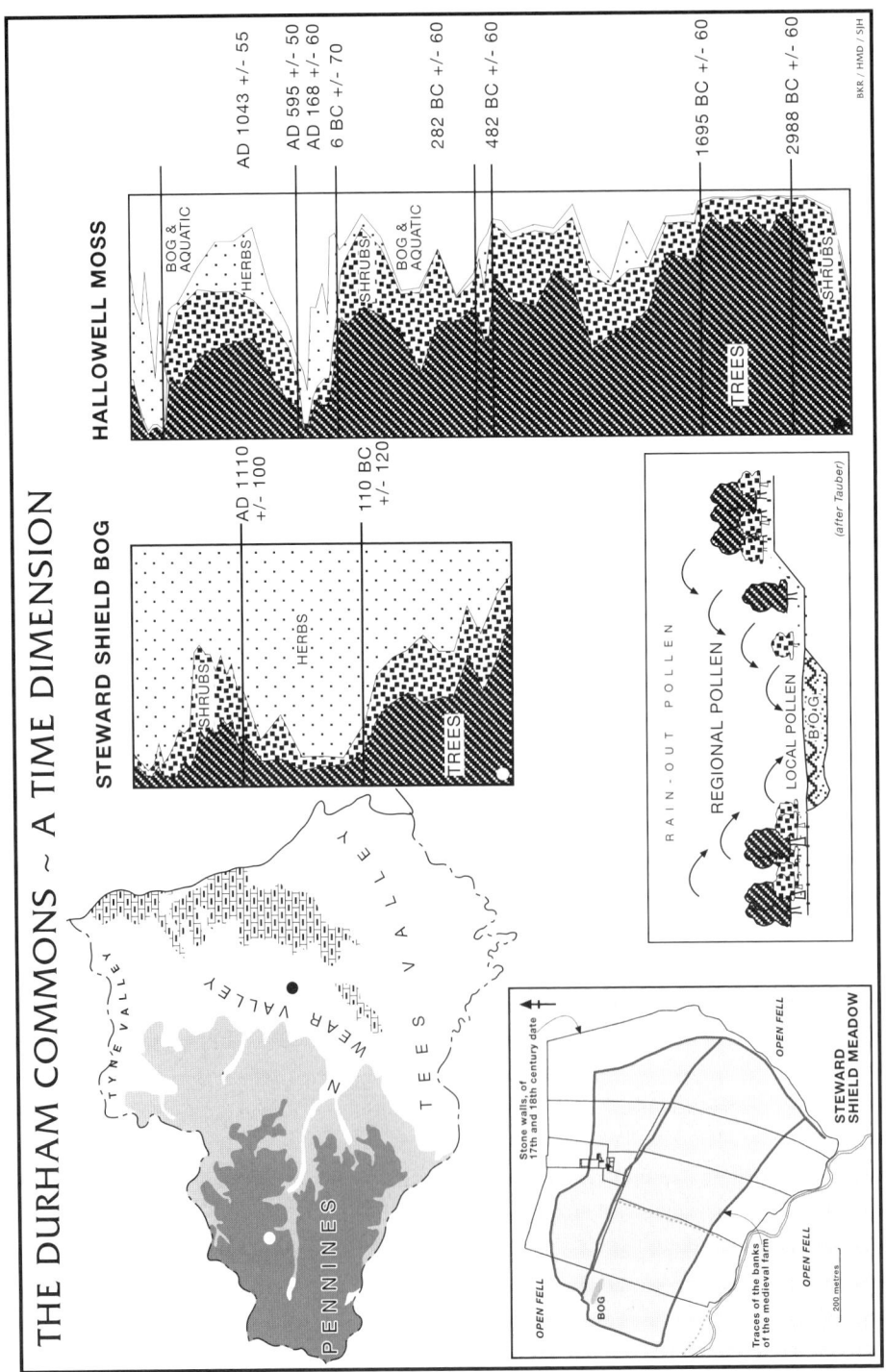

Fig. 6.6 The Durham commons: a time dimension

of Staindropshire, Aucklandshire and Heighingtonshire (Hart 1975, 127; Fig. 7.1 below).

In Figure 6.5.a the detail of Aucklandshire has been projected upon a background that shows the extent of the waste and the farmsteads carved from this between 1150 and 1350 (see Fig. 2.5). Admittedly the focus is by no means sharp for 1150, but the distinction between the lowland core of the shire and the massive tract of the upland section is wholly evident, a glimpse of settlement reality. A pollen diagram from Steward Shield Meadow shows that by the later Iron Age the rolling swells and plateau surfaces of the uplands had largely been cleared of their Scots pine forest (Fig. 6.6). As the diagram from Hallowell Moss suggests it is probable that the foothill zone and dale sides of western Durham were more wooded in 1150 than they had been in the Roman period or are at the present day. In Boldon Book the listing of 'turners' at Wolsingham, the locating of the great hunt in the dale to take the deer, and the presence of the eyries of hawks in the care of Ralph the Crafty at Frosterley provide sharp but indirect images of this. Many centuries earlier wild boar had been taken in Bollihope valley, while the presence of wild cattle is possible. In Figure 6.5.b the tenurial structures of the vills are summarised, emphasising the contrast between those at the core of the estate and those in its body.

The first known list of Aucklandshire vills appears in an entry referring to the Bishopric of Ealdhun, 995 x 1006 and records the granting of two groups of villages, probably two small shires, to St. Cuthbert (Hart 1975, 125). One is based upon Gainford, the other, Aucklandshire, and comprises '*Aclit ij* (two Aucklands), *Copland* (Copeland in West Auckland), *Weardseatle* ('the guarded seat', possibly the ridge top site of the later palace at North Auckland and *not* Warsall near Yarm), *Bynceastre* (Binchester), *Cuthberteston* (concievably the church site at South Church, Auckland rather than Cotherstone in North Yorkshire, see Watts 2002, 32)), *Thicclea* (Thickley, part of the debateable ground between Aucklandshire and Heighingtonshire, see Fig.7.1), *Ediscum* (Escomb, the site of a standing seventh century church, Fig. 3.4), *Wuduton* (Witton le Wear), *Hunewic* (Hunwick), *Newatun* (Newton Cap), and *Healme* (Helmington)'. These settlements are confined to the lower lands around the junction of the Wear and Gaunless, the most westerly being Witton-le-Wear (Fig. 6.5.b). The vills of this list are shown by a means of a small black dot at the centre of the other symbols. Several of these identifications differ from those made by the editor of the *Historia de Sancto Cuthberto* and Cyril Hart, but this interpretation is fully in accord with the evidence and creates a structural coherence in the list that is otherwise absent.

Turning to the services incumbent upon the chief vills of this estate, the entry for Bishop or North Auckland can be summarised as follows:

North Auckland
Twenty-two villans, full status farmers, each holding 1 bovate (each 20 acres of land, but probably measured with a twenty-one foot land rod, in all about 32 statute acres).

These render – we must assume collectively:
1. 2 chalders (measures) of oat-malt,
   one *wheit* of malt by exchequer measure
   one *wheit* of meal,
   one *wheit* of oats.
   > By 1380 these measures of grain above are recorded as '*buz. cumulatam*', probably implying 'heaped bushels', and as late as the first two decades of the twentieth century a 'weigh' or 'wey' was equal to 40 bushels (McConnell, 1904, 38; *ibid.* 1922, 43).
2. 8 pence of *averpenny*, a commutation of carriage for the lord by horse or ox
3. 19 pence of *cornage*
4. one hen and ten eggs
5. 3 cartloads of *woodlades* (presumably 'man sized' bundles of fuelwood) if they are carted to Auckland but 2.5 cartloads if they bear them to Durham.
6. The whole vill renders one *milch cow*.
7. Work service, from the Feast of St. Peter in Chains (1st August) to the Feast of St, Martin (11th November) 2 days each week, and from the Feast of St, Martin to the Feast of St, Peter in Chains one day a week, plus four days of boon work in the autumn, 'with all the house except the housewife'.
8. Every one of the ploughs of the town (*i.e.* the vill) ploughs and harrows two acres and a half over and above their work.

These are heavy grain renders, while the heavy labour services support the lord's home farm, the demesne. While this nominally lay in Coundon, where in 1183 the bishop had six ploughs with pasture and sheep, in practice the boundaries of this township and that of Bishop Auckland were interwoven (Greenwell 1857, 36–38, 41–43). In both Escomb and Newton Cap the villans – they are called bondagers by 1381 – hold, render and work 'as the villans of North Auckland', and the Hatfield Survey of 1381 that tells us they also paid cornage and milch cow. In all these cases it appears that heavy work services (items 7 and 8) have been grafted into renders that were more allied to ancient food renders and services (items 1 to 6) making very heavy burdens indeed.

At this point it is worth a brief review of the services of servile peasants. Seebohm summarises three categories of these:

- first, *gafol*, *i.e.* 'tributes in money and in kind and in work at ploughing etc., and in the nature rather of rent, rates and taxes than anything else' (Seebohm 1896, 140–1);
- second, *precariae* or *bene* (boon) work for the lord of the estate, extra and special services, agricultural, building and the like, and
- third, regular week work, generally limited to certain days a week according to the season.

He demonstrates that these three categories are present in the services rendered by villan holders of post-Domesday virgates, in the *Recitudines Singularum Personarum* of the eleventh century, and that there are echoes of the same differentiation in earlier centuries, for instance a law of Ine of Wessex, of about AD 690, states that

> If anyone covenants for a yardland or more at a fixed rent (*gafol*), and ploughs it, if the lord wishes to increase for him (the rent of the) land by demanding service (*weorc*) as well as rent, he need not accept it, if he (*i.e.* the lord) does not give him a dwelling: and he is to forfeit the crops.
> (Seebohm 1896, 142–3; Whitelock 1955, law 67)

It seems inherently probable that Seebohm's simple list represents a gradation from the personal services due to the 'chief', however he be styled, to the rents payable to the landlord, of whatever status. The accretion of individual elements must have a temporal context, and was probably extremely variable in both time and space. All three elements are found in the North Auckland list. This hypothesis suggesting accreted layers is in no way at variance with the gradual increase in the burdens upon the peasantry nor indeed with the assimilation of many and varied types of localised renders, service and tenure into the categories finally recognised by the Anglo-Norman lawyers. Sir Paul Vinogradoff in his study of *Villeinage in England* (1892, reprinted 1963) recognised varied categories of

- cash payments, these latter often, perhaps even normally, representing the commutation of older renders (*ibid.* 288–312). He was acutely aware that this plethora of work services, renders and rents represented elements 'which belonged to different localities and perhaps to different epochs' (*ibid.* 295);
- renders in kind, corn, honey, ale, stock, poultry and eggs, and noted that these were 'the most archaic form of arranging the relationship between a lord and his subjects';
- agricultural labour services, including several types of ploughing, reaping and carriage duties.

What is undoubtedly needed is a broad analysis of the variability of villan, villein and bondage services not only between manors but in varied geographical localities and at varied periods of time. These were not themes that Seebohm, nor indeed Vinogradoff, were able to pursue in any great detail, a comment that too easily dismisses these vast and impressive pioneer foundation works. It seems to the present author that the periods during which there were social pressures bringing tenurial change are the same crucial periods during which settlement may also have been undergoing rapid development. The decades after the Norman Conquest must have been one such time, but the Viking raids and settlement and the advent of new forms of taxation and royal control must have been another. Even if one only alights on one factor that may have increased the use of '*weorc*', labour, as a form of rent for land, the extraction of vast amounts of bullion, either directly as loot and eventually as more formal Danegeld must at least be considered. To carry the argument forward, this may account for the imposition on the Cuthbertine estates of the standardised 'and they work as they of Boldon'. A possible chronology for the establishment of this formula will be considered in the Chapter 8.

To return to the Durham scene, Auckland must incorporate the British name of the estate. '*Allt clüd*' is identical with the name given by Bede to Dumbarton rock, 'the cliff on the river Clyde'. Victor Watts makes the rational suggestion that this is the pre-Scandinavian name for the Gaunless, because the name of the Wear is itself also a pre-Anglo-Saxon river name (Watts 2002, 9–10). The place-name must apply to the high ridge that now bears the Bishop's palace. Escomb, with its ancient church and enigmatic circular churchyard, incorporates an Old English dative plural *ediscum,* and the exact meaning of *edisc* in Old English is unclear: 'Park', 'deerpark', 'pasture' and 'estate', even perhaps 'fallow' are all possible (*ibid.* 40; Seebohm 1896, 376–80). The present author would opt for 'at the pasture' – which may show signs of former tillage – as the most likely derivation, *i.e.* the settlement placed between an area dominated by inby land, cultivated and improved, and the vast sea of waste, a temperate savanna, extending up and up to the high ridges of the Pennines. In effect the church is sited on the edge of the hunting ground, to be resorted to by a seventh century local ruler when the demands of the church drew him and his entourage from the pleasures of the chase.

But is *Newton Cap* a settlement paying ancient renders? The adjective *neowe* is wholly clear, 'new', 'newly built', 'newly acquired', 'newly cultivated', 'newly reclaimed from the waste', a solid Old English word still in common currency. "Newton" implies a 'new settlement'; the second element reflects a thirteenth century tenant. Ekwall shows that the word *neowe* is documented in AD 956, 943 and 938 (Ekwall 1960, 341–2). There are two possibilities here. First, that the name was a replacement name for an older one, perhaps generated when formerly tenants were congregated at a single locus, or second, tenants may have been moved out of an original location, to Newton. One possibility is from *Weardseatle,* 'the guard house', the watch house', often implying a lofty location, which must surely apply to the high ridge on which Auckland Castle, the great hall of the Bishops of Durham still sits. Perhaps this also involved the expansion of the demesne. However, there are other possible explanations to be explored below, but postulating a move shows that there need be no conflict here with the 'new village' being north of the Wear: the tenants merely moved to fields that had already been taken from the waste. Do we have a date? The Boldon Book entry is concise: 'In Newton are 13 villans (a curious number), who hold, render and work in all ways as the villans of North Auckland'. In this case there are no clutters of extra tenancies, the holding of individuals with special ministerial duties and the like. All is crisp and sharp and we can argue, in the light of this updated administrative record, that the move took place not that long before the creation of Boldon Book in 1183, and may have been linked with the construction of the Norman hall of the Bishop's palace on the old site. The present structure appears to have been built for Bishop Hugh du Puiset, later in his episcopate and may not have been completed before he died. Stone fragments from a building dating from the 1160s and 1170s have been recovered. An earlier Norman hall, perhaps of timber, may be assumed (Cunningham in Fernie and Crossley, 1990, 82, 87). The fact that *Neowatun* appears in a lost charter of 995 x 1006 cited by Symeon of Durham, the published copy being of the late twelfth century, need not be fatal to this argument (Craster 1954, 177). In the period between 1068 and 1183 the arrival of Newton only needed a wholly 'legitimate' adjustment made to an older settlement listing!

However, there is a second possibility, perhaps more feasible than a move from *Weardseatle*. Little Coundon, a settlement of cotmen, 'cottagers' owes heavy works, each tenant having only six acres of land of their own, but owing the work services of North Auckland (item 7) and in addition a render of one hen and 100 eggs. No cornage and no milch cow are due from this place, and we must presume that these are labourers whose primary duties were to serve the demesne and supplement the labour force needed on the home farm. Once again, the entry in 1183 lists no other tenures, although free tenures and exchequer tenancies do appear by *c.* 1380. This again implies a 'new' development somewhat before 1183. However, the demesne already occupied the whole township of Coundon, termed Great Coundon, in 1183. The place-name may mean 'cows hill', a perfectly sound name for the limestone pastures on which the settlement sits, that were certainly used for sheep in 1183. However, as Victor Watts points out the name could be primitive Welsh in origin, **cöned*, of unknown meaning. In the light of this, it is distinctly possible that the inhabitants of Newton Cap were moved from an earlier settlement at Great Coundon at some date between the 1070s, the effective Norman Conquest of the region and 1183. This could have been done in order to substantially expand the demesne, a demesne that eventually spread into North (now Bishop) Auckland township. While the distance between Coundon Grange and Newton Cap is of the order of four or five miles, the author has met former miners who regularly walked seven miles to work and back again, day in and day out! New fields could have been opened, preparatory to a move, particularly if the labour services of the rest of the core vills were brought to bear. A move could have been achieved in perhaps two or three years and the ancient renders were translated with the tenants.

This picture possesses a convincing coherence. But there are other ancient core vills. West Auckland is one and its services are listed below:

West Auckland
1. 18 villans with 18 oxgangs render for each oxgang 5s.
2. they all find in the autumn from each oxgang 3 men in a week to mow, and they cut the whole meadow and make hay and lead it: for this they have a corrody, *i.e.* food, sustenance.

3. they carry corn for two days, and
4. render 18 hens and 180 eggs and
5. they render one milch cow
6. carry three cartloads (perhaps of grain; Greenwell 1857, 31, although wood is also possible) between Tyne and Tees.
7. Lodge building services, noted earlier, were incumbent upon the four core vills of the shire.

There are in addition numerous subsidiary tenures, the holders of which clearly offer ministerial or special services to the Bishop. These will be considered later. Overall these renders and services are significantly lighter than those owed by the other core vills and the week work is notably absent. A possible reason for this is to be found in the fact that in 1031, a single *Alclit*, was part of a vill list associated with Staindrop and its appendages and at this time the Gaunless was probably the boundary between the two estates (Hart 1975, 127). The transfer of vills between Staindropshire and Aucklandshire has already been noted and a reminder of this earlier link is to be found in 1381, for the Hatfield Survey notes that part of the Staindrop glebe, one messuage and sixteen acres of land, no doubt one bovate, lay within West Auckland. In this case, only a milch cow is paid by the tenants, and the week work has a different quality to the heavy grain renders and lighter work services owed by the tenants of North Auckland. Is this variation a product of acquisition of 'already settled land' in West Auckland – implied by the glebe land – for a new but expanding foundation and hence the imposition of a cash rent and light services on each tenant. In passing, one hopes the 180 eggs were fresh! Not all were for eating of course, the white having uses in manuscript production. Overall, however, the contrast between the two tenurial profiles raises important questions. The contrasting spectra of renders, services and work must in some way relate to the evolution of settlement, and if in the same time horizon the renders from West Auckland seem more 'primitive' than those of North Auckland and the other core vills, then part at least of the answer must be found in its peripherality.

One further lowland vill needs considering; the services are as follows:

Binchester
1. *Cornage* and *milch cow* and one castleman.
    The latter represents an element of military service that often runs with cornage (Reid 1920, 187–88).
2. A render of 4 scatchalders of malt,
    4 scatchalders of meal,
    4 scatchalders of oats
    (a volumetric grain measure used by the Bishop's exchequer, literally *scat-chalder*)
3. Work services: each villan ploughs and harrows two acres at Coundon, and makes

3 boon days in the autumn, with one man for each oxgang, and
4. carts one ton of wine and a millstone to Auckland.
5. Finally,
'The dreng feeds a dog and a horse, and attends the great chase with 2 greyhounds and 5 ropes and follows the pleas (*i.e.* attends court) and goes on messages'.

We may note how this pattern of services locks into the support of the demesne at Coundon and the great hunt in the dales, while retaining the two perhaps most ancient renders of cornage and milch cow. However, the name gives a clue to the importance of this place. Lying no more than a mile to the north of the medieval estate centre at North (Bishop) Auckland, Binchester was an important Roman site. The place-name implies the 'settlement within the Roman fort' or 'the cattle-stall fort'. There may be a link between the Roman name, *Vinovia* and the later name but it would be unwise to labour this. Recent finds at the site have produced a 6th century pagan Anglo-Saxon burial (Watts 2002, 9). It is noted by the Greek geographer Ptolemy as *Vinovium* or *Vinnovium* (Rivet 1979, 504–5), who terms it a 'city' of the Brigantes (Dobson in Dewdney 1970, 195). There is evidence that a *beneficarius consularis* lived within the fort, a posting that often took place along roads leading to frontier regions, as if their responsibilities included the transmission of intelligence to military headquarters and perhaps also the supervision of supply (Frere 1996, 185, 202). The fort was at one stage occupied by the *ala Vettonum*, a cavalry unit, whose medical officer left an altar providing us with the information (Johnson 1983, 161). In short, Bishop Auckland and its immediate vicinity represent, to use Everitt's evocative term, a 'seminal place', and a place 'where things happen'. Curiously enough, neither Bishop nor West Auckland possess an important church: the church focus of the estate lies about two miles to the south-east of the palace site, at a location now enigmatically termed 'South Church', properly St. Andrew's church of Auckland' (Watts 2002, 115). As Watts notes the *Cuthbertstun* of the pre-Conquest charter is not in fact Cotherston. Looking for this lost place within the orbit of the reconstructed Aucklandshire, South Church offers the most likely solution. The present impressive structure was begun in 1292 as a collegiate church, but contains fragments of a late eighth or ninth century decorated stone cross, perhaps with stylistic affinities to Midland examples (Pevsner 1985, 413; Cramp 1984, 37–41).

The remaining vills of the lowland section of Aucklandshire (Figure 6.5) comprise Lutterington, Whitworth, Hunwick, Byers Green and (Greenwell 1852, 27, 62–63). However, a second group of villages present in 1183 can be attributed to 'Aucklandshire' on the grounds that the tenants of one of them, Stanhope, also owe lodge-building services, and these services complement those of the four named vills of the shire. All are found to the west, in Weardale comprising Wolsingham and Stanhope with their subsidiary hamlets such as Thornley, Rogerley, and Frosterley. As different levels of work services are appended and as none pays cornage or milch cow, there is a strong indication that, as villages, these are relative latecomers to the rural scene. The Old

English place-names imply, however, that there were more ancient roots. At Wolsingham the villans pay for their 300 acres a substantial fixed rent, *i.e.* their lands are 'at farm', but they also owe mowing services, carting services, and an unspecified 180 days of other 'work', a substantial burden. There are in addition numerous other holdings, held for ministerial services, forest service, bee-keeping, going on errands, acting as bailiff, shepherd, pinder, carpenter for ploughs, and wood turning (Greenwell 1852, 27, 63). It is clear that three demesne at Wolsingham, Rogerley and Broadwood were being serviced; although by 1183 the first two were being leased out, and were producing wheat, barley and oats. Wolsingham is Old English, implying 'the place called after Wulfsige'. Stanhope – 'the stony side-valley' – was in 1183 inhabited by 20 villans or bondsmen (Watts 2002, 141–2, 118). Their works involved only 16 days, with one man, between Whit Sunday and November 11th, with some boon works and carting and carrying, between Stanhope and Wolsingham, carrying venison to Durham and Auckland and carrying provisions to the lodges, presumably when the great hunt was in progress. With the tenants of Aucklandshire these tenants construct the great lodge for the hunts, and also construct the mill dam and cart the millstones. These are by no means light services, but they are not the heavy week work of the core villages of the shire. There is an emphasis on carting items the Bishops needed down the dale. The cartage duties to Auckland and Durham were no doubt often onerous, but they did give the tenants involved a view of the wider world that would have otherwise remained unseen. The new Norman cathedral and castle must have been a revelation to the rustics of the dales and woodlands. The remaining tenants are mainly, as at Wolsingham, ministerial, offering to the Bishop a variety of services: various sorts of forest service, some works, smith service, weaving, acting as bailiff, and even marble cutting, no doubt exploiting the dark fossiliferous pseudo-marble of Frosterley. Ralf the Crafty, the falconer who kept the eyries of the hawks, held Frosterley – 'the forester's portion of a clearing called the Lee' (Watts 2002, 46) – and also had 12 acres of arable land in Stanhope. However, a significant proportion of the miscellaneous entries mention toft holders, tenants who merely hold a house-plot and sometimes a few acres. Widows hold three of these tofts, but four without houses are in the Bishop's hand, although they render a few pence, presumably for their grazing or garden cultivation. Scammell in his short but vivid description of west Durham, 'where mountain pasture alternated with wolf ridden forest' captures the setting of these upland settlements (Scammell 1956, 212). Figure 2.5 can only serve to emphasise his fundamental point.

Aucklandshire Core Villages: Plan Morphology

North or Bishop Auckland emerged into history as a market town (Beresford and Finberg 1973, 105). The 'castle' site, still the Bishop's palace, forms a separate enclave, the putative *Weardseatle* of the early document. To the west of this along the ridge, is a square, a planned market space, but further west lay a green village, a regular two row plan. Still called Bondgate it is undoubtedly where the villan tenants once had their farmsteads. A new suburb, Newgate extends southwards along the line of the Dere Street, *i.e.* the paved Roman road running southwards to Deira, a polity based upon the Yorkshire Wolds and one locus of the territory that eventually became Northumbria. These plan components are impossible to date although the temporal sequence is clear, but there is no inherent reason why they should not be Norman, associated with the post-Conquest development of the estate centre around the Bishop Hugh du Puiset's great hall. In contrast, the form of South Church is uncertain, but the churchyard is essentially oval, although with a vastly elongated tail, set on a small ridge above the Gaunless. Escomb also focuses upon its oval churchyard, with a ring-way around it, so that the church appears set upon a green. Nineteenth century maps and air photographs hint at an underlying structural radiality, closely paralled in Celtic sites that are regarded as ancient (O'Sullivan in Baldwin and Whyte 1985, 31–2). Escomb, arranged around the curvilinear churchyard (Fig. 3.4), may in fact be one of the oldest surviving plans in the county. There is no nucleation at Newton Cap and air photographs show no traces of earthworks. Coundon survived onto nineteenth century maps as a rather irregular two row street plan, and is now overbuilt completely. West Auckland is the dramatic site. It is the biggest green village in the county, vast, with a six hectare (15 acre) green, wedge-shaped, with a marked head-row at its western end. It has the look and the feel of a market town that has failed to develop. The tenurial structure in 1183 was already so complex that comment on this arrangement must be deferred to a later chapter.

The Old English names suggest that none of these settlements were in any complete sense 'new' in 1183. Foci for eventual growth had long existed, but what could be new were the actual village plans. Thus, the tofts, particularly those without houses and still in the Bishop's hands, hint that the settlement at Stanhope was being expanded at the time of the compilation of Boldon Book. How does this relate to the general morphology of the upland settlements? At Stanhope and Frosterley it appears that the forms are based upon rows, strung along terraces, with tofts of the order of 200 metres in length rising up the well-drained south facing slopes behind. In the case of Stanhope, however, the sheer number of individuals listed in 1183 suggests that the place had already moved beyond this simple structure to something more complex. A perceptive suggestion by Peter Bowes that the present back lane may then have been a toft frontage line, and that development down slope of this, including the Norman church and its churchyard, appeared upon a former broad open green that may even have extended to the river. Wolsingham is much more complex because it did achieve, as did Stanhope, market town status (Whelan 1894, 413, 431–2).

Finally, there is an as yet unmentioned element associated with the core vills of Aucklandshire, the neat little village of St. Helen's Auckland, just north of the Gaunless and West Auckland's great spread. Nevertheless, the place cannot be 'found' either in Boldon Book or the Hatfield Survey. Three things are quite remarkable about it. First, nineteenth century maps suggest that the plan was at least as regular as that at East

Boldon (Fig. 2.7). Second, a later twelfth century church is built into the northern compartment of the plan, suggesting that it is contemporary with the layout. Third, St. Helens is not documented by name until 1242 (Watts 2002, 107). Nevertheless, it is possible that St. Helen's Auckland was in fact a planned settlement for the villans. This probably took place in the middle decades of the twelfth century, while West Auckland represents a subsidiary accretion, south of the Gaunless and rather marginal to Episcopal lands, where free tenancies could multiply after 1183 (Greenwell 1857, 29–30, where 13 messuages are described as *Tenentes in Dringagio* in 1381 yet are not listed in 1183). This development took place around a tract of open common, perhaps accounting for the vast 15 acre (6 ha.) green at West Auckland.

Turning finally to the remaining settlements lying in Aucklandshire as defined in Figure 6.5 but not all mapped, these fall into several categories:

Present in 1183 in the shire core:
> Lutterington, Henknowle, Whitworth, Binchester (already discussed), Byers and Harperley.

Listed in 1381 in the shire core:
> Binchester, Hunwick, Byres (Geffrey – later 'Green'), Whitworth, Aldpark, Henknowll (all being part of North Auckland), Witton le Wear (including Fychewacke and Ednesknolle), Lynsack, South Bedburn (including Mayland, East Shipley, West Shipley, Little Mayland, Bitforth, and Hopyland), North Bedburn (with MacNiel, Little Mayland, Harperley and Wodingfield).

> Hamsterley, part of the parish, and surrounded by South Bedburn, Lynesack and Softley, and Evenwood and Barony, the last being treated as a separate entity in 1381 and in the hands of Lord Neville.

At this point in the argument, the most important thing to note is that with few exceptions, the colonisation of the vast wastes after the later twelfth century was undertaken generally without planting new villages. To mention only one of the possible cases; Byers Green has already been discussed. The assart or clearing of 1183 had the formal village plan intruded before 1381, and probably during the earlier decades of the twelfth century (Fig. 3.4). Witton-le-Wear is now a rather irregular green village but had no bondsmen, with the free tenures and exchequer tenures coming into being largely after 1183 (Fig. 6.5.b). Victor Watts explains the name of Witton as 'wood settlement', implying a settlement which depended on the felling and processing of timber for building, fuel and possibly the constituent of a larger multiple estate' (Watts 2002, 141). Appearing in the charter of 995 x 1006 as *Wudutun*, along with *Hunewic* and *Healme* there is nothing in these arguments not to support Witton's existence as a named, perhaps settled place, with a special function. Nevertheless the village of Witton is a latecomer to the settlement scene. Whitworth may have been a nucleation in the later twelfth century but later became deserted, for the name *Tofts* appears as a field name to the west of the present parkland of Whitworth Hall on the mid-nineteenth century 1:10,560 Ordnance Survey map. At Lutterington, air photographs taken in the mid-1940s, show traces of earthworks adjacent to the farmstead of that name and are indicative of the existence of a small hamlet. Both of these will be discussed more fully in Chapter 8. In many senses Aucklandshire is not the most typical of the Durham small shires, being far larger than most, but it is clear that the colonising movement which took place after 1183 led to the establishment of scatters of single farmsteads rather than villages. This is evident from Simon Harris' work (Figs 2.5 and 6.5).

In conclusion, in the case of the small shire of Auckland we can argue that the middle decades of the twelfth century saw a shift from earlier colonisation based on villages and hamlets to later colonisation that led only to the appearance of single farmsteads. Furthermore, there are substantive indications that revision of the local settlement structure was taking place in the period before 1183, involving the expansion of the demesne, movements of tenant populations, the planning of some new settlements and the restructuring of others. The chapter to follow continues an exploration of the implications of some of the tenurial variations recorded in Boldon Book, for it is the dynamism inherent in this record, confirmed and enhanced by the Hatfield Survey and by Offler's analysis, that is crucial to understanding settlement evolution, not only in County Durham, but also throughout the north of England.

Chapter Seven

Village Plantation – Problems and Questions

The preceding chapters have laid a foundation for the study of the links between tenures and settlement characteristics, and identified contexts both spatial and temporal within which these can be explored. This chapter considers further the main question: is it possible to use tenurial evidence to document and explore medieval village plantation and planning in the North of England? In 1183 there were in County Durham a small group of settlements, we dare not yet call them villages or hamlets, generally considered to be held 'in drengage', that is to say held by an individual tenant who rendered to the Bishop particular and specified services. These will provide a focus for discussion in both this and the chapter to follow. The documents suggest that these places varied greatly in character. To recapitulate the Aucklandshire cases (Fig. 6.5): Binchester is a fascinating problem, for on or near the major Roman site there appears to have been a vill, whose bondmen owed ploughing services on the demesne at Coundon and whose *dreng* kept a dog and a horse for the Bishop and attended the great hunt with two greyhounds and five ropes. In Lutterington Walter de Lutterington rendered for 'his vill' twenty shillings, harvest work 'with all his men', carried messages for the Bishop, found oxen to cart wine and attended the great hunts, in fact a drengage tenure. At Byers, never described as a drengage, there was a clearing (later Byers Green Fig. 3.4) for which an unnamed person paid half a mark – six shillings and eight pence. In this we have a complex group of settlements, ranging from the very old (Binchester) to the very new (Byers Green). Lutterington, as was noted previously, is today a single farmstead, but air photographs reveal earthworks nearby and show that it was once larger. Whitworth was, in 1183, a substantial village of sixteen bondage tenants and held of the Bishop by drengage tenure, but by the episcopate of Bishop Philip (1197–1208) it was converted to a manorial holding of one quarter of a knight's fee, a feudal tenure (Greenwell 1852, xliii). Today there is only a hall bearing the name, but nineteenth century maps record the field name 'Tofts', a term usually indicative of former house plots. Any physical evidence is now wholly ploughed out. However this is not the entire story of the Aucklandshire villages, and Figure 6.5 incorporates a diagrammatic impression of the varied plans present in about 1800, together with a reminder of their setting within a broader framework of enclosed land and rough grazings. From what has already been said about Aucklandshire that it is clear that before 1200 there had already been a long history of settlement development and that the settlements present at the end of the twelfth century were far from homogeneous in character.

Heighingtonshire abuts Aucklandshire but lies further to the south and east, on better quality undulating land on the north side of the Tees valley (Fig. 6.3 bottom). The chief village is remarkable one, having the dimensions of a small town and possesses a very large green (Fig. 1.3). In 1183 Heighington contained 16 villan tenants whose services were as follows:

Heighington – The Bondsmen (Villans) and Their Renders
1. 10 scatchalders of malt,
   10 scatchalders of meal,
   10 scatchalders of oats,
   64 scatchalders of oat malt after the measure of Heighington Hall.
   32 hens and no eggs.
2. 8 cartloads of woodlades, *i.e.* loads of fuelwood.
3. 36 shillings of cornage and one milch cow and one castleman.
4. Weed all the Bishop's corn.
5. Find every week in autumn one man every day from each oxgang to mow.
6. Villans and cotmen render 4 boon works with 'all the house except the housewife', for which they have subsistence.
7. Each villan ploughs and harrows half an acre of oat stubble (averere), and for each plough belonging to the town they plough and harrow one acre, and then they have subsistence,
8. they make one boon work one day with all the harrows of the town.
9. The aforesaid 16 villans render 16s for michelmet (perhaps a Michaelmas render when stock were killed and derived from *met*, 'meat'; Michaelmas reaping seems improbable, Greenwell 1852, lxiv–lxv: *ibid.* 1857, 281) and 26s for yolwaiting – perhaps connected with yule, Christmas, but a service of an uncertain nature, perhaps involving entertainment. In Lothian Duncan notes that the dues rendered to thanes – *ministeralis* – were known as wayting or hospitality (Duncan 1975, 76) placing them into an ancient group of tenant renders to the lord or his officer.
10. The villans also, along with the cotmen, mow the Bishop's meadows, lead the hay, and enclose the court of Heighington and the copse. They also lead the corn of the demesne wherever the Bishop pleases between the Tees and the Wear, and find one rope for the great chase.

We can only speculate upon the labour required to weed all the Bishop's corn! Five cotmen share many services with the villans, but owe week work for either the whole year or part. There are the usual ministerial rents and dues, sometimes for land specified, sometimes not. Thus, while the keeper of the pound (for stray cattle) – the pinder – held only six acres, and rendered 80 hens and 500 eggs he also appears to receive for his duties 'thraves', *i.e.* sheaves of grain, 'like the others', an enigmatic and unexplained phrase. It probably implies that there was a standard payment for this duty and in fact the Hatfield Survey shows that one thrave came from each carucate of land 'there', *i.e.* within the shire (Greenwell 1857, 18). The pinder's duties meant that he could not be a normal farmer and had to be supported by the community. These are heavy demands from the bondsmen, literally food renders, and the week work only lies upon the cotmen, cottagers, who may be newcomers to the community, perhaps even folk taken as slaves, or perhaps younger sons, who had not yet been able to find a widow to marry! The ancient services, cornage and milch cow appear, again with a hint of military service – the castleman – while the demesne was run with the assistance of all the villan and cottage tenants. In the rendering of chalders, vats of grain, there are echoes of ancient Irish, Norse and Danish practices (Patterson 1994, 172).

In fact, within Heighingtonshire are the remains of an earthwork of a form suggestive of a small Iron Age hill fort set amid the shire's pastures (Fig. 7.1). This draws this small shire closer towards the 'lowland estate' modelled by Glanville Jones, with the hall and church centre at Heighington itself, whose name means 'the settlement, village or estate at the high ground', a local perspective viewed from the lands of the Tees valley (Watts 2002, 57). The church of St. Michael appears to have comprised a 10th or 11th century aisleless nave and chancel, and possibly the lower portion of the west tower, but was extensively altered *c.* 1160–70 (Pevsner 1985, 321). In 1183, although the demesne was at farm, it is clear that this had been, and indeed was still, an important centre of agrarian production, an episcopal chief vill, with a hall, the focus of numerous services. The presence of "Simon the doorward (*hostiarius*)' holding 'the old land (*terram veteram*), that another version of the manuscript describes as 'the land that was Utred's (*terram quae fuit Utredi*), together with the 60 acres that were added to it by the Bishop, suggests the presence of an official of substantial status. In fact as Hatfield Survey tells us, this was a holding of six bovates (Greenwell 1857, 16). The enigmatic 'castleman' is clearly associated with the bondage tenants (Greenwell 1852, 20, 57 and liv) having a duty involving 'watching'. While there is no way of assuring an indisputable correlation, there are here undoubted parallels in the office of *hostarius*, howsoever it be translated, with the officials of the Welsh royal court, the steward (Jenkins 2000, 12–14), the usher (*ibid.* 20–21), the doorkeeper (*ibid.* 25–26), and in the case of the castleman, with the watchman (*ibid.* 36–7). Effectively, both 'doorward' and 'castleman', resident in Heighington, must have been concerned with the care of the hall in the absence of the peripatetic lordly household.

All of the Heighington tenancies present in 1183 are discernible in the account appearing in the Hatfield Survey of 1381 but in addition there are a number of free tenants and tenants of exchequer land. Many hold tofts, and we are told that they also bear a portion, 4s, of the cornage payment. We can only speculate, but it is possible that these freeholds and toft holders were located around the westernmost of the two elements of the green, for the hall appears to have been on the eastern side, making this likely to have been the older element (Fig. 1.3). In contrast, the geometric order of the western side of the plan betokens a more formal layout. There is a more general question emerging from this argument: if a village was 'set up', howsoever and whenever this took place, and a suite of works, rents and services was defined, then what took place when additional population accreted? Did newcomers merely take on the established pattern? This seems improbable in the light of the emphasis in the record between 1183 and 1381 of the retention of long-established arrangements. Clearly, if newcomers held only small holdings then they could appear in the records as cotmen or cottagers, and in Heighington by 1381 there were in addition to other holders of small pieces of land, nine 'toft holders', paying exchequer, *i.e.* cash rents (Greenwell 1857, 18–9). However, before the datum of 1183 we face a problem, for in Heighington there are two issues: first, the cotmen's holdings, with some work services appended, could be interpretable as 'newcomers'. Second, we are faced with sixteen villans, itself a suspiciously round number, all with unified services. Had this tenurial structure been imposed only a short time before 1183, a structure that had had no time to devolve and become irregular? That it was effectively fossilised by the record of Boldon Book cannot be gainsaid, for it is still present in the survey of 1381. The broader question here is can the nature of a settlement's tenurial profile be a guide to its temporal and physical development?

On this point Welsh evidence once again throws up some interesting issues. Rees makes an interesting comment that the class of non-tribesmen (*i.e.* tribesmen were the kinsmen, associated with hereditary land, the group being termed the *gwely*) as seen in the laws, consisted in the main of two groups, first, hereditary bondsmen (*taeogs*) living in separate bond vills or *taeogtrefs* and holding *tregyfrif* (or *tir cyfrif*, reckoned land (Rees 1924, 218–21). Secondly, there were 'strangers' (*alltudion*), each of whom was required upon entry into a district to place himself under the protection of the lord. An *alltud* (*i.e.* stranger) family that remained on the same soil for four generations became permanently attached to its lord, although *alltuds* might also hold in *gwelys*, as did free tribesmen. Both groups after the conquest (by the English) were relegated to the class of *native*, *i.e.* rustics bound to the soil, sharing many characteristics with bondsmen (Rees 1924, 218–9). Seebohm records that in the 1293–4 'Record of Caernarvon' the surveyor noted that in two manors (Kemmys and Penros) there were 'people paying *mal*, or money tribute, people doing services or work and people on 'board land' *i.e.* the mensal or table land of the estate's lord. In Rosfair three classes of tenants were identified, (a) the 'pure *nativi*' of the *maerdreve*, pure bondsmen of the reeves' hamlets, (b) other *nativi* who termed themselves 'free' *nativi*, and (c) other *nativi* termed *Gardymen*, 'garden-men' (Seebohm 1904, 4). Seebohm, focussing upon the Welsh system, rather dismisses these and suggests they result from the imposition of Norman perceptions. In this he may be right, but there is an interesting general point here; the unfree tenantry are not a homogeneous group. Ancient relatively servile groups will accrete others to their class, the utterly impoverished, prisoners captured and enslaved though war, those enslaved as punishment for crimes, and those poor souls who suffer the slings and stones of bad fortune. Each element forms a potential breeding population amongst whom differences in rents and duties, at first carefully maintained, will gradually tend to merge (Pelteret 1995, 252). It follows that custumals as diverse as the Record of Caernarvon or Boldon Book may retain within their structure traces of irregularities of tenants and services which reflect the origins of a social class to which unifying terms, *taeogs*, *nativi*, villans, or bondsmen, cotmen or *firmarii* are eventually applied. In his analysis of the 'sorts of men' in Scotland Duncan demonstrates the rich diversity of social groups present amongst the lower social orders, a diversity that must be concealed beneath the formal tenantry of the great surveys (Duncan 1975, 326–48).

On a European scale, work by McCormick has revealed the importance of the slave trade in the developing economy between AD 300 and 900 (McCormick 2001, 752–77). We may recall that when the Northumbrians raided Northampton in 1065, they seized 'many hundreds of men and led them off north with them' (Swanton 2000, 193; see below), while Richard of Hexham lays some emphasis on the Scots taking north 'noble matrons and chaste virgins together with other women' (Stephenson 1988, 63; Douglas and Greenaway 1981, 342). The role of these unfortunates as breeding stock for a generation of slaves within the recipient society can be imagined, as can their subtler role as agents for the transfer of language and culture. Not kin, their offspring formed a new social nexus. David Pelteret has shown how slavery, at first endemic in Anglo-Saxon society, gradually gave way to praedial tenancies, a transition between the community of the kindred to the community of the estate in the context of the rise of co-operative farming and the rise of estate custom (Pelteret 1995, 177). The expansion of bookland between the seventh and the eleventh century, and the particularly strong developments from the tenth century onwards, passed power from the tribe and from kin to individuals and institutions (*ibid.* 172). Week work for *ceorls* can be documented in about 900, soon after the death of Alfred (*ibid.* 178–9: Seebohm 1896, 162–3). From the estate grew settlement structuring and the rise of communally organised field systems, and peasant obligations passed from the tribal to the manorial sphere (Pelteret 1995,172) As noted earlier as early as the 690s the laws of Ine of Wessex imply the possibility of settlement structuring when they state:

> If a man agree for a yardland or more land at a fixed rent (*gafol*) and plough it, if the lord desire to raise the land to him to work and to rent (*gafol*), he need not take it upon him, if the lord do not give him a dwelling, and he is to forfeit the crops.
>
> (Seebohm 1896, 142–3)

Patrick Wormald translates this as

> 'if anyone comes to terms about a yard of land or more at an agreed payment and ploughs, if the lord wishes him to increase that land for him as regards either labour or payment, he need not accept it from him if he does not give him a house'

and interprets this as Ine 'reacting to a particular case'. If this is accepted, then the pragmatic issues raised by the doom remain. If 'x' had taken place, and Ine reacted in this way, then he was nevertheless responding with a judgement in a manner that appears to possess wide implications (Wormald 1999, 104–5). It does appear from some of Wormald's analysis there was a fundamental division between royal, written law – church driven – and what may best termed 'folk law', for one hesitates to use the word 'common' law (Wormald 1999, 143). Perhaps 'vernacular legal traditions' or 'rustic law' may be more appropriate circumlocutions. That the two interdigitated cannot be doubted, so that royal law, treating wergilds and the peace, manslayings and fornication, land occupation and service to the crown, eventually absorbed elements of 'rustic law', concerned with the practicalities of settlement and farming routines. This interface, extending through time from Æthelberht, to Ine and Alfred, and eventually Æthelstan, shows a complex pattern surfacing most clearly in the Dooms of Ine.

Time and new lordship gradually eroded earlier social distinctions: these changes are part of the dynamics of population growth, settlement evolution and changing economy. If circumstances permitted, then the imposition of a unified set of tenurial demands could be intimately linked to the allocation of aliquot shares in the land resources of the community, perhaps with some re-evaluation of status. This is a concept to which we will return, but is to be seen in the status variations between villans (later bondsmen), cottagers and other tenants in both Aucklandshire and Heighingtonshire. On the other hand, such social distinctions can run very deep: the author remembers being told with pride some forty years ago 'Oh yes, my father was a Durham hind', *i.e.* a farm-labourer, different and distinct from those incomers who arrived as a result of mining colonisation. To return to Heighingtonshire: Killerby and Middridge are smaller settlements. In 1183 the former had 12 (or 14) villans, and the second 15 villans, who rendered in kind proportionately 'as those of Heighington', *i.e.* as the villans of Heighington. The tenurial structure of Middridge has been analysed in Chapter 3 and here attention must again be drawn to two particular holdings, namely that of Vekeman, described as half a ploughland, interpreted as four bovates, and Anketill's two bovates. Both men pay cash rents, do relatively light works, boon day or obligatory works, a little ploughing and harrowing (one day), mowing (one day), carting hay and corn (two days). Vekeman is 'over the boon days' and must be a village official, while Anketill pays a proportion of the grain rent, but goes on the Bishop's errands. These men are undoubtedly of rather higher status than the rest of the farmers. They offer specific services, and are set apart from their fellows. Both holdings can be identified in 1381, as *Ukemanland* and the land *quondam Anketill*, formerly Anketill's. By that date they are free holdings, and so have a status distinct from that of the bondage tenants (Greenwell 1852, 20; Fig. 7.8). Interestingly enough, the single bovate of the cottager, Ulkill, present in 1183, can also be detected in 1381, when it is also of free status. The point is that in 1183, a sector of the village's assessed land, *i.e.* that measured in bovates, was separate, special, and in the hands of tenants whose social attributes differed from those of the normal villans or bondsmen. In this case they are of higher status. There is a hint of the same at Killerby, where in 1183 Simon the Doorward holds one ploughland, although in this case any older obligations have already been converted to knight service, paralleling the case of Whitworth noted earlier (Greenwell 1852, 21, 59).

Middridge, as Figure 3.1 shows, is a regular two row green village, while Killerby is the same. The former, sited on a heathy plateau lies to the north of small group of fields on a limestone ridge still known in the nineteenth century as Old Towns, and forming a small island set amid the demesne township of Middridge Grange. The presumption is clear: at some date before 1183, the demesne had been expanded, and the tenants moved to a new and planted regular green village. It is tempting to assume a post-Conquest date for this development, contingent upon an expansion of the demesne. Were the services and rents then unified, or do they pre-date the move? As cornage and milch cow were paid, we must assume that pre-Conquest dues were indeed collated within any new bundle. The next vill listed in 1183 is Thickley, and this gives much trouble, for no village of this name survives. In 1183 eight villans held by services proportionate to those of Heighington. The render of half of a milch cow shows that this payment had already been commuted to cash, but the other half cannot be accounted for. In 1381 the farmstead of West Thickley accounts for 3s instead of the normal 6s of payment for milch cow (Greenwell 1857, 28) indicating the site of the earlier hamlet. The demesne of Middridge and Thickley emerges as the township of Middridge Grange, with in 1381 some 21 bovates each of 15 acres, in all 315 acres of arable, more if the Durham rod of 21 feet was used. In 1183 there was pasture, at Shakleton and at Redworth, where the Bishop ran sheep flocks (Greenwell 1852, 59). There are hints here of woodlands being cleared: in Heighington, Killerby, Middridge and Thickley we read of 'woodlades'; the place-name *Thicceleia* appears in 995 x 1006 as part of the Aucklandshire group of vills, and in 1031 as part of the Staindropshire group (Hart 1975, 125 and 127) and the name implies 'clearing amid dense undergrowth' (Watts 2002, 124). In this case it appears that the demesne grew amid countryside in a process of active change and re-definition. Redworth lies close by, in 1183 a vill inhabited by 16 farmers or leaseholders (*firmarii*) who held between them 16 oxgangs or bovates, but in this case Heighington is not cited as the model for services. Each two oxgangs render 5s and 2 hens, and 'each bovate owes three boon works in the autumn with one man, and mows one day with eight [men] – one version excludes the housewife – and carry hay with eight carts and plough one day'. In addition three cotmen hold 12 acres and do week work from 1st August to 11th November for one day in every week. The eight men are surprising; how were they to be mustered, for the burden is laid upon each bovate and that would imply the muster of 128 men, an improbable number, although the same figures are cited in 1381 (Greenwell 1857, 26). The text is surely at fault here, and either one man per bovate was involved, or more probably the 16 bovates were expected to muster eight men. By 1381 the *firmarii* appear in the Hatfield Survey as *tenentes in dringagio*, tenants in drengage, an interesting collective use of a term so far only met in a ministerial context. There is also some exchequer land, *i.e.* land colonised between 1183 and 1381. Redworth itself pays neither cornage nor milch cow, and may be taken to be a younger settlement than those places that do, namely, the larger core vills of Heighingtonshire. Redworth is today a rather indeterminate sort of plan, irregular, and lacking a proper green, and dominated by a recent hall. The place-name is nevertheless Old English implying 'the enclosure where the reeds grow' (Watts 2002, 103), redolent of former wasteland. That a regular plan has not survived in this case need occasion no great surprise: all settlements are subject to the vicissitudes of changes, some small, others cataclysmic and in this case the expansion of parkland around a hall has been destructive of the plan.

How is this complexity to be comprehended? At this point Boldon Book becomes interesting, for it continues:

> Guy de Redworth holds the new vill near Thickley in exchange for Redworth, and renders one marc (13s 4d, two thirds of a pound sterling), and finds 12 men one day or one man 12 days to mow in autumn, and he ploughs one day, and works at the mill dam, and goes on the Bishop's errands and carts wine with four oxen.

It is quite clear that Guy had a relationship with Redworth: this is evident in both his name and in the clear statement of the exchange. What was this relationship? Surely he had already been the mentor of a 'new' settlement at a place bearing an older name (Watts 2002, 103). The regular tenemental structure of the new vill at Redworth, containing sixteen leaseholders, suggests this newness. In 1381 his second new vill at Thickley appears as Newbigging (*i.e.* 'the new buildings', Watts 2002, 84), and is now no more than a farmstead. In 1381 it was all in the hands of one man, John of Nottingham while Henry Staynesby held certain land of new assart, and William of Heighington also held one plot in Newbigging Moor. Why, then, did Guy de Redworth make the exchange? Perhaps he was induced to do this, but the alternative labour demands makes one point wholly clear: he had the option – and we must put it no stronger than this – of creating a new village at Newbigging, indeed the Latin text speaks in these terms, he received the *novam villam*. Newbigging itself does not render cornage or milch cow. It is a new creation. By 1381 it is described as being a drengage.

As if all this were not complex enough, a note attached in Boldon Book records that 'Old Thickley, which was made of the land of Redworth yields 1 mark for cornage at the feast of St. Cuthbert in September'. In 1381 this appears under the entry for Redworth, when a William Lilburn held the vill (villam) of Old Thickley. This must be the site of the oldest settlement in the Thickley area, still retaining an ancient rent, while one half of a milch cow was due from the settlement that became West Thickley. The location of Old Thickley, presumably paying the other half of the milch cow is unknown. The most reasonable interpretation of these topographical and settlement complexities is that an area of woodland and moorland was being developed. Within this there were traces of older settlements, of which there were sufficient records to ensure that some older rent forms were carried forward, and the revitalisation of these and attempts to establish some new vills is concealed within the complexities of the working document that Boldon Book represents. We see in effect a shatter zone within the settlement system.

However, this documentary analysis leaves us with an interesting pattern. It appears that the core vills of the shire, Heighington, Killerby, Middridge and one of the several settlements termed Thickley had already been established before 1183, but the evidence suggests that attempts to create new vills were not singularly successful in the later twelfth century. Figure 7.1 takes the argument further. It began as a simple map of Heighingtonshire and was cut out of the county map seen in Figure 2.6: the thick dotted outline draws together the territories of the later parish and the core vills listed in 1183. The large amounts of common waste serve to emphasise the earlier geographical context of the shire. The core of cultivated land, focussing upon Heighington, was in about 1150, surrounded by a sea of waste. In the north there had been some pre-Conquest settlement within the 'thick wood' of Thickley, but recession took place – hence Old Thickley and the complexities discussed above. By 1183 the area was being re-colonised, establishing a newly planted vill at Redworth with a wholly new plantation at Newbiggin. Walworth's Old English place-name indicates – via a medial 'e' in the earliest form – that distinctively British folk, *wealas*, survived sufficiently long to be seen and identified as distinctive and separate (Watts 2002, 131–2). At a later stage a large village was planted, a village comparable in plan with Heighington itself and perhaps half its size. Nothing is known of its history or depopulation, and the great and splendid earthworks seen on air photographs remain as one of the major enigmas of Durham settlement. The sheer density of buildings emphasises its former success. School Aycliffe, now suburbanised, will not be discussed, although it probably incorporates the Scandinavian name of Skuli or Skula (Watts 2002, 108) and was once part of an ancient estate linked with Aycliffe – including Heworth, Rykenhall, and Brafferton – but appears to have become attached to Heighingtonshire. Finally, it will be noted that after 1183, there was insufficient common waste within the shire for the Bishops' officers to encourage the planting of single farmsteads in Heighingtonshire, in marked contrast to Aucklandshire to the northwest.

Killerby is an outlier of the shire, and bears a Scandinavian place-name, but why the detachment? Local place-names give important clues. The adjacent Summerhouse means what it says, a grazing area used in the summer months; Morton, incorporates the word for moor, while Headlam incorporates the word for heather; Hilton and Houghton imply, respectively, settlements associated with a slope and a hill spur, while Ingleton incorporates a personal name that could be Old English or Old Danish. Bolam implies land cleared and forming smooth round hills, or possibly 'land with tree stumps' (Watts, 2002, passim). The map makes the context clear. Before 1183 there had been a block of common waste to the south east of the core of Heighingtonshire and between it and the adjacent small shires of Gainford and Staindrop, and this was colonised

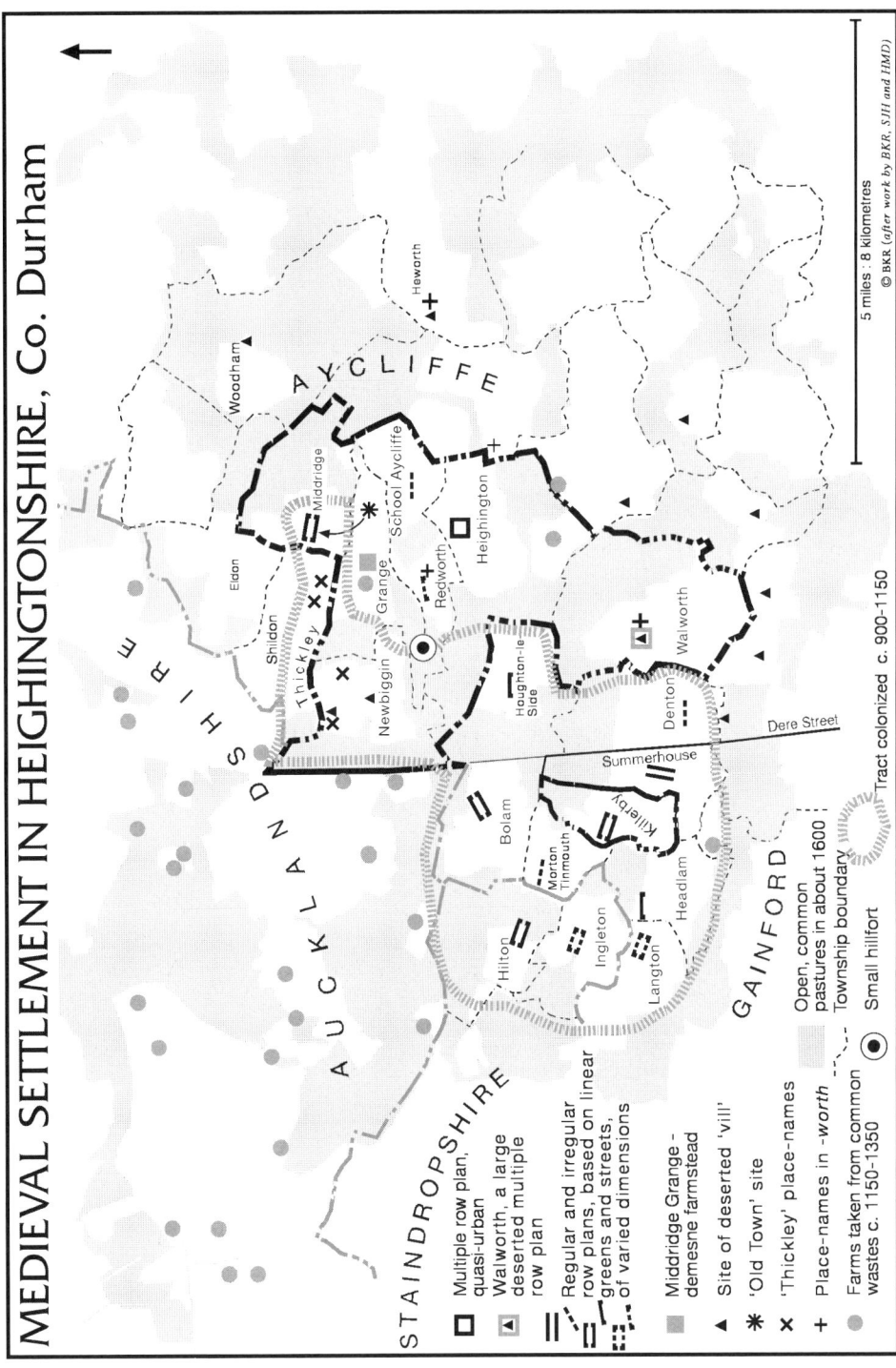

Fig. 7.1 Settlement in Heighingtonshire, County Durham

with small regular villages. The place-names of this block, many of them meaningful in topographic terms, are a mixture of Old English and Scandinavian. Victor Watts, in his analysis of Scandinavian names in the county reached the interesting conclusion that 'a not insignificant part of this name-giving took place in the eleventh and twelfth centuries', and notes that Killerby is first documented in a charter of William I dated 1091 x 1092 (Watts 1988–9, 45–6). Given that Ingleton, Langton, and Morton are mentioned by name, possibly between 995 and 1031, and certainly before 1040, this could be the date before which active colonisation was initiated in this zone, a process leading to the appearance of regular village plans (Watts *passim*). There can be no absolute proof, but the author is increasingly drawn towards the possibility, in this case, that the village plans and unitary Heighington type services seen at Killerby, and present by 1183, point to a phase of village plantation and service definition before 1040, and possibly earlier. By the twelfth century the wastes of this small shire were not sufficiently extensive to encourage the massive single-farmstead colonisation that took place further north and west. The presumption is that by the twelfth century, village communities of this zone were already sufficiently established to leave insufficient rough grazing reserves for individual colonisation.

We are now faced with a dilemma: it is clear that the post-1183 colonising movement in western and central Durham did not generate regular village plans, indeed landtaking largely took the form of establishing single farmsteads (Fig. 2.5). On the other hand, there are clear indications from west of the Pennines that active colonisation after the Norman take-over of the late eleventh century did result in villages with long and strip tofts. There are indeed some grounds, in the form of similar distinctive plans, for arguing that instances of this did take place in some parts of west Durham (Cockfield, Frosterley, Stanhope and Iveston). Nevertheless, we are still not close to the circumstances in which the widespread and repetitious regularity of the county's planned villages evolved, although this analysis of Heighingtonshire hints that these could be pre-Conquest. The argument must now turn yet again to a re-assessment of the role of a powerful force other than that of colonisation, namely, devastation, deliberate wasting created by military activity.

Devastation and Medieval Settlement

In a chapter originally drafted before 1936 Sir Clifford Darby noted that repeated devastation, the deliberate destruction of cornfields, houses and the stealing and killing of both stock and people, was 'an ingredient of no mean importance in the life of England during the earlier Middle Ages' (Darby 1951, 173). The Anglo-Saxon Chronicle for the year 1065 describes such an attack by earl Morcar and the men of the north of England upon the county of Northampton, where

> they both killed men and burned houses and corn, and seized all the cattle that they could come at, which was many thousands: and they seized many hundreds

of men, and led them off north with them, so that the shire and the other shires which were near there were for many years the worse.

(Swanton 2000, 193)

Even if this is exaggerated, and it probably isn't, then this passage is full of meaning. The cattle and people represented movable wealth: the cattle would expand northern herds, while the men, and no doubt the women, would add to the stock of true slaves. In time these would extend the numbers of servile tenants on northern estates, those tenants with a heavy burden of services and only a small amount of land. Richard of Hexham indicated the subtleties of such raiding in a description of a Scottish raid before the Battle of the Standard in 1138. As he wrote before 1154, and is nearly contemporary with the events he describes, the narrative is valuable. He describes the Scottish army 'over-running the province and sparing none' and ravaging

> with fire and sword almost all Northumberland as far as the river Tyne, excepting the towns (*i.e.* vills) and the sea-coasts on the eastern side, but this they designed to devastate on their return. One part of that army also crossed the Tyne, and massacred numberless persons in the wilds, laying waste in the same way the greater part of the territory of St. Cuthbert on the west side.

Later on in the campaigning season the Scots returned to devastate

> first the seacoast and the county [of Northumberland], which on the former occasion had been left unravaged, and after that the greater part of the territory of St. Cuthbert, on the eastern side, between Durham and the sea. And both on this and the former occasion he [the Scottish king] in like manner destroyed, together with the husbandmen, many farms of the monks who served god and St. Cuthbert day and night.

(Douglas and Greenaway 1981, 340 and 342).

From Craven we are specifically told that they carried off 'noble matrons and chaste virgins' into slavery. Women, like cattle, were a transportable commodity. We should remember that in Irish law a *cumal* or female slave was of the value of three milch cows (Kelly 1998, 592). Later on in September the Scottish king and his army crossed Durham and

> destroyed crops as far as the river Tees, and according to his usual practice caused the towns and churches which had previously escaped unharmed to be dismantled, plundered and burnt

(Douglas and Greenaway 1981, 344).

The devastation continued into Yorkshire, and while the precise chronology is by no means certain, according to Richard the battle of the Standard near Northallerton took place on Monday 22nd August, *i.e.* before the September date given for the crossing of

Durham, the essential account of the devastation rings true. Furthermore, an army on the move would consume milled grain, cattle, sheep and pigs, poultry and all other stored consumables, and steal iron goods, gold and other ornaments and fabrics. The impact was literally devastating.

Figure 7.2 draws together as a series of simple national maps some of the areas known to have been devastated between 902 and 1156. This is a bald and perhaps unconvincing synopsis, and assessing the real impact of devastation is difficult. It is, interesting to note that the wasting of Northamptonshire recorded in the Anglo-Saxon Chronicle under the year 1065 left few traces to appear in Domesday Book in 1086. The county had essentially recovered within twenty years. These are cold words, for the human suffering must have been acute. Those led off were to become hostages or more probably slaves, and must eventually have been absorbed into northern English society, for the raiders came from 'Northumberland and Yorkshire'. This evidence for rapid recovery supports David Palliser's point concerning the dangers of exaggerating the impact of the Harrying of the North in 1069–70 (Palliser 1993). However, Figure 7.3 records the waste noted by the Domesday account for the north of England. In this account we must set aside all of the complexities of detailed interpretation of the term *vasta* in 1086, and there are many, and recall that the Domesday Commissioners, whatever the circumstances in detail were able to create for Yorkshire a data-set in which – unlike Lancashire – a large number of places are named and thus 'on the record'. Is it possible to take the distribution at face value and think about the distribution rather than merely describe it? There are regional contrasts within Yorkshire that indisputably transgress the boundaries of the ridings. We can see that 'partial wasting' is much more common in the East Riding, and as the woodland superimposed in Figure 7.3 suggests, these were open landscapes, the productive core of the ancient kingdom of Deira. The superimposed shading is based upon the distribution appearing in Figure 1.5, and while it can, and indeed should be challenged in detail, it does suggest that, excluding the dales of the North Riding, the greatest levels of 'waste' appear in the foothills and wooded areas. Why should this be? Here one must reflect that cattle and people can disappear into woodland, locations where the Commissioners and their representatives may have been reluctant to tread, although this is also one possible reason for penetrating them with fire and sword. T. A. M. Bishop postulated that this wasting of more marginal land represented a movement of population to the lowlands to repopulate thoroughly devastated areas (Bishop 1948).

Figure 7.4 extends this argument by using later sources: it is based upon a series of maps produced by Colm McNamee (1997, figs 5–10). Essentially this generalises his analyses of a series of raids between 1315 and 1322, but includes also some evidence for a raid into Cumberland in 1345 (Winchester 1987, fig. 12). For the shaded northern portion of the distribution it is not possible to plot the course of the raids in detail, except for Cumberland, but for Yorkshire McNamee has been able to record the specific villages that suffered in the varied raids. At this time raiders from the north characteristically swept southwards down the richer eastern lowlands and then swung westwards, booty-laden, to take a shorter route northwards through what were then the western marches.

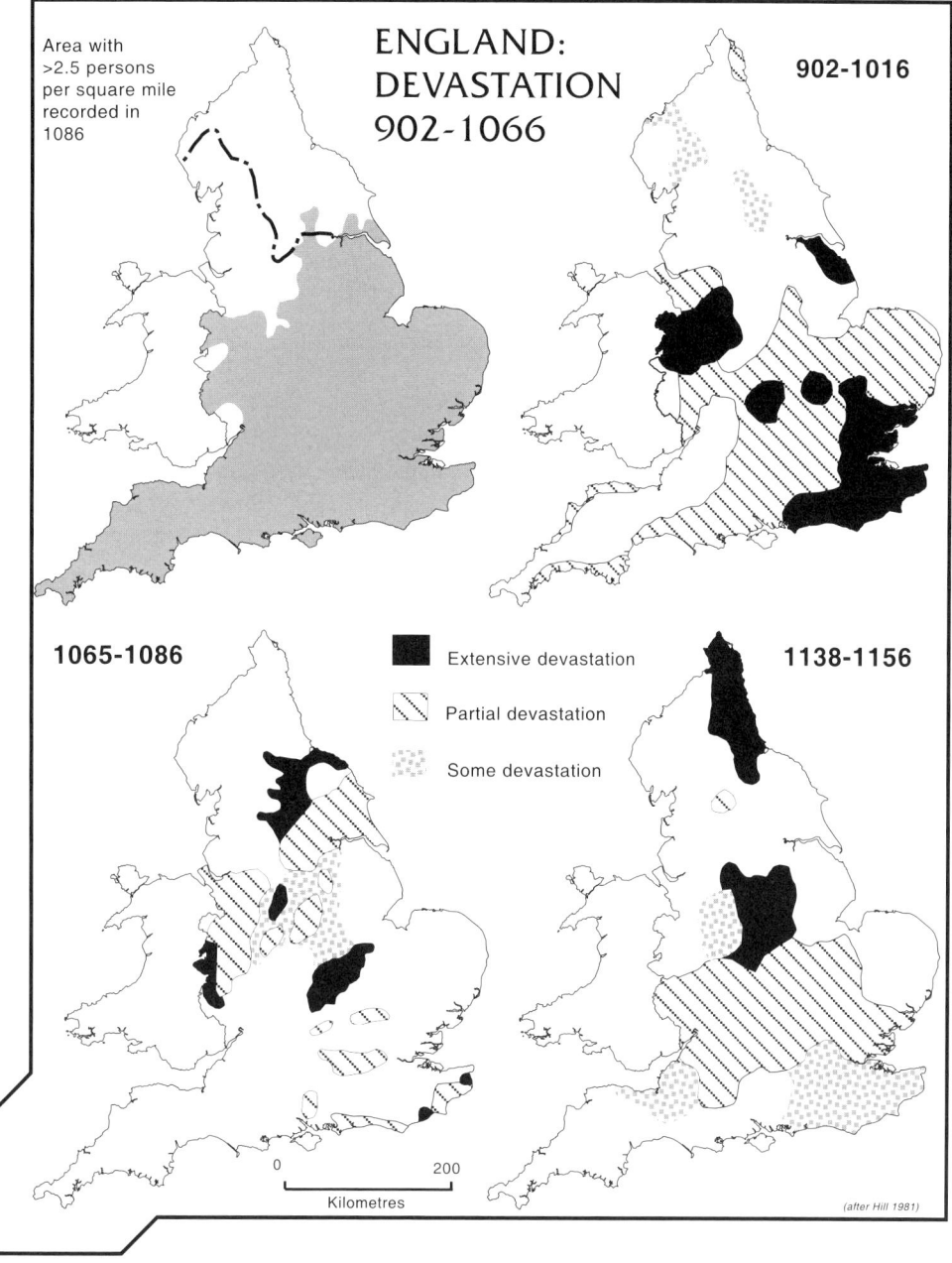

Fig. 7.2 Devastation in England 902–1086

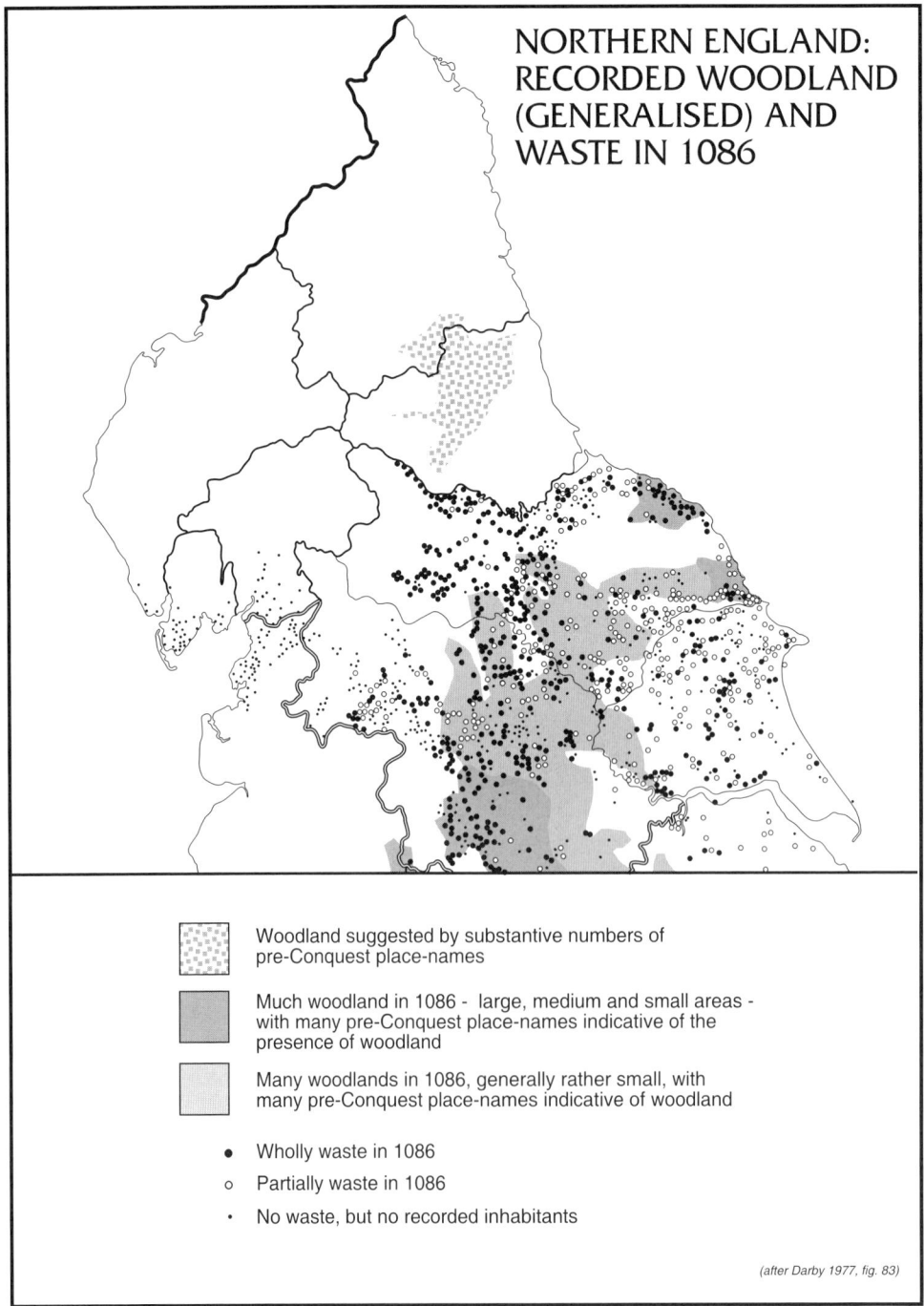

Fig. 7.3 Woodland and waste in northern England in 1086

Village Plantation 203

Effectively this was a U-shaped trajectory. That such raids did have an impact is shown by the graph appearing in the lower portion of Figure 7.4 that correlates raids with rent levels (McNamee 1997, 113, see also 72–122). This is by no means a simple link; thus the raid of 1326–7 did not prevent the upswing of rents, any more than did the changing climatic conditions of the period. Nevertheless the broad correlations are clear, and this argument is forwarded to emphasise the sporadic and capricious nature of raiding. What we can re-create from the records is only a very partial picture, but Darby's conclusion that devastation was 'an ingredient of no mean importance in the life of England during the earlier Middle Ages' remains correct. Settlements in some locations were more prone to be affected than others, necessitating *in situ* reiteration, rebuilding and redevelopment when population and economy were able to recover. This is not a conclusion applicable only to the period when we have some documentation: as Figure 7.2 implies it has always been an ingredient of settlement evolution, and in this fact we may see one source for reconstituted planned settlements.

The table that follows attempts to catalogue for Durham the likely devastation during the period between the later tenth century and the mid-twelfth century:

Table 7.1 Devastations in County Durham 969–1138

969 (1006)	Durham besieged; Barmton, Skerningham, Elton, Carlton by Stockton, School Aycliffe and Monk Hesleton laid waste by the Scots (Hart 1975, 146–7; Kapelle 1979, 240, n.30: but see Stephenson 1988, 97–100).
994	Scots plundered 'Saxony' (i.e. England) as far as Stainmore and 'the lakes of Deira' (Fletcher 2002, 73)
1006	Scots devastated the province of the Northumbrians by fire and slaughter, laid waste the land and besieged Durham (Fletcher 2002, 53)
1038 +	Second wasting of Barmton etc. (Hart 1975, 150)
1039/40	Durham besieged (Hart 1975, 146, n. 2; Kapelle 1979, 25, n.62; Fletcher 2002, 134)
1067–70	Devastation in Yorkshire and parts of Durham, associated with the initial Norman conquest (Kapelle 1979, 118, n.87; *idem* 280, 66: Fletcher 2002, 181).
1070	Scottish pillaging in Teesdale and Cleveland, reaching Wearmouth in Durham (Fletcher 2002, 185)
1080	Devastation by Odo Bishop of Bayeux following the murder of Walcher; a 'large body of troops ... reduced nearly the whole land into a wilderness' (Stephenson 1988, Symeon, chap. LIX,83). Siege of Durham (Bonney 1990, 20–22).
1088	Temporary dispossession of the Bishop of Durham by royal command; some devastation? (*EHD* II, 653)
1091	Scottish incursion reaching as far south as Durham (Kapelle 1979, 149).
[1093–1133 Building of Durham cathedral]	
1138	Scottish devastation recorded by Richard of Hexham; (a) to the east, between Durham and the sea, 'the husbandmen and many farms of the monks destroyed' (*EHD* II, 342), and (b) devastation of swathe of land from the Tyne, to Durham and thence to the Tees (*EHD* II, 344) involving the destruction of crops and 'causing towns and churches to be plundered and burnt'.

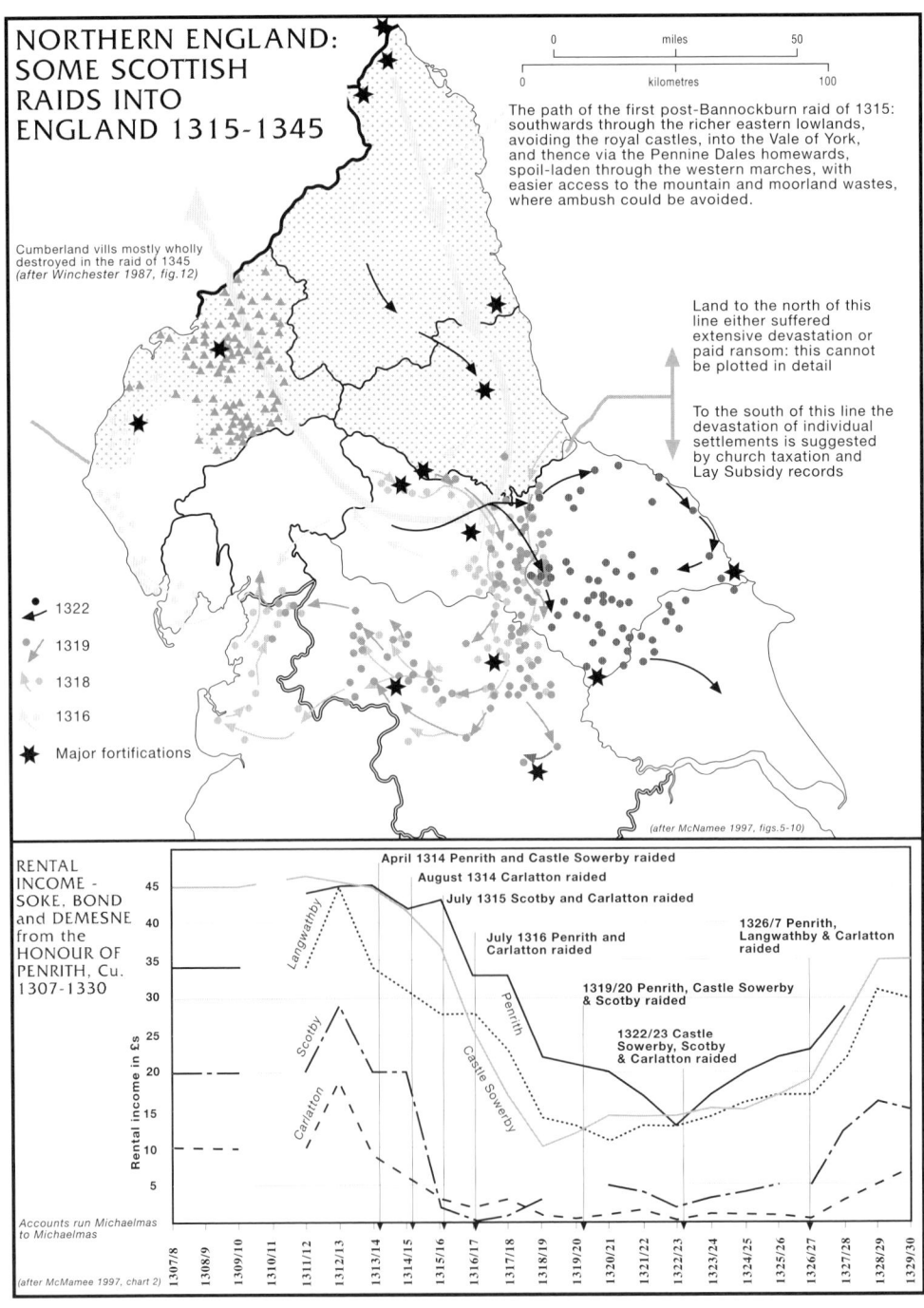

Figure 7.4 Scottish raids into northern England 1315–1345

We cannot know the full extent of wasting in Durham in the years between 1067 and 1070. The county, as a result of the intervention of St. Cuthbert or not, escaped the worst of the king's vengeance (Stephenson 1988, Symeon Chap. L, 70). This may imply that the community reached an accommodation with the Normans as they had with the Vikings, for there is no doubt that the *Haliwerfolc*, the Community of St. Cuthbert, were flexible survivors! A similar interpretation must be placed upon the story of Ralph, whose task was to compel 'the saint's people to pay tribute to the king'. As a result of a saintly visitation which rendered poor Ralph incapable, we are told primly by Symeon that the king 'by his own assent and authority confirmed the laws and customs of the saint, which had been established by the direction of ancient kings and commanded they should be carefully observed by all' (Stephenson 1988, Symeon Chap LV, 75–6). However, this is not to say that Durham did not experience some devastation. As the table indicates, there are good grounds for believing it did. Symeon does not dwell upon the impact of Odo's activities, but he dismisses the devastation of Yorkshire in a short phrase 'King William came to York and devastated all the circumjacent districts' (Stephenson 1988, Symeon Chap. L, 70–1). Nevertheless, we can only conclude that in spite of Symeon's monastic calmness, the life of the average husbandman of the period was fraught with deep fears. It will be noted from the table that the building of Durham cathedral took place after the devastations of the 1080s and 90s, and precedes those of the late 1130s and later. We must presume that there was a period of economic prosperity allowing Bishop and monks to sustain the level of income to sustain a building campaign, even if Bishop William de St. Calais did contribute from his own purse. This income can hardly have come from a devastated countryside, or indeed countryside in progress of a major recovery.

This digression is important for understanding some of the economic and social forces active within the tenth, eleventh and twelfth centuries. The rather uncomfortable implications involved in this conclusion are summarised in Figure 7.5 which deals with the problem in a theoretical way. It is included to reinforce two points: first, the problem of using documentation in settlement history, and second, the complexity of change within a settlement system through time and space. It is clear from all that has gone before that neither settlements nor settlement plans need established at one and the same time. A few may appear first, then a greater number, followed by a gradual trail off. This is expressed in Figure 7.5 section I. In most cases, we can talk only of plan types, we have no idea of the shape of this developmental curve. It may be skewed, with the bulk of new plans appearing very rapidly, followed by a gradual tail off, or the reverse may be true. Given the quantity of plans and the problems of documenting them we have no way, other than speculation, of dealing with such temporal trends. Furthermore, precise evidence is so rare and so precious that we tend to over-emphasise it. All the few dated examples can do is establish a *terminus ante quem*, the date before which some, but not necessarily all, of the plans we can place in time were present.

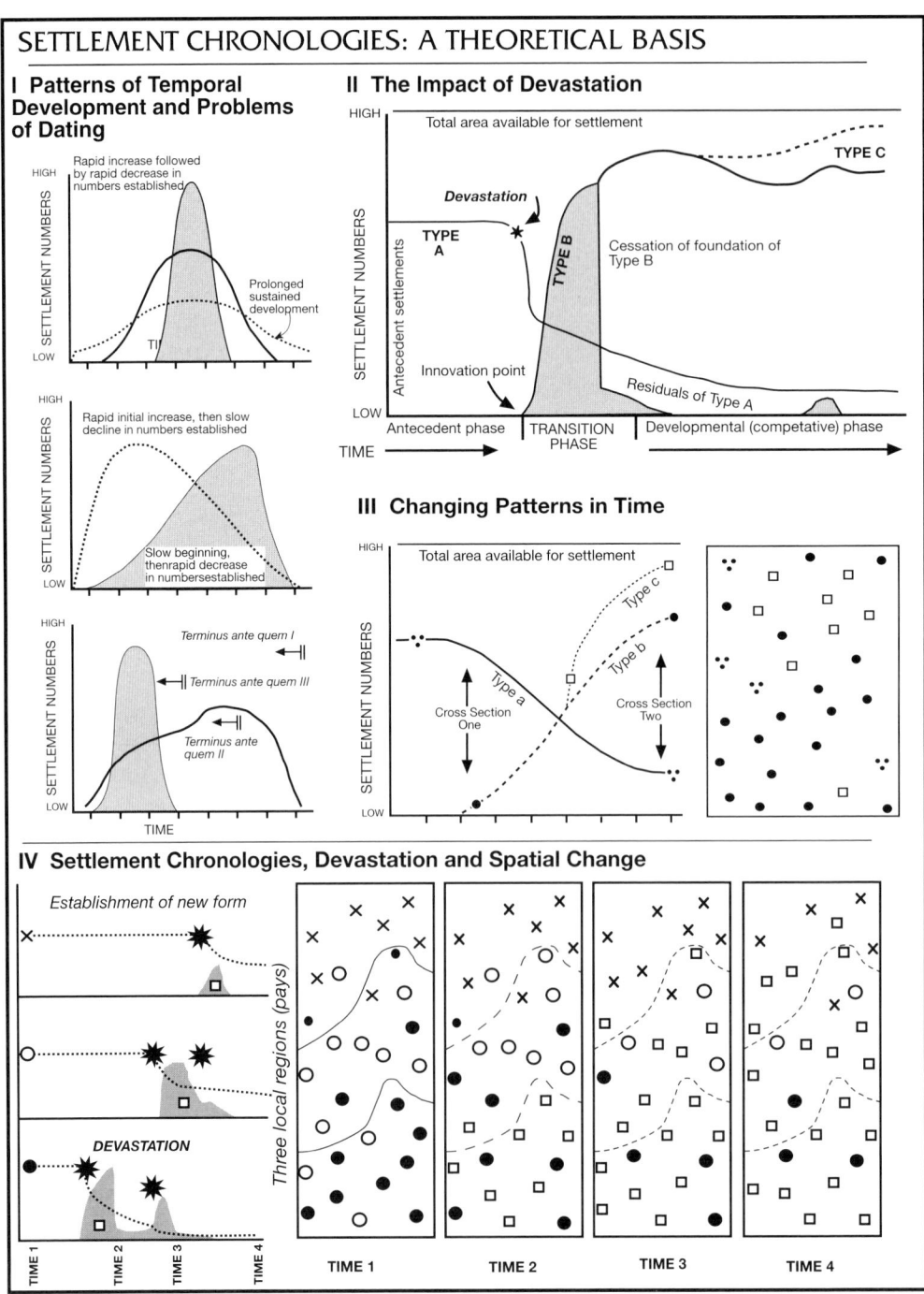

Fig. 7.5 A theoretical basis for settlement chronologies

Graph II suggests what happens in a single simple pattern, through time, if devastation is seen as the sole generator of change. At first settlement Type A dominates, and accounts for about two thirds of the land surface occupation. Catastrophic devastation could reduce settlement by at least fifty percent, and regeneration brings a new plan type. This expands spatially and eventually may fill all or more of the territory previously occupied (Type B), while other forms, Type C, may eventually take up all potentially good land, infilling all but the least desirable settlement niches. Graph III brings us to geographical ground. Let us imagine a settlement type, we will call it Anglo-Saxon so as not to make the argument too abstract, expressed by the three pips – perhaps linked hamlet clusters to be specific (Type A). Devastation occurs over a period of time, and is so complete that the surviving inhabitants are drawn together into new concentrations, planned settlements (Type B), and these are established in great numbers as population recovers. Most are successful, but some are not, causing a slight recession. Type C, wholly new plantations appear later. Throughout there are some survivors from the antecedent, pre-devastation, situation, appearing on the map as three pips. We have here simple analysis, with a single prime cause, and the resultant pattern is shown as a diagrammatic map. But no human activities or events are like this and the problem is to establish the temporal phasing of the events. Do the divisions on the horizontal time axis represent, years or decades?

Figure 7.5 Graph IV shows a more realistic and an inevitably more complex picture. At Time 1 the diagrammatic map shows a mature settlement system, with three clear local regions, each possessing the characteristic feature of a particular type of settlement, symbolised by the closed circle, the open circle and the cross. Extensive devastation occurs in the southernmost region, leading to the introduction of a new form, appearing as a small open square, which brings changes by Time 2. Of proven success, this is introduced to the middle region after it is devastated in Time 2, so that by Time 3 the new form has further diffused. By Time 4 the whole area tends to be dominated by whatever form the small open square represents, and the regional contrasts of Time 1 have become culturally different by Time 4. Here we must reiterate that this abstract argument, largely free of loaded terms relating to location and chronology, is put forward to emphasise the complexity of the changes we are attempting to recover by limited historical and archaeological analyses. This level of intricacy underlies all of the distribution maps of settlement types and these models draw directly from empirical experience. However, while the issues are complex, they are not beyond grasp. To some readers these graphs may appear tedious; nevertheless, the fundamental point is quite crucial. While it would be wrong to attribute village planning to a single catastrophic event such as the Harrying of the North in 1069–70, repeated local devastations, in the full destructive sense of this world, gradually had an cumulative effect on settlement, affecting both the peasantry and those seeking a living from their labours. In this, and in the increasing need to levy tax, lay powerful forces engendering change. Nevertheless, this schematic hypothetical graphic analysis – to create a measure of criticism of the technique – ignores the issue of landownership and estates. It is at this point we must now return to more specific materials concerning questions of the links between settlement chronology, settlement forms and the signature of the rents and services incumbent upon them as revealed by the specific Durham evidence.

Of Drengs and Village Plans

In short, the following discussion postulates that throughout northern England *drengs*, in addition to other duties, may also have acted in much the same capacity as did the *locators* of the Continent (Duby 1968, 79, 391–6; Postan 1966, 461–72). Drengs, whatever their ultimate origin, could operate as land agents, officers, who on behalf of a superior lord supervised the plantation of new villages. The underpinnings of this proposition are based upon a continuation of an evaluation of settlement and tenure on St. Cuthbert's estates, concentrating on that portion which passed into the hands of the Bishops of Durham after the Norman Conquest where a coherent, if limited, body of data allows a structured model to be developed.

The ministerial or service character of drengage as revealed by twelfth and thirteenth century sources is clear (Maitland 1887; Vinogradoff 1911, 1908; VCH Du, i, 259–326 1905; VCH Cu, i, 295–335; Jolliffe 1926; Barrow 1969 and Barrow 1973). As Jolliffe pointed out the tenure has been classified in every category from knight service to villeinage (1926, 16). Its origins remain opaque but Campbell has established a likely context by identifying a class of Anglo-Saxon tenants concerned with secular administration (in Holt 1986, 210–218, particularly 213–4), while Vinogradoff perhaps touched the truth when he talked of 'statesmen farmers'(1908, 409–10) and noted their 'squires services' (1908, 62–64). Furthermore, there is a need to distinguish between the words – 'dreng' and 'drengage' – as well as the precise form, or forms, of tenure with which these were associated. We are in fact not dealing with a single, unitary idea but *a form of tenure*, a concept that changed through time. In practice no close, single, all-embracing definition is possible, and the tenure was characterised as much by variation as by uniformity. Paradoxically this variation is significant and important, for as well as reflecting imperfections in the documentary record, the discrepancies may derive from two factors, first, evolution through time and, second, origins in particular bargains struck with individuals. That drengage has pre-Conquest roots is not debated, but Campey's view that drengage holdings in settlements imply a pre-Conquest origin for their plans must be examined critically (Campey 1989, 85–6). There are three possibilities: either some of the village plans are pre-Conquest, or they are indeed Norman and post-Conquest, or they spanned a period extending before and after the Norman Conquest. The latter now appears inherently more likely. Nevertheless, to achieve an understanding of the chronology is important, and in this matter the appearance of drengage holdings may offer a clue. The evidence from Boldon Book, 1183, on which this argument is based, is summarised in the Appendices as a series of tables, and this material has been supplemented by evidence from the Hatfield Survey of 1381 (Greenwell 1852 and 1857).

Primary Evidence: Drengage in 1183 and 1381
Figure 7.6 lists a distinctive group of vills that, in 1183, were recorded as containing a dreng. Great Usworth is characteristic of this group:

> Great Usworth renders 30s of cornage, and one cow in milk and one castleman, and eight scatchalders of malt and as many of meal, and as many of oats, and each plough, except the demesne ploughs and harrows two acres. And the villans make three precations (obligatory boon-works) in autumn with 26 men and these works, which they were used to perform at Washington, they now perform at Gateshead, and they cart one cask of wine and a millstone to Durham. The dreng feeds a dog and a horse, and attends the great chase with two greyhounds and five ropes, and follows the pleas (does court duty), and goes on messages. The mill of the same town renders 10s.
>
> (Greenwell 1852, 35–6, 69–70)

Here it is possible to distinguish between services incumbent upon the vill and services rendered by the individual dreng. The latter are surely not in addition to the other vill-based services? Thus, at Sheraton, although a named person is said to be responsible for the vill-based services of cornage, milch cow and castle-guard, it is 'his villans' who plough, harrow and perform the boon works, and it is reasonable to see this named individual, Thomas, as *the dreng*. In this case he holds a half-drengage; the other half of the vill, and half of the drengage, is specifically quit of works and services, part of an agreement by which John, the other 'half-dreng', relinquished his claim to Crawcrook (Greenwell 1852, 36, 70). In these and similar cases, the division between collective services centering on the vill and personal services owed by the dreng is sharp, and is emphasised in the table by the vertical double line. The tabulation confirms the essential similarity of settlements in this group, but also incorporates in part B less-certain cases that may contain drengages passed over silently by Boldon Book. It is notable that by 1183 some of these tenures were already subdivided, with services converted to cash payments, but they were not heavily fragmented. The case of Sheraton has already been noted, while at Herrington, Boldon Book records only two parts of the vill, noting that the dreng attends the great chase with two parts of two greyhounds, implying commutation for cash. Perhaps the fun was sufficiently great for him to go with two dogs in any case, although one might have served! The services incumbent upon vills are diverse; cornage and milch cow, with renders of malt, oats and flour, ploughing, harrowing and boon works, and usually carting wine and/or millstones. These work-services are noticeably light, comparing favourably with the heavy week work, three days per week, rendered by villans of Boldon and the core vills of Aucklandshire, while the food renders are significantly lighter than those found in villages such as

Heighington. Significantly, in all but two of the cases in Figure 7.6 the works were performed at another vill, where demesne lands were present. The distances involved are generally of the order of two miles, although Gateshead is over four miles from Great Usworth Washington is closer. In contrast, the drengs themselves owed more honourable services, the keeping of their lord's dogs and horses, carrying his messages and attending his great chase on the open fells and in the wooded vales of Weardale. In only two cases in Figure 7.6, part A were carting services due from the dreng, and in neither settlement were these services performed by the villans. Nevertheless, the evidence summarised in this table provides grounds for arguing that vill and dreng were separate although closely interrelated. The dreng was part of the vill, perhaps answerable to the Bishop for its renders, yet separate and somewhat raised above the general level by the distinctive character of his services.

Although the services present in this group in 1183 did survive to be recorded in the Hatfield Survey of 1381 certain changes had taken place. It is not the present purpose to examine these completely; some may be more apparent than real, but as the compilers of the Hatfield Survey undoubtedly took careful note of the text of Boldon Book (*e.g.* Greenwell 1857, 11, 34, 46), sharp differences are likely to be significant. Comparison of the two sources shows that the earlier patterns had in some instances been transmitted wholly unchanged. In other cases 'adjustment' had taken place, notably at Binchester, Hunwick, Great Usworth, Hutton Henry and Urpeth, where the term *servitium forinsecum* – forinsec service, itself a term not lacking ambiguity – has replaced drengage (Vinogradoff 1908, 39; Kapelle 1979, 53). At Binchester and Hunwick, however, it is specifically noted in 1381 that they were formerly drengages, while at Sheraton traces of the drengage persists, half the vill being held *pro redditu dringagii*, for a drengage rent. In this context it is instructive to compare the entry for Urpath in 1183 with that of 1381

> 1183: Urpeth renders 60s rent at the four terms, and ploughs and harrows 8 acres at Chester le Street, and does 3 precations (boon or obligatory days) in the autumn, each precation with 24 men and the fourth precation with 12 men. The dreng feeds a dog and a horse and attends the Great Chase with 2 greyhounds and 15 ropes, and carts one cask of wine and a millstone for the mill at Durham and follows the pleas (does court duty) and goes on messages and repairs half of the mill-pond and mill-house of Chester with the men of Chester.
>
> (Greenwell 1852, 37–8).

> 1381: Thomas Grey of Hetton holds the lordship of Urpeth with the water-mill and one assart, for forinsec service (per servitium forinsecum) and renders at the four usual terms 8 pounds. The same Thomas renders for the works of 20 bond tenants due on the demesne land at Chester at the feast of St. Martin yearly 20s. And he carries each year one cask of wine. He owes suit of court to the county of Durham.
>
> (Greenwell 1857, 82).

Village Plantation 211

VILLS	Carting wine	Great Chase with n Greyhounds & n Ropes	Keeping dog and horse	Errands for Bishop	Suit of Court	CORNAGE in shillings	MILCHCOW	CASTLEMAN	CARTING WINE	CARTING MILLSTONES	MALT	MEAL	OATS	PLOUGHING & HARROWING (acres)	BOON WORKS in autumn	NOTES concerning BOLDON BOOK entry	PLAN TYPE	PAGES BB / Hatfield Survey
PART A		SERVICES SPECIFIC TO DRENG				SERVICES SPECIFIC TO VILL												
BINCHESTER	*	2G / 5R	*	*	*	5	1	1	*	*	4	4	4	2 Specifically 'the villans'	3	Works at **COUNDON**	▲	37, 71 / 34
BRAFFERTON		2G / 5R	Excluded	*	*	24s 3.5p	1	1			5	5	5			Dreng named	[ ]	37, 71 / 34
BUTTERWICK		2G / 5R	*	*	*	32	1	1	*	*	8	8	8	2 Specifically 'the villans'	4 with one man from each house	Works at **SEDGEFIELD**	▲	37, 70 / Abs
HERRINGTON 2 parts only	*	2G	*	*	*	20	0.66	0.66			8	8	8	4	* 'with 12 men'	Works at **NEWBOTTLE**	[ ]	36, 70 / 157
HUTTON HENRY	* +Millstone	2G / 5R	*	*	*	35	1	1			8	8	8	2	3 with one man from each oxgang	Richard and Ucted plough at **SHOTTON**, 2 ac. in addition	[ ]	36, 70 / 153
SHERATON a moiety		1G / 2R + 2 men	*	*	*	30	0.5	-	*	*	4	4	4	2 Specifically 'the villans'	3	2nd. moiety quit of works and services for 3 marks	[ ]	36, 70 / 152
URPETH	Mill repairs	2G / 15R (sic)	*	*	*	-	-	-						8	3 each with 24 men; 1 each with 12 men	Works at **CHESTER**; 60s farm rent paid	×	37, 71 / 82
USWORTH, GREAT		2G / 5R	*	*	*	30	1	1			8	8	8	2	3 'with 26 men'	Works formerly at **WASHINGTON**, now at **GATESHEAD**	[ ]	35, 69 / 102
PART B																		
CORNSAY & HEDLEY		5R														Renders 2 marks	[ ] ×	31, 66 / 121
CRAWCROOK							1	1			4	4	4			At farm; renders 11.5 marks; assize rent 4 marks	[ ]	35, 69 / 90
HUNWICK																8s of farm rent. Termed former drengage in Hatfield Survey	[ ]	27, 63 / 50
IVESTON	*	2G					1								1.5	Renders 2 marks. Works at **LANCHESTER**	[ ]	31, 66 / 119
WHITWORTH																Drengage converted to knight's fee	▲	31, 66 / 34

{ *VCH Durham*, I, 333; *Boldon Book*, xliii}

Fig. 7.6 Durham vills with a dreng, Boldon Book 1183

The drengage service has, by 1381, become a cash render – a pointer to what the terminological change to forinsec service really implied – but only fifteen years earlier an Inquisition *post mortem* recorded that

> 1365: Thomas de Urpeth held of the Lord Bishop on the day that he died the manor Urpeth, for homage and fealty and for the service of 40s to the exchequer of the Lord Bishop... and for the mill there £4.13s.4d... and he ploughed and harrowed at Chester 8 acres of land.... item 3 boon-days in the autumn, that is to say each one with 24 men... item he made other service to the said Lord Bishop after the manner of drengage (*Item faciet alia servicia dicto episcopo more drengagii*) keeping a dog and a horse for the Lord Bishop and attending the Great Chase... with 2 hunting dogs and 15 ropes... And he carried l cask of wine once yearly between the Tyne and the Tees, and he made suit to the county of Durham regularly.
>
> (Jolliffe 1926, 17).

In all three cases there is a subtle separation between services incumbent upon the vill and the services due from the dreng. Jolliffe suggested that drengages originated as a ministerial office, the dreng being responsible for the services of the township, in a capacity resembling that of a steward. In this example, by the late fourteenth century, this responsibility has become lordship and this would appear to be a common trend, found in many of the vills listed in Table I.

Before leaving Figure 7.6 the case of Whitworth should be noted for it confirms an assumption made earlier. One manuscript of Boldon Book states that in 'Whitworth there are 16 villans, every man of whom holds one bovate of 20 acres and renders and works in all things...' with the entry terminating at this point. A different manuscript, however, noted that 'Thomas de Acley holds Whitworth for the free service of the fourth part of one knight' (Greenwell, 1852, 27, 63: VCH Du, i, 333; Austin 1982, 38, 39, 82 n.38.17) and a surviving charter issued by Bishop Philip (1197–1208) records formal adjustment of the tenure from drengage to knight service (Greenwell 1857, xliii). Here the drengage holding was clearly a block of land, probably the 1586 statute acres of the township. By 1381 it was held by *forinsec service.* The distinction would seem to be that while the tenant of the quarter fee rendered appropriate service or payment to the Bishop for his land, the dreng was seen as receiving from the territory renders for which he was answerable to the Bishop, a form of more personal service. In return he had freedom from the more onerous services on the villans. Indeed, if the fortunes of the tenants of some of the vills, including Thomas de Ackley at Whitworth, are a guide, a twelfth century dreng could be in possession of a considerable opportunity for personal advancement. Further, his surname name implies that he originated in a vill on the estates of the Cathedral Priory.

The case of Hunwick suggests that Boldon Book could indeed pass over a drengage silently. To counter this problem Figure 7.7 lists all Bishop's vills in Boldon Book

Village Plantation

VILLS	TENANT NAME	CASH shillings	CARTING WINE n Oxen	ERRANDS	GREAT CHASE n Greyhounds	WORKS and NOTES pertaining to 1183	Entry in Hatfield Survey 1381	PLAN TYPE	PAGES BB / Hatfield Survey
BURDON, LITTLE	John de Houghton	10	4					×	6, 47 / 145
GREENCROFT	None given	16	4			Villans 'of the same town' construct mill dam at LANCHESTER and cart wine	Described as drengage	×	31, 66 / 119
HENKNOWLE	Peter	8	4					▲	27, 62 / 44
HULAM	None given	20	4				Possibly a drengage	▲	36, 70 / 153
LUTTERINGTON	Walter de Lutterington	20	4	*	*		Described as drengage	▲	27, 62 / 30
NEWBIGGIN	Guy de Redworth	13/4	4	*		'3 boon works in the autumn, with his men except his own house'	Described as drengage	▲	42, 74 / 28
PLAWSWORTH	Simon Vitulus	20	8		2G	'finds 12 men 1 day or 1 man 12 days to mow in autumn, and he ploughs one day'		▲	2, 44 / 84
TWIZELL	Walter Buggethorpe	30			1G	when a common aid shall arise he ought to give 2s. at the most'. Exchanged with CLAXTON		×	9, 49 / 108
USWORTH, LITTLE	William	10	8		2G			▲	22, 44 / 102
WASHINGTON	William de Hertburn	80			2G	'excluding the church and the land belonging to the church'. In exchange for HARTBURN. Ought to give 13s 4d at most in common aid.		[ ]	3, 44 / 102

PLAN TYPES

■ (a) towns, with complex morphologies, but often originally based upon basic row plans, with or without greens; vennels are often well developed, and there aretraces of infilled open spaces.

[·] (b) settlements retaining village-like plans and strong row-layout, but with some intensification of building plots

◊ (c) composite/polyfocal plans, containing two or more plan types

☐ (d) regular multiple row plans, often around a large green

[ ] (e) regular two row green plans

[ ] (f) part-regular and irregular two row green plans

= (g) regular two row street plans

= = (h) part-regular and irregular street plans

— (i) regular one row plans

● (j) irregular agglomerations without green

○ (k) irregular agglomerations with green

▲ (l) deserted / very shrunken village or hamlet

× (m) no nucleation known

Fig. 7.7 Durham vills with a probable dreng, Boldon Book 1183

with services in some way resembling those in Figure 7.6. A first point to establish is that, given the broad similarities that are present between the services of the vills, how many of those in Figure 7.7 were in fact drengages? Greencroft, Hulam, Lutterington and Newbiggin are all described as drengages in the Hatfield Survey, giving reasonable grounds for arguing that all of the vills of the table had a dreng in 1183, indeed each of the specifically named tenants may surely be interpreted as being 'the' dreng. Certain distinctive patterns of service emerge; all the vills pay some cash and all but two of them cart wine. No vill in this group renders cornage or milch cow, while in all but two instances works are absent. This is an important point. The emphasis on cash and the absence or cornage and milch-cow payments, must imply either that these are *younger* settlements than those in Figure 7.6 or that silent commutation has already occurred. Newbiggin was, in 1183, indisputably new, and in 1382 the settlement appears as a drengage holding, but still in the hands of one tenant. The entry in Boldon Book has already been cited, but

> Guy de Redworth holds the new town near Thickley (*i.e.* Newbiggin) in exchange for Redworth, and renders one mark, and provides 12 men one day, or one man 12 days, to mow in the autumn, and he ploughs one day and works at the mill-dam, and goes on the Bishop's errands and carts wine with four oxen
>
> (Greenwell 1852, 23).

The regularity of 'twelve' may be noted, and this is also present in the Urpath documentation noted above. Here surely, is a newborn tenurially regular settlement and a newly born drengage? This Newbiggin entry throws light on the precise nature of one of the dreng's fundamental services to the Bishop, *that he could be the mentor of new settlements*. Success would mean twelve men to mow; failure – or perhaps a conscious decision by the dreng to work the land with his immediate household and farm servants – would mean that one man had to be sent to mow for twelve days. It was argued earlier that Guy de Redworth had already successfully nurtured another new vill, or perhaps a newly regulated vill at Redworth itself. Redworth, as will be shown below, is an important link in the chain of argument.

We must now ask, can all of the vills in Figure 7.7 be regarded as 'new'? The case of Lutterington appears to be wholly fatal to this hypothesis, for the vill is mentioned in the *Historia de Sancto Cuthberto*, (Hodgson Hinde 1868, 151) when it is described as a dependency of Staindrop and ascribed to a grant of Cnut (Hart 1975, 132). However, while its place-name is indeed Old English, it is not in fact an *-ington* form but implies 'the farmstead or settlement on the *Hluting*' or clear stream (Watts 2002, 74). At the heart of any new village foundation there could be the cleared lands of an existing farmstead. At Washington the place-name and the existence of a twelfth century font would also imply the presence of an older settlement (Pevsner 1985, 487; Watts 2002, 132). Significantly there is a clear hint of a change in status of this place in the Boldon Book entry for Great Usworth (Fig. 7.6), where it is noted that works formerly undertaken at Washington were, by 1183, performed at Gateshead. In both these cases it seems reasonable to invoke estate reorganisation, perhaps following devastation, as a causal factor: the settlement system was inevitably in flux. Nevertheless, and this must be emphasised, the broad similarity of services shown in Figure 7.7 suggests that the service characteristics of this group of settlements may, in some way, have had a common origin and that they represent a narrow chronological phase. Furthermore the active changes in status lie within the period of the administrative notes from which Boldon Book was compiled, *i.e.* in the decades, or perhaps half century, before 1183. Some emerge as green villages: for example, in Figure 7.6 Brafferton, possibly Herrington (obfuscated by the fact there are two settlements of this name), Sheraton, Great Usworth, Crawcrook, Hunwick, and Iveston. In Figure 7.7, however, a surprising number emerge as single farmsteads and/or deserted villages, sometimes with ambiguous earthworks, or with no known settlement focus. Why?

We can suggest that by the later twelfth century the drengs had an option, as the cases of Newbiggin and Redworth show, and the balance of economic opportunity was shifting away from tenanted vills towards different modes of land exploitation based upon labourers, hinds, rather than bondage tenants based in vills. There is a strong presumption that while some of these were indisputably on new sites, others were long occupied, while others, and Washington is one case, were sites where factors were present that necessitated redevelopment and moving the estate centre to a new locus. If this cannot be proved, the probability is nevertheless high. However, while there are strong implications in this argument that new drengages appeared right up to 1183, at which date they were already being converted into newer forms of land-based rather than service-based tenures, other drengs do appear in Boldon Book to carry the story backwards from 1183.

Drengs, Split Drengages, Firmars and Molmen

The entries documented so far by no means exhaust all references to drengs or drengages in Boldon Book, and Figure 7.8 completes the picture. Although the vills owe broadly similar services to those found in so far, those of this group tend to be more complex, more variable in character, and their renders and services had already been subjected to considerable change before being noted in Boldon Book. In this case, the criteria for inclusion include references to a dreng or drengage in either 1183 and/or 1381. For instance, Carlton appears not to possess a dreng in 1183, but the Hatfield Survey identifies a drengage holding. Figure 7.8 includes in part B two vills lacking such clear confirmation. However, before analysing this group it is necessary to digress and consider briefly a further category of tenant appearing in 1183, *firmarii*, or leaseholders (Fig. 7.9). Lapsley's conclusion about this class of tenant is worthy of recall

> in the case of vills composed of farmers [*firmarii*] only we should see relatively new communities allowed or encouraged by Bishop to grow up on his demesne

lands… and …where farmers occur in connection with villans we discern something that resembled rather an offshoot from the older vill than the creating of a new one.

(VCH Du, i, 282).

The essential point concerning the services rendered by this group of tenants is that, as Figure 7.9 shows, the heavy week work of the long-established vills was absent. This was surely a logical arrangement when new land was being broken or once-cultivated land reclaimed? However, if the linkage between new vills and drengage postulated above is indeed correct, then we might expect a dreng to be present in 1183 in all of the vills containing *firmarii*.

In this respect, the results are only partly conclusive; at Wardon and Morton there are no signs of a dreng; South Sherburn has none of the usual signs, but there is a rather distinctive larger holding of four bovates, described separately from the rest. In Carlton the dreng's holding of a carucate appears in 1183 as the holding of William son of Orm, but eight bovates held freely 'by charter' in 1381 are in fact a drengage holding – they appear under the heading *Tenentes in Dringagio*. No dreng is mentioned in Redworth, but this is to be expected, because the entry for Newbiggin – already cited – shows that Guy de Redworth had 'held' this village before acquiring Newbiggin. Paradoxically, in the Hatfield Survey the entry for Redworth begins with the heading *Tenentes in Dringagio*, listing a number of tenants holding a total of 16 messuages to which are attached highly irregular holdings expressed in acres. In this case the *firmarii* of 1183 have 'become' drengs by 1381, surely a misuse of this latter term and an interesting confusion in the mind of the medieval clerks. Because of Guy de Redworth's move, the dreng's men – all seen as *firmarii* – answer directly to the Bishop and become tenants in drengage by 1381. Of Newton by Boldon we know nothing, because in 1381 Lord Neville held it. Another pattern of change can be seen in Carlton and Wardon, where between 1183 and 1381 the *firmarii* 'become' bondsmen (*bondarii*).

These arguments aid the analysis of Figure 7.8. For the great village of West Auckland Boldon Book is quite unequivocal: Elstan, formerly the dreng, held four bovates for specified services. Turning to the Hatfield Survey no less than seven separate holdings appear under the heading *Tenentes in Dringagio* but Elstan's holding is not identifiable. In fact these 'drengages' of 1381 clearly originate in a separate group of holdings in the hands of named individuals whose services are in fact listed in Boldon Book but which are not at that stage described as drengages. They may more properly be viewed as *firmarii*, and, as at Norton, Sedgefield, Stockton, Cockerton and Darlington, such tenants were appended to an older vill, whose existing administrations could have directed expansion. West Auckland was for some reason an exceptional case. On the ground this is a vast green village, to this day a quasi-town, although it never achieved urban status. In fact, with the exception of Cockerton, all these settlements with similar groups of leaseholder tenants grafted on to them either become towns or

Village Plantation

PART A VILLS	CARTING WINE	Great Chase with n Greyhounds & n Ropes	Keeping dog and horse	Errands for Bishop	CASH in shillings	BOON DAYS	OVERSEEING WORKS	PLOUGHING & HARROWING (acres)	LAND HELD	NOTES concerning Boldon Book entry	NOTES concerning Hatfield Survey entry	PLAN TYPE	PAGES BB / Hatfield Survey
Services dues from DRENG													
WEST AUCKLAND	*			*	10	3 'with all his men except his own house'		2	4 oxgangs	Formerly held by Elstan, the dreng		[·]	25, 61 / 29
CARLTON		1G			10				8 oxgangs	William son of Orm, specifically quit of all other services	Described as drengage	[ ]	15, 53 / 177
HOUGHTON-LE-SKERNE				*	2		*		40 acres	Gilbert and Aldred, in exchange for land held by father in drengage		[ ]	18, 56 / 7
HOUGHTON-LE-SKERNE				*	2		*		40 acres				
NORTON					10	4				Alan de Normanton, he finds 4 carts 1 day, or 2 carts 2 days to carry corn	Described as drengage	[·]	12, 51 / 172
OXENHALL Service of ONE QUARTER part of a DRENGAGE	*		0.25 of year			3 'with all his men except his own house' AND	1 'with one man per house except his own house'	4 'and sows it with the Bishop's seed'		Makes UTWARE when it is laid in the Bishopric		x	17, 55 / 9
WHESSOE	*			*	10s 8p	4 'with all his men except his own house'	*	1.5	8 oxgangs	Robert Fitz-Meldred holds one quater part of one drengage. Makes UTWARE.		▲	19, 57 / 9
PART B													
LANCHESTER		1G		*	16				60 acres	Liulf		[·]	30, 65 / 109
MIDDRIDGE					6	3	*	1 day; mows 1 day	4 oxgangs	Vekeman; carts hay and corn 2 days		[ ]	22, 59 / 20

Fig. 7.8 Durham vills with a dreng, Boldon Book 1183

VILLS	CASH in shillings	CARTING corn and hay	BOON WORKS in autumn	HENS & EGGS	PLOUGHING & HARROWING (acres)	REAPING & MOWING	ERRANDS	WORKS	LAND HELD (TOTAL)	NUMBER OF FIRMARII	FIRMARII only	NOTES	PLAN TYPE	PAGES BB / Hatfield Survey
In each case the services listed are for each individual firmar														
BLACKWELL	5						*		4 oxgangs	5		Services 'as they of DARLINGTON'	⊡	17, 54 / 11
CARLTON	10	6 days							46 oxgangs	23	*		[ ]	15, 53 / 177
COCKERTON	5						*		3 oxgangs	4		Services 'as they of DARLINGTON'	⊡	17, 55 / 14
DARLINGTON	5			*			*		12 oxgangs	12			■	16, 54 / 1
MORTON	16.6	6 days		*			*	20 days Ploughing at HOUGHTON	25 oxgangs	16	*	8 cartloads a year to Durham or 4 to Auckland	∷	8, 48 / 197
NEWTON BY BOLDON	5		4 for every 2 oxgangs, with 2 men						24 oxgangs	12 mallmen	*		◂	5.45 / Abs
NORTON	6s 8p	*	4 with all the house except the housewife		half acre per oxgang	*			40 oxgangs	20		CORNAGE not paid for want of pasture Named dreng; drengage in Hatfield Survey	⊡	12, 51 / 172
REDWORTH	5	*	3 with one man	*	*	*			16 oxgangs	16	*		○	23, 59 / 25
SEDGEFIELD	5	*	4 with all the house except the housewife		half acre per oxgang	*			40 oxgangs	20			⊡	11, 50 / 186
SOUTH SHERBURN	2		4	*	1	*			60 acres	5			◂	10, 49 / ?
STOCKTON	6s 8p	*							9 oxgang	6		CORNAGE not paid for want of pasture	⊡	13, 52 / 164
WARDON	8p	*	20 (sic) includes, 4 with all the house except the housewife	*	half acre per oxgang				18 oxgangs	9	*		◂	7, 48 / 157

Figure 7.9 Durham vills with firmarii, Boldon Book 1183

show signs of abnormal development when compared with more characteristic vills, *i.e.* they are generally larger places, of enhanced importance. What then of Elstan's drengage in West Auckland? In Hatfield Survey, under the heading *Liberi Tenentes* two tenants hold *per servitium ringagii* (*sic*), in all forty acres of land. This is surely Elstan's drengage holding? Norton is a very similar case, but here in 1381 a sharp distinction was preserved between the ploughland held originally by Alan de Normanton in drengage and the land held by *tenentes vocati Malmen sive Firmarii*. Here, heavy work services of the Boldon type were rendered by the bondsmen, but the *firmarii* owe far lighter services. Boldon Book shows that by 1183 the drengage at Haughton le Skerne (already split in two) had been exchanged for freehold lands, and no trace appears in 1381. Carlton has already been mentioned, the dreng's holding in fact forming one-eighth of the sixty-four bovates of land in the vill in 1183. The cases of Whessoe and Oxenhall remain. In both cases a drengage has apparently been subdivided into four parts, and the information is not complete; in Oxenhall the dreng keeps a dog and a horse for one quarter of the year, but this is not specified at Whessoe. Both entries concern complex situations, and there are surely omissions and textual distortions in what were in effect administrative notes.

In summary, in none of these cases are there grounds to suggest that the dreng's original relationship with the vill need have been in any way different from that postulated already. Namely, that the normal arrangement was for one tenant to be of this status, of higher status than the majority of the tenants be these bondsmen or leaseholders. In such cases the dreng is seen in a new role, acting as the mentor of new extensions to older vills. The considerable internal variations of services within the tenures of this group suggest underlying processes of bargaining between the Bishop's officers and the individual concerned, as well as the passage of time. There are evidently old and new drengages but there is nothing in this analysis to suggest that these tenancies originated more than two or three generations before 1183, or certainly, in these particular cases, before the Norman Conquest. The fact that the drengages were in 1183 mainly listed separately from the other distinctively organised vill groups implies they were already, at that date, perceived as something separate (Austin 1982, 6–9; Offler 1996, XII, 13 ff.).

Conclusions

This analysis has raised important questions about the temporal and spatial variations in the character of drengage tenure and the relationship in Durham between the dreng and settlement development. The broad thrust of the argument has been that there was normally one dreng present in one vill, serving an administrative role, but often acting as a mentor for local development. In the earlier cases it appears that his status was one above the normal tenant farmers, just above, so that he was in danger of merging with them. This personal holding could either be fragmented or converted to other forms of tenure. In the decades before 1183, however, new opportunities were achieved and, paradoxically, a dreng could take advantage of his mediate position to establish a family who were seen to possess 'lordship' over the vill. In this the naming of the dreng is an important element in the historical record: the name was a reminder of his personal responsibilities. Nevertheless, there is a contrast between 'ministerial drengages', in which service to the Bishop was the hallmark of the tenure and a humbler group, perhaps 'praedial drengages', in which the dreng undertook humbler agricultural works, even if in the role of overseer. In none of these cases are there grounds for seeing any of these as ancient tenures or indeed necessarily pre-Conquest.

The essential conclusions can be summarised as a series of propositions. Figures 7.6 to 7.9 imply that three four categories of circumstance may be identified:

Type I (Fig. 7.6), in which a single drengage holding is associated with a populated vill from which renders in kind and work are demanded. Most, but not all, of these render cornage and milch-cow, and may thus have been settlements of ancient foundation, even if subsequently subjected to redevelopment. 'Devastation' is perhaps too much of a catchall explanation, but warfare and slave raiding may have been crucial factors in causing local depopulations. Figure 7.10 is a reminder that established settlements containing traces of drengages also appear on the estates of Durham Cathedral Priory, estates severed from the Episcopal estates in the later eleventh century. The earthwork traces at Woodham suggest that this settlement was a single row regular plan. The drengages present seem comparable to those in Figure 7.6.

Type II (Fig 7.7), in which a single drengage holding held by a named individual dominates the settlement, so that any villan tenants and their services remain largely concealed by Boldon Book. In general vills of this type do not render cornage and milch cow. We postulate that these represent new foundations, most of which were retained 'in hand' by the named drengs to which the lands were allocated.

Type III (Fig. 7.8), in which a drengage holding, sometimes already fragmented, appears as part of a thriving, tenanted successful settlement of older foundation.

Type IV (Fig. 7.9), in which in some cases extra tenants, *firmarii*, 'rent payers', are in process of being grafted onto older centres, some of them the centres of small shires, as at Darlington, Sedgefield and Norton, while in others such as Redworth and Newton by Boldon, new and tenurially regular entities are being established. There is evidence that in the minds of the clerks these new tenures could sometimes be described as drengages.

Two additional groups of tenurial profiles must be added to this listing:

Type 01 (Appendix I), thriving tenanted villages, producing renders in kind and cash

Village Plantation 221

VILLS	TENURE	LANDS	MERCHET	HERIOT	CORNAGE	MILCHCOW	AID	MILL WORKS	MOWING	REAPING	PLOUGHING & HARROWING (acres)	HENS & EGGS	CASH (Shillings)	SUIT of COURT	PLAN TYPE	PAGES F.P.D.
BILLINGHAM	Freely Military Service	3 oxgangs	*	*					1 day with 1 man	1 day with 1 man	4 days with 1 man	*	13s 4d	*	[·]	40
FERRYHILL	?	3 oxgangs	*	*		*	*	*		4 days, with 1 man; over works	* dependent on team size		10s	*	[ ]	66n
KIRK MERRINGTON	Freely Military Service	4 oxgangs	*	*		*	*	*					13s 4d	*	[ ]	68n
SHELOM	Freely Military Service	4 oxgangs								1 day with 1 man	half acre		4s 8d	*	[ ]	68
MIDDLESTONE	Freely Military Service	4 oxgangs	*	*		*				1 day with 1 man	half acre		8s	*	[ ]	69-70n
MONKTON	Freely ?	30 acres	*	*	*		*			*	*		2s 8d		= =	114-5n
WOODHAM	Freely Military Service	Whole vill					*	*		*				*	▲	68
WOLVISTON	Freely Military Service	Whole vill	*				*	*		*			3s 9d	*	[·]	64

F.P.D. = W. Greenwell, *Feodarium Prioratus Dunelmensis* (Surtees Society 58, 1872)

Figure 7.10 Durham vills with a probable dreng on the estates of the Cathedral Priory

and owing heavy works for the villans or bondsmen, many of which contain holdings which are 'abnormal', *i.e.* held by a named individual, larger than the norm or rendering services reminiscent of a drengage, even if not described as such. Boldon is a classic example, but Blackwell, Darlington and Morton amongst others fall into this category. We must presume that these represent an even older generation of 'drengages', a generation already subjected to the traumas of time.

Type 02 (Appendix I), settlements held at farm, with the tenants paying an agreed fixed sum to the Bishop. These are quite simply leased, to provide a fixed income in cash, and provide only an impenetrable barrier to further speculation, although it may be worthwhile asking why they are at farm. What qualities have ensured this? No answer is yet forthcoming.

Of course, none of these are wholly watertight self-contained categories. This is further emphasised by the fact that each of the settlement sets identified have an inevitable tendency to contain one or more individuals that exhibit features found within other sets. The classifications are not, and indeed, cannot be perfect and wholly mutually exclusive. Neither need they be. This is a crucial point when dealing with document/landscape correlation: the documented variations must reflect varied stages in ongoing temporal processes as well as spatial variations deriving from land quality and settlement history. This is to be expected, and it is not special pleading to argue that all explanations and generalisations must recognise and accept that slight discrepancies are inevitable, even if we ignore the inevitable problem of imperfections and downright errors in the documentary record. Appendix I contains full details of this classification, categorising individual places and drawing attention to some anomalies. For comparison two other attempts to group Durham villages by Lapsley and Kapelle also appear. The chapter to follow returns to the possible implications concerning the chronology and character of this tabulation for understanding the development of settlement, and the place of these conclusions in the wider context provided by the other vills of the Cuthbertine estates.

Chapter Eight

Of Drengs and Plans

This analysis of tenurial profiles shows that these do have a bearing upon the dating of Durham settlement plans, and within this chapter we must both reassess this question, and draw many threads together. Ultimately it is not possible to do more than arrive at a balance of probabilities, but two themes underlie what is suggested. First, the analysis of many individual plans in this study points towards their presence by the twelfth century and conceivably by the tenth century. Second, Figure 5.5 suggested a close general correlation between 'on ground' settlement characteristics recorded in the nineteenth century and the tenurial status of each settlement recorded in the great surveys of the lands of the Bishop of Durham. Vills containing drengs and drengages discussed in the previous chapter form only a limited proportion of those listed, and it is to the remainder, indeed the majority, that we must return.

Settlement Sequences and Settlement Cycles

To recap, Figure 7.7 – arguably the latest phase – rather uncomfortably groups together settlements with indisputable Old English place-names with a 'new' name like Newbiggin. In these cases the heterogeneity of the place-names, plus their wide geographical dispersal, must mean that the tenurial homogeneity of the settlements is not a direct reflection of their ultimate origins, but results from subsequent changes. None pay cornage or milch cow, but their Old English place-names imply earlier settlement 'presences', although we cannot now determine their character. Specifically, it seems probable that the places listed include devastated estate centres being brought into production (*e.g.* Washington – perhaps itself once a small shire focus), as well as a wholly new plantation at Newbiggin. In addition there must have been single farmsteads being lifted to hamlet or village level. This work was being undertaken by a named dreng. From this it is but one short step to suggest that it was the dreng's task to undertake this revitalisation, although in the longer term, the Bishop's officers were prepared to accept the specified work or rent, however it was generated. In this argument we are temporally close, in 1183, to the agreements that established these tenures, and significantly, placed the name of each dreng firmly on record. Of course, some of the places still retained or had acquired some villan tenants, but the assumption must be that the mediate tenant, the dreng, possessed an element of choice and in most of these particular cases, at a time of economic and social change, chose not to develop the classic nucleated village divided between a lordship farm and tenancies.

In contrast Figure 7.6 differentiates sharply between the services of the dreng and the services of the tenants, and in a number of these cases these tenants are described as villans, who often perform services at other places, estate centres in whose territory they lie. The place-names, and the payment of cornage and milch cow indicate Old English or even older settlement roots, but once again this uniformity of rents and services in a group of vills spread widely throughout all elements of the Cuthbertine estates, must be interpreted as deliberately imposed. Some pay and some do not, and this is hardly likely to be random. It is possible that the settlements of Figure 7.6 represent an earlier set than those of Figure 7.7, but as has been shown, perhaps no more than a generation earlier. Proof of this is seen in Herrington and Sheraton whose drengage holdings have by 1183 been split once, but not further fragmented. The group in Figure 7.7 overlaps with those of Figure 7.6 in as much as one settlement, Brafferton, contains a named dreng and it is notable that this is the settlement that also breaks the distinctive and regular pattern of grain renders. It is likely that villan tenants were present in five out of the eight cases, but Brafferton apparently possesses no bondsmen. The settlements of Figure 7.6 part A are best interpreted as rent-producing vills, owing works to sustain lordship farms at Coundon, Sedgefield, Newbottle, Shotton, Chester, Washington and Gateshead (the substitute for Washington) and re-founded after devastation or re-development. Nevertheless, we must assume that circumstances were such that memory of older cornage and milch cow payments had not been wholly erased, indeed that some tenants or some records survived to bring memory to reconstruction and reconstitution so that these rents were sustained within the re-planted settlements. Sufficient population may have pre-existed upon or near the site to term this process 'revitalisation' rather than re-foundation although this leaves open the question of the origins of any new tenants. Nevertheless, a dreng was the agent employed, and in these cases nine out of fourteen proved to be successful plantations.

The vills of Figure 7.8 may represent the earliest group of drengages to be specifically recorded as drengages in 1183. It will be noted that the services listed are only those due from the dreng; the villan services are separately enumerated and are, as might be predicted, only moderately heavy when set against those of Boldon or Heighington. In contrast to those of Figure 7.7, the settlements of Figure 7.8 were notably more successful. All lie on the better agricultural lands of the south of the county. In this context the dreng is, to borrow Mark Twain's splendidly neutral term, seen as 'the boss', supervising the works of the other tenants and the fragmentation into halves and quarters suggests that they are earlier than those of Figures 7.6 and 7.7. But by how much? At West Auckland the land of the drengage is in the Bishop's hand 'until Elstan's son shall be grown up' (Greenwell 1852, 62). At Oxenhall and Whessoe the quarter drengages appear to have been recently established. In 1183 the 'whole drengage' is no more than one or two generations earlier and these drengage holdings, with a clear tendency to be divided amongst sons, are by no means utterly fragmented. We can conclude that the sequence of development postulated here extends back at the most no more than two generations, to perhaps the first quarter of the twelfth century, or at the most the last quarter of the eleventh century. More particularly, there are no grounds for suggesting that these are ancient tenures, but have come into being to serve a particular need.

It seems probable that the settlement categories defined in this and the previous chapter fall in a chronological sequence as follows:

Table 8.1: Relative sequence of tenurial types on the bishopric estates County Durham as revealed by an analysis of Boldon Book, based on Figures 7.6–7.9 and Appendices I and II

Types:	
I	= Single drengage holding in populated vill (Fig. 7.6)
II	= Single drengage holding with named dreng (Fig. 7.7)
III	= Drengage holding, sometimes fragmented, is part of larger settlement (Fig. 7.8)
IV	= Group of rent paying *firmarii* attached to larger vill (Fig. 7.9)
01	= Villages without a dreng, with villans and cottars (Appendix I)

Oldest	*Intermediate*	*Youngest*
Type 01 →		
	Type IV →	
	Type III →	
	Type II →	
		Type I →
Possible chronology	1080	1183

If the argument concerning the place of the dreng within the vill groups in is indeed correct, then all of these tenures could have evolved in the century between the Norman take-over of about 1070 and the survey of 1183. Whatever the situation that faced William de St. Calais when he obtained the Bishopric of Durham in 1080, the commencement of the cathedral in 1093 suggests that a measure of stability had been achieved by that date in spite of variations in his personal fortunes (Douglas and Greenaway 1981, 652–669; Chaplais in Holt 1987, 65–77). What then was happening to settlement and tenure in earlier times?

As was noted in the previous chapter there may be examples of older, 'decayed' drengages. A glance down Lapsley's table of Boldon Book tenants not included under the headings villans, cottars and *firmarii* reveals a complex group, many of whom render services that echo the demands upon drengs found in Figure 7.6 and 7.7 (*ibid.* 1905, 317–21). Thus in North Sherburn, Cassop and Shadforth, all villages possessing regular two-row plan structures, Boldon Book picks out a tenant paying cash and going on the Bishop's errands; in each case the holding survives as the only freehold within in each village in 1381. Given that the drengages of 1183 can be seen mutating rapidly even in the face of a written survey, it is hard to believe that this process had not been equally active before that date. Thus, in Heighington and Shotton, Easington and Wolsingham certain individuals have the duty of 'errands' while others owe boon days, duties that differ from those undertaken by the reeve (VCH Du, i, 317–321). It is reasonable to suggest that these holdings may represent traces of yet an earlier generation of ministerial holdings (Campbell in Holt 1986, 201–18), giving us a glimpse of cycles of imposed tenurial unity followed by devolution and decay, cycles which may reflect differing generations of settlement planning. There is however one futher way of sifting the vills listed in 1183.

Settlement and Tenure: The Core Vills of Small Shires and Estates

Much of the preceding long argument has necessarily concerned minutiae, which have already been generalised by using Figure 5.5. This is repeated, and modified, in Figure 8.1 and must now be re-considered in the light of the conclusions reached so far. The settlement icons used all consist of the parish and township foci that appear as names in Boldon Book and the Hatfield Survey, plus others that can be identified as 'of some status' in Hatfield Survey. A remarkable fact with this matrix is that that data derived from both medieval and post-medieval sources, generate such clear divisions, so emphasising the strong causal links between twelfth century tenurial characteristics and the settlement forms still visible in the nineteenth century. Three isochrones have now been inserted, one of *c.* 1000 and one of 1183, and may be interpreted as defining development sequences broadly extending from top left to bottom right of the graph. It is deduced that the more complex plans developed before 1080, indeed possibly even before 1000.

Group A (largely Type 01 in Appendix I) comprises those Bishopric villages that both appear in the documentary record and have survived as successful villages since the medieval period. This group is dominated by settlements with regular plans, mostly based upon two rows, but also including more complex types such as the multiple row plans of Easington and Heighington. If these had been devastated – and this is not improbable, for they were central places before the Norman conquest and hence the more attractive for large numbers of raiders – they nevertheless differ substantially from those vills with drengs and were surely established and thriving substantively before 1183. In this context the implications of the group of these villages which are described in Boldon Book as rendering 'as they of Boldon' must now be considered, paying particular attention to possible contexts in which such a uniformity of obligations could have been imposed. In fact 'as they of Boldon' is probably no more than an accident deriving from the sequence of the record, for Boldon was the first 'standard village' whose renders and services were listed, and the phrase 'as they of Boldon' was a way of shortening the compilation of the work. There must be a strong suspicion

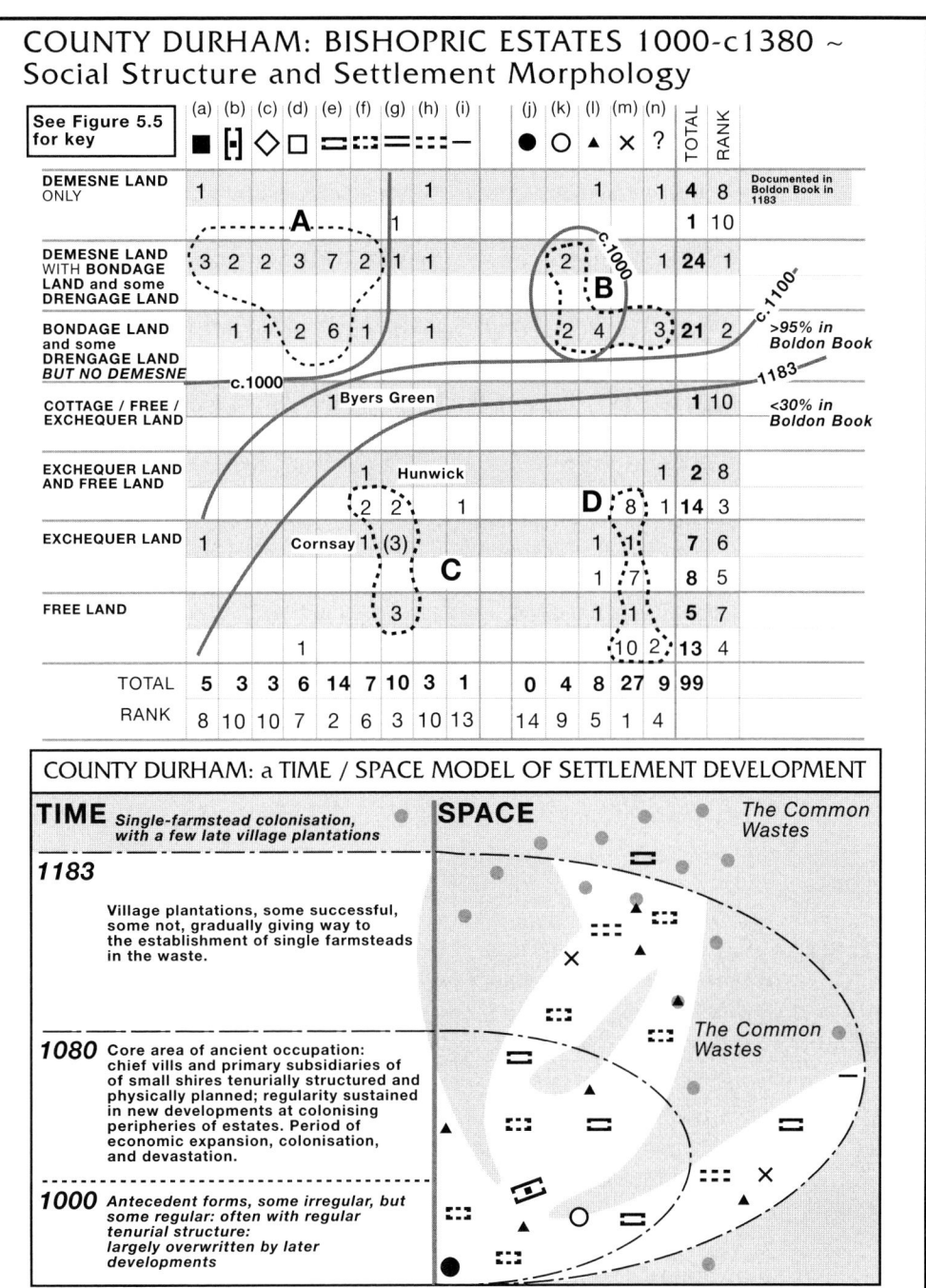

Fig. 8.1 Settlement and social structure in Bishopric vills, county Durham

that had the services of Chester-le-Street, the centre of the whole Cuthbertine estate before the move to Durham in 996, been listed, then this place would have been the exemplar, and the document would have been known as the 'Chester Book'. In addition the Heighingtonshire, Aucklandshire and Darlington vills form distinct and separate groups, with the services of their dependencies being modelled on the services of the estate centre (Fig. 6.3). Nevertheless, the vills that render 'as they of Boldon' throughout the county are associated with the settlements of the core east Durham properties of St Cuthbert, extending southwards from Whitburn and Cleadon to Wearmouth and Easington, and also up the Tyne Valley to Whickham. Boldon services are also found in the Sedgefield group, purchased in 901 x 915, and at Stockton and Norton, a gift of about 994 (Hart 1975, 1140, 125). Either the 'Boldon obligations' are part of an extremely ancient substratum of service, or, as seems the more likely, they were defined, or perhaps re-defined, as an element of the estates *after* these dates. This redefinition could have gone hand in hand with the establishment of new village plans as paradigms of the new tenurial arrangements.

There appears to have been a significant assembly of land by St. Cuthbert's bishops and community in what was to become County Durham in the late ninth century, both before and after the death of the Danish King Guthred in 894 (Craster 1954, 189). This collation is mapped in Figures 6.2 and 6.3 and tabulated in Figures 8.2 (a) and (b). To simplify the presentation the tabulation is proffered merely for reference and will not be directly integrated into the discussion but it summarises much essential evidence and has been crucial to the formulation of this argument. Substantive grants of land took place in the north and centre of the putative county and as far west as the Roman road called Dere Street (Fig. 6.2). This limit is meaningful in that these grants included wastes with some settlement, while the land west of the road comprised open upland pastures with woodlands on valley sides and few permanent settlements. We can note that subsequent colonisation of this zone did not bring Boldon type services, and indeed Aucklandshire in 1183 still possessed the most 'primitive' set of renders, echoed most closely in Welsh sources. Great estates at Gainford, and further south and east at Billingham in *Heortenesse* (Hartness) were granted to the community by Bishop Ecgred between 830 and 845 (Hart 1975, 138). In the former case, the land extended from the Tees to the Wear and from the Dere Street to the hills, a suitably vague definition applied to the largely unsettled wastes of the west (Craster 1954, 186). Unfortunately, none of these lands appear in Boldon Book, then being in Priory hands and were probably already subinfeudated to the Fitz Meldred family (Offler 1996, XIII, 3–4). However, Symeon, writing in the twelfth century, is quite specific about Billingham. In a passage emphasising Ecgred's role as a donator of goods and property to the church of St. Cuthbert, he specifically mentions 'the church and vill which he had built at Gainford… and two other vills, namely *Ilecliffe* and *Wigecliffe*, and also Billingham in *Heortenesse*, of which he had been the founder' (Stephenson 1988, Symeon XX, 37; Aird 1998, 26). We have perhaps no reason to do other than take Symeon's claims at face value and conclude that Ecgred was initiating the planting of villages in the 830s and 840s. Certainly the nave of Billingham church is dated by Harold Taylor to the period AD 800 to 950 (Taylor 1965, vol. I, 66–70), and in spite of appearances the place-name is not an early folk-name (Watts 2002, 8).

Another grant from King Athelstan comprising Bishop (South) Wearmouth and its dependencies is significant. We do not know when this land was acquired, but it was eventually appropriated by Onlafbold. He was a Viking, who swore by Thor and Odin, and after his subsequent, inevitable, and no doubt justly painful and deserved death – probably of heart failure rather than divine intervention – the estate was forfeited to king Athelstan, before being restored to the church in 934 (Hart 1975, 118: Aird 1998, 147 n. 25). In 1183 the husbandmen of this estate also rendered 'as they as Boldon', and in fact we are dealing with a small shire. As Craster summarises:

> one way or another the See of Chester le Street had come in the early years of the tenth century to own a considerable portion of the present county of Durham – that region between the Tyne and the Tees which came to be pre-eminently known as the Bishopric
>
> (Craster 1954, 190).

The community had moved to Chester-le-Street in 883 (Aird 1998, 36), a location that because of its Roman roots was a convenient high status administrative centre for the community of St Cuthbert and its growing landed estate. The site also lies near one of the important north-south Roman roads through the region, as does the Sedgefield estate which was added in 901 x 915 (Hart 1975, 140), purchased by Bishop Cutheard (Aird 1998, 116, note 72) and by 1183 these tenants were again rendering 'as they of Boldon'. Given that Cutheard's purchase (Fig. 6.2) was made from the funds of the see (*de pecunia S. Cuthberti*) then revenues from all estates, including those north of the Tyne, south of the Tees, and between the Tyne and the Wear, were flowing in to supply the treasury. Aird notes that the word *pecunia* implies livestock or cash, and opts for the latter (Aird 1998, 116, note 72). This early tenth century context, for Cutheard was Bishop between 900 and 915, may have been when the bondsmen of the estate were initially being brought under the defined body of works, renders and services antecedent to those eventually performed by those 'of Boldon'. In time, the bishops, with the approval of the Community of St. Cuthbert, made leases of the accumulated estates to great noblemen, on defined conditions, namely that the lessee swore fealty to the bishop and the community of St. Cuthbert and rendered full service, which included payment of rent (Aird 1998, 115, and note 70). This undoubtedly represents one possible context for a formalisation of rents and services that were so necessary to support the developing community (see Aird 1998, 108–123). More kindly, it was one way of ensuring that the 'leased' tenantry were not too oppressed by the lessee. In this, the payment of cornage, milch cow and lodge-building services may be seen as survivals from more ancient obligations attached to the accumulated lands of the Cuthbertine

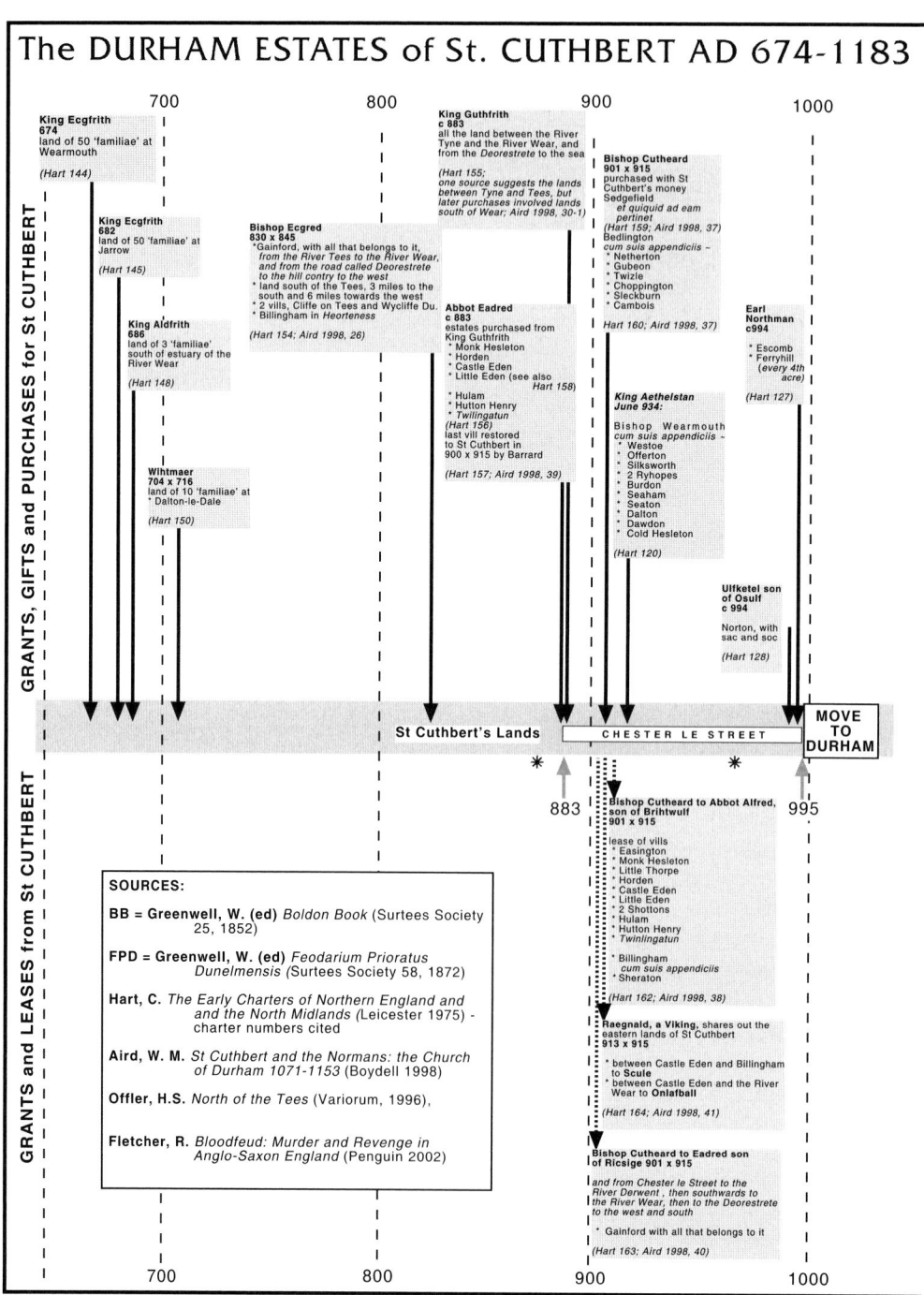

Fig. 8.2.a The Durham estates of St. Cuthbert 674–1183

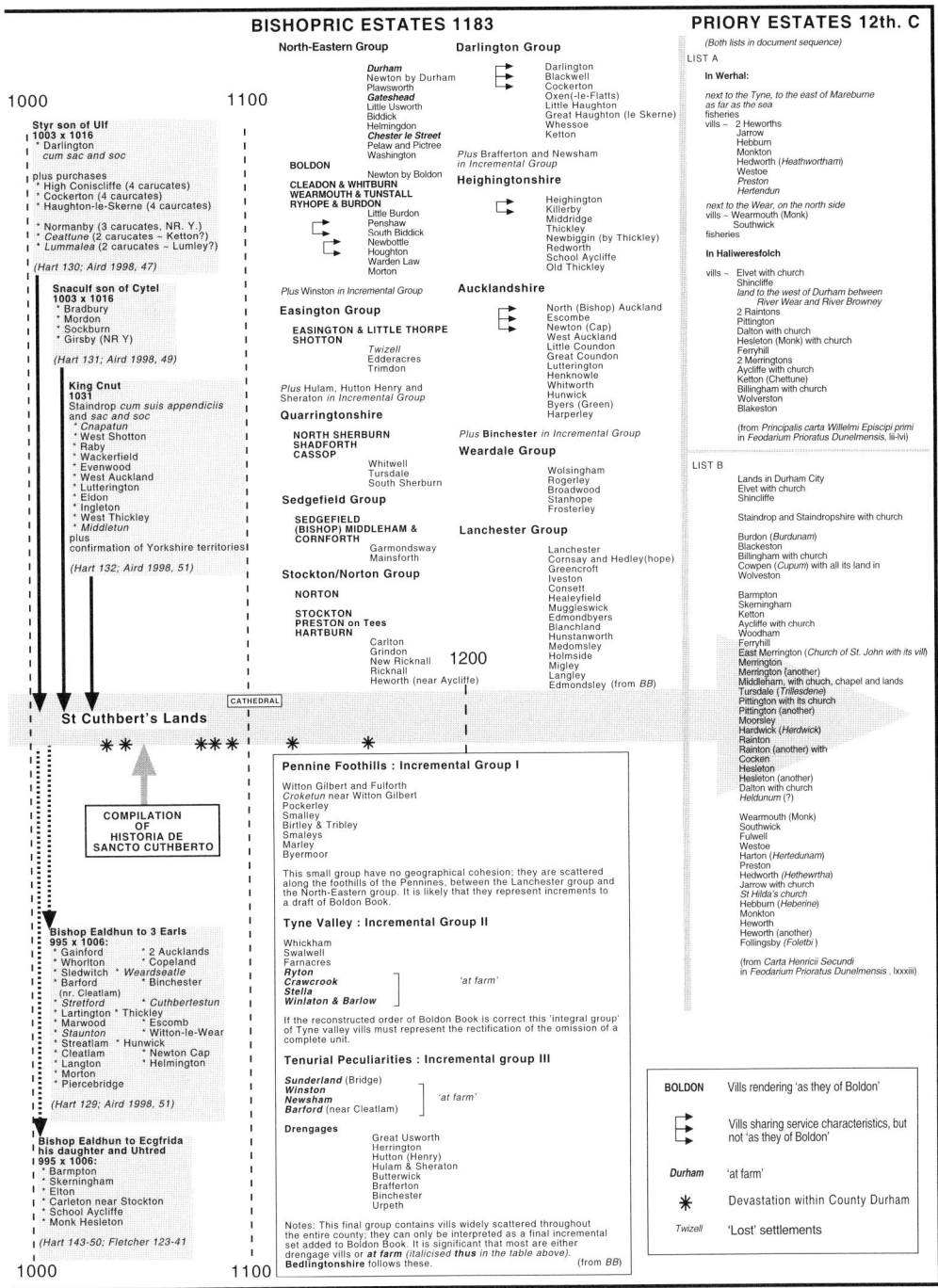

Fig. 8.2.b The Durham estates of St. Cuthbert 674–1183 (contd.)

estates, as no doubt were the food renders, work services and cartage. Their roots, no doubt as 'royal' obligations, are probably concealed amid the lands of the fifty *familiae* granted to Wearmouth in 674 and the lands of the forty *familiae* granted to Jarrow in 682 (Hart 1975, 132 and 133). They must once have been owed to King Ecgfrith himself (Aird 198, 135, note150); they were services due to the local ruler. In short the renders and services of the Boldon tenants themselves represent a set of accumulated layers; they were by no means merely inherited from time immemorial

The end of the tenth century saw other important grants to St, Cuthbert. First, we may take note of Norton, granted by Ulfketel in *c.* 994 with sake and soke (Fig.6.2; Hart 1975, 125). This grant is likely to have included Stockton and perhaps Hartburn and Preston and eventually Carlton – thus in 1381 the bondsmen there owed building services at Stockton (Greenwell 1857, 177). By 1183 the husbandmen of these vills rendered 'as they of Boldon'. In fact cornage, the payment due from the semi-wild herds of the larger pastures, was excused the tenantry of this group 'for want of pasture', implying that the lower Tees Valley was already a more densely settled region, lacking the vast tracts found in the north and west of the proto-county. However, a further estate, Darlington, was acquired by the church as a gift from Styr son of Ulf in 1003 x 1006. In 1183 the Darlington group of vills comprised Darlington itself, plus Blackwell, Cockerton, Oxenhall, and Little Haughton, and possibly Great Haughton, Whessoe and Ketton. Of these, Blackwell, Cockerton, Oxenhall and Little Haughton, are linked by specific references in their services to Darlington, while the remaining three, Great Haughton, Whessoe and Ketton follow in sequence in Boldon Book. It is significant that none of this group pays cornage or milch cow, and none render 'as they of Boldon'. Here, on some of the best agricultural and thus more desirable land of the county, the break with the past was substantial and had taken place at an even earlier date.

There has been a qualified tendency in discussion to treat small shires as transferable entities, but the case of Auckland shire and a close examination of the exceedingly intricate land transactions of the Cuthbertine community suggest that both fragmentation and re-assembly could take place. Darlington is another case and must be considered. Styr granted Darlington to St. Cuthbert with jurisdictional rights, sake and soke, possibly with other unnamed vills. He adds 'And I purchased with my own money and gave to St. Cuthbert four carucates of land in Coniscliffe and four in Cockerton and four in Haughton le Skerne and three in Normanby and two in Ketton with sake and soke and two in Lumley' in the presence of King Aethelred and ecclesiastical signatories (Aird 1998, 47, note 139). Of these only Haughton le Skerne, Cockerton and Ketton appear as part of the Darlington estate in 1183, rendering 'as they of Darlington' so that we must infer that the definition of this particular set of services post-dates this purchase, grant and estate assemblage in 1003 x 1006. The possibility exists that all of these vills were part of a post-Roman polity to which the name *Catreath* – Catterick – may legitimately be given (Higham 1986, fig 6.2). Furthermore, the vills purchased by Styr were not measured in hides but in the carucates adopted by Scandinavian settlers for land-measurement (Craster 1954, 193: Hart 1975, 126–7). The enigmatic phrase used in 1183 that the 48 oxgangs of Darlington, 'which, as well as of the old villanage as of the new, the villans hold' also implies substantial changes noted by the twelfth century clerks. In this case 'Boldon' was not used as an exemplar, probably because the estate already had a defined set of renders and services. Neither was the Boldon exemplar used for Aucklandshire, acquired at an unknown date before 995 x 1006 when it was leased to three earls (Hart 1975, 125). Cnut finally confirmed possession by St Cuthbert in 1031 (Hart 1975, 127), and in this case, in an estate set in more marginal lands, dominated by woodland and waste, ancient services survive. It is the date of *c.* 994 for the Norton grant, including also Stockton (Hart 1975, 125), both of which may have been restorations, and the Darlington gift of 1003 x 1016, that hint at when we must look for a regularisation of the Boldon renders and services, namely before the end of the tenth century.

The Cuthbertine estates assembled before 994 comprise the group that 'work as they of Boldon' and this date brings us towards the move of St. Cuthbert's community to Durham in 995 (Aird 1998, 113). The new site we are told was 'covered on all sides by dense forest' and that 'a multitude of people from the whole area between the River Coquet and the River Tees readily came to help not only with this task (*i.e.* clearing the wood) but also afterwards with the construction of the church' (Aird 1998, 46–7). This sounds very like a redirection of the building services owed by many of the tenants of the ancient vills, and drawn together at the behest of 'Uhtred, Earl of the Northumbrians'. This argument by no means dates village plans, but the set of rents, renders and services could well date from definitions gradually achieved during the previous troubled period of leasing and recovery, namely, during the tenth century between about 900 and 994, with village plans being formalised as occasion demanded. Two dates stand out, 883, when considerable resources were needed to establish an estate focus at Chester le Street, and 996, when the community moved to Durham. Both could well mark administrative surges that led to the documentation of the estates, the formalisation of the services and the re-planning of some settlements. This view qualifies and extends back in time the period during which tenurial regulation was taking place. The end of the tenth century also saw the curious 'gift' of Escomb by Earl Northman to St Cuthbert, which settlement was soon after leased with the Aucklandshire and Gainford estates back to three earls, Northman, Aethelred and Uhtred (Craster 1954, 193–4; Hart 1975, 125). Escomb remains an utter enigma; all other known structures of the seventh century are monastic sites, and yet no monastery is known at Escomb (Fig. 3.4). The suggestion made in Chapter 6 that this was a special 'royal' church linked with dales-based hunts remains a possibility and the site may be compared with a chain of sites with Anglo-Saxon stone sculpture or churches extending from Whittingham to Hexham, and from Escomb to Staindrop, and from Wycliffe, and perhaps Romaldkirk, to Masham. These are all liminal sites, set between the great wastes to the west, largely devoid of permanent settlement, and the old-settled areas to the east with larger islands of cultivated land (Fig. 2.6; Cramp 1984, fig. 1 and 2; Lang 2001, fig. 4). In conclusion, Cnut, in 1031, granted to St. Cuthbert a western small shire that was not included in the great Gainford grant, namely Staindropshire and its appendages. This estate had by 1200 long been out of the direct control of the Bishops, at first in the hands of the Priory and subinfeudated by them to Dolfin son of Uhtred, so that no early surveys are available to dissect the tenures (Aird in Appleby and Dalton 1997, 31, Aird 1998, 147, note 28; Offler 1996, XIII).

This lengthy digression postulates the presence of an estate-wide system of renders and services already in existence by about 1000 and already to some degree standardised. However, in *c*. 994, when Earl Northman granted to St. Cuthbert Escomb, as noted above, he included '*the fourth acre at Feregenne*', the 'fourth acre at Ferryhill' in the heart of County Durham (Hart 1975, 125). This specific reference undoubtedly implies a field system organised in such a way that the abstraction of the rent, revenue or produce of every fourth acre was possible. It is tempting to see these as strips, but this need not be so, for the term could imply 'furlong', often termed 'x-acre' and the like. Nevertheless, such a description could equally well be applied to the model seen in Figure 3.5. The original document is enigmatically brief. One further reference suggests that a further concomitant of an organised field system was indeed present as a concept in the land of the Haliwerfolc in the tenth century. Following the move to Durham in 995 Symeon notes that the members of the community each had a residence assigned by lot (Aird 1998, 116 note 73). While this took place in a quasi-urban context, the idea of a careful allocation of house plots, as part of achieving aliquot shares, underlies Figure 3.5. In the light of the discussion it is now possible to turn to an earlier source. Bertram Colgrave's study of the *Two Lives of St Cuthbert,* one written by an unknown monk of Lindisfarne between 699 and 705, the other by Bede some small time before 721 provides some information. Bede's straightforward account of the life of St. Cuthbert, based in part upon the anonymous life, was in fact 'read for two days before the elders and teachers' of the congregation of St. Cuthbert on Lindisfarne (Colgrave 1985, 145 and 143) 'in order that it might be corrected if false'. These men, of religious persuasion, and in modern eyes of narrow perspective, had, nevertheless, roots in the countryside of late seventh century England. Place-names and precise localities are too rarely provided, but in measure a generalised picture of settlement in Northumbria at that remote time is given. People live in villages, to which the terms *vicus, villam, viculum* are applied (Colgrave 1985, 169, 171, 186, 195, 187, 117 etc.). We can only speculate about the subtle distinctions here. Only two sites are named: first *Bedesfeld,* an unknown location, although one might note that the river name Bedburn contains the same personal name (*ibid.* 1985, 117). There is also the curiously named *Medilwong,* a name probably meaning 'middle furlong' and not wholly compatible with a village name (*ibid.* 1985, 119: Colgrave 1977, 97 and 101). Villages do appear as far north as the Tweed (*ibid.* 1985, 121). In contrast, on a journey between Hexham and Carlisle, amid a mountainous and wild region, people gathered together to see Cuthbert from widely scattered little hamlets (*villulas*), in a region where the bishop and his party had set up tents (*ibid.* 1985, 117, 259). In even greater contrast, we are told of Cuthbert travelling from the south in winter, reaching the Wear, and turning aside because of rain and storm to seek shelter in shepherd's huts (*turgaria*). These had been roughly built during the summer time, and were then lying open and deserted but *in eo loco ubi Kunacester,* 'a place called Chester-le-Street' (*ibid.* 1985, 171). Colgrave in his notes makes the statement that 'this story emphasises the fact that a large part of County Durham was deserted until well on into the Anglo-Saxon period' (*ibid.* 1985, 314), but all accounts fail to address the question of why the Bishop deliberately turned aside from Chester itself, that must surely have been inhabited? Its hagiological intent we cannot doubt, but there is here much more here than the account reveals. Nevertheless, we have a clear picture of the summer use of some of the vast reserves of waste, and a contrast to the populated areas with their villages.

None of this speaks of settlement forms. One story however raises questions. Cuthbert was in the house of a woman he visited frequently because 'she had brought him up from his boyhood years and was therefore called mother by him' (Colgrave 1985, 200–203). The Leader Valley is specifically described by the author of the *Anonymous Life* as the location of his boyhood (*ibid.* 1985, 68–9). Revisiting his foster mother Cuthbert entered her dwelling when 'a house in the eastern quarter of the same village caught fire owing to carelessness and began to burn fiercely. Moreover a great wind arose from the same quarter, which tore away the blazing thatch of the straw roof and carried it far and wide throughout the same village'. The flames could not be dowsed, but Cuthbert prayed, and the winds changed, and 'blowing from the west removed all danger of the fire attacking the house which the man of good had entered'. In this, as Bede himself states, there was emulation of other miracles and he himself was following an account of the same incident in the *Anonymous Life*, (Colgrave 1985, 89–91), where the village is named, although greatly corrupted (Barrow in Rollason *et al.* 1994, 312, n. 18). His boyhood association with the Leader Valley places his foster-mother in the far north, but well within the orbit of Bernician influence (Nicholaison, 1976, figs 2 and 3). Nevertheless, the scene must have been commonplace, and there are few things more terrible than the sight and smell of a recently burned-out dwelling. Such wind changes could have been disastrous in a village like West Heslerton (Fig. 5.1), but no modern reader, aware of the strong tendency of the planned villages of the north to lie in an east-to-west orientation, can fail to take note of this story (Colgrave 1985, 201–3; Thorpe 1951). On balance, the author would not place undue emphasis on this frail craft, but the story must be told.

This discussion provides no clear-cut answers to the origins of village plans. It does however suggest that the tenurial signatures of the individual vills form a useful set of data for thinking about the centuries before 1183. There is much indirect evidence to show that devastation, plantation and re-organisation were a part of the life of the northern husbandman. We should recall that when William I restored the estate at Billingham *cum suis appendiciis* during his stay in Durham in 1072, the confirmation specifying that it be 'for the provision of food for those who ministered in the church to God and to St Cuthbert' was no meaningless formula (Stephenson 1998, Symeon LV, 75). Land without tenants produced no food. It can be no accident that these good lands bear the clearest signs of organised villages.

The Peripheral Vills of the Bishopric Estates

Cornsay, Byers Green and Hunwick, strays attached to no village group in 1183, form useful and well-documented pivots (Fig. 8.1). Cornsay is set high on a bleak sandstone ridge – the 'cranes hill-spur' of the name – above the Browney valley in the Pennine foothills of west Durham (Watts 2002, 30). This exposed site would be the very last place for any sensible peasant farmer to locate a village. It was held, along with Hedleyhope, by Simon the Chamberlain in 1183, perhaps a man of higher status than the normal dreng, for a basic drengage service involving a cash rent and the duty of carting wine with twelve oxen and providing five ropes for the Bishop's great hunts. This was waste land when given to Simon (Greenwell 1857, xliv) and the drengage was converted to one twentieth of a knight's fee by a charter of Bishop Hugh (1153–1195). In this case by 1381 there were only three messuages listed as exchequer land, plus other sundry small pieces of land, but other tenures – by then in the hands of tenants of Lord Neville – were unmentioned. What now appears is a large interior green, rectangular, around which straggle a few farmsteads and cottages set square to the open space. Hunwick, 'Huna's dairy farm', was held by Thomas de Binchester in 1183, a personal name significantly derived from an older, well-established settlement, who held Hunwick 'at farm', while an enigmatic Robert held an assart, again indicative of a context of reclamation (Watts 2002, 64). We are here moving towards contexts in which grants of waste led to the establishment of single farmsteads. Byers Green, already discussed, appears in Boldon Book as 'one assart of Byers' held for half a mark. By 1381 it was described as a manor, with Richard Park holding two carucates of free land, and six cottage tenants with cottages. The development of this settlement involved the founding of a regular two-row street-green village, with a north-to-south orientation. Largely post-1183 in development, this village was also post-drengage in its tenurial characteristics. It remains exceptional as a village of medieval foundation because it incorporates the place-name element 'green'.

In Figure 8.1 Group C shows that a few village settlements continued to be founded after 1183, while of the settlements of group D, some survive as halls, but others may never have been more than congregations of scattered farmsteads. In fact, the bulk of the places in these two groups, 33 out of 44, are not documented in 1183, and – as their tenures suggest – represent subsequent reclamations. None contain drengages, and all appear amid the woods and wastes of the foothills flanking the mountain wastes of the western dales of County Durham. They are part of the post 1150 colonising movement more fully manifest in Figure 2.5.

Settlement Cycles in Durham

When evaluating the forces that generated regular tenurial structures and regular village plans within Durham several contextual factors must be taken into account. First, between 1095 and 1133 the new Durham cathedral and monastery were constructed, together with Durham castle, to mention only the two buildings to have an immediate impact upon the local region. The Bishops were responsible for the construction of the cathedral and the castle, while the community of Benedictine monks were responsible for their own conventual buildings (Aird 1998, 174, note 139). Both of these projects speak of estate stability and a steady income from land, and together of lifestyles and buildings that embodied seigniorial power. Second, the personalities of the individual Bishops and Priors can in no way be excluded from the equation. The energy and talent of William de St Calais is beyond doubt, and while Rannulf Flambard may have a mixed reputation both of these men were active upon a stage larger than Durham, indeed Roffe argues that Flambard was the progenitor of Domesday Book itself (Roffe 2000, 242–7).

It is to individuals with a direct interest in the Durham lands that one turns, and the eye alights upon Prior Turgot. He was clearly an exceptional man, so much so that Rannulf Flambard saw to his removal in 1106 by promoting to the see of St Andrews! He was Prior from 1087 to 1106, nineteen crucial years in the development of Durham, its buildings, its institutions and its estates (Aird 1998, 152, 167, 172). In fact Turgot was more than prior, he was archdeacon, *i.e.* the deputy to the Bishop, and charged with overseeing the church and the parishes. He had been the constant companion of the preceding prior, Aldwin, since arriving in the northeast in the mid 1070s. He was of noble birth, having been a hostage of King William the Conqueror to guarantee the good behaviour of all of Lindsey, had spent time at the court of King Olaf in Norway, and eventually, after some sharp changes of fortune, entered monastic life at Jarrow. He was clearly a man of talent and energy and his activities might explain one slightly puzzling fact about Durham villages: there are no sharp contrasts detectable between the plans of the priory vills and the Bishopric vills. This would be immediately explicable if in fact there was no fundamental division between the two administrations at a critical period. What is being suggested here is not that Turgot suddenly and completely and single-handedly reorganised all Durham villages, but that, building on roots already well-established by 994 when the community moved from Chester le Street to Durham, he reinforced and reiterated earlier tendencies. The roles of earlier more shadowy figures such as Ecgred (830–845), Eadred (*c.* 883), Cutheard (901–915) and Ealdhun (987–1006) and those around them cannot easily be assessed (Fig. 8.2). However, the mindsets encouraging the conscious ordering of terrestrial space may be compared with the careful arrangement of ritual space within the great churches. The arrangement of altar, choir, ambulatory, nave, transepts with their additional chapels, and even the porches, had meaning within the ritual cycles of the church. The allocation of terrestrial space, each to each in appropriate proportion to status was also an expression of divine order. Finally, the tenantry must not be forgotten: the regular village plans, linked with regular tenemental systems formed a permanent memory of what *was and should be*. Boldon Book and Hatfield Surveys were meaningless to the illiterate husbandmen, but the logically conceived layouts of settlement and fields created vast mnemonic structures that would survive even the worst of human devastation. This concept would arise easily, perhaps even naturally, amongst those deriving a living from land resources, where the capacity to achieve equity in shares was also necessary for maintaining social harmony amongst tenantry. This was a context with no maps and with only elemental written surveys. Any initial allocation of aliquot shares would create a stable situation, but within a generation or so the vicissitudes of fortune and the processes of expansion of both population and arable fields could lead towards pressures towards a redefinition of the initial arrangements. In this respect there were advantages for both landlord and tenant in a logical ordering of economic space and in episodic reiteration and restructuring. The documented case of Acklington shows what was possible (Fig. 3.2).

This study of tenure and settlement has raised two general questions, which must now be addressed briefly. The first concerns the chronology of settlement development, the other the scale of settlement planning. It must be admitted that the evidence to date individual plans is limited to a few percent of the total and arguments based upon establishing contexts, particularly when using map sources tend to occlude perceptions by compressing events into a limited temporal plane. In County Durham the period after the Norman Conquest of the seventh decade of the eleventh century appears to be one phase, imposing new plans, new tenures and new documents upon older settlements. Some of these had surely been devastated, but doubtless some were simply being subjected to reorganisation. However, there is no doubt that the Normans built upon earlier antecedents, thus the chief vills of the pre-Norman charters tend to be the chief vills of sections of the post-Conquest estates. Furthermore, to think in terms of a single cycle of innovation and change would be wrong. In fact Figure 8.1 is, it can be argued, itself evidence for the presence of at least four cycles of settlement development – represented by groups A to D. Groups A and B each contain a sharply defined core, where the close links between the type of settlement plan and internal tenurial arrangements are particularly strong. The existence of a penumbra of rather less clear-cut relationships is an indicator that each group probably contained several sub-cycles of development. These are concealed by the limitations of the evidence, and we should not forget the small size of the sample even within County Durham, and even more so when set against the numbers of villages and substantial hamlets throughout the north.

These arguments are a basis for understanding what may be concealed within the written survey and the landscape, and, eventually, the distribution map. It is probable that each cycle of settlement development involved an initiating phase, when new ideas were introduced, perhaps in estate centres, followed by a phase of innovation and diffusion, when idealised forms were established in numerous other settlements, and a dwindling phase, when a few last cases were created. These ideas were explored in the discussion of Figure 7.5 and these events may have lasted no more than a decade or two for each cycle. Once established, each settlement then followed its own individual temporal trajectory. This dynamic view of settlement, remoulding an even darker Anglo-Saxon base, is uncomfortably complicated, yet undoubtedly touches reality. It follows that the distribution maps of northern settlement – indeed all distribution maps of settlement – compress these cycles into one plane, with the added complication that the plans visible on maps and in the landscape have been filtered through many centuries of later use and adaptation. Of course, regular settlement plans are found in many parts of the country and their development has not been examined here: what is unusual in the north is their vast numbers.

Conclusions in Durham

In many senses Durham is a special case, but before applying the ideas developed in this discussion to Cumbria, a summary of the basic conclusions is necessary:

- by 1183 the planned green villages were already a part of the Durham landscape; this is suggested by clear links between settlement layouts and the regular and part-regular tenemental structures recorded in Boldon Book, the 'gillycorn' rental relating to the Priory vills and the fact that an exploration of the 'late foundations' evidenced by ministerial drengages does not suggest more than the *finis* of a process already well under way;

- praedial drengages, those involving agricultural work, effectively boon works, are deeply embedded within the tenurial signatures of the core vills of the shires and ministerial drengages, involving higher status services, what were later 'serjeanty' services, and associated tenures normally present in reconstituted or new settlements, also appear as elements grafted on to the tenemental structures of these vills, suggesting accretions to well-established arrangements;

- the fact that the Darlington group of vills, acquired by the Cuthbertine estates between 1003 x 1016, do *not* render 'as they of Boldon', is a indication that this element of tenurial signatures pre-dates the earlier eleventh century, suggesting that a mature system of estate management had appeared by that time;

- similarly, the fact that West Auckland, acquired by the Cuthbertine estate in 1031, after the acquisition of the remainder of Aucklandshire (before 995 x 1006) does *not* render as they of Auckland is a pointer in the same direction, namely that the suite of villan services 'as they of Boldon' were defined before AD 1000;

- from this we may conclude that definition took place before AD 1000, during, or even before, the tenth century. Logically this took place at the time of the creation of extensive leases, voluntary or enforced which were applied to the lands making up the Cuthbertine estates.

- While an explanation of the fact that Bedlington does not render 'as they of Boldon' can perhaps be found in the location of these estates, peripheral to the core lands focussing upon Chester le Street. Norton, acquired *c.* 994, does render as they of Boldon, suggesting a formal definition of services between this grant and 1003 x 1016, the date of the Darlington grant, or, and this must be admitted, that a simple decision was taken not to impose Boldon type services on this sector of the estate.

- Nevertheless, these dates approximate to the episcopate of Bishop Ealdhun (987–1016) and as this tallies with the move from Chester le Street to Durham in 995, the definition of services becomes meaningful in this context, the more so if these services were originally 'as they of Chester', a pattern unfortunately concealed by the fact that Chester was in 1183 at farm, presumably to the villans themselves.

- This is not to say that all Durham, still less all northern, villages were planned at one time, still less that tenemental regularity need imply plan-regularity or *vice versa*. The process of tenemental regulation may have preceded settlement regulation. Only gradually were the two elements completely fused, when three factors, settlement plantation, devastation and the expansion of long-established nuclei provided opportunities. In this the transition from a hallgarth focus, a small hamlet with some ministerial holdings, perhaps even of slaves, to a tenanted village, is a crucial step, and once taken the 'original' site was simply absorbed into the arable of the village. Cockfield is example in which the separation of the two entities has been fortuitously preserved (Fig. 4.1).

- It could be that the integration of tenemental structure and village plan represented an ordering of terrestrial space and earthly society, much as the houses of the community of St. Cuthbert and the seating of the community in church represented an expression of divine order.

- Into these patterns could be integrated the logical procedures adopted by the farmers for the disposition of field strips. There is no need to envisage the regulated village emerging suddenly or in a complete form. Experiment and time must have been crucial ingredients.

This analysis of the Bishop's vills between 1183 and 1381 establishes a firm framework linking tenure to settlement types. A convergence of evidence suggests that the visible plans reflect ancient antecedents, roots, to be found in the troubled decades both before and after the Norman Conquest. The arguments presented show the dreng as an officer of the Bishop directly concerned with what can be termed a 'settlement re-vitalisation policy'. To go further would be to speculate, but comparison with the locators of

Continental Europe is appropriate (Bartlett 1993, 133–44) and will be pursued in the final chapter. A careful reading of the substantial literature on drengage shows no conflict between the interpretation of the dreng's role presented here and the role presented by other scholars. None of this is to deny that drengage had a long history.

Beyond County Durham

The hypothesis that the dreng was acting virtually in the capacity of a locator appears to fit the recorded facts of Boldon Book satisfactorily. However, it also offers a new dimension for appreciating the possibilities inherent in evidence such as the classic Domesday entry relating to Newton Hundred, *Inter Ripam et Mersham*, where in the time of King Edward '15 men called *drenchs*' held land in this manor for 15 manors, but they were berewicks (outliers) of this manor' (Morgan 1978, R1–2, 269d; Welldon Finn 1963, 148–9). Neither is there any conflict with the view than the thane differed from the dreng only in the fact that he owned more than one vill (Graham 1927, 93). Of course, the planting of new settlements on or near internal and external frontiers, of both kingdoms and estates, was of sustained importance during and before the centuries discussed here (Hallam 1988, 1–12, 245–59). A fundamental point is that the processes being explored were not of a limited scale or import: there are very large numbers of settlements, covering large tracts of northern England and probably other regions, where concealed regularity is often present. Seen overall, on a national scale, the establishment of regular plans bears comparison with the enclosure movement of the eighteenth and nineteenth centuries, and the economic importance of the latter is hardly in doubt.

The *Rectitudines Singularum Personarum* provides another perspective. This document, while lacking exact date and provenance, may have been compiled under the influence of Archbishop Wulfstan in the second half of the eleventh century and have as its subject the extensive holdings of the Worcester church (Pelteret 1995, 172 and n. 45; Hadley 2000, 80; Harvey 1993, 1–33). Seebohm provides both text and translation and here the services of the *geneat* are selected:

> The geneat's services are various as on the land is fixed. On some he shall pay landgafol and grass-swine yearly, and ride and carry, and lead loads; work and support his lord, and reap and mow, cut deer-hedge and keep it up, build and hedge the burh, make new roads for the tun: pay kirkshot and almsfree; keep headward and horseward: go errands far or near wherever he is directed.
>
> (Seebohm 1896, 130)

There is, as Finberg notes, nothing servile in this position. He offers his lord personal services, often in a supervisory category, and his status originated from the fact that being a companion of the king or other lord he had been made a gift of land in recognition (Finberg 1972, 439 and 514–5). In the West Midlands he appears in Domesday Book as the *radcniht*. The parallels with the services of the northern dreng are wholly clear and it is perfectly possible that one of his duties was to assist in the plantation and development of new settlements, for much may lie behind the phrases *build and hedge the burh, make new roads for the tun*. The phrase *various as on the land is fixed,* surely implies the same levels of variability as seen in the Durham drengages

West of the Pennines, as has already been shown (Figs 4.3, 4.4 and 5.6), the landscapes of lowland Cumbria are replete with similar but not identical village and hamlet plans, and in this case a possible datum is provided by the reference in the Anglo-Saxon chronicle of the conquest of the region in 1092. In fact to cite this without comment distorts the picture, for between 1135 and 1157 the area was again is Scottish hands, and Aird touches a complex issue when he also notes that the twelfth century the Anglo-Scottish frontier was 'permeable to the extent that it was almost negligible' (in Appleby and Dalton 1997, 28–9, 32). Thus it is no surprise to find regular village and town plans in the upper Clyde valley (Roberts 1987, fig. 3.1). Cumbria however lacks both Domesday Book and extensive early customals such as Boldon Book so that difficulties of linking the available documentation with the on-ground circumstances are thus considerable. However, an entry in a *Curia Regis* roll of 1201 provides an initial step by citing a writ of Henry I (1100–1135) by which he granted to Hildred of Carlisle and Odard his son the land of Gamel son of Bern and the land of Glassam son of Brictric, *drengorum meorum*, 'my drengs'. The subsequent history of the estate shows that the villages of Gamblesby and Glassonby must derive their names from these two individuals, and this allows two important inferences (Wilson 1901, 313, n. 2). Firstly, place-names terminating in *-by* were still being formed – or perhaps reformed – in the period 1100–1135, and secondly that such place-names can give only a tenuous guide to the origins of their founders, for while Gamel is Old Norse and Bern is possibly so, Glassan is Old Irish and yet his father possessed an Old English name.

There are a number of *-by* names in Cumberland with prefixes derived from non-Old English or non-Scandinavian names (Armstrong *et al.* 1952, 192; Fellows Jensen 1985, 10–24; Roberts 1989, 25–40; Fellows-Jensen 1989, 41–60). They are Irish, French, Flemish and even Breton in origin. When these are mapped they are found to concentrate in two areas, first around Glassonby and Gamblesby, near the Eden-Eamont confluence, with an outlying scatter further west, while a second group quite literally forms a ring around Carlisle. Not to associate these coherent groups with the consolidation of Norman power after the take-over of 1092 would be stretching scepticism too far. Both Gamblesby (Fig. 4.4) and Glassonby have 'normal' Cumbrian plans, part regular rather than wholly regular, with long-tofts, a type seen to be normal throughout the region. One might infer that Gamel and Glassan were not only drengs, but also *locatores*, holding their lands by gift of the king and bringing in colonists in furtherance of royal policies. The case is a reasonable one. Within the township of Gamblesby the place-name Addingham is probably 'one of the most ancient Anglian place-names in Cumberland' and was the focus of a large parish containing Unthank, Glassonby*, Maughanby*, Hunsonby*, Farmanby*, Robberby*, Winskill and Little

Salkeld, the asterisks denoting 'late' *-by* names established within the older territory. Addingham lay close to the Eden and its medieval church has now been swept away. The township name of Hunsonby, the 'dog keeper's *-by*', hints at a link with one characteristic of drengage tenure, the keeping of dogs. Gambleby's rise as a parish centre, and probably its foundation, must fall between 1092 and 1135. Once again, the settlements of this group fall into two essential classes, large successful villages and what were by the mid-nineteenth century no more than farmsteads. As in Durham this may reflect an element of choice, the grant could either be stocked with men or retained in hand. Maughanby ('Maffanby') is a case in question, for the earthworks of what may have once been a toft compartment of a small hamlet are present. Field evidence suggests that Farmanby was never more than a single-farmstead, but at another 'late' *-by*, Dolphenby, near Penrith, five or six long-houses are visible as earthworks as well as a mound that may well have been a small castle motte. More pragmatically, the present author, working upon putative prehistoric and Romano-British steadings in the upper valley of the Eden found unidentified long rectangular buildings upon many of them (Roberts 1993a). This discovery, when linked with anomalous radio-carbon dates from the few excavated sites in the north-west, allowed the hypothesis that the final desertion of the steadings came with the development of nucleated villages in the Norman period, a result of the concentration of once scatted local populations (O'Sullivan and Dickinson in Baldwin and Whyte 1985, 21, 86; Roberts 1993a).

This evidence for the presence of a distinctive block of early twelfth century colonising activity north of the Eamont-Eden confluence poses a question. Why here? The answer must lie in military strategy, settling colonists straddling the main north to south communications in the valley. Carlisle was the key regional fortress from which William Rufus dislodged Dolfin to gain control of the area. Gilsland, on the northeastern flank of the Eden valley, was not taken from the native ruler, Gille, until around 1156 (Kapelle 1979, 200). The castles at Appleby and Brough were present by 1130 (Beeler 1966, 400, 418; Renn 1968, 90, 118–120). Men settled in the Gamblesby-Melmerby zone were ideally placed to become aware of the progress of raiders southwards via the Fell Edge lowlands, to the east of the Eden, for even the most hardy were unlikely to attempt passage across the peat hags of the Cross Fell ridge. Carlisle itself is ringed by a second group of *-by* names: Botcherby and Rickerby, Etterby and Tarraby, Upperby and Aglionby, with which may be associated Willow Holm, derived from Guerri the Fleming. Botcherby and Rickerby – in which the names Burchard and Richard can be detected – are particularly significant, for both men gave their names to streets within the town and to the gates at the end of these (Jones in Clack and Gosling 1976, 180–5). In fact both Etard and probably the same Richard appear in the Pipe Roll of 1130. We have here a situation in which specific sectors of the frontier city were in the charge of men who also gave their names to both quarters within the town and to agricultural rural settlements beyond the gates. Some of these colonists were no doubt those peasants brought northwards as described in the Chronicle, not only by William

Rufus, but perhaps also by Henry I, and by those knights who formed the cutting edge of the conquest. The very mix of 'nationalities' and languages implied by the personal names suggest the opportunities upon the frontier for those with ambition, horse, mail and a lance. There were also perceived opportunities for those with 'cattle and wives', and no doubt also for those with a craft or trade, for the masons who worked upon the new Norman cathedral were part of the movement. The presence of Irish and French quarters within the town, a *vicus hibernicorum* and a *vicus francorum.* only serve to emphasise the mixture. If there is a grain of truth in this argument then we are here identifying strategic footholds established between 1092 and 1135.

However, as in Durham, to see all Cumbria's village plans as of the same date would be incautious. At first sight it seems that this side of the Pennines most are likely to be post-Conquest (*i.e.* 1092). Nevertheless, a writ of 1041 x 1064 issued by Cospatric refers to a block of territory that can 'be roughly defined by the Derwent, the Eamont, the Lakeland mountains and the marshes at the head of the Solway'. The writ concerns privileges bestowed upon his freemen and dependants, including freedom from the geld, or royal taxation. This is an important document, generally taken as implying that territory in the neighbourhood of Carlisle was politically connected to Northumberland for a period during the eleventh century, subject to Northumbrian law and ruled by a Northumbrian earl, Cospatric, the father of the ruler of Carlisle in 1092 (Aird in Appleby and Dalton 1997, 31). Amid the shifting mosaic of local political alliances his ejection by William Rufus need occasion no surprise. In their analysis of this document Wilson and Allinson comment upon the varied persons named. They consciously link *Thorfynn* with Torpenhow, *Melmor* with Melmerby, *Wygande* with Wyggonby, *Wyberth* with Waberthwaite or Wyberthwait, *Thore* with Thoresby or Thursby (and one might add possibly Kirkby Thore), *Gamel* with Gamelsby, noting that he was a different man and this is a different place to the Gamblesby established by Gamel son of Bern discussed earlier (Wilson 1901, 231–4; Harmer, 1952, 410–424, 531–36; Fletcher 2002, 147). These correlations can hardly be accidental: we are dealing with a distinctive social group, by no means peasants, but not necessarily of the upper aristocracy by birth, and men who were concerned, *inter alia*, with the planting of villages in this frontier zone between kingdoms. This appears to have been taking place by the middle decades of the eleventh century and *before* the Norman conquest of the area. The formal clause at the beginning of the document includes 'all my dependants (*wassennas*) and each free man, free and dreng'. The term *wassenas* is a rare one: it may be a British word, a form of the Welsh *gwassan*, deriving from the Frankish *vassalus,* although the obvious link to the term 'vassal' cannot be a direct one (VCH Cu.II, 232, note 3: Harmer 1952, 420). It implies a dependant or retainer. The freedoms are granted 'in wood, in heath, in enclosures and as to all things that are existing on the earth and under it'. This is reasonably interpretable as both an affirmation of a peace agreement, purporting to end local tensions, and an encouragement to colonisation while the links between the individuals named in the document and surviving settlements is a reminder of the practicalities of settlement. There can be little doubt that in this troubled border not only were there ample opportunities for replanning and refounding settlements, but men, settled on the land by trusted retainers, represented political power. These men were the progenitors of those border tenants who in later centuries formed the van of an army moving north into Scotland and the rearguard of an army moving south.

Concluding Remarks

The material presented in the last three chapters is full of pitfalls. There are pitfalls of language, for even the 'original' documents, normally in Latin, have been brought to us in varied ways. There are pitfalls in concepts, for, as any perusal of the literature shows, historians are by no means unanimous about the precise meaning of many of the technical terms. Above all there are pitfalls in attempting what must quite honestly be seen as linkages between an inadequately documented medieval past and the more fully documented but matured landscapes of the nineteenth century and today, and the evidence of those limited areas where fieldwork has been done. The leap from the morphological analyses, which if properly documented, using a map, can be evaluated and tested by all readers, to the obscurities of rents and renders is not easy; all that can be established is a broad hypothesis that others must test in detail. All interpretations can be overlain by prejudices, but a balance of probabilities must be attempted.

We can conclude that many – but not all – of the regular village plans of northern England are likely to date from before 1200. Only rarely is the evidence conclusive, but cumulatively it is impressive. On both sides of the Pennines detailed investigations suggest that some village plan foundation, as distinct from the establishment of settlements that eventually became villages, took place after the Norman Conquest of the later eleventh century. The plantation of new villages was fading by the early decades of the thirteenth century, indeed, in many areas, by or before 1150. This is part of the national scene (Hallam 1988, figs 3.1–3.5, 3.7–3.9). Furthermore, in both regions there are ambiguous hints that amid the large numbers of plans there could be significant numbers of pre-Conquest settlement plantations. The author began this study firmly of the view that the planned villages were all post-Conquest, but as he has worked though the material his suspicions have grown that there were also phases of village planning in the eleventh century, the tenth century and conceivably even earlier. In many instances there are indications of the presence of ministerial tenures supporting officers, whose task it was to oversee in some manner the 'vill'. They are by no means a homogenous body, and the tenure associated with them, drengage, which undoubtedly has pre-Conquest roots, was pragmatically sustained in the century after the Conquest in the face of advancing feudal tenures. There are reasonable grounds for suggesting that these tenants could act the mentors of vills, so that the term *locator*, to be discussed again in the next chapter, seems appropriate.

As with the growth of complex field systems the process of settlement planning is largely undocumented, but again and again one returns to a doom of Ine of Wessex (688–694) cited earlier, which states:

> If anyone covenants for a yardland or more at a fixed rent (*gafol*), and ploughs it, if the lord wishes to increase for him (the rent of the) land by demanding service (*weorc*) as well as rent, he need not accept it, if he does not give him a dwelling: and he is to forfeit the crops.
>
> (Seebohm 1896, 142–3; Whitelock 1955, law 67)

To the author this law appears to span an important bridge, between having access to the use of land for renders, either in kind, service or even cash, and holding land for a rent and other services. In the original document the term used is *weorc,* a less neutral term than *service* (Seebohm 1883, 142–3). Agricultural work services could be meant. The important point in the present argument is that the acceptance of a dwelling, provided by the lord, meant that work could be demanded, with all that this implies in terms of changing social status. In this there are two points to be made. First, this makes sense in a context of land reclamation, colonisation, pushing the head-dyke back into the waste, and second, what could be more logical that a lord could provide a group of people with dwellings, perhaps by initially stripping the timber off the land with his own men. The endemic warfare of the period must have provided a flow of potential colonists, of free status or slave. Already we are on the edge of reading too much into the text, yet the frontier between cultivated land and the open and wood pasture was an essential part of early landscapes on both macro- and the micro-scales. We can say, however, that the reference to a yardland, a yard of land, presumably measured with a land-yard, a rod, pole or perch, was already present as a concept, and presumably as an on-ground reality. This is a remarkably sophisticated concept and ultimately underlies complex arrangements such as those shown schematically in Figure 3.5. The survival of this code is no more than a fortunate accident that came about when it was attached to the later laws of King Alfred, and although it relates to a southern portion of the English realm, it reveals the presence of important concepts in that remote time.

England is not of course an island, and some recognition of this fact has appeared in the use of Welsh and Irish sources in the arguments. As Barrow has shown, the small shire and renders similar to those of northern England and Wales do occur in Scotland. By way of specific illustration, a letter, sent by Thor Longus, to Earl David, later David I of Scotland (1124–53), provides a fascinating insight into the process of establishing villages.

> Know, my lord, that King Edgar (of Scotland, 1097–1107) your brother gave me Ednam (near Kelso, Roxburghshire) when it was uninhabited, which with his assistance and my capital (*pecunia*) I have settled, and built there from its foundations a church which your bother the king caused to be dedicated in honour of St. Cuthbert and endowed with one carucate of land.
>
> (*Early Scottish Charters* ed. A. C. Lawrie, Glasgow 1905, no. xxxiii, 25–6; no. xxiv pp.19, 259).

The 1863 OS six inch map shows that this village had a short east to west row plan. Unfortunately, as is so often the case when relating documentation to landscape, great change has taken place, for by the mid-nineteenth century the village had been deformed by re-modelling. Two cottage rows, eaves orientated and continuous had been added, while at the eastern end of the south row a brewery had been inserted. Nevertheless, to the practiced eye, the basic skeleton of the older plan is visible: two short east to west rows with a short north to south head row at the western end. What the document reveals of the plantation process is fascinating: the grant from the king, his assistance (perhaps tenants?), capital investment (perhaps stock?), and the building of a new church are all important steps in bringing a new settlement into being in an uninhabited place. The prior existence of the Old English place-name may be taken as a hint that Ednam had already been lived in and named (Nicolaisen 1976, 21, 23 and 76). In general, however, by the later twelfth century the pattern of village and hamlet settlement was firmly established, with the landscape being largely replete, *i.e.* economically incapable of supplying the land resources to accommodate any more agriculturally based and communally organized settlements. Indeed from as early as the middle decades of the twelfth century a process of single-farmstead infill had been taking place. However, as Eric Bylund showed, diffusion and colonization are messy businesses (1960). In detail geographical diffusion responds not only to variations in terrain and land quality, but also to random, stochastic factors, so that precursors of what historically must be seen and simplified as a logical movement by no means always appear where they are to be most expected. Planned settlements may have appeared in colonising contexts long before they were imposed upon older foci. As with the fossil record in evolution, the surviving record, both documentary and landscape, does not in itself provide a continuous narrative. Continuity and discontinuity have to be imaginatively perceived and expressed through existential, empirical models. These provide a vision of the past, and can be readily adapted and changed in the light of new discoveries. Overall, however, this rather complex view must inform any analysis of local settlement circumstances; each ten by ten kilometre square of the national grid contains many layers of such accretive complexity (Roberts 1987, fig. 6.4)

Chapter Nine

Planned Villages in Europe and England

This chapter must allow pause for reflection and then look outwards to consider the experience of the northern English village in the wider context of Europe. The discussions forming the substance of this book have built towards the conclusion that planned settlements, and probably their planned field systems, were indeed developing both before and after the Norman take-over of the north, and this conclusion has wider implications. We must conclude that there was no one idea, no single point of origin followed by a clear-cut, logical and hence easily interpretable, diffusion pattern and that no single cause, be this the Harrying of the North, nor the Scandinavian incursions, nor the Norman conquest, need be invoked. An understanding of the vast complexity of settlement processes excludes all mono-causal simplicities. In this matter village plans have much in common with the architectural styles associated with the great churches and castles, a phraseology which neatly by-passes the troubled questions of vernacular architecture found in the homes of the illiterate peasantry. Furthermore, peasant pressures, indeed needs, for equality in the shares of each community's resources, and in the equitable definition of services must also have played a part, pressures providing direct linkages to population levels within key local regions. Village plans and systematised field arrangements represent the meeting-ground between two flows of ideas. On the one hand are scholastic ideas, emanating from the world of literacy, travel and fashion, while on the other are the needs, and perhaps demands, of the tenantry to assist the everyday pressures of negotiating with nature, and with landlord demands, the economic necessity of wresting a living, indeed, a surplus from the land, and the incidents of warfare. The melting pot, as it were, must surely be *custom*, in which vessel were accomplished complex balances derived from that which was normal practice from time immemorial and set in the mind of men, and that which was new and imposed. Solve Göransson used very prescient words in his paper on solskifte published in 1966 and already quoted:

> The bulk of the evidence suggests that the Scandinavian *solskifte* was in fact derived from England during the period of close political, ecclesiastical and cultural contact between these countries (10th to 12th centuries). By the time the system as well developed in Denmark and Sweden, however, it was already, as Homans suggests, in full decay in England, vanishing in consequence of land subdivision, transfer and consolidation. It origin lies in the obscure organisational processes of the Dark Ages.
>
> (Göransson 1961, 101)

It is clear from the varied arguments concerning regular planned settlements that they are likely to be a product of a society in which there are kings, landholders and tenants rather than chiefs and clansmen, where there was taxation rather than renders and personal ministrations. They presuppose developments associated with polities that are developing levels of sophistication attendant upon a conscious organisation of taxation in the form of labour and coin rather than cattle and grain. This change has a spatial impact in the rise of settlements which in an essentially pre-literate society, leading to a formalisation of the taxable entity, the basic peasant holding, and emphasising the links between land and its productive capacity rather than numbers of men and their ability to fight.

However tempted we may be to seek bridges, it is possible the planned settlements emerging in early medieval Europe owed little or perhaps nothing to the direct transmission of Roman concepts. The two compartment cell arranged along a street or green can be viewed as two conjoined halves of the chequer or quarter found in town plans, and there may indeed be a link to the writings of Vitruvius (Morgan 1960, Book I, ch. VI, 1, 7; Book VI, ch. VI, 1), but this link cannot be proven. Nevertheless, the planning of great churches, the keeping of records by the clerks, at first for their own benefit, but eventually on behalf of royal masters, through the demands they placed upon tenants established new concepts of tenure rather than service. The presence of classical texts in ecclesiastical libraries led to an indirect transmission of antecedent concepts of order and record keeping, and informed the transition from the mnemonics of tribe and clan to the written record. Further, it cannot be stressed sufficiently that the viewpoint of the tenantry rights to, and shares in, the land and its produce were more fundamental than any of us can now imagine. One of the more thrilling swift insights achieved by the author was when Ulf Sporrong took him to a Swedish farm and from behind the porch door the housewife produced 'the farm'. This took the form of a great necklace of small wooden shingles, and on each was stuck a piece of paper on which was written details of each field. These could just as easily have been mnemonic symbols, and while a normal working farmer doubtless carried in his or her head the details, a record to convince non-literate neighbours and sceptical administrators must, particularly in troubled times, have been a common need. In short, a planned settlement and systematised field arrangements provided numerous advantages. These can be listed as follows:

- they encouraged the landholding possessor of rights – the lord – to define standard 'family-supporting holdings';

- they allowed the integration of newcomers, indeed strangers, new tenants and not kin, into a settlement's physical and social structure, without conflict, simply by adding new units or compartments, at least while reserves of potential arable land and pasture were available;

- they provided a means of defining rents and services in a essentially pre-literate society, for both the possessor and the tenant; thus, the layout of both settlement and fields became a paradigm for the tenancies;

- this provided a means of 'documenting' shares upon the ground in a way that would survive repeated episodes of devastation;

- in a pre-map context the more elaborate systems of land distribution provided a way of accurately locating shares within the lands of what eventually emerges as a heterogeneous community, no matter how homogeneous it was when created;

- for the holder of the land they provided an easy way of reckoning, of knowing, how many tenants were present, of providing a view of the land's productive capacity and hence its capability to bear tax;

- planned settlements arose from two fundamental contexts, on one hand the creation of new plantations amid the common wastes and woodlands, and on the other, the reorganisation of older nucleations, a process sometimes involving the aggregation of hamlets into a single large cluster. Retrospectively it is difficult to differentiate between these.

Finally, deeper psychological levels may be present: planned, organised settlements provided a tangible link with the immediate past, a mnemonic device which, in Layton's words 'to some degree parallels the function of written records', something that can be seen and experienced, a signifier, a tangible embodiment of shared values and ideas for a community (Layton 1989, 10–11). A visit to any well-preserved Romanesque church, large or small, reveals the importance of symbols in the world of the medieval mind, and the more churches that are seen the more observation generates amazement over the constant reworking of a set of ideas derived from the Bible – seen as the word of God. Admittedly, there are no injunctions to plan settlements in the Bible, but in Leviticus 25 verse 31 we are told that 'the houses of the villages which have no wall round about them shall be counted as the fields of the country'. As Helen Waddell reveals with startling clarity, not only were the writings of the 'ancients', pagan or not, part of the Christian *corpus* of texts, but that scholars and administrators of the eighth and ninth century with access to classical literature sustained contacts over great distances. Charlemagne, writing to Paul the Deacon at Monte Cassino created a marvellous image of this transit and transmission:

> *Across the hills and through the valley's shade,*
>   *Alone the small script goes,*
> *Seeking for Benedict's beloved roof,*
>   *Where waits its sure repose.*
>
> (Waddell 1982, 141)

In these points there is no single causal factor, no single uniform imposition of one idea, no completely sustained rigidity, and as Göransson noted, land subdivision, transfer and consolidation all played a part. At root is a pragmatic idea, a paradigm, carried in the heads and books of both scholars and administrators and found in the need for aliquot shares amongst the peasants. If this conclusion is less than precise, then the generic discussions in this volume provide a gauge against which to measure studies of particular places.

An Overview of European Settlement

A brief analysis of European rural settlement will begin with spatial distributions suggested by the work of generations of European scholars, and continue with some specific cases that have bearings on the contexts and chronology of the appearance of planned villages and hamlets. It concludes with a discussion of the varied linkages underlying the diffusion and implementation of the 'village idea' though time. This creates the possibility of integrating the detailed evidence from Great Britain into the wider context of Europe, and ultimately the Mediterranean.

Figures 9.1.a and 9.1.b build upon a splendid map of continental Europe compiled by Schröder and Schwarz, and work by many others, to create a view of rural settlement throughout the zone north of the Alps. (Schröder and Schwarz 1978, maps 1 and 2, endpapers; Smith 1967, fig. 5.1; Houston 1963, fig. 16; Roberts and Wrathmell 2002, fig. 1.14) The *date* of the map cannot be closely defined. Essentially it shows 'traditional' settlement forms, namely those that existed before the accretions and changes of the twentieth century and are visible on cadastral maps and estate surveys, but the original German data integrates material considered to range between the eighth and the later eighteenth century! The data for England and France are notably more schematic than that for Germany, and the seams are obvious. The challenge in the case of materials not included within the original Schröder and Schwarz map was to create a general key that was in accord with that constructed for Germany, so that a spatial picture of the varied types is developed. The map embraces great varieties of terrain, but this has been generalised in Figures 9.3.a and 9.3.b by using a model cross-section, running approximately between the Alps and the Baltic coast of Jutland via the valley of the Elbe. This has not been constructed with precision, but distinguishes six broad categories of terrain as follows:

- *coastal wetlands*, at or near sea-level,
- the *North European plain*, from which rise
- *forested interfluve ridges and uplands*, which are intersected by
- *valley lowlands*, associated with the upper courses of rivers.
- *Alpine Forelands* rise gradually southwards to
- the *Alps* proper.

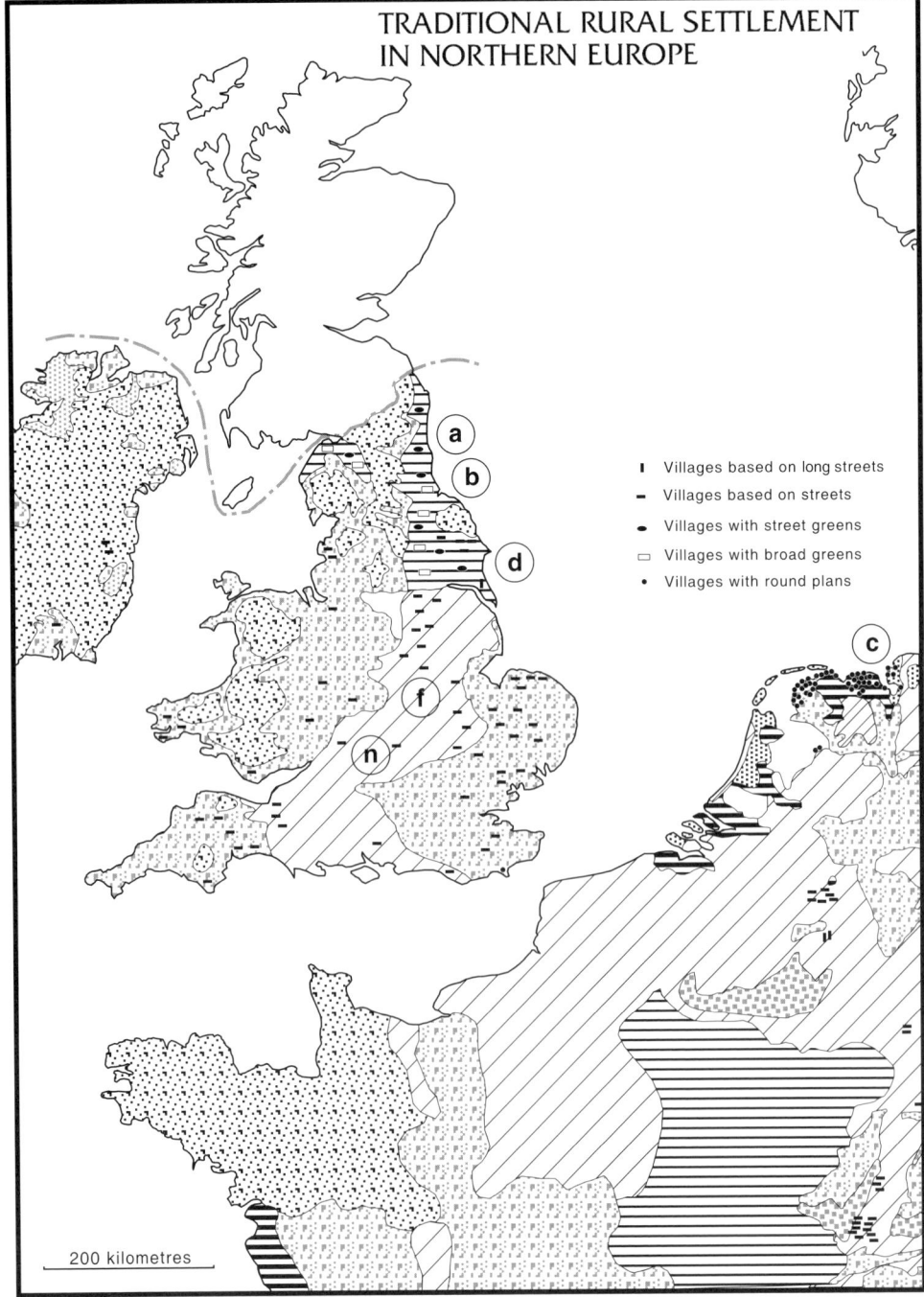

Fig. 9.1.a Traditional rural settlement forms in northern Europe

Planned Villages in Europe and England 253

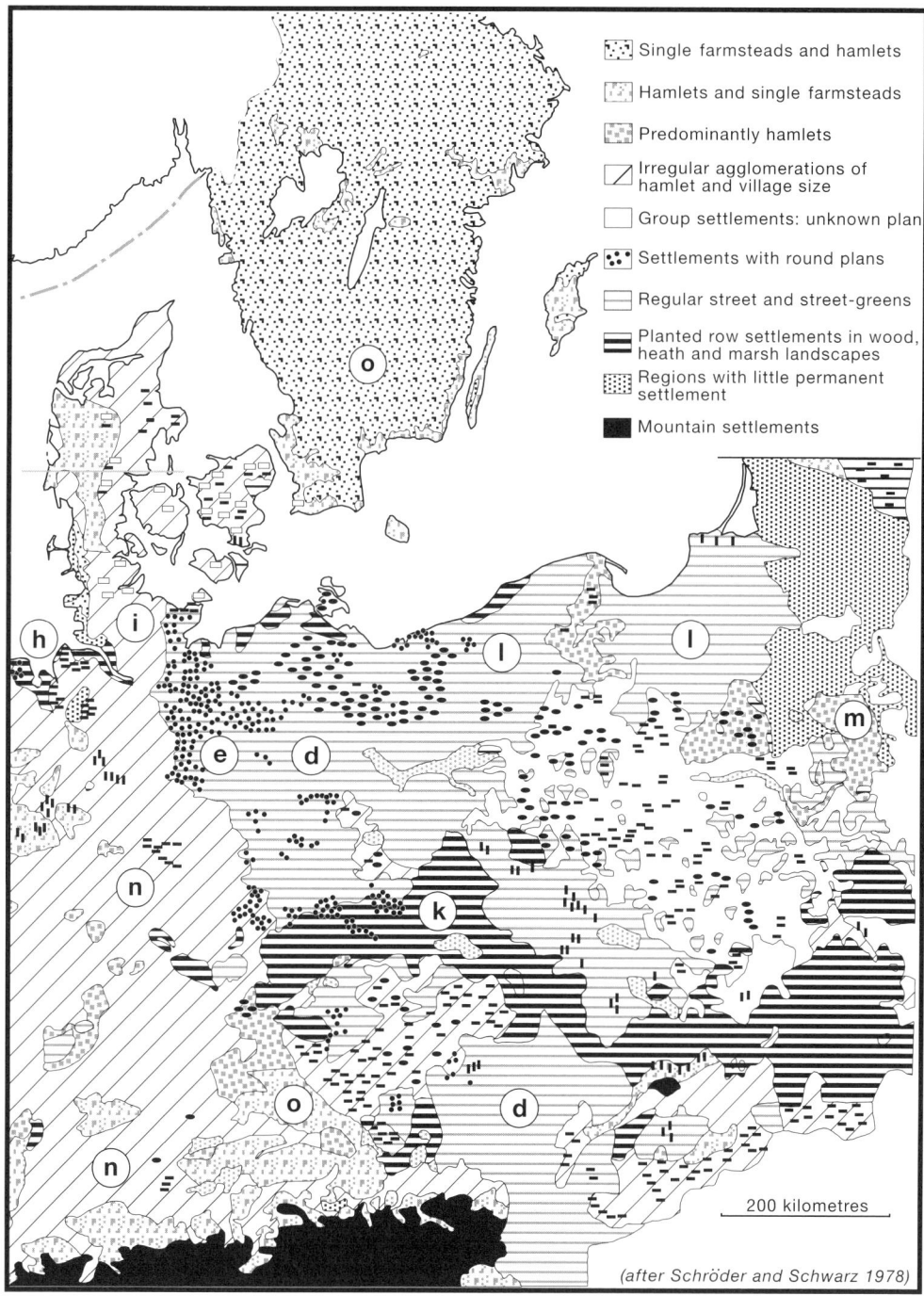

Fig. 9.1.b Traditional rural settlement forms in northern Europe (contd.)

Cutting across these terrains, and following boundaries running broadly slantwise from northeast to southwest, there are a series of well-marked edaphic zones. There are tundra and boreal lands in the far north, Atlantic conditions in the west where the influences of the Atlantic, North Sea and Baltic penetrate, while Central European conditions appear in the continental interior to the east and south east, with the Alps intruding more elements of boreal and tundra into the interior. These are merely ways of describing the broad conditions of climate vegetation, and thus pointing towards the negotiations farmers needed to make with terrains and soils (Polunin and Walters 1985, 9–21). In general, on the North European Plain, rolling lowlands are involved, flat near the rivers, rising to well-drained terraced lands and the lower interfluves set above these. Higher still, on the interfluves between the great rivers, are areas that long retained their wood pastures and open pastures (Darby in Thomas 1956, fig 60) and that were associated with hamlet and even single-farmstead settlement. Figures 9.3.a and 9.3.b show a number of specific cases that are keyed to the map in Figure 9.1 as well as the cross-section, but to avoid the complexities of dealing with particular cases Figure 9.2 presents a simple set of models that allow the generalities of European settlement and field systems to be readily grasped.

In settlement terms the actual line of the transect in Figure 9.3 is important, because, as the Schröder and Schwarz map shows a fundamental break in settlement characteristics occurs along the line of the Elbe, effectively dividing Western Europe from Eastern Europe. Gutkind in 1964 (104–5) identified this line as follows:

> The line of the Elbe, the Saale, the Thuringian Forest and the Fichtelbirge was roughly the structural divide. To the west of this line the structure of settlement rested upon Germanic influences ... and on Frankish elements introduced from outside Germany: other influences, above all those of Roman origin, were absorbed into the pattern of settlement. To the east of this line the structure of settlement may be called secondary. It had Germanic and Frankish characteristics and spread over the existing and thin Slavic layer. It remained secondary because the combined Germanic and Frankish conquest had at its disposal colonial methods and agrarian organisation incomparably higher than those of the Slavs.

Nevertheless, he emphasises that these variations were not conditioned by ethnological factors. The variations should be sought in first, the different relationship of the community to the system of cultivation, and second, in the different ideas about what was more important, the social equality of the village members or the economic rationalism of the village community. Further,

> the layout of the village alone is meaningless; only the plan of the village and the plan of the field system together can explain the functional structure of the settlement as a whole. Time was essential as a formative power. A slow development was often accompanied by a greater adaptation to the existing conditions... while a fast development often led to a ruthless disregard of men and nature... Slowly growing [unsystematic] settlements were less subject to the stylistic influences

Planned Villages in Europe and England 255

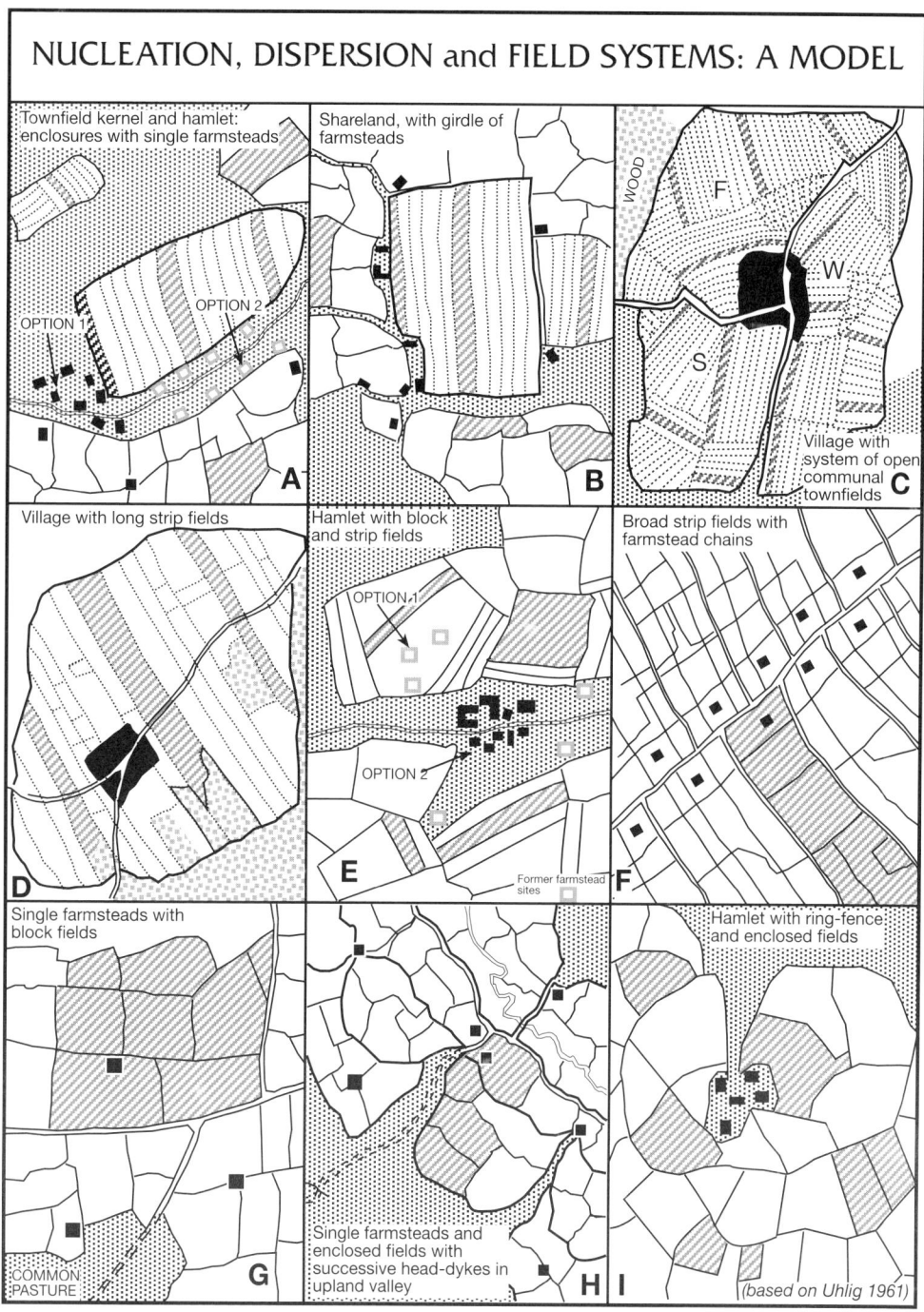

Fig. 9.2 Nucleation, dispersion and field systems: a model

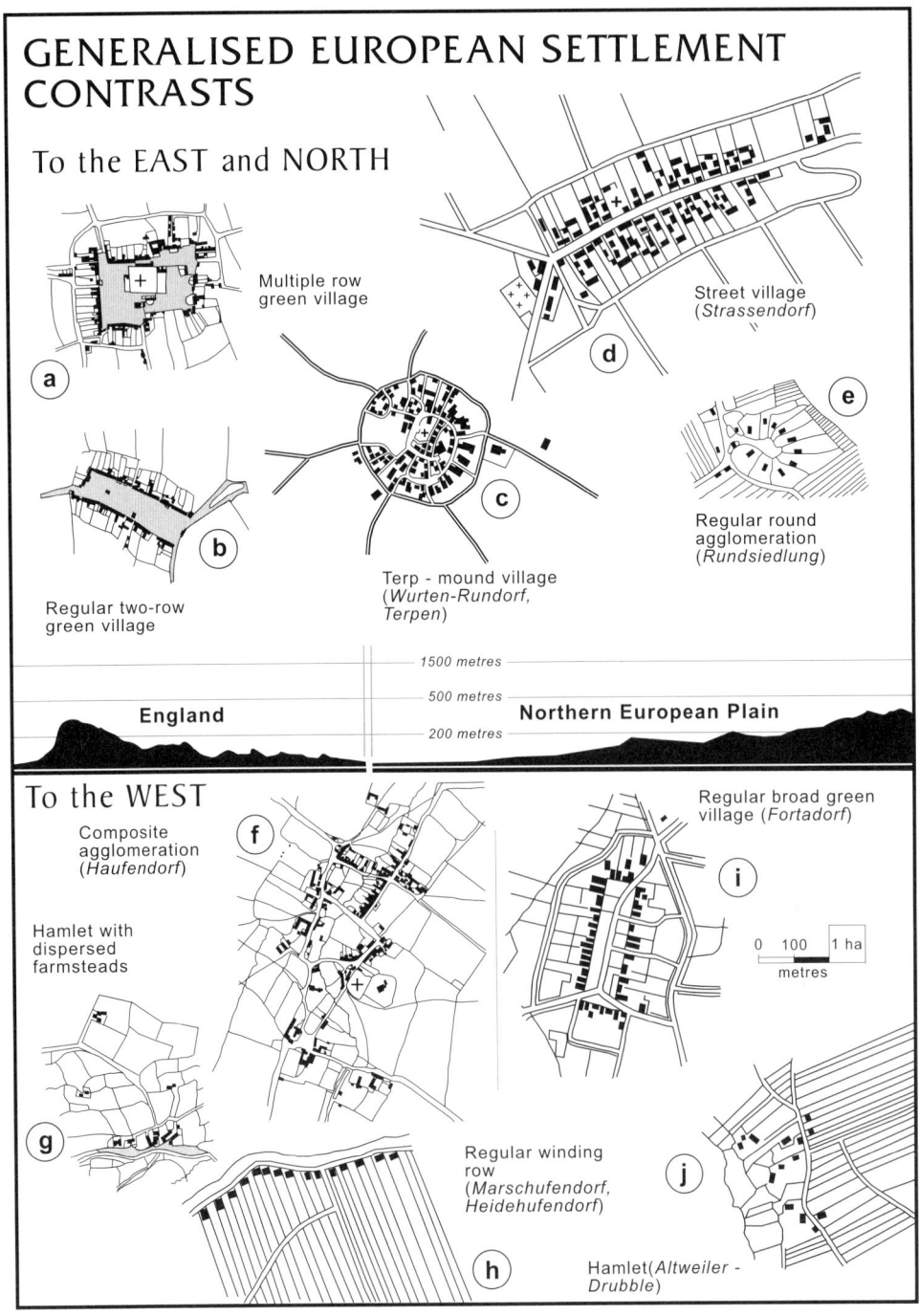

Fig. 9.3.a Generalised European settlement contrasts

Planned Villages in Europe and England

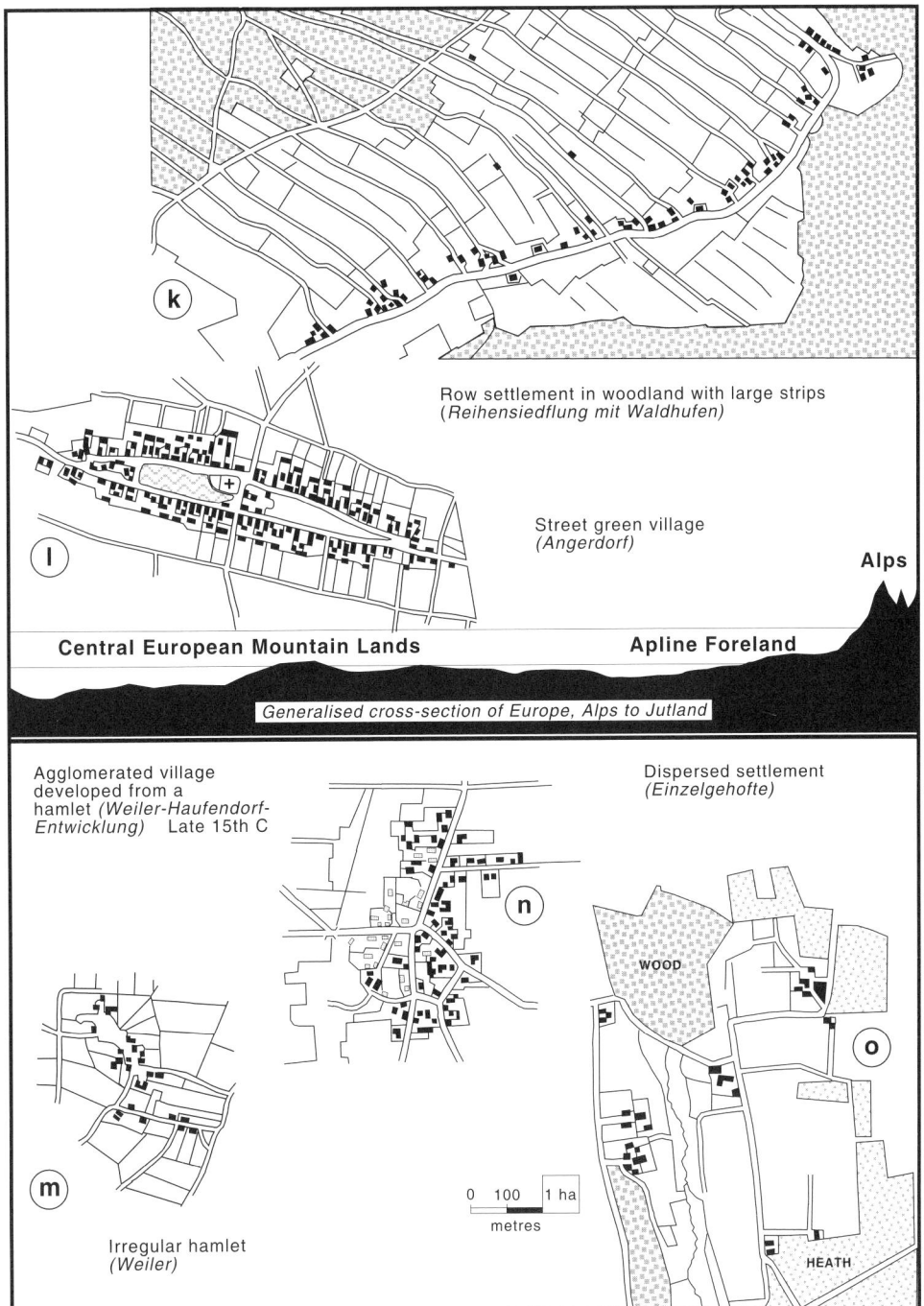

Fig. 9.3.b *Generalised European settlement contrasts (contd.)*

of the time than were those founded by territorial princes. In these latter cases every transformation or expansion was detrimental to the original conception and invariably spoiled the essence of the plan.

He touches difficult and largely unprovable ground in a later discussion, arguing that the Franks used Roman camps and the street *vici* attached to these formed 'prototypes for their fortified villages'. This occurred especially when decisions on how new villages were to be founded began to pass from the folk community to the individual person of a feudal lord… 'a street village in front of the fortified manor replaced the *vicus*'…and …the adaptation of military prototypes for a semi-military purpose …for colonial conquest and colonial settlement – was obvious' (Gutkind 1964, 111). He points out that the row of dwellings, in the Roman fashion, had the advantage of defining street space, giving a clear definition to what otherwise could be no more than nondescript 'interspaces'. One of the heritages of Rome, still visible in the centuries between the fifth and the eighth centuries, was the fact that their large colonial ventures imparted to their colonisation an almost modern rationalisation and a high standard of efficiency. Further (Gutkind 1964, 112):

> They used methods that could easily be organised and mastered anywhere by those who had to apply them. The street village was therefore the obvious form of settlement. It made possible the solution of the social problem by association and of the economic problem by a combination of house and fields, as far as this was feasible. At the same time the village was related without any difficulty to the road system.

These are wise and measured words, encompassing a vast, yet largely unprovable vision within a few elegant phrases and concise sentences. They offer prescient comment on the many questions about the classical roots of planned villages in Europe.

Looking at the broad pattern in more detail, there is to the west of the Elbe a core zone, extending from the North Sea to the Alpine Foreland where irregular agglomerated settlements, from small hamlets to large villages prevail. In contrast, to the east of the Elbe, regular forms predominate, associated with Frankish and Germanic colonisations and the 'drive to the east' (Koebner in Postan 1966, 1–91; Smith, C.T. 1967, 163–188; Pounds, 1974, 165–87; Mayhew 1973, 37–90). The former core zone, of older Germanic settlement, extends from the plains of north-western Europe, the middle and upper Rhine, and its tributaries, the Mosel, the Main, the Neckar and the Lahn, to the valleys of the Maas-Saône. Such settlements appear as far east as the Elbe and the Saale, and to the south as far as the Danube valley; to the west they are present in the valleys of the Marne and the Seine, and into central England, as far north as the Humber. This vast tract is of course far from homogeneous in landscapes, economy, peoples or settlement characteristics. Most notably, in central and southern Germany, and west as far as the valley of the Saône and indeed extending eastwards into the Hungarian Plain, are rather large agglomerated villages, *Haufendorfer*. In general these are supported by a form of sub-divided townfields, divided into strip parcels, although varied stages of development from block fields, more regular in form, to highly subdivided systems based upon strips are found. These are intermixed with hamlets, and a developmental sequence, from hamlets with a simple field system based upon blocks and some strips gives rise in areas of high agricultural potential to more complicated field arrangements and larger, well-populated villages as population increases. This distinction has both a temporal and a spatial import and is modelled as Types E and C in Figure 9.2 and exemplified in Figure 9.3 as case 'n'. It is characteristic of villages that they have a tendency to settle upon their sites for long periods, while the hamlet systems from which they evolved were inherently less stable. German evidence places these developments broadly between the ninth and the twelfth centuries AD. Further north, on the sandy lands of the Low Countries and northern Germany, hamlets with less structured plans were supported by smaller but intensively manured arable cores. These were often divided into a limited number of great strips. Type A in Figure 9.2 models this, while further north and west, amid the Atlantic fringes of the continent, in Brittany, Cornwall, Ireland, Wales and Scotland permanently manured infields, linked with settlement girdles or clusters, claimed footholds where land suitable for arable was available. Depending upon land quality Scandinavian settlement roots reflect Type C on the better soils, with variants of Types C, B and E in the more intractable environments.

Along the coast marsh colonisation landscapes took two characteristics: earlier forms comprise hamlets on mounds constructed of brushwood, clay, gravel and animal dung, to lift the steadings rather precariously above the level of the highest tides. These round or oval settlements, in a few cases reach four or five metres above the surrounding land but are generally lower. A wholly special case, these 'tump-hamlets' and 'tump-villages', *Wurten*, *Terpen* or *Waerften*, have not been included in Figure 9.2 but an example appears in Figure 9.3.a, item 'c'. They are seen developing during the ninth and tenth centuries AD, but in many cases occupation continues to the present day. Later marshland colonisation, between the eleventh and the fourteenth centuries, results in broad settlement ribbons, based upon levees set above the floods, from which great strip holdings extended in each direction into the heaths and marshes, to give each farmer a share of each type of land. This resulted in many subtle variants, one to be seen in Type F, Figure 9.2, with the most striking, and possibly the latest, taking on a rigidly formal linear geometry (Fig. 9.3.a, item 'h').

Essentially the core zone of western Germany, and indeed much of north-eastern France was a region of communally organised townfield systems. At first these were not necessarily wholly open, not necessarily wholly common, not necessarily wholly sub-divided and not necessarily unenclosed. Nevertheless many, through the course of time, eventually approached the norm of the classic two- or three-field systems – Type C in Figure 9.2 – which permeated into and eventually came to dominate the lands of western Europe possessed of the better agricultural soils. These are agriculturally well-developed and populous regions, and provided core-areas from which emerged the enduring political entities, focussing upon areas such as the Paris Basin, the Mark of Brandenburg, the Prague lowlands, the island of Sjaelland, and the lowlands of southern and central England (Pounds 1994, fig. 3.1). Within them emerged the urban concentrations, industrial development and trade links of early modern states. A classic map in Seebohm of local names in *-heim*, *-ingen* and *-ingaheim* and German patronymic names in France provides a powerful reminder that a zone of Germanic settlement sprawls westwards across the limes of the former Roman empire. Thus the emergence of these nucleated villages and hamlets and communally organised field systems antedates the emergence of the modern states whose names have necessarily been used in this discussion. It is the result of the movement of Germanic peoples (Seebohm 1896, between 256–7; see also Smith 1967, fig. 3.1 for another version). In England these appear as names with *-ing*, *-ingham* and *-ham* terminations and as the zone of hamlet settlement in the extreme south east of England. Irregular agglomerated villages and hamlets in the Central Province extending from the English Channel to the Humber, with planned settlements concentrated at the northern periphery, echoes what is found extending from west to east in continental Europe.

All this is useful generalisation, but in detail matters are inevitably much more complicated. Occupying locations that were essentially peripheral to these cores and the great river valleys with which they were associated were numerous other landscapes: some appeared as physical inliers, some along ethnic and political frontiers, while others were marginal in terms of patterns of movement. Generally characterised by hamlet and single-farm settlements the inliers often represent rather higher interfluval zones and are set away from the main rivers. In all such areas hamlets and enclosed block-fields of Types E, G, H and I appeared. Some of these were exceedingly ancient and longstanding, while others emerged within a generation or two at a time of active colonisation between the eighth and the thirteenth centuries. In some of these, notably in Types E and I, we glimpse something of the character of ancient pre-village settlement roots, while Types H and G are more specifically the result of late medieval and post-medieval individual colonisation. Layouts such as are modelled in Figure 9.2 D, long strips extending across a whole township, are intermediate between Type C, the classic nucleated village with open, subdivided communally worked townfields, and Type F, the classic high medieval forest, marsh or heath clearing settlement, divided into long broad strips that extend as much as several kilometres. There are clear links with plans such as are seen in Figure 4.6.

Thus, to turn to eastern Europe, the Schröder and Schwarz map (Fig. 9.1) shows two other major zones, a first is characterised by 'planted row settlements in woodland, heath and marsh', generally considered to date between the 11th and 12th centuries, and represent ventures in Europe's internal frontiers. The marshland colonisations are placed in this group, but the large majority are linked with woodland colonisation of mountain lands of central Europe, and are present in south-eastern Germany and the uplands of the Erzgebirge, the former Czechoslovakia and southern Poland, and northern Hungary, where great tracts of woodland remained to be colonised. In measure these same zones represented external frontiers, as was eastern Germany, east of the Elbe, where across the great plains of Europe regular street and street-green plans were established during the drive to the east by German colonists during and indeed after the twelfth and thirteenth centuries. They were often substantively reorganised in post-medieval centuries when the areas became famous for the export of grains crops via the Baltic ports. Such settlements, with their great planned villages and associated regular open field systems extend deep into Poland and the Baltic states. Reflecting their origin as planned ventures these layouts show great regularities, and Types D and F in Figure 9.2 reflect this, without notably emphasising the degree to which individual village plans could be geometrically formal (Postan 1966, 86, 462–3, 470–2, 501–3; Duby 1968, 79, docs. 36, 39). Often organised by *Lokators* or land agents these regular plans, it may be noted fall essentially into a period ranging in date from between the eleventh and the fourteenth century but some are as late as the two centuries between 1600 and 1800. Others may be significantly earlier (Fig. 9.5 below).

Of course, the whole question is much more complex than any small-scale map can show. The over-printed symbols, for 'street green plans', 'broad green plans', 'street plans', 'planted row plans' and even 'settlements with round plans', are reminders that each and every settlement pattern contains varied intrusions, some of which vary significantly from the dominant type. Furthermore, the underlying chronologies of local regional development, so confidently generalised above, present many research questions. Finally this brief synoptic overview may be compared with Figure 9.4, a wholly European-wide picture created by Meeus, Wijermans and Vroom for the major landscape types, again showing a break along the Elbe line. The linkages between settlement types and field systems are manifold and complex. However, such synoptic views have two purposes: they present vast challenges in their creation, demanding that local information be integrated and literally keyed into the wider picture, and raise questions about the trustworthiness of local generalisation. Second, their existence creates contexts within which local regional data can, indeed should, be assessed and evaluated. While it is true that both processes may tell as much about the scholars involved as the historical situation, broad context mapping is a wholly necessary step to move from local regional introversion to wider questions.

Antecedents and Roots

These sweeping pictures permit one conclusion: the planned villages of Northern England undoubtedly appear to be earlier than the main tranche of German high medieval planned settlements established during the drive to the east. However, comparisons may be taken forward in several directions: first, in Germany work by Nitz

262 *Landscapes, Documents and Maps*

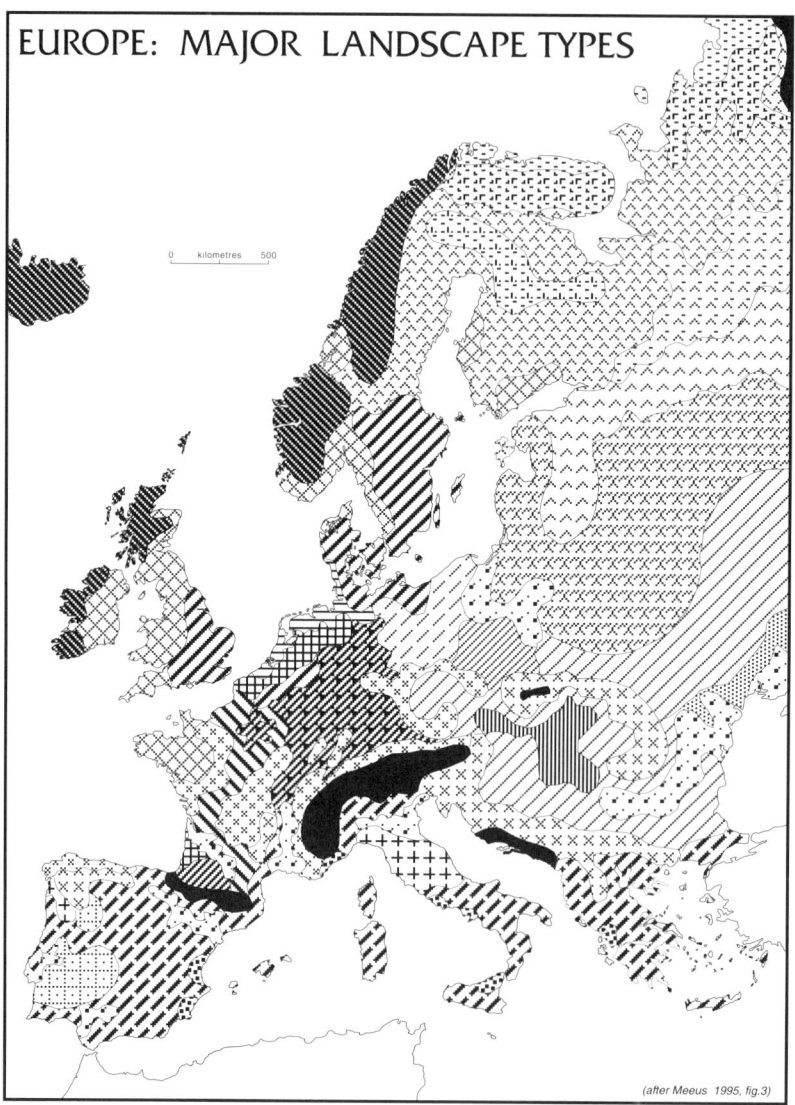

Fig. 9.4.a Major landscape types in Europe

and others has revealed the presence of lineally arranged settlements arising from even earlier Frankish colonisation. These are to be found along the middle Rhine, the rising lands west of Mainz, Worms and Speyer; between Augsberg and Mindelheim in the Alpine Foreland, as well as in other smaller zones, and to the east of the Mosel and north and east of Nancy in the Départments of Merthe-Mosel and Mosel. Second, there is archaeological evidence from a number of sites concerning early plans. In making these

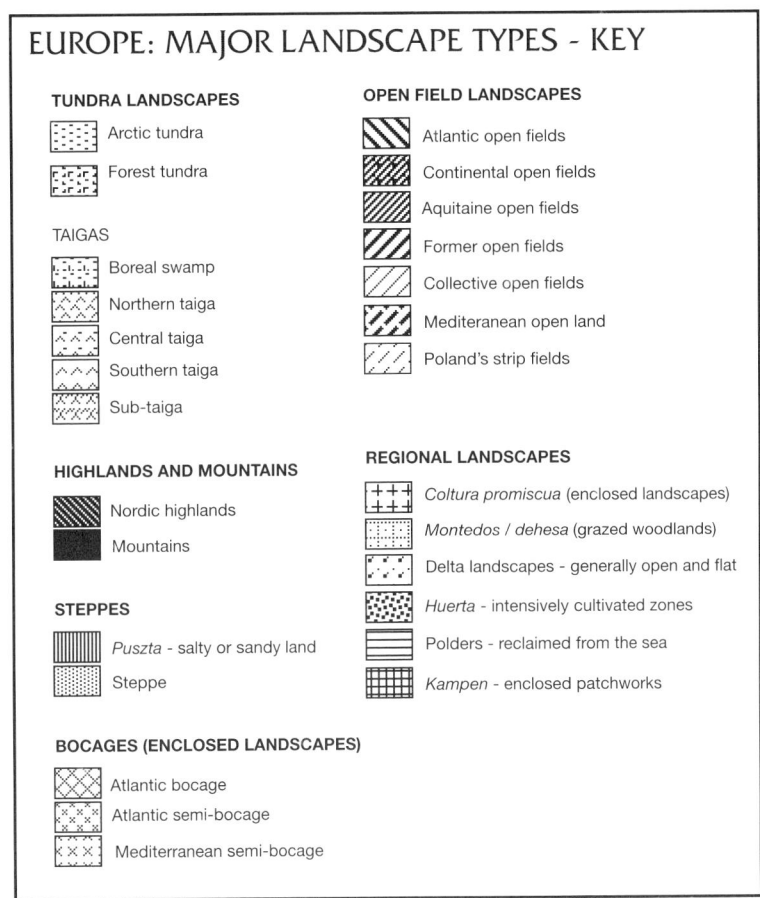

Fig. 9.4.b Major landscape types in Europe – key

comparisons the author must confess that where retrogressive analysis is often involved, moving from plans documented in the post-medieval period to interpreting them in the light of earlier, often fragmentary documentation and archaeological recovery, he retains a level of scepticism that is profound! As is always said in these circumstances, while many scholars are close friends, historians, geographers and archaeologists, the fact remains that in all fields professional judgement must be exercised. In a field as yet lacking the fine-grained arguments of art history or historical documentary or historical architectural analysis, landscape interpretation can often involve leaps of faith as well as scholarly weighing. In all such matters it is too easy to find what one is looking for and effectively overlook whole phases of development that may simply not be documented. The well-documented case of Acklington, discussed in Chapter 3, is severe warning of the problems. The fortuitous survival of *one* map of circa 1800 and

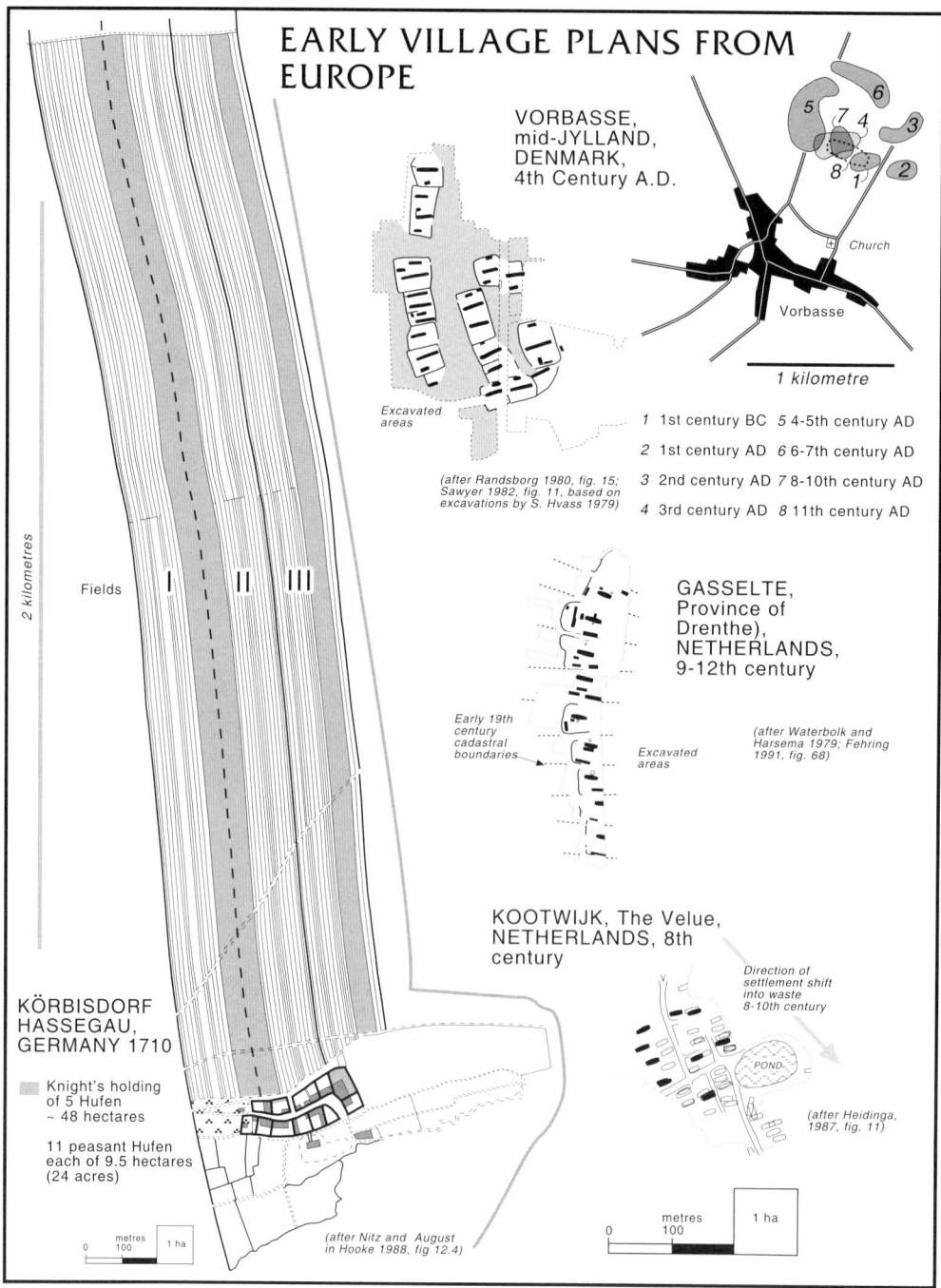

Fig. 9.5 Early village plans from Europe

the documentation of a major tenemental reorganisation in the later fifteenth century made two unexpected and cataclysmic events in the history of the settlement and its field system clear. In most cases this evidence would be absent.

Frankish Colonisation

Jürgen Nitz has argued that field layouts, comprising regular, long rather broad strips – *Langstreifenflur* – were being established in the eighth and ninth centuries as part of Frankish colonisation, involving the planting of soldier colonists under the Merovingians, Carolingians and Ottonians. His work is based on place-names, township shapes, the presence of royal vills or manses, services, terms indicative of particular groups, dedications to St. Martin, and the presence of royal highways. The strips were of the order of 20–30 metres in width and up to as much as 3 kilometres or even more in length. Between 741 and 768 Frankish power was being extended into this part of Alemannia by Pepin III, at first as mayor of the palace and then, after 751, as king (MacKay and Ditchburn 1997, 18–19). As Nitz stresses, these are important foundations, occurring no less than 500 years before the classic east-German developments of the High Middle Ages (Nitz 1974, 334–360). In detailed analysis of villages in the Hassegau, extending between the Harz and the Saale, he argues that there is evidence for a regular disposition of the strips of individual holdings, *Hufen*, throughout the fields (Nitz in Hooke 1988, 249–73). Furthermore, three-field systems were imposed, certainly before 1121 and possibly before 979, and he recognises that village planning continued into the eleventh century (see also Hildebrandt in Hooke 1988, 275–290). He suggests that the original plantation has mid-eighth century roots and that standardised regular two-row planned settlements were an integral part of the system. There are even back lanes! An example, Körbisdorf, is incorporated into Figure 9.5, where the strip width-length proportion is 1:44, and the strips are in fact some 1400 metres in length. There are striking parallels in form between the great strips seen at Middleton by Pickering (Fig. 4.6) and these German examples. The village and field layouts are variants of those modelled in Types D and F in Figure 9.2 and as example k in Figure 9.3.b. Further north in Germany between the lower Elbe and Weser rivers and amid heath lands developed on glacial outwash, poor sandy soils were traditionally maintained by the intensive manuring of a permanently cultivated core field termed the *Esch*. This arrangement is modelled as Type A in Figure 9.2, and Nitz argues that such forms are also the result of Frankish military occupation. In these cases the accompanying settlement is sometimes grouped in a circle, sometimes in a row. Fields tended to be regularly divided, and significantly a common place-name element associated with these forms, *-loh,* is related to the Old English *-leah*. He shows that these Geesteland settlements were integrated into estates that comprised functionally and tenurially distinct entities that were given coherence by the varied demands imposed upon them by control from royal centres, an arrangement not dissimilar to the small shires discussed in Chapter 6.

In fact, a close English parallel to the township frameworks within which the Hassegau settlements are found is to be seen in the well-known strip parishes of Dorset, Wiltshire, Berkshire, Lincolnshire and Yorkshire. However, it is the existence of regular plans, regulated planned field systems, and regular shifts within these fields that are germane to the arguments of this study. It is no criticism of Nitz that he cites neither archaeological evidence nor landscape-topographical evidence in support of his arguments for the antiquity of landscapes effectively first recorded only on eighteenth and nineteenth century maps. Correlations between these late sources and medieval estate documents are supported by documented glebe strips and other assessed holdings. Scepticism is easy, for there are certain circularities of argument, interpreting the documents from the maps and the maps from the documents. On balance, however, it is the convergence of the map evidence within the broader contexts provided by place-names and the limited documentary record, when handled by such a scholar as Nitz, that is convincing. His conclusion that the 'very regular and almost standardised villages ,field and township patterns, along with the dominance of place names in *-dorf*, can only be understood as being created under one single planning institution, and the only one allotting land in the region (Harz-Saale) between the eighth and ninth centuries was the royal administration. During the tenth century and even earlier, the crown gave many villages away as grants and fiefs to various ecclesiastical and lay grantees' (Nitz in Hooke 1988, 260). In fact, the field arrangements of the type described by him are recorded in later documentation, providing a bridge between these earlier arrangements and the villages planted in the twelfth and thirteenth century. Thus Duby cites a document dated 1106 by which Frederic, Bishop of Hamburg, grants to men 'from beyond the Rhine, called Hollanders', land 'now uncultivated and marshy and useless to the inhabitants of the country, to put it under cultivation'. Each manse, or 'Hufen' was to be 720 royal rods in length and 30 in width, with the streams crossing the land, a ratio of 24:1. These holdings are of similar proportion to those at Körbisdorf (Fig. 9.5), comprising great, broad strips (Duby 1968, 392–3). In his own consideration of similar field arrangements in the north of England the present author gave attention to the problems of ploughing such strips, and the arrangements at Middleton-by-Pickering – also 1400 metres long – show that vast aratral curves have been imposed on the terrain (Roberts 1996c; Fig. 4.6 above). There are explicit and important questions here for the genesis of the English planned forms.

Archaeological Evidence
Archaeological evidence is inevitably limited in quantity, because of the expenses involved, but three particular cases provide relevant material to support the questions being formulated here (Fig. 9.5). Kootwijk, in the Veluwe, west of Appledoorn in the Netherlands comprised a hamlet of between six and eight farmhouses that between about 750 and 1000 developed into a village of some 20 steadings. In addition there were an unknown number of other scattered farmhouses (Heidinga 1987, 34 ff). The agglomeration focussed upon a pond, a vital water supply in these sandy dry lands,

and a north-south road formed the axis of the earliest settlement plan. The larger homesteads were each separated from other by trackways and open spaces. Buildings comprised substantial post-built hall houses, between 17 and 22 metres long, with a width-length proportion of 1:3. Barns and sunken huts provided service structures. In the history of the site there were signs of a steady migration of new buildings out into uncultivated land accompanied by an absorption of former dwelling sites, with an improved soil structure and fertility resulting from the occupation, into the arable fields. The excavators' reconstruction of the middle of the eighth century – the earliest phase – shows a simple two-row structure, with eight steadings, comprising buildings and tofts. Seven of these were arranged in a small two-row plan, with the eighth added to the rear of the east row. Is this layout planned? At least it is not haphazard: it is organised and structured. Subsequent changes destroyed the simplicity of the initial plan, as Gutkind predicted, but this settlement with its strip fields, at least by the later stage of its history, represent an informal prototype for the planned layouts of later centuries. In fact, a complex series of phases and sub-phases were recognised, but dating these with precision was difficult. Significantly the excavators summarise the qualities of the site as follows:

> it has been assumed that the orderly structure of Kootwijk 2 must have been due to control exercised by a (preferably Frankish) ruling authority, but there is no evidence for this: local native farmers must also be considered capable of establishing order in their home environment. As a result of later developments in these settlements (Kootwijk and a nearby hamlet, Horst) the original structure has changed considerably. Moreover, at Kootwijk 2 and Horst the strict rule of east-west orientation was no longer adhered to… Settlements were dynamic organisms.
>
> (Heidinga 1987, 44–45).

It must be noted that the 'east-west orientation' referred to above concerns not the plan-orientation, which was north to south, but the fundamental orientation of the long farmhouses, containing dwelling and byre. One can only speculate that this orientation may reflect cosmological attitudes such as are manifest in the *solskifte* system of field layout.

In a nutshell, this painstakingly excavated material, on a large scale, and meticulously reported, puts before us the conundrum of settlement history. The excavated material, from a settlement deserted by about AD 1000, cannot be documented, while even if excavations were undertaken within living, documented settlements the archaeological material would be even more fragmentary. Nevertheless, this is an exciting and stimulating site. At the least it shows that what one can call latencies towards planning were indeed present by AD 750. We must accept that this is a period when Charles Martel (mayor of the palace 717–41) and Pepin III (mayor 741–51 and king 751–68) were establishing the dominance of the Arnulfing/Carolingian family in Francia. This was supported by their military success against the Arabs, Aquitanians, Frisians and various peoples east of the Rhine and they achieved these conquests by creating networks of aristocratic support and by forging a close alliance with the church. From this base they established, not without vicissitudes, control over substantial areas of western Europe, while Charlemagne (768–814) made further territorial gains and became powerful enough to be crowned emperor by the pope on Christmas day in the year 800 (MacKay and Ditchburn 1997, 18–19).

Another regular settlement, summarised in Figure 9.5, and probably itself an addition to an older core, has been excavated in Gasselte, Drenthe, the Netherlands, comprising a series of eight or nine long farmsteads set along a north-to south street (Waterbolk and Harsema, 1979, 228–299; Fehring 1991, 168–71). Each steading was surrounded by a 40 metre wide toft, and was separated from its neighbour by a narrow vennel, or *throughgang*, to use Cumbrian terminology. There are convincing signs that plots appearing on a cadastral plan of 1813 are the lineal successors of the plots of the excavated farmsteads (Waterbolk and Harsema 1979, fig. 24), because their property boundaries are precisely in accord. The settlement ranged in date from the ninth to the twelfth century. More startling is a settlement at Vorbasse, in mid-west Jylland, Denmark, excavated by Sven Hvass, which produced a planned village containing a series of well-built long-houses, up to 44 metres in length and divided into several rooms, including a living-room, a stall and possibly a barn (Fig. 9.5). Each long-house lay adjacent to one or two minor buildings and each individual group was surrounded by fences defining a square plot or toft (Randsborg 1980, 61–66). There is a tendency for two farmsteads to share a toft, and the tofts are set in rows, facing across a street-green, all orientated north to south. The regular plan originates in the fourth century A.D., and subsequent developments saw an increase in the numbers of steadings in the fifth century. By the tenth and eleventh centuries, a separation had taken place between three larger magnate farmsteads, some with boat-shaped sides, set in large tofts, together with an associated less regular cluster. In fact, as a map published by Sawyer shows, fourth century Vorbasse was only one of a whole succession of settlements extending from the Roman period into the tenth century, and all lay on sites distinct from the medieval and modern village (Sawyer 1982, fig. 11). As at Kootwijk it is possible, indeed likely, that the manured and trampled soils of the settlement site offered rich productive capacities. In a land of short-lived timber structures, when any rebuilding took place there was a tendency for the settlement to shuffle – the sum total of a series of individual decisions – towards the waste. This was by no means universal, for at Sædding, in West Jylland, Denmark, an open green lay at the centre of the site, occupied in the tenth and eleventh centuries, while the long-houses changed orientation from east-west to north-south. We need not expect consistency in settlement evolution (Randsborg 1980, 61–9). In conclusion, Randsborg hints that some settlement reorganisations may have taken place as the result of the military organisation of the country, the so-called 'leding', where each 'herred' (territory) had to man one or more warships. The single village and farm contribute according to their size, and it is clearly in the interest of the administration to create standard measures. Such a development can be seen as a strong indicator of the arrival of the 'state' as an active element in the organisation of space (Randsborg 1980, 69: Mead 1981, 27–9).

Archaeological evidence is wholly material in character, and must be interpreted to establish arguments about the economic and social contexts from which these particular planned settlements appeared. The comments from Heidinga cited above admirably summarise the issues. But what general conclusions can be drawn? We can argue that the settlements sufficiently regular to be called 'planned', or at least 'conceptually organised' are indeed present in parts of continental and peninsular by the second half of the eighth century, indeed even as early as the fourth century AD. The plan of Vorbasse with a street green rather over 300 metres in length would not be exceptional if placed within a group of smaller village plans found on nineteenth century British Ordnance Survey maps. What differs is the character of the buildings. Even if such plans are indeed merely established by farmers themselves to create order in their home environment, then these are forms 'capable of improvement' to use Lancelot Brown's words applied to landscapes a millennium later. New plantations, perhaps established under aristocratic patronage, could adopt, regenerate and redefine existing vernacular ideas.

Finally, evidence from Scandinavia concerning settlement regulation and its chronology raises, as Göransson noted, crucial questions about trans-North Sea links, both with Scandinavia and the continent proper. In turn these take the argument into new realms: of royal demands and the imposition of taxation, the travels of churchmen and the role of individuals, the diffusion of styles of architecture, concepts and even of language. Finally, there are questions about the role of complex interactions between local polities and formal states and vice versa, and the degree to which classical concepts of landscape organisation and taxation were filtered into the early medieval world.

A 'Romanesque Society'?

At an architectural conference in Durham in 2003 the author used in public the term 'Romanesque society'. He was courteously, and of course quite rightly, taken to task by an eminent scholar in the architectural field. An art historical term cannot be used to define a society. With this there can be no disagreement … and yet, the term 'Norman', also an art historical term, is used quite freely in other contexts. What it actually means is very much the subject of debate (Davis 1976). Admittedly we can discuss 'the Normans' who gave their name to a region – Normandy – and in England to a distinctive architectural style, to a specific conquest and at the very least to social attitudes. While Patrick Wormald (1999, 39) in a scholarly and magisterial review has used the term 'Romanesque law', the term 'Romanesque world' appropriately characterises a reality comprising more than a series of discrete parts. Beneath the very relative homogeneity of Romanesque art styles, from the opulence of the Mediterranean manifestations to the northern starkness of Durham, Dunfermline and even Kirkwall in Orkney, there are, throughout temperate and continental transalpine Europe, certain strong unities of economy and society. This is no more clearly expressed than in the economic base. Agriculture was based on ploughs, wagons and carts, sustaining yields of grain crops in fields by fallowing the soils as well as using animal dung. The larger implements were supplemented by a variety of wooden hand tools, which when needful were shod or edged with iron. Four basic crops, wheat, barley, rye and oats were grown to support a host of at first rather small and often rather scattered communities, while beans and other legumes gave variety and vegetable protein to the diet. Cattle, horses, sheep, pigs and chickens were kept, with the two former used for traction as well as food and hides. This farming was successful and supported growing populations during the period between the barbarian invasions and the advent of the fourteenth century plagues not least the Black Death. Of course, this was not a continuous flow of growth; there were setbacks, but regionally discrete surges in population created conditions for change and migration, processes complicated by the dynastic struggles of aristocratic kings, warriors and holy men. In effect this foundational agricultural order which had appeared in the later centuries of prehistory – the Iron Age – and with some rationalization, modification and development of specialisms, was to persist until a series of cumulative 'agricultural revolutions' in the sixteenth, seventeenth and eighteenth centuries (Orme 1981, 273–84; Van Bath 1963a; b). Of course there were regional differences and of course this is vast generalisation, but Van Bath's careful tabulation of yield ratios emphasizes the fundamental slowness of agricultural change and the way that innovations only gradually led to significant jumps in yield ratios (Van Bath 1963a; b). None of this is to deny the importance of woodland, heath, marsh and upland colonisation in diversifying the medieval economy, but this is important detail within an underlying unity.

If we take the period between 800 and 1200, some four hundred years, the fundamental system of agricultural support in the areas of transalpine Europe within which Romanesque art styles blossomed, was remarkably homogeneous as well as varied in detail. It was sufficiently productive and flexible to sustain increasing populations. To what degree the continent's long settled and well-developed agricultural zones saw marked increases in population is a more open question than might at first seem the case. Although increased numbers of tenancies point to substantial rises between 1200 and 1300 this was often the result of population pressures upon limited numbers of tenements in productive agricultural zones, and a virtually finite amount of productive arable. The fact that new lands were undoubtedly colonized and settlement was in general intensified between 800 and 1200 implies both the appearance, and migration, of population surpluses created within the long settled territories. Towns also expanded, by both indigenous growth and by immigration from the countryside. In these contexts people were a form of crop, sustained by mixed farming in all its possible variations, but, because they were mobile, they moved to other less populous regions, to the growing towns, or to join armies and crusades. Further, the same agricultural system was producing food surpluses sufficient to sustain secular and ecclesiastical elites, armies, merchants and the craftsmen needed to provide both basic and luxury goods for consumption. In short agriculture was remarkably successful throughout the Europe that gave birth to the Romanesque. To describe these labouring folk – the *laboratores* – peasants and artisans – as 'Romanesque' would be sheer parody, yet their labours lay at the roots of the Romanesque architectural styles as surely as the great Romanesque *Porta Gloria* at Compostella, whose jambs are based upon the backs of crouching and subdued chthonic beasts.

Medieval society also contained the *bellatores* and *oratores*, those who fought and those who prayed. Here again, distance in time affords views of other traces of underlying homogeneities. First, throughout what we will term Atlantic and Central Europe, leaving aside the classically rooted complexities of Mediterranean Europe, there was the emergence of new polities. In fact long before AD 800 Europe north of the Alps was divided into two fundamental portions: to the west lay former imperial provinces, while to the east, beyond the Roman limes lay the territories of the free barbarian peoples. Of course, reality was infinitely subtle, with the frontier zone subjected to varying degrees of Romanisation, while the limes, essentially the Rhine and the Danube, formed a military and political frontier. The collapse of imperial control and some westward movement of barbarians created an even more complex mixture, yet at root the fundamental imperial contrast permeated the development of the nascent barbarian polities. Because of the longstanding classical heritage three critical civilising tendencies, towns, taxation and record-keeping, lay nearer to the surface in the west of Europe than in the north and east, although Barford's recent study is a reminder that we must never under-estimate the early Slavic peoples (Barford 2001).

Socially the period between 800 and 1200 saw in the west a transition from the tribalism that emerged from the folk movements – recognising that in themselves these tribes were in no manner homogenous – to feudally organised states. Social structures in which the bonds of kin and locality, intermixed with the rootless enforcements of slavery, gradually but surely gave way to customarily defined tenancies linked to the estates of landowners and landholders. Kings and aristocratic families – once tribal leaders – took control of land resources, and exploited these with the labour of the *laboratore*s. Because of the slow birth of a cash-based exchange system, personal services and gifts of land and goods were a key means of wealth transfer. However, as personal services became formalised and as renders and services defined by long-standing custom, the written text and increased amounts of coinage, personal service was eventually replaced by taxation. The written word replaced memory and custom and gradually cash replaced services and renders.

The period 800–1200 saw the continuation of the conversion of the barbarians. Charlemagne's coronation by the Pope in 800 marked less a return of an emperor in the west than a public and permanent bonding of embryonic but eventually enduring

European polities to the political, social and economic life of the states, towns and church of the Mediterranean world. From this link flowed and diffused the styles and attitudes associated with what art historians have termed the 'Romanesque', the 'Roman-like' stone structures and portable artefacts. The importance of this link cannot be over-emphasised, for the travel to and from Rome by churchmen and aristocratic pilgrims brought them to contact with classical culture, structures and values. Books, relics and reliquaries, textiles and other works of craftsmanship flowed in each direction, but it is particularly in book illustration and church architecture that we detect the intangible flows of ideas and mental models. A classic case is to be seen in the use of spiral columns, in Repton, England, in the Low Countries, in Lanfranc's Canterbury and eventually in Durham and in other churches of imitation. St Peter's ciborium columns and marble are considered to be the exemplars, but the Romanesque world – a less challenging concept than Romanesque society – took the Mediterranean exemplar and absorbed it into art, iconography and physical structures.

This general unity of both plebeian and aristocratic culture in transalpine Europe is important, and it is both the simple contention and conclusion to this study that planned settlements, both towns and villages, are as much a product of 'the Romanesque' as are the churches and castles. They are part of taking possession of space and then imposing cultural organisation upon it, involving social, economic and psychological dimensions. Settlement planning derives from a mutuality of interest and a state of mind. On one side was a tenantry, both free and servile, facing increasing pressures upon land resources, not only on the precious arable, but also on fuel-wood, fodder, building wood, honey, fruits of the forest – for wild strawberries are unimaginably delicious. On the other were the demands placed upon them by aristocracy and church for renders, services and labour and, eventually, cash (Glacken 1976, 320–322). For the tenantry, amid a world of intermittent warfare and changing masters, settlement planning and an associated definition of services and renders involved offered a degree of security. Both planning and reorganisation, provided contexts of definition, oiled by concepts of custom and memory, and offered at least a measure of constraint upon excessive seigniorial demands.

On the other hand there were the lords; it was the church estates where written records first began to supplement custom and memory, closely followed by royal estates. While the focus of church and monastery provided fixed loci for estate administration, royal power was exercised from rural centres, royal vills. Some of these lay upon the circuits of these peripatetic rulers, regularly visited to consume the produce assembled there and hence often associated with Roman roads. Others were in the hands of royal officers, officials, some of whom tended to be more static and tied to a locality by virtue of the services they rendered and the nature of the local power they exercised. Gradually this system of production and consumption was replicated on estates granted to retainers and followers. The emergence of the standard tenement, the *Hufen*, the *Bol*, the *virgate*, the *bovate*, the *Morgan* and the like, was closely linked to settlement standardisation and to the imposition of taxation and dues rather than food renders. Such concepts could also be applied to existing structurally unplanned settlements, but the movement of people, either voluntarily or enforced, was a stimulus to formal settlement planning.

The English Dimension

In an attempt to grasp and define the broad scale issues Figure 9.6 draws together in a single diagram some of the points that can be made about the English and Continental roots of settlement planning. The time frame emphasises how isolated are the points that can be made, while the hatched background is a reminder of the seamless matrix of events, the warp and weft of time, some elements of which can be documented while most can not. Given the strong formal parallels between the English and Scandinavian planned settlements, and in the light of Göransson's comments noted above, Figure 9.7 shows the empire of Cnut, king of England and Scandinavia. The links to classical roots through observing surviving remains and through writings such as Vegetius and Vitruvius, the former certainly known at the court of Charlemagne, need not be pursued here (Haywood 1999, 144–5 *passim*). The king and his agents were certainly engaged in the construction of forts, fortified royal vills and planning villages (Phillips 1944, 141). One rather startling example of the way in which Roman order could be combined with the 'vernacular' curvilinearity of Iron Age constructions is to be seen at the fortress of Eketorp on the Swedish island of Öland, where a series of forts were apparently constructed by groups of villages and experienced occupation until the end of the thirteenth century. Circular in form, Eketorp was divided radially into a series of wedge-shaped blockhouses, with an interior central block. There are resonances with the great royal fortresses in Jutland, of the reign of Sven Forkbeard, but the parallels are superficial, not close and the dating is quite different (Wegraeus and Näsman sd, 34–60; Lawson 2004, 22).

Strong links existed between Kentish and East Anglian kings and Franks in the mid-7th century and artefacts were exchanged (Fletcher 1998, 160–1–2; 184–5). It was Charlemagne who formalised the link between secular and spiritual conquest, adding imperial purpose to the regular, successful, predatory warfare of his predecessors, necessary to reward and earn the gratitude of his aristocratic followers (*ibid*. 193–195). Ruling from 768–814 Charlemagne acquired land, plunder and tribute on a large scale for distribution to loyal followers, and eventually, divided into two, his vast conquests formed the later kingdoms of Germany and France. A rather ramshackle administration, operated through existing aristocratic families and, we must presume, existing systems of raising basic tribute, for instance there had been annual render in *circa* 660 of 500 cows by the Saxons to the Frankish kings since the time of King Chlothar I, the son of Clovis (*ibid*. 213). The Christianisation of his conquests was in the hands of a few intellectuals and there were strong and sustained links between the clergy of England and the 'conversion' of the emergent Frankish realms (*ibid*. 204 ff). Thus, Lul, archbishop of Mainz between 754–786

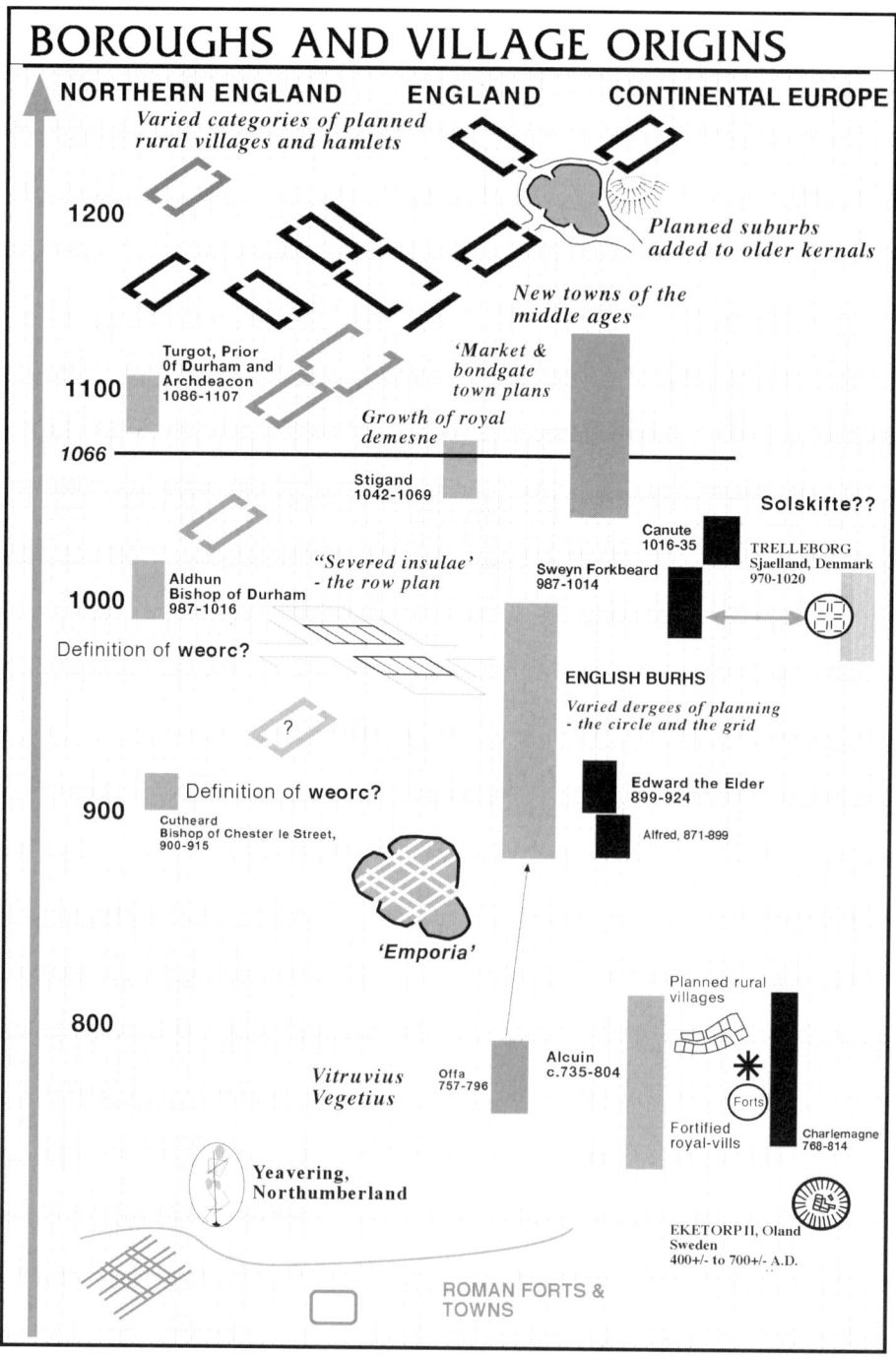

Fig. 9.6 Boroughs and village origins

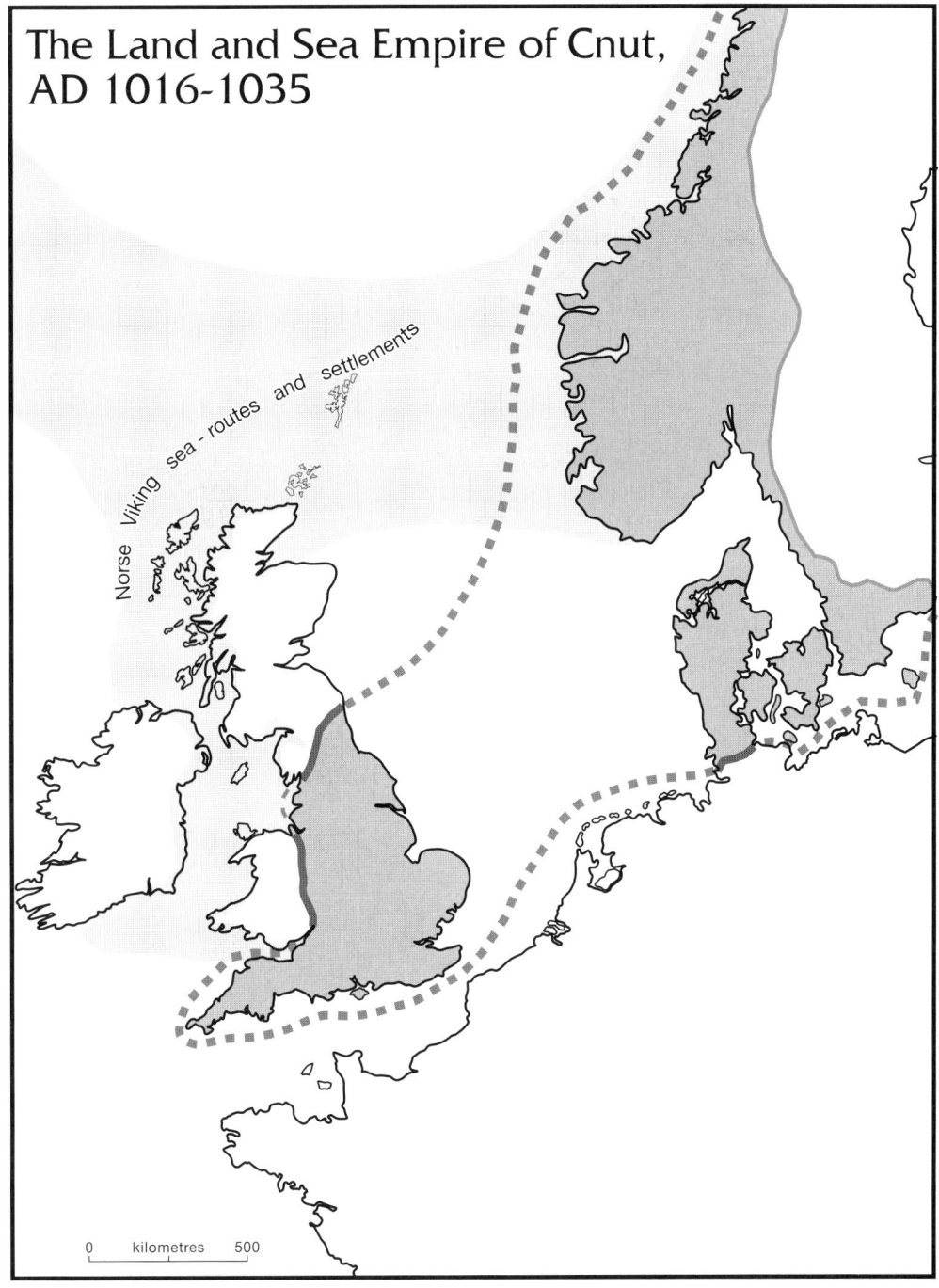

Fig. 9.7 The land and sea empire of Cnut

(*ibid.* 215 and 217), was deeply implicated in the forced conversion of the Saxons in the 770s and 780s and was in correspondence with Abbot Cuthbert of Wearmouth in 764 and requested *inter alia* Bede's prose and verse *Lives of St Cuthbert* (*ibid.* 217). With such contacts, ideas must also have flowed, for it was an essential part of the enforced conversion that new churches in Frisia were to be endowed with land and buildings (*ibid.* 215). Fletcher touches key issues when he talks of the diffusion of Christianity in some shape or form beyond the imperial frontiers – wherever these might be – in terms of 'seepage'. This can take many forms 'transfer of goods and fashions by means of raiding or trading, recruitment and return of soldiers, cross-border movement of peddlers, vagrants, exiles, escaping slaves, brides, explorers, ambassadors, arms dealers' (*ibid.* 229). 'Being educated into the duties of Christian kingship… and … their missionary and teaching responsibilities' (*ibid.* 242–4), were hardly good and sufficient reasons for a predatory war-leader to adopt Christianity. At base lay the degree to which barbarian ambassadors were impressed by the wealth and ritual of more sophisticated courts. Power, magic, and perceived advantages – the wealth others possessed – lay at the roots of conversion. 'Magic' may seem to imply cheap tricks, but the cultivation of hagiological accounts depicting missionaries controlling the weather, emphasises the important role of agriculture in sustaining early medieval society. As was noted earlier, the work by Helen Waddell on the literature of the period shows both a familiarity with classic sources and strong ties sustained by scholarly travellers and letters.

Hodges (1989a, 117ff) comments on the vast problems of administering Charlemagne's conquests, and notes that English monks helped him formulate a policy. Social and economic transformations allowed taxes to be raised while modifications of underdeveloped traditions were used. A key ideological revolution was a keystone of policy: Charlemagne manipulated the church so that Christianity became the basis of a 'reborn' society. After his anointing as Emperor he possessed the theocratic status of a Roman emperor. Public ritual to enforce the role of the church was a central theme. Hodges suggests that as summer military campaigns decreased, so long distance trade increased, notably the Carolingian-Abbasid trade. This suffered a sharp decline after 820, threatening the stability of the elite. However, by the early 790s the minting of reformed coinage took place, while Roman technology, building skills and agrarian practices, perhaps including the development of open-townfield systems (Hodges 1989a, 120) and recovered craft skills were given new form. Alcuin and his pupil Fridugis, played central roles in the management of the Carolingian empire, and they were Anglo-Saxons. These developments had repercussions in England. Hodges concludes that a ninth-century Mercian architect was striving (at Northampton) to emulate a Carolingian model. New coinages, and rural sites in which there was an emphasis on storage of hay and grain, and the specialist production of meat were coming into being (Hodges 1989a, 134–139) and there are indications that the kinship to tenancy transition was taking place at this time (*ibid.* 139).

In the light of the appearance of planted and planned colonising settlements in Charlemagne's realms it is worth looking briefly at the career of a figure such as Alcuin (*c*. 735–804) which illustrates the important intellectual linkages between England and the court of Charlemagne. He originated in England, was a kinsman of Willibrord, one of the founders of the Frisian church, and between 767 and 780 he was the focus of a group of scholars in the school of York and in that period he took two journeys to Rome. In 780, having become Archbishop of York he travelled again to Rome to get his pallium, but on the journey he met Charlemagne who offered him a permanent place at the Frankish court. By 782 he was head of the palace school of scholars, where he was joined by many of his English contemporaries. This placement established secure links between the Frankish court at Aachen and England, and while the flows undoubtedly emphasised doctrinal issues and church practice, Alcuin seems to have been the focus of intellectual activity. He was at the heart of the Carolingian renaissance in speculative thought (Stenton 1971, 188–91). Jim Lang in an article on four unusual Anglo-Saxon shafts from Yorkshire, at Otley and Dewsbury in the West Riding and Masham and Easby in the North Riding, with one at Halton in the Lune Valley, Lancashire, reached several interesting conclusions. He suggests that they are not 'normal' crosses but may have been markers for baptismal locations on adjacent rivers, and that not only are their iconic programmes of classical origin, but are symbols of apostolic power deriving from exemplars to be found in Rome and Ravenna. He associates them with links between early English church contacts with the papal court. An important intermediary in these links may have been Alcuin himself, who also made gifts of heavy ornamental stones to those English centres that cherished or aspired to metropolitan status. With these contacts we can suggest that there flowed more ephemeral materials including ideas, moving with the sophisticated, literate and well-travelled ambassadors of the church of York (Lang 2000, 109–119).

That planned villages owed something to the development of planned towns and fortresses is probable but at the moment unprovable. Some of the Alfredian burhs, for instance Lyng in Somerset, show signs, in their surviving plans of being morphologically indistinguishable from the regular village plans of later centuries. This brings us to the troubled question of the Vikings and their impact on English settlement. As David Sturdy notes, the Vikings arrived as mercenary freebooters as much as mere raiders; loot, the returns from blackmail, and 'taxation' were one and the same thing to them, and they intruded into regional politics wherever they penetrated. They met an Anglo-Saxon nobility that was based upon a set of aristocratic clans, any member of which could be king, governor, minister or senior churchman (or woman). The senior members of each clan all possessed household warriors, often junior relatives, and the bulk of local populations were not involved in warfare, except as victims, for much savagery took place both within and without each and every temporary polity. Peasants were not expected to fight (Sturdy 1995, 107). They were expected to work the land. This aristocratic power centred on 'royal vills', church foci and monastic sites, and these were often associated – throughout Europe – with fortifications. Trading settlements tended to be separate, and while often destroyed by raids, normally quickly recovered. The aristocratic centres were only periodically or seasonally occupied; they represented centres where stores were accumulated and where cattle and other rents were rendered, this activity occurring within spatial systems that resembled small shires. By the ninth century these centres were becoming more sophisticated, centres of power and regional influence. This process began in Carolingian times and continued into the tenth century. Forts and the supporting systems that accompanied them, were part of the aristocratic strategy in response to Viking raiding, and involved three elements, (a) defence (b) a local organisation for manning and maintenance and for assembling a field army and (c) a place in an overall national or regional strategy. Sturdy indicates that these were universal in the ninth century citing cases in Denmark, Rome, France, and emphasises the role of planning and measurement (Sturdy 1995, 178–192). Plantation could be accompanied by the movement of both peasant and mercantile populations, who were translated, often deported, from one locality or one region to another (*ibid*. 179 and 214).

Sturdy's study, reviewing European contexts and being rather iconoclastic in character, draws a strong view of the period. Many of the fort developments post-date Charlemagne's activities, suggesting that Frankish developments at the end of the eighth century acted as a stimulus to the later developments, even those in Rome. If Charlemagne was indeed planting and planning settlements, then Frankish planned rural settlements were some of the earliest in post-Roman Europe. The links between fiscal settlement and settlement and planning emerged most easily in contexts of colonisation, particularly when enforced migrations were involved. The case of Cumbria discussed in this study fits in well with this hypothesis, for while there is indeed a little evidence to support what is suggested, this is really only just sufficient to establish a possible context. Permanent occupation of fort sites was clearly encouraged, but Sturdy argues that they were not in any sense planned towns. He throws out the astringent comment that 'roads and lanes of various dates running off approximately at right angles to a spine road do not constitute "planning" and no indisputable evidence for ninth-century trade or manufacture has yet been found at any of the places in the *Burghal Hidage*' (*ibid*. 191). To this, one can only add that spine roads and coaxial lanes imply something more than haphazard development.

To draw together these wide ranging speculations and the materials from the north of England, two interlocking issues now warrant attention, the impact of the Viking raiding on society and settlement, and the possible role of the royal demesne. As yet the author hesitates to attempt to assemble a continuous narrative, and what follows undoubtedly skirts the zone between formal analysis and speculation in a marcher zone between history, archaeology, landscape studies and a host of related disciplines. By dispensing with the object of creating a narrative, issues can be more freely explored, and the discontinuities provide pressure points for further enquiry, questions and challenges. If the narrative is a subtle way of concealing what is not known, and this is often the case, then the mode of analysis to follow frankly admits that 'Here be dragons'… creatures unknown and perhaps even unsuspected.

Chapter Ten

Planned Villages in England – a National Perspective

In 1986, exactly one thousand nine hundred years after Domesday Book was compiled, Elizabeth Hallam created a superb national map of royal demesne between 1066 and 1086 (Hallam 1986, 74–113), a general distribution that is striking for both its voids and for its concentrations (Fig. 10.1). These are effectively royal vills and each monarch was in possession of two broad categories: on one hand there were those inherited from predecessors, the fixed capital of royal power. On the other there were those acquired by right of conquest. In the case of William the Conqueror this latter category is particularly to be found in those vills not possessed by Edward the Confessor and his close relatives. As Elizabeth Hallam points out, some of the symbols represent full manors, some parts of manors and others are merely outlying soke as well as lands administered by the crown for others and in 1086 listed as *terra Regis*. Thus the map conflates several, possibly many, distributions only three of which are differentiated by the symbols: there are the lands held by Edward the Confessor, both those granted by 1086 to others and those still in royal hands, and those lands acquired by William as a result of the conquest and held by him in 1086.

Of Royal Demesne

Hallam links her maps to a discussion of the special privileges possessed by the villein tenants – generally termed villein sokemen – of the royal demesne. Such tenants were subject only to fixed and usually nominal labour services, and did not have to attend county or hundred courts, to serve on juries, to pay taxes with the county, or to contribute to the expenses of members of parliament. They had direct access to royal courts, and while they were free of tolls and customs the king could tax them at will. These privileges have been the subject of much discussion by historians and views vary. Vinogradoff suggested that in them we have 'clues to the condition of the Saxon peasantry' (1892, 136). In contrast, Hoyt argued that such tenants originated as ordinary villeins who, possessing access to the financial and judicial resources of the crown, were able to win 'special privileges which set them apart from men on other manors (Hallam 1986, 75 ff.; Hoyt 1950, 171–207). These theses cannot be evaluated here, but two caveats can be added: first, the analysis of the Durham tenures suggests that complex shifts could and did take place in the centuries between 1150 and 1350. Lawyers' definitions by no means always fit reality and the gradual shifts occasioned by common law judgements do not necessarily reflect the real origins of ancient demesne.

In essence this is Hoyt's view. Second, it is clear from Hallam's map that the large scale acquisition by the Crown after 1066 must have initiated a fresh wave of colonisation, the planting of men, both major and minor tenants, on the new royal lands. In this step lay a consolidation of political power. Furthermore, there are no grounds for not assuming that something akin to this process must have been operating in the decades and centuries before the conquest of 1066. Royal demesne itself, whatever it precisely implied, must always have been part of ongoing settlement processes.

In King Edward's estates – and without descending to the detail Hallam's fine maps deserve – we can see a thin scatter throughout the Wessex heartlands, extending into East Anglia and the West Midlands, fading away in Devon and being thin on the ground in the London area and the extreme south-east. These are reasonably explained as a residual distribution reflecting royal progresses, at first for the consumption of food renders, but eventually when dealing with administrative and military matters (Hill 1981, 82–91). In contrast, there are eight noteworthy concentrations of this royal demesne:

- at the southern end of the Cotswolds, north of Bristol;
- south of the small ports along the northern Norfolk coast;
- in eastern Leicestershire and in
- northern Nottinghamshire;
- in north-western Derbyshire;
- in the western portion of the West Riding of Yorkshire
- with a smaller concentration in the Pennine foothills between the Ure and the Swale;
- finally, there is a small concentration along the Ouse, north of Goole, where the great Humber estuary becomes a river.

Why should this be? Hill's mapping of the hidation of King Edward's lands serves as a reminder that the vast weight of agriculturally productive estates lay in the heartlands of Wessex, and south of the Midlands, but the three Yorkshire foci stand out as economically significant in terms of hidage (1981, 100–101). In fact they comprise lands focussing on Howdenshire on the lower Ouse, a great estate centring on Wakefield, later part of the Honour of Pontefract, and another centring on Knaresborough, later the Honour of Knaresborough (Fig. 10.2). The history of the acquisition of each of these lands and an analysis of their settlement content constitutes a major research topic, not to be undertaken here, but one is left with the suspicion that these areas of royal control provided the seeds for settlement developments which reached full fruition after the events of 1066–1070. A preliminary re-analysis of June Sheppard's map of regular and part-regular plans in Yorkshire indicates that the most regular plans have tendency to concentrate in the best lands of Knaresborough and further north in the land of Count Alan, later the Honour of Richmond (Fig. 10.2). The pre-Conquest Yorkshire royal estates straddle or control key routes, the Humber

Planned Villages in England – a National Perspective 281

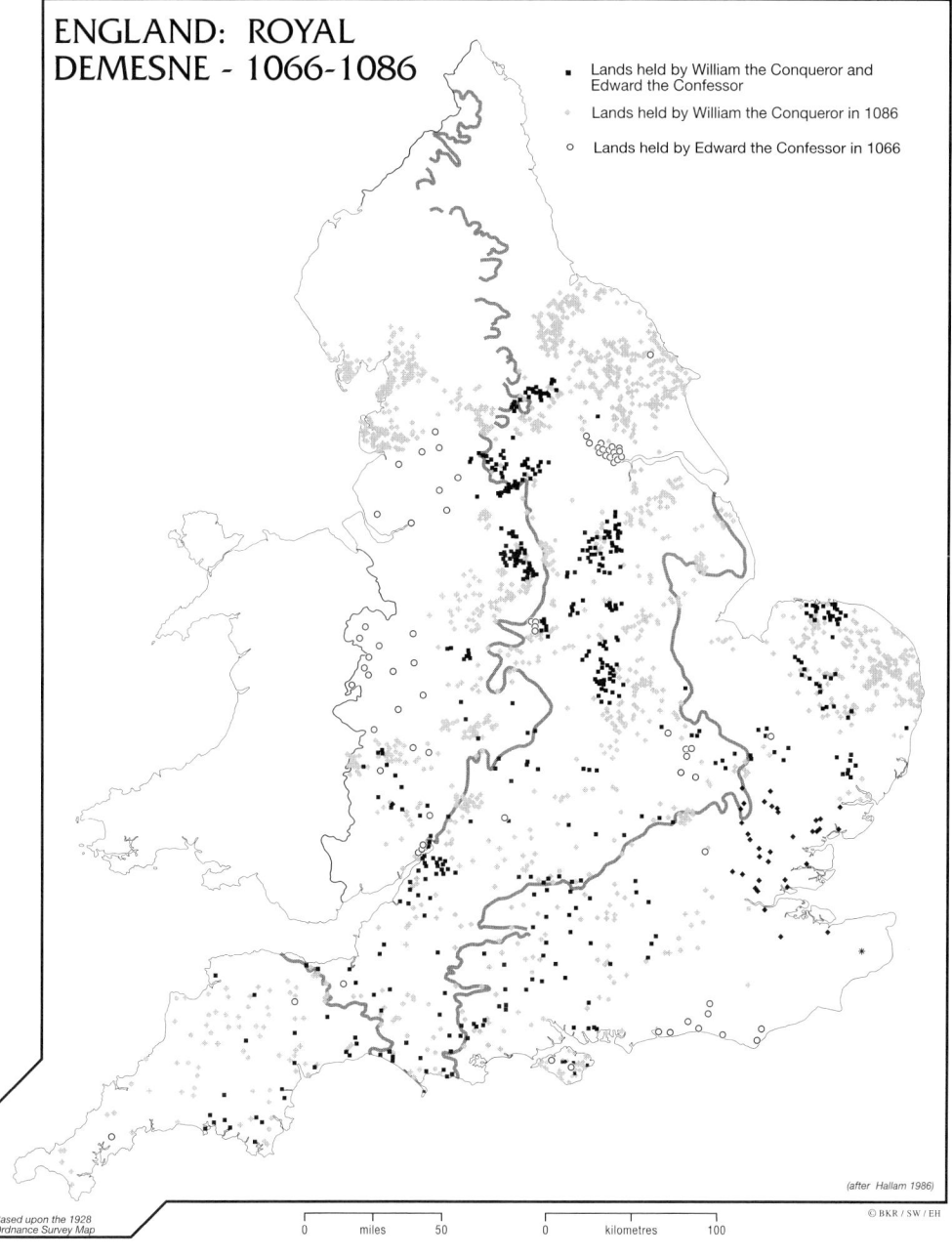

Fig. 10.1 *The distribution of royal demesne in England 1066–1086*

282 *Landscapes, Documents and Maps*

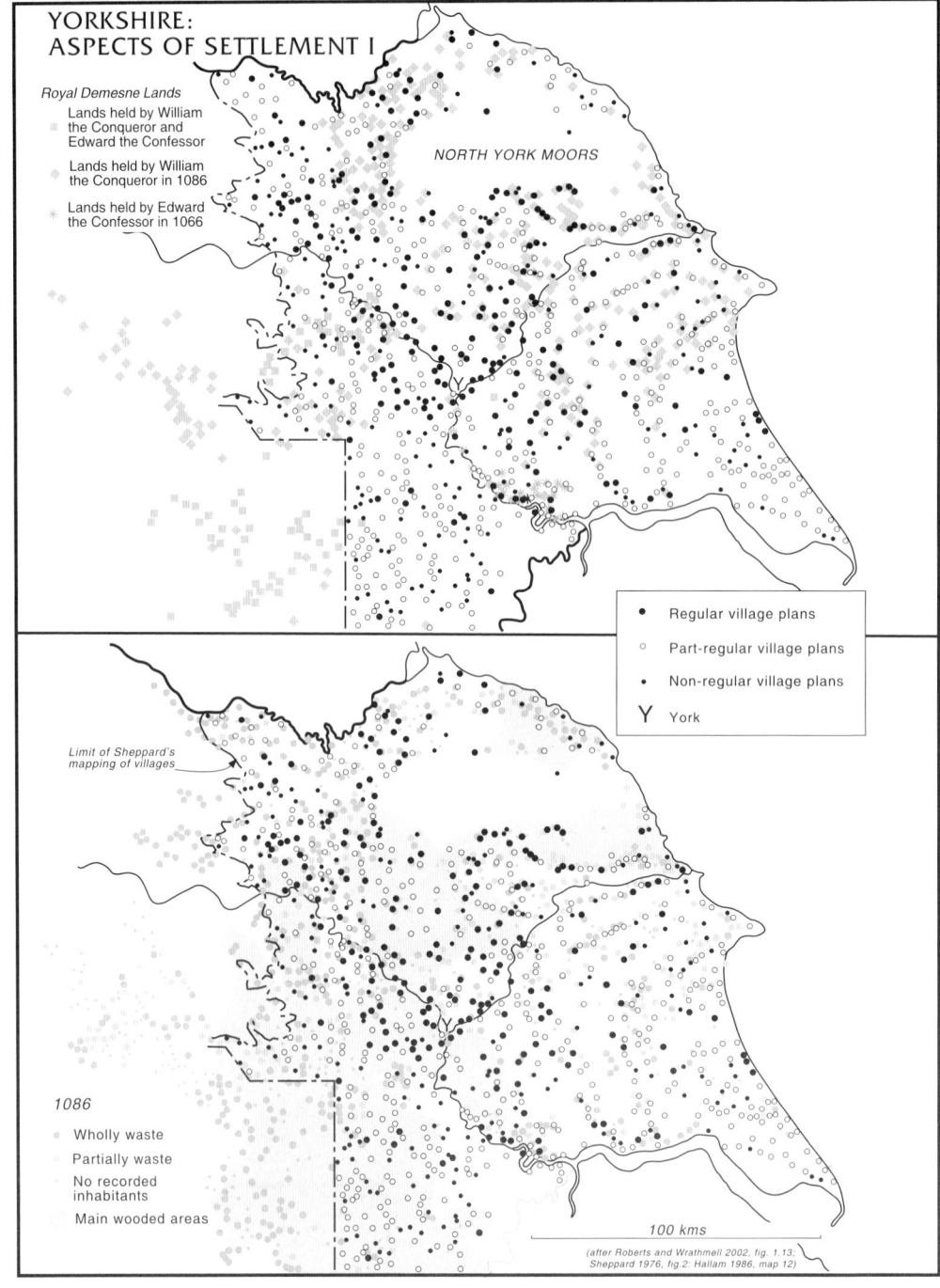

Fig. 10.2.a *Aspects of settlement in Yorkshire*

Planned Villages in England – a National Perspective 283

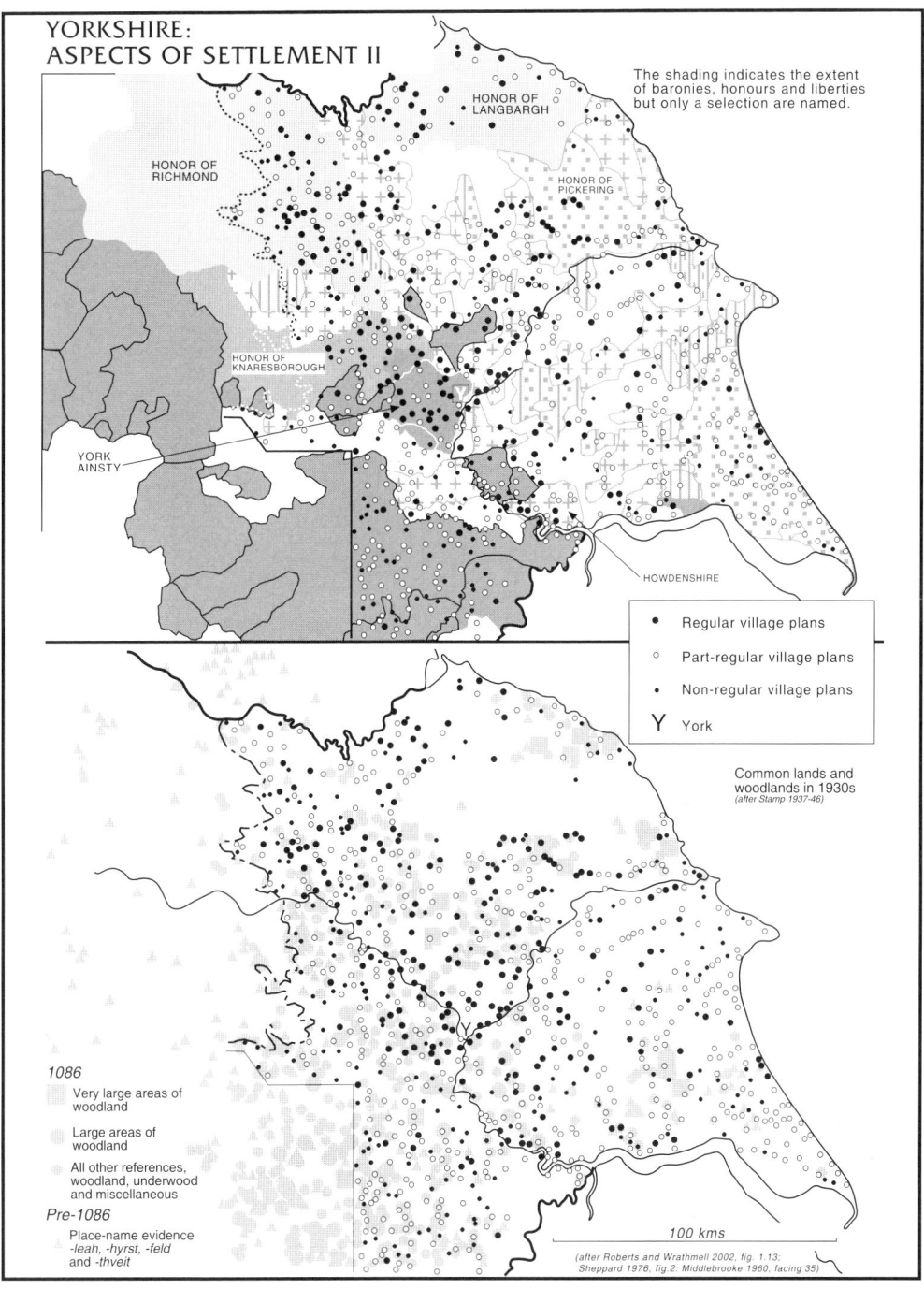

Fig. 10.2.b Aspects of settlement in Yorkshire (contd.)

entry and the north to south links along the Pennine foothills and west to east cross-routes. Glanville Jones suggests in his short study of the Knaresborough estate that it was once part of an even larger unit, focussing on Aldborough, the site of *Isurium Brigantum,* formerly the administrative centre for the whole of the Brigantian tribe (Jones in Dussart 1971, 257–9). It is possible that royal control from Wessex may have come after the campaigns of Athelstan in the 920s and 930s (Hill 1981, 60, 87), the royal grantor of significant estates in what was to become County Durham to the Community of St. Cuthbert (Fig. 6.2).

Amid all the raids, counter raids and warfare of the later tenth and earlier eleventh century, culminating in the emergence of Cnut as king of all England (Hill 1981, 65–71), local cultivation, stock-production, taxation and administration all needed to be sustained (Loyn 1977, 92–5). In this matter we can recall that Stigand, archbishop of Canterbury in 1066, may have run the Confessor's administrative machine. Barlow thought he may have been of 'Norse trading stock, indeed the name *Stígandr* is Old Norse (Barlow 1963, 77–81, 78 n. 1; Harmer 1952, 542–73). He was, as Harmer claims, 'a priest of Cnut'. His possessions, and hence wealth, were immense, as Domesday Book attests. He died in 1070 and if he was born somewhat before 1000, then he would have been in his mid- to late-60s in 1066, and indeed an age of somewhat over seventy would not have been unreasonable. He was a survivor, and seemingly indispensable to the state, appearing as one of a small group of royal priests who witness Cnut's later charters and to one charter of his successor Harthacnut (Harmer 1952, 564). Eric John notes acerbically that 'Stigand first appears in history as the head of a community Cnut founded to celebrate his victory at *Assandune*' and that Stigand 'had a fair claim to be the worst bishop in Christendom' (John 1996, 174). This is documented by the *Anglo-Saxon Chronicle* for the entry for 1020 notes that Stigand was the priest in charge of the new minster at Ashingdon (Swanton 2000, 154–5, n. 9). Hart suggests that *Assandune,* a debated name, was in fact Ashdon in Essex, and notes that Stigand was the young priest put in charge of the new minster built by Thurkil the Tall, whom Cnut made Earl of East Anglia (1992, 262, 563, chapter 20 *passim*). Under the year 1042 (1043) the Chronicle records that Stigand the priest was blessed as bishop for East Anglia (the same period as the coronation of Edward the Confessor). Another version adds that 'soon after Stigand was put from his Bishopric and all that he owned was taken into the king's hands because he was his (Edward's) mother's closest advisor'. There are suggestions that the lady, not being a supporter of the house of Godwin, was willing to give her treasure to Magnus king of Norway if he were to invade the country (Swanton 2000, 162, n. 9). Stigand as Hart notes 'was the protégé of Queen Emma, Cnut's widow and Edward the Confessor's mother' who was the widow of Æthelred when she married Cnut. The conflict between Edward the Confessor and his mother Emma is well described by Sir Frank Stenton (1971, 426–7; Hart 1992, 91). In 1051 he is described as 'the king's advisor and chaplain' (Swanton 2000, 181, n. 12) and in the same year he succeeded to the archbishopric of Canterbury (*ibid.*, 183). This period corresponded with the ejection of the Norman Robert of Jumièrges. His tenure of this office was, however, never without problems, not least because of the Conquest, and in 1066 was taken to Normandy as hostage by William. He was deposed, by the Pope, in 1069 (Loyn 1962, 320) and died a year later.

Here, in the *persona* of a single man, we have a glimpse of one possible link between the wider realms of Cnut, the often-antagonistic aristocratic families of Anglo-Scandinavian England, the management of royal estates and, above all, the levying of taxation throughout his empire. While there are no concrete pointers to Stigand's role in financial matters, his capacity to ride political storms suggests a remarkable astuteness. James Campbell concludes that it is possible that Stigand ran Edward the Confessor's administrative machine (2000, 225). Further, Patrick Wormald suggests that the post-Conquest administrative regime was 'not run by equivalents of Cromwell's Major-Generals, but by the machinery, and at lower levels presumably the personnel, of the vanquished. If the levers of power were in good enough order to work for William I and Henry I, the likelihood is that they worked quite smoothly for Cnut, Edward the Confessor and Harold II' (Wormald 1999, 19). For the years 1040–1042 the chronicle makes it clear that Harthacnut, Cnut's son, imposed substantial taxation upon England, for which administrative mechanisms must have long existed (Loyn 1977, 97). Indeed James Campbell emphasises the degree to which many of the organisational elements of Anglo-Saxon England are to be found in the Carolingian empire (Campbell 2000, xv), indeed there a slight hints that even 'mayors of the palace' – royal administrative officers – may have existed in eighth century Northumbria (*ibid.* 91). An important wild card exists in the form of Brian Hope-Taylor's excavations at Yeavering: not only does he argue cogently for an intermixing of British, Roman and 'Saxo-Frisian' building traditions and concepts, he derives these from a meticulous excavation that demonstrated the presence of carefully measured great halls, focussed upon a west-to-east axis. Ritual and practicality were conjoined in the entrance to one hall, on the site axis, where there was a burial containing an implement resembling a Roman *groma,* for the laying out of right angles. Gatekeeper this individual might also have been, but he was in possession of unusual powers (Hope-Taylor 1977, 267–275, 200–203, 1124–147, 67–69). Even if all the details of this interpretation are not correct, the archaeological facts suggest that a 'regard for geometry and precise measurement in quasi-Roman feet' was an important part of the planning of this 'Anglian' royal vill (Hope-Taylor 1977, 273).

When we turn to the royal estates of the Conqueror, the scale of post 1066 acquisition is great; the properties owned by Edward the Confessor and passed either to King William or the others were approximately 576 in number (counted from the map), and must be set against a further 1483 properties acquired by King William. Predominantly these lie in three areas: in Norfolk, in the North Riding and east Riding of Yorkshire and in Lancashire and southern Westmorland. Smaller concentrations of acquisition appear in Lincolnshire, in Northamptonshire, in northern Derbyshire and in northern Herefordshire. No one explanation is acceptable, but the links between the circumstance of Yorkshire in 1086, be the 'waste' real or a fiscal fiction, and the frontier marginality of northern Lancashire must surely be key factors (Fig. 10.2). Such observations carry the argument to the administrative machinery of pre-Conquest England, a grimpen where even angels fear to tread. In a generally necessarily oblique account Campbell discusses possible references to the post-Conquest survivals of administrative elements of the Anglo-Saxon state. *Ministri, servientes*, and *taini* appear, along with *serjeants* (Campbell in Holt 1987, 201 ff, and 208, 210–211; Roffe 2002, 40, 213). His argument is that traces, and only faint traces, of Anglo-Saxon administrative arrangements survive into post-Conquest records, and that within these there may here be an echo of Carolingian arrangements, where *missi* helped execute the royal will. Royal officials, royal messengers and royal reeves all played a role and their perquisites may have absorbed up to 50% of the actual tax collected. And England appears to have been a heavily taxed country. Here is a group, not obviously aristocratic, who are the king's intermediaries, taking the argument back to the mediate tenure of drengage discussed earlier in this study. Campbell sketches the context: 'behind the achievements of the Northumbrian church lay great wealth; and that the 'Northumbrian renaissance like the Carolingian renaissance, may have depended largely on the fruits of conquest'… 'Northumbrian kings plundered in the north and levied tribute there'. This would have comprised cattle, slaves and treasure, bullion. While 'it is true that in the eighth century Northumbrian kings ceased to conquer… it is worth noting that if they did not conquer, neither were they conquered and made tributary by other kings' (Campbell, 2000, 87–89). If the eighth century was indeed a time of prosperity and growth north of the Humber, then internal colonisation as opposed to external conquest must have been a powerful force, laying foundations for what followed in the ninth century.

The Genesis of Villages

Figures 10.3, 10.4 and 10.5 take root in a speculative map published in 1987 by the author, and are now much modified in the light of subsequent investigations (Roberts 1987, 212–3). In striving to fashion a general picture from fragmented evidence perceptual leaps are undoubtedly needed and the title of this map series, *The Genesis of the English Village – a Testable Hypothesis,* is a deliberate challenge. These complex and multifaceted maps, and three are used to make the multilayered originals intelligible, were brought together using a computer. In fact these maps represent the 'cabling effect' of assembling varied and often very imperfect evidence in a situation where close-linked chains of logic are either impossible or premature. Citing work by Alison Wylie, a philosopher of science, David Lewis-Williams has applied this way of thinking to a recent re-analysis of Palaeolithic rock art. He points out that while intertwining multiple strands of evidence can overcome a discontinuous record, each strand is both *sustaining* and *constraining*: sustaining in that it may compensate for a gap in another

Planned Villages in England – a National Perspective 287

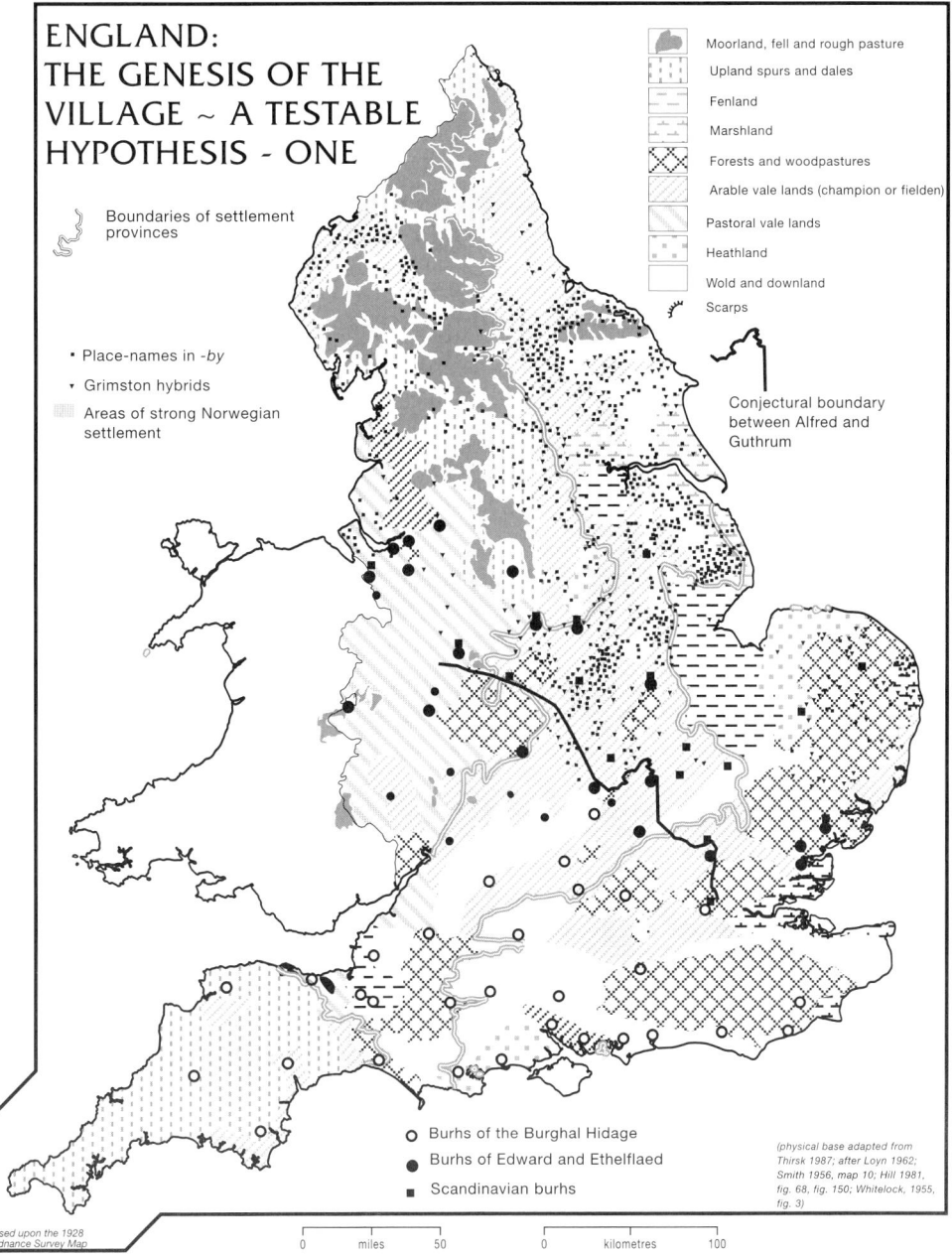

Fig. 10.3 The genesis of the English village – one

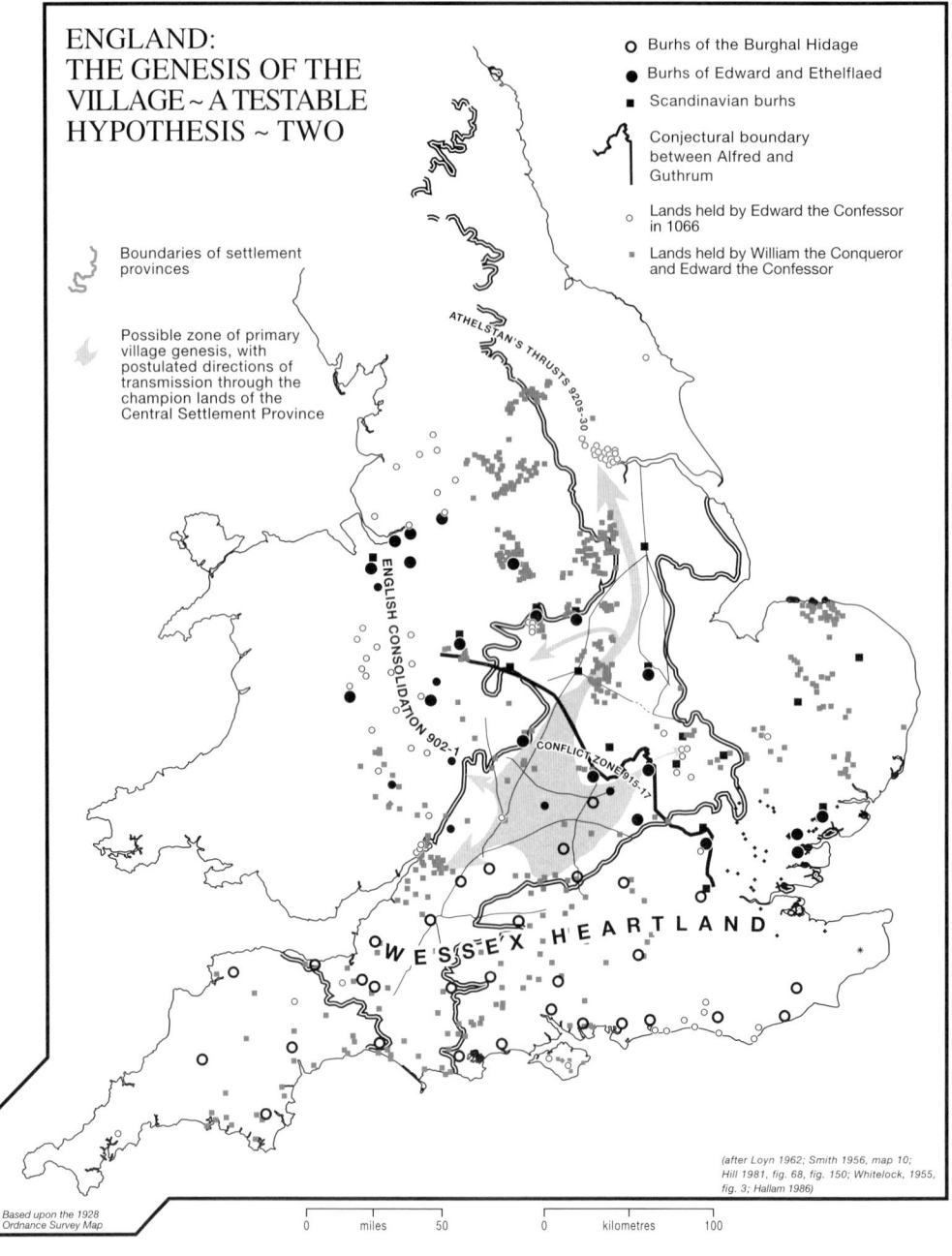

Fig. 10.4 The genesis of the English village – two

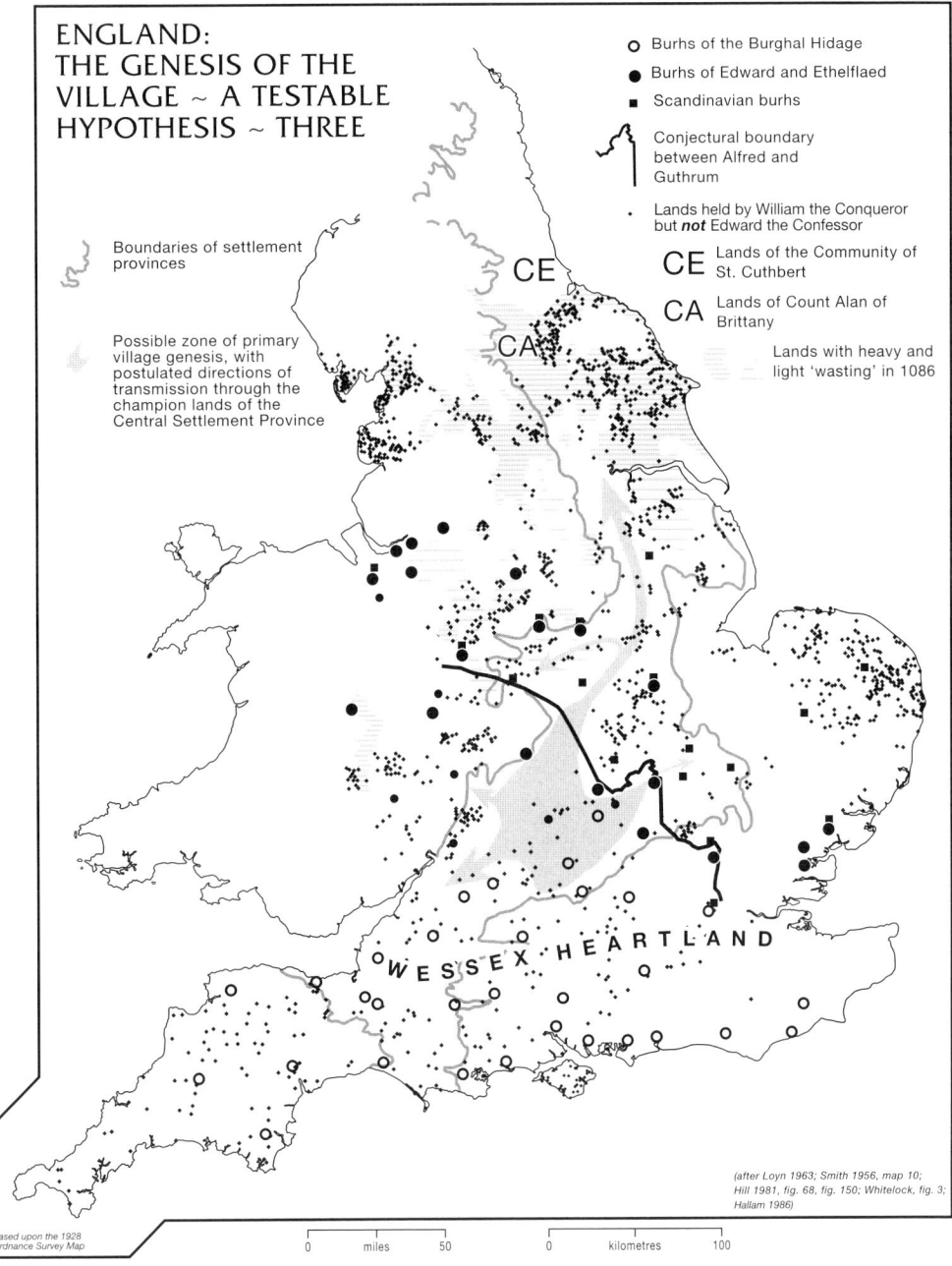

Fig. 10.5 *The genesis of the English village – three*

strand, and constraining in that what does exist restricts wild hypotheses which may take the researcher far from the archaeological record as it exists (Lewis-Williams 2002, 102–4). Thus Figures 10.3–5 construct a broad hypothesis framed by the varied strands, pockets and patches of evidence and argument used throughout this study. Each map draws together several distributions; in Figure 10.3 these consist of:

- a base map, a greatly simplified version of a national terrain map;

- upon this are lines showing the zone containing the greatest concentration of nucleated villages, the 'Central Province' as defined by the present author and Stuart Wrathmell (2002, fig.1.1).

Superimposed upon this base are three further distributions:

- the distribution of Wessex *burhs,* and other *burhs* and fortifications associated with the English reconquest between 902 and 921 (Hill 1981, 56–9);

- the distribution of names using the Scandinavian element *-by* and the Grimston hybrids, names with a mixture of Old English and Scandinavian elements (Fellows-Jensen in Crawford 1995, fig. 33);

- those boroughs associated with Viking defences, which overlap in part with the *burhs* of Old English origin, as the tides of conquest and re-conquest occasioned (Hill 1981, 56–9; S. R. H. Jones 1993, 672).

Finally, the line created between the English kingdom of Alfred and the Danelaw of Guthrum is appended (Whitelock 1955, fig. 3).

What does this map tell us? While the overall pattern of Danish settlement is well known and much discussed, two observations are immediately striking: first, the vast preponderance of Scandinavian place-names fall within the Central Province, *i.e.* a settlement zone already long-cleared, probably always relatively well populated. This in no way excludes the possibility that the Scandinavian farmers were occupying land of rather poorer quality and relative peripherality within this zone than the long-established English settlements (Cameron 1965). Furthermore, a map published by Gillian Fellows-Jensen, but originally created by Peter Sawyer, shows how the distribution of names in *-by* is reinforced but little expanded when the names in *-thorp* are added (Fellows-Jensen in Crawford 1995, fig. 33). The overall concentration within the limits of the Central Province is striking. Why should this be? The lateral boundaries of the province, defined in terms of the concentration of villages and hamlets, are, of course, infinitely permeable (Roberts and Wrathmell 2002, 126, *passim*), so that we must conclude that the bulk of Danish Viking settlement was essentially concentrated within the anciently cleared lands. Of course, the Norwegian settlements of the northwest were quite another matter.

Second, the Scandinavian or Scandinavianised place-names are by no means uniformly distributed. There are very marked variations in their numbers, and the individual clusters within the overall distribution are by no means easy to explain. Gillian Fellows Jensen's monumental studies undoubtedly provide the foundation for further work, but so far as the author can discover, no scholar has addressed the questions *at this scale of analysis,* and so penetrated the distribution as a potential research tool, since Ken Cameron framed the basic arguments in his inaugural lecture of 1965. There is much more regionally based work to be done on this onomastic-geographical threshold, although the existing volume of local studies is so great that it is perfectly possible that a key study, already in existence, has escaped the attention of this author.

Figure 10.4 is partly abstracted from 10.3, but also adds new data:
- the lands held in 1066 by Edward the Confessor;
- lands held in 1086 by King William, which had also been held by Edward the Confessor.

In effect this is, in its essentials and subject to some caveats, a map of late Anglo-Saxon royal demesne. The distribution acquires more significance when it is compared with Hill's map of the hidage of the varied elements (Hill 1981, 101). The real concentration of wealth lies in Wessex, extending northwards to the Thames valley and westwards into the Cotswolds and Severn valley. Further north there is a strong scatter through the West Midlands, a concentration in south Huntingdon, in north Nottinghamshire, in north-central Derbyshire, but there are three small concentrations with high hidages in Yorkshire. While a glimpse of the time-depth in this distribution is possible in Hill's maps of royal itineraries between the later ninth and the first three decades of the eleventh centuries, the 1066 distribution of royal estates demands lengthy and detailed study that cannot be undertaken here. A final layer on Figure 10.4 comprises four short notes and a few details: the Wessex heartland is indicated, as is the general thrust of the English re-conquest between 902 and 916 as detailed in Hill's maps. Edward of Wessex defended Mercia from Scandinavian attacks, attacks that could come from either York or from Norwegian settlers pouring into the coastal lands of Northumbria west of the Pennines. Defence and eventually re-conquest seem to have first taken place in the west Midlands, focussing on Chester and the Mersey, with forts at Chester, Eddisbury, Runcorn and Thelwall protecting from attack from the Irish Sea flank. These dispositions ensured to some degree the safety of the heartlands of Mercia in the rich valleys of the Severn, the upper Trent and the Warwickshire Avon (Smyth 1975, 76–77). It is difficult to perceive how contemporaries saw this, but it appears as a strong flanking build-up, between the Welsh to the west and the Vikings to the east, consolidating Mercian hold on the varied countrysides of the western Midlands. In 910 (Swanton 2000, 97, 95, n. 12) a host of Northumbrian Danes were slaughtered after a raid into Mercia, and this took place at Tettenhall, near Wolverhampton, as they were marching homeward, 'rejoicing in rich spoil', presumably laden with booty and slaves. Many of their aristocracy were slain, including three named kings, who were 'hastened to the hall of the infernal one'. Tettenhall is set well within the wooded zones of the West Midlands, as is Wednesfield, another name linked either to the same engagement or to a concurrent one, and it seems possible that they were attempting to by-pass the fortresses and field armies of the champion valley lands. This loss of leadership was probably a factor allowing the Viking leader Ragnall to conquer York, certainly by 919 and possibly as early as 910 (Smyth 1975, 103). It was after 914 that Ragnall seized the estates of the Lindisfarne monks at Chester le Street, and granted them, or some of them, to Onlafball and Scula (Smyth 1975, 98).

The period between the summer and the late autumn of 917, and extending into 918, saw a series of actions focussing upon the East Midland portion of the Central Province, with the most intense activity concentrated in the zone where the boundary drawn by Alfred and Guthrum was eventually to emerge (Hill 1981, 56–9). Undoubtedly this is varied countryside, but it eventually emerged as grain producing champion, with open townfields and villages, and it was already well-cleared in by the tenth century, probably already substantively cleared by Roman times, and possibly by the Iron Age. A few Roman roads are included in Figure 10.4 to provide a perspective on some lines of movement which could be followed. The present author and Stuart Wrathmell noted that the easternmost lobe of the Central Province was an anomalous area, with rather more surviving woodland in 1086 than the valleys to the north and west (Fig. 1.5). Before attempting to interpret what these distributions may mean, it is necessary to follow the bridge provided by the so far unexplained presence of the shaded area in this inner Midland zone into Figure 10.5.

While containing many common elements to the previous maps Figure 10.5 is subtly different. The tiny scattered dots represent Elizabeth Hallam's mapping of those lands held in 1086 by King William, land he took by right of conquest. To gain a full picture of royal lands in 1086 these would have to be added to the estates appearing in Figure 10.4, as seen in Figure 10.1. The concentrations of these post-Conquest acquisitions appear several zones:

- first, in eastern England, notably north of the more wooded zones of Suffolk and Essex, particularly in Norfolk;

- second, smaller concentrations appear throughout the Midland, largely in wood-pasture areas, one within the Central Province, but with the remainder lying further west;

- third, the greatest concentrations of 'new' royal lands appear in the north, in Yorkshire and in the northwest.

This is not the place to embark on a detailed consideration of the full meaning of this national distribution, but in Yorkshire there is a broad but clear correlation between the royal land and the areas returning 'waste' in 1086 (Fig.10.2.a). Several observations can be made about this third map:

- Sheppard's mapping of regular and part-regular village plans in Yorkshire shows

- that they do correlate, in broad terms, with the zones of recorded 'waste' in 1086, particularly her category of 'regular' plans (Sheppard 1976: above Fig. 10.2.a);

- the most regular village plans tend to correlate with areas where Domesday Book also shows the presences of either woodland or brushwood and the like (Fig. 10.2.b). These are probably colonising ventures, even if older settlements were being expanded;

- the notation 'CA' on Figure 10.4 approximates the area of the Honour of Richmond, in 1086 in the hands of the trusted Count Alan of Brittany (Middlebrook 1968, map facing 35; above Fig. 10.2.b). The lowlands of this great estate, probably originating in an amalgamation of several 'small shires' are, according to June Sheppard's mapping, particularly rich in regular plans;

- finally, the 'CE' indicates the County Durham area of the Cuthbertine estates, where there are, as has been shown in previous chapters, reasonable grounds for postulating the appearance of regular regulated village plans with formalised tenurial profiles in the period between approximately 900 and 1150.

Thus, Figures 10.3, 10.4 and 10.5 provide the basis for a number of interlocking hypotheses about the development of villages not only throughout the north but also on a national scale. The period during and following the Viking invasions of England was a time of social, economic, tenurial and landscape ferment. Pelteret has argued for a gradual merging of the peasantry of both free and slave origin in the tenth and eleventh centuries into a spectrum of unfree categories; in effect they became the bondsmen and villeins of later sources (Pelteret 1995, 252). While he adopts a slightly despairing view of the present knowledge of the evolution of settlement and field systems he does see evidence for a concurrency of development (*ibid*. 183–4). The village with its extensive communally organised field system represents a concentration of people, of tenants, of lordly control and of the capacity to sustain grain yields under all but the worst conditions of warfare and weather. We can reflect on the implications of the fact that the 40,000 Anglo-Saxon coins known from finds in Scandinavia represent a larger total than the number known to have survived in England. As James Campbell notes 'even this figure fades into insignificance when it is appreciated that the *Anglo-Saxon Chronicle* records that England paid in gelds between 991 and 1014 at least £150,000, a sum equivalent to thirty-six million coins' (in Farrell 1982, 35; see also Sawyer 1971, 86–119 and S.R.H. Jones 1993, 674). This sum must be set against the issues between *c*. 973 and *c*. 1059 that varied between 47 million and 2.5 million coins, and the amount in circulation from 12 million to 1.3 million (Campbell 2000, 181). These complex questions are reviewed by M.K. Lawson and Richard Fletcher; the tenth and eleventh century Viking attacks, royal plundering expeditions rather than mere raids, initiated fundamental changes in what was in effect a rich and well-exploited country. The urban economy was booming, silver was available to mint vast quantities of coin, and even after extended periods of warfare and attrition Cnut was able to extract great amounts of tax when he became king (Fletcher 2002, 107, and 96–101; Lawson 2004, 173–188).

Hamlet, Village and Burh

The heavy taxation of accumulated wealth and the withdrawal of bullion from circulation, even if it was not immediately transported to Scandinavia and the Continent, must have had a significant economic impact. It implies that landowners, as part of the processes of re-settlement and colonisation, were more inclined, indeed perhaps even compelled, to accept the render of produce and work rather than coin. Tenants were offered holdings on the basis of food renders and work, sometimes sweetened by the provision of stock and tools, for as the *Rectitudines Singularum Personarum* records, on that land where week work was demanded:

> it pertains to the *gebur* that he shall have given to him for his outfit 2 oxen and 1 cow and 6 sheep and 7 acres sown on his yardland. Wherefore after that year, he must perform all the services which pertain to him. And he must have given to him tools for his work, and utensils for his house. Then when he dies his lord takes back what he leaves.
>
> (Seebohm 1896, 131–3)

A second translation, subtly different, and provided by Douglas and Greenaway (1981, 876) is as follows:

> On the same land to which the customs apply a farmer (*gebur* in Seebohm's version of the Old English text) ought to be given for his occupation of the land 2 oxen, 1 cow, 6 sheep and 7 acres sown on his rood of land. After (or possibly 'during' – the Latin word, in Seebohm, is '*post*') that year let him perform all the dues that fall to him, and let him be given tools for his work and utensils for his house. When death befalls him let the lord take charge of what he leaves.

The date and context of this document are much debated. Paul Harvey places it securely in Wessex, and all we can be reasonably certain of is that the *Rectitudines* originated in south-west England, 'very likely in west Wiltshire or east Somerset', and while Glastonbury is one possible place of origin, he notes that we 'may well wonder whether the *Rectitudines* was written for royal estates' (Harvey 1993, 1–21). A mid-tenth century date seems possible, although the document appears to incorporate material from an even earlier exemplar. Harvey suggests that it was designed as much to establish, as to record, estate custom. Chris Dyer opts more confidently for a Worcester revision of an earlier document, conceivably by Bishop Wulfstan I (1002–16) (Dyer in Brooks and Cubitt 1996, 183). He regards the view that the lord provided a *gebur* with equipment as a 'feudal myth' (Dyer in Brooks and Cubitt 1996, 189). Surely, however, at an earlier time and in contexts of devastation and colonisation, such provision would have been one way of attracting extra men, extra tenants, to an estate, and at a faster rate than could be reasonably expected from the natural increase of *in situ* tenants and slaves? The provision of stock and tools, an outfit, what Seebohm terms a *stuht* (Seebohm 1896, 61, 133 and 139), was one practical way of settling or resettling tenants on land.

In this way, where land was available for resettlement or colonisation, even destitute refugees could be given a new beginning. From arguments presented earlier, it is clear that village development could involve many things: on one hand, accretive expansion from an pre-existing nucleus, the growing together of a number of pre-existing small nuclei or hamlets could take place. On the other, the deliberate creation of a new and structured system, integrating settlement plan, tenancies, social status variations and the potential for man and horse-supporting grain production into a coherent whole. In practice these represent a clutch of subtly variable possibilities, a gradient of possibilities. That the processes were complex in nature and variable in impact need occasion no surprise. There must be strong suspicions, if no more, that the stresses of the Viking raids, subsequent warfare and eventual settlement, sharpened tendencies that had already been present in Anglo-Saxon society. The assumption, subtly built into Figures 9.6 and 10.5, is that even before the re-conquest of north-eastern England by English kings, planned villages may well have accompanied the establishment of planned *burhs*, used in fact as instruments of reconquest, throughout the inner Midlands (S. R. H. Jones 1993, 668; Smyth 1977, 53–4). The shading on the maps suggests that from this potential 'central zone of origin' the concept migrated outwards. There are practical problems in testing this hypothesis. There is no doubt that excavations, particularly of high status sites, will continue to produce material falling between the sixth and the eleventh centuries, but the normal problem is to place what are inevitably keyhole explorations within the context of even a two or three hundred year slot. Work as competent that at Raunds by Graham Cadman and Glen Foard, with all the fascinating questions it raised and the impressive level of interpretation, nevertheless failed to show the chronological sequence of plan development in a polyfocal or composite plan which emerged around what appear to be two Anglo-Saxon manorial nuclei (Erskine and Williams 2003, 73–6). The problems are not insoluble, but their solution, as the work at Wharram Percy showed, will be expensive and time-consuming (Beresford and Hurst 1990).

However, there is nothing intrinsically impossible in the same ideas emerging semi-independently within the northeast of England itself, for even through the worst of the Viking period churchmen and noble households sustained links and ideas flowed in many directions (Brown 2003, 98 and n. 44 and 45). As has been emphasised repeatedly in this study, we must not assume that our model need be a simple one. It is too easy to assume linear temporal developments. For instance, the Anglo-Saxon chronicle itself records for the year 1088 that a group of conspirators, including William de St. Calais, Bishop of Durham, 'raided, burned and laid waste the king's home farms' (*feorme hams*) and 'the lands of those men who were in the king's service' (*eallra thaera manna land hi for dydon the waeron innan thaes cynges holdscipe*: Plummer and Earle 1892, 223*)*. After describing wasting in Gloucestershire and around Bristol, and raids into Worcestershire the entry continues 'The bishop of Durham did what harm he could in the north', surely amongst the royal estates of Yorkshire (Swanton 2000, 222–3). Each and every raiding episode, graphically yet succinctly described here, created potential for a local new beginning. What we cannot easily discern is the intensity and the regional variations in such activity.

Vikings in the North of England

This takes the argument back to the north of England: the involvement of the regional ecclesiastical communities, particularly at York and Durham, and the Vikings was extraordinarily intricate and delicate. The Viking king Halfdan is often seen in terms of his dividing up the land of Northumbria in 874/5 so that his warriors began 'ploughing and providing for themselves', as the Chronicle records (Swanton 2000, 74–5). Prior to this, however, in 874, he and his men had wintered on the Tyne, and 'the raiding army conquered that land' (Swanton 2000, 72–5). Using Irish, Scandinavian, and Durham sources, Smyth argues that having settled his warriors Halfdan himself remained a *herkonugr,* a warrior-king, and fell out with his settled followers, deserted them and fled the Tyne with three ships, choosing according to Saxo Grammaticus, to 'dispeople [his Northumbrian province], and leave its fields, which were matted in decay, with none to till them. He covered the richest land of the island with the most hideous desolation, thinking it better to be lord of a wilderness, than of a headstrong country'(Smyth 1977, 260–3). Why? Halfdan needed movable wealth, bullion, weapons, ships and women to attract warriors to his warband, but we cannot ascertain what complex factors drew him back to Dublin, where he had a dynastic claim, and led him to burn his boats. His death in battle in 877 need not concern us further. Saxo Grammaticus implies a degree of regional devastation.

Clearly, the on-ground political circumstances were intricate. Thus, Wulfhere Archbishop of York from 854 seems to have come to terms with the Viking Great Army soon after its arrival and during the worst of the warfare retreated to Addingham in Wharfdale (Smyth 1975, 46). He died *c.* 895 but in his younger life this is a man who would have been close to men who had known Alcuin, a confident of Charlemagne (*ibid.* 44). Furthermore, the Community of St. Cuthbert itself certainly had an accommodation with the Vikings: the move from Lindisfarne, the subsequent wanderings, the settlements at Chester-le-Street and eventually Durham were moves to 'embrace the challenges' of the Viking threat, moves towards new power centres and political centrality (Brown, 2003, 113–4). Eardwulf, Bishop of the Community, was deeply involved in the inauguration of one Scandinavian king, Guthrith son of Harthacnut, in a ceremony on the hill of *Oswigsdune*, and involving the body of St.

Cuthbert, which was then lodged at Chester-le-Street (Smyth 1975, 43–5). Guthrith also died in 895. Alfred Smyth suggests that the earliest likely date for the return to more settled conditions in Northumbria is 880. It was in this context that the plantation of the Cuthbertine Community at Chester le Street took place in 883, and the acquisition from the newly elevated king, Guthrith, with further intervention of Eadred abbot of Carlisle, of 'the whole territory between the Tyne and the Wear' (Smyth 1975, 42–3). Although the Cuthbertine lands do not appear to have been extensively settled by Scandinavians (Watts in Crawford 1995, 206–13) it appears likely that the warfare focussed upon the Tyne valley, perhaps around Corbridge, where Ragnall probably fought two battles (Smyth 1975, 93–116); the Durham estates of St. Cuthbert were sited in a broad region of conflict. In fact the loss of Northumbrian leadership at Tettenhall was probably a factor allowing Ragnall to conquer York, certainly by 919 and possibly as early as 910, and indeed may itself have opened a door for the English advances in the southern Danelaw after 916. It is tempting to ask if the royal estates held by Edward the Confessor in 1066 originated in the campaigns of Aethelstan in the third decade of the tenth century (Hill 1981, 60–61) and were still in royal control at the coronation of Edgar in 973. In Edgar's monetary scheme, involving the introduction of a uniform type of coin for all England and an extensive and large-scale programme of monastery founding, we can see a large scale innovatory programme crucial to which were centralisation and a wealthy economy. Secular and religious centralisation went hand in hand (Hill 1981, 61–2; Campbell 2000, 162). Nevertheless, throughout the two centuries between 800 and the advent of more stable conditions in the earlier eleventh century, the life of a northern peasant farmer, the basic producer in early medieval society can hardly have been comfortable. Defined services, a measure of protection from St. Cuthbert – even if it took the form of clerics protecting their own interests and estates – or even the control of a Scandinavian lord and/or overlord, must have created welcome if chancy protection from hazards created by sporadic raiding and episodic warfare. Taxation was, of course, always as certain as death. Necessary 'negotiations' with soil, climate, weather, pests and health must have already been ample burdens for the cultivators of the soil without the additional hazards of warfare, raids and slave taking.

Envoi
Planned settlements have deep roots in Europe. They were part of creating ordered productivity in which planning of all aspects was a deeply embedded. This was a fundamental ingredient of the Romanesque world. In northern England in the period between about 800 and 1150 several threads came together that were neither wholly indigenous nor wholly alien. At root we have the possibility that village planting and village planning disseminated from royal lands, where at first only the estate centres may have been involved. In this there were close links with *burh* plantation. Royal officers, ecclesiastical in training and thought, are likely vectors and from these beginnings the

exigencies of taxation and colonisation diffused the ideas throughout wider society. The creation of towns added greatly to the wealth, strength and stability of Anglo-Saxon England, enabling the kings not only to defend the population against further attacks, but also to sustain a long and largely effective campaign against the Vikings. Three or four hundred years of development, for the last villages were placed soon after 1200, may seem a long time, but we should recall that it took four hundred years of enclosure movements between the mid-fifteenth century and the early nineteenth century to enclose and eliminate the great townfields which once dominated the Central Province. We can document these latter developments (Roberts and Wrathmell 2000, 118) and their complexity is both revealing and, given the richness of the later documentation, daunting. Furthermore, as with the later enclosure movements in the complex and attenuated process of village planning the role of the individual is problematic: that it was present can hardly be doubted, but in the absence of specific documentation cannot be proved and analysed. Even in the case of Battle Abbey, Sussex, where the chronicler records that once possession had been secured and the building of the church commenced:

> a great many men were recruited, many from the neighbouring districts and even some from across the channel. The brethren who were in charge of the building began to apportion to individuals house sites of definite dimensions near the boundary of the (abbey) site. These, with their customary rent and service, can be seen to have remained to this day just as they were then arranged.
>
> (Searle 1980, 51–9)

The chronicler follows this with a detailed citation of a house-by-house rental to which a date between *c.* 1102 and 1107 can be assigned. This is, nevertheless, a generalized picture, although it does suggest that the Norman clerks were wholly familiar with the procedures needed for the laying out of settlement plans.

Further speculation is likely to remain dangerous, but speculate we must. Hadley put the problem succinctly: 'little progress has been made in our understanding whether such processes as the emergence of nucleated villages and the development of manorial sites preceded the Scandinavian settlements or were subsequent to them. If it was the latter, it is not apparent whether the Vikings were 'catalysts for or coincidental to change' (Hadley 2000, 33, citing R. A. Hall). As is so often the case with these issues the answer is 'Well, yes and no … and perhaps maybe!' Nevertheless, there can now be no doubt that the imprint upon the landscape of settlement planning was at once powerful, enduring and revealing. Essentially the 'village concept' had to be formulated, detailed and then implemented. This took place within an evolving society, while on the ground the process is likely to have involved at least two or three individuals, probably descending the social gradient from king or lord to a craft operative on site. The diffusion of the concept and the decision to implement it must have derived from social intercourse, discussion, recognition of potential, but only rarely from reading, although this is not a completely impossible root source. Advantages and difficulties must have been weighed and assessed, involving other individuals, while implementation fell to another individual, in Germany termed the *Lokator*, in Latin *locator*, while in England the terms *thegn* or *dreng* were applied, ministerial terms that undoubtedly had more ancient roots and wider meanings. In the analysis of the Durham situation certain individuals haven been named as conceivable initiators, but more generally, the king and his senior offices could have performed the same role. In the case of the northern village, unlike the twelfth and thirteenth century colonisations in eastern Europe, direct and unambiguous documentation is rare, but the analysis of drengage suggests that this is the level at which practical implementation took place. Barrow catches a wholly pragmatic view when he notes

> Neither 'thane' (thegn) nor 'dreng' was a strict term of art, for at the lower end of the scale thanes might overlap or be confused with drengs. Their essential characteristic lay in their being ministers or officers acting as estate managers for the kings and greater lords.
>
> (Barrow in Bartlett and Mackay 1989, 15)

While post-Enlightenment perspectives will always tend to seek an economic explanation for village planning and regulation, it should always be kept in mind that many others are possible:

- the imposition of a divinely ordained order on this earth;
- the definition of peasant shares as a pragmatic yet ritual gesture;
- the imposition of a form of physical definition of usufruct in uncertain times in which documentation, even when created, was prone to be ephemeral, and where even the record of local memory was prone to annihilation in the aftermath of a large scale raid.

All of these offer alternative explanations. The problem of the northern village is not one of lack of evidence. There is ample evidence. On one hand there is the landscape itself, bearing traces of many hundreds of examples of planned villages and hamlets. On the other, sufficient documentary evidence may survive to permit the construction of hypotheses about origins and development, and in a proportion of such cases the local landscape detail can be related, at least in general terms, to a fragmentary documentary record. Furthermore, as has been shown, such vignettes afford cumulative evidence for building generalisations at both local and regional scales.

Each of these approaches is wholly valid, but serious difficulties arise when attempts are made to bring the imprecisions of landscape history into close correlation with the documentary records. Both architectural history and archaeology have been wrestling with the same issues for nearly two centuries. Like strands of DNA the two parts have to be brought together ... and the problem is that both strings, as noted earlier, tend to be fragmentary. Village plantation must have taken place over time, perhaps with several peaks and troughs, and the landscape evidence, without impossibly extensive and detailed examination, is inadequate to reveal these. We can speculate, infer and construct hypotheses, but these are not evidence. Above all, the establishment of a taut and reliable time line for settlement development is, and will in all likelihood continue to be, impossible. While architectural dating is often sufficiently close to allow some correlations with persons to be made, correlations between village planning and individual initiators can only be tentative. Nevertheless, not to attempt a measure of explanation via simple correlation would be cowardly, for there are undoubtedly concepts and models involved in settlement regulation, *i.e.* the interlocking of settlement plan, field system and tenurial and fiscal arrangements. In such cases some one, or some corporation and perhaps even some communities, have said 'Let this be done!' as surely as any patron involved with a great church-building venture. In writing about this field at all decisions must be taken about the probabilities inherent a given body of material. Any conclusions arrived at must then hedged with appropriate caveats and qualifications. Varied options need to be identified and assessed. This book represents one attempt to discuss the un-discussable.

If as has been argued it was the tenth century which saw in Durham the emergence of formalised tenurial profiles such as 'they of Boldon', possibly linked with settlement regeneration and/or plantation, then the twin poles of ecclesiastical control and royal control must also have been powerful generative forces elsewhere. It was King Alfred who touched upon a crucial underlying factor when he wrote:

> a man cannot work on any enterprise without resources. In the case of the king, the resources and tools with which to rule are that he have his land fully manned; he must have praying men, fighting men, and working men… he must have the means of support for his tools, the three classes of men. These then are the means of their support: land to live on, gifts, weapons, food, ale, clothing, and, whatever else is necessary.
>
> (Keynes and Lapidge 1983, 132).

Hamlets and villages represent concentrations of men and their wives, children and cattle settled on good quality and productive land. They were a taxable resource. If Oderic Vitalis felt able to state, a view presumably meaningful to his contemporaries, that Rannulf Flambard had 'measured all the ploughlands, which in English are called hides, with a rope', then both Flambard and his agents were capable of ordering the laying out of planned villages (Roffe 2002, 245). So too were men in the tenth and eleventh centuries.

Appendices

APPENDIX I

The Settlements of Boldon Book by Tenurial Type

(a) = Aucklandshire
(h) = Heighingtonshire
(q) = Quarringtonshire
(v) = recorded villeins

Settlements Associated with Drengs and Firmars, discussed in Figures 7.6 to 7.9.

Type I, in which a drengage holding is associated with a populated vill from which renders in kind and work are demanded:

Butterwick(v); Brafferton; Binchester(v); Urpeth; Whitworth(v); Hunwick; Cornsay; Iveston; Hedley(hope); Great Usworth; Two parts of Herrington; Hutton Henry(v); Sheraton(v)

Type II, in which a drengage holding is held by a named individual, who appears to dominate the settlement, and any tenants and their services remain largely concealed:

Plawsworth; Little Usworth; Washington; Little Burdon; Twizell; Lutterington; Henknowle; Greencroft; Hulam; Newbiggin (by Thickley);

Type III, in which a drengage holding, sometimes fragmented, is a part of a thriving tenanted settlement:

(West) Auckland (a); Norton; Carlton; Oxen (-le-Flatts); Great Haughton (le Skerne); Whessoe; [Lanchester]; [Middridge]

Type IV, thriving tenanted settlements to which a group of *firmarii* (+F or +M) have been added, or in which *firmarii* (=F) or *malmen* (=M), are wholly dominant;

Newton by Boldon (=M); Warden Law (=F); Morton (=F); Sedgefield (+F); Norton (+F); Stockton (+F); Carlton (=F); Darlington (+F); Blackwell (+F); Redworth (=F);

Principal Settlements of Episcopal Estates in 1183

Type 01, thriving tenanted settlements, producing renders in kind and cash and owing works; many contain holdings which are in some way 'abnormal', larger, or rendering services reminiscent of a drengage:

Services as Boldon:
Boldon; Cleaburn; Whitburn; Wearmouth; Tunstall; Ryhope; Burdon; Easington; Shotton; North Sherburn(q); Shadforth(q); Cassop(q); Tursdale; Sedgefield; (Bishop) Middleham; Cornforth; Norton and Stockton (except for cornage); Preston; Hartburn;

Services as Heighington:
Heighington (h); Killerby (h); Middridge (h); Thickley (h)

Services as North Auckland:
North (Bishop) Auckland (a); Escomb (a); Newton Cap (a)

Services as Darlington:
Darlington; Cockerton; Blackwell

Others:
Wolsingham; Stanhope; Lanchester; Witton Gilbert; Fulforth; Whickham; New Ricknall;

Type 02, settlements held at farm, with the tenants paying an agreed fixed sum:
   Gateshead; Chester le Street; South Biddick; Ryton; Crawcrook; Winlaton; Westoe

Type 03, settlements comprising cottagers only:
   Newbottle; Houghton; Little Coundon;

Type 04, settlements held for knight service:
   Biddick

Type 05, settlements held in free alms:
   Trimdon

Type / – all other recorded settlements:
   Durham (urban); Pelaw; Picktree; Penshaw; Edderacres; Quarrington; Whitwell; Garmondsway; Mainsforth; Frosterley; Consett; Muggleswick; Edmondbyers; Hunstanworth; Medomsley; Migley; Langley; Isle of Bradbury; Crookhall; Pockerley; Smalley; Birtley; Marley; Byermoor; Swalwell; Farnacres; Stella; Sunderland; Newsham; Barford; Grindon; Heworth; Little Haughton; School Aycliffe; Old Thickley

Settement Types in Durham after Kapelle
(1979, 279–80, ns. 51–58).

Bondage vills of the Butterwick type:
  Butterwick; Binchester; Herrrington; Hutton; Oxenhall; Sheraton; Urpath; West Auckland.

Bondage vills apparently lacking drengs:
  Brafferton; Iveston; Little Burdon; Lutterington; Mainsforth; Tursdale.

Vills with malmen:
  Carlton; Morton; Newton by Boldon; Redworth; Wardon.

Centres of groups of bondage vills 'in days gone by':
  Crawcrook; Great Usworth; the vills of Heighingtonshire; Lanchester; Witton; and perhaps Stanhope.

'Boldon' type villages:
  Cleadon and Whitburn; Easington and Thorpe; Hartburn; Middleham and Cornforth; North Sherburn, Shadforth and Cassop; Norton, Preston, Ryhope and Burdon; Sedgefield; Shotton; Stockton; Wearmouth and Tunstall;
  Whickham may also have been a Boldon vill.

'Non-Boldon' Type 'manors' where the villeins did week work:
  Haughton; New Ricknall, Whessoe; North Auckland, Escomb and Newton (Cap) have defective descriptions.

Villages with Cottars owing week work
  Houghton; Little Coundon; Newbottle.

Settlement Types in Durham after Lapsley
(VCH II, 270, 271, 272, 289)

'Pastoral vills' (based upon payment of cornage);

Chester Ward: Boldon, Newton, Cleadon, Whitburn, Whickham, Crawcrook, Great Usworth,
Easington Ward: Wearmouth, Tunstall, Ryhope, Burdon, Easington, Thorpe, Shotton, North Sherburn, Shadforth, Cassop, Herrington, Hutton (Henry), Sheraton
Stockton Ward: Sedgefield, Middleham, Cornforth, Norton, Stockton, Hartburn, Preston, Butterwick
Darlington Ward: Heighington, Killerby, Middridge, Thickley, North Auckland, Escomb, Newton, West Auckland, Brafferton, Binchester

Bedlingtonshire: Bedlington, West Sleckburn, Netherton, Choppington, Cambois, East Sleckburn
Also possibly including Whitwell, Herrington, Sheraton (VCH, 272, note 2)

Note: The vills of Bedlingtonshire seem to have compounded for many or most of the Boldon services (in fact there is no evidence to prove they ever owed these precise services). North and West Auckland with Newton and Escomb had certain obligations that place them half way between the Boldon and Stanhope types.

'Agricultural vills', (so described because of an absence of cornage payments):
Darlington, Blackwell, Cockerton, Great Haughton and Whessoe.

'Forest vills' (characterised by service at the great hunt):
Darlington Ward: Stanhope, North Auckland, Escomb, Newton
Chester Ward: Lanchester, Iveston, Marley, Britley (Birtley), Tribley, Holmside

'Vills held by knight service or in free alms':
Pencher, Edderacres, Trimdon, Muggleswick, Byermore (not Ryermore), Farnacres.

'Fractional knight's fee':
Ulkill's Biddick, (Bedlingtonshire: Tillmouth, Heton, Twysell, Duddoe)

'Drengage vills':
Plawsworth, Little Usworth, Washington, Little Burdon, Twizell, Heworth, Oxenhall, Thickley, (Newton), Lutterington, Henknoll, Cornsay, Edmondbyers, Hunstanworth, Herrington, Sheraton.

'Fee farm, by favour or upon sufferance':
Newton by Durham, Pelaw, Picktree, Newton by Boldon, Hardwick, Grindon, Ketton, Hunwick, Frosterley, Heley (Healey), Migley, Langley, Smallees, Stella

'Money payment only':
Chester, School Aycliffe, Old Thickley, Harperley, Medomsley, Edmondsley, Crook, Pokerley, Newsham, Barford, Hulam, (in Bedlingtonshire: Cornhill, Newbiggin, Upsetlington [Ladykirk]).

'Boroughs'
Durham, Wearmouth (Sunderland), Gateshead, Darlington, (Bedlingtonshire: Norham); Chester le Street, Stockton and Auckland are of later creation (VCH II, 306–309)

APPENDIX II

The Structural Arrangement of Settlements in Boldon Book – Settlement Groupings.

Notes:

1. In spite of Offler's criticisms (Offler 1996, XII) David Austin's suggested re-arrangement (Boldon Book, Appendix I, 73) provides an important foundation for further work, with the designations below as Block {I},{II},{III},{IV}, indicating the sections making up the restructured sequence and (a), (b), (c), or (d) noting the original arrangement (Austin 8–9 and 73).

2. On the assumption that the original substance of Boldon Book reflected the existence of spatially coherent village groupings rather than a random order – and there are internal signs that this is indeed the case – the sequential list created by this rearrangement was then progressively subdivided, to try to isolate likely coherent settlement groups. These are designated by geographical terms.

3. Each group isolated by this procedure is then documented from Hart (1975) and Craster (1954).

    The interpretation of this material must take note of the fact that the Cuthbertine estate never existed as a total unity; it was assembled by gift and purchase between the seventh and the twelfth century but also subjected to fragmentation by leasing and conquest, and final division between the Bishop and the Cathedral Priory in about 1080.

    Further, as Offler has shown beyond all doubt, Boldon Book as it survives was a working record and subject to all the varied small errors and corrections this implies. This is important because of the dynamic dimension it imparts to the record.

4 The list concludes with a list of the village groupings and 'shires' recorded in both Boldon Book and the pre-Conquest documentation of the Cuthbertine estates.

Key to table:

[01, III, etc.] Settlement type as designated in Appendix I above.

SF = Shire focus   EF = Estate focus   LF = Lordship farm

    < >   Single vill or group which shows sequential discordance.
    *   Linked by charter Hart (1975), 120
    +   Linked by charter Hart (1975), 129
    o   Linked by charter Hart (1975), 130
    x   Linked by charter Hart (1975), 162

North-Eastern Group (Chester-le-Street)

Block {I} (a)

Durham [U];
Plawsworth [II];
Gateshead [U]; Little Usworth [II];
Biddick [04]; Chester le Street [02/LF];

Pelaw and Pictree [/]; Washington [II];
Boldon [EF: 01/LF]; Newton (East Boldon)
[IV];
Cleadon and Whitburn [01/LF]; *Wearmouth and Tunstall
[01/LF];
*Ryhope and *Burdon [01/LF]; Little Burdon [II];
Penshaw [/]; South Biddick [04];
Newbottle [03/LF]; Houghton [03];
Warden Law [IV]; Morton [IV];

Plus: Westoe in Incremental Group III

Note: With the possible exception of Plawsworth this group lies wholly to the east of the Roman road (*Deorestrete*) between the Durham area and Chester le Street and thence to Gateshead; it may fall into four sections:

(1) set north of the Wear: this corresponds to the properties of Jarrow and (Monk)Wearmouth (Hart 1975, 155),
ACQUISITION pre-700

(2) south of the Wear and adjacent to the coast are such survivors of the *appendicia* of South (Bishop) Wearmouth as remain in the Bishop's hands; originally it comprised South Wearmouth (*australem*); Westoe, Offerton, Silksworth, two Ryhopes, Burdon, Seaham, Dalton le Dale, Dawdon and Cold Heslerden
(Hart 1975,120 = *)
ACQUISITION by estate: Unknown   RECONSITUTED 934

(3) inland, but south of the Wear lies a group of settlements which appear to have focused on Houghton le Spring;
ACQUISITION by estate: Unknown

(4) finally, the ancient settlement focus of Chester le Street must have lands associated with it (Hart 1975, 163).
ACQUISITION by estate: Unknown   LEASED 901 x 915

It is significant that there are only fragmentary traces of the internal structure of this large territory; Monkwearmouth and Jarrow (Hart 1975, 144 and 145) had long been destroyed, and by 1183 both new arrangements and new vills were appearing.

Appendices

As has been argued in the text, it is probable that Chester le Street represented one original estate centre for some, or indeed all, of this group of vills.

Block {I} (a)

Easington Group

xEasington and Little Thorpe[01/LF];
xShotton [01/LF];   Twizell [II];   Edderacres [/];
<Trimdon [05]>;

Plus: Hulam, Hutton Henry and Sheraton in Incremental Group III.

Note: Hart 1975, 162: this is the Bishop's remnant of an estate once comprising Easington, Monk Heslerton, Thorpe, Horden, Castle Eden, two Shottons, Little Eden, Hulam, Hutton Henry, *Twinlingatun* and Billingham with its appendages and Sheraton.
The estate had a troubled history (Hart 1975, 164) and became much fragmented.
ACQUISITION by estate: Unknown   *LEASED* 901 x 915

Block {I} (a)

Quarringtonshire Group

Quarringtonshire, *i.e.*   Quarrington [?/LF]
North Sherburn [01/LF];   Shadforth [01];
South Sherburn [/]   Cassop [01];
Whitwell [/];   Tursdale [01];

Note: If the doubtful *Queornington* of Hart 129 is excluded (it is probably Whorlton, near Gainford, on the Tees, Craster 1954, 194, note 7), there is no reference to this territory earlier than Boldon Book,
ACQUISITION by estate: Unknown

Block {I} (a)

Sedgefield Group

Sedgefield [IV];
(Bishop) Middleham and Cornforth [01/LF];
Fishburn [?]   Garmondsway [/];   Mainsforth [/];

Note: Hart 1975,159; Craster suggests that this purchase for the Cuthbertine estates, 'Sedgefield with its appurtenances', included Bishop Middleham.
ACQUISITION by purchase: 901 x 915

Block {II} (d) / Block {I} (a)

Stockton/Norton/ Darlington Groups

Norton [EF/IV]; Hardwick [/]

Note: Hart 1975,128; Craster (1954, 193) thought that this included Stockton.
ACQUISITION by estate: Gift *c*.994

Block {II} (d)
Stockton [IV/LF];   Preston [01];
Hartburn [01/LF];   Carlton [IV];
Grindon [/];   New Ricknall [01];
Ricknall [/];   Heworth [/];
ACQUISITION by estate: Possibly *c.* 994

Block {II} (d)

Darlington

oDarlington [IV];   Ketton [/];
Blackwell [IV];   Baydales [/];
Cockerton [01];   Oxen(-le-Flatts) [III];   Little Haughton [02/LF];Burdon [/];

Great Haughton (le Skerne) [III/LF];
Whessoe [III/LF];

Plus Brafferton and Newsham: see Incremental Group III.

Note: Darlington, granted *cum omnibus suis appendiciis* (Hart 130: Craster 1954, 193, note 1). In addition the grant included a territory assembled by purchase, High Coniscliffe, Cockerton, Haughton le Skerne, Normanby (near Middlesbrough) and Lumley.
ACQUISITION by estate: 1003 x 1006

Block {II} (d)

Heighington Group

Heighington [01/LF];
Killerby [01/LF];   Middridge [01];
Thickley [01/LF];   Newbiggin (by Thickley) [II]; Redworth [IV];
                        School Aycliffe [/];

+Old Thickley [/];
ACQUISITION by estate: Unknown

Appendices

Block {II} (d)

Aucklandshire Group

Aucklandshire *i.e.*
+North (Bishop) Auckland [01];   +Escomb [01];
+Newton (Cap) [01];

Block {III} (c)

West Auckland [III];	Little Coundon [03];
Great Coundon [?/LF]	
Lutterington [II];	Henknowle [II];
Whitworth [I];	+Hunwick [I];
Byers (Green) [/];	Harperley [/];

Plus: Binchester in Incremental Group III

Note: Hart 1975, 129: two Aucklands, Copeland, Weardseatle (lost), Binchester, Cuthberteston (lost), Thickley, Escomb, Witton le Wear, Hunwick, Newton Cap, Helmington.
Hart 1975,154, records the acquisition of some of this estate; only Newton Cap lies north of the Wear.
ACQUISITION by estate: 830 X 845?   LEASE 995 x 1006

Block {III} (c)

Weardale (Upper Aucklandshire?)

Wolsingham [01/LF];	Rogerley [?/LF];	
Broadwood [?/LF]	Stanhope [01];	Frosterley [/];

Note: This dales sub-group is associated with the Aucklandshire group though lodge-building services recorded in Boldon Book. Hart 1975,154 may record acquisition.
ACQUISITION by estate: 830 x 845

Block {III} (c)

Lanchester Group

Lanchester [01/LF];	
Cornsay and Hedley(hope) [I];	Greencroft [II/LF];
Iveston [I];	Consett [/];
Hedley(hope) [I];	Muggleswick [/];
Edmondbyers [/];	Blanchland [/];
Hunstanworth [/];	Medomsley [/];
Migley [/];	Langley [/];

Edmondsley [/];

Note: Hart 1975, 163 may record the lease of some of this territory, implying acquisition before 901 X 915
ACQUISITION by estate: pre 901 x 915

Block {III} (c)

<Incremental Group I>

<Witton Gilbert and Fulforth [01/LF];
Crockhall (Crookhall) [/];   Pockerley [/];
Smalley [/];   Birtley [service to Great Chase];

Marley [service to Great Chase];   Gildford [04];>

Note: This small group have no geographical cohesion; they are scattered along the foothills of the Pennines, between the Lanchester group and the North-Eastern group. It is possible that they represent a first increment to the first draft of Boldon Book.

Block {III} (c)

Tyne Valley: Incremental Group II

Whickham [01/LF];   Swalwell [/];
Farnacres [/; lost];   Ryton [02/LF];
Crawcrook [02];   Stella [/];
Winlaton [02/LF];

Note: If the reconstructed order of Boldon Book is indeed correct this 'integral group' of Tyne valley vills must represent the rectification of the omission of a complete small shire unit in an early draft of Boldon Book.

Block {III} (c)

Incremental group III

Sunderland [02];
*Westoe [02/LF];   Newsham [/];
Barford [/];   Great Usworth [I];
Herrington [I];   Hutton (Henry) [I];
Hulam [II] and Sheraton [I];
{IV} (b)
Butterwick [I];   Brafferton [I];
+Binchester [I];   Urpeth [I]

Note: This final group contains vills widely scattered throughout the entire county; they can only be interpreted as a final incremental set added to Boldon Book. It is significant that most are either drengage vills or at farm.

It is probable that Bedlingtonshire – Block {IV} (b) – that follows in the sequence was upon a separate folio.

Identifiable Village Groups from Supplemental Sources

Craster (1954), writing on the *Historia de Sancto Cuthberto*, notes that the term *appendicia* occurs frequently in the *Historia* and equates it with the Anglo-Saxon term *geburatunas*, i.e. 'the hamlets and farmsteads of the farming population', and notes that the 'use implies the grouping of vills around an administrative centre' (*ibid.*, 192). They were also termed shires.

Durham vills with appendages or appurtenances.
The references in Hart 1975 are in this case to the document numbers, *not* pages.

> Wearmouth with appendages (Hart 1975, 120)
> Darlington with appendages (Hart 1975, 130)
>
> Billingham with appendages (Hart 1975, 162)
> Billingham in *Heorteness* (Hart 1975, 154)
> Sedgefield with appurtenances (Hart 1975, 159)
> Jarrow with appurtenances (Craster 1954, 192; *Historia* para 21, p.208; see Hart 1975, 145; NB. Hart144 for (Monk) Wearmouth)
> Easington (this could be an 'assembled' group (Hart 1975, 162)
> Staindrop with appurtenances   (Hart 1975, 132)
> Aycliffe with dependencies (Hart 1975, 165)
> Bishop Wearmouth with appendages (Hart 1975, 120)
> Bedlingham with appendages (Hart 1975, 160)

'Shire' groups (indicated by the specific use of the word).

> Quarringtonshire
> Heighingtonshire
> Aucklandshire
> Staindropshire (Rabyshire)
> Bedlingtonshire

APPENDIX III Historic County Boundaries

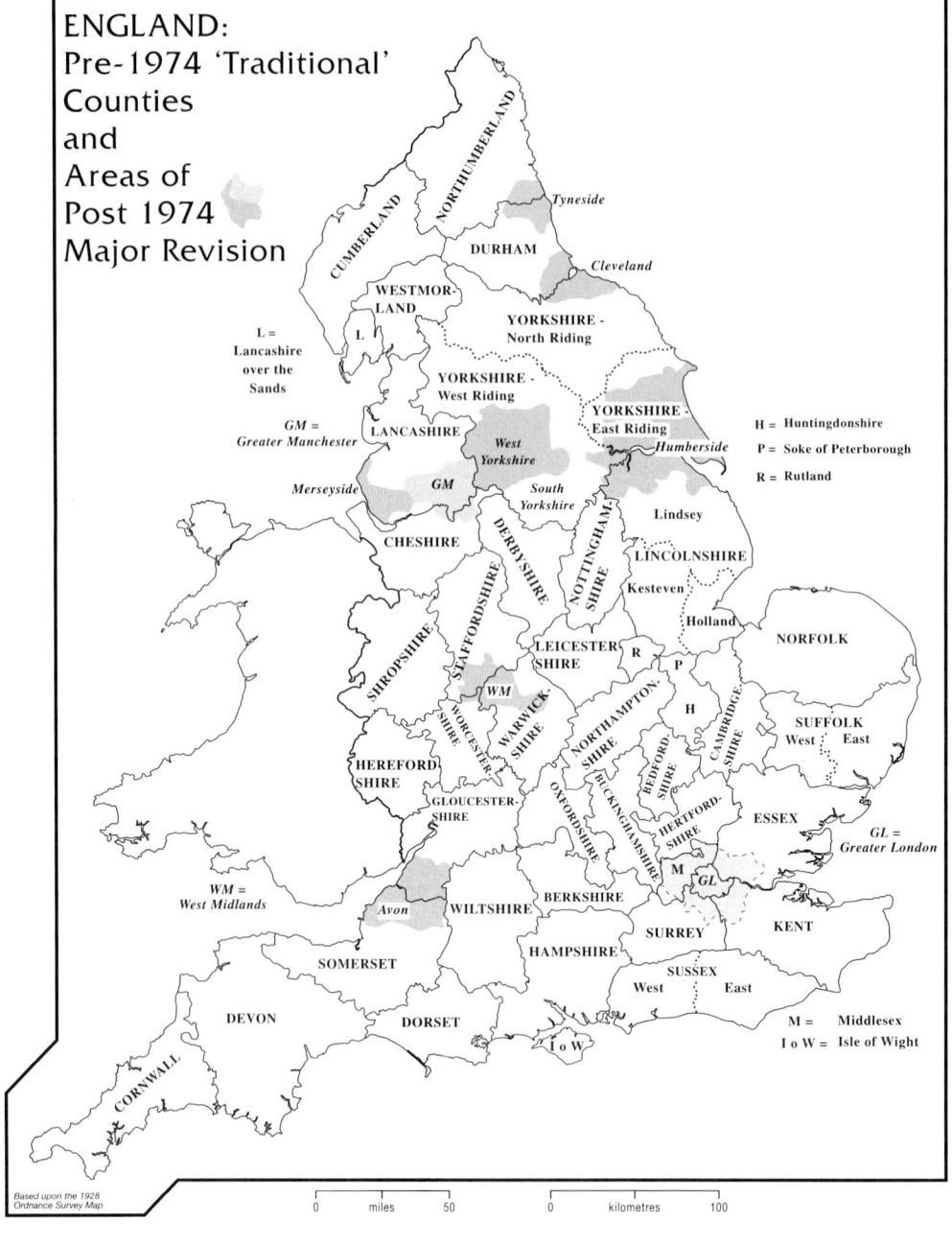

Bibliography

Aberg, A. (ed.) 1978 *Medieval Moated Sites* (Council for British Archaeology Research Report No. 17).

Adams, I. H. (ed.) 1976 *Agrarian Landscape Terms: a Glossary for Historical Geography* (Institute of British Geographers, London).

Aird, W. M. 1998 *St Cuthbert and the Normans – the Church of Durham, 1071–1153* (The Boydell Press, Woodbridge, Suffolk).

Allerston, P. 1970 'English Village Development', *Transactions of the Institute of British Geographers*, 51.

Allison, M. 2003 *History of Appleton-le-Moors* (Privately Produced, ISBN 0904775429).

Appleby, J. C. and Dalton, P. (eds) 1997 *Government, Religion and Society in Northern England 1000–1700* (Sutton Publishing).

Armstrong, A. M., Mawer, A., Stenton, F. M. and Dickens. B. 1952 *The Place-Names of Cumberland* (English Place-Name Society 20–22, 3 vols, University Press, Cambridge).

Aston, T. H. 1958 'The Origins of the Manor in Britain' *Transactions of the Royal Historical Society*, 5th series, VIII, 59–83.

Aston, M. A. and Costen, M. D. (eds) 1994 *The Shapwick Project – a Topographical and Historical Study, 5th. Report* (University of Bristol, Department of Continuing Education).

Austin, D. (ed.) 1982 *Boldon Book* (Phillimore, Chichester).

Austin, D. 1989, *The Deserted Medieval Village of Thrislington, Co. Durham* (monograph 12, Medieval Archaeology, London).

Baker, A. R. H. and Butlin, R. A. (eds) 1973 *Studies of Field Systems in the British Isles* (University Press, Cambridge).

Baldwin, J. R. and Whyte, I. D. (eds) 1985 *The Scandinavians in Cumbria* (The Scottish Society for Northern Studies, University of Edinburgh, Edinburgh).

Barford, P. M. 2001 *The Early Slavs* (The British Museum Press, London).

Barlow, F. 1963 *The English Church 1000–1086* (Longman, Green and Co. Ltd., London).

Barraclough, G. (ed.) 1960 *Social Life in Early England* (Routledge and Kegan Paul, London).

Barrow, G. W. S. 1969 'Northern English Society in the Twelfth and Thirteenth Centuries' *Northern History* vol. IV, 1–28.

Barrow, G. W. S. 1973 *The Kingdom of the Scots* (Edward Arnold, London).

Bartlett, R. 1993 *The Making of Europe: Conquest, Colonisation and Cultural Change 950–1350* (Allen Lane, The Penguin Press, Harmondsworth).

Bartlett, R. and MacKay, A. (eds) 1989 *Medieval Frontier Societies* (Clarendon Press, Oxford, pb. 1992).

Bassett, S. (ed.) 1989 *The Origins of the Anglo-Saxon Kingdoms* (University Press, Leicester).

Bassett, S. 1989 'In Search of the Origins of Anglo-Saxon Kingdoms' in Bassett, S. (ed.) 1989 *The Origins of the Anglo-Saxon Kingdoms* (University Press, Leicester), 3–27.

Beeler, J. 1966 *Warfare in England* (Cornell University Press, New York).

Beresford, M. W. 1954 *The Lost Villages of England* (Lutterworth Press, London).

Beresford, M. W. 1988 *New Towns of the Middle Ages: Town Plantation in England, Wales and Gascony* (Alan Sutton, Gloucester, first published 1967 by Lutterworth Press).

Beresford, M. and Finberg, H. P. R., 1973 *English Medieval Boroughs: a Handlist* (David and Charles, Newton Abbot).

Beresford, M. W., and Hurst, J. G. 1971 *Deserted Medieval Villages* (Lutterworth Press, London).

Beresford, M. W. and Hurst, J. G. 1990 *Wharram Percy: Deserted Medieval Village* (B.T. Batsford Ltd / English Heritage, London).

Beresford, M. W., and St Joseph, J. K. S. 1979 *Medieval England: an Aerial Survey*, 2nd edition, Cambridge).

Bishop, T. A. M. 1934 'The Distribution of manorial demesne in the Vale of York', *English Historical Review* 49, 386–407.

Bishop, T. A. M. 1935 'Assarting and the growth of open fields' *Economic History Review* 6, 13–29.

Bishop, T. A. M. 1948 'The Norman Settlement of Yorkshire' in E. M. Carus-Wilson, *Essays in Economic History II* (Edward Arnold Publishers, London 1962, reprinted 1966).

Bonney, M. 1990 *Lordship and the Urban Community – Durham and its overlords 1250–1540* (University Press, Cambridge).

Bouch, C. A. L. 1948 *Prelates and People of the Lake Counties* (Titus Wilson, Kendal).

Brooks, C., Daniels, R. and Harding, A. (eds) 2002 *Past, Present and Future: the Archaeology of Northern England* (Architectural and Archaeological Society of Durham and Northumberland, Research Report No. 5).

Brooks, N. and Cubitt, C. (eds) 1996 *St Oswald of Worcester – Life and Influence* (University Press, Leicester).

Brown, M. P. 2003 *The Lindisfarne Gospels* (The British Library, London).

Bylund, E. 1960 'Theoretical considerations regarding the distribution of settlement in inner north Sweden', *Geografiska Annaler*, 42, 255–49.

Cadman, G. and Foard, G. 1984 '*Raunds; Memorial and Village Origins*' in Faull, M. L. (ed.) Studies in Late Anglo-Saxon Settlement (Oxford).

Cam, H. 1944 *Liberties and Communities in Medieval England – Collected Studies in Local Administration and Topography* (Merlin Press reprint 1963).

Cameron, K. 1965 *Scandinavian Settlement in the Territory of the Five Boroughs: the Place-Name Evidence* (University of Nottingham, Inaugural Lecture; reprinted 1975 by the *English Place-Name Society, in Place-Name Evidence for the Anglo-Saxon Invasion and the Scandinavian Settlements*, assembled by Margaret Gelling).

Camille, M. 1998 *Mirror in Parchment: the Luttrell Psalter and the Making of Medieval England* (Reaktion Books, London).

Campbell, J. G. 2000 *The Anglo-Saxon State* (Hambledon and London).

Campey, L. 1989 'Medieval Village Plans in County Durham: an Analysis of Reconstructed Plans Based on Medieval Sources', *Northern History*, vol. XXV, 60–87.

Charles-Edwards, C. 1989 'Early Medieval Kingship in the British Isles' in Bassett, S. (ed.) 1989 *The Origins of the Anglo-Saxon Kingdoms* (University Press, Leicester), 28–39.

Clack, P. A. G., and Gosling, P. F., 1976 *Archaeology in the North: Report of the Northern Archaeological Survey* (Northern Archaeological Survey, with permission of Her Majesty's Stationary Office).

Clancy, T. O. (ed.) 1998 *The Triumph Tree: Scotland's Earliest Poetry AD 550–1350* (Cannongate Classics, Cannongate Books, Edinburgh).

Coates, B. E. 1965 'The Origin and Distribution of Markets and Fairs in Medieval Derbyshire', *Derbyshire Archaeological Journal* 85, 92–111.
Cohen, A. P. (ed.) 1982 *Belonging: Identity and Social Organisation in British Cultures* (Manchester University Press).
Colgrave, B. 1985 *Two Lives of Saint Cuthbert* (Cambridge University Press).
Conzen, M. R. G. 1960 *Alnwick, Northumberland: a Study in Town Plan Analysis* (Institute of British Geographers, Publication No. 17, George Philip and Son. Ltd., London).
Cramp, R. 1984 *Corpus of Anglo-Saxon Stone Sculpture, vol. I, County Durham and Northumberland* (Published for the British Academy by Oxford University Press).
Craster, E. 1954, 'The Patrimony of St. Cuthbert', *English Historical Review*, CCLXXI, April, 177–99.
Crawford, B. E. 1995 *Scandinavian Settlement in Northern Britain* (University Press, Leicester).
Cunningham, J. 1990 Auckland Castle: Some Recent Discoveries', in Felnie, E. and Crossley, P. *Medieval Architecture and its Intelligent Context* (The Hambledon Press, London).
Darby, H. C. 1951 *An Historical Geography of England before A.D. 1800* (Cambridge University Press, Cambridge).
Darby, H. C. *et al.* (ed.) 1952–77 *The Domesday Geography of England* (7 volumes, University Press, Cambridge): *Eastern England* (1952); *Midland England* (1954); *South-East England* (1962a); *Northern England* (1962b); *South-West England* (1967); *Gazetteer* (1975); *Domesday England* (1977).
Davis, R. H. C. 1976 *The Normans and their Myth* (Thames and Hudson, London, reprint 1997).
Davis, W. (ed.) 2003 *From the Vikings to the Normans* (University Press, Oxford).
Defoe, D. 1724–6, edited and abridged by P. Rogers, *A Tour through the Whole Island of Great Britain* (Penguin Books Ltd., Harmondsworth 1971).
Denman, D. R. 1958 *Origins of Ownership* (George Allen and Unwin Ltd., London).
Denman, D. R., Roberts, R. A. and Smith, H. J. F. (1967) *Commons and Village Greens* (Leonard Hill, London).
Dobson, B 1970 'The Roman Period' in Dewdney, J. C. (ed.) *Durham County and City with Teeside* (British Association for the Advancement of Science, Durham).
Dodgshon, R. A. and Butlin, R. A. 1978 *An Historical Geography of England and Wales* (second edition, Academic Press, London).
Dornier, A. (ed.) 1977 *Mercian Studies* (University Press, Leicester).
Douglas, D. C. and Greenaway, G.W. 1981 *English Historical Documents 1042–1189* (Eyre Methuen and Oxford University Press.
Duby, G. 1968 *Rural Economy and Country Life in the Medieval West* (Edward Arnold, London).
Duncan, A. A. M. 1975 *Scotland – The Making of the Kingdom* (The Edinburgh History of Scotland, vol. I, reprinted in paperback 2000, Mercat Press, Edinburgh).
Dunsford, H. and Harris, S. J. 2003 'Colonisation of the wasteland in County Durham, 1100–1400', *Economic History Review* LVI, No. 1, 34–56.
Dussart, F. 1971 *L'Habitat et les Paysages Ruraux d'Europe* (University de Liege, Les Congres et Colloques de l'University de Liege, vol. 58).
Eckwall, E. 1960 *The Concise Oxford Dictionary of English Place-Names* (4th. edition Clarendon Press, Oxford).
English, B. (1979) *The Lords of Holderness 1086–1260* (University of Hull, published by the University Press, Oxford).

Erskine, R. W. H. and Williams, A. (eds) 2003 *The Story of Domesday Book* (Phillimore, Chichester).
Evans, D. H. and Jarrett, M. J. 1987 'The Deserted Village of West Whelpington: Third Report, Part One', *Archaeologia Aeliana*, 5th Series, Vol. XV, 199–308.
Evans, D. H., Jarrett, M. J. and Wrathmell, S. 1988 'The Deserted Village of West Whelpington: Third Report, Part Two, *Archaeologia Aeliana*, 5th Series, Vol. XV, 139–192.
Everitt, A. 1967 'The Marketing of Agricultural Produce' in Thirsk, J. (ed.) *The Agrarian History of England and Wales 1500–1640*, vol. IV (Cambridge University Press, Cambridge).
Everitt, A. 1985 *Landscape and Community in England* (Hambledon Press, London).
Everitt, A. 1986 *Continuity and Colonization: the Evolution of Kentish Settlement* (University Press, Leicester).
Everson, P., Taylor, C. C. and Dunn, C. J. 1991 *Change and Continuity: Rural Settlement in North-West Lincolnshire* (Royal Commission on the Historical Monuments of England, HMSO, London).
Faith, R. 1997, *The English Peasantry and the Growth of Lordship* (the University Press, Leicester).
Farrell, R. T. (ed.) 1982 *The Vikings* (Phillimore, London and Chichester).
Fehring, G. 1991 *The Archaeology of Medieval Germany: an Introduction* (trans. R. Samson: Routledge, London).
Fellows-Jensen, G. 1985 *Scandinavian Settlement Names in the North-West* (C. A. Reitzels Forlag, Copenhagen).
Fellows-Jensen, G. 1989–90 'Scandinavians in Southern Scotland?' *Nomina* XII, 40–61.
Finberg, H. P. R. 1964 *Lucerna: Studies of Some Problems of the Early History of England* (Macmillan and Co. Ltd, London).
Fletcher, R. 1998 *The Barbarian Conversion: from Paganism to Christianity* (Henry Holt and Company, New York).
Fletcher, R. 2002 *Bloodfeud – Murder and Revenge in Anglo-Saxon England* (Penguin Books, London).
Fraser, C. 1955 'Gillycorn and the Customary of the Convent of Durham', *Archaeologia Aeliana*, 4th series, vol xxxiii, 35–60.
Fraser, D. 1969 *Village Planning in the Primitive World* (Studio Vista, London).
Fraser, G. MacDonald 1971 *The Steel Bonnets* (Barrie and Jenkins, London, paperback edition, reprinted 1995, Harper Collins, London).
Frere, S. 1987 *Britannia* (reprinted 1996, Pimlico, London).
Frodisham, P. (ed.) 2004 *Archaeology in Northumberland National Park* (CBA Research Report 136; Council for British Archaeology, York).
Gamble, C. 1996 *Timewalkers – the Prehistory of Global Colonisation* (Harvard University Press, Cambridge, Massachusetts)
Gelling, M. 1978 *Signposts to the Past* (J.M. Dent and Sons Ltd., London).
Gelling, M. 1992 *The West Midlands in the Early Middle Ages* (University Press, Leicester).
Getmapping 2001, *Photographic Atlas of England* (Harper Collins Publishers, London).
Gibson, E. 1695 *Camden's Britannia* (Facsimile edition, Times Newspapers Ltd. 1971).
Glacken, C. J. 1976 *Traces on the Rhodian Shore* (paperback ed., University of California Press, Berkeley).
Glasscock, R. E. 1975 *The Lay Subsidy of 1334* (British Academy Records of Social and Economic History, New Series II, University Press, Oxford).
Göransson, S. 1958 'Field and Village on the Island of Öland: a Study in the Genetic Compound of an East Swedish Rural Landscape' *Geografiska Annaler*, 40, 101–58.

Göransson, S. 1961 'Regular Open-field Pattern in England and Scandinavian *Solskifte*', *Geografiska Annaler* 43, 80–104.
Graham, T. H. B. 1927 'Cornage and Drengage' *Tranactions of the Cumberland and Westmorland Antiquarian Society*, vol. XXX, 1927–8, 78–95.
Graham, T. H. B. 1934 *The Barony of Gilsland: Lord William Howard's survey taken in 1603*, Cumberland and Westmorland Antiquarian and Archaeological Society, Extra Series, 16 (Titus Wilson, Kendal).
Greenway, D. E. 1972 *Charters of the Honour of Mowbray* (British Academy, The University Press, Oxford).
Greenwell, W. (ed.) 1852 *Boldon Buke* (Surtees Society 25, 2).
Greenwell, W. (ed.) 1857 *Bishop Hatfield's Survey* (Surtees Society 32, 1856, reprinted 1967 by Wm. Dawson and Sons Ltd. London).
Greenwell, W. (ed.) 1872 *Feodarium Prioratus Dunelmensis* (Surtees Society 58, II).
Grierson, P. 1972 *English Linear Measures* (The Stenton Lecture, University of Reading).
Gutkind, E. A. 1964 *Urban Development in Central Europe* (Free Press of Glencoe, Collier – Macmillan Ltd., London).
Hadley, D. M. 2000 *The Northern Danelaw: its Social Structure, c. 800–1100* (University Press, Leicester).
Hallam, E. M. 1986 *Domesday Book Through Nine Centuries* (Thames and Hudson, London).
Hallam, H. E. (ed.) 1988 *The Agrarian History of England and Wales, Volume II 1042–1350* (Cambridge University Press).
Harley, J. B. *Historian's Guide to Ordnance Survey Maps* (The Standing Council for Local History for The National Council of Social Service. London).
Harley, J. B. 1975 *Ordnance Survey Maps: a Descriptive Manual* (Southampton Ordnance Survey).
Harmer, F. E. 1952 *Anglo-Saxon Writs* (University Press, Manchester).
Harris, A. 1961 *The Rural Landscape of the East Riding of Yorkshire 1700–1850* (University of Hull and the University Press, Oxford).
Harrison, W. 1994 *The Description of England* (The Folgar Shakespeare Library, Washington D.C. and Dover Publications, New York).
Hart, C, 1975 *The Early Charters of Northern England and the North Midlands* (University Press, Leicester).
Hart, C. 1992 *The Danelaw* (Hambledon Press, London).
Harvey, M. 1982 'Regular open-field systems on the Yorkshire Wolds', *Landscape History*, 4, 29–39.
Harvey. M 1983 'Planned field systems in Eastern Yorkshire: some thoughts on their origin', *Agricultural History Review* 31, 91–103.
Harvey, P. D. A. 1980 The *History of Topographical Maps* (Thames and Hudson, London).
Harvey, P. D. A. 1993 'Rectitudines Singularum Personarum and Gerefa', *English History Review* 108, 1–22).
Harvey, P. D. A. 1994 'Boldon Book and the Wards between Tyne and Tees' in Rollason, D., Harvey, M. and Prestwich, M, (eds) 1994 *Anglo-Norman Durham, 1093–1193* (The Boydell Press, Woodbridge, Suffolk), 399–405.
Hawkes, J. and Mills, S. (eds) 1999 *Northumbria's Golden Age* (Sutton Publishing, Frome, Somerset).
Haywood, J. 1999 *Dark Age Naval Power* (Anglo-Saxon Books, Hockwold-cum-Wilton, Norfolk, England).
Heidinga, H. A. 1987 *Medieval Settlement and Economy North of the Lower Rhine* (Van Gorcuin, Assen/Maastrict).

Helmfrid, S. 1994 *Landscape and Settlements* (National Atlas of Sweden, Royal Swedish Academy of Sciences, Stockholm).
Hemming, J. 2002 '*Bos primigenius* in Britain: or, Why Do Fairy Cows Have Red Ears?', Folklore vol. 113, 71–82.
Higham, N. 1986 *The Northern Counties to AD 1000* (Longman, London).
Higham, N. 1992 *Rome Britain and the Anglo-Saxons* (Seaby, London).
Hill, D. 1981 *An Atlas of Anglo-Saxon England* (Basil Blackwell, Oxford).
Hillaby, J. 1993 *The Sculptured Capitals of Leominster Priory* (Friends of Leominster Priory Church, The Priory. Leominster, Herefordshire).
Hilton, R. H. 1966 *A Medieval Society* (Weidenfeld and Nicolson, London).
Hodges, R. 1989 a The *Anglo-Saxon Achievement* (Duckworth, London).
Hodges, R. 1989 b *Dark Age Economics* (second edition, Duckworth, London).
Hodges, R. 1991 *Wall-to-Wall History – The Story of Roystone Grange* (Duckworth, London).
Hodgson, J. C. 1899 *A History of Northumberland*, vol. V (Andrew Reid and Co. Ltd. Newcastle upon Tyne and Simpkin, Marshall, Hamilton, Kent and Company, London).
Hodgson, R. I. 1989 *Coalmining, Population and Enclosure in the Seasale Colliery Districts of (Northern) Durham, 1551–1810* (Unpublished Ph.D. thesis, University of Durham).
Hodgson Hinde, J. 1868 *Simeon of Durham* (Surtees Society, 51).
Holt, J. C. (ed.) 1986 *Domesday Studies* The Boydell Press, Woodbridge)
Homans, G. C. 1941 *The English Villagers of the Thirteenth Century* (Russell and Russell, New York, reprinted 1960).
Hooke, D. 1988 *Angko-Saxon Settlements* (Basil Blackwell, Oxford).
Hooke, D. 1998 *The Landscape of Anglo-Saxon England* (University Press, Leicester).
Hope-Taylor, B. 1977 *Yeavering: An Anglo-British Centre of early Northumbria* (Her Majesty's Stationary Office, London).
Houston, J. M. 1963 *A Social Geography of Europe* (Gerald Duckworth and Co. Ltd., London).
Howell, C. 1976 'Peasant Inheritance Customs in the Midlands 1280–1700', in J. Goody, J. Thirsk and E. P. Thompson *Family and Inheritance: Rural Society in Western Europe 1200–1800* (University Press, Cambridge).
Howell, C. 1983 *Land, Family and Inheritance in Transition – Kibworth Harcourt 1280–1700* (University Press, Cambridge).
Hoyt, R. S. 1968 *The Royal Demesne in English Constitutional History, 1066–1272* (Greenwood Press Publishers, New York).
Huddart, D. and Glasser, N. F. 2002 *Quaternary of Northern England* (Geological Conservation Review Series, no. 25, Joint Conservation Committee, Peterborough).
Ingleson, S. 1972, *Settlement, Agrarian Systems and Field Patterns in Central Durham 1600–1850: a Study in Historical Geography* (unpublished MA thesis, University of Durham).
James, E. 1989 'The Origins of Barbarian Kingdoms: the Continental Evidence' in Bassett, S. (ed.) 1989 *The Origins of the Anglo-Saxon Kingdoms* (University Press, Leicester), 40–52.
Jenkins, D. 2000 *Hywel Dda – The Law* (Third impression, Gomer Press, Llandysul, Ceredigion).
John, E. 1996, *Reassessing Anglo-Saxon England* (University Press, Manchester).
Johnson, A. 1983 *Roman Forts* (Adam and Charles Black, London).
Jolliffe, J. E. A. 1926 'Northumbrian Institutions', *English Historical Review* vol. XLI, no. CLXI, 1–42.
Jolliffe, J. E. A. 1935–6 'A Survey of Fiscal Tenements', *Economic History Review,* VI, 157–171.

Jones, A. 1979 'Land Measurement in England, 1150–1350', *Agricultural History Review*, 17.1, 10–18.

Jones, G. R. J. 1971 'The Multiple Estate as a Model Framework for Tracing the Early Stages of Settlement Evolution', in F. Dussart (ed.), *L'Habitat et les Paysages Rureaux d'Europe* (Les Congres et Colloques de l'Universite de Liege, Liege).

Jones, S. R. H. 1993 'Transaction costs, institutional change and the emergence of a market economy in later Anglo-Saxon England', *Economic History Review* xlvi, 4, 658–78.

Jarvis, R. A., Bendelow, V. C., Bradley, R. I., Carroll, D. M., Furness, R. R., Kilgour, I. N. L. and King, S.J. 1984 *Soils and their use in Northern England* (Soil Survey of England and Wales, Bulletin No. 10, Hapenden).

Kapelle, W. E. 1979 *The Norman Conquest of the North* (Croom Helm, London).

Kelly, F. 1988 *A Guide to Early Irish Law* (Early Irish Law Series, vol. III, Dublin Institute for Advanced Studies, Dublin).

Kelly, F. 1998 *Early Irish Farming* (Dublin Institute for Advanced Studies, Dublin).

Keynes, S. and Lapidge, M. (eds) 1983, *Alfred the Great* (Penguin Books, London).

Kirby, D. A. 1971 *Parliamentary Surveys of the Bishopric of Durham* (Surtees Society, 183 1968, Northumberland Press, Gateshead).

Koch, J. T. 1997 *The Gododdin of Aneirin: Text and Context from Dark-Age Britain* (University of Wales Press, Cardiff and Celtic Studies Publications, Andover, Massachusetts).

Lang, J. 2000 'Monuments from Yorkshire in the Age of Alcuin', in Geake, H. and Kenny, J. *Early Deira: Archaeological Studies of the East Riding in the fourth to ninth centuries AD* (Oxbow Books, Oxford).

Latham, R. E. 1965 *Revised Medieval Latin Word-List* (Oxford University Press for the British Academy, Oxford).

Latham, L. C. 1960 'The Manor and the Village' in G. Barraclough (ed.) *Social Life in Early England* (Routledge and Kegan Paul, London).

Lawson, M. K. 2004 *Cnut – England's Viking King* (Tempus, Stroud, Gloucestershire, England).

Layton, R. (ed.) 1989 *Who Needs the Past – Indigenous Values and Archaeology* (Unwin Hyman, London).

Lewis, H. 1963, *Angles and Britons* (O'Donnell Lectures. University of Wales Press, Cardiff).

Lewis-Williams, D. 2002 *The Mind in the Cave* (Thames and Hudson, London).

Leighly, J. (ed.) 1963 *Land and Life – A Selection from the Writings of Carl Ortwin Sauer* (University Press, California).

Liddy, C. D. and Britnell, R. H. (eds) 2005 *North-East England in the Later Middle Ages* (The Boydell Press, Woodbridge, Suffolk).

Lockhart, D. G. 1980 'The Planned Villages' in M. L. Parry and T. Slater (eds) *The Making of the Scottish Countryside* (Croom Helm, London).

Loyn, H. R. 1962 *Anglo-Saxon England and the Norman Conquest* (Longmans, London).

Loyn, H. R. 1977 *The Vikings in Britain* (Book Club Associates, London).

MacKay, A. and Ditchburn. D. 1997 *Atlas of Medieval Europe* (Routledge, London).

Maitland, F. W. 1897 *Domesday Book and Beyond* (University Press, Cambridge: reprinted 1960, Fontana Library, London).

Margary, H (publisher), 1975–1981 *The Old Series Ordnance Survey Maps of England and Wales* (Harry Margery, Lympne Castle, Kent).

Mayhew, A. 1973 *Rural Settlement and Farming in Germany* (B. T. Batsford Ltd., London).

McConnell, P. (1904 and 1922) *The Agricultural Notebook* (reprinted many times – First Edition 1883; Crosby Lockwood and Son, London).

McCormick, M. 2001 *Origins of the European Economy: Communications and Commerce AD 300–900* (Cambridge University Press).

McNamee, C. 1997 *The Wars of the Bruces, 1306–1320* (Tuckwell Press, East Linton, Scotland).

Mead, W. R. 1981 *An Historical Geography of Scandinavia* (Academic Press, London).

Meeus, J. H. A., Wijermans, M. P. I. and Vroom, M. J. 1990 'Agricultural Landscapes in Europe', *Landscape and Urban Planning,* 18, 289–352.

Meeus, J. H. A. 1995 'Pan-European Landscapes', *Landscape and Urban Planning* 31, 57–79.

Middlebrook, S. 1968 *Newcastle upon Tyne – Its Growth and Achievement* (First published in 1950 by the Newcastle Journal Limited by arrangement with Horace Cox Limited, London, and reprinted by S. R. Publishers Limited, Wakefield).

Morgan, H. L. 1960 *Vitrivius, the Ten Books of Architecture* (Originally published 1914; reprinted by Dover Publications, Inc., New York).

Morgan, E. 1978 *Domesday Book, Cheshire* (ed. J. Morris, Phillimore, Chichester).

Morris, J. 1973 *The Age of Arthur* (Weidenfeld and Nicholson, London).

Nicolaisen, W. F. H. 1976 *Scottish Place Names* (B. T. Batsford Ltd., London).

Nitz, H-J. 1974 'Regelmässige Langstreifenfluren und Fränkische Staatskolonisation', in Nitz, H-J. (ed.) *Historisch-Genetische Siedlungsforschung,* (Wirrenschaftliche Buchgesellschaft, Darmstadt).

Nitz, H-J. 1988 'Settlement Structures and Settlement Systems of the Frankish Central State in Carolingian and Ottonian Times', in Hooke, D. (ed.), *Anglo-Saxon Settlements* (Basil Blackwell Ltd., Oxford).

Nørland, P. 1968 *Trelleborg* (Nationalmuseet, Copenhagen).

O'Brien, C. and Miket, R. 1991 'The Early Medieval Settlement of Thirlings, Northumberland', *Durham Archaeological Journal* 7, 57–91.

Offler, H. S. 1996 *North of the Tees* (Variarum, Ashgate Publishing Ltd., Aldershot).

Oliver, R. 1991 *Ordnance Survey of Great Britain, England and Wales, Indexes* (David Archer, The Pentre, Kerry, Newtown, Montgomeryshire).

Ordnance Survey, 1992, *Gazetteer of Great Britain* (3rd edition, Southampton).

Orme, B. 1981 *Anthropology for Archaeologists* (Duckworth, London).

Palliser, D. M. 1993 'Domesday Book and the "Harrying of the North"', *Northern History*, vol. XXIX, 2–23.

Palliser, D. M. (ed.) 2000 *The Cambridge Urban History of Britain*, vol. I, 600–1540 (University Press, Cambridge).

Palmer, L. R. 1998 *The Interpretation of Mycenean Texts* (Oxford University Press 1963: special edition Sandpiper Books 1998).

Parson, W. and White, W. 1829 *A History and Gazetteer of Cumberland and Westmorland* (republished 1984 by Michael Moon, Whitehaven).

Patterson, N. T. 1994, *Cattle Lords and Clansmen: the Social Structure of Early Ireland* (University of Notre Dame Press, Notre Dame and London).

Pelteret, D. A. E. 1995 *Slavery in Early Medieval England from the Reign of Alfred to the Twelfth Century* (reprinted 2001, The Boydell Press, Woodbridge).

Pennar, M. (1988) *Taliesin Poems* (Llanerch Enterprises, Lampeter).

Perriam, D. R. and Robinson, J. 1998 *The Medieval Fortified Buildings of Cumbria* (Cumberland and Westmorland Antiquarian and Archaeological Society, Extra Series 39).

Pevsner, N. 1966 *The Buildings of England: Yorkshire, The North Riding* (reprinted 1985, Penguin Books, Harmondsworth).

Pevsner, N. 1967 *The Buildings of England: Cumberland and Westmorland* (reprinted 1980, Penguin Books, Harmondsworth).
Phillips, D. 1985 *Excavations at York Minster, II* (Royal Commission on Historical Monuments of England, Her Majesty's Stationary Office, London).
Phillips, T. R. 1944 *The Roots of Strategy* (Harrisburg).
Piper, A. J. and Doyle, A. I. (eds) 1996 *North of the Tees: Studies in Medieval British History* (Variorum, Aldershot, England).
Plummer, C. and Earle, J. (eds) 1892 *Two of the Saxon Chronicles Parallel* (2 vols., re-issued in 1952 by D. Whitelock, Clarendon Press, Oxford).
Polunin, O. and Walters, M. 1985 *A Guide to the Vegetation of Britain and Europe* (Oxford University Press, Oxford).
Postan, M. M. 1966 *The Cambridge Economic History of Europe, vol. I, The Agrarian Life of the Middle Ages* (The University Press, Cambridge).
Postan, M. M. 1972 *The Medieval Economy and Society: an Economic History of Britain 1100–1500* (Weidenfeld and Nicolson, London).
Postan, M. M. 1973 *Essays on Medieval Agriculture and General Problems of the Medieval Economy* (University Press, Cambridge).
Pounds, N. J. G. 1974 *An Economic History of Medieval Europe* (Longman, London).
Powlesland, D. 1999 'The Anglo-Saxon Settlement at West Heslerton, North Yorkshire', in Hawkes, J. and Mills, S. (eds) *Northumbria's Golden Age* (Sutton Publishing).
Rackham, O. 1986 *The History of the Countryside* (J. M. Dent and Sons Ltd. London).
Rahtz, P. 1976 'Buildings and Rural Settlement' in D. M. Wilson (ed.) *The Archaeology of Anglo-Saxon England* (Methuen and Co. Ltd, London).
Ramm, H., McDowall, R. W. and Mercer, E. 1970 *Shielings and Bastles* (Royal Commission on Historical Monuments of England, Her Majesty's Stationary Office, London).
Randsborg, K. 1980 *The Viking Age in Denmark* (Duckworth, London).
RCHM Royal Commission on Historical Monuments, England 1936 *Inventory of the Historical Monuments in Westmorland* (His Majesty's Stationary Office, London).
Rees, W. 1924 *South Wales and the March 1284–1415: a Social and Agrarian Study* (Cedric Chivers, Portway, Bath).
Rees, W. 1953, *A Survey of the Duchy of Lancaster Lordships in Wales 1609–1613* (University of Wales Press, Cardiff)
Rees, W. 1968 'The Medieval Lordship of Brecon' *Transactions of the Honourable Society of Cymmrodorian*, Session 1915–16 (reprinted in *An Address Presented to Professor Emeritus William Rees by the Brecknock Society, 12th October 1968*, Brecknock Museum Publication).
Reid, R. R. 1920 'Barony and Thanage' *English Historical Review* vol XXXV, no. CXXXVIII, 161–99.
Renn, D. 1968 *Norman Castles in Britain* (reprint 1973, John Baker, London; Humanities Press, New York).
Rivet, A. L. F. 1979 *The Place-Names of Roman Britain* (B.T. Batsford Ltd., London, reprinted 1981, Book Club Associates, London).
Roberts, B. K. 1972 'Village plans in County Durham: a preliminary statement', *Medieval Archaeology* 16, 33–56.
Roberts, B. K. 1973 'Planned Villages from Medieval England' in Baker, A. R. H. and Harley, J. B. (eds) *Man Made the Land* (David and Charles, Newton Abbot).
Roberts, B. K., Turner, J. and Ward, P. F. 1973 'Recent Forest History and Land Use in Weardale,

Northern England' in Birks, H. J. B. and West, R. G. *Quaternary Plant Ecology* (Blackwell Scientific Publications, Oxford).

Roberts, B. K. 1975 'Cockfield Fell', *Antiquity*, XLIX, 193, 48–50.

Roberts, B. K. and R. G. Glasscock (eds) 1983, *Villages, Fields and Frontiers: Studies in European Rural Settlement in the Medieval and Early Modern Periods* (British Archaeological Reports, International Series, 185).

Roberts, B. K. 1987 *The Making of the English Village* (Longman Scientific and Technical, London).

Roberts, B. K. 1989 'Nucleation and Dispersion: Distribution Maps as a Research Tool' in Aston, M., Austin, D. and Dyer, C. (eds) *The Rural Settlements of Medieval England* (Basil Blackwell, Oxford).

Roberts, B. K. 1989–90, 'Late *-by* Names in the Eden Valley, Cumberland', *Nomina*, vol. XIII, 25–40.

Roberts, B. K. 1990 'Back Lanes and Tofts, Distribution Maps and Time; Medieval Nucleated Settlement in the North of England' in Vyner, B. (ed.) *Medieval Rural Settlement in North-East England* (Architectural and Archaeological Society of Durham and Northumberland, Research Report No. 2).

Roberts, B. K. 1993a 'Some Relict landscapes in Westmorland: a Reconsideration', *The Archaeological Journal*, 150, 433–455.

Roberts, B. K. 1993b 'Five Westmorland Settlements: a Comparative Study' *Transactions of the Cumberland and Westmorland Antiquarian and Archaeological Society*, xcii, 131–143.

Roberts, B. K. 1996a 'A Field Survey of Maulds Meaburn, Westmorland', *Transactions of the Cumberland and Westmorland Antiquarian and Archaeological Society*, xcvi, 45–50.

Roberts, B. K. 1996b *Landscapes of Settlement: Prehistory to the Present* (Routledge, London and New York).

Roberts, B. K. 1996c 'The great plough: a hypothesis concerning village genesis and land reclamation in Cumberland', *Landscape History* 18, 17–30.

Roberts, B. K, and Wrathmell, S, 2001 *Atlas of Rural Settlement in England* (English Heritage).

Roberts, B. K. and Wrathmell, S. 2002 *Region and Place* (English Heritage. London).

Roberts, B. K., Dunsford, H. and Harris, S.J. 'Framing Medieval Landscapes: Region and Place in County Durham', in Liddy, C. D. and Britnell, R. H. (eds) 2005 *North-East England in the Later Middle Ages* (The Boydell Press, Woodbridge, Suffolk), 222–37.

Roberts, B. K. 2007 'Between the brine and the high ground': the roots of Northumbria' in R. Colls and W. Lancaster *A New History of Northumbria* (Phillimore, Chichester 2007).

Roffe, D. 2000 *Domesday: The Inquest and the Book* (Oxford University Press, Oxford).

Rollason, D., Harvey, M. and Prestwich, M, (eds) 1994 *Anglo-Norman Durham, 1093–1193* (The Boydell Press, Woodbridge, Suffolk).

Ryder, P. 1993 *Medieval Churches of West Yorkshire* (West Yorkshire Archaeology Service, Whitley Press, Hunstanton, Norfolk).

Sawyer, P. H. 1971 *The Age of the Vikings* (2nd edition, Edward Arnold, London).

Sawyer, P. H. (ed.) 1976 *Medieval Settlement* (Edward Arnold, London).

Sawyer, P. H. 1978 *From Roman Britain to Norman England* (Methuen and Co. Ltd. London).

Sawyer, P. H. 1982 *Kings and Vikings* (Routledge, London and New York).

Scammell, G. V. 1956 *Hugh du Puiset* (University Press, Cambridge).

Schröder, K. H. and Schwarz, G. 1978 *Die Ländlichen Siedlungsformen in Mitteleuropa* (Forschurgen zur Deutschen Landeskunde, Band 175, Trier).

Searle, E. (ed.) 1980 *The Chronicle of Battle Abbey* (Clarendon Press, Oxford).

Seebohm, F. 1896 *The English Village Community* (Longman's Green and Co., London).
Seebohm, F. 1904, *The Tribal System in Wales* (Longman's Green and Co., London).
Seebohm, F. 1911 *Tribal Custom in Anglo-Saxon Law* (Longman's Green and Co., London).
Sheppard, J. A. 1966 'Pre-enclosure field and settlement patterns in an English township', *Geografiska Annaler*, 48, ser. B, 59–77.
Sheppard, J. 1974 'Metrological Analysis of regular village plans in Yorkshire', *Agricultural History Review* 22, 2,118–35.
Sheppard, J. A. 1976 'Medieval village planning in northern England: some evidence from Yorkshire', *Journal of Historical Geography*, 2, 1, 3–20.
Skaife, R. H. 1866 *The Survey of the County of York taken by John de Kirkby – 'Kirkby's Inquest'* (Surtees Society 49, Andrews and Co., Durham).
Smith, A. H. 1928 *The Place-Names of the North Riding of Yorkshire* (English Place-Name Society V, The University Press, Cambridge).
Smith, A. H. 1964 *The Preparation of County Place-Name Surveys* (English Place-Name Society, University Collage, Gower Street, London).
Smith, A. H. 1956 *English Place-Name Elements* (English Place-Name Society XXV. parts i and ii, University Press, Cambridge).
Smith, A. H. 1967 *The Place-names of Westmorland* (English Place-Name Society 43, 2 vols, University Press, Cambridge).
Smith, C. T. 1967 *An Historical Geography of Western Europe before 1800* (Longman, London).
Smith, D. 1988 *Maps and Plans* (B.T. Batsford, London).
Smyth, A. P. 1975 *Scandinavian York and Dublin* (Templekieran Press, Dublin).
Smyth, A. P. 1977 *Scandinavian Kings in the British Isles, 850–880* (University Press, Oxford).
Snooks, G. D. 1996 *The Dynamic Society: Exploring the Sources of Global Change* (Routledge, London).
Sømme, A. (ed.) 1968 *A Geography of Norden* (Heinemann, London).
Sporrong, U., Elkstam, U. and Samuelson, K. 1995 *Swedish Landscapes* (Swedish Environmental Protection Agency, Stockholm).
Stamp, L. D. (ed.) 1937–44 *The Land of Britain*, County Fascicles (Royal Geographical Society and Geographical Publications Ltd., London).
Stamp. L. D. (ed.) 1962 *The Land of Britain: its Use and Misuse* (Longmans Green and Co. Ltd. with Geographical Publications, 3rd, edition, enlarged, London).
Stephenson, J. 1988 *Contemporary Chronicles of the Middle Ages* (Llanerch Enterprises, Dyfed).
Stenton, F. M. 1971 *Anglo-Saxon England* (Clarendon Press, Oxford, 3rd edition).
Stewart-Brown, R. 1936 *Serjeants of the Peace in Medieval England and Wales* (Manchester University Press).
Sturdy, D. 1995 *Alfred the Great* (Constable, London).
Swanton, M. 2000 *The Anglo-Saxon Chronicles* (Phoenix Press, London).
Sylvester, D. 1969 *The Rural Landscape of the Welsh Borderland* (Macmillan, London).
Taylor, H. M and Taylor, J. 1965 *Anglo-Saxon Architecture*, 2 vols, (Cambridge University Press, paperback 1980)
Thomas, W. L. (ed.) 1956 *Mans Role in Changing the Face of the Earth* (University of Chicago Press).
Thorpe, H. 1951 'The Green Villages of County Durham', *Transactions of the Institute of British Geographers* 15, 150–80.
Thorpe, H. 1964 'Rural Settlement' in. J. Wreford Watson and J. B. Sissons, *The British Isles; a Systematic*

Geography (Nelson, Edinburgh).

Turner, M. E. (ed.) 1978 *A Domesday of English Enclosure Acts and Awards – the Work of W.E. Tate* (The Library, University of Reading).

Uhlig, H. 1961 'Old Hamlets with Infield and Outfield Systems in Western and Central Europe', *Geografiska Annaler* XLII, nos. 1–2, 285–312

Uhlig, H. (ed.) 1972 *Rural Settlements* (in German, English and French, Lenz-Verlag, Giessen).

Van Bath, S. 1963a *The Agrarian History of Western Europe AD 500–1850* Edward Arnold, London).

Van Bath, S. 1963b *Yield Ratios 810–1820* (Afdeling Agrarische Geschiedenis Bijdragen 10, Wageningen).

Van der Veen, M. 1992 *Crop Husbandry Regimes: an Archaeobotanical Study of Farming in northern England, 1000BC – AD 500* (Sheffield Archaeological Monographs 3, Department of Archaeology and Prehistory, University of Sheffield).

Vico, G. 1744 *New Science* (3rd. edition, translated by David Marsh, Penguin Books, 2001).

Vinogradoff, P. 1892 *Villainage in England* (Clarenden Press, Oxford).

Vinogradoff, P. 1908 *English Society in the Eleventh Century* (Clarendon Press, Oxford).

Vinogradoff, P. 1911 *The Growth of the Manor* (1904, revised 1911, George Allen and Unwin Ltd., London).

Waddell, H. 1982 *Songs of the Wandering Scholars,* edited with preface by Dame Felicitas Corrigan (The Folio Society, London).

Waterbolk, H. T. and Halsema, O. 1979 'Medieval Farmsteads in Gasselte (Province of Dreuthe)', *Palaeohistoria* 21, 228–65.

Watts, V. 1988–9 'Scandinavian Settlement-Names in County Durham' *Nomina* XII, 17–63.

Watts, V. 2002 *A Dictionary of County Durham Place-Names* (English Place-Name Society, Popular Series 3, Nottingham).

Wegraeus, E. and Näsman, U. s.d. *Eketorp – Fortification and Settlement on Öland, Sweden: The Monument* (Royal Academy of Letters, History and Antiquities, Stockholm).

Welldon Finn, R. 1963 *An Introduction to Domesday Book* (Longmans).

Whelan, F. 1894 History, *Topography and Directory of the County Palatine of Durham* (Ballentyne, Hansen and Co. Ltd, London).

Whitehand, J. W. R. 1981 *The Urban Landscape: Historical Development and Management: Papers by M.R.G. Conzen* (Institute of British Geographers Special Publication, No. 13, Academic Press, London).

Whitelock, D. (ed.) 1955 *English Historical Documents, c. 500–1042* (Eyre and Spottiswoode, London).

Wilson, J. (ed.) 1901 *A History of Cumberland*, vols. I and II (Victoria History of the Counties of England, University of London, Institute of Historical Research: reprinted 1968 by Dawsons of Pall Mall, London).

Winchester A. J. L. 1987 *Landscape and Society in Medieval Cumbria* (John Donald Publishers Ltd., Edinburgh).

Winchester, A. J. L 1990 *Discovering Parish Boundaries* (Shire Publications Ltd., Princes Risborough).

Winchester, A. J. L 2000 *Discovering Parish Boundaries* (2nd edition Shire Publications Ltd., Princes Risborough).

Winchester, A. J. L. 2000 *The Harvest of the Hills* (University Press, Edinburgh).

Wormald, P. 1999 *The Making of English Law: King Alfred to the Twelfth Century vol. I* (reprinted, 2001, Blackwell Publishers, Oxford).

INDEXES

INDEX OF PLACES

With only slight modifications English counties are designated with the codes used in E. Ekwall, *The Oxford Dictionary of English Place-Names* (Clarendon Press, Oxford)

Aberchirder, Bnf, 13; fig. 1.3
Acklington, Nb, 73 ff, 74, 76, 81, 124, 208, 263; fig. 3.2
Addingham, Cu, 243
Aglionby, Cu, 243
Airy Hill, NR.Y, 37
Airy Holm, NR.Y, 32, 37
Aislaby, NR.Y, 67
Aldborough, NR.Y, 158, 284
Aldpark, Du, 185
Allertonshire, 158
Alnwick, Nb, 124
Ampleforth, ER.Y, 103, 111, 118; fig. 2.1.a, 4.8, 4.10
    Ampleforth Birdforth, 113 ff
    Ampleforth Oswaldkirk, 113 ff
    Ampleforth St. Peter, 113 ff
Amerston, Du, 35
Amounderness, 158
Angram Grange, NR.Y, fig. 4.8, 4.9
Appleby, We, 41, 43, 107, 118, 243; fig. 11.2
Appleton-le-Moors, NR. Y, 13, 40, 61, 65 ff; fig. 1.3, 2.1.b, 2.3
Ashdon, *Assandune*, Ess, 284
Ashingdon, Ess, 284
Auckland, Du, 157 ff, 171 ff, fig. 6.3, 7.1
    Auckland Castle, 179
    Bishop (North) Auckland, 24, 41, 48, 52, 139, 154, 173 ff; fig. 2.4, 2.5, 2.6, 6.5
    St. Andrew Auckland, 173 ff
    St. Helen's Auckland, 71, 173 ff; fig. 6.5
    West Auckland, 154, 176 ff, 180 ff, 216 ff, 239; fig. 6.5, 7.8

Aucklandshire, Du, 157, 158, 172 ff, 188, 228, 232; fig. 7.1
Aycliffe, Du, 133, 139, 196

Bamburgh/Dingayroi, fig. 1.8
Barony, Du, 173 ff
Barmton, Du, 203
Barnard Castle, Du, 48, 50, 139; fig. 2.4, 2.5, 2.6
Baschebi, NR.Y, 67
Battle Abbey, Sx, 298
Baxby, ER.Y, 103, 110
Beaumont, Cu, fig. 1.3
Beaurepayr, Du, 90
Bedale, NR.Y, 107
Bedesfeld, 234
Bedlington, Nb, 240
Bedlingtonshire, 158
Bernicia/Brynaich, fig. 1.8
Billingham, Du, 133, 139, 228 ff; fig. 6.3, 7.10
Billinghamshire, 157
Binchester, Du, 176 ff, 210; fig. 6.5, 7.6
Birdforth, NR.Y, 113 ff; fig. 4.8, 4.9
Bishop Auckland, Du (*see* Auckland)
Blackburnshire, 158
Blackwell, Du, 222, 232; fig. 7.9
Boldon, 71 ff, 221, 223, 225 ff; fig. 6.3
    East Boldon (Newton by Boldon), 71ff, 123, fig. 2.7
    West Boldon, 72 ff
Bolam, Du, 195; fig. 7.1
Botcherby, Cu, 243
Brafferton, Du, 196, 215, 224; fig. 7.6

Bramley, WR.Y, 61
Brancepeth, Du, 40
Bristol, 296
Brough, We, 243
Burdon, Little, Du, fig. 7.7
Burgshire, 158
Butterwick, Du, fig. 7.6
Byers Green, Du, 12, 80 ff, 146, 188, 236; fig. 3.4, 6.5
Byland, NR.Y, 107; fig. 4.8, 4.9
Byland Abbey, NR.Y, 103; fig. 4.8

Canterbury, 272
Cardington, Sa, fig. 1.3
Carlatton, Cu, fig. 7.4
Carlisle, 33, 40, 147, 234, 242, 243
Carlton, 106, 146
Carlton, in Cleveland, NR.Y, 40, 61, 68 ff; fig. 2.1.a, 2.3, 3.1
Carlton, Du, 69 ff, 91, 142, 203, 215 ff, 230; fig. 3.1, 7.8, 7.9
Carlton Husthwaite, NR.Y, 109 ff; fig. 2.1.a, 4.8, 4.9
Cassop, Du, 225
Castle Sowerby, Cu, fig. 7.4
Catterick, NR.Y, 25, 232
Catraeth, see Catterick, NR.Y, fig. 1.8
Chester, 291
Chester-le-Street, Du, 48, 52, 139, 157, 210 ff, 224, 228, 229, 233, 234 ff, 293 ff; fig. 2.4, 2.5, 2.6, 6.3, 9.6
Chillingham, Nb, 171
Cleadon, Du, 228
Cockerton, Du, 216, 232; fig. 7.9
Cockfield, Du, 60, 88 ff, 97, 147, 198, 240; fig. 4
Cold Kirby, ER.Y, 109
Compostella, Spain, 271
Coniscliffe, Du, 232
Copeland, Du, 173 ff; fig. 6.5
Cotherstone, NR.Y, 176
Corbridge, Nb, 24
Cornsay, Du, 236; fig. 7.6
Coxwold, NR.Y, 103; fig. 2.1.a, 4.8
Coxwoldshire, 103 ff
Coundon, Du, 177, 224; fig. 6.5
Craven, WR.Y, 199

Crawcrook, Du, 209, 215; fig. 7.6
Cuhawalda, see Coxwold
Cumwhitton, Cu, 94; fig. 4.3

Darlington, Du, 40, 157, 216, 220 ff, 228, 232 ff, 240, fig. 6.3, 7.9
Danzey Green, Wa , 12
Deira, 200; fig. 1.8
Denton, Du, fig. 7.1
Dere Street, 157, 184, 228; fig. 7.1
Dewsbury, WR.Y, 277
Dolphenby, Cu, 243
Driffield, ER.Y, 158
Dumbarton, Dnb, 179
Dunfermline, Fife, 270
Durham, 33, 40, 45, 50, 118 ff, 123, 139, 159 ff, 172 ff, 203, 205 ff, 233 ff, 237, 270, 272, 293, 296, fig. 2.4, 2.5, 2.6, 4.13, 5.5

Easby, NR.Y, 277
Earsdon, Nb, 52; fig. 2.7
Easington, Du, 226 ff; fig. 6.3
Easingwold, NR.Y, 41
East Boldon, *see* Boldon
East Hartburn, Du, 52; fig. 2.7
East Thirston, Nb, 63
Edderacres, Du, 34
Eddisbury, Chs, 291
Ednam, Rox, 246
Ednesknolle, see Aucklandshire
Eketorp, Öland, Sweden, 273; fig. 9.6
Eldon, Du, 173 ff; fig. 6.5, 7.1
Elmet, fig. 1.8
Elton, Du, 203
Embleton, Nb, fig. 1.3
Escomb, Du, 154, 172 ff, 233 ff; fig. 3.4, 6.5
Etterby, Cu, 243
Europe, 251 ff, 270; fig. 9.1, 9.4, 9.5, 9.7
Evenwood, Du, 173 ff, 185; fig. 6.5

Fadmoor, NR.Y, 109; fig. 2.1.a
Falsgrave, NR.Y, 37
Farmanby, Cu, 242
Fenny Compton, Wa, fig. 1.3
Ferryhill, Du, 24, 52, 138 ff, 234; fig. 2.7, 5.3.b, 7.10
Frisemareis, ER.Y, 61

Frosterley, Du, 91, 173, 198;
Fychewacke, Du, *see* Aucklandshire

Gainford, Du, 157, 228; fig. 6.3, 7.1
Gamblesby, Cu, 13, 94, 97, 139, 150, 242; fig. 1.3, 4.4, 5.6
Gamelsby, Cu, 244
Gasselte, 268; fig 9.5
Gateshead, Du, 48, 210, 214, 224; fig. 2.4, 2.5, 2.6
Gilcrux, Cu., fig. 3.3
Gillamoor, ER.Y, 109; fig. 2.1.a
Gillingshire, 158
Gilsland, Cu, 26, 243
Glassonby, Cu, 139, 149, 242
Glastonbury, So, 294
Great Asby, We, 93, 99; fig. 4.2
Great Ayton, NR.Y, 37
Great Haughton, Du, 232
Great Thirkleby, NR.Y, fig. 4.8, 4.9
Great Usworth. Du, 209 ff, 215; fig. 7.6
Greencroft, Du, 214; fig. 7.7
Grewelthorpe, WR.Y, fig. 1.3
Greysouthen, Cu, fig. 1.3

Hallamshire, 158
Hallowell Moss, Du, fig. 6.6
Halton, La, 277
Hamsterley, Du, 185; fig. 6.5
Hamsterley Castles, Du, 89
Harperley, Du, 185
Hartburn, Du, 232
Hartside, Nb, 94; frontispiece
Harwood Dale, NR.Y, 37
Haughton le Skerne, Du, 232; fig. 7.8
Hayton, Cu, 93, 94; fig. 4.3
Headlam, Du, 13, 196; fig. 1.3, 7.1
Hedley (hope), Du, 236; fig. 7.6
Heortenesse, Du, 228
Heighington, Du, 13, 139, 189 ff, 210, 224, 226; fig. 1.3, 7.1
Heighingtonshire, Du, 172ff, 188 ff, 228; fig. 7.1
Henknowle, Du, 185; fig.7.7
Helmington, Du, 176 ff
Helmsley, NR.Y, 32, 37, 43, 117; fig. 2.1.a, 4.12

Herrington, Du, 209, 215, 224; fig. 7.6
Heworth, Du, 196; fig. 7.1
Hexham, Nb, 199, 203, 233 ff
Hilton, Du, fig. 7.1
Holderness, 89
Hood, ER.Y, 102; fig. 4.8
Horenbodbi, ER.Y, 114 ff
Houghton-le-Side, Du, 196; fig. 7.1
Houghton-le-Skerne, 220; fig. 7.8
Howdenshire, 158, 280
Huggate, ER, Y, 60
Hulam, Du, 214; fig. 7.7
Hunsonby, Cu, 242
Hunwick, Du, 210 ff, 236; fig. 7.6
Husthwaite, NR.Y, 109, 110; fig. 4.8, 4.9
Hutton Buschel, NR.Y, 32, 101; fig. 4.7
Hutton Henry, Du, 210; fig. 7.6
Hutton-le-Hole, NR.Y, 132; fig. 2.1.a
Hutton Rudby, NR.Y, 40, 41; fig. 2.1.a, 2.3
Hutton Sessay, NR.Y, 114 ff; fig. 2.1.a, 4.8, 4.9, 4.11
Hunwick, Du, 176 ff, 214
Hurworth, -Black, -Burn, -Red and -White, 35

Ilecliffe, NR.Y, 228
Ingleton, Du, 196; fig. 7.1
Ireton, NR.Y, 107
Islandshire, 158
Iveston, Du, 91, 198, 215; fig. 7.6

Jarrow, Du, 237

Kelso, Rox, 246
Ketton, Du, 232
Kilburn, NR.Y, 107, 110 ff; fig. 2.1.a
Kilham, ER.Y, 158
Killerby, Du, 193 ff, 198; fig. 7.1
Kirkbampton, Cu, 94; fig. 4.2
Kirby Grindalythe, ER.Y, 30
Kirby Malzeard, WR.Y, 158
Kirk Merrington, *see* Merrington
Kirkby Thore, Cu, 244
Kirbyshire, 158
Kirk Merrington, *see* Merrington
Kirkwall, Ork, 270
Knaresborough, WR.Y, 280, 284

Kootwijk, 266, 268; fig 9.5
Körbisdorf, 265; fig 9.5

Lanchester, Du, 139; fig. 6.3, 7.1, 7.8
Langwathby, Cu, fig. 7.4
Laskill, NR.Y, 37
Leominster, He, 2
Leyland, 158
Lindisfarne, Nb, 154, 157, 234, 292, 296; fig. 9.6
Linthorpe, NR.Y, 61
Little Asby, We, 97; fig. 4.5
Little Haughton, Du, 232
Little Salkeld, Cu, 242
Little Thirkleby, NR. Y, fig. 4.8, 4.9
Little Usworth, Du, fig. 7.7
Liverton, NR.Y, 61
Longhirst, Nb, 124; fig. 2.7
Long Lawford, Wa, fig.1.3
Low Kilburn, *see* Kilburn
Lutteringtun, Du, 173 ff, 214; fig. 6.5, 7.7
Lumley, Du, 232
Lyng, So, 277
Lynsack, Du, 185
Lyvennet, River, We, 38, 76

Martin Garth, NR.Y, 101
Masham, NR.Y, 233, 277
Maughanby, Cu, 243
Maulds Meaburn, We, 77 ff, 93; fig. 3.3
Meaburn Hall. We, 78
Medilwong, 234
Melkinthorpe, Cu, 63, 64 ff; fig. 3.1
Melmerby, Cu, 97, 139, 243, 244; fig. 4.4
Merrington, Du, fig. 5.3.a
    Kirk Merrington, 57, 132; fig. 5.3.a
    Middle Merrington (*Middlestone*), 132, 138 ff; fig. 2.7, 5.3.a, 7.10
    Westerton (*West Merrington*), fig. 2.7
Merringtonshire, 138
Middle Merrington, *see* Merrington
Middlestone, *see* Merrington
Middleton, by Pickering, NR.Y, 67, 99, 265; fig. 2.1.b, 4.6
Middridge, Du, 13, 69 ff, 91, 147, 193 ff; fig. 3.1, 7.1, 7.8
Milburn, Cu, 67

Monk Hesleton, Du, 203
Monkton, Du, fig. 7.10
Morton, Du, 216, 222; fig. 7.9
Morton Tinmouth, Du, fig. 7.1

Newbottle, Du, 224
Newcastle upon Tyne, 24
Newbiggin, Du, 214 ff, 223; fig. 7.1, 7.7
Newby, near Scalby, NR.Y, fig. 2.1.b, 3.4
Newby, in Cleveland, NY.Y, 40, 63 ff; fig. 2.1.a, 2.3, 3.1
Newburgh, NR.Y, 110 ff
Newcastle, 40
Newstead, NR.Y, 107 ff
Newton Bromswold, Np, 63
Newton, 72, 101
Newton Cap, Du, 154, 172 ff; fig. 6.5
Newton, by Hutton Buschel, NR.Y
Newton by Boldon (East Boldon), 220
Newton Garths, Du, 72
Newton Hundred, 241
Newton Reigny, Cu, 97; fig. 4.4
Newton on Rawcliffe, NR.Y, fig. 2.1.b, 3.4
Normanby, NR.Y, 101, 232; fig. 2.1.b
North Auckland, *see* Auckland
North Bedburn, Du, 185
North Sherburn, Du, 225
Northumbria, 285, 296
Norton, Du, 216, 220, 228, 232; fig. 6.3, 7.8, 7.9
Nun Coton, Y, (deserted?), 60

Oldstead, ER.Y, 107; fig. 4.8, 4.9
Old Thickley, Du, 195 ff
Old Towns, Middridge, Du
Ormsby, 81
Osgodby, NR.Y, 103, 107; fig. 4.8, 4.9
Oswaldkirk, NR.Y, fig. 4.8, 4.9
Otley, WR.Y, 274
Oulston, NR.Y, 107 ff; fig. 4.8, 4.9
Oxenhall, Du, 219, 224, 232; fig. 7.8

Penrith, Cu, 40, 7.4
Pickering, NR.Y, 32, 40, 101; fig. 2.1.b
Piercebridge, Du, 24
Plawsworth, Du, fig. 7.7
Pocklington, ER.Y, 158

Preston, NR.Y, 101
Preston, Du, 232

Quarringtonshire, 157

Rabyshire, 158
Raunds, Np, 295
Rauensykschales, Cu, 99
Ravenna, 274
Redworth, Du, 194 ff, 216 ff, 220; fig. 7.1, 7.9
Rheged, 38; fig. 1.8
Richmond, NR.Y, 89, 279, 291
Rickerby, Cu, 243
Riponshire, 158
Robberby, Cu, 242
Romaldkirk, NR.Y, 232
Rome, 277 ff
Rothbury, Nb, 124
Roxby, NR.Y, 37
Runcorn, Chs, 291
Rykenhall, Du, 197

Sædding, 268
Salford. La, 158
Saxstead Green, Sf, 12
Scailhouses, Cu, 99
Scale Houses, Cu, 99; fig. 4.5
Scales, 99
Scaling, NR.Y, 37
Scotby, Cu, fig. 7.4
School Aycliffe, Du, 196, 203; fig. 7.1
Sedgefield, Du, 157, 216, 220, 224, 229; fig. 6.3, 7.9
Settrington, ER.Y, 60
Shadforth, Du, 225
Shakleton, Du, 194
Shap, We, 78, 91
Sheffield, WR.Y, 158
Shelam (*Shelom*), Du, 134; fig. 5.3.a, 7.10
Sheraton, Du, 215, 224; fig. 7.6
Shildon, Du, fig. 7.1
Shotton, Du, 224, 226
Skerningham, Du, 203
Softley, Du, 185
South Bedburn, Du, 185
South Church, *see* Auckland

South Sherburn, Du, fig. 7.9
St. Andrew Auckland, *see* Auckland
St. Helen's Auckland, *see* Auckland
Staindrop, Du, 173, 233
Staindropshire, 158, 173 ff, 194 ff
Stanhope, Du, 139, 172 ff, 198; fig. 2.2, 6.5
Statheleg, Du, 90
Stainmore, 203
Steward Shield Meadow, Du, 37, 176; fig. 6.6
Stockley, Du, 40
Stockton, Du, 216, 228, 232; fig. 6.3, 7.9
Stokesley, NR.Y, 63; fig. 7.1
Swaythorpe, ER.Y, 60

Tallentire, Cu, fig. 1.3
Tarraby, Cu, 243
Tettenhall, St, 291
Thelwall, Chs, 291
Thickley, Du, 173 ff, 194 ff; fig. 6.5, 7.1
Thirkleby, (*see* Great and Little), 103, 107
Thirley Cotes, NR.Y, 32, 37
Thirsk, NR.Y, 41; fig. 2.1.a, 2.3
Thoresby, Cu, 244
Thornton-on-the-Hill, NR.Y, 107; fig. 4.8, 4.9
Thorp-le-Willows, NR.Y, fig. 4.8, 4.9
Trimdon, Du, fig. 5.6
Thrislington, Du, 125; fig. 5.1
Thursby, Cu, 244
Tile Green, Wa, 12
Tollesby, NR.Y, 60
Torpenhow, Cu, 244
Troutsdale Hall, NR.Y, 37
Twattleton, NR.Y, 107
Twizell, Du, fig. 7.7

Unthank, Cu, 242
Upperby, Cu, 243
Urpeth, Du, 210 ff
Usworth, Du, *see* Great and Little

Vorbasse, 268 ff; fig. 9.5

Waberthwaite, Cu, 244
Waitby, We, 94, 97; fig. 4.4
Wakefield. WR.Y, 280
Walbottle, Nb, fig. 1.3

Walworth, Du, 196; fig. 7.1
Wardon, Du, 216; fig. 7.9
Warkworth, Nb, 44, 73
Wasdale Head, Cu, fig. 1.3
Washington, Du, 214, 215, 223, 224, fig. 7.7
Wass, ER.Y, 107, fig. 4.8
Weardseatle, Du, 176 ff, 179 ff, 182, fig. 6.5
Weardale, Du, 37, 172, 182, 210, fig 2.2
Wearmouth, Du, 157, 203, 228 ff, 232 ff, 276
    Bishop (South) Wearmouth
Wednesfield, St, 292
Welbeck, Nt, 124
Werhale, fig. 6.3
West Boldon, *see* Boldon
West Derby, 158
West Heslerton, ER.Y, 125, 128, 235; fig. 5.1
West Whelpington, Nb, 53, 125 ff, fig. 2.7
Westerton, *see* Merrington
Wharram Percy, ER, Y, 125 ff, 295; fig. 5.1
Wheldrake, ER, Y, 139 ff, 142; fig. 5.4
Whessoe, Du, 219, 224, 232; fig. 7.8
Whickham, Du, 228
Whitburn, Du, 72, 228
Whittingham, Nb, 233
Whitworth, Du, 182 ff, 194, 212; fig. 6.5, 7.6
Whorlton, Du, 44
Wilberfosse, ER.Y, 60
Wildon, ER.Y, 107, 110
Willow Holm, Cu, 243
Winlaton, Du, fig. 2.7
Winskill, Cu, 242
Witton-le-Wear, Du, 176 ff, 185
Wolsingham, Du, 139, 172 ff, 182 ff, 226; fig. 6.5
Wolviston, Du, 132, 139 ff; fig. 7.10
Woodham, Du, 220; fig. 7.1, 7.10
Worcester, 241, 294
Wrelton, NR.Y, 67
Wyberthwaite, Cu, 244
Wycliffe (*Wygecliffe*), NR.Y, 228, 233
Wyggonby, Cu, 244

Yarm, NR.Y, 41, 83, 176
Yearsley, NR.Y, 103, 107 ff; fig. 4.8, 4.9, 4.10
Yeavering, Nb, 129, 285; fig. 9.6
York, 33, 118, 205, 296

INDEX OF PERSONS

Aberg, A., 34
Adams, I. H., 82, 234
Aird, W. M., 154, 160, 228, 229 ff, 237, 242, 247
Allinson, M, 65 ff
Appleton, J.C., 244
Armstrong, A. M., 97, 99, 149, 242
Aston, T. H., 168
Aston, M. A., 122
Austin, D., 125 ff, 126 ff, 212, 219

Baker, A. R. H., 17
Barford, P. M., 271
Barlow, F., 284
Barrow, G. W. S., 152, 157 ff, 161, 163, 208, 235, 246, 299
Bartlett, R., 241, 299
Bassett, S., 163
Beeler, J., 243,
Beresford, M. W, 3, 34, 43 ff, 65 ff, 107, 118, 121, 123, 125, 138, 183, 295
Bishop, T. A. M., 33, 200
Bonney, M., 121
Bouch, C. A. L., 139
Brooks, C., 119
Brooks, N., 294
Brown, M. P., 293
Butlin, R. A., 17
Bylund, E., 247

Cam, H., 152
Cameron, K., 290 ff
Campbell, J. G., 152, 159, 208, 227, 283 ff, 293, 297
Campey, L., 133ff, 138 ff, 208

Camille, M., 44, 82
Chaplais, P., 225
Charles-Edwards, C., 166
Clack, P. A. G., 121, 243
Clancy, T. O., 163
Coates, B. E., 44
Conzen, M. R. G., 43, 119
Colgrave, B., 234 ff, 235
Cohen, A. P., 4
Costen, M. D., 123
Craster, E., 157, 160, 180, 228, 229, 233
Cramp, R., 182, 234
Crawford, B. E., 290, 297
Cubitt, C., 294
Cunningham, J., 180

Dalton, P., 234, 242, 244
Daniels, R., 119
Darby, H. C., 142, 198, 203, 254
Davis, R. H. C., 269
Davis, W., 142
Defoe, D., 19
Denman, D. R., 12, 159, 168
Dickinson, D., 38, 243
Dobson, B., 182
Dornier, A., 121
Douglas, D. C., 192, 199, 225, 294
Duby, G., 208, 261, 266
Duncan, A. A. M., 189, 192
Dunsford, H., 45f, 152
Dussart, F., 284

Earle, J., 296
Ekwall, E., 179
Everitt, A., 182
Everson, P., 3
Evans, D. H., 127

Faith, R., 158
Farrell, R. T., 293
Fehring, G., 268
Fellows Jensen, G., 107, 127, 149, 242, 291
Finberg, H. P. R., 3, 43, 67 ff, 107, 118, 138, 166, 183, 241 ff
Fletcher, R., 143, 203, 244, 273, 276, 293
Fraser, C., 132, 138

Fraser, D., 10
Fraser, G. MacDonald, 50, 62
Frere, S., 182
Frodisham, P., 94

Gamble, C., 122
Gates. T., frontispiece, 94
Gelling, M., 123
Getmapping , 3
Gibson, E., 26
Glacken, C. J., 272
Glasscock, R. E., 65
Göransson, S., 61, 76, 82 ff, 149, 249, 251, 269, 273
Gosling, P. F., 121, 243
Graham, T. H. B., 241
Greenaway, G.W., 192, 199, 225, 294
Greenway, D. E., 104 ff, 109
Greenwell, W., 50, 72, 80, 123, 133, 144, 160, 168, 172 ff, 177, 181, 182, 189 ff, 193 ff, 209 ff, 212 ff, 224
Grierson, P., 66
Gutkind, E. A., 254 ff, 267

Hadley, D. M., 241, 298
Hallam, E. M., 279 ff, 292
Hallam, H. E., 241, 245
Harris, A., 34
Harris, S. J., 48 ff, 154, 187
Harrison, B., 37
Harrison,W., 17
Harley, J. B., 19
Harmer, F. E., 244, 284
Harsemsa, O., 268
Hart, C. R., 107, 154, 160, 173 ff, 181, 194, 214, 228, 229 ff, 232 ff, 284
Harvey, M., 101
Harvey, P. D. A., 122, 144, 241, 294
Hawkes, J., 128
Haywood, J., 273
Heidinga, 266 ff, 269
Helmfrid, S., 129, 248
Hemming, J., 171
Higham, N., 23, 28, 232
Hilderbrandt, H., 265
Hill, D., 121, 280, 281, 290, 297

Hilton, R. H., 151
Hillaby, J., 2
Hodges, R., 38, 121, 276
Hodgson, R. I., 45 ff, 50, 71 ff
Hodgson Hinde, J., 214
Homans, G. C., 81 ff, 151, 161, 248
Holt, J. C., 208, 225, 226 ff, 285
Hooke, D., 10, 265, 266
Hope-Taylor, B., 84, 285
Houston, J. M., 251
Howell, C., 4, 122
Hoyt, R. S., 279 ff
Huddart, D., 52
Hurst, J. G., 34, 123, 125 ff, 295
Hvass, S., 268

Ingleson, S., 40
Innes. J., 52

James, E., 166
Jarrett, M. J., 127
Jenkins, D., 173, 190
John, E., 284
Johnson, A., 182
Jolliffe, J. E. A., 158 ff, 161, 208, 212
Jones, G. R. J., 152, 158 ff, 161 ff, 165, 171, 190 ff, 284
Jones, S. R. H., 60, 121, 290, 293

Kapelle, W. E., 33, 108, 210, 222, 243
Kelly, F., 170, 199
Keynes, S., 300
Kirby, D. A., 171
Koch, J. T., 162
Koebner, R., 258

Lapidge, M., 300
Lapsley, 215 ff, 225 ff
Lang, J., 234, 277
Latham, R. E., 143
Latham, L. C., 167
Lawson, M. K., 273, 293
Layton, R., 250
Lewis-Williams, D., 286 ff
Lockhart, D. G., 13
Lloyn, H. R., 282, 284
MacKay, A., 265, 268, 299

Maitland, F. W., 208
Margary, H., 14
Mayhew, A., 258
Mead, W. R., 269
Meeus, J. H. A. etc., 261
McNamee, C., 200, 203
McConnell, P., 177
McCormick, M., 192
Middlebrook S., 293
Miket, R., 129
Mills, S., 129
Morgan, H. L., 241, 249
Morris, J., 169

Näsman, U., 273
Nicolaisen W. F. H., 247
Nitz, J., 261 ff, 263

O'Brien, C., 128
O'Sulliva, 38, 184, 243
Offler, H. S., 40, 152, 158 ff, 187, 219, 228, 234
Orme, B., 270

Palliser, D. M., 121 ff, 142 ff, 200
Palmer, L. R, 157
Patterson, N. T., 171, 190
Parson, W., 94
Pelteret, D. A. E., 192, 241, 293
Pennar, M., 38
Perriam, D. R., 91
Pevsner, N., 3, 33, 139, 183, 190, 214
Phillips, D., 33
Phillips T. R., 273
Plummer, C., 296
Postan, M. M., 123, 167 ff, 208, 258, 261
Pounds, N. J. G., 258, 260
Powlesland, D., 128

Rahtz, P., 10, 121
Ramm, H., 37
Randsborg, K., 268 ff
Rees, W., 168 ff, 191
Reid, R. R., 168 ff, 181
Renn, D., 41, 43, 243
Rivet, A. L. F., 182
Robinson, J., 91

Roffe, D., 237, 286, 300
Rollason, D., 235
Ryder, P., 62

Sawyer, P. H., 122, 268, 290, 293
Scammell, G. V., 183
Schröder, K. H., 251, 260
Schwarz, G., 251, 260
Searl, E., 298
Seebohm, F., 161, 177 ff, 191 ff, 241, 246, 260, 294, 295
Sheppard, J. A., 10, 139, 140 ff, 280, 293
Skaife, R. H., 68, 110, 113
Snooks, G. D., 132
Sømme, A., 87
Smith, A. H., 19, 35, 40, 63 ff, 80, 99, 107, 157
Smith, C. T., 251, 258, 260
Smith, D., 122
Smyth, A. P., 291 ff, 292 ff
Sporrong, U., 129, 249
St Joseph, J. K. S., 64
Stamp, L. D., 26
Stephenson, J., 192, 203, 228, 236
Stenton, F. M., 147, 277, 284
Sturdy, D., 10, 277 ff,
Swanton, M., 142, 147, 192, 199, 284, 291, 296
Sylvester, D., 6
Symeon of Durham, 180, 205, 228, 234, 236

Taylor, H. M., 33, 229
Thomas, W. L., 254
Thorpe, H., 3, 13, 45
Turner, M. E., 66

Uhlig, H., 13

Van Bath, S., 270
Van der Veen, M., 172
Vinogradoff, P., 84, 178, 208, 210, 279

Waddell, H., 250, 276
Waterbolk, H. T., 268
Watts, V., 34 ff, 45 ff, 50, 81, 123, 160, 172 ff, 179 ff, 182 ff, 185 ff, 190, 194 ff, 198, 214, 229, 236, 297
Wegraeus, E., 273
Welldon Finn, R., 241
Whelan, F., 184
White, W., 94
Whitehand, J. W. R., 43, 119
Whitelock, D., 129, 178, 246, 290
Whyte, I. D., 37, 38, 184
Wilson, J., 169 ff, 170, 242 ff
Winchester, A. J. L., 6, 19, 37, 152, 200
Wormald, P., 192 ff, 269, 285
Wrathmell, S., 12, 18 ff, 35, 110, 125, 127, 143, 251, 290, 298

Zaluckyj, S., 121

GENERAL INDEX

agglomerated plans, 8, 12 ff, 36, 41 ff, 73, 146, 255, 258, 260, 264
agriculture, 172, 270 ff, 276
Alan of Brittany, Count, 280, 293
Alcuin, 276 ff, 296
Alfred, king, 193 ff, 246, 275, 285, 290, 297, 300, fig. 10.4, 10.5
alltud(ion), 191
Anglo-Saxon Chronicle, 147, 198 ff, 242 ff, 284, 293, 295

antecedence, 17, 23 ff, 33, 101, 103, 108 ff, 114, 125, 129 ff, 149, 207, 229, 238 ff, 249, 261 ff; fig.1.2
archaeological evidence, 32, 38, 42, 62ff, 122 ff, 125 ff, 143, 172, 207, 262, 266 ff, 285 ff; fig. 5.1
Athelstan, 229 ff, 285

back lanes, 61 ff, 65, 78, 92 ff, 109, 265; fig. 4.2 , 4.11
Bede, 158, 179, 234, 276

beltancu, *see* cornage
Beltane cow, *see* cornage
bondsmen, xi ff, 71ff, 123, 161 ff, 169 ff, 183 ff, 189 ff, 216 ff, 220 ff, 229 ff, 293
burh, 45, 241 ff, 277, 290, 294 ff, fig. 9.6, 10.4, 10.5
Burghal Hidage, 278

Central Province, 17 ff, 260, 290, 298
ceorls, 68, 129, 166, 192
Charlemagne, 250, 268, 271 ff, 276 ff, 296 ff
Charles Martel, 267 ff
Chlothar I, 273
churchyard (kirkgarth), 4, 11, 43, 54 ff, 101, 108, 111, 179, 184
Cnut, king, 170, 214, 233 ff, 273, 284 ff, 294, 297, fig. 9.7

colonisation, 38, 43, 91, 110, 113, 119, 149, 150, 160, 185 ff, 193, 198, 244 ff, 258 ff, 259 ff, 265, 278 ff, 286, 294 ff
commons, 12, 18, 26, 48 ff, 52, 103, 144, 166, fig. 1.5, 2.4, 2.5, 2.6
commorth, commortha, 166
communal fields, *see* townfields
Community of St Cuthbert, 157, 205, 229 ff, 240, 284, 297; fig. 8.2
compartment, 1
components of settlement patterns, 33, 151, 158
    dispersed elements, 17 ff, 34 ff, 38, 50, figs. 1.4, 1.6, 2.1, 2.2
    villages and hamlets, 38 ff; figs. 1.4, 1.6
    towns, 38 ff, 43 ff, 194, 199, 204
cornage, 149, 168 ff, 171 ff, 177, 180 ff, 189 ff, 194 ff, 209 ff, 214, 223 ff, 229 ff
cougeld, *see* cornage
couma(e)le, *see* cornage
cowgeld, *see* cornage
cumal, 169 ff, 199
Cuthbert, bishop and saint, 114, 154, 160, 170 ff, 173 ff, 194, 205, 228, 232 ff, 234 ff, 240 ff, 246, 296
Cuthbertine estates, 138, 144 ff, 154 ff, 157, 160 ff, 179, 199, 224, 228 ff, 239 ff, 293; fig. 6.2, 6.3, 8.2

devastation, 32, 40, 68, 87, 108, 109, 111, 142 ff, 147, 198 ff, 203 ff, 215, 220 ff, 235 ff, 240, 250, 293 ff; fig. 7.2, 7.3, 7.4; table 7.1
diffusion, 45, 87, 121, 239, 247 ff, 251, 269, 276, 298
Domesday Book, 18, 32 ff, 38, 63, 78, 99, 101 ff, 111 ff, 118, 122, 142 ff, 151, 200, 237, 242, 279, 284, 293
drengs / drengage, 69 ff, 97, 133, 149, 182, 188, 195, 208 ff, 223 ff, 237 ff, 241 ff, 286, 296; fig. 7.6, 7.7, 7.8

Eardwulf, bishop, 296
Edgar, king, 246, 297
Edward the Confessor, 279, 284, 291, 297, fig. 10.4, 10.5
Edward of Wessex, 291
exchequer land (terra scaccarii), 80, 123 ff, 144 ff, 177, 180 ff, 185, 190 ff, 195, 212, 236

feorma hams, 295
feudal structures / tenures, 103 ff, 107, 111 ff, 118, 159, 166 ff, 188, 245, 258, 271; fig 4.9, 4.10, 4.11, 10.2.b
field systems, 10, 17, 34, 54, 74 ff, 81, 99 ff, 151, 192, 245 ff, 254, 259 ff, 276, 293, fig. 4.6, 4.7, 5.4, 9.4, 9.5
firmarii (leasholders), 69, ff. 192 ff, 194 ff, 215 ff, 220, 225; fig. 7.9, 7.10
food rents, 159, 169; fig. 6.4
foothold furlong, 90, 94 f, 132, 146 ff; fig. 4.5

Gardymen, 191
garth (*see* toft), 1
gebur, 157, 294 ff
geburatunas, 157
graphical analyses, 144 ff, fig. 5.5, 7.5, 8.1
'great plough', 93 ff
greens, 1, 3, 8, 11 ff, 40 ff, 54 ff, 62 ff, 76 ff, 84, 90 ff, 94 ff, 107 ff, 128 ff, 149, 183 ff, 194 ff, 215 ff, 236, 239, 249, 261, 268 ff
Guthrith, 297
Guthrum, 290; fig. 10.4, 10.5
gwely, 169, 191

gwestfa, 169

Halfdan, king, 296
hallgarth, *see* manor house
Harold II, king, 283
Harrying of the North, 142 ff, 146, 200, 207, 248
Harthacnut, 284, 297
Henry I, king, 97, 149, 242, 244, 285
Henry II, king, 81, 118
Historia de Sancto Cuthberto, 160, 176, 214
Honour of Mowbray, 103 ff
horngeld, *see* cornage

kirkgarth, *see* churchyard

llys, 161 ff

maenor, 161 ff
maerdref, 162 ff, 169
mal, 191
manor house (hallgarth), 11, 40, 41, 54, 64, 67 ff, 90 ff, 107, 125 ff, 133, 135
Mayors of the Palace, 285
maps:
    as sources, 124 ff
    as tools, 26, 147, fig. 5.6
    distribution maps, 45 ff
market towns, 1, 4, 18, 32, 44; fig. 1.4
metride, *see* milch cow
methreth, *see* milch cow,
metrological analysis, 115 ff, 122 ff, 139 ff; fig. 4.11, 5.4
milch cow, 81 ff, 135 ff, 170 ff, 177, 191
ministry, 286
missi, 286
molmen, 215 ff
morphology, total, fig 1.2
multiple estate (*see* shire), 158, 161, 163, 185; fig. 6.4

nativi, 191 ff
noutgeld, *see* cornage
Norman Conquest, 10, 14, 18 ff, 151, 159, 178 ff, 203, 207 219, 226, 238, 240, 244 ff, 248

North Yorkshire Moors, 24 ff, 29 ff, 37, 45, 67, 101; fig. 2.1

Oderic Vitalis, 300
Onlafball, 293

parish(es), 6, 12, 17 ff, 33 ff, 63 ff, 67 ff, 94, 109 ff, 113 ff, 152 ff, 163 ff, 173, 185, 196, 226, 242, 263; fig. 6.1
patterns, *see* settlement
Paul the Deacon, 250
Pepin III, 265
Photographic Atlas of England, 3 ff
place-names and elements, 19, 45 ff, 154 ff, 166, 174 ff, 185 ff, 196 ff, 242 ff, 259, 265
plan elements, *see* settlement
polities, 269 ff; fig. 1.8
polyfocal, see composite
processes of change, 52 ff, 124; fig. 2.7

Ragnall, 292, 297
Rectitudines Singularum Personarum, 241 ff, 294 ff
regulated villages, 61, 81 ff, 87, 151, 214, 240, 266, 293
renders and rents, 167 ff, 177 ff, 189 ff, 195 ff, 209 ff, 249 ff, 280 ff; fig. 7.6. 7.7
retrospective model, 22
Romano-British, 18, 23 ff, 27, 32, 38, 94, 159, 166, 172, 244
'Romanesque society', 269 ff
royal demesnes, 279 ff; fig. 10.4, 10.5

Saxo Grammaticus, 296
serjeants, 286
servientes, 286
settlement:
    chronology, 37, 122 ff, 135
    classification, 1 ff, 6–11, 41, 53 ff, 60 ff, 101, 171, 222
    cycles, 23, 223 ff, 237 ff
    definitions, 2 ff, 6 ff; fig. 1.2, 9.2
    forms / morphology, 3 ff, 8, 58 ff, 183 ff; fig. 1.1, 1.3, 9.2
    function, 14

patterns, see components, 3ff, 32 ff, 183 ff; fig. 1.1, 1,2, 1.5, 1.6, 6.5.a
plan categorisation, 220 ff, 225 ff, 239 ff; fig. 5.5, 7.5, 8.1, 9.2
plan elements, 10 ff, 52 ff; fig. 1.1, 5.2
plans, see forms
plan antecedents, see antecedent
row plans, 62 ff
scales of study, fig. 1.1
sites, 56 ff; fig. 2.8
space (s), 10
territories, 6, 8; 22, 32, 153, 158 ff, 173, 196, 270 ff; fig. 1.1, 1.2

Scula, 292
shealings, scales, etc., 26
shielings, *see* shealings,scales
shire (s), small, 103, 107 ff, 114, 138, 142, 151 ff, 157 ff, 161 ff, 167 ff, 172 ff, 181 ff, 186 ff, 196 ff, 223 ff, 229 ff, 234, 246, 263, 278, 293; fig. 6.3
slaves, slavery, 129, 143, 166 ff, 170, 172, 190 ff, 199 ff, 220, 240, 246, 271, 276, 286, 291 ff
Stigand, Archbishop, 284 ff
sun division, solskifte, 82 ff, 150, 248 ff, 267, fig. 3.5, 3.6
Symeon of Durham, 228 ff

taeogs, 170, 173, 191 ff
taini (*see* thane)
tenures, 159, 180 ff, 185 ff, 209, 215, 219 ff, 225 ff, 232 ff, 245 ff, 278
Terpen, *see* Wurten
terrain (s), 14, 23 ff, 45, 52, 56, 251 ff, 266, 290, fig. 1.7, 6.1
thane (thegn), 241, 299
tithing, 6
tir cyfrif, 191
tofts (*see* garths), 1, 82 ff
tofts, types, 58 ff; fig. 4.5
toft vennels, 64 ff, 91

townfields, 17, 50, 70 ff, 82, 259, 260, 292, 298
towns, 38 ff, 43 ff, 118 ff; fig. 4.12, 4.13
township(s), 6 ff, 12, 17 ff, 34 ff, 63 ff, 72, 83, 94, 99 ff, 103, 107, 110 ff, 118 ff, 127, 140 ff, 146, 152 ff, 166, 177, 180, 194, 212, 226, 242 ff, 260 ff, 261 ff; fig. 6.1
tref, 161, 170, 191
trefgordd (lawful hamlet), 161
tregyfrif, 191
Turgot, Prior and Archdeacon in Durham, 237

villages:
    villages, classification, 10 ff; fig. 1.3, 5.2
    villages, composite / polyfocal plans, 12, 37, 43, 56, 67, 118 ff, 292; fig. 5.3.a
    villages, plan families, 13 ff
    villages, polyfocal, see composite
    village ideas, 1; fig. 5.2
    villages, genesis, 266, 286 ff; fig. 10.3, 10.4 10.5
    villages, regulated, 61, 81 ff, 87, 151, 214, 240, 266, 293
villans, xi ff, 71, 154, 173 ff, 179 ff, 185 ff, 189 ff, 192 ff, 209 ff, 212 ff, 220 ff, 233 ff
villeins, see villans
Vitruvius, 249

Waerften, see Wurten
Weorc, 178, 246; fig. 9.6
wasting, *see* devastation
William de St. Calais, 205, 225, 237, 296
William the Conqueror, 142, 169, 237, 279, 285 ff, 291 ff; fig 10.4, 10.5
Willibrord, 277
woodland, 14 ff, 17 ff, 26 ff, 35, 44 ff, 50 ff, 56, 80, 81, 101, 107 ff, 113, 129, 159, 166 ff, 183, 194 ff, 200, 228 ff, 233, 250, 260, 270, 292 ff; fig. 1.5, 1.6, 1.8
Wulfhere, bishop, 296
Wurten, 259